'Many histories of psychology recount events, biographies and id
thoughtfully in context in the way this book does. Students will g
psychological concepts and historical narratives were powerfully sha
intellectual traditions from which they sprung, with the lessons learn ....vance
today.' – **Aiden Gregg, Associate Professor, University of Southa...,.pton, UK**

'In his latest text, Hughes has set the bar for a textbook on conceptual, historical and philosophical
issues in psychology. It stands apart, not just in making the sub-field topic accessible to tutors and
students, but also in bringing together far more nuanced and critical literature that has been
missing from traditional textbooks in this field. In short, this is a book I wish I had written!' –
Gareth Hall, Senior Lecturer in Psychology, Aberystwyth University, UK

'Finally, we have a comprehensive and detail-orientated introduction to the history of psychology
which brings in a range of non-Western perspectives to challenge all the given tenets from 20th-
century Western psychology.' – **Sven Hroar Klempe, Professor in Psychology, Norwegian
University of Technology and Science, Norway**

'This volume is a must-read for Psychology students seeking an insight into the origins and
evolution of the discipline. Unlike many books which detail the history of psychology, Brian
Hughes' clear and engaging writing style, and use of examples from popular culture, literature and
modern politics make this an entertaining and insightful text. It is noteworthy that Hughes has
delved beyond typical Westernized accounts of the history of psychology, exploring perspectives
from across cultures and giving a voice to minority scholars who played important but somewhat
forgotten roles in shaping current psychological knowledge and understanding.' – **Michael Smith,
Associate Professor of Psychology, Northumbria University, UK**

'Throughout its history, psychology has incorporated a large number of highly varied and at times
incongruous theories, opinions, and philosophical and religious views about human nature – while
ignoring many others. In this tour-de-force, Brian Hughes provides a comprehensive overview of
the checkered history of psychology, emphasizing both its enduring limitations and its continuing
potential contributions. This book is a must-read for anyone interested in gaining a broader
perspective on psychology and broader ideas about human nature.' – **Hans Pols, University of
Sydney, Australia**

A Conceptual History of Psychology

The Mind Through Time

by
Brian Hughes

BLOOMSBURY ACADEMIC
LONDON · NEW YORK · OXFORD · NEW DELHI · SYDNEY

BLOOMSBURY ACADEMIC
Bloomsbury Publishing Plc
50 Bedford Square, London, WC1B 3DP, UK
1385 Broadway, New York, NY 10018, USA
29 Earlsfort Terrace, Dublin 2, Ireland

BLOOMSBURY, BLOOMSBURY ACADEMIC and the Diana logo
are trademarks of Bloomsbury Publishing Plc

First published in Great Britain 2023

A catalogue record for this book is available from the British Library.

Library of Congress Cataloging-in-Publication Data
Names: Hughes, Brian, author.
Title: A conceptual history of psychology: the mind through time / Brian Hughes.
Description: New York: Bloomsbury Publishing Plc, 2023. | Includes
bibliographical references and index.
Identifiers: LCCN 2022022214 | ISBN 9781350328198 (hardback) |
ISBN 9781350328204 (paperback) | ISBN 9781350328228 (epub) |
ISBN 9781350328211 (pdf) | ISBN 9781350328235 (XML)
Subjects: LCSH: Psychology–History.
Classification: LCC BF81 .H797 2023 | DDC 150.9–dc23/eng/20220614
LC record available at https://lccn.loc.gov/2022022214

ISBN: HB: 978-1-3503-2819-8
         PB: 978-1-3503-2820-4
         ePDF: 978-1-3503-2821-1
         eBook: 978-1-3503-2822-8

Typeset by Integra Software Services Pvt. Ltd.
Printed and bound in Great Britain by Bell and Bain Ltd, Glasgow

To find out more about our authors and books visit www.bloomsbury.com
and sign up for our newsletters.

To Louis and Annie, as history unfolds.

BRIEF CONTENTS

CONTENTS

PART IV FUTURE: Limitations and legacy

BOXES

ALMOST FAMOUS

HISTORICALLY (IN)ACCURATE?

HISTORY IN STORIES

ILLUSTRATIONS

IMAGES

FIGURES

ACKNOWLEDGEMENTS

Good practice in historiography demands that we try to avoid relying on 'Great Person' narratives (or their traditionally more gendered equivalents). Nonetheless, it behoves me to acknowledge the input of very many people who, more and less directly, influenced the content and context that have led to what you see on these pages.

I am especially grateful to everyone at Bloomsbury for their work on this book, in particular Jenna Steventon for her input and guidance, and Becky Mutton for vital support. I would also like to thank Luke Block for his role in the book's early stages, and Verity Rimmer. The inputs of several (anonymous) reviewers were extremely valuable along the way, and I wish to record my appreciation here.

It is a fallacy to imagine that history is past-facing. In fact, the importance of history is to enable us to understand the *present*, and to protect us as we explore the *future*. I have benefited for many years from colleagues and peers whose wisdom, ideas and collaborative inputs have combined to shape the way I think about my field. I would like to acknowledge some of those here, especially: Krys Kaniasty, Esther Greenglass and Albert Sesé; Ad Kaptein; David Tuller, Steven Lubet and David Marks; Annette Burns, Suzanne Guerin, Marie Loughman, Dean McDonnell, Nuala Whelan, Eimile Holton and Vincent McDarby; Nóirín Buckley and Paul O'Donoghue; Anna Whittaker, Douglas Carroll, Annie Ginty, Michael Smith, Lukasz Kaczmarek and Suchitra Pal; and Chris Curtin, Páraic Ó Súilleabháin and Séamus McLoone. I would wish to add special thanks to Siobhán Howard, Jack James and Donncha O'Connell.

Some of those whose influence has been especially valued are no longer here to read these words, but their role is no less appreciated for that fact. I remember, with great fondness, Martin F. McHugh, Lynn Myers, Noel Sheehy, Johan Denollet and Graham McPhee. History reminds us how quickly time passes.

It may seem sentimental, but I also wish to express sincere gratitude to all the students I have had the pleasure of encountering in the classroom and beyond. I am extremely privileged to have shared these journeys with you, and constantly inspired by your curiosity.

And as ever, I pay tribute to those whom destiny has required to join me in enduring my plight, namely, Marguerite, Louis and Annie.

B. M. H.

Part I

FOUNDATION: THE ROOTS OF PSYCHOLOGY

PEOPLE, HISTORY AND THE CONCEPT OF *PSYCHOLOGY*

1

In this chapter, we will ...

- consider the scope of psychology, beyond its academic and laboratory-based stereotypes
- evaluate the many meanings of the term 'psychology' and, thus, what counts as psychology's subject matter
- address the debate about whether psychology is a modern Euro-American university subject area or an ancient international intellectual pursuit
- examine the various ways in which historical knowledge is produced, and how history itself is shaped by psychological factors
- explain why the history of psychology is nearly always best approached by looking at the emergence of psychological concepts instead of the exploits of individual psychologists
- consider how the *psychology of history* affects our appreciation of the *history of psychology*

At the outset

Being human requires that we form views about what people in general are *like*: how they think, feel and behave in different situations; how they perceive life and are shaped by those experiences; and what kinds of personalities and aptitudes emerge within human populations. These ideas about what human beings are like comprise a body of human knowledge that we refer to as 'psychology'.

Our understanding of psychology shapes the way society engages with itself and so is relevant to all aspects of human culture, including our intellectual, social, educational and political systems. Psychology is a continually expanding field of knowledge about human thoughts, feelings and behaviour, and exists as such whether or not historians attempt to document its development.

Historians sometimes debate whether psychology is 'old' or 'new', often overlooking the way human culture has accumulated this type of knowledge for thousands of years. Detailed psychological insights were contemplated throughout the world long before the first university psychology departments were opened in Europe in the nineteenth century.

History is written from the perspective of the present and so there is a danger of assuming that only recent events are valid in shaping the modern world. We should be careful of judging historical events in terms of modern social attitudes and norms. That said, even though our social attitudes and value systems shift over time, the present remains connected to the past. The onus is on historians to try to account for the social context of each period when considering the relevance of its history.

It can be tempting to resort to clichéd narratives when describing history, such as the idea that human affairs reflect a trajectory of constant improvement and refinement. There is also a risk of assuming a continuous thread of influences from ancient to modern times. In reality, historical development does not always conform to our expectations.

Psychology itself shows us how people are prone to various reasoning errors that might skew their interpretation of history. People have preferences when it comes to explaining their past. Historians of psychology are no exception, and so they need to be mindful of their own biases.

Psychology is a set of concepts that are endemic and omnipresent in culture. The history of psychology should reflect this evolution of knowledge, rather than simply presenting a series of compelling discoveries or an incremental story of preordained intellectual achievement.

Key concept: Psychology

Psychology is easier to discuss than to define. This chapter will consider a number of different meanings for the term 'psychology'. 'Psychology' can be said to be a field of knowledge about the mental – that is, non-physical – aspects of the human condition. These non-physical aspects include thoughts, feelings, behaviours, personalities, temperaments, aptitudes, afflictions and well-being. 'Psychology' can represent the accumulated knowledge about such things, or the active study of them. It can also consider the way such attributes emerge in non-human animals, although often still with a view to shedding light on human beings.

For many commentators, including several major international associations and organizations, psychology is a science. It is also an academic subject area and, for that matter, a profession. Finally, the word 'psychology' can also refer to the combined non-physical factors that relate to a person or group or activity or situation. In that sense, human beings are often said to 'have' a psychology. Likewise, social issues or experiences can also be said to 'have' a psychology, whether or not any psychologist has yet studied or written about them (for example, 'the psychology of chatbots' or 'the psychology of *Rick & Morty*').

POPULAR PSYCHOLOGY

Around the world, *psychology* is a subject of mass public fascination. This is especially clear in academic settings, where psychology courses are always extremely popular. For example, in British universities, three times as many students take psychology as take biology, and five times as many take psychology as take physics (Higher Education Statistics Agency (HESA), 2019). By this reckoning – and without getting sucked into the *Is-psychology-a-science?* quagmire just yet – official statistics suggest that psychology is by far the most popular science subject in the UK.

Even so, universities offering psychology degrees usually have to turn away students, as demand for places almost always outstrips supply. The market for psychology is vastly oversubscribed. This pattern is repeated in virtually every country where psychology is taught in higher education.

But it is not just in academic contexts that psychology thrives. Psychological topics permeate society and culture. Beliefs about why people behave the way they do, why they feel the emotions they feel, and how they might be affected by their experiences, either positive or negative, are at the core of nearly all human interactions and activities. Whether explicitly acknowledged or not, psychological issues penetrate nearly every political and societal concern, placing psychology itself at the heart of daily culture.

In short, human beings have been intrigued by one another's psychologies for centuries. They have long sought to formulate clear and reliable explanations for one another's thoughts, feelings and behaviours. The ways humans depict, describe and discuss psychological concepts – ideas such as *emotions, instinct, rationality, intelligence, personality, maturity* or *autonomy* – have been part of the human experience since the earliest humans formulated their first thoughts.

Efforts to account for how memory works, what intelligence is made of, or why temperament runs in families (or, allegedly, in races) did not simply appear from nowhere when universities began to teach psychology in the late nineteenth century. Nor were European and North American societies the only ones interested in providing formal and reliable explanations for the human condition.

Psychology has been part and parcel of human civilization wherever civilization has emerged, and throughout its history. Indeed, our approaches to explaining ourselves have changed as civilization itself has evolved. The development of civilization has spanned thousands of years, during which human culture as we know it has been gradually organized and structured. Civilization is visible not just in logistics, but also in logic. How we think is more important than what we do. Civilization is not simply the building of buildings, the drawing of maps, or the invention of inventions. Civilization reflects the capacity of humans to *be* civilized. Technology is an emblem of civilization only insofar as it reflects the ingenuity that produced it.

Civilization is thus a psychological process. It is propelled by human psychology, and it creates a feedback loop that helps to shape the contours of that same human psychology. Civilization is dependent on people having implicit theories regarding human psychology that are shared across societies. For a species to become whatever it is we choose to refer to as 'civilized', it requires the creation of a coherent non-random ecosystem within which a majority can thrive.

Human beings are not isolated biological machines, they are social animals. Part of being human – an essential part – is that we operate with a consensus about how human beings in general are likely to think, feel and behave in different situations, about how they perceive life and are shaped by those experiences, and about how different types of personalities and aptitudes are likely to emerge within human populations.

In other words, civilization demands that people develop widely agreed ideas about what human beings are actually *like*.

These widely agreed ideas about what human beings are like comprise an enormous body of human knowledge that has been accumulated over thousands of years. This field of knowledge is what we refer to as 'psychology'.

As psychological concepts have been embedded in human thinking since the dawn of human history, we can be sure that the way human beings have handled these concepts has evolved over time. The human understanding of psychological concepts is not confined to those humans who study psychology in universities.

Interest in psychological concepts is central to human life. How humans explain each other's behaviour – and how they have arrived at their current explanations – is therefore central to understanding human life itself.

Our psychological world

Psychological concepts pervade all of human existence. While we don't always think about things this way, it can be argued that all political issues, all social issues and all cultural issues are, fundamentally, psychological. In other words, our daily lives are governed on the basis of the way we presume to know psychology.

One example of this is the fact that psychological concepts regularly attract the attention of politicians and political commentators. The people responsible for running our societies, and those citizens who are governed by them, frequently find themselves having to grapple with psychological challenges.

Many such challenges are negative, attracting attention precisely because of the alarm they cause. Consider, for example, the issue of interpersonal violence. When a major violent crime makes the news, or if rates of violent crime are perceived to have risen, the many psychological questions relating to violence will be pushed firmly into the public spotlight: *What makes people violent towards each other? How can we predict when violence will occur? What can be done to prevent violence? Can you rehabilitate a person who is violent and turn them into a pacifist? Or do we need to lock them up for life?*

On other occasions, psychological topics will feature prominently in political debate because of lobbying by special interest groups who want to shape the way that relevant policies are developed. Many advocates and campaigners spend their lives garnering attention for topics such addiction, suicide, mental health and intellectual disability. There is frequently widespread public concern about these issues. Once again, the focus tends to be on causes, on consequences, and, where relevant, on 'cures'.

Sometimes political decisions are evaluated in terms of their psychological consequences. The prospect that an economic or social policy might cause unintended distress or danger to the emotionally vulnerable is commonly raised. Such concerns are reflected in the now much-parodied expression '*Won't somebody please think of the children!*' Politically, mental well-being is everybody's concern.

The way people seek reasoned explanations for their own and others' mental health is another sign of the long-standing universal interest of humans in their own psychology. Essentially, mental well-being is seen in terms of norms. The fact that such norms change over time, and differ across cultures, is another reason why it is informative to explore the history of psychological concepts.

Beyond dealing with explicitly psychological concerns, daily politics often reveals universal psychology in more implicit ways. Everyday political issues – such as the economy and public finances, healthcare and public health, law and order, or education – also centre on how people view and understand psychology.

Economic policy rests on how we believe people understand and react to such factors as wealth, taxation and fluctuating cost. Decisions about the economy cannot be made without some kind of working assumptions about how 'normal' humans deal with reward, punishment or material contentment, or the extent to which they are willing to prioritize the welfare of others over that of their own. All these considerations rely on beliefs about human psychology. They rely equally on a consensus about such beliefs being widely held across the population. Governments simply cannot operate unless politicians and voters share a fair degree of psychological understanding – or, at least, that they *believe* they understand how human beings think, feel and behave.

Virtually every political topic coheres around working theories of psychology:

- Debates about healthcare rely on a shared consensual view of such psychological issues as well-being, risk aversion and pain.
- Debates about education depend on beliefs regarding child development, the nature of talent and skill, and ageing.
- Debates about law and order will rest on perceptions of the nature of personal culpability, competence and compassion.
- Climate change is a behavioural challenge.
- Racism is intrinsically social-psychological.
- War would not happen were it not for the human willingness to inflict full-scale carnage on out-groups.

Governed societies are intrinsically human. As such, every area of government will require an understanding of a range of psychological concepts. Such concepts affect our approaches to political challenge in virtually endless ways.

Even the way governments are formed will rely on there being agreed social assumptions about human psychology. For example, open democracy assumes that human beings are capable of exercising free will and choice, of evaluating the merit of propositions, of recognizing and deciding what they want, and of collaborating with other like-minded people to pursue their objectives. Implicitly, democracy also assumes that people possess a social identity and that humans tend towards altruism.

Even the belief that social order is a good thing assumes much about human psychology. For example, it assumes that most humans prefer order to chaos, and will care enough about this that they are willing to obey laws. Living among other people requires that we implicitly accept such assumptions. As such, how we live our lives is highly influenced by the way we perceive, understand and explain the psychology of humans.

Views on psychology are communally shared, but are subject to shifting interpretations over time. They are shaped and fashioned by observation, experience, precedent, analysis and formal speculation. How we design our political system is not random or based on guesswork. The required understanding is methodically formed.

Our psychological lives

From an early age, human beings are concerned with relationships. By extension, they are receptive to relationship advice. Guidance on how to deal with others is not just passed down from parents to children, it is circulated throughout the adult population. Even many high-brow broadsheet newspapers and fashionable magazines carry advice columns from relationship experts.

Rigid cultural conventions shape the sequence of activities that allow tentative pubertal dalliances to flower one day into marriages, civil unions or other types of permanent life-partnerships. In many places, strict laws govern what is, or is not, permitted, with many prescriptions reflecting taboos and beliefs that are more visceral than logical.

All of this daily life is driven by collectively held theories of what is appropriate, desirable or 'normal' for human beings. Such determinations rest on accumulated beliefs about human psychology. They reflect a view that human nature is a certain way and not another.

In short, the very shapes and structures into which we assemble as human populations reflect prevailing beliefs about how humans do – and should – think, feel and behave.

Our inherent human fascination with what goes on in each other's minds can be inferred from these interactions. These days, with the ubiquity of social media, our psychological curiosity is exhibited instantaneously in digital form, for all the world to see. From Facebook, Twitter and Instagram, to TikTok, WeChat, Weibo and Baido, to QQ, VK and Cloob, and even to LinkedIn, social media platforms have proven transformatively popular. This is because they offer users a way to tap into the thoughts and feelings of their fellow human beings on a massive scale.

Whenever a celebrity shares their views on a given topic – perhaps a political event, a new product or, most tantalizingly, another celebrity – the chance to experience their inner thoughts on a moment-by-moment basis can, within minutes, grab an audience of literally millions.

It is arguable that our social-media age represents a true turning point for humanity precisely *because* a means has been found by which psychological communion can at last be achieved. Short of telepathy, this is as close our species has ever come to having other people's thoughts and feelings made available on demand.

But despite the availability of free social media, people also pay money to learn other people's psychological perspectives. Some of the bestselling non-fiction books of all time are books about psychological topics. Among these are texts on decision-making, consumer behaviour, evolution and the implications of genetics. Many classics of the genre are self-help or advice books, manuals that formally guide readers towards recommended ways to think, behave and even *feel*.

Even humans who consider themselves utterly uninterested in others will find it hard to live their lives without a functional theory of psychology. Some people relish spending time alone with their thoughts, never having to socialize. However, those thoughts with which they spend their time – the inner monologues with which they talk to themselves – take the form of language, which is a social code.

People cannot think their own thoughts without drawing on a skill that they only learned in the first place so that they could affiliate with others (Hughes, 2019). Thoughts are inherently linguistic, and thus communicative. In this way, thinking is inherently social. Words have meaning only insofar as they mean something to someone else. Having your own thoughts relies on your ability to perceive the thoughts of others.

For every conscious human being, psychology comes naturally.

HISTORY REPEATING ITSELF: SELF-HELP MANUALS

Interest in codified life advice dates back to the earliest days of commercial publishing. One of the first examples was a book called *Self-Help* by Samuel Smiles, a political writer from Scotland. It appeared in 1859, a year that proved to be a good one for publishers: two of the most famous books ever written in English – John Stuart Mill's *On Liberty* (Mill, 1859) and Charles Darwin's *On the Origin of Species* (Darwin, 1859) – also appeared that year. However, while Mill and Darwin are credited with producing masterpieces of scholarly culture, Smiles's work was far more successful commercially.

Self-Help sold more copies than *On Liberty* and *On the Origin of Species* combined. Even Darwin himself bought a copy of Smiles's book. Another purchaser was Sakichi Toyoda, the Japanese inventor whose family business eventually spawned the Toyota Motor Corporation. Toyoda's personal copy of *Self-Help* is now on permanent display at the museum that commemorates his birth site.

Smiles's book offers us a glimpse of how our perceptions of psychological concepts evolve over time. His version of self-help was typical of the nineteenth century, emphasizing hard work and self-sacrifice as keys to human happiness. This seems a far cry from the more gentle approaches of today's self-help gurus, whose booklists are much more likely to feature titles like *The One Minute Manager* (Blanchard & Johnson, 1982) or *Meditations for Men Who Do Too Much* (Lazear, 1992).

Nonetheless, while perspectives on human happiness might shift across time, the human appetite for self-awareness remains.

Once again, the very fact that such perspectives *do* shift – in other words, the fact that with passing time, our understanding of what constitutes a constructive or healthy way of thinking actually *evolves* – is precisely one of the reasons it is so important to consider the history not just of psychology, but of psychological *concepts*.

BUT WHAT EXACTLY IS 'PSYCHOLOGY'?

Indeed. What exactly *is* this thing called 'psychology'? Answering the question is not as straightforward as you might think. 'Psychology' can mean different, but interrelated, things in different contexts.

Nonetheless, to keep things simple for now, we can note that *psychology* is made up of two underlying words: *psycho* and *logy*.

The suffix '-logy' denotes a field of knowledge relating to a given subject matter. Technically, 'logy' comes from the ancient Greek term λογία (or logia in the Roman alphabet), which means 'words' or, more precisely, 'that which has been said'.

In this case, the subject matter is therefore, effectively, *psycho*. In the history of English-language usage, *psycho* derives from the ancient Greek word ψυχή (psūkhḗ), a word that was used to discuss many different concepts. We can say that ψυχή has been used to describe each of the following:

- the state of being alive, of being able to breathe;
- the immortal part of a person that survives physical death (e.g. the 'soul');

- the ghost of a person after their death (e.g. their 'spirit');
- the intangible part of a person where thinking occurs;
- the human capacity for reason;
- the temperament or individual character of a person.

It is important for us to always remember that ancient Greek is a somewhat alien language that developed long before the modern English that exists today. As such, translating ψυχή into English is not easy. However, it seems fair to summarize the overall term 'psychology', at least loosely, as follows:

- knowledge about the mental aspects – that is to say, the *nonphysical* aspects – of human beings.

The nonphysical aspects of human beings have been conceived of in many different ways, and, indeed, this central concept of psychology has changed a lot over time, making a conceptual history of psychology all the more intriguing.

Some textbooks translate ψυχή as 'soul', rather than 'mind', but it would be misleading to suggest that only one satisfactory English-language translation can be used. In addition, defining ψυχή as 'soul' begs the question: What exactly is 'soul'? When engaging in retrospective interpretation, it is always wiser to hedge your bets.

It is perhaps most useful to consider ψυχή as referring to those features of an individual human's life that are not purely physical. Examples of such features include emotions, thoughts, memories, personality traits, tastes, attitudes, aptitudes, mental afflictions and behaviours. Accordingly, all these things are part of what we call 'psychology'.

The *physical-versus-nonphysical* distinction provides a starting point, but clearly it does not explain everything. It sets up an oversimplified dichotomy. After all, some things are *both* physical *and* nonphysical. The study of the human brain, for example, involves many physiological and biochemical processes that are undeniably physical. However, insofar as studying the brain helps to explain some of those nonphysical phenomena – emotion or cognition, for instance – then it counts as a way of 'doing' psychology. Of course, it is also a way of doing neurology or biochemistry – as we will see, scientific and scholarly areas often overlap.

Layers of psychology

There is another way in which the word 'psychology' has multiple meanings. As with many sciences or academic subject areas, the term 'psychology' is frequently applied not just to the 'study of' the issues concerned. It is also used as a word that denotes those very issues themselves.

The word 'psychology' is frequently used to refer to the nonphysical factors that relate to a person or group or activity or situation, in the same way that 'physiology' refers to the physical factors of living beings, or 'chemistry' refers to the way elements and compounds are composed of atoms, molecules and ions.

In this sense, we can talk about ideas like the 'psychology of crowd behaviour', or the 'physiology of molluscs', or the 'chemistry of high-carbon steel'. High-carbon steel 'has' a chemistry, in the sense that it is composed of atoms and molecules. Molluscs 'have' a physiology, in the sense that they are living organisms. And crowd behaviour 'has' a psychology, in the sense that it relates to the nonphysical aspects of what human beings are *like*.

At one time or another, scientists will have conducted detailed and formal research into each of these topics. The relevant specialists – psychologists, physiologists and chemists – will have applied their skills to do so. However, such concepts are part of our world whether or not there are scientists who study them. Molluscs 'have' a physiology *whether or not any physiologist has bothered to look*. High-carbon steel 'has' a chemistry *even if no chemist has ever thought about it*. And crowd behaviour 'has' a psychology, *regardless of whether psychologists have ever said that it does*.

Sometimes a topic will be discussed in culture long before formal investigations or analyses have been pursued. For example, before there were any modern scientific studies of crowd behaviour, there were many ideas about how people's behaviour in crowds differed from their behaviour in isolation. In the fifth century CE, the Greek playwright Euripides (480–406 BCE) made the unique social dynamics of crowd behaviour a crucial plot-point in several of his plays, once noting that 'a packed crowd of wise men is weaker than an inferior mind with sole authority' (Schwab, 2011).

The accumulated human wisdom concerning the psychology of crowd behaviour should not be ignored when thinking about the formal scientific study of crowds by modern psychologists (a field that began to take shape in the mid-twentieth century). For one thing, the ways in which crowd behaviour was described, depicted and deciphered in everyday culture will have shaped the starting beliefs of those modern researchers. They will also have influenced how those psychological findings would have been interpreted by readers, and perhaps even whether are believed by policymakers.

Irrespective of whether research is done by psychologists in psychology departments or published in psychology journals, human culture will accumulate knowledge on a wide range of psychological topics. Unlike chemistry or physiology, however, this accumulated knowledge will bear directly on how human society functions, and on how humans lead their lives.

In essence, psychology will exist with or without psychologists.

Psychology as a field of knowledge, about psychology, known by psychologists

It is useful to remember that all words are after-the-fact labels concocted by human culture to describe entities that may or may not exist. It is difficult to reflect on a concept, or to study it, until there is at least a *word* for it. Therefore, when words are first invented, the concepts they refer to are often only loosely understood. Their precise dimensions become clear only over time, as knowledge about them is accumulated. The implication of this is that, ironically, words *can often be a poor guide* to what people are actually talking about!

'Psychology' is a case in point. 'Psychology' is an example of a word that was adopted in order to talk about something that was at first only vaguely identified. Meaning was refined gradually as consensus about meaning emerged.

In any given era, people who used the term understood, generally, what was being referred to. However, its inherent latitude often meant the word could be used to refer to a number of different, but overlapping, concepts, allowing its definition to evolve over time. The word 'psychology' has ended up having quite different meanings at different times, exhibiting what linguists some-times refer to as *semantic shift*.

As outlined above, in its modern usage (in English), the word 'psychology' is commonly employed to denote *both*:

(a) the nonphysical factors that relate to people and groups; *and*
(b) the body of knowledge that has been accumulated, formally and informally, with regard to those factors.

As the latter use of the term involves a *body of knowledge*, it requires people to do the *knowing*.

Accordingly, you could say that 'psychology' is the body of knowledge *about* psychology, as known by psychologists.

The distinction between 'psychology' in the first sense – *a set of topics* – and in the second sense – *a body of knowledge* about those topics – is important. This is because sometimes commen-tators argue that 'psychology' in the first sense doesn't really count. An implication of this is that we shouldn't talk about the 'history of psychology' unless we are referring to *the body of knowledge about psychology as it is known by psychologists*.

A related perspective is that 'psychology' can hardly be said to exist if people do not *say* that it exists, or if people do not use the word 'psychology' (or an equivalent) in that particular sense. This raises a question akin to the old riddle about a tree falling in a forest with no one around to hear it. 'Does it make a sound?' the riddle asks.

Can we say that psychology existed before people actually started to refer to it by name?

IS PSYCHOLOGY MODERN OR ANCIENT?

For some historians of psychology, it is pointless to talk about 'psychology' as existing before the eighteenth or nineteenth centuries. According to this view, the eighteenth century was when the topic of psychology began to be mentioned by scholars, paving the way for the concept to be taught in (Western) universities. Before that, nobody in the world talked about psychology as a field of study per se. Like the tree alone in the forest that is deemed not to have made a sound, psychology was absent from human awareness and so is deemed not to have existed. If nobody alive *perceived* it as existing before the 1800s, the argument goes, then it is folly for historians of psychology to talk about it as if it were there all along.

The German-born South African historian of psychology Kurt Danziger is a proponent of such a view, and possibly its most famous advocate. Danziger has written extensively about how the subject of psychology – 'in the modern sense' – was constructed across the 1700s and 1800s. He identifies two trends as being important in this regard.

Firstly, scholars began to group together a set of concepts and problems that previously had been studied by a disparate range of unconnected philosophers and physiologists. Secondly, a number of formal research practices that had been developed for other sciences were then adapted to suit the study of these psychological issues (Danziger, 1990).

Danziger argues that, until these trends emerged, there was no domain of knowledge that could be referred to as 'psychology'. While there were 'theological, philosophical, moral, rhetorical, medical, aesthetic, [and] political categories' of interest, there were 'no psychological categories' of knowledge per se (Danziger, 1997, p. 37). As such, he argues that the appropriate historical timeline of psychology should be seen as beginning with 'its institutionalisation as a modern discipline' (Danziger, 2013, p. 830).

Among the reasons Danziger offers for this view are:

(a) the study of psychological topics lacked an 'identifiable conceptual unity' prior to the eighteenth century;

(b) the modern forms of empirical and experimental science used to study psychological topics did not become prevalent until then; and

(c) professional structures for psychology, such as learned societies and, especially, university psychology departments, had not been established before this time.

In other words, psychology did not exist until recent times. According to Danziger, therefore, any discussion of the history of psychology as predating the eighteenth century is historically flawed – notwithstanding the fact that, by giving historians more to write about, the antiquarian approach seems 'welcome in the well-established introductory textbook market' (Danziger, 2013).

Fortunately, not all historians of psychology are satisfied with this assessment.

Psychology is ancient

For many historians of psychology – and perhaps the majority – psychology really is a field of great antiquity. The process of using reason and evidence to build defensible knowledge about psychological concepts can be seen across several very old intellectual traditions. Such approaches predate modern scientific methods and are traceable to ancient times. Most importantly, they coalesce thematically in a recurring way, allowing us – perhaps *compelling* us – to discuss them in terms of a coherent inclusive history.

A leading proponent of this view has been the American historian of psychology Daniel N. Robinson. According to figures like Robinson, psychology has been part of intellectual culture since the earliest human civilizations (D. N. Robinson, 1989).

For example, in the fourth century BCE, the Greek philosopher Aristotle (384–322 BCE) wrote considered treatises that sought to explain emotions, personality, consciousness, cognitions and the nature–nurture debate. The Classical Greek philosophers did not just speculate about the human condition, they were methodical in their approach, advising caution when facts were unavailable (D. N. Robinson, 2013).

Similar discipline was apparent with other intellectual traditions. In ancient Chinese philosophy, for example, the third-century BCE philosopher Xun Kuang (荀況; 310–235 BCE) taught that human temperaments should be studied as a part of nature, and that the exercise should be informed by empiricism rather than by superstition (D. B. King, Viney & Woody, 2009).

In short, for as long as there have been humans curious enough to investigate the natural world, there have been humans using those same intellectual methods to evaluate psychological experience.

The modernist fallacy

Scholars such as Robinson are not convinced by the Danziger view that the history of psychology dates only from the eighteenth century. They are unswayed by Danziger's three main arguments regarding the absence of conceptual unity in antiquarian psychology, the emergence of scientific experimentalism, and the importance of psychology's institutionalization in universities (e.g. D. N. Robinson, 2013).

Firstly, while it is reasonable to claim that psychology lacked 'conceptual unity' before the eighteenth century, it is wrong to imply that this disunity is decisive. In other words, the statement is true but moot. Lots of sciences were conceptually fragmented throughout most of their histories. In many respects, they continue to be fragmented today. The fact that psychology lacked conceptual unity for most of its history does not differentiate it from other sciences. Nor does it disqualify it from existing.

In any event, 'conceptual unity' is a somewhat vague notion. What exactly *is* conceptual unity? There is a danger that terms like *conceptual* and *unity* can be interpreted arbitrarily in order to make whatever case you wish. But on the face of it, few sciences can easily be said to possess true unity in conceptual terms.

Science is far more diverse than you might think. Contrary to the common belief that there are a relatively small number of different sciences, analyses of the scientific research literature suggest that there are in fact very many. According to one such analysis, modern science comprises around 200 different clusters, or silos, of free-standing research activity (Leydesdorff & Rafols, 2009). Each silo contains a global community of scientists who collaborate intensively among themselves, who meticulously read and cite each other's works, but who largely ignore the work that goes on in all the other silos.

For example, physicists who conduct research in the area of optics rarely have cause to cite the work of physicists who conduct research in astronomy. Optics and astronomy thrive as separate scientific communities, and both optics scientists and astronomers consider themselves to be 'physicists'. Both communities adhere to common assumptions about the scientific method (such as the value of empiricism) and the nature of the universe (such as the distinction between what is real and what is imaginary), but then so do most psychologists. Logic and reality are concepts that 'unify' all sciences.

The point here is not that physics and psychology are the same. Optics researchers and astronomers arguably have more in common than, say, psychoanalysts and neuroscientists.

The point here is that the existence of a wide range of target subjects, theoretical models, key concepts, investigatory methods, desired applications – or communities of scholars who act and interact more or less independently of each other – does not deprive a field of unity to an extent *that negates its very existence.*

Moreover, the claim that psychology somehow acquired a critical form of 'conceptual unity' in the eighteenth century is also a bit confusing. This is because such a claim implies that psychology will have enjoyed this 'conceptual unity' ever since. In reality, as we will go on to see, psychology has been – and remains – a highly disparate and fragmented field. If anything, its current range of subfields and specialisms is far more disparate, complex and internally diverse than it was in the 1700s.

Some psychologists work with fundamental ideas, or paradigms, that are entirely incompatible with the ideas used by psychologists in other subfields (Hughes, 2018a). It is true that this fragmentation threatens to undermine psychology's claim to be a strong science, and we will return to this issue later. However, for now, the most important point is that this fragmentation – this lack of conceptual unity – is very much a present-day problem. It seems therefore wrong to suggest that psychology became 'conceptually unified' back in the eighteenth century, or indeed at any subsequent time.

For similar reasons, the argument that there was no 'psychology' until there were modern forms of empirical and experimental science is also unsatisfying. The counterargument is of a similar structure to before. Firstly, it is in fact wrong to say that there was no scientific experimentation until the eighteenth century. As Robinson points out, Archimedes had cause to shout 'Eureka!' long before then (D. N. Robinson, 2013). And secondly, the implication that all of *today's* psychology is based on such 'modern' forms is simply incorrect. Much of today's psychology is non-experimental. Quite a bit of it is non-empirical. (Indeed, some modern psychologists are avowedly *anti*-experimental, and even anti-empirical.)

Areas such as qualitative research, discourse analysis, idiographic methods, philosophical psychology, psychoanalysis, phenomenological psychology and critical psychology are all non-experimental forms of scholarship. They might be seen as minority pursuits, but each is uncontroversially part of orthodox psychology. If modern non-experimental approaches are included as part of psychology today, then why should we exclude those non-experimental forms of psychology that predated modern experimentalism (D. N. Robinson, 2013)? Why should we make experimentalism a precondition for recognizing psychology's historical starting point?

Finally, the argument that psychology cannot have existed at all before it existed in institutions also seems unconvincing. Linking the birth of psychology to its academic professionalization seems to equate intellectual culture with bureaucracy. It also begs the question: if the field did not exist until the required professional structures were established, then what exactly did the founders think they were establishing those structures *for*? Why would you decide to open a university psychology department if there was no such thing as 'psychology'? How could you form a learned society for a subject area that didn't exist?

In one sense, the Danziger case seems to rest on a favourable definition of terms. So long as psychology is *defined* as a field that exhibits an eighteenth-century conceptual structure, *defined* as experimental, and *defined* as institutional, then you can sustain the argument that psychology did not truly exist before these criteria were fulfilled. The argument is true by definition, and so is effectively not an argument at all. It is an assertion.

Robinson points out that the weakness in the assertion is apparent from the phrase Danziger uses to make the case. Danziger talks repeatedly about psychology 'in the modern sense'. This specification – 'in the modern sense' – is the problem. It reduces Danziger's claim to a tautology: 'Psychology in the modern sense is *modern*.'

While Robinson's own arguments have attracted some rebuttals (e.g. Brock, 2014), it would appear that the Danziger view involves a certain degree of circularity. There is no compulsion on historians of psychology to restrict themselves to the study of psychology 'in the modern sense', just as there is no compulsion on historians of any other area to restrict themselves to modern events.

As outlined above, the majority of historians recognize that psychology has been an object of human attention since the earliest civilizations. Psychology 'in the *non*-modern sense' is as legitimate to consider. In fact, it would be difficult to properly appreciate the significance of psychology 'in the modern sense' without considering its historical context.

This, after all, is what history is *for*.

The hazard of false lineage

The debate about when psychology did or did not come to exist is borne out of a concern over historical continuity. In the eighteenth century, Italian philosopher Giambattista Vico (1668–1744 CE) warned of 'scholastica successionis civitatium', or *the error of scholarly succession*. This error arises when historians falsely presume that a modern idea owes an intellectual debt to an older one.

For example, if a modern psychologist develops a theory of behaviour that historians say resembles a theory that was popular in ancient Rome, it may be tempting to conclude that the psychologist was familiar with the antiquarian view. However, if the psychologist was actually *unaware* of the original idea, then such a historical explanation would be inaccurate. It would represent an error of scholarly succession.

Public domain, via Wikimedia Commons / {PD-US}

Image 1.1   Ivan Pavlov

Sometimes scholars and scientists develop the same 'new' ideas at different times. Who ultimately gets the credit can result from cultural privilege, historical timeliness or even chance.

For example, in the early twentieth century, the Russian physiologist Ivan Pavlov (1849–1936) was acclaimed for identifying the behavioural concept of *classical conditioning*, in which a person or animal learns to produce a biologically natural response whenever they perceive a neutral stimulus. Famously, Pavlov demonstrated that dogs could be trained to drool at the sound of a bell, by teaching the dogs to associate the sound of the bell with the smell of food. This demonstration is so famous that the idea of 'Pavlov's dog' has become something of a modern-day meme, figurative shorthand for any situation where a person is trained to respond by reflex to a simple prompt.

However, while the Oxford English Dictionary now offers the word 'Pavlovian' to describe such conditioning, Pavlov was not, in fact, the first person to record the concept. An American physiologist published data that demonstrated classical conditioning a year before Pavlov. An Austrian physiologist did so a decade before that. A fellow Russian physician referred to it in the 1880s. In fact, mainstream physiologists appear to have been talking about classical conditioning throughout the nineteenth century. And some scholars even suggest that the French physician François Rabelais (1483–1553) described classical conditioning, in thorough detail, as far back as in the sixteenth century (Jarius & Wildemann, 2017).

Older variations of classical conditioning were often presented in less accessible academic formats. For example, Rabelais's sixteenth-century work was not only written in French, at a time when most serious Western scholarship was written in Latin, he also couched his ideas within some wide-ranging literary outputs. Even though he was a physician and a professor of anatomy, his explanation of classical conditioning was presented as part of a satirical novel. It was embedded in tales of fantastical characters, surrounded by scatological humour and bizarre expletives (the College de la Sorbonne decided to censor much of the work on the grounds of its obscenity).

We should remember that the methods by which scientists and scholars promote their ideas have varied considerably over the centuries. Intellectual work did not always flow as freely as it can do today. Indeed, the idea of the 'information age', in which the circulation of information became a driver of social evolution, is very much a late-twentieth-century concept. While it is true that universities, in particular, have maintained a type of global knowledge-sharing cooperative for a very long time, it has had many limitations for most of its history. We should not assume that the way knowledge is produced and circulated today is directly comparable to how it was produced and circulated in the past.

Pavlov's questionable status is consistent with what American mathematician Stephen Stigler (1941–) has called the 'law of eponymy' (Stigler, 1980): that virtually no scientific discovery ever comes to be named after, or associated with, its original discoverer. The fact that Pavlov is credited with identifying classical conditioning is at least partly due to the culture of academia that existed during his lifetime. The social context in which he found himself empowered him to share his insights, whereas his predecessors simply did not have the same opportunities. They published similar ideas, but their circumstances were very different. Their theories evaporated upon contact with obscurity, slipping into an intellectual abyss.

In the same way, according to some critics, psychology should not be described as if it can trace an unbroken intellectual lineage back to antiquity. The fact that ancient scholars, such as Aristotle, discussed issues that *resemble* the issues discussed in modern psychology does not, in and of itself, constitute proof of heritage.

Different people can have the same ideas at different times. Modern thinkers can be entirely uninfluenced by their ancient predecessors, and even unaware of their work. They might develop their modern ideas all by themselves.

Similarities to previous ideas could simply be coincidental.

LOGOPHILIA: 'ADUMBRATIONISM'

Adumbrationism is the retrospective attribution of an idea or insight to an original work that was not actually intended by the author of the work. The problem of adumbration can arise when historians attempt to identify insights about modern concepts in ancient literatures. Sometimes, an ancient scholar might provide an explanation of a concept that resembles a modern concept, but does so by coincidence. Presuming the ancient scholar to have had knowing foresight about the concept would be a mistake.

ALMOST FAMOUS: EDWIN TWITMYER

Edwin B. Twitmyer (1873–1943) was the American scholar who reported data on classical conditioning a full year before Ivan Pavlov presented his now-famous findings. That Pavlov is credited as the person who made the discovery is likely related to the fact that he was already an esteemed scholar when he published his work in 1903, presenting the findings at a high-profile international conference in Madrid. By contrast, Twitmyer was still a PhD student at the University of Pennsylvania when his own data were recorded a year earlier, in 1902.

Twitmyer included his findings in a doctoral dissertation. His thesis focused on the knee-jerk reflex (also commonly referred to as the patellar reflex) and, especially, on the way emotions can interfere with the response. Twitmyer collected data from volunteers who attended his laboratory. In order to collect the data, he devised an apparatus that would tap each volunteer just below the knee, thereby eliciting a knee-jerk reflex. When it became apparent that his unsuspecting volunteers were getting alarmed at the way the apparatus would suddenly strike their leg without warning, he added a feature where a bell would ring just beforehand to let them know the apparatus was about to engage. Eventually, Twitmyer discovered that for participants who had undergone the procedure several times, ringing the bell on its *own* would actually elicit the knee-jerk response. He had successfully conditioned the reflex.

A year later, when Pavlov presented evidence for the very same conditioning effect, it was met with great acclaim. But when Twitmyer submitted his work at a local conference of the American Psychological Association, he was given an unfavourable late-afternoon speaking slot (not unusual for a PhD student) and, after his presentation, nobody in the audience asked any questions. Twitmyer's lowly professional status ensured that his groundbreaking insight went unnoticed.

Pavlov's personal fame ensured wide visibility for all of his ideas, and almost immediately his version of classical conditioning was the one to be acclaimed and popularized. Even though Twitmyer had recorded his findings a full year before Pavlov, it was Pavlov who, in 1904, was awarded the Nobel Prize for the 'discovery' of classical conditioning.

Depressed at the lack of interest in his experiments, Twitmyer did not conduct any further research into conditioning (Irwin, 1943). Instead, he pursued a career of relative academic obscurity, teaching clinical psychology students in Pennsylvania until his death in 1943.

HISTORY AS DISTINCT FROM HISTORIANS

According to British historian of psychology Graham Richards, 'no discipline calling itself Psychology existed prior to the mid-nineteenth century' (G. Richards, 2010, p. 20). Such an observation puts a lot of store in linguistics.

We might also note that no discipline calling itself Telephony existed prior to 1876, the year Alexander Graham Bell was awarded a patent for an 'apparatus for transmitting vocal or other sounds telegraphically'. It would seem odd, however, to suggest that historians of telephony should omit Bell's work from their consideration.

The fact that a particular word is or is not used as the name for a discipline seems peripheral to determining matters of historical relevance. The fact that 'no discipline calling itself Psychology existed prior to the mid-nineteenth century' tells us something about how and when academic psychology became organized into a bureaucracy. But the history of psychology is distinct from the history of technical nomenclature, professional guilds or university departments.

An irony with this is that many of the historians of psychology who caution against historical overreach are concerned about the matter of *presentism*. This is the habit of incorporating anachronistically modern notions into an explanation of history. Scholars are guilty of presentism whenever they describe past events using modern frames of reference. Examples of presentism include the following:

- *Hindsight bias:* This is where the outcomes of past events are discussed as more predictable than they really were, and so people's decisions are unfairly judged on the basis of the desirability of those outcomes. We display hindsight bias when we blame entire societies for failing to foresee the rise of despots or the devastating consequences of war. For one thing, this falsely implies that today's societies are somehow wiser and, thus, less likely to make similar 'mistakes'.
- *Survivor bias:* This is where a history is shaped by people who thrive enough to become educated or to otherwise participate in the recording of events. We display survivor bias when we focus our historical accounts on successful groups in the population, while ignoring the experiences of the less privileged. This can skew history by making successes, such as scientific breakthroughs, look easier than they really are.
- *Affluence bias:* This is where the past is evaluated without regard to the fact that most human societies lived in what would now be seen as dire economic and cultural poverty. In the absence of material prosperity, and without access to technology, entire societies were organized in ways that allowed them to survive very harsh realities that would be seen as intolerable today. We display affluence bias when we depict traditional communities as somehow primitive or underdeveloped, and contrast them with today's (Western) living in ways that suggest a form of cultural advancement or 'progress' has been achieved.
- *Moral relativism:* This is where historical developments are evaluated on the basis of contemporary standards of moral behaviour. We display moral relativism when we assume that past behaviours that would today be classed as immoral are infused with malevolent intent. For instance, many early researchers exhibited attitudes that would today be considered unambiguously racist. However, in many historical societies, such attitudes, while truly causing enormous human misery, were often shaped more by ignorance than by hostility.

The irony is that, in their effort to avoid presentism, the historians who say that psychology is a purely modern thing often seem to fall into an intellectual trap. Psychology 'in the modern sense' is used as the benchmark against which the relevance of historical forerunners is to be judged. They discuss psychology not in terms of its existence at a particular time, but only insofar as how it compares with the psychology we have today.

Moreover, these historians seem less concerned with whether psychology truly exists in the world (independently of psychologists), and more interested in how psychology is depicted in human affairs. In warning against cultural bias, they rely on a cultural construct. It is as though the way psychology is *talked about* (by the European or American academic mainstream) determines whether or not it is a coherent subject worthy of historical review.

For example, these historians attach considerable importance to the label-word 'psychology'. Some attempt to distinguish 'psychology' from 'Psychology' (e.g. G. Richards, 2010), where 'little-p' psychology refers to the *subject matter*, while the 'big-P' version refers to the *discipline that studies that subject matter*. One problem with this approach is that there are more than two senses in which the term 'psychology' is used (a third sense, for example, is in 'psychology' the *profession*).

A more perplexing problem is that the distinction is heavily grounded in the English language. The nuances of little-p and big-P psychology do not apply easily to other tongues (such as German, in which *all* nouns begin with a capital letter). This is important to bear in mind when we recall that English is just one of 7,000 current human languages (Clingingsmith, 2017). It is spoken natively by fewer than half the number of people who speak Mandarin Chinese.

The reality is that presentism cuts both ways. It is true that modern ideas do not always apply easily to past contexts. However, it is also a mistake to assume that the present is disconnected from the past. The idea that older scholarship might not count as true psychology (or Psychology) because it does not adhere to a modern definition of what such an academic subject area should look like is itself a form of presentism. The human endeavour to explain psychological concepts has taken different forms at different times, and the way we 'do' psychology today might offer some clues about how we have done it before. But the way we do it today is not the only way to do it.

Writing history is not easy. History is always, by its nature, a *social construction*. It is a narrative written in modern times that is agreed, by some, to represent a useful explanation of the past. There is no complete, contemporaneously compiled record of universal human experience. Therefore, all historical works are incomplete in their coverage, partial in their perspective, interpreted under the influence of contemporary norms, and cobbled together retrospectively with varying degrees of corroboration.

There is no one true history, and historical consensus should be viewed with caution. History should be expected to be cacophony, not chorus.

Historiographically speaking

The process of producing history – the methods and strategies by which histories are investigated, assembled and interpreted – is known as *historiography*. As we can see, historiography is not an exact process. History is not just a chronology of past occurrences. Nor is it a self-serving story inspired by real events. Historiography is partly empirical and partly explanatory (D. B. King et al., 2009). It involves both investigation and interpretation. As well as science, it is art.

As with all forms of scholarship, historiography is improved when it is objective. However, objectivity is a matter of degree rather than kind; it is not an all-or-nothing concept. No matter how much we aspire for history to be written objectively, there will always be a subjective dimension. Objectivity is something that can be attempted but never fully achieved.

Presentism is one form of unavoidable subjectivity. Even though the documents and records scrutinized by a historian might originate from the distant past, the synthesising of their implications into a 'history' will take place in the present. As such, the perspective of the present is unavoidable. The best thing for a historian to do is to acknowledge the effects of presentism, and to make a comprehensive effort to interpret and explain its influence. A naïve course of action would be to imagine oneself as unassailably objective and immune to the presentism bias, or to pretend that presentism doesn't really matter.

Psychologically, our ability to extract meaning from experience or observation is fraught with different kinds of error. At a basic level of logic and reasoning, human beings are prone to use a variety of mental shortcuts, or *cognitive heuristics*, when piecing things together. One example is confirmation bias. This is our habit of focusing on evidence that supports our prior beliefs, while paying insufficient attention to equally valid information that might suggest our prior beliefs are mistaken. All humans – including all historians – are liable to be lulled by confirmation bias much of the time, especially where they make no conscious effort to avoid it.

A large body of psychological research has shown how cognitive biases affect human decision-making and our interpretations of events. For example, they can influence how historians make sense of the past from the perspective of the present.

Psychological research also highlights how we are inclined to extract more meaning from what we see and hear than is justified by the facts. Often we have access to just a fragment of what is relevant. Nonetheless, we are quick to recognize patterns where they exist. Sometimes we recognize patterns where they do not exist. We interpret random sequences to be meaningful, and unconnected events to be intertwined. This feature of human perception is called *pareidolia*, and it accounts for most cases of misperception (such as optical illusions or false memories). It is as though our brains are overly tuned to detect patterns, and resultingly prone to derive meaningful narratives from events that are, in effect, meaningless.

When considering history, there is always a strong temptation to describe centuries' worth of events as though they belong to a single plotline or narrative. We tend to interpret events as reflecting a kind of historical logic, as if they relate to an inherent order in the passage of time (Hughes, 2019). We are intolerant of randomness. We dislike the idea that history might be, in the words of British historian Herbert Butterfield, 'just one bloody thing after another' (Hytner, 2004).

History as storytelling

Historians often choose to interpret events in terms of *metanarratives*. This means that history is construed as reflecting some comprehensive overarching theory about the nature of the human world and how all its events unfold.

HISTORICALLY (IN)ACCURATE?: CONDEMNED TO REPETITION

There are many reasons to study history, but one of the most frequently cited justifications is that doing so helps us to avoid making the same mistakes over and over again. In this regard, a quotation by American philosopher George Santayana (1863–1952) has become particularly famous. In his treatise on philosophy, *The Life of Reason: The Phases of Human Progress* (1905), Santayana states: 'Those who cannot remember the past are condemned to repeat it' (p. 284). This sentence is often used to argue that a poor understanding of history will inevitably lead humanity into a pattern of recurring error. Famously, a version of the statement appears on an inscription at the Auschwitz concentration camp. Its lesson seems to be that ignoring history can have disastrous consequences for the world.

However, Santayana's aphorism is not so clear-cut. It is very frequently misquoted, sometimes in ways that cloud its exact meaning. In *The Life of Reason*, Santayana uses the statement to describe how the human capacity for logic is addled by deficient remembering at different times. Babies are unable to learn from experience, and, because 'old age is as forgetful as youth', the elderly too become inattentive to their surroundings and incorrigibly repetitious in their thoughts.

In contrast, the rephrased versions of Santayana's warning are often intended to emphasize the specific problem of historical ignorance. For example,

when extolling the advantages of studying the history of psychology, a number of textbooks have rendered his advice as 'Those who do not know history are doomed to repeat it' (Thomas, 2007). Replacing 'cannot remember' with 'do not know' and changing 'the past' to 'history' both alter the meaning of the statement. The emphasis is now on the wilful ignoring of historians, rather than on the parlous nature of memory.

The fact that *precisely the same rephrasing* appears across multiple textbooks suggests that authors may have relied on a single inaccurate source (Thomas, 2007). The commonness of this particular misquotation highlights how misinformation can seep into our historical record and, in the process, distort our understanding of old ideas.

The claim that ignoring history leads humanity to repeat its mistakes might seem at first to be wise counsel. However, there is a downside. The assertion implies that simply *being aware* of history will somehow *prevent* humanity from repeating its errors. This idea is something of a conceit. History itself shows us that many historically literate societies – countries with a very keen interest in their past, for example – frequently find themselves mired in crises that they have experienced several times before. Simply being aware of history does not inoculate a population against the likelihood of repeating its mistakes.

One example of this is the Marxist metanarrative, where human affairs are described as conforming to the predictions of Marxist theory. From a Marxist perspective, historical periods such as the European Reformation or the Industrial Revolution can always be better understood if considered in a Marxist way. The theory predicts endless cycles of social and economic upheaval where capitalism is initially embraced but ultimately found to be self-defeating, thereby creating periodic crises for global structures of ownership, production and political governance.

One of the more common metanarratives in historical storytelling is the 'Great Man theory', named after terms used by nineteenth-century Scottish philosopher Thomas Carlyle (1795–1881). This approach describes history in terms of prominent characters and their impacts on events (Carlyle, 1841). These characters are seen as benefiting from superior intellect, heroic courage, divine inspiration and good breeding. In addition, as the terminology suggests, they are usually men.

Image 1.2 'The Great Man Theory' depicts history as a series of successes by heroic figures such as Napoleon Bonaparte (painting by Jacques-Louis David, on display at the Musée National de Malmaison et Bois-Préau, France).

When historical accounts are handed down through the generations in the form of folklore, they usually take the form of the Great Man theory. For many centuries, virtually all human histories were written in this way.

The problems with the Great Man approach are many. Apart from the in-built sexism (presumably, history can be influenced by great women too), there is the problem of presuming that historical events are ever 'caused' by individuals. In reality, such events are usually shaped by several people, most of whom never achieve name recognition in the eyes of future generations.

For example, the moon landing of 1969 is often described as an important landmark of human history. The American astronaut Neil Armstrong has certainly achieved name recognition in the eyes of future generations, having been the first human being ever to walk on the lunar surface. However, when reflecting on how profound this moment was, it seems reasonable to ask whether Armstrong himself did anything particularly historical. For sure, he walked on the moon. However, had he not been available, another astronaut would have been deployed in his place.

Surely, the achievement of the first moon landing was the fact that human beings – *other* human beings – had developed a means to get him there. Hundreds, if not thousands, of other people had worked in various ways to make it happen. As well as the scientists and administrators working for NASA, there were the policymakers and educators who shaped their work. The social context of the time – where the United States competed against the Soviet Union in what was to become known as the Space Race – was also critical. The Space Race was propelled not just by science, but also by politics. It was part of the Cold War, itself an after-effect of the Second World War, and thus the consequence of emerging irredentist nationalism in European states, the proliferation of military technologies, the development of novel political systems and theories, and many other factors (we will further discuss the impact of the Cold War in Chapter 8).

All in all, the moon landing of 1969 reflected a confluence of technological developments, political dynamics and social pressures, and was itself a transitory moment within a longer series of cultural events that is arguably continuing to this day – all of which have had very little to do with Neil Armstrong and his life or achievements. Characterizing Armstrong as a key figure might help us to describe the moon landing in the form of a dramatic story. However, in doing so, it also serves to *distract* us from fully understanding the significance of the moon landing in the context of human history, and how – or why – it happened.

Individuals can only 'make' history if they have the opportunity to do so, if they are in the right place, and if they live at a time when their activities and skills are relevant. Therefore, as explanations of history, all Great Man (or 'Great Person') theories miss the point. History is multicausal and context-dependent. Opportunity, place and time have to be 'great' too (assuming we leave aside the question of whether 'greatness' is an appropriate quality to describe any human happening).

Today, the Great Man approach is often described as obsolete. However, perhaps it is not as obsolete as is commonly suggested. In the history of science – and, in particular, the history of psychology – developments are frequently discussed in relation to the work of individual scientists and innovators, figures who are typically identified, and acclaimed, by name.

The gallery of 'great' figures in psychology contains names that will be familiar to all psychology students: the likes of James, Wundt, Freud, Piaget, Watson, Maslow, Rogers and Skinner. Historical figures loom large, and yet all their achievements are as much the product of circumstance as they are of individual greatness.

When history focuses on the achievements of great figures who work within the field, we sometimes refer to this type of historiography as *internalist*. By contrast, historiography that considers the wider social and cultural context as primary driving forces is referred to as *externalist*. Many historians will argue that not only is externalism superior to internalism, but that internalism is always wrong.

Another important notion is that of the *Zeitgeist*, a term derived from German, which refers to the characteristic spirit or mood of a particular historical period. It is sometimes argued that the opportunity for individuals to affect history depends on the prevailing Zeitgeist. The fashions and fads of a particular era might, or might not, create the circumstances necessary for historical events to happen. However, many historians disapprove of this term. They believe that talk of Zeitgeists could be interpreted as a form of predeterminism. This is the idea that certain historical events are inevitable, and thus that history is subject to 'hidden' forces that cause these events to happen, regardless of who is alive at the time.

While often presented as an alternative to the Great Man theory, the idea of Zeitgeists could be just another way of portraying history as a heroic narrative. It describes human ingenuity as a force that consistently liberates humanity from the restraining shackles of ignorance. Knowledge and sophistication are seen as triumphing over primitivism and callowness. The 'Dark Ages' are supplanted by 'The Enlightenment'. Any or all suffering faced by humanity will be worth it in the end, because the beneficence of the human spirit will eventually shine through.

Getting better all the time

Another common metanarrative is that of *linear progression*. According to this perspective, human history is an experience of continuous technological, cultural and social improvement. It is believed that humanity is inclined towards learning from the past, building upon existing knowledge, and benefiting from prior intellectual investment. This metanarrative also assumes that human beings are motivated to seek their own comfort, are naturally innovative and curious, and are somewhat altruistic.

In historiography, the linear progress narrative is sometimes referred to as 'Whig history', a term named after the early-twentieth-century British Whig political movement (Butterfield, 1931). The Whigs espoused a philosophy of displacing traditional power structures and replacing them with more democratic ones. The power of this historical narrative is reflected in the way political figures have sought to commandeer it. The Chinese revolutionary and leader Mao Zedong (毛泽东; 1893–1976) explicitly demanded that his country's history be written with a linear progress narrative, declaring that China must 'use the past to serve the present' (Chen, 2010, p. 206).

Some political historians use a psychological argument to support their Whig worldview. They believe that human styles of behaviour and thought are naturally productive and guarantee societal improvement over time. People's tendencies to learn from experience, their drive to always seek out ways to be comfortable, and their innate sense of altruism are said to yield a net benefit for humanity. Within political systems, it is argued, these psychological attributes encourage a natural yearning for democracy; undemocratic societies, therefore, are inherently unstable and doomed to eventual decay. According to this metanarrative, the spread of democracy, with its associated 'free-doms', to all parts of the world is not just politically inevitable – it is something that represents the climax of history itself.

In the late 1980s, after the fall of the USSR, the American political scientist Francis Fukuyama took this approach to a memorable extreme. Fukuyama suggested that the conclusion of the Cold War marked 'the end point of mankind's ideological evolution and the universalisation of Western liberal democracy as the final form of human government' (Fukuyama, 1989, p. 4). He famously proclaimed that these events had brought about 'the end of history'.

The linear progress hypothesis is sometimes employed by psychologists too. Some psychologists concur that humankind has experienced a trajectory of continuous betterment, with fewer people living in misery, danger or ill health today than during any past period (e.g. Pinker, 2011). The case made is that while human nature does not inherently change over time, the cumulative cognitive effects of civilization shape society and culture in pacifying ways and lead to a decline in malevolence and violence.

The problems with the Whig approach are both empirical and ethical. Empirically, as no history contains a complete account of past events, there will almost always be some missing counterexamples to contradict any narrative. The risk is that Whig historians are guilty of cherry-picking – of selecting particular examples that suit their narrative well and ignoring or discounting those that fit it poorly.

Because of the perils of confirmation bias, a historian in this situation might not even recognize a particular counterexample as being relevant. For example, histories arguing that humanity is becoming less violent over time tend to rely on a narrow definition of violence. They overlook the way contemporary power structures produce shorter life expectancies and greater physical misery for much of the world's socio-economically deprived populations. The fact that this system-generated suffering is built into today's social structures could be said to represent a modern expression of collective callousness that has displaced older methods of violence. Its deadly consequences for the world's poor are not captured by psychologists' analyses of battlefield deaths or murders (e.g. Laws, 2012). In essence, therefore, the empirical problem with the linear progress narrative is *presentism*.

The ethical problem is that Whig narratives portray history in terms of winners and losers in a way that is factually questionable, but nonetheless consequential. When peace and happiness are deemed to be the products of intellectual advancement, it implies that strife and sadness must be signs of intellectual deficiency. Many parts of the world are war-torn, conflict-riven or politically unstable. The Whig narrative implies that such places are primitive and unenlightened. In reality, however, the evidence for linear progress has been widely challenged (e.g. Lewis & Lewis, 2017), and, in any event, human beings are rarely personally responsible for the political histories that they live through. It is therefore ethically dubious to blame the people who live in problem-riven societies for somehow lacking the attributes necessary to become advanced.

The ethical implications of Whiggism are not confined to academia. Politicians too frequently criticize their geopolitical adversaries by declaring entire countries, or cultures, to be backward, underdeveloped, and unsophisticated. Such dismissals serve to delegitimize the humanity of the people who live in these places. It is a form of victim-blaming, a way of holding the downtrodden responsible for their own plight. Whiggism provides the powerful and wealthy with a coping strategy to help them avoid the guilt that might otherwise arise from their many privileges.

In psychology, the Whig narrative conspicuously fails to account for the field's replication crisis (Hughes, 2018a). During the past decade, several rigorous studies have revealed a range of problems with psychology's research base, suggesting that, methodologically at least, continuous improvement has been far from assured. In fact, in some key respects, it can be argued that modern research practices promote several forms of continuous *dis*improvement (Smaldino & McElreath, 2016). We will return to this challenge in Chapter 12.

It is perhaps unsurprising that Whig narratives have been especially prevalent in the history of science. After all, science itself is a process of continuous exploration and, we hope, continuous discovery. It seems convincing to imagine that human understanding can only ever go forward, or that scientific bodies of knowledge can only ever be refined. It seems less obvious that understanding might regress, or that a larger volume of knowledge might lead to greater confusion. However, both these eventualities are possible, making the Whig version of history an arbitrary one.

The narrative of continuous linear improvement continues to affect the way we think and talk about our world and our activities. For example, in psychology, it is very common for newer subfields to be discussed as though they are inherently more 'advanced' than older ones, even when they are not. A good example of this is neuroscience. Psychological studies that avail of brain images, or other neuroscientific technologies, are often presumed to represent the cutting edge of psychological science. However, as we will see in Chapter 12, in terms of intellectual depth, these studies are often far simpler than they appear. Their underlying questions, their use of evidence, and the conclusions they draw are often very rudimentary. There is little to suggest that neuroscience – simply by virtue of being *new* – represents a type of science superior to that conducted in other psychological subfields.

The linear progress approach is not the only way to depict historical change. Some historians have instead invoked *declinism* (Zanchetta, 2015), believing that all cultural movements eventually collapse. Others have argued for a *cyclical hypothesis* (Modelski, 1987), where cultural movements gradually rise and fall, and then rise and fall again. Meanwhile, others have argued for a *chaos hypothesis* (Koch, 1969), where historical events follow no identifiable trajectory at all. Any of these frameworks could be applied to the history of psychology.

In summary, historical narratives are arbitrary, and can be said to reflect the preferences and presumptions of the people who decide to write them. However, historical narratives don't just affect the

Alejandro Lecuna / Wikimedia Commons / CC BY-SA 4.0

Image 1.3   Linear progress?
Historians often debate whether today's world really is characterized by less danger, misery and violence than in the past.

HISTORY IN STORIES: *IDIOCRACY* (2006)

Whig history, which posits inevitable improvement in the progress of civilization, represents a common way in which people think about the passage of time. As such, theories that present the opposite scenario – namely, inevitable *dis*improvement in the progress of civilization – can seem striking. This possibility of societal decay has been the inspiration for several artistic works, especially in literature and cinema.

A number of renowned English-language novels have depicted dystopian futures, including *Brave New World* by Aldous Huxley (1932), *Nineteen Eighty-Four* by George Orwell (1949) and *The Handmaid's Tale* by Margaret Atwood (1985). Many dystopian novels have been made into movies.

Indeed, there is a very long cinematic tradition of portraying the different ways in which civilization can decline. Prominent cinematic examples include *Things to Come* (Menzies, 1936), *Planet of the Apes* (Schaffner, 1968), *Blade Runner* (Scott, 1982), *The Hunger Games* (G. Ross, 2012), and *Alita: Battle Angel* (Rodriguez, 2019).

One of the most comprehensive twenty-first-century depictions of anti-Whiggism was the movie *Idiocracy* (Judge, 2006). The story is set 500 years into the future, and shows (American) society to be a scene of unmitigated environmental, cultural, political and economic collapse. Instead of the ever-flourishing growth in knowledge and scientific achievement that a Whig perspective would predict, there is rampant anti-intellectualism and technological deterioration, fuelled by political malaise and endemic social irresponsibility.

The story is told as humorous satire. The population are addicted to coarse slapstick sitcoms and egregious junk food (even society's water supply has been replaced with fizzy soda). TV news channels have become so sensationalized that newscasters are dressed like professional wrestlers and include swearwords in their reports. Commercial corporations also use profanities in their advertising, with their billboards appearing everywhere in society, including on the speaker's podium in parliament. People have become so

dependent on automation that they are unable to fend for themselves in any way.

Idiocracy is regarded as an insightful social commentary, if albeit at times a controversial one. It provides a humorous evaluation of today's world by extrapolating current cultural trends to project a dystopian future, arguing that, contrary to the Whig view, decline might in fact be inexorable.

By showing how civilization might regress instead of progress, dystopian storytelling can serve as a warning against cultural complacency. It also shows how art can be used to highlight weaknesses in academic scholarship, by debunking such narrative frames as Whiggism in a vivid and entertaining way.

writing of histories. They also determine how we view the contemporary world, and what *value* we attach to our activities.

Therefore, historiography needs to be more than just empirical and explanatory. It also needs to be *ethical*.

THINKING HISTORICALLY

The belief that history is best constructed as a story of gradual progress itself reflects a peculiar bias in human reasoning that has been extensively studied by psychologists. In short, human beings are unduly inclined to think positively about the future.

In predicting the future, people tend to expect success. Sometimes success will be glorious, at other times it will be modest, but, however it happens, people generally feel that all will be well in the end. Everything will work out. Justice will be done. Good things come to those who wait.

This bias towards optimism is not always rational. In many cases, it is clearly irrational. The human tendency to overestimate the odds of success is one of the reasons bookmaking is such a lucrative business. A perceived immunity to misfortune helps explain why so many people take risks, whether it be driving dangerously, spending recklessly or leading unhealthy lifestyles. Through rose-tinted spectacles, the future always looks bright. We feel that everything is destined to get better and better, rather than worse and worse. In this context, there is nothing untoward about Whig history. In fact, it makes a lot of sense.

The idea that human affairs are destined to resolve themselves is linked to a form of fallacious reasoning known as *just-world thinking*. This is the tendency to anticipate a kind of moral balancing across events. We feel that, over time, injustices will even themselves out. For this to happen, there would need to be some universal record of actions and consequences, so that after any series of 'bad' events, a series of offsetting 'good' events can be precipitated. There would also need to be some cosmic 'prime mover' who controls the universe and ensures that the correct events happen. In reality, though, there is no such universal record. Nor is there any omnipotent prime mover.

After something bad happens, there is simply no guarantee that anything good will ever happen again. Our expectation that good days must return is not even a 'belief' in the strict sense of that term. It is a 'wish'. And a wish is certainly a poor basis on which to interpret historical change.

As we will see in Chapter 2, humans also tend to interpret changes in the physical world as reflecting some kind of intelligent influence, often ascribing unwarranted agency to inanimate concepts. Human societies have long viewed the world as subject to divine intervention, where some or other sentient being can 'cause' hurricanes, infestations or wars. We are prone to consider events in terms of the agents that must have caused them.

Our disposition to think this way can make us overconfident when interpreting historical sequences. We apply an orderly pattern to events in an effort to construct a coherent historical account, even if the events are effectively random or chaotic. This desire for coherent explanations – and the concomitant distrust of uncertainty – relates to a psychological need for 'closure' (Kruglanski & Webster, 1996). We would rather attribute events to some intangible force, such as 'culture' or 'imperialism', than conclude that the causes are actually unknowable. This tendency, known as *teleological thinking* (Wagner-Egger et al., 2018), is probably why so many people believe conspiracy theories, even when they are logically tenuous and unsubstantiated (Marchlewska et al., 2018).

We can also note that history itself, and its significance, can be viewed in psychological terms. Human beings appreciate history because they possess what is known as *historical consciousness*. This is the understanding that each person's finite lifetime is part of a much longer set of experiences that incorporates humanity's past, present and future. Most species lack historical consciousness, and even human societies developed it only gradually, once they found ways to sustain themselves and could safely reflect on issues other than on immediate survival (Gilderhus, 1992).

Overall, psychological factors steer our historical thinking, skew how we observe and record our history, and determine our motivation to think historically. Our tendency to veer towards Great Man theories, internalist histories and Whiggist narratives highlights how history itself is a product of human habits of thought.

In this book, our primary interest will lie in *the history of psychology*. However, given the complexities of historiography, we will also need to bear in mind *the psychology of history*.

History of psychology as an emotional endeavour

Philosophers who talk about psychology sometimes warn of a problem called *reflexivity*. This relates to the fact that all reasoning about human psychology will include an element of subjectivity (Bannister, 1966). Researchers are human beings. This means that they will have a personal interest in the outcome of their own research. In principle, their findings should shed light on the psychology of people in general. But as the researcher is themselves a person, this means that their findings will shed light on *them*.

Not only this, but the participants being studied are human beings too. They are *aware* that they are being studied. Anything they do in a study – any behaviour in a laboratory or response to a questionnaire – will be the action of a person *who is aware they are being studied*, rather than the action of a person *in general*.

Philosophers who are concerned about reflexivity feel that all this self-referencing means psychology cannot be a science. It makes it impossible for psychological research to truly meet the scientific requirement of objectivity. The persons *conducting* the research will always feel an intuitive pull of subjective bias when they interpret the behaviour of the persons *being* researched. And the persons *being* researched will moderate their behaviour precisely because they are conscious of the persons *conducting* the research. Psychology is the study of human behaviour; but psychology also *is* human behaviour.

Of course, historians are human beings too. This means that similar questions can be raised with regard to historiography. Historians will have prior beliefs about the nature of human events that are derived from their own human consciousness. They will find it extremely difficult to avoid perceiving history other than through the lens of such perspectives. Historians of psychology, likewise, will have beliefs also about *psychology*, derived simply from being human themselves.

Historians of psychology often position themselves as psychologists first and foremost, rather than historians per se (e.g. Brock, 2017). They claim that their work advances our core understanding of human behaviour, and is just as valid a means of doing so as any population survey, laboratory experiment, randomized controlled trial, or brain imaging study. They believe that their evaluation of historical evidence is as much a part of mainstream empirical psychology as is the scrutinizing of statistical datasets. Occasionally, they make this point in the form of an appeal for recognition: the academic work produced by historians of psychology, they say, should be seen as materially equivalent to that produced by cognitive psychologists, clinical psychologists or developmental psychologists.

In fact, some historians of psychology argue that the history of psychology is more a branch of psychology than it is of history. Therefore, they say, a thorough training as a psychologist is a necessary prerequisite for being able to write about the history of psychology. They believe that 'ordinary' historians are ill-equipped to do the job correctly.

That being noted, some historians of psychology also appear deeply sceptical of those psychologists who choose to write about the history of psychology without first being properly trained *in* the history of psychology. As such, 'ordinary' psychologists too are seen as ill-equipped to perform the task.

Such a guarded approach might reflect a degree of appropriate precaution. However, it might also reflect a dollop of academic protectionism. It would be unusual for it to be said that the history of science can only be written by a scientist, or that the history of politics can only be written by a politician, or that the history of art can only be written by an artist. Surely it would also be tenuous to claim that the history of art itself constitutes a piece of art.

Of course, because of reflexivity, we can always single out psychology as a special case. It is the study of behaviour that itself constitutes a behaviour. However, the inherent problems of subjectivity only serve to highlight the importance of incorporating multiple perspectives.

In many ways, what we might refer to as 'traditional' history of psychology can often seem extremely self-referential. One of the problems with reflexive scholarship is that it can be very poor at incorporating diverse sources of knowledge, at revising its perspective, at broadening its scope, or at acknowledging its own biases. We often end up with histories that are overly focused on narrow in-group concerns, such as those of Western academia. Such histories ultimately produce, and perpetuate, unsustainable metanarratives (we will examine the *history of* the history of psychology in Chapter 3).

Attempting to restrict the writing of psychology's history to a guild of accredited practitioners ironically subjects the enterprise to its own form of Great Man theory: one in which the Great Historians of Psychology are seen as unique leaders, heroically driving the field forward. Such idolatry is acutely and arbitrarily normative, and serves only to exacerbate the problems of subjectivity.

Psychology, ultimately, is a set of concepts. We cannot consider the history of psychology without considering the history of these concepts. The famous figures of the field – Wundt, Skinner, Freud, and so on – might be impossible to ignore. The very fact that they are so closely associated with how we *talk about* the history of these concepts intertwines them with the concepts themselves. But they are not the only people in history who have had beliefs about human thoughts, feelings and behaviours.

Pondering, portraying and purporting to explain human psychology has always been part of our culture. Arguably, our culture would not even be possible without the universal endeavour to explicate the human condition using reason and, where appropriate, evidence. The way human beings have understood each other over the centuries has shaped the experience of our species.

WHERE TO FROM HERE?

The history of psychology extends far beyond modern Western academia. It encompasses the human view of personhood and uniqueness, normality and xenophobia, autonomy and aggression, rationality and reality, science and ethics, and many other domains.

In the next chapter we will examine a profound example of psychology's ancient heritage, a spiritual quest that predates the dawn of civilization itself. For thousands of years, human beings have employed a multitude of means – myths, mystics, magic and, ultimately, scientific methods – in their attempts to explore the one great enigma of their intellectual experience: *the nature of their very own minds.*

DISCUSSION QUESTIONS

1. Does it matter whether psychology is seen as ancient or modern?
2. Why do people think differently about the history of psychology compared to the history of other sciences?
3. When writing a history of psychology, is it a help or a hindrance for the writer to themselves be a psychologist?
4. Why do humans like to think about history as a series of stories involving 'great' people?

RECOMMENDED READING

- **Burman, J. T. (2018). What is history of psychology? Network analysis of journal citation reports, 2009–2015. *SAGE Open*, *8*(1), 1–17.** In this analysis, the author attempts to define the range of topics relating to the history of psychology based on the content of academic journals.
- **Jarius, S., & Wildemann, B. (2017). Pavlov's reflex before Pavlov: Early accounts from the English, French and German classic literature. *European Neurology*, *77*, 322–6.** In this essay, the authors examine a number of (nearly) forgotten accounts of classical conditioning that were published long before the purportedly pioneering work of Ivan Pavlov.
- **Lovett, B. J. (2006). The new history of psychology: A review and critique. *History of Psychology*, *9*, 17–37.** In this review, the author questions whether contemporary historians of psychology really have succeeded in improving on the more limited historiographies used in the past.
- **Robinson, D. N. (2013). Historiography in psychology: A note on ignorance. *Theory & Psychology*, *23*(6), 819–28.** In this essay, the author examines the limits of attempting to distinguish between 'old' and 'new' forms of psychology.

SPIRITUALITY, PHILOSOPHY AND THE CONCEPT OF *THE MIND*

2

In this chapter, we will …

- consider how psychological factors underpin the common cultural belief that human individuals are composed of more than just their physical bodies
- explore why, in most societies, this non-physical version of the self has become associated with profound religious and mystical belief systems
- compare and contrast the ways in which the non-physical version of the self was described and explained in the major cultural communities of the ancient world
- examine how, during the Middle Ages, European Christendom established a cultural norm for explaining human souls that would prove globally influential for centuries
- consider how pre-existing assumptions about the non-physical human self informed the earliest modern attempts to produce scientific explanations for the existence of human minds

---

At the outset

The idea that every person is composed of *more than just a physical body* has emerged in virtually all recorded human societies. There is a strong cultural belief that each person possesses a special kind of inner self, where thoughts, decisions, temperaments and identities are created. This 'non-physical version' of human beings is often seen as existing separately from their 'physical version'.

People in general are 'common-sense' dualists. This means they intuitively believe that the psychological part of a person is different to, and separate from, the physical part. Moreover, it means that most people default to the view that a person's non-physical self is somehow special, and that its independent existence might even allow it to continue to exist after a person has physically died.

Throughout history, this non-physical version of the self has been described in many ways, including as mind, soul, psyche, intellect and spirit. For long periods, people felt that all objects in the universe were animate rather than inanimate. Later they concluded that the entire universe was subject to mechanical principles. The way scientists employed these concepts was often influenced by prevailing religious views regarding *souls*.

The core debate about the non-physical self is referred to as the 'mind–body problem', wherein dualism (the belief that mind and body are separate) is contrasted with monism (the belief that they are unified). Archaeological evidence suggests that dualism is very old and that belief in souls was a core part of shamanic practice in prehistoric societies. Consideration about the detailed nature of souls flourished once language, and thus civilization, arrived.

The earliest civilizations developed extensive ideas about the non-physical self, framed in terms of religion but often grounded in empirical observation. A variety of related worldviews developed across several ancient civilizations, including those of Egypt, India, China, Greece and Rome.

Monism declined with the fall of the Roman civilization and the arrival of the Middle Ages, reflecting an increasing dominance of religion over the state. In Europe, political superstructures disappeared, and religion became a unifying focus for the population. Christian ideas about souls became culturally dominant, although scholars in each of the Abrahamic religions (namely, Christianity, Islam and Judaism) found ways to ensure that establishment views of the human mind were consistent with religious teaching.

Religious views on souls framed the context in which early scientific assessments of the human mind were conceived of and conducted. Even when the arrival of the modern age stimulated new vigour in science and scholarship, the influence of dualistic thinking remained strong. It was felt around the world, as geopolitical trends (such as colonialism) produced a rampant form of cultural imperialism that allowed European ideas to exert a domineering influence on global culture.

It is often assumed that scientific thinking leads to a diminution of religious mysticism, at least with regard to specific issues like the existence of tangible souls. But that has not been always obvious from the history of scientific research on the mind. Today's practitioners and producers of psychology are themselves inheritors of several centuries' worth of culturally crafted attitudes concerning minds, souls and psyches.

Key concept: The human mind

You could argue that the entire point of psychology has been to define, describe and delineate *the human mind*. In common language, a person's 'mind' is said to be the part of them that enables them to think. However, this explanation itself involves many complex ideas.

In English, for example, the word 'mind' is used to refer to a range of different psychological concepts, including: memory ('*It slipped my mind*'); attention ('*I kept my mind on the task*'); intelligence ('*You have a very sharp mind*'); intention ('*I can do it if I set my mind to it*'); analytic deliberation ('*I will run it through my mind*'); sanity ('*That person is not of sound mind*'); emotion ('*I went out of my mind with worry*'); self-control ('*It was an act of mindless violence*'); cognitive style ('*You have the mind of a scientist*'); perception ('*How it appears in my mind might not be the same as how it appears in yours*'); and the inexplicable nature of personal autonomy ('*Who knows what was going through their mind when they did that*').

Each conceptualization of the 'mind' illustrates a fundamental challenge in trying to explain it. The core question is: Does the mind even exist? What we refer to as the 'mind' could be the entity that produces our mental processes – or it could just be *the combined end product* of these processes, *a strongly held impression* of individual personhood based on a mosaic of our behaviours, characteristics and other attributes. This non-physical version of personhood has always drawn the attention of humans, and has been described in many different ways – sacred, secular and scientific – over several centuries.

PSYCHOLOGY OF THE SELF

Human beings are everyday psychologists. We are so accustomed to considering each other in psychological terms that we don't even realize when we are doing it. Unlike other animals (as far as we can tell), human beings differentiate 'minds' from 'bodies'. We understand that every person possesses their 'own' mind – a personal consciousness that exists in its own right.

When we interact with someone, we seldom take account of their heart rate, or height, or hair colour. But we do try to focus on what they are thinking. Our ability to navigate a social interaction will depend on what we see as the other person's 'mind'. Arguably, our ability to be *human* will require it.

The idea that every person is composed of more than just a physical body has emerged in virtually all human societies that historians have ever studied. Millions of people believe that humans possess a special kind of inner self, where thoughts, decisions, temperaments and identities are created. The idea that this 'non-physical version' of human beings is substantive in nature – that it exists and is separate from the 'physical version' – is nothing less than profound.

It is also extremely contentious. It is a source of deeply polarizing social politics, bitter cultural divides and intense moral controversies.

For example, worldviews relating to such practices as abortion or euthanasia are frequently propelled by wildly differing beliefs about the existence or non-existence of the 'non-physical self'. *Is a foetus conscious? Is a brain-dead patient on life support still really 'alive'? Where does our mind go when we die?* Despite thousands of years of analysis, scholarship and science have produced few clear answers to such questions.

The belief that human beings possess a 'non-physical' self – one that is capable of independent, deliberate and private thought – has existed for centuries, but has taken many forms. In the English language, the concepts of 'mind', 'spirit', 'intellect', 'consciousness', 'being', 'essence' and 'psyche' are just a few examples.

Throughout history, however, for many people the concept is best encapsulated in spiritual terms. As we saw in Chapter 1, the *psyche* (ψυχή) that gives 'psychology' its name is often translated in such a way.

For millions of human beings, this thing – this special, mystical and sacrosanct thing – is their *soul*.

I know you got soul

Views on souls tend to come in two types. In some philosophical systems, the soul is an immortal human essence that exists beyond the realm of ordinary nature. It is said to be infused with a divine (or perhaps 'quantum') quality that transcends the banal vicissitudes of biological life.

In other ways of thinking, the soul comprises the sum mental activities of a living being, a version of what a person is like as viewed by others, and an ephemeral synthesis of personal attributes that becomes obsolete once that person dies.

The fact that the concept of 'soul' has emerged across every culture and historical period could have resulted from one of two possible causes. The first is that independent souls do, in fact, exist, and the ability of humans to comprehend their existence is based on reality. The other cause is that independent souls do *not*, in fact, exist, and so the tendency of humans to believe in their existence is based on subjective impression. In the latter case, what human cultures refer to as the 'soul' is effectively a social construction – a notion that exists only in the sense that people *refer* to it as existing.

The fact that humans seem attracted to this social construction is often attributed to our craving for comfort. Belief in souls is consoling. For most people, the idea of having but a few decades of life to live is quite unpleasant. The prospect that death will be followed by an unstoppable and everlasting *non-existence of our own minds* is even more disturbing. In contrast, having an immortal soul offers *hope*.

The contemplation of death affects our perceptions and behaviours in the present moment. We are permanently encouraged to avoid thinking about mortality. The potency of this thought process is encapsulated in the title of a theory that one group of psychologists developed to explain it. Vividly, they call their approach 'terror management theory' (Greenberg, Pyszczynski & Solomon, 1986). According to this thesis, every human being is aware of their own mortality *all the time*. They spend *every day of their lives* managing the resulting 'terror'.

Believing that physical death, in effect, does *not* mark the end of personal life helps to provide solace in the face of such terror. Therefore, it should be no surprise that ideas about souls are so quickly transmitted throughout culture. Belief systems that posit the existence of robust and immortal personal consciousnesses are keenly embraced by human beings, because every human being is consoled by the idea that they themselves might possess such a thing.

But belief in souls is not driven by wishful thinking alone. According to some psychologists, such beliefs are more likely because of the peculiar circumstances in which our thinking has evolved. Our perceptions tend to become skewed by a number of situational factors, including the following:

- *Simulation constraint:* Humans find it extremely difficult even to *imagine* a universe without souls. This is because our daily patterns of thought are shaped exclusively by experiences we have *while we are alive*. In other words, we simply cannot *know* what it is like to be dead. When we try to imagine death, we can only think of it in ways that *resemble being alive*. Belief in everlasting souls results from this 'simulation constraint' – our inability to simulate the experience of not being alive (Bering, 2008).
- *Offline social reasoning:* Humans tend to know lots of other people, but to meet only a few of them with any regularity. In other words, it is normal for us to be separated from our acquaintances: we are physically apart from *most* people we know, *most* of the time. Despite this, whenever we meet someone after a period apart, we continue our social interactions with them quite seamlessly. We benefit from a habit of thought known as 'offline social reasoning' (Bering, 2006), a powerful feeling that their *non-physical* identity remains stable. Even if they look physically different (perhaps they have got older), we know that psychologically they are the same person. Offline social reasoning is an important element of our ability to engage in meaningful social interaction over time. But one consequence is that when a person we know dies, we find it difficult to believe that they no longer exist. We revert to our usual way of

thinking about them, as merely physically absent – we know that they are *not here*, but we imagine they must be *somewhere*. Our underlying experience of how people can physically change but remain psychologically the same encourages us to consider that their 'souls' might be everlasting.

- **Illusion by design:** A third theory of why belief in souls is so common relates to the promotion of pro-social behaviour. The idea that souls endure after death encourages the living to feel like they are never truly alone. The spirits of the dead – be they saints or lost loved ones – are forever watching over, a reminder to us to always do the right thing. Even when people are physically alone, the feeling of being watched discourages them from behaving immorally. It has been argued, therefore, that a collective belief in immortal souls capable of everlasting consciousness is helpful to the species in *survival-of-the-fittest* terms. It is an 'illusion by design' (Boyer, 2001), common in humans for the same reason that all other evolved traits are common – because it is *adaptive*.

'Common-sense' dualism

It is often presumed that religious people become religious because of cultural exposure. In other words, they come to believe in souls, in afterlives and – by extension – in deities, only after such ideas are *presented to them* by others. Before this, it is said, people are natural atheists.

However, a lot of psychology research suggests that this might not be true at all. It would seem that, in several ways, our innate cognitive architecture predisposes us to formulate religious ideas all by ourselves. Far from being naturally atheistic, people in fact are *intuitively* inclined towards religiosity.

One way researchers have approached this topic is by examining how children talk about metaphysical issues. Such studies show that young children make what appear to be a number of automatic assumptions. They believe that the self is non-physical in nature, and that consciousness continues after death.

For example, when young children are told that a (fictitious) animal character has just been 'killed', they will continue to discuss the animal as though it were still psychologically alive. They will happily describe its ongoing experiences. In their minds, even after death, a cartoon mouse will continue to feel hunger, to 'know' things, and to have thoughts (Bering & Bjorklund, 2004). They will acknowledge that the mouse's body is no longer 'working', but this does not seem to matter. The mouse still exists, psychologically.

When older children are studied using the same approaches, they are much less likely to describe the mouse in this way. It seems that although young children *start off* by assuming that a dead mouse can continue to think, as they get older they *learn* that this is not the case. As such, if anything, exposure to cultural knowledge would appear to *dampen* children's innate belief in souls, rather than to plant such ideas in their otherwise atheistic minds.

More broadly, young children tend to see *agency* in everything. They tend to describe *all* objects as having thoughts, feelings or intentions – in other words, as having a kind of soul. For example, they explain that rocks are pointy in order to protect themselves ('so that animals won't sit on them'), as if rocks were able to fear pain and take evasive action (Kelemen, 2004). To young children, there is no such thing as a truly 'inanimate' object.

As revealed in the attitudes of very young children, humans appear to have a natural propensity to imagine that *everything* has a capacity for consciousness. Moreover, they imagine this consciousness to be unencumbered and unconstrained by physical processes. No biology is required.

The thought styles of children suggest that, from birth, human beings think about minds as existing separately from bodies. The view that minds and bodies are separate is known as *dualism*. As such, the way young children (and many adults) intuitively and unquestioningly believe in the existence of free-standing souls has been described as 'common-sense dualism' (Bloom, 2004). This tendency to consider minds as separate, free-standing and everlasting does not appear to result from cultural teaching. Rather, it seems to be our default cognitive setting.

The concept of the non-physical version of the self – typified by notions such as 'mind', 'soul' and 'psyche' – is therefore extremely old, perhaps as old as humanity. Accordingly, curiosity about what *exactly* these things are – how they work, where they come from, what happens to them after we die – has an extremely long history.

The process of defining, describing and even deifying the human mind represents the first form of psychology. It remains one of humanity's ongoing intellectual quests, and thus psychology's oldest endeavour by far.

THE ANIMATED UNIVERSE

Humanity's default cognitive architecture is reflected in its earliest worldviews. For example, for much of history, people in general – adults as well as children – believed that *all* objects in the universe had agency. In other words, they felt that everything around them had the potential to act of its own accord and, thus, to behave in non-random ways.

Whenever a rock fell from a cliff edge, it was because the rock *wanted* to do so. The rock possesses a spirit or soul that enabled it to form, and act upon, an intention. The rock's inner psychological presence *caused* it to fall. This worldview is known as *animism*, the belief that all objects possess a spiritual essence that makes them somehow alive. According to anthropologists, animism formed the basis of ancient religious belief. The idea may even be the spark that led to the emergence of formal religion as part of human culture.

Today, animism remains part of some of the world's oldest belief systems, including Shintoism in Japan, as well as the religions of many indigenous communities. It is frequently discussed as an example of 'primitive' thinking, an attitude that dates back to the early days of modern anthropology.

For example, British scholar E. B. Tylor first coined the term 'animism' in his book *Primitive Culture* in 1871. Later, in 1910, French anthropologist Lucien Lévy-Bruhl elaborated on the concept in a book called *Les Fonctions mentales dans les sociétés inférieures*. Clearly, these scholars viewed animism as intellectually regressive and a deficient form of thinking.

However, dismissing animism as 'primitive' provides us with a very good example of presentism, the historiographical bias we discussed in Chapter 1.

Science of spirits

Presentism involves interpreting the past with reference to present-day norms. The early anthropologists claimed that animism was the preserve of ancient superstition and exotic religion, and that it lagged behind more 'advanced' forms of thought. They declared it to be an obsolete way of thinking, whose existence in tribal religions reflected the legacy of prehistoric times. In doing so, they overlooked animism's influence on their own society, in their own purportedly modern age.

At the time of the early anthropologists, animism's influence could be detected widely in scientific scholarship, including in the works of renowned scientists. For example, for much of history scientists would discuss gravity by saying that weighty objects fall to the ground because they 'want' (or are 'compelled') to move closer to the centre of the earth, as though the object fulfils a 'purpose' by falling.

In fact, according to some philosophers, animism continues to influence science even today. Modern scientists claim that they no longer attribute agency to objects, but they still frequently employ animist narratives to explain their concepts.

Scientists often refer to 'proteins that *regulate* cell division', 'muscle cells that *harvest* energy', or 'genes that *dictate* the production of enzymes' (Riskin, 2016, p. 5). Such language does not presume that proteins or cells or genes 'want' to act in particular ways. Nor does it imply that they are psychologically conscious or emotionally intelligent. Nonetheless, animist metaphors describe these entities as exhibiting *purposeful* action, thus belying the idea that they are truly 'inanimate'.

Scientists who describe non-conscious objects as pursuing a goal or objective usually say that they are employing a kind of scientific shorthand. The metaphor is intended to be figurative rather than literal. It provides a convenient way to describe events that are highly complex, or which are not yet fully understood. Thus, when a biologist talks about proteins that 'regulate' cell division, they do not mean that these proteins are independently minded beings possessed of their own souls.

However, in many sciences, these metaphors are used so frequently, it is often forgotten that the processes they are intended to depict are, in fact, not yet fully understood (Riskin, 2016). Through persistent use, the metaphor of animism has become internalized as the explanatory norm.

The reason scientists use animist narratives is precisely because, psychologically, human audiences like them. They make it easier for us to understand processes that would otherwise be impossibly obtuse. The idea that cancer cells are tiny little *beings* playing individual roles within a broader choreography brings the scene to life. We can easily imagine a 'follower cell' following a 'leader cell' because, after all, it is its *leader*. Adopting the perspectives of microscopic entities – seeing things from their 'point of view' – helps us to comprehend the way they act, react and interact.

From children talking about the thoughts of dead mice to immunologists describing how white blood cells hunt down dangerous antibodies, the human inclination to attribute agency to all types of objects, small or large, tangible or intangible, is extremely powerful. It should be no surprise, therefore, that we are also inclined to presume that – whether mind, soul or psyche – human beings too possess their own purposeful agency.

Mechanical nature

In many ways, the emergence of modern science marked a significant cultural shift away from animism. Ordinary people are no longer comfortable attributing agency to inanimate objects. When a rock falls, we understand that this is a consequence of gravity, erosion, friction and structural disturbance. When we watch a river flow, we know that the water is moving because of physical forces acting upon it. We do not believe the movement is inherent in the water itself. And when a hurricane occurs, we appreciate that this has many complex causes, none of which involve spirits or gods. Overall, we feel as though science has taught us that animism is indeed a primitive form of thought.

However, modern scientists were not the first people to see the flaws in animism. To presume that they were is just another example of presentism. Even in the most ancient civilizations, sophisticated scholars expressed doubts about claims that objects could possibly have their own animating force. These doubts predated modern science by many centuries. Rather than saying that modern science led us to become sceptical of animism, it would be more accurate to say that *scepticism of animism led us to modern science.*

As we will discuss in Chapter 3, what we now refer to as 'modern science' first began to appear in the sixteenth and seventeenth centuries. The combined cultural shifts that caused this emergence are often referred to as the 'Scientific Revolution'. A prominent intellectual theme of this period was a widespread rejection of the idea that individual objects could possess their own independent agency.

Instead, progressive scholars viewed events as adhering to *mechanistic* principles. The universe was seen as a huge machine, a passive apparatus in which all elements were interconnected. No component could move unless a physical force acted upon it, and no force could be applied except when actuated through mechanical linkages. The challenge for science was not to account for mysteries or miracles, it was to reverse-engineer the machine.

Reflecting the cutting-edge technology of the era, many scientists compared the universe to the workings of a mechanical clock (Dolnick, 2011). On the surface, a clock looks like a self-animating device, capable of performing intelligent functions. Based on what it 'tells' us, a clock could even seem like it 'knows' the time. Similarly, the universe itself comprises a totalizing system that, under the surface, incorporates a multitude of interlocking cogs, gears and hairsprings, all operating together to produce the constant *tick-tick-tick* of life.

In this view, the universe is best explained by charting its mechanical properties. There is no need to talk about intention, desires or agency.

Divine clockwork

If anything, the scientists of the sixteenth and seventeenth centuries took mechanism to the extreme. According to them, it was not only rocks and rivers that lacked agency. Animals too, even human beings, should be analysed as mechanical devices.

This mechanistic approach – where all creatures are treated as a composite of discrete biological, chemical and physical events – has become the dominant standard in modern science (Riskin,

Image 2.1 Mechanical universe
Many early scientists compared the universe to the workings of a mechanical clock.

2016). However, when used as a basis to describe the human experience, the mechanistic approach has proven controversial. Critics see it as an example of unwarranted *scientism.*

Scientism is a philosophical view that argues that all forms of reality can be explained using science. It sees science as the only source of objective truth, and considers other types of knowledge to be inherently flawed. According to scientism, science is the best way to decide what is, and is not, important in life. In fact, it is the only way.

Critics of scientism feel that it misapplies the scientific method. They argue that using science this way leads to reductionist explanations that largely miss the point of a range of alternative worldviews, including ethical, moral, philosophical and cultural perspectives.

For example, subjectively, many people believe that agency is a key ingredient of the human experience. They feel that all human beings possess *free will*, the power to make autonomous choices and decisions. We will consider the concept of free will in more detail in Chapter 8.

For now, however, we should reflect on the point that depicting human beings as biological machines is sometimes said to be – literally – *dehumanizing.* It is accused of ignoring, if not denying, one of the key aspects of being human.

In ancient Rome, the philosopher Lucretius (99–55 BCE; also known as Titus Lucretius Carus) was regarded as one of the greatest scientific geniuses ever to have lived. However, in later centuries he was condemned as an enemy of religion. This was because he portrayed the human mind as a mechanical by-product of physiology, something that ceases to exist at the end of biological life (Bergson, 2014). Because of the prevailing culture of religiosity, Lucretius' scientific logic and astute empirical reasoning were treated as forms of heresy.

Perennial concerns about scientism have meant that mechanistic approaches to psychology always attract a certain degree of disapproval. Indeed, as mechanistic accounts are seen as 'scientific', the very idea of using *science* in psychology is itself frequently criticized.

However, there is a certain paradox at the heart of such complaints. This is because, historically, mechanistic ideas were grounded in attitudes that were deeply theological. Lucretius, for example, was very religious for his time. He argued that several gods certainly existed, and even that they were the source of human morality. He simply believed that the gods existed in a godly realm, whereas humans existed in a human one. Only in the human realm did mechanistic principles apply.

Likewise, the scientists of the Scientific Revolution assumed that a passive universe, lacking its own agency, could be effective only if it were guided by a supernatural god. The cosmic clock required not just a designer to create it, but also a controller to wind it regularly and to keep everything in motion.

Many historians of science conclude that the Scientific Revolution was itself a consequence of the Protestant Reformation. The Reformation, which swept across Europe during the sixteenth and seventeenth centuries, was a cultural revolution that saw open revolt against the political and social authority of the Catholic Church. The more superstitious elements of Catholic teachings were challenged and reinterpreted. Animistic explanations for nature were dispensed with. As a consequence, virtually *all* agency in the universe was redirected away from things like rocks and rivers, and towards the supreme single god of Christendom.

The mechanistic models that emerged from the Scientific Revolution were not irreligious or atheistic, but were instead intended to *strengthen* claims that there must exist a supreme universal deity. To early scientists, the smooth running of the universe was far from a rejection of religion. Rather, it was strong evidence for the existence of this all-powerful, infallible, Christian god (Riskin, 2016).

Contrary to some stereotypes, science and religion do not always produce competing views of nature. Throughout the history of psychological concepts, many scientists have been very religious, and many religious people have been champions of science. Across the world, religious traditions have proven to be deeply influential on scientific thought.

There are few more vivid examples of this than the way religions have depicted the nature of human souls.

DUALISM AS DOGMA

We have seen how human psychology is predisposed to recognize the 'non-physical version' of human beings. People think of human minds as somehow everlasting, unconstrained by physical realities. Part of this is driven by a simple fear of death. Some of it is shaped by the way our 'offline' relationships teach us to think of people as existing even when they are not physically present. Young children consider minds to outlast bodies, and to not even require a physical body per se.

Innately, we are common-sense dualists. We default to seeing minds as robust entities that exist separately from bodies, and, thus, from the mechanical dimensions of nature.

Theological virtue

The idea that this 'non-physical version' of the self somehow transcends the physical world – such that it might even survive biological death – brings with it many implications. A mind like this would represent a type of entity that is qualitatively unlike anything else in this world. Were it to exist, it would be nothing short of miraculous.

Therefore, it should be no surprise that for most of human history the mind has been discussed with religious veneration. Quite literally, concepts of the mind – in other words, *psychological* concepts – have been the stuff of theology.

As we discussed in Chapter 1, the *psyche* – or ψυχή – that gives psychology its name is often translated in English-language textbooks as 'soul'. However, we must recall that a word like 'soul' will have had different meanings at different times, in different places, and, of course, in different languages.

The word ψυχή was originally used by the ancient Greeks. In the sixteenth century, it was reworked into Renaissance Latin by a Croatian-speaking poet, Marko Marulić (1450–1524), who coined the word *psychologia* (Krstić, 1964). This word was eventually appropriated into French, where it became *psychologie*, and from there it was translated into many other languages. When Anglicized, it became 'psychology'.

Given this variety of contextual factors, spanning history, geography and linguistics, it would be especially perilous for twenty-first-century English-speakers to overconfidently restrict its nuances. To declare that ψυχή can be translated directly as 'soul' would be a flagrant oversimplification.

Nonetheless, it seems entirely reasonable to acknowledge the theological roots of 'ψυχή'. After all, religious worldviews have dominated human cultures throughout history. For centuries, formalized religions have been politically intertwined with cultural power structures all over the world. Religion has always been significant in the evolution of politics, with spirituality and mysticism central to the formation and recognition of social power. Some examples of this include:

- the way ancestor worship enabled shamans to rise to positions of tribal protectors in prehistoric societies (Strathern, 1994);
- the use of cults and temples to further the political agendas of the ruling classes in Pharaonic Egypt (Wellendorf, 2008);
- the establishment of an Islamic State in Medina in 622 CE by the prophet Muhammad (Effendy, 2008);
- the 'god-kings' that ruled over the Inca, the Aztecs and Imperial Japan (Conrad & Demarest, 1984; Garon, 1986);

- the 'divine right of kings' invoked to legitimize the many monarchies of medieval Europe (Burgess, 1992);
- the dual role of the modern-day British monarch as both head of state and supreme governor of its established church (Eberle, 2016); and
- the evangelical political bases that comprise decisive voting blocs in many present-day democracies (D. E. Campbell, 2006).

In short, nearly every society's view of psychological personhood is intertwined with politics, power and propaganda. Alongside everyday explanations and social speculations are 'official' accounts of the nature and status of ψυχή. How average citizens have viewed and talked about the human mind has never been a trivial matter.

Consider, again, a divisive social issue such as abortion. In all societies, the regulation of abortion is recognized as presenting a complex and controversial challenge. The controversies stem largely from conflicting views about whether, or at what point, a foetus is capable of having a soul, or mind, or consciousness, or some other form of self-animating personhood. The central ethical question rests largely on what is seen as the true nature and status of the 'non-physical version' of a human being.

In even so-called sophisticated societies, scepticism towards the establishment view of souls can attract harsh community disapproval. It can be seen not just as religious heresy, but also as political subversion.

Dualism as the prehistoric default

The basic debate about whether the mind is separate from the body, or whether it is a by-product of that body, is often referred to as the *mind–body problem*. As discussed above, the view that minds and bodies are separate is known as *dualism*. The corresponding term for the alternative, the view that minds and bodies are unified, is *monism*.

While often discussed as though they are incompatible, sometimes dualism and monism are described in ways that appear to overlap. In addition, both dualism and monism come in many different forms. Not all dualists agree with one another, and neither do all monists. It is somewhat ironic that the mind–body problem cannot easily be reduced to two free-standing worldviews. What seems at first glance to be a simple *either/or* debate is actually far more convoluted and confusing.

The concept of the 'mind–body problem' reflects a range of related ideas that have emerged, time and again, since the dawn of humankind.

Although never definitive, archaeological evidence has long suggested that belief in an afterlife was common in the earliest prehistoric communities. Up to 80,000 years ago, in what is now Iraqi Kurdistan, Neanderthals formally interred their dead, reposed their remains in a foetal position, and apparently buried them with flowers (Pomeroy et al., 2020). The cave paintings in Lascaux, France, which date back some 17,000 years, include a scene where a human figure, apparently trampled to death by a bison, is shown next to a bird, a traditional shamanic symbol for passage into the afterlife (Lewis-Williams, 2006).

As far as we can tell, many of the earliest formal religions revolved around the notion of ancestor worship. Prehistoric societies believed that long-dead ancestors continued to exist in a non-physical form, with the power to exert influence on current events. The souls of the dead were often believed to reappear in the bodies of newly born babies, a process known as *transmigration* (although in popular culture, it is more commonly referred to as *reincarnation*). In some religions, souls could even transmigrate from humans into animals.

Believing in a life after death is a form of dualism. The permanent survival of consciousness requires a worldview that sees souls as separate from biological bodies. As such, afterlife beliefs reflect a fixed theory of human minds – specifically, the theory that human minds exist of their own accord, and are not bound by physiological processes.

Perhaps rooted in common-sense dualism and the associated proliferation of ancient religious belief, the idea that souls remain alive after physical death represents the first major theory of the human mind to be widely accepted. While dualism is still defended by some religiously minded philosophers, the theory of a free-standing human mind fundamentally departs from the modern understanding of how brain functions are involved in cognition.

Image 2.2 Prehistoric dualism
The 17,000-year-old cave paintings in Lascaux, France, include a scene where a human figure, trampled to death by a bison, appears next to a bird, a traditional shamanic symbol for passage into the afterlife.

The Good Place (Schur, 2016–2020) was an American television comedy series that explored the implications and possible nature of an afterlife. In the series, lead character Eleanor discovers that she has survived death and entered the 'Good Place', specially reserved for people who have led moral lives. The Good Place is a sunlit traditional village with amenities provided to cater for everybody who lives there, all overseen by its architect, an immortal being named Michael.

The problem for Eleanor is that she feels that her life had in fact been morally very questionable, and so she becomes convinced that she has been sent to the Good Place by mistake. She feels it is only a matter of time before the error is discovered and she is instead despatched to the Bad Place, a corresponding community reserved for people who behave unethically during their lives.

Eleanor meets several other characters, each of whom has their own doubts about their suitability for the Good Place. In the season 1 finale, there is a twist. Eleanor discovers that in fact this is not the Good Place after all, but the Bad Place. Michael is a demon who created this place as an experiment in torture. His plan was to punish the various characters by having them emotionally torment themselves, and each other, with their doubts, guilt and foibles.

The Good Place is a modern depiction of some ancient ideas about life after death. It deliberately critiques traditional philosophical and religious approaches by showing an afterlife that is not all that it seems, and where moral boundaries are uncertain. The audience are invited to engage seriously with the characters' plights and to grapple with some challenging conundrums. They need to suspend their disbelief only with regard to the plot's core assumption of dualism.

For example, in this afterlife, all the characters retain their living personalities, temperaments and habits, as well as their physical state (such as their age) when they died. This form of dualism, where a person's dead body is reproduced in the afterlife *minus whatever injury caused their death*, could raise questions about plot coherence. However, the writers are able to rely on the traditional familiarity of common-sense dualism to keep the audience engaged.

The writers of *The Good Place* craft several story-points from moral dilemmas commonly discussed in conventional academic philosophy (at times citing prominent philosophers by name). The overall plot presents a deliberate critique of the fundamental premise of afterlife beliefs and their moral implications. The storyline works so long as the audience accepts its presumption of dualism. As such, the show is a vehicle for portraying a wide range of philosophical concepts, offered within a light-hearted version of a dualist universe.

THE PSYCHOLOGICAL SELF IN EARLY CIVILIZATION

Most human adults can speak, read and write. Indeed, the ability to use language is often argued to be a defining feature of humanity. However, relative to the history of our species, language is a very modern thing. For most of the time, humans could not even talk, never mind write. Verbal communication is a trick that humans learned to perform only recently.

Homo sapiens emerged around 400,000 years ago, its lineage splitting from previous humanlike species that had existed in one form or another for millions of years. Such splitting is known as *speciation*. The speciation of *Homo sapiens* occurred when a subpopulation of extant hominids began to intermingle in isolation, eventually reproducing in sufficient numbers to survive together. This process gradually resulted in a new population with enough uniqueness to be classifiable as its own distinct species.

Homo sapiens was not the only lineage to spring up in this way. *Homo neanderthalensis* similarly evolved through speciation, always existing in small numbers but proving resilient enough to persist for hundreds of thousands of years. A lesser-known lineage known as *Homo denisova* also appeared, spreading through eastern Asia and, at times, interbreeding with *Homo sapiens*. Both *Homo neanderthalensis* and *Homo denisova* became extinct between 15,000 and 40,000 years ago.

Homo sapiens had speciated for some 300,000 years before language emerged. In other words, it took us the first three-quarters of our existence to learn how to talk (Hughes, 2016). After that, we were talking for a further 95,000 years before we came up with the idea of writing things down. The earliest systems of writing were invented just in the last 5,000 years.

In short, although today's humans are genetically indistinguishable from those who lived nearly half a million years ago, our species has been using written words for just fifty centuries. (Even then, it took several millennia for written communication to become widely adopted.) While we might consider written language to be distinctively 'human' – or even a *defining feature* of humanity – for the vast majority of its history, *Homo sapiens* has in fact been an illiterate, and mostly non-verbal, species.

Nonetheless, the invention of writing had a profound impact on the experience of humankind and, by extension, the world. Writing permitted the communication of intentions, the transmission of knowledge, and the ability to develop complex ideas that would otherwise exceed what human attention spans could follow. Most of all, writing changed the world because it allowed for the keeping of records. Societies could audit their affairs, organize their activities and, importantly, document their histories.

Writing fundamentally changed the way humans collectively understood their past. For this reason, historians see the invention of writing as a threshold event. It marked the transition from 'prehistory' to 'recorded history' (or to just plain old 'history').

The prehistoric age lasted hundreds of thousands of years, but without written language it produced only gradual cultural change and, of course, few records. Effectively, the prehistoric age bequeathed less material for modern historians to consider.

The period subsequent to the invention of writing has been quite different. While much shorter than prehistory, the era of 'recorded' history has not just produced an enormous quantum of material for historians to scrutinize. It has also overlapped with an exponential explosion of cultural development, fuelled by the almost limitless computational, communicational and cognitive capacity unleashed by the invention of writing.

Polypsychism in Ancient Egypt: North Africa and the Nile Valley (4000–3000 BCE)

One of the earliest formal writing systems was developed in northern Africa, by the ancient Egyptians, between 4000 and 3000 BCE. Comprising a set of around 1,000 pictographic symbols, the system has become known as 'Egyptian hieroglyphics'. Ancient Egypt was an extremely influential civilization, existing for over 3,000 years. Its writing system is believed to be the ancestor of

Image 2.3   Polypsychism
Ancient Egyptian funerary practices included a post-mortem examination, where the deceased person's heart would be weighed.

several modern scripts and alphabets, including that used for Latin (which is also used for English), as well as those for Greek, Cyrillic and Arabic.

The archaeological evidence shows how the ancient Egyptians developed elaborate theories about the nature of human minds. It was obvious, for example, that they believed in an afterlife, and thus in dualism (Wilkinson, 2017). More importantly, they explicitly divided human person-hood into two distinct categories of components: the physical and the non-physical.

According to the ancient Egyptians, the non-physical version of the self was composed of five separate elements, *Ba*, *Ib*, *Ka*, *Ren* and *Sheut* (Santoro et al., 2009). *Ba* represented an individual's unique personality, their traits and defining attributes; *Ib* comprised the person's emotions and emotional thoughts; *Ka* was the vital force that animated physical life and differentiated it from death; *Ren* was the person's self-identity, self-concept and name; and *Sheut* was the person's shadow, something that was always present and so would protect the person in the afterlife.

The idea that human minds are composed of multiple components is known as *polypsychism*. Polypsychism has been a recurring theme in the history of psychology. One important implication of this view is that different parts of the mind will often be driven by different motivating factors. As a result, each individual's ultimate behaviour will be shaped by the way these conflicting influences eventually combine. In some instances they might compound each other's effects. In other cases they might cancel each other out.

For example, the ancient Egyptians described how a person's *Ba* might tempt them towards self-destructive habits, whereas their *Ib* might help them lead a more moral life. The person's eventual behaviour will be determined by whether their *Ba* or *Ib* is stronger. Such polypsychic reasoning closely echoes the theories of modern psychoanalysis, where the resolution of mental conflicts is seen as an important determinant of human functioning (Wickramasekera II, 2014). We will discuss psychoanalysis in detail in Chapter 7.

The ancient Egyptians believed that the physical and non-physical versions of the self could affect each other. Specifically, if a person's *Ib* was weak, they could end up leading an immoral life, which would cause their heart to be inhabited by the demon Ammit and so become heavier (Santoro et al., 2009). For this reason, ancient Egyptian funerary practices included a post-mortem examination, during which the deceased person's heart would be weighed. The weight of the heart would determine the person's fate in the afterlife.

It is worth bearing in mind that the ancient Egyptians conducted many sophisticated anatomical studies and had relatively advanced knowledge of human physiology. Their belief that the heart served as the interface between the physical and the non-physical reflected their understanding of the centrality of the cardiovascular system. The idea that there exists a particular body part which serves as a physical site for the psychological self is another recurring theme in the history of psychology.

The life force *Ka* was said to be represented by human breathing. It entered the body at birth and left it forever upon death. This metaphor of *consciousness-as-respiration* was to emerge in several psychological worldviews throughout history. We can recall how, in ancient Greece, the word ψυχή was used to refer not just to soul or consciousness, but also to the act of breathing. Similarly, the ancient Hebrew concept of *nephesh* (נֶפֶשׁ) had the same double meaning (Mix, 2018), as does the Hindu concept of *prana* (पुराण).

The Vedic soul: Northern India and present-day Nepal and Pakistan (2000–500 BCE)

The original Vedic notion of *Ātman* (आत्मन्), today associated with Buddhism, Hinduism and Jainism, was also used to refer to both consciousness and respiration (Deshmukh, 2011). The *Vedas* are the oldest scriptures of Hinduism, the earliest of which were written between 2000 and 1000 BCE. One of the most well-studied Vedas is a series of writings known as the *Upanishads*, which were written from around 700 BCE onwards in a variety of regions in or near what is now northern India (Olivelle, 1998).

The Vedas include many elaborate depictions of the non-physical human self. In particular, the Upanishads promote a polypsychic model based on the *chakra system*. In this system, different parts of the body are said to be the locations of different 'chakras', centres that regulate major aspects of the mind. For example, the throat chakra, *Vishuddha* (विशुद्ध), is said to process higher cognition, creativity and self-expression, as well as to regulate negative experiences, such as guilt and jealousy.

According to the Vedic system, the non-physical self is said to exist on two levels. Each human being possesses a primordial soul, *Paramatman* (परमात्मन्), which is infused with the supreme deity and exists separately from the physical body. They also possess a separate animating life force, *jiva* (जीव), which comprises their body-bound self-identity and exists only while they are physically alive. After a person dies, their *jiva* is destroyed but their Paramatman continues to exist (Rao & Paranjpe, 2016).

These concepts have been influential throughout Asian culture, and have infused generations of Indian, Chinese, Japanese and Tibetan traditions (Wickramasekera II, 2014). Over the centuries, the associated religious philosophies have become more complex. While orthodox Hinduism and Jainism retain the view that humans have individualized souls, Buddhism and some streams within Hindu Indian philosophy have come to reject this possibility.

Overall, the world's oldest writings show how ancient cultures embraced a number of recurring societal views about the non-physical version of the self. These include:

- a view that the psyche is best construed as some kind of polypsychic system (i.e. as a system comprised of multiple interacting components);
- a belief that human consciousness interacts with the physical body but somehow nonetheless stands separate from it; and
- the hypothesis that such individualized consciousness allows the human mind to exist apart from the physical world, and perhaps even to outlast biological death.

These initial theories about minds and souls were among the first topics to be written about by humanity's earliest literate cultures. They reflected profound presumptions about human psychology that went on to resonate throughout succeeding centuries. Their basic tenets endure as influential ideas to this day.

The non-physical self in Ancient China (1600–400 BCE)

China, one of the oldest continuously existing countries in the world, is home to one of history's great civilizations. The original Chinese civilization emerged around 1600 BCE in the valley of the Huang He (黃河), also known as the Yellow River, a region that today includes such megacities as Xi'an and Zhengzhou. Chinese philosophy is very diverse but is often regarded as having a focus on the human condition, as opposed to, say, on metaphysics or logic.

Ancient Chinese theories of the mind often reflected a dualistic model, involving two types of personal selves: *hún* (魂), a thinking and feeling capacity that leaves the person after death, dispersing into the universe; and *pò* (魄), a motor and sensory capacity that remains within the deceased body and thus returns to the earth (Baldrian-Hussein, 2008). It appears that *pò* was the original concept of soul to become common in Chinese thought, with the dualistic *hún–pò* approach not emerging until around the sixth century BCE (Yü, 1987). These ideas became pillars of early Chinese religions, such as Daoism.

The *hún–pò* model was part of a wider natural philosophy that explained the function of all existence in terms of two interacting forces, *yin* (陰) and *yang* (陽). (In the *hún–pò* model, *hún* was seen as yang, whereas *pò* was seen as yin.) Broadly speaking, everything in the universe was best served whenever yin and yang were in harmonious equilibrium. As such, human well-being was believed to depend on a balance of yin and yang. This view was to become the basis for a wide range of medical and therapeutic practices, including acupuncture and Tai Chi, which aimed to optimize a person's yin–yang balance (Tong, 2003).

While *pò* could exist separately from the body after death, the yin–yang approach required that *hún* and *pò* be seen as interacting and somewhat interdependent. As such, the ancient Chinese approach stressed the biological integration of thoughts and feelings in the living body. This was reflected in the associated medical practices, where physical treatments were frequently used to address emotional health. Overall, the ancient Chinese view of the human 'soul' anticipated several subtleties that were later to become central in modern scientific psychology.

Chinese philosophy went through something of a golden age with the work of the celebrated ancient philosopher K'ung-fu-tzu (孔夫子; 551–479 BCE), known in the West as Confucius. Confucius developed extensive teachings on the nature of human harmony, ethics and politics that were to become hugely influential around the world. However, although promoting ancestor worship and revering the sacredness of human bodies, Confucius' spiritual humanism did not develop detailed new ideas regarding the nature of souls.

Life, the universe and everything: Souls in Greece, Asia Minor (Turkey) and Persia (600–400 BCE)

At around the same time, a similar golden age of intellectualism was beginning to emerge in and around what is now modern Greece. The period from 600 to 300 BCE is often seen as the pinnacle of the ancient Greek civilization.

Archaeologists have shown that Greece had been populated for many thousands of years previously, and it has never been clear why this rocky Mediterranean peninsula suddenly yielded so many great philosophers. It seems likely that economic conditions, trading routes and plain good fortune all helped to cultivate a unique combination of opportunities and resources that fuelled many different types of productivity. At its peak, the Greek state had colonized several nearby territories, including the Aegean coast of present-day Turkey, then known as Asia Minor.

Many of the early Greek philosophers attempted to account for the status of human souls as part of a wider effort to explain the physical nature of the entire universe. One such line of reasoning was introduced by Thales (624–548 BCE), a philosopher who lived in the city of Miletus in Asia Minor. Thales believed that everything in the universe – including human souls – was made of water. Later, one of his students, Anaximander (610–546 BCE), concluded that everything was derived from a mysterious and formless substance that human senses could not comprehend, which he called *apeiron* (ἄπειρον). In turn, one of Anaximander's own students, Anaximenes (586–526 BCE) came to believe that this fundamental substance was actually air.

Eventually, such theories were refined when a number of philosophers concluded that the basic material of the universe was, in fact, a kind of fire. Heraclitus (535–475 BCE), a philosopher from Ephesus, then a city of the Persian Empire (and now part of Turkey), was one of the first to propose this view.

If everything is composed of fire, then water or moisture must be seen as dangerous, especially for such complex entities as human minds. In Heraclitus' view, all forms of wetness were indeed a threat to the human soul. According to him, this was why drunkenness interfered so much with people's judgements (Burnet, 1930). Such views were echoed in the work of the legendary medical pioneer Hippocrates (460–370 BCE), who also believed that human consciousness contained fire: Hippocrates taught that excessive water resulted in mental slowness.

All this theorizing about the composition of the universe might seem abstract, if not strange, to modern readers. However, we must again try to avoid the problem of presentism. In its time, explaining what the universe was made of – or, more precisely, what the universe *was* – presented a logically important scientific challenge.

The ancient Greeks may have been proficient engineers, but they had little understanding of what we now call 'materials science'. They knew almost nothing about the structure and properties of matter. The polytheistic religions of the time filled this explanatory vacuum with superstition, encouraging popular acceptance of animism. Against this backdrop, explaining the composition of the universe in terms of *physical* components, such as water or fire, reflected an early intellectual attempt to replace superstition with science.

This materialist view sparked a whole new way of thinking about physics. It set in motion an intellectual endeavour that eventually led to the approach scientists still use today when they talk about elements – namely, the classic periodic table.

While ancient Greek philosophy was innovative in several respects, it was clear that many of its views reflected a context of historical intellectualism. Either directly or indirectly, several of its ideas mirrored those of other cultures that had thrived previously. For example, the view that human souls might possess a physical form resembling some kind of gas – such as Anaximander's concept of *apeiron* or Anaximines' idea that the universe was made of air – brings to mind the ancient concept of *consciousness-as-respiration*. It resembled the much older Egyptian and Hindu ideas of *Ka* and *prana*.

Similarly, the ancient Greek philosophers echoed their much older Egyptian counterparts (and common-sense dualism) when they presumed that human consciousness was able to exist in the physical world while managing also to transcend it. An important example of this was the work of the renowned mathematician Pythagoras (570–495 BCE). Pythagoras taught that reason and intelligence occurred in the brain (Prioreschi, 1991), but also that human souls transmigrated to other living beings after death (Luchte, 2009).

The mind in multiple dimensions: Athens (400–300 BCE)

The claim that there were multiple realms of existence proved hugely influential in ancient Greek philosophy. Once again, the work of Pythagoras offers an example. Pythagoras became famous for developing complex mathematics, and was particularly interested in geometry. But he was also interested in souls. He consistently sought to provide mathematically informed explanations for spiritual matters.

Pythagoras was struck by the difference between mathematical perfection and real-world fallibility. While it was possible for humans to *imagine* geometrically perfect shapes, angles and trajectories – and even to codify them using mathematics – all this perfection was in fact illusory. In reality, humans were unable to recreate such geometric perfection *in the real world*. Human handiwork would always contain blemishes: lines drawn by hand would never be perfectly straight; circles produced by humans would never be exactly round. Mathematical perfection existed only in the mind's eye.

For Pythagoras, the very fact that human beings could visualize mathematical perfection suggested that they could 'see' into some non-earthly realm. They could mentally access a higher world of numbers that could help them make sense of the chaos in their earthly human existence.

Perhaps the most famous multi-realm approach was the *theory of forms*, a perspective proposed by the Athenian philosopher Plato (428–348 BCE). Plato argued that the ability of humans to imagine a perfectly straight line without ever having seen one in reality suggests they must have experienced such straightness *in a previous life*. He believed that this previous life occurred in a special realm in which perfect objects could be found. He called these perfect objects 'forms'.

In Plato's view, this realm of perfect forms truly exists. However, it exists in a different dimension to our own so-called real world. Our world is a secondary replica, a flawed imitation of the perfect realm. The entities and concepts that surround us are recognizable but inexact, in the same way as hand-drawn geometry falls short of the mathematical ideal.

Plato hypothesized that, before being born, each human being exists in the realm of forms. This is where they experience perfection directly, acquiring the ability to visualize it later. After they are born, they are able to benefit from the knowledge that they gathered in the perfect realm. Whenever they learn a new concept, they are not really 'learning' it for the first time. Instead, they are *recalling from memory* their initial experience of the concept, which they encountered in its ideal form during this prior existence.

Plato was a student of Socrates (470–399 BCE), who is often described as the founder of Western philosophy. Socrates developed new methods of critical thinking, such as the use of argumentative dialogue as an approach to teaching. His ideas are credited with having revolutionized philosophy's approach to the validation of knowledge, a subfield of philosophy known as *epistemology*.

However, Socrates himself produced no written work and so most of what we know about him is inferred from the writings of Plato and his other students. This can sometimes make it difficult to distinguish Plato's own ideas from those of his mentor. As a result, Plato's theories can sometimes seem inconsistent.

For example, Plato sometimes uses the word ψυχή to refer to the religious notion of soul, the type of soul that can predate (and postdate) physiological life and exist in a perfect, even heavenly, realm. In other contexts, he uses ψυχή to refer to mental functions, in a manner more akin to secular discussions of the mind, such as when he describes concepts like executive control and metacognition (Worley, 2018).

Plato's contributions to psychology were wide-ranging. He was one of the first thinkers to describe reasoning as a conflict between rationality and irrationality, drawing attention to the human tendency towards error. He also spoke of three different types of mental function involving different physiological systems: acuity in the brain, affect in the heart, and appetite in the gut.

However, it is Plato's student Aristotle (384–322 BCE) who is widely regarded as perhaps the most influential ancient philosopher in the history of psychology (D. N. Robinson, 1989). Aristotle was something of a specialist on human souls. His major work on the subject was a treatise called Περὶ Ψυχῆς (Peri psychēs), usually translated into English as 'On the soul'. The antiquarian Greek version of this work was translated into Arabic, and eventually into Latin in the twelfth century CE. The Latin version, *De anima*, has been the basis for much scholarship on Aristotle ever since.

It is notable that even after spending twenty years as Plato's student, Aristotle developed a significantly different view on souls (D. N. Robinson, 1989). Importantly, he defined the soul as an intrinsic feature of a living being. He argued that a soul does not exist before or after a person is alive. The soul is, in essence, the very property of being alive. This principle is referred to as *hylomorphism*.

As ever, of course, things are not simple. Although Aristotle described the soul as a property of being alive, he had previously written that cognition – the end product of intellectual function – did not occur in the body. So while Aristotle's view of the unity of souls and bodies is often described as monist, his earlier view on the immaterial nature of thought seems to imply a form of dualism.

Quite how we should interpret Aristotle's take on the mind–body debate has been argued over by philosophers for centuries. It remains controversial even to this day. Some scholars suggest that Aristotle's inconsistency simply reflects how he changed his mind over time. They say his writings on intellect were immature, influenced by his early-career contact with Plato; in contrast, his later writings on hylomorphism reflect a more thoughtful view on the subject (Frede, 1987). According to this assessment, Aristotle's naïve dualism was superseded by a more considered monism.

By most historical accounts, the death of Aristotle saw the beginning of the end of this period of exceptional Greek scholarship. An important feature of subsequent Greek philosophy was a shift of focus away from traditional broad questions and the pursuit of knowledge for its own sake. Instead there emerged a new emphasis on practical outcomes. For example, philosophers began to explore ways to promote personal happiness and achieve material well-being (Stace, 1962).

LOGOPHILIA: 'HYLOMORPHISM'

Hylomorphism is the idea that our perception of every object depends on a combination of its 'matter' and its 'form'. For example, a wooden stool could be seen as just a piece of wood, which is its *matter*. However, we understand that it is more than a piece of wood because of its *form* – in other words, its shape or design. Its form leads us to perceive the object as a stool. Hylomorphism is often invoked to explain that while the human body is a living being's *matter*, the human mind is its *form*, and so completes the person. The concept of hylomorphism is usually associated with Aristotle. However, the word *hylomorphism* was introduced only in the nineteenth century. Despite its Greek styling – it combines the Greek words for *matter* (hyle or ὕλη) and *form* (morphē or μορφή) – the term was never used by Aristotle himself.

Philosophy thus became less profound and more self-centred – or, to use modern terms, less 'basic' and more 'applied'.

The decline and fall of monism: Rome (550 BCE–400 CE)

The Kingdom of Rome emerged in around the sixth century BCE, comprising a number of settlements near the Tiber river in central Italy. By 509 BCE, the monarchy was overthrown and the Roman people began to rule themselves as a republic. There then began a period of expansionist cultural dominance by the Roman civilization.

According to some estimates, at the peak of their influence the Romans exerted political control over nearly half of the world's population: 70 to 100 million people lived inside the Roman Empire (Scheidel, 2009) at a time when the total global population was around 180 million (McEvedy & Jones, 1978). Rome's borders stretched from Hadrian's Wall in Scotland to the Nile Delta in Egypt, and from the Atlantic shores of Portugal all the way to where the Persian Gulf touches the coastline of modern Kuwait.

The Romans established Europe's civic infrastructures, codified its languages, and paved the way for Christianity to become its dominant religion. In underpinning many of the social and cultural norms that have come to characterize the modern Western outlook, it is true to say that the Romans have had nothing less than a profound impact on the course of human history.

The Roman approach to the mind was influenced by medicine, philosophy and, significantly, religion. During the period of Roman dominance, polytheistic and indigenous religions gave way to Christianity, with animistic views gradually being displaced by orthodox Christian spirituality.

But prior to the arrival of Christianity, Roman philosophy appeared to have settled on a monist position that mind and body are unified. The philosopher Lucretius, who we mentioned previously, was a prominent advocate of this outlook. Lucretius openly mocked the idea that souls entered human bodies from outside. For one thing, he noted, this would involve bodiless spirits wandering the ether just waiting for human beings to have sex, so that they could be on hand whenever conception produced a 'mortal frame' for them to inhabit (Potkay, 2019).

Lucretius had been a follower of the Greek philosopher Epicurus (341–270 BCE). Like all Epicureans, he promoted monist views that denied the existence of immortal spiritual souls. As mentioned above, these ideas were later vigorously criticized by Christian leaders.

The renowned physician Galen (129–200 CE) was also a very prominent advocate of monism. Galen lived and worked in the Roman city of Bergamon, located in what is now İzmir Province in Turkey. He developed an influential model of personality based on the circulation of fluids within the human body. We will discuss the psychology of personality further in Chapter 11. For now we can note that Galen promoted a range of theories based on the premise that mind and body were unified, specifically in the brain.

Galen adapted and promoted Plato's tripartite theory of mental function, considering the brain to be the site of rationality, the heart the place of emotions, and the gut the source of desire. Each mental function was described as comprising a type of vital energy called *pneuma* (πνεῦμα), which translates as 'air' or 'breath', once again invoking the idea of *consciousness-as-respiration*.

Galen based his views on careful research. For example, he correctly identified and described the structure of the human spinal cord and its connection to the brain. In Galen's time, it was difficult to complete detailed human anatomical studies because it was considered socially unacceptable to interfere with a dead body. It is believed that Galen managed to complete this work by studying the bodies of people who had died accidentally or violently, and who had been mutilated in a way that allowed him to see their brains.

Galen also carried out experimental research. In a number of animal studies, conducted on pigs and oxen, he found that touching the live heart had no effect on sensation or consciousness. This conclusively falsified claims that the heart was the centre of the mind (Crivellato & Ribatti, 2007).

Galen became extremely famous within his own lifetime, even earning the declared praise of the Roman emperor of the day, Marcus Aurelius (121–180 CE). His medicine became the standard throughout the Roman world, and indeed far beyond. As the Eastern Roman Empire included Syria and surrounding regions, Galen's writings were soon translated into Arabic. As a result, his ideas were assimilated into Middle Eastern medicine and thrived in the Islamic world even after Roman influence had abated.

However, the monism of Roman philosophy did not endure. An important shift came with the work of Plotinus (204–70 CE), a spiritual philosopher who was certainly able to draw on a wide range of cultural influences. Plotinus was born in rural Egypt, moved to Alexandria where he was educated in the Greek tradition, and then travelled widely in the east, where he became familiar with Persian and Indian thought. He later settled in the city of Rome, and lived there for a number of decades, interacting with an eclectic coterie of students that included politicians, poets and doctors. He produced most of his written works in his old age, cobbling together several existing ideas into a style of reasoning that became known as *Neoplatonism*.

Plotinus concluded that the soul was derived from a transcendent source, entered the body temporarily, and returned to this transcendent source after death. This worldview echoed both Pythagoras and Plato, but it also reflected the Vedic approaches of Hinduism. These ideas were to become deeply influential on the then emerging Christian tradition of philosophy, which was to dominate succeeding centuries.

It is often said that the reason for Rome's eventual decline was the extent of its success. As its territory became more and more vast, its political realities and structures became increasingly complex. The economic costs of managing – and of militarily defending – such a realm grew beyond what was sustainable. The Roman world declined rather slowly, across the fourth and fifth centuries CE. Historians still argue about the precise causes (Bowersock, 1996).

In terms of the history of the Western world, the fall of Rome was significant not only because it marked the end of the Roman era. It also saw the rise of Christianity, and a sustained period of religious hegemony in Europe.

THE MIDDLE AGES: THEOLOGY CLAIMS THE SOUL

In Europe, the period from the fifth to the fifteenth century CE is often referred to as the Middle Ages. This rather arbitrary label is part of a three-stage model of European history, in which the years before the fifth century CE are seen as 'classical' and the era subsequent to the fifteenth century CE is seen as 'modern'. The intervening period, therefore, is seen as the 'middle'. A traditional word used when describing this period is 'medieval', based on the phrase *medium aevum*, which is Latin for 'middle ages'.

The Middle Ages began with the decay of the Roman political structures that had shaped everyday life in Europe, North Africa and western Asia for several centuries. Religion became a unifying focus for the region's otherwise multicultural population. However, although the Emperor Theodosius I (347–95 CE) had made Christianity the official state religion for all of Rome, there were still variations in how it was practised in different parts of the continent.

In the eastern part of the Roman Empire, churches used the Greek language, banned religious icons and images, and allowed married men to become priests. By contrast, churches in the western empire used Latin, embraced and promoted iconography, and insisted that priests be celibate. There were theological points of difference too, as well as differences in how the various churches organized themselves politically. Ultimately, it was the western Christian church that grew to be dominant in European affairs.

Christianity and the medieval soul

In many ways, this pan-continental church filled the power vacuum created by the erosion of the Roman state. Civilian deference to the secular government was now redirected to church leaders. For a time, the Christian church operated as a de facto state in its own right, defining borders around its territory and operating its own military. However, for the most part it exerted its influence through existing monarchical, feudal and political structures. Over time, its political leverage became all-encompassing. The Christian pope would eventually claim an absolute right to depose any king in Europe should he wish to do so.

This period is sometimes referred to as the 'Dark Ages' of European history, a phrase chosen to depict an atmosphere of intellectual and cultural malaise. However, many historians object to such a dismal assessment. They argue that the 'Dark Ages' label underestimates the achievements and vitality of medieval times (Harper, 2017). But there is no doubt that intellectualism in the Middle Ages was severely constrained by a widespread culture of religious dogmatism. Across Europe, the Christian church was uncritically revered as sacred, beyond reproach, and holding supreme authority with regard to people's social and individual lives.

The way early Christian theologians discussed the human soul typified this ascendancy of dogma, and its marginalization of empirical scepticism. Monist views, such as those of the Epicureans, were discarded (and indeed often condemned as heresy), while dualist approaches, such as Neoplatonism, were embraced.

Debates shifted away from the central challenge of the mind–body problem. Instead of focusing on *whether* the soul existed, philosophers argued about *what* the soul was, *what* it was capable of, and *how* it behaved before and after death. In terms of formal scholarship, the existence of independent non-corporeal souls was no longer in question.

Given the dominance of theology over philosophy, the Christian view of souls became the main culturally approved explanation for human consciousness throughout Europe, for literally centuries. The 'non-physical version' of a person was assumed to be a spiritual phenomenon. It arrived in the body through a process of *ensoulment*, departed it after death, and ultimately fulfilled a divine destiny by joining an ever-growing population of righteous souls in heaven.

HISTORY REPEATING ITSELF: ABORTION AND THE 'RIGHT TO LIFE'

Abortion is the use of medication or surgery to deliberately end a pregnancy, such that an embryo or foetus is then unable to survive. The procedure is considered very safe in medical terms, and is considered by many to be a fundamental right for all people who might become pregnant. The World Health Organization recommends that, for public health reasons, every person should have ready access to abortion services. Nonetheless, abortion is often seen as controversial. For example, in many societies, critics believe that abortion is used to favour the selection of sons over daughters, and thus to reinforce inherently sexist social structures and attitudes.

However, perhaps the greatest tension relates to the core question of whether it is intrinsically ethical to terminate a pregnancy when it would otherwise lead to the birth of a living human being.

Even in countries where abortion has been legal for many years, there tend to be several restrictions on its availability, as well as ongoing legal debate. A particular point of concern is whether an abortion can be conducted early or late in a pregnancy. By and large, late-term abortion is considered more contentious than early abortion. For this reason, the relevant laws tend to specify a particular cut-off time, after which abortion is considered unacceptable. The precise time frame for this restriction varies from country to country.

The core consideration seems to be one of when, exactly, an embryo or foetus becomes a living being in its own right. Medical specialists often refer to the point of viability, which is when a foetus would be able to survive outside the uterus. However, this point of viability is determined more by medical technology than by ethics. As technology has improved, the point of medical viability has

shifted. In the future, it may shift again. As such, during any given period in medical history, the point of medical viability will be contingent on the technology available at the time, and so is unrelated to the arrival of souls into bodies.

Accordingly, ethicists argue about a different time point, the one at which an embryo or foetus assumes the status of an independent living entity. Although such debates take place today, they seem largely unchanged from those that consumed the minds of theologians at the beginning of the Middle Ages. At that time, these dualist philosophers needed to account for how and when each soul came to occupy its designated human body.

Theologians such as Basil of Caesarea (329–79 CE) and John Chrysostom (349–407 CE) argued that the soul entered the embryo as soon as conception occurred. By implication, any procedure that causes an abortion was therefore said to constitute a form of murder.

Later theologians, such as Augustine of Hippo (354–430 CE), formulated a different view. Augustine argued that the soul could not enter the body until the foetus was completely formed. In effect this allowed abortions to be conducted until the beginning of the second trimester of pregnancy. (However, while not considering first-trimester terminations to be 'murder', Augustine nonetheless objected to *all* abortions, on the basis that unfettered procreation was a religious duty for all married Christians; Bauerschmidt, 1999.) This remained the effective view of Christianity until the sixteenth century.

In debates about abortion, the fundamental psychological question of when the non-physical version of human beings comes to exist within the physical version continues to be disputed today.

The medieval mind in Islam and Judaism

Although European Christian culture came to exert an almost hegemonic influence on science, scholarship and politics, other major world cultures also thrived during the Middle Ages. Islamic scholarship, for example, produced significant contributions to medicine and philosophy. These developments rarely occurred in isolation. Islamic thinkers were extremely well read and their work reflected a mix of intellectual traditions and influences.

With regard to the human mind, Islamic philosophy inherited its major concepts from Aristotle. Many Islamic scholars cited Aristotle directly and wrote extensively about him in their own work. One important example was al-Kindi (short for Ya'qūb ibn 'Isḥāq al-Kindī; 801–73 CE), a philosopher from the city of Kufa, which is now part of Iraq. Al-Kindi is often credited as being one of the founders of the Islamic philosophical tradition.

Al-Kindi was an expert mathematician and physician as well as a philosopher. He played an important role in adapting the Indian numeral system to create the Arabic numerals that the world uses today. He also devised advanced methods for estimating probabilities based on projected outcomes, from which later mathematicians would formalize modern techniques of statistical inference (Broemeling, 2011). Al-Kindi was renowned for applying statistical approaches to medicine and physiology, from which he developed a number of theories about the soul, viewing it as immortal, tripartite and divine.

The philosopher Rhazes (Latinized name of Muhammad ibn Zakariya al-Razi; 854–925 CE) also derived his theories of the mind from a prodigious expertise in medicine. Rhazes, from Shahr-e Ray near Tehran in Iran, adopted a modern experimentalist approach to the Galenic medicine that was prevalent in his time. He developed new methods and concepts that ultimately had a huge influence on the evolution of Western medical practice (Tibi, 2006). In many respects, his work pre-empted modern psychosomatics, paediatrics, medical chemistry, pathology, virology and the conducting of clinical trials (Zarrintan, Shahnaee & Aslanabadi, 2018).

Although arguing against quackery, superstition and medical mysticism, Rhazes nonetheless promoted a

Public domain, via Wikimedia Commons / (PD-US)

Image 2.4   Avicenna
The Islamic philosopher Avicenna is regarded as one of the founders of modern medicine. He rejected the idea of transmigration but supported the view that souls were immortal.

religious view of souls. To him, human minds were created by a divine being, who would reward or punish people in heaven based on their moral behaviour while on earth (Druart, 1996). To complicate matters, Rhazes concluded that souls would transmigrate several times – from person to person, or even from person to animal – before ultimately entering the afterlife.

In the Islamic philosophical tradition, the Kazakh-born scholar al-Farabi (short for Abū Naṣr Muḥammad ibn Muḥammad al Fārābī; 872–950 CE) is often considered the 'Second Master' after Aristotle (Netton, 1992). Importantly, al-Farabi viewed souls as having an imaginative faculty that was intertwined with cosmic spirituality. He saw the human intellect as capable of receiving knowledge from divine sources. Al-Farabi's belief that information could flow from deities into human minds was to acquire great cultural significance, because it served to reconcile philosophical views of the mind with religious teachings about prophesy.

One of the most prolific philosophers in the Islamic tradition was Avicenna (Latinized version of Ibn Sina; 980–1037 CE), a Persian polymath from Bukhara, now part of Uzbekistan. Avicenna is yet another Islamic scholar to be considered a founder of modern medicine (McGinnis, 2010). In his philosophy of souls, Avicenna largely followed Aristotle's view. He specified a tripartite model, and linked the soul to the human heart. Avicenna rejected the idea of transmigration but supported the view that souls were immortal. According to him, the souls of the dead live permanently in the afterlife, where they continue to display all their earthly personality traits.

The influential Syrian physician Ibn al-Nafis (short for Ala-al-Ddin abu al-Hasan Ali ibn Abi-Hazm al-Qarshi al-Dimashqi; 1213–88 CE) largely endorsed Avicenna's approach. However, as an expert on cardiology, al-Nafis could not agree with Avicenna that the soul resided only in the heart. Al-Nafis was the first scientist to accurately describe how blood circulates throughout the cardiovascular system. Duly, he concluded that this meant that the soul could be found everywhere in the body.

Islamic scholars were prodigious innovators, communicators and translators. The philosopher Averroes (Latinized version of Abū l-Walīd Muḥammad Ibn ʾAḥmad Ibn Rušd; 1126–98 CE), from Córdoba in southern Spain, proved especially influential. He wrote many commentaries about the works of Aristotle, which proved crucial in broadening the audience for Aristotle's theories.

Among those inspired by Averroes' commentaries were a number of scholars in the Jewish philosophical tradition. These included a fellow citizen of Córdoba, the philosopher Moses ben Maimon (1135–1204 CE), commonly known as Maimonides. Maimonides appropriated Aristotle's approach to reflect the rabbinical teachings of Judaism, affirming that the immaterial part of the human soul was created by the deity. Others who relied heavily on Averroes' commentaries were the French-Jewish scholar Samuel ibn Tibbon (1150–1230 CE) and the Spanish-Jewish philosopher and poet Shem-Tov ibn Falaquera (1225–90 CE).

Ultimately, throughout the Middle Ages, philosophers in all the major Abrahamic religions found common ways to ensure that the establishment view of the human mind was consistent with religious teaching.

HISTORICALLY (IN)ACCURATE?: THE ISLAMIC WORLD'S CONTRIBUTION TO MEDICINE

Western scholars – and politicians – often consider the realm of European Christianity to have been a unique hub of intellectual and scientific progress throughout history. By implication (and sometimes by explicit acclaim), such observers dismiss non-European and non-Christian cultures for having contributed little or nothing to our contemporary technological world.

These views tend to overlook the fact that Islamic culture has been the source of several important scientific advancements, especially in medicine. Many elements of modern medicine – including medical devices, surgical procedures and the design of hospitals and medical schools – were first introduced in the Islamic world. As we have discussed, pioneers such as Rhazes and Avicenna are considered founders of modern medicine. For hundreds of years, Islamic medicine was far ahead of what was practised elsewhere.

In the tenth century, Islamic medicine was acknowledged to be the most sophisticated ever seen in the world. Islamic scholars tended to be multilingual and so were capable of combining knowledge from a variety of sources, including Greek and Latin texts. Such was the status of their work that Arabic itself came to be seen as an important language of science. Avicenna's medical encyclopaedia, *al-Qānūn fī al-ṭibb* (*Canon of Medicine*), which he completed in 1025 CE, was studied by European medical students right up until the eighteenth century.

Another influential encyclopaedia – *Kitab al-tasrif* (*The Method of Medicine*) – was produced by the Spanish Muslim physician Al-Zahrawi (short for Abū al-Qāsim Khalaf ibn al-ʿAbbās al-Zahrāwī al-Ansari; 936–1013 CE). Comprising thirty volumes, it took Al-Zahrawi more than fifty years to complete. Its final volume, *On Surgery and Instruments*, was used by surgeons until well into the nineteenth century. The book describes a huge variety of medical conditions, as well as dozens of surgical procedures and devices.

Al-Zahrawi is credited with inventing a number of instruments that are still used for surgery today, including scalpels, catheters, forceps, pincers and cauteries. He devised the method of surgical stitching using catgut (a cord made from animal intestines that can dissolve harmlessly in the human body) that continues to be widely used in modern surgery.

Islamic medicine also introduced the concept of the hospital. Previously, physicians would see patients in their homes. Islamic societies were the first to open public hospitals where the sick could be treated and recover. They introduced several principles of modern hospital care: the best doctors would treat the poorest as well as the richest patients; student doctors would participate in the life of the hospital in order to learn their trade; mental illness would be treated as well as physical illness; and there would be different wards for each disease category, as well as special sections for the elderly, whose care needs would often require a tailored approach.

In the modern world, medical and healthcare systems are often viewed as among the most valuable of all social assets, and an important achievement of human civilization. Modern medicine's traditions, technologies and training methods reflect a lasting legacy of Islamic intellectualism, in which education, humanitarianism and public service are valued as much as scientific excellence.

SETTING THE SCENE FOR MODERN MINDS

Most historians view the fifteenth century as marking the end of the Middle Ages and thus the beginning of modernity. This was a time known as the 'Renaissance' of Europe, a period named after the French word for 'rebirth'. Over the next 200 years, European culture began to rediscover an intellectual freedom that was said to be reminiscent of the golden age of classical antiquity. Inspired by classical Greek tradition, among other influences, Renaissance scholars applied fresh thinking to architecture, philosophy, science, technology, literature, music and the fine arts.

This era coincided with a period of extensive overseas exploration, sometimes referred to as the Age of Discovery. New seafaring technologies enabled European powers such as Portugal and Spain to commission exploratory voyages, charting what was then to them a 'new' world. They ultimately established extensive empires in the Americas, as well as in Africa and Asia.

Overseas colonialism became a national policy ambition for many European states. French colonization of the Americas began. The Dutch Republic embarked on military exploits to defend its traders in Africa and Asia from Spanish and Portuguese rivals, going on to establish its own colonial empire. Further trading rivalries emerged involving Britain, who after the (Protestant) Reformation had become enemies of a number of European states. The great Spanish and English armadas clashed on the seas off western Africa.

Of course, for many people living outside Europe, this was a dark period of recurring invasion and, in many cases, brutal subjugation. The sixteenth century also saw the beginning of the so-called slave trade, in which millions of African people were abducted, imprisoned and then forcibly transported to the Americas by European traffickers (we will return to the long-lasting consequences of this activity in Chapter 6).

As well as *political* imperialism, the modern age ushered in rampant *cultural* imperialism, where the economic and political might of the European continent led it to exert a domineering influence on global culture. Perspectives of scholarship, science and communication became skewed, and Western (or European or Christian) standards were increasingly presented as the norm for humanity as a whole.

The Renaissance lasted just two centuries, and is often uncritically lauded as a cherished turning point in the history of civilization. Nonetheless, it set the scene for a modern era of culture, intellectualism and science that, in a number of ways, gave rise to global structures of injustice and inequality that remain problematic in today's world.

'Renaissance Man'

Many fifteenth-century technical innovations relied on mathematics and science to enhance our cultural experiences. One example was the use of geometric perspective to add realism to paintings. This ability to combine and appreciate disparate fields of knowledge became especially valued during the Renaissance. The notion of a 'universal' education was popularized and a plethora of new universities established, along with numerous academies, institutes and other places of learning.

Today the term 'Renaissance Man' is used to describe someone who epitomizes this spirit of learning – a person unusually talented in multiple fields of culture (and also, presumably, a man).

Of course, human history does not just suddenly shift from one cultural period to the next. Social transitions are far more fragmented than they might appear in hindsight. Renaissance thinking might often seem more complex than medieval thinking, but that does not mean that Renaissance *thinkers* were intellectually superior. After all, they had the advantage of standing on their predecessors' shoulders. As we discussed in Chapter 1, to presume a narrative of inevitable progress is to succumb to the fallacy of Whig history.

Nonetheless, one of the key cultural figures of the Renaissance was indisputably precocious. Born in Florence, Italy, Leonardo da Vinci (1452–1519) is widely regarded as having been a true universal genius. He is often presented as the archetypal example of a 'Renaissance Man'. Considered one of the great artists of all time – producing such classic works as the *Mona Lisa* and *The Last Supper* – his renown as a painter endures to this day, even though only fifteen or so of his paintings survive.

As well as being a legendary artist, Leonardo was a prodigious scientist and engineer. Among his inventions were the helicopter, the parachute, the armoured car, the diving suit and the machine gun. He developed plans for a functional robot, a driverless car and solar panels. He wrote thousands of pages of scholarly notes, detailing complex observations on optics, botany, engineering, physics, geology, fluid mechanics, architecture and astronomy. He was a supremely talented analyst of human physiology and anatomy, producing a number of diagrams – such as *Vitruvian Man* – that have become icons of global culture.

Perhaps unsurprisingly, Leonardo eventually applied his considerable talent to the investigation of human souls. He endeavoured to establish what part of anatomy might be the point of contact between soul and body (Del Maestro, 1998). His evaluations led him to conclude that it lay in the middle of the human brain, specifically just above the optic chiasm, close to the anterior of the third ventricle (Santoro et al., 2009). That one of the greatest geniuses ever to have lived would invest effort in such a study illustrates how the non-physical version of the self has long been seen as a central human concern, attracting universal curiosity.

The mind thinks, therefore it exists

From the sixteenth and seventeenth centuries onwards, European scholars began to take tentative steps to consider the secular dimensions of their universe. We will consider the impact of their endeavours on science as a whole in Chapter 3.

One of the most lasting contributions to the study of the non-physical self was offered by the seventeenth-century French philosopher and scientist René Descartes (1596–1650). Descartes was interested in the promotion of philosophical scepticism, focusing on the distinction between 'that which is true' and 'that which can be proven'. In doing so he was taking a brave step. He was effectively implying that church teachings on philosophical matters might not be 'true' unless they can be 'proven'. This step towards scepticism is often credited as marking the starting point of modern (Western) philosophy.

A polymath, Descartes was interested in the apparent autonomy of physiological systems. He was particularly fascinated by a series of decorative mechanical statues he encountered while visiting the Parisian district of Saint-Germain-des-Prés. These statues were installed by the city's fountain-makers, and had been plumbed with intricate systems of internal piping. Whenever passers-by walked past, water would shoot up inside the statues, causing them to move (Fancher, 1996). For Descartes, these statues demonstrated how living organisms could be made to function without needing to have a conscious mind.

Image 2.5 Adi Shankara (painting by Raja Ravi Varma, c. 1904)

Descartes's reasoning about the non-physical self was to become a landmark in the history of philosophy – and of psychology. He noted that human perceptions do not always conform to reality, and so can always be doubted. Crucially, he felt that in order to be able to doubt one's own perceptions, each human being must have *a mind that does the doubting*. Descartes saw this line of argument as proving that while everything we perceive could actually be an illusion, the one thing that could not possibly be illusory is *the very act of thinking* itself. Therefore, the reality of one's own mind is unassailable.

Descartes's conclusion – *I think, therefore I am* – is famously recalled in its Latin form, *Cogito ergo sum*. During the Middle Ages, Latin had become the standard written language of European scholarship, reflecting its role as liturgical language of the Christian church. 'Cogito ergo sum' appeared in Descartes's scholarly volume, *Principia philosophiæ* (*Principles of Philosophy*; 1644), a book written entirely in Latin as it was intended for an academic readership.

However, nearly a decade before, Descartes had presented the exact same conclusion in his native French ('Je pense, donc je suis'). He included it in his treatise, *Discours de la méthode* (*Discourse on Method*), a book that was part philosophy and part autobiography (Descartes, 1637). As very few ordinary European citizens could read Latin, it was probable that far more readers encountered the French version before they ever heard the Latin one. Nonetheless, reflecting how the transmission of history can often be adulterated by the filters of arbitrary privilege, it is the Latin version that went on to become renowned.

Like other dualists before him, Descartes sought to argue that the mind and body must interact in a truly physical sense. Otherwise, he felt, the human mind would simply float away, disconnected from the body where its thoughts and feelings were experienced. Descartes identified the pineal gland as the point of contact, largely on the basis that it was a single component not duplicated within the brain's anatomical symmetry. Descartes's physical explanation did not discount the existence of a deity. Indeed, it was reliant on it. The pineal gland was said to be where sensations and experiences of the mind were transmitted to a non-material spirit.

Descartes's dualistic account became so influential that the separation of mind and body is now often referred to as 'Cartesian dualism' (*Cartesian* being the adjectival form of *Cartesius*,

ALMOST FAMOUS: ADI SHANKARA

Adi Shankara (short for Adi Shankaracharya; 788–820 CE) was a renowned eighth-century Indian philosopher, who remains largely undiscussed in the modern West. Born in the town of Kalady, in present-day Kerala in southern India, Shankara expressed interest in philosophy from an early age. According to the traditional story of his life, at the age of eight, he convinced his reluctant mother to allow him to become a hermit after a crocodile attacked him while he was bathing in a river. When the crocodile grabbed him, he cried to his mother that he would be killed unless she allowed him to leave home. After she reluctantly agreed, the crocodile released the boy, enabling him to begin his ascetic life.

Shankara travelled widely throughout India, studying under a guru and participating in philosophical debates. He became an influential thinker and garnered a number of disciples who joined him on his travels. He produced several texts, including commentaries on a number of Upanishads, as well as his own original philosophical works. He is considered to be an influential promoter of Advaita Vedanta, a school of Hinduism.

Shankara sought to critique Buddhist ideas about the momentariness of mental states, and thus the ephemeral nature of existence. To do so he presented an elaborate argument based on the implications of personal thought. He described how it was impossible to speak of oneself as not existing. He wrote that 'No one thinks, "I am *not*"', thereby demonstrating that certainty in such statements as 'I *am*' proves that nobody can doubt their own existence (Krishnan, 2004). 'Even when the object of knowledge alters,' he explained, 'the knower does not alter, for he is the past, present and future as his essence is eternally present' (Radhakrishnan, 2009).

This argument is effectively the Hindu equivalent of *Cogito ergo sum*. In this way, Shankara's philosophy anticipated that of Descartes by some 800 years. However, while *Cogito ergo sum* is one of the most recognizable phrases in Western intellectual culture, few in the West – even few Western philosophy students – will be aware of the writings of Adi Shankara.

At the age of thirty-two, Shankara moved to a Hindu pilgrimage site located deep in the Himalayas. One day he went missing while walking in the mountains. His disciples last saw him walking in the direction of a cave, but his body was never found. Presuming him dead, they declared the cave to be his final resting place. In his short life, Shankara produced many ideas that would filter throughout Hindu philosophy for centuries.

which was Descartes's name in Latin). While dualism had been contemplated for millennia before him, Descartes's specific approach was bold and persuasive. As such, he is credited with elevating the 'mind–body problem' in importance, making it a topic worthy of the closest philosophical attention.

THE NON-PHYSICAL SELF: FROM ANCIENT TO MODERN

Since its earliest beginnings, human culture has sought to understand the nature of the non-physical version of the self – be it soul, mind, intellect, consciousness, essence, spirit or psyche. The quest has produced a variety of views about this thing's existence, nature and location, views that have emerged from several philosophical – and theological – origins.

We can consider these ideas to have fallen into two main categories. To some observers, the mind is immaterial, immortal and inviolable. To others, it is a biological by-product of existence, a consequence of physiological life, and as ephemeral as any other organic quality that decays after death. Culturally, and to many scholars, the former position has been preferred, despite the fact that (in the purely technical sense of these terms) the latter is more consistent with the available evidence.

For those for whom the soul must exist within the anatomy of the human body, opinion has varied with regard to the precise details. Broadly speaking, again there are two types of approach. Some intellectual traditions hold that the soul is housed in, or accesses the body through, a specific anatomical structure (such as the brain or the heart). Others hold that the spirit is more endemic in physiological terms, and infused throughout every part of the body.

From our vantage in the twenty-first century, it often appears as though historical narratives are liable to produce certain cycles. The human quest to understand the nature of souls might be an example. After millennia of prehistoric superstition and shamanism, the invention of writing unleashed a prolific means by which humans could generate and share their insights. To the early global civilizations animism appeared mystical and incomplete, a 'just-so' story that raised more questions than were answered. Ancient scholars were keen to find rational explanations for their world, and to them the universe made more sense when viewed in mechanistic terms. Human minds were no exception. But as time passed, the mechanistic explanations that replaced prehistoric animism were *themselves* gradually displaced by a new type of mysticism – a mysticism derived from the dogmatic doctrines of hegemonic religion.

This intellectual journey shaped the cultural context within which humanity today thinks, talks and argues about the human mind. For example, the historical interweaving with theology has propelled a certain mood of reverence and attached considerable tension to this topic. In our modern world, human minds are frequently discussed as though they are mysterious, qualitatively distinct, unique within the universe and truly sacred in nature.

Such quasi-religious deference towards human minds is far from anachronistic. Even in the throes of modernity, these ideas define how human societies view the difference between life and death. The ensoulment of foetuses, the right to life of comatose patients, the morality of suicide, and the ethics of capital punishment – these and many other issues are profoundly influenced by prevailing social norms about what the human mind actually is, where and when it becomes alive, and whether its reach extends beyond the banalities of human biology. Whether scientific psychology has been genuinely useful in progressing a resolution to such debates is, to put it mildly, far from clear.

It is often assumed that scientific thinking leads to a diminution of religious mysticism, at least with regard to specific issues like the existence of tangible souls. But that has not always been obvious from the history of scientific research on the mind, even in its modern institutionalized form.

For example, in the nineteenth century, prominent scientific psychologists invested significant effort in researching the existence of independent and autonomous human souls. Among the equipment procured by the American psychologist William James for his laboratory at Harvard University was a Ouija board, a device for contacting dead spirits (we will explore James's pivotal contributions to the development of academic psychology in Chapter 3). James discussed with colleagues the possibility of using scientific evidence of an afterlife as the basis for establishing a new secular religion, and completed many studies of psychic mediums as they conducted seances (Coon, 1992). The prospect of communicating with the dead was pursued by many notable scientists, including the American inventor Thomas Edison (1847–1931), who for many years attempted to build a 'spirit phone' capable of allowing conversations with 'personalities which have left this earth' (Penn, 2002).

Others sought ways to physically measure aspects of the spirit world. In 1907, the American physician Duncan McDougall (1866–1920) achieved national newspaper attention for his efforts to calculate the weight of human souls. His method was to place critically ill patients on weighing scales before and after they died. After five failed attempts, he eventually produced a successful measurement for the sixth patient he examined. That person, he recorded, was 21.3 grammes lighter after they died compared to when they were alive. He concluded that this therefore must be the precise weight of that patient's soul (Wiseman, 2011).

In the same year, the French doctor Hippolyte Baraduc (1850–1902) photographed his own wife as she lay dying in her bed, hoping to capture an image of her spirit as it departed her body (Pethes, 2016). He concluded that what seemed to be wisps of gaseous material appearing in the pictures taken shortly after she passed away were in fact elements of his dead wife's spirit.

The search for souls has undoubtedly helped to propel the success of science. From ancient to medieval to modern times, efforts to define the nature of the non-physical self have uncovered vast reservoirs of knowledge about human physiology and anatomy, insights that otherwise might have forever remained untapped. Universal curiosity about human souls, and a firm belief that such things are uniquely special within the universe, have provided a constant momentum to these efforts, and a ready audience who attach immediate value to whatever knowledge gets produced. The search for souls has also served to propel the field of psychology in precisely the same way, even if psychologists themselves are often reluctant to acknowledge this influence.

WHERE TO FROM HERE?

Formally, contemporary psychology stands within the mainstream of the natural sciences, and so – by implication, at least – promotes a secular materialist worldview. However, only a minority of psychologists directly study the question of selfhood or consciousness. Meanwhile, all psychologists are immersed within the same cultural norms that shape the rest of humanity's ethical (and religious) perspectives.

In other words, today's practitioners and producers of psychology – that science of the mind – are themselves inheritors of several centuries' worth of culturally crafted attitudes concerning minds, souls and psyches. Simultaneously, as human beings, they are just as predisposed as anyone else towards common-sense dualism.

The mind–body problem is not just an esoteric philosophical topic for psychologists to ponder. It is a distorting lens through which psychologists must view their data, develop their theories and experience their environments. Whenever psychologists attempt to formulate an understanding of the human mind, they must grapple with profound cultural assumptions about the very existence of humanity.

Insights are never formed in a vacuum. All scientists must grapple with assumptions. The process of producing knowledge on any subject is fraught with peril, and never as straightforward as we might at first believe. In our next chapter, we will examine how humans developed various methods, means and measures to try to make sense of their world, including their efforts to deal with a deceptively difficult initial intellectual challenge: deciding what it is that actually counts as 'knowledge'.

DISCUSSION QUESTIONS

1. How might current psychological views on the mind be influenced by social value systems and religious beliefs?
2. Why has the non-physical version of the self attracted so much attention from thinkers and scholars across all civilizations?
3. Are there significant cross-cultural differences in the way that the non-physical self has been depicted and explained? If so, then what are these differences and why did they emerge? If not, then why not?
4. Has humanity truly made progress in understanding the nature of the non-physical self? What could psychologists do to ensure that discourse on this subject is productive?

RECOMMENDED READING

- **Bering, J. (2008). The end? Why so many of us think our minds continue after we die.** *Scientific American: Mind, 19,* **34–41.** In this article, the author explains the psychological influences that lead many people to believe that human minds continue to exist after physical death, and thus that minds exist separately from bodies.
- **Crivellato, E., & Ribatti, D. (2007). Soul, mind, brain: Greek philosophy and the birth of neuroscience.** *Brain Research Bulletin, 71,* **327–36.** In this review, the authors show how ancient Greek philosophers and physicians insightfully discussed the properties of human minds and the ways in which localized brain function can lead to neural disorders.
- **Santoro, G., Wood, M. D., Merlo, L., Anastasi, G. P., Tomasello, F., & Germanò, A. (2009). The anatomic location of the soul from the heart, through the brain, to the whole body, and beyond: A journey through Western history, science, and philosophy.**

Neurosurgery, *65*, 633–43. In this review, the authors survey the philosophical and scientific ideas of several Western civilizations to show how each viewed the nature, and location, of human souls.

- **Tibi, S. (2006). Al-Razi and Islamic medicine in the 9th century.** *Journal of the Royal Society of Medicine*, *99*, 206–7. In this essay, the author examines the wide-ranging medical and psychological work of the ninth-century physician Al-Razi (or 'Rhazes'), within the broader context of early Islamic-world medicine.

KNOWLEDGE, EMPIRICISM AND THE CONCEPT OF *SCIENCE*

3

In this chapter, we will …

- examine how the history of psychology is often portrayed in terms of a traditional schema that is based on narrow and incomplete perspectives
- compare the different ways in which human societies evaluate knowledge-based claims
- trace the development of formal science as a method of generating reliable knowledge, and the gradual process by which science eventually gained mainstream acceptance in wider society
- consider the contextual factors that shaped nineteenth-century university education and, by extension, the establishment of the first university departments and laboratories to use the title 'psychology'
- evaluate the factors that make 'creation myths' psychologically attractive, including in professional and academic contexts

At the outset

It is common to summarize the history of psychology in terms of its emergence in nineteenth-century universities, with roots in philosophy and physiology. This schema owes much to a textbook written by Harvard psychologist Edwin G. Boring in 1929. However, many historians find Boring's version of psychology's history to be very selective, and in the subsequent century there has been a wider appreciation of how psychology evolved.

Central to the history of psychology is the developing way in which human beings have made sense of the world around them. Over centuries, the standards by which people agree that something is 'true' (or 'factual') have changed. Humans have moved from relying on 'knowledge from authority' to attaching greater credence to knowledge that is based on logic and, especially, evidence.

The combination of logic and evidence to produce knowledge is the central premise of the human activity we now call 'science'. Science dates back to the ancient world, but was initially an obscure practice, with most people in society continuing to rely on authority. During the Middle Ages, wider society gradually began to embrace empiricism as an acceptable, and worthy, way to validate claims.

After the Renaissance, science began to flourish, especially in Europe. A great many new science-based organizations were established, including university departments. The opening of a laboratory at Leipzig University in Germany is often credited as a starting point for the history of psychology.

In reality, psychology existed in universities long before the laboratory at Leipzig, and outside universities for centuries. Moreover, the psychology taught at Leipzig was very narrow. While many Leipzig graduates went on to set up laboratories in other universities, they were far outnumbered by departments based on other areas of psychology that, collectively, now make up a field we might call 'university psychology'.

Psychologically, all groups in society are liable to be lulled by 'creation myths'. Creation myths help human beings to rationalize their own place in the world, and to justify their current privilege. Creation myths in psychology are an example of Great Man historiography and professional propaganda. Human activities evolve from context; the real myth is that an area of science would ever have a single 'moment' of creation.

Key concept: Science

Science is a word that seldom means what people think. For many people, *science* is the name of a subject taught in schools and universities, alongside *history*, *geography*, *mathematics*, and so on. This is to use the word as a category heading, part of the logistics of education delivery.

For other people, *science* is an activity performed by a particular profession, namely that of the *scientist*. In this sense, *science* is 'what scientists do' in the sense that *engineering* is 'what engineers do'.

Some uses of the term 'science' are more sociological, and almost political. For some audiences, *science* is just one of a number of available belief systems: one that says that decisions should be taken on the basis of the consensus of professional scientists, rather than on the basis of, say, values. In this sense, *science* is tribal: its proponents defend it as a set of mutually supportive beliefs about why the world is the way it is; its

critics dismiss it as the dogma of a self-interested, elitist and control-obsessed cult. Both proponents and critics of science defend their own worldview as a matter of tribal loyalty, construing their duty to do so as an important moral obligation.

But at its core, science is more than just a subject area or professional title, and less than a political conspiracy to portray the events of the world as conforming to a preferred template. Rather, science is *a process by which objectively defensible knowledge is produced and handled by humans*. Over time humans have discovered that certain ways of doing this are more successful than others, which is why most modern science draws on the same set of processes and tools (such as controlled experimentation or quantitative analysis). In this sense, science is not a body of information that human society knows, it is *the way that human society truly 'knows' anything at all*.

WHERE SHALL WE BEGIN?

As discussed in Chapter 1, some historians take the view that psychology 'in the modern sense' did not exist until the 1870s. Some textbooks even refer to the opening of a laboratory at Leipzig University in 1879 as psychology's 'formal founding' (D. W. King et al., 2009) – as if no psychology existed in the world prior to that event.

However, also as noted in Chapter 1, the notion of 'history of psychology *in the modern sense*' is arbitrarily limiting. The history of anything 'in its modern sense' will not stretch back very far. Indeed, the very fact that reference is made to a 'modern sense' is an explicit acknowledgement that there are other – older – senses that could be discussed as well. After all, it would not be necessary to limit conversation to the 'modern' sense if there was nothing else to talk about.

The history of psychology *in all its senses* stretches back far beyond 1879. For this reason, the majority of histories acknowledge the antiquarian roots of the field. That being said, there often appears to be a somewhat rigid view of what such histories should contain. The textbooks, syllabi and websites devoted to the field all tend to follow the same traditional schema. It is possible to sketch out the dimensions of this schema in just a few paragraphs.

The traditional 'history of psychology' schema

The traditional schema for the history of psychology will acknowledge that its roots can be found in ancient philosophy and historical physiology. Psychology's roots in philosophy are depicted as dating back to the Greco-Roman world, progressing up to Descartes's seventeenth-century *rationalism* and then to later movements, such as the *empiricism* of John Locke (1632–1704) and the *materialism* of J. S. Mill (1806–73). Its physiological roots involve work by Johannes Peter Müller (1801–58) on the nervous system, Paul Broca (1824–80) on the brain, and Hermann von Helmholtz (1821–94) on *psychophysics*, among others.

From these roots, psychology 'in the modern sense' emerged (although, as we will see, this 'modern sense' itself comprises many different, often conflicting, traditions and activities). For some, this version of psychology consists exclusively of the scientific research traditions, which tend to be discussed in terms of *structuralism* and *functionalism*. The structuralists, such as Wilhelm Wundt (1832–1920), focused on the simplest measurable experiences of the mind, whereas the functionalists, such as Edward L. Thorndike (1874–1949), concentrated on the processes and purposes of behaviour. This latter approach went on to spawn a number of significant specialist subfields of psychology, including *behaviourism* and *Gestalt psychology*.

Alongside these explicitly scientific developments came several forms of psychology that could be described as more 'person-centred'. These include major sub-disciplines like *psychoanalysis*, most notably associated with its founder Sigmund Freud (1856–1939), and *humanistic psychology*, which largely emerged from the work of Carl Rogers (1902–87).

Then, from the latter half of the twentieth century onwards, there have been a number of so-called scholarly 'revolutions'. In the *cognitive revolution*, scientific methods were applied to the study of human thought, giving rise to a new interdisciplinary field of activity known as *cognitive science*. Similarly, in what is sometimes referred to as a *neuro-revolution* (Jarrett, 2014), a substantial number of psychologists have become specialized in collaborating with molecular biologists, neurophysiologists, geneticists and scientists from other fields that study the human brain and nervous system. For many observers, such research into DNA and brain anatomy represents the cutting edge of modern psychology, and thus the current culmination of its history.

Broadly speaking, this traditional schema relates to psychology as a Euro-American endeavour. Each of the 'great men' named above are either German (Müller, von Helmholtz, Wundt),

American (Rogers, Thorndike), British (Locke, Mill), French (Broca, Descartes) or Austrian (Freud). Insofar as other parts of the world are concerned, it is common for the history of psychology timeline to include, say, the establishment of the International Union of Psychological Sciences in 1950, under the auspices of the United Nations (UN) and largely reflecting that organization's Western worldview (Staeuble, 2006), or the publication in 1899 of the 'earliest' Chinese-language psychology book: namely, the translation from English of a previously published American one (Blowers, 2006).

One modern textbook even contains the following statement: 'During the imperialist era [i.e. 1870–1920] Westerners and some indigenous scholars imported Psychology to Asian societies' (R. T. G. Walsh, Teo & Baydala, 2014). It is as though, prior to the twentieth century, there was no history of psychology worth recording in these places.

The history of the history of psychology

One challenge for those historians of psychology who assert that psychology itself did not exist until 1879 is the fact that the first discussions of the *history* of psychology were themselves written long before then.

For example, the British psychiatrist Henry Maudsley (1835–1918), describing the history of psychology in 1865, outlined the way that verifiable observation had superseded introspection as a means of improving scientific psychology over time:

> Nay more: if any one will be at the pains to examine into the history of the development of psychology up to its present stage, he may be surprised to find how much the important acquisitions of new truth and the corrections of old errors have been due, not to the interrogation of self-consciousness, but to external observation, though it was not recognised as a systematic method. The past history of psychology – its instinctive progress, so to speak – no less than the consideration of its present state, proves the necessity of admitting the objective method.
>
> (Maudsley, 1865, p. 258)

Maudsley was adamant that the history of psychology had led to a distinct approach to studying the mind, beyond what the relevant branches of philosophy had to offer. This approach drew on the natural sciences, especially physiology, in providing methods for both theory and research (Maudsley, 1868).

As an experienced physician, Maudsley also highlighted the importance of studying psychopathology as a way to gain better insights into the range and scope of human cognition and behaviour. In this regard, he highlighted how the history of psychiatry and mental illness was inextricably part of psychology's history too, despite being frequently marginalized or even overlooked by historians of psychology. We will return to this issue in Chapter 4.

Some years before this, the British educationalist John D. Morell (1816–91) discussed the history of psychology in his book *Elements of Psychology*, published in 1853. Morell starts by defining psychology as 'the science which investigates the central properties of the human mind'. He then proceeds to offer a 'historical sketch' of the field, 'a brief outline of the history of psychology, so far as it has assumed the form of a distinct science' (Morell, 1853, p. 3). This brief historical out-line, which explicitly separates psychology from philosophy, extends to some seventeen pages.

Much earlier, the German philosopher Freiderich Carus (1770–1807) wrote an extensive volume, *Geschichte der Psychologie* (*History of Psychology*), posthumously published in 1808 (Carus, 1808). Even Aristotle's treatise *De anima*, which was written in the fourth century BCE, starts with a discussion on the 'History of Psychological Theories' (Littman, 1981). In short, the history of psychology is itself a very old field of scholarship.

Nonetheless, it is indisputable that the late nineteenth century saw the arrival of psychology as a free-standing subject in the university system, with the establishment of psychology departments in a number of countries. It should be borne in mind that this development was related to the diversification of subject offerings in higher education more generally. One consequence of this flux was that many psychologists felt a strong need to promote the merits of their discipline when describing it to their academic colleagues.

As universities were opening more and more departments in new subject areas, there was considerable competition for attention and, not least, for resources. As such, the opportunity to write a history of one's discipline was not merely a chance to record events or to reflect upon its evolution. It offered an enticing potential to define, or even to *redefine*, the field whose history was being written – an important way to advertise one's wares to the public, to peers, and to the powers-that-be.

'A History of Experimental Psychology'

In the 1920s, one young American academic found himself very much mired in this type of university politics. Edwin G. Boring (1886–1968) had accepted an offer of employment at Clark University, a modern research university in Massachusetts, only to find his position threatened when the university's new president expressed a wish to update the curriculum by replacing psychology with geography (Boring & Lindzey, 1967). When Harvard University offered him a job as associate professor in 1924, he very gladly accepted.

Boring had long aspired to work at Harvard, but not just because it was one of the world's most prestigious universities. He had become concerned at the direction that Harvard's psychology faculty had taken. Specifically, he felt that the teaching there focused too much on abstract philosophical issues, and insufficiently on what he saw as the science of psychology. He later wrote that his mission was to 'rescue Harvard psychology from the philosophers' (Boring & Lindzey, 1967, p. 36), as their teaching of psychology had been 'vulgarized' and 'needed to be dragged back into science and made worthy' (S. S. Stevens, 1973, p. 46).

At Harvard, Boring became unhappy with the poor financial support available for scientific research in psychology, and somewhat concerned that this would impede his own ability to be productive (Samelson, 1980). When he did finally publish his first book (Boring, 1929), it was unrelated to his own laboratory work, which at the time focused on visual sensation and perception. Instead, his book was entitled *A History of Experimental Psychology*. Boring based it on more than 200 lectures he had helped to prepare during his graduate student days at Cornell University, where he had studied under Titchener, the founder of functionalism. It was destined to become a classic textbook used by teachers of psychology for decades to come.

Boring's book depicted experimental psychology as an offshoot of physiology, and thus, by extension, of physics: 'Scientific physiology developed because physics had provided a method for it, and physiology was scientific because it held to this method. Later we shall see that physiology gave birth to experimental psychology, at first called "physiological psychology," in much the same way that physical science gave birth to physiology' (Boring, 1929, p. 23). Boring described the emergence of science within human civilization, and what he termed the 'origin of modern psychology within science' (p. 25), which centred largely on nineteenth-century research into the nervous system. There was extensive coverage of brain physiology, perception and even hypnotism. His discussion of philosophy focused on rationalism and empiricism.

All this formed a basis for what he called 'the founding of experimental psychology' (p. 263), a development culminating in the opening of the Institut für experimentelle Psychologie (the Institute for Experimental Psychology) by Wundt in Leipzig in 1879.

A History of Experimental Psychology was a publishing success and became widely adopted as a history book for students of psychology. A second edition appeared in 1950 (Boring, 1950), augmented by new coverage of Kantian philosophy, behaviourism, psychoanalysis and elements of applied psychology.

However, despite its standing and influence – or perhaps because of them – Boring's book soon became a target of some considerable controversy. A common complaint noted in early reviews (e.g. Weld, 1931) related to the alleged narrowness of its coverage; Boring tended to respond to such put-downs by emphasizing that his was a history of *experimental* psychology, rather than of psychology in all its forms (Samelson, 1980).

In later years, however, other critics were more damning. Many suggested that Boring's selective approach resulted from deliberate bias, and that he was less interested in writing a fair history of psychology than in projecting his own preferred vision of the field.

Some argued that Boring was especially keen to boost the type of psychology he was pursuing at Harvard, and to denigrate those activities that he saw as its competition. For this reason, they say, Boring's version of history privileged laboratory-based experimentation in an effort to disparage areas of applied psychology, such as educational psychology and psychotherapy (O'Donnell, 1979). University politics also encouraged him to emphasize the independence of scientific psychology from academic philosophy (Samelson, 1980).

A common observation is that Boring seemed especially selective when describing the contribution of Wundt. By excising Wundt's more amorphous scholarship, Boring made it look as though the early psychophysicists were more single-mindedly devoted to empirical laboratory work, and less interested in philosophy, than in fact they actually were (Leahey, 2001).

Boring's style of scholarship has also been criticized, given that he emphasized personal agency more than wider cultural influences. Boring is said to have glamorized experimental psychology by casting its development in terms of 'hero-and-demon legends' (Blumenthal, 1998), based largely on sequences of biographical sketches.

In summary, Boring is accused of having broken all the rules of modern historiography. His emblematic textbook – one that served as the model for dozens of others throughout the twentieth century – was internalist, Whiggish and presentist, and replete with Great Man narratives.

New history, old problems

Today, Boring's textbook is seen as a product of its own time, and as representing an old-fashioned approach to the writing of history. Modern histories of psychology are expected to avoid its flaws, and in the late twentieth century, many historians of psychology began to explicitly use the term 'new history' in order to differentiate their approach. This new history of psychology would be 'critical rather than ceremonial' and would seek to avoid 'the passing down of anecdotes and myths from one generation of textbook writers to the next' (Furumoto, 1989, p. 18).

However, as we discussed in Chapter 1, the writing of history is always hampered by both the limits of human judgement and the unavoidable nature of perspective. In other words, adhering to the aspirations of 'new history' is easier said than done (Watrin, 2017). All history is written retrospectively, and so is structured in terms of its relevance to the present. This makes it virtually impossible to eliminate presentism completely (Baltas, 1994), especially where history-writers are themselves involved in the field whose history is being written.

For example, while modern critics are able to discern from Boring's *History of Experimental Psychology* a bias in favour of laboratory approaches to research, it can often seem that most 'new histories' of psychology are written by authors who have their own preferences as to what constitutes 'good' (or 'proper') psychology.

In the main, most such histories are written from the perspective of a type of social science scholarship known as *critical theory* (Lovett, 2006). Proponents of critical theory argue that our ability to understand the human experience tends to be hampered by an undue focus on individual perspectives and psychological factors. Instead, critical theorists argue, we can only garner true insights by taking account of societal power structures and cultural assumptions. As such, critical theory is not just a way to write history, it is also a way to 'do' psychology. However, it is by no means the case that all psychologists would agree that it is the best way.

There is no doubt that critical theory perspectives enhance the writing of histories in many crucial respects. However, insofar as they generate a *preference* for certain types of psychology more than others, they can strain our efforts to achieve historiographical objectivity. By influencing what does, or does not, constitute 'real' psychology, such preferences begin to resemble a kind of bias that is not entirely unlike that of which Boring himself has so frequently been accused.

SCIENCE AS A WAY OF KNOWING

One of the effects of rejecting 'old' history – with its implicit ambition of depicting psychology as an ever-improving science – is to make 'new' histories appear as though they are *sceptical* of psychology's scientific status (Lovett, 2006). From a critical theory perspective, the Boring-era progress narrative is dismissed as simply naïve: psychology's ambition to be a science will be forever futile, because social factors and cultural assumptions will always get in the way of scientific objectivity.

At the same time, arguing that psychology has a 'modern sense' that is attributable to the invention of experimental methods – in other words, that all historical non-experimental forms are not truly 'psychology' – would appear to make it *compulsory* for psychology to be a science. In this worldview, psychology must be scientific *by definition*, because non-scientific efforts at exploring the human condition are customarily deemed to be irrelevant.

The relationship between science and psychology – and the role of science in psychology's history – have proven to be somewhat nebulous. The issues do not readily lend themselves to easy summary.

Firstly, as we have discussed, the claim that scientific experimentation is an intrinsic element of true psychology (or of psychology 'in the modern sense') belies the fact that many areas of modern psychology eschew experimentation, or even renounce it.

Secondly, the implication that scientific methods are exclusively a 'modern' thing is itself quite tenuous. While it has changed and developed a lot over the centuries, science is in fact quite ancient. Science is not defined by its superficial features; not all scientists inhabit laboratories, wear white coats, crunch numbers or are men (Hughes, 2016). Science is a *way of knowing*. It is the practice of gauging the merit of claims based on logic, on reason and, most importantly, on empirical evidence.

As we will see, humans have been adopting this type of approach to the gathering of knowledge for thousands of years, long before scientists started wearing lab coats or completing science degrees in universities. Their consideration of knowledge about psychology – about how human minds work and how people think and behave – has been no exception.

A third complication is the idea that science itself is an 'all-or-nothing' affair, or that a particular approach to knowledge generation must be *either* entirely scientific *or* completely unscientific. This viewpoint places too much store in the infallibility of human endeavours. It ignores the fact that most attempts at science betray human frailties. The end product of scientific investigation is often much fuzzier than we might expect it to be.

Even the most dedicated professional scientist will be susceptible to reasoning errors. They will also be bound by the pragmatic limitations of what can and cannot be achieved with circumscribed research grants and finite human lifetimes.

It is wrong to think that, given enough time, the human scientific endeavour will eventually produce an exhaustive encyclopaedia of all possible knowledge. This hope assumes that human beings will be minded to study everything. In reality, the range of topics that scientists investigate is skewed. It reflects the broader population's whims and curiosities, and, more distally, the interests and priorities of whatever bloc in society exerts the most power and influence. And how their work is greeted in the public square frequently depends not on its scientific rigour, but on its perceived relevance.

Of course, most human beings are not dedicated professional scientists. For the majority, a scientific outlook is just one of a number of options with which to evaluate the world. As we will see, human civilizations have gathered their knowledge within a milieu of cultural influences, only some of which involve the valorization of empirical rigour and purity. The way people think about science – especially the science of behaviour – is frequently shaped by preference, prejudice and piety.

Advocates of science argue that the scientific approach produces cumulative benefits by default. Science involves the gathering and filtering of knowledge. It uses logic and evidence to exclude bad ideas in favour of better ones. As time passes, they suggest, you end up with fewer of the former and more of the latter. Therefore, describing the history of psychology in terms of an ever-improving knowledge base is not 'Whiggism' per se, it is simply an acknowledgement of psychology's scientific character.

That being said, science is seldom straightforward. Not all of it takes place in laboratories or under the auspices of universities. As mentioned above, science is not an industry or an academic subject area, it is a way of knowing. It is less a product, more a process. It is something that has evolved over time. This is because human societies have not always agreed on *what it is that actually constitutes 'knowledge'*.

Psychology involves the accumulation of knowledge about how human beings think, feel and behave. But knowledge like this does not arrive out of nowhere. If psychology is (even partly) scientific, then the history of psychology will be intertwined with the history of 'knowledge' as a concept, and thus with the history of science.

The appreciation of *what knowledge is* – of how facts are different from opinions, suppositions, superstitions or hearsay – is certainly something that has improved over the centuries.

HISTORY REPEATING ITSELF: COVID-19 AND 'KNOWLEDGE FROM AUTHORITY'

In late 2019, a new infectious disease was identified in Wuhan, China. Titled Covid-19, the disease soon spread around the world, becoming a global pandemic. Millions of people became infected without there being any specific antiviral treatments or vaccines to protect them. The disease was very contagious and highly dangerous, leading many sufferers to develop acute respiratory syndrome and pneumonia. A relatively large minority of those infected experienced multi-organ failure and, ultimately, death.

In the United States, the virus was not detected until early 2020. At first, the sitting president, Donald J. Trump, voiced public scepticism about the seriousness of the threat it posed. A member of the conservative Republican Party, the president offered a view similar to that of political commentators who were publicly critical of scientific advice on a wide range of matters in American politics.

While there were many underlying reasons for debate, American politicians would often argue over scientific advice where it had implications for government regulation or taxation. A long-running example was the debate about climate change. The scientific advice was that the government needed to impose restrictions on certain types of trade in order to protect the environment; by and large, the Republican Party position was to question the merit of this advice, and the need for consequent action.

When Covid-19 began to be detected in the United States, President Trump dismissed warnings as politically motivated, and as constituting a political hoax. Contrary to the statements of his own official scientific advisors, he suggested that the disease would soon disappear and would result in few or no deaths in the United States. Not only did such statements offer (misplaced) comfort to the population, they also resonated with the wider anti-scientist scepticism of many Republican Party voters.

Accordingly, when opinion polls were conducted, they showed that Republican voters were much less likely than their Democratic opponents to consider the new virus to be a genuine threat. They also declared a much greater unwillingness to take avoidant action, such as working from home, wearing face masks, or even washing their hands more regularly. It was notable that, on average, Republican voters included a much larger subgroup of older citizens, precisely those most at risk of death if infected by Covid-19. This reality gave new meaning to a traditional observation that, in the United States, Republican voters very often seemed willing to vote against their own interests (Lexington, 2020).

The lack of a committed and coordinated government response to suppress the virus no doubt contributed to its lethal effects in the United States, at least in comparison to its effects in many other countries. Far from avoiding the impact of the Covid-19 pandemic, the United States in fact quickly became riven with the illness, accumulating more than a million infections. By May 2020, the United States had by far the largest number of infections in the world, with more than six times the number of the next most infected country. Close to 60,000 Americans had died in the first three months, more than had lost their lives in the country's twenty-year involvement in the Vietnam War.

Unlike debates on climate change – where the consequences of decisions would become apparent only after years, if not decades – the impact of hesitation regarding the Covid-19 pandemic was immediate. Voters could see, in real time, the consequences of anti-science rhetoric and reliance on appeals to authority. However, in November 2020, President Trump was very nearly re-elected to the presidency of the United States, attracting the highest ever number of votes for a Republican candidate. Opinion polls continued to suggest that his supporters were relatively unconcerned about Covid-19, illustrating the powerful effects of 'knowledge' from authority.

Where people are psychologically motivated to hold particular beliefs, evidence and rationality are not always as persuasive as they logically should be. The basis on which 'knowledge' is formed and then shared in the modern world is not always different to how it was produced in the pre-scientific age. Knowledge from authority remains a powerful cultural concept, to which some people, literally, are willing to entrust their lives.

Multiple ways to know

As mentioned above, science is not merely a product, it is a *process*. It is not just a collection of knowledge, it is *the means by which believable knowledge is generated*. The separation of factual knowledge from opinion, hearsay, superstition or supposition does not come naturally to human minds. The process of distinguishing justified belief from unjustified belief is harder than it sounds.

Philosophers have examined the very nature of knowledge – of what exactly it means to 'know' something – for centuries. This branch of philosophy has its own name: it is referred to as *epistemology*.

Essentially, when we think about how knowledge is formed, we can do so in two ways. We can consider the way individuals personally gather knowledge during their own lives. More broadly, we can also consider how societies accumulate stores of collective knowledge that can then be passed on to individuals. To an extent, these two contexts are interlinked. People often gather personal knowledge by consulting formal sources, where they can get reliable information that has been compiled by others. But the information in these sources did not just appear from nowhere. All of it has been gathered, interpreted, and filtered – independently – by other individuals.

For centuries, human beings have shared knowledge directly and indirectly, actively and passively, deliberately and inadvertently, formally and informally, and in both structured and unstructured ways. The spread of ideas through civilization is largely organic, propelled by social communication, and sustained by credulity and trust.

To begin with, children acquire most of their knowledge from watching and listening to trustworthy adults. In fact, receptiveness to this type of information is an important survival skill. Were children to lack such credulity, they would find it extremely difficult to navigate even the simplest of situations. Child-rearing and education as we know them would be virtually impossible if children required primary tangible evidence for every factual assertion they encountered.

As such, human beings grow up to be naturally trusting of what they see and hear. They are predisposed to believe. It is a basic convention of human communication that people speak the truth, and that you should duly believe what they say (Grice, 1975). While we understand that what people say might sometimes be honestly mistaken, we are accustomed to accepting most information as believable entirely on the basis that we think it comes from a reliable source. As individuals, most of our knowledge is acquired second-hand.

This is what is referred to as *knowledge from authority*. We accept the things we are told when we believe the source to be authoritative. The problem, of course, is that sometimes the source will not be authoritative at all. It will be unreliable. If we falsely believe a source to be authoritative when it is not, then we will end up accepting as fact 'knowledge' that is actually incorrect. It seems reasonable to suggest that most of the misinformation that spreads through society does so as a result of this problem.

However, there is a further psychological dimension to this effect. After all, human beings do not always believe *everything* they hear. They weigh up various factors other than the authority of the source alone. For example, humans are persuaded by information that conforms to their prior beliefs (the problem of confirmation bias, which we discussed in Chapter 1). They more readily accept information that is consistent with their worldview. This can often involve a social dimension – people might attach greater credibility to a weak claim if it furthers the interests of their in-group, as might happen when blameless members of an out-group are scapegoated or stigmatized.

Research in cognitive psychology has shown that people also draw a number of erroneous conclusions about knowledge in everyday situations. People are unduly swayed by the first information they encounter (McCann, Higgins & Fondacaro, 1991), by information that is specific rather than vague (Gigerenzer & Gaissmaier, 2011), by numbers and photographs (McCabe & Castel, 2008), and by information that reminds them of something they can easily remember (B. Mitchell & Roberts, 2012).

Self-serving biases and systematic errors of cognition are why intuition is inherently a poor source of knowledge. Nonetheless, human beings default to intuition when they need to judge whether a particular source is authoritative. They don't just believe everything they hear, they also judge information on the basis of whether it 'feels' true to them. In short, most people believe that they know quite a lot of things. However, most of what they *think* they know rests on very weak foundations.

Reasoning methodically

Of course, human beings are entirely capable of recognizing the fragility of their own intuition. They are well aware that authorities can be unreliable. It was precisely because they knew about these problems that they began to look for ways to circumvent them. It is the reason they created what we now often refer to as the *scientific method*, the process of using logic and evidence to objectively establish the truth or falsity of claims.

The scientific method seeks to apply an accuracy check to assertions. It does so by combining rationality with observation. The principles of rationality have been discussed for millennia and relate largely to the use of logic in reasoning. While there are many different types of reasoning, three main categories are particularly relevant to the scientific method: deductive reasoning, inductive reasoning and abductive reasoning.

Deductive reasoning is the combination of true statements of successively lessening generality to produce an irrefutably true conclusion (Hughes, 2012). An example of deductive reasoning is the claim that because all human beings are mortal, and because René Descartes is a human being, then this must mean that Descartes is mortal. (As it happens, Descartes expanded on the use of deductive reasoning for science in his treatise *Discourse on Method*, which we discussed in Chapter 2.) We can note that deductive reasoning involves generalizing from the broad ('all human beings') to the specific ('Descartes'), and that the conclusion drawn is always correct.

Inductive reasoning refers to the combination of true statements concerning samples from a larger group, the identification of a pattern across the statements, and a conclusion about the larger group that assumes this pattern will continue (Hughes, 2012). An example of inductive reasoning is the claim that because Descartes's first name is René, and because Descartes is French, then this must mean that all French people are called René. By contrast to deductive reasoning, inductive reasoning involves generalizing from the specific ('Descartes') to the broad ('all French people'). Unlike with deduction, the conclusion generated by induction is *not* always correct. Not all French people *are* called René. However, the fact that many French people do have this name shows how, over time, inductive reasoning can *help* us to uncover knowledge that is *likely* to be correct.

Even though inductive reasoning does not always produce the correct conclusion, it is very helpful to the process of science. It supports the notion of sampling, where large-scale knowledge is inferred from small selections of information. Inductive logic is used whenever a scientist draws conclusions about nature based on a small number of cases. Induction is not perfect, but some inductions are better than others. We can improve induction by improving the representativeness of our sample of cases. And we can remember to bear the representativeness of our sample in mind whenever we judge the quality of an induction. All of this enhances the ability of science to generate useful knowledge.

Finally, *abductive reasoning* is the combination of true statements about a given outcome and its possible preconditions in a way that concludes that the outcome was directly caused by those preconditions (Hughes, 2012). An example of abductive reasoning is the claim that because Descartes had a beard, and because many philosophers have beards, then the reason Descartes grew a beard is because he was a philosopher. The conclusion drawn by abductive reasoning does not hold a particular likelihood of being true; rather, it reflects a person's judgement of the 'best' explanation available. It is a way to consider new possibilities that can then be investigated, or tested, in other ways, and so serves as a basis for generating new scientific theories.

Deductive reasoning was discussed by Aristotle, while inductive reasoning is often associated with the seventeenth-century English philosopher Francis Bacon (1561–1626). Abductive reasoning is a relatively modern concept, having been introduced in the late nineteenth century by the American philosopher Charles Sanders Peirce (1839–1914). While each type of reasoning is inherently useful to science, it is important to remember that our methods of scientific reasoning have emerged slowly, and sporadically, throughout history.

Both induction and abduction are intertwined with the notion of observation. The philosophers and scientists who promote their use do so from a theoretical position called *empiricism*. Empiricism is the assumption that all knowledge is ultimately derived from what we can detect with our senses. In other words, all real knowledge should be traceable back to experience (either your own or someone else's). There is no such thing as an innate idea, or an inherently irrefutable claim, or things that are true because we 'just know'. Evidence matters.

While often associated with the eighteenth-century Scottish philosopher David Hume (1711–76), the empirical approach has been promoted since ancient times, in many different civilizations. However, because of the psychological power of knowledge from authority and intuition, the idea of empiricism has not always met with universal approval in society.

We often presume that scientific knowledge is inherently objective and reliable. However, this presumption is itself an example of knowledge from authority. Our assumption of accuracy relates to our belief that scientific sources are authoritative. We seldom enquire about the quality of the underlying empirical evidence, the logic applied by the researcher, or the merit of the methodologies that were used to gather and analyse the data. However, it might not always be the case that infallible standards have been met. The intrusion of human failings into science serves as a perennial reminder of the need for the scientific method itself.

In addition, we often presume that when the idea of science was introduced to the world, the world embraced it in all respects. A Whiggish version of history would have us believe that the sheer usefulness of scientific thinking must have been immediately celebrated. However, history shows us that this was not the case. For largely psychological reasons, intuition, superstition and mysticism continued to dominate the way people thought about their lives.

LOGOPHILIA: 'HIPPOPOTOMONSTROSESQUIPPEDALIOPHOBIA'

Hippopotomonstrosesquippedaliophobia is a quasi-figurative term used to describe a fear of long words. It is itself a compound of several terms: *hippopoto-*, meaning 'hippopotamus'; *monstro-*, meaning 'monster'; *sesquipedalis*, meaning 'one-and-a-half feet in length'; and *phobia*, meaning 'fear'. While the origins of the word are unclear, its own length is likely intended to serve as self-referential parody: people who suffer from this fear will no doubt be terrified of its extremely lengthy label.

Long words are typically coined to encapsulate complex, multifaceted concepts. Some of the longest words in the English language are scientific terms. The longest word that appears in a major dictionary, *pneumonoultramicroscopicsilicovolcano-coniosis*, denotes a respiratory disease caused by dust particles (Oxford Dictionaries, 2020). The more specialized *Student's Dictionary & Gazetteer* (Dictionary Project, 2011) includes the name of a chemical compound that contains 1,909 letters. According to the standard system for naming chemicals, the correct term for describing the protein encoded by TTN genes in humans would have nearly 200,000 letters if (ever) fully spelled out (Panico, Richer & Powell, 1993).

While the use of long words is common in science, this does not mean that long words are *themselves* necessarily scientific. For example, *hippopotomonstrosesquippedaliophobia* is not particularly scientific, as it contains several prefixes that convey the same meaning and are thus unnecessary. Their inclusion is for rhetorical effect, and not for clarity or precision. However, the use of cumbersome and impenetrable language is a common stereotype of science. Scientists are perceived as regularly using language in ways that ordinary people struggle to understand (Mendrick & Francis, 2012).

Many scientists do resort to jargon more often than seems strictly necessary. While their aim is to communicate exactitude, the outcome is often the opposite. An over-reliance on jargon can create a creeping problem, where the general population comes to see science as obscure, disconnected from everyday life, or ridiculous.

Another consequence of jargon is that it facilitates the imitation of science by imposters. The language used by purveyors of pseudosciences (such as homoeopaths, astrologers or past-life regression therapists) is often replete with meandering multiclausal sentences and tongue-twisting polysyllabic terms. However, despite conforming to a popular stereotype of science, the use of such language is not in itself scientific. The problem, of course, is that casual observers are unlikely to be able to tell the difference.

The scientific reasoning that influenced the course of human civilization reflects a way of approaching knowledge that relies on logic and evidence, and has little to do with superficial features such as terminology. A preponderance of jargon in psychology could be a legacy of its scientific origins, but it could also be a side effect of an impulse to *imitate* science in order to garner a positive professional reputation. In short, there is more to science than appearances or sounds. The historical emergence of science is not the same as the historical emergence of laboratories.

THE HISTORICAL PURSUIT OF KNOWLEDGE

The English-language word *scientist* was not coined until the nineteenth century. William Whewell (1794–1866), an academic at Cambridge University, introduced the term in an anonymous essay, in which he attributed the suggestion to an otherwise unnamed 'ingenious gentleman' (Merton, 1996). Before coming up with *scientist*, Whewell considered a number of alternatives, including *savans* (which he rejected because it was French), *naturforscher* (likewise, for being German), and 'cultivator of science' (which was just too cumbersome). He formally acknowledged the coinage of his neologism in 1840: 'We need very much a name to describe a cultivator of science in general. I should incline to call him a *Scientist*' (Whewell, 1840, p. 113).

Whewell's new word attracted resistance, primarily because it hybridized a Latin root (*scient*) with a Greek suffix (-*ist*), a move immediately impugned for its 'linguistic barbarity' (Merton, 1996, p. 230). Purists felt there was nothing wrong with retaining the terms 'men of science' or 'scientific men', which were then in common usage. But Whewell's new word eventually caught on, and it seems fair to say that it has stood the test of time.

Of course, while there was no such word as *scientist* until the nineteenth century, that is not to say that there were no such things as scientists. In fact, human beings have been cultivating science since the dawn of humanity.

Science in the ancient world

Arguably, the earliest innovations of prehistoric humans – such as the discovery of fire or the invention of the wheel – constituted an elementary form of science. These developments produced new wisdom: knowledge that was derived from observation, crafted by trial and error, transmitted socially, and then widely adopted. The fact that these innovations were employed by humans and not by non-human animals suggests that they benefited from, and required, a non-trivial amount of intelligence and rationality. They represented real intellectual knowledge rather than recurring idiosyncratic happenstance.

In the sense that this knowledge was empirical and logical – its success depending on people's ability to test it for themselves and to agree about its merits – then it certainly amounted to, at least, a *type* of science.

However, the humans who discovered fire or those who invented the wheel were unlikely to have seen themselves as cultivators of science. Most likely, they made their discoveries by accident, without ever intending to generate knowledge (and without ever consciously attempting to do so again). It is probable that multiple human societies discovered fire and 'invented' the wheel in separate places and at different times. Nonetheless, the ability of the earliest human societies to adopt such technologies, and thus their ability to share useful observations, highlights a very important aspect of our species.

A key part of what makes human beings so highly adaptable is their inherent curiosity for information, their appetite for knowledge, and their capacity for intellectual growth. The inclination to garner, accumulate and then share insights allowed humans to experience a rapid exponential escalation in their understanding of the world.

From our twenty-first-century perspective it can be difficult to fully appreciate the profound power of these human capacities. Consider the fact that many highly complex insights were widely shared by humans *before the invention of writing*. Human beings domesticated farm animals and engaged in crop rotation, created pottery and ceramics, compiled astronomical charts, spun rope, baked bread, fermented alcohol, developed methods of irrigation, and fixed each other's teeth using dental drills, all without any written information to guide them. Relying solely on an oral tradition they were able to construct elaborate communities that thrived for centuries. Some of these early settlements continue to be inhabited today, having evolved into cities such as Aleppo, Damascus, Erbil, Jericho, Luoyang, Plovdiv, and the Shahr-e Rey suburb of Tehran.

Of course, as we discussed in Chapter 2, the emergence of writing systems served to bolster the collective power of human intellectual enquiry. The earliest literate societies were burgeoning centres of knowledge discovery. The ancient Egyptians and Mesopotamians developed complex systems of astronomy and formed a detailed understanding of metallurgy and physiology. Ancient Indian scholars understood the nature of planetary ellipses and the spherical shape of the earth (Riepe, 1982). In Asia Minor, within the realm of ancient Greece, the Miletian scholar Thales (who we discussed in Chapter 2) achieved widespread fame in the sixth century BCE for promoting non-supernatural explanations of natural phenomena, and in later centuries would become regarded by many as the 'father of science' (French, 1994). In the second century CE, Chinese scientists invented a highly accurate working seismoscope, capable of detecting earthquakes up to 500 kilometres away (Feng & Yu, 2006).

As was the case with the invention of writing, the human capacity for science was also enhanced by the development of mathematics. Many modern mathematical concepts date back to the ancient world. As described in Chapter 2, our current system of numbers is based on the Hindu-Arabic numeral system developed between the first and fourth centuries CE. Chinese mathematicians devised the ideas of fractions and negative numbers in the first century, while the Greek scholar

Euclid of Alexandria developed geometry in the fourth century. In the seventh century CE, Indian mathematicians introduced the concept of 'zero'.

For a time, the fragmentation of western European society after the fall of Rome allowed eastern Europe and Asia Minor to become leading global centres of learning. With easy access to Greek texts and scholarship from Indian sources, Islamic scholarship in particular thrived. We saw in Chapter 2 how Islamic medicine and physiology represented the cutting edge of science, and above, how similar advances were achieved in various areas of mathematics. Scholars of the so-called Islamic Golden Age, said to have occurred from the eighth to the fourteenth century CE, produced sophisticated scholarship across the full gamut of scientific fields, including astronomy, biology, engineering and physics.

One of the distinctive features of Islamic scholarship was the way it actively incorporated a diversity of influences and inputs. High value was attached to knowledge that could be assimilated from other cultures. Christian and Jewish intellectuals and physicians were employed in Islamic schools, royal courts and hospitals. Scholarship from ancient Greece, Egypt, Persia, China and India were translated into Arabic, Turkish and Hebrew, and thus preserved for the world's future generations (Gergorian, 2003). The philosophy of Aristotle and Plato, especially their teachings on deductive reasoning, was very influential. Scholars such as the Iraqi physicist Alhazen (Latinized form of Ḥasan Ibn al-Haytham; 965–1040 CE) wrote extensively about the use of controlled experimentation, promoting the importance of experiments in science centuries before Western philosophers did so (Rashed, 2008).

Public domain, via Wikimedia Commons / {PD-US}

Image 3.1 Al-Khwarizmi
The Islamic polymath Al-Khwarizmi was a mathematical genius who established the field of algebra in the eighth century. The term 'algorithm' is a phonetic version of his name. Born in what is now Uzbekistan, he is memorialized in this statue in the city of Khiva.

The Islamic Golden Age is said to have receded as a result of the Mongol conquests, which saw the aggressive expansion of the Mongol Empire across large parts of Eurasia from the thirteenth century. This period saw the destruction of libraries, hospitals and universities that had flourished in the Byzantine world following the fall of the Romans. The end of the Islamic Golden Age is traditionally linked to the destruction of Baghdad in 1258, but some scholars argue that this period of Islamic flourishing continued until the fourteenth or fifteenth century (Saliba, 1994). One consequence of its eventual demise was a large westward migration of scholars and scientists, many of whom would settle in northern Italy in the decades leading up to the Renaissance.

ALMOST FAMOUS: AL-KHWARIZMI

The ninth-century Persian polymath al-Khwarizmi (short for Muḥammad ibn Mūsā al-Khwārizmī; 780–850 CE) was born in what is now modern-day Uzbekistan. After the Muslim conquest of Persia, al-Khwarizmi joined many other scholars from across Asia who travelled to the city of Baghdad in order to make their living.

Al-Khwarizmi proved to be a mathematical genius. He developed methods for systematically solving linear and quadratic equations, which he described in his book *Al-kitāb al-mukhtaṣar fī ḥisāb al-ǧabr wa'l-muqābala* (*The Compendious Book on Calculation by Completion and Balancing*). The book is credited with popularizing this area of mathematics, uniquely treating it as an independent field in its own right.

Although rarely spoken about in the West today, al-Khwarizmi's legacy lives on in the technical language used by virtually every student of mathematics from high school onwards. Two everyday terms relate to him directly. The first is 'algebra', the field of mathematics in which he specialized: the word is a derivation of *Al-ǧabr*, the shortened version of the (very long) title of his most famous book.

The other term that relates to al-Khwarizmi is 'algorithm'. In fact, this word relates to him very directly: it is a phonetic version of the pronunciation of his name (Brezina, 2006). So, while few Western high-school students know who al-Khwarizmi actually was, nearly all of them are able to pronounce his name, in its vernacular form, with perfect fluency.

Europe as epicentre

From ancient times to the Middle Ages and beyond, Europe has exerted a considerable influence on global culture. As we saw in Chapter 2, the European Renaissance spawned marked developments in the arts and sciences, but also in technology, politics and warfare. Advances in shipbuilding and munitions helped European powers to engage in overseas colonialism. There emerged a culture of imperialism whereby, in general, European powers competed to establish global empires in which large numbers of the world's population were forcibly subjugated.

Europe had previously been the cradle of Greek and Roman civilization. After the Renaissance, it would see the emergence of modern science and philosophy, and then become the epicentre of the Industrial Revolution. While its colonies would gradually dissipate, its influence on global affairs would remain disproportionate, largely fuelled by its accumulation of wealth and resources.

The fact that Europe experienced this history of dominant influence on global culture is sometimes said to reveal a peculiar ingenuity in European people, and the inherent inventiveness of its civilization. However, various sociological studies suggest that this verdict results from a misleading illusion of perspective. In reality, Europe's inhabitants benefited from a number of unique and compelling opportunities that had little to do with innate intelligence. Fortuitous conditions enabled them to capitalize on otherwise universal human propensities. Pot luck and geography propelled their capacity for creativity, but also unleashed their belligerence and greed.

Some of the factors that are believed to have advantaged European development and favoured its expansionism include climate and geography, and their self-compounding consequences. In Neolithic times, the European climate was temperate enough to allow rich diversity in edible vegetation, and to make it easy to store food for long periods.

The environment also provided a large number of animals that were sufficiently docile to be domesticated and bred by humans. Of the large animals currently used in farming, at least thirteen species are indigenous to Eurasia (including cows, horses, pigs and sheep), compared to just one from the Americas (the llama), and *none* from the rest of the world (Dartnell, 2020). The domestication of animals provided food, milk, fertilizer, and (literally) horsepower for the pulling of ploughs, thereby further increasing the availability of food. Ultimately, the availability of more consumable calories ensured a densely accelerating population growth. Another consequence, it is argued, is that close proximity to all those farm animals exposed Europeans to a wide variety of pathogens, and thus allowed for the natural selection of greater immunity to disease (Diamond, 1997).

It has also been suggested that the particular geography of western Europe assisted its agricultural practices to develop. The fact that Europe is oriented in an east–west direction gave it advantages over, say, the Americas or Africa, which are oriented in a north–south direction. This is because climate is generally stable by latitude, but variable by longitude. In Neolithic times, when the early Americans and Africans migrated, they tended to move north or south and thus to encounter sometimes extreme differences in climate, for which their lifestyles and agricultural practices were ill-suited. However, when the Europeans migrated, they moved east or west, into areas where the climate stayed the same.

Within Europe, the local physical geography offered further advantages. The presence of mountain ranges, rivers, coastlines and islands encouraged the emergence of multiple free-standing tribal societies in relatively close proximity to each other. This is believed to have encouraged a greater competition for resources – and thus more innovation – than was seen in larger more unitary societies, such as China. For example, in the fourteenth and fifteenth centuries, while European powers were competing to embark on overseas imperialism, the Chinese empire adopted policies which *banned* the production of ships and prohibited maritime trade. The isolationist approach of the monolithic Chinese state aimed to preserve their internal trading practices, rather than to adapt to the changing external environment.

In short, the fact that today's European society (along with its offshoots in the wider Western world) controls disproportionate amounts of the world's wealth, trade and political power has little to do with the intelligence or innate abilities of Europeans. Instead, it is a consequence of circumstantial conditions that were favourable to population growth at an opportune time, out of which a spiral of feedback loops emerged to create an ever-increasing advantage.

Critics of such assessments note that geographical and economic factors ultimately explain just part of this story. They do not explain why Europeans used their advantages to reach out and seize the resources and populations of other continents, with often remarkable cruelty and callousness (Errington & Gewertz, 2010). This human motivation to subjugate foreign populations in order to bolster domestic wealth is a psychological issue, rather than a geographical (or historical) one. The human tendency to rationalize their own motives, and to discount the relative merits of foreigners, is an important psychological concept with a long and at times dark history. It continues to underpin many current debates concerning wealth inequality, immigration and global justice. We will return to this issue in Chapter 6.

Superstition versus science

We saw in Chapter 2 how many historians disapprove of the term 'the Dark Ages' as a description of medieval times. The period between the fifth and fifteenth centuries was one of intellectual disruption rather than decline. Foreign tribes that the Romans dismissed as 'barbarians' were often highly sophisticated populations with complex social structures, as well as innovators of useful technologies such as blacksmithing. As the Roman superstate disappeared, the densely populated European continent began to encounter many new influences and infusions.

Nonetheless, it is important again to remember that for most of human history – and certainly for much of the Middle Ages – rigorous information just did not flow as freely as it does today. Inhabitants of a medieval village would have had little direct knowledge about what life was like on the other side of the mountain, never mind in other countries or cultures. During the Middle Ages, it was common for people to believe that nearby regions were home to tribes of weird and wonderful creatures, such as twelve-foot tall humans, dog-headed men, or headless people with faces in the middle of their chests (Mittman & Kim, 2017). There was no customary method of fact-checking new claims or testing the accuracy of accounts, nor was there an appreciation that this regularly needed to be done.

As we saw in Chapter 2, many psychologists have argued that human beings are heavily influenced by an awareness of their own mortality. According to terror management theory (Greenberg et al., 1986), anything that *reminds* us that we are all going to die will be particularly addling. The medieval world was very much full of such reminders. Death and disease were commonplace, and life was often compromised and curtailed. Malnutrition, plague, childbirth complications, food contamination, poor sanitation and weather events were familiar deadly threats. In a world where life expectancy was short, most people were happy to accept whatever aid was available, even if much of what was on offer at the time was supernatural (D. Wilson, 2017). Credulity for mysticism tends to thrive in communities where death is a frequent visitor.

Common-sense dualism also ensured that for many medieval citizens, belief in an afterlife was sacrosanct. As well as reinforcing particular views about the human mind, such beliefs also influenced the way people understood and interpreted claims about nature.

In an effort to secure passage into heaven, people would adhere to strictures that amounted to little more than superstition: gathering relics, visiting holy sites, invoking incantations and accumulating 'indulgences' – rewards for good behaviour that allegedly reduced the amount of punishment a person would receive in the afterlife (Shaffern, 2006). Pagan lore about goblins, fairies and 'little people' was appropriated into mainstream religious observance, where such beings became regarded as fallen angels or souls of the dead that occasionally trespassed into the world of humans (Newman, 2018). In short, most people were completely open to a wide range of ideas about other dimensions of existence, without wanting empirical evidence of any kind.

Indeed, claims that a miracle had taken place – quite common in the Middle Ages – did not tend to raise suspicions about the credibility of religious teaching. Rather, such events were often seen as *evidence* for the existence of the divine, a 'proof' of Christian truth (D. Wilson, 2017). The performance of miracles by priests and religious clerics became a routine part of the job: the weekly Christian mass incorporated prayers that were said to transform bread and wine into human flesh and blood.

Pre-scientific superstition was part and parcel of everyday medieval society. Norms of reasoning did not demand formal logic or empiricism; knowledge by authority and intuition reigned supreme. Within the confines of their cloisters, philosophers certainly speculated about a material universe, and theologians harboured scepticism towards the more miraculous tales that had been incorporated into ecclesiastical history (S. Justice, 2008). However, for ordinary citizens, the vicissitudes of daily life encouraged endless epistemological promiscuity.

Knowledge within limits

Science, such as it was, was the preserve of scholars. But even then, the influence of superstition and mysticism could be found. As described earlier, the fall of Rome saw organized religion become the central structure around which European society gathered. In the east, there were free-standing libraries, the Islamic Golden Age, and the transcribing of ancient knowledge for future posterity. In the west, where society fragmented, scholarship retreated into monasteries. Scientific thinking was promoted, but primarily as a way to understand the divine nature of the universe.

Astronomers contemplated what they saw as, literally, the heavens. In the thirteenth century, Frederick II (1194–1250), ruler of a central European territory known as the Holy Roman Empire, challenged one of his court philosophers to address a number of scientific questions:

> explain to us the foundations of the earth, that is to say how it is established over the abyss and how the abyss stands beneath the earth, and whether there is anything else than air and water which supports the earth, and whether it stands of itself or rests on the heavens beneath it. And how many heavens there are and who are their rulers and principal inhabitants, and exactly how far one heaven is from another, and by how much one is greater [i.e. higher] than another, and what is beyond the last heaven if there are several; and in which heaven God is in the person of His divine majesty and how He sits on His throne, and how He is accompanied by angels and saints, and what these continually do before God.
>
> (Haskins, 1922, pp. 689–90)

In terms of what was known about the universe at the time, such questions reflected a reasonable expression of curiosity. The task of medieval science in Europe was often precisely this, to establish where and how far away heaven was, and what exactly the angels and saints did all day.

Institutionally, the hegemonic organized religions did much to promote the development of science. The founding of the first universities is often attributed to the medieval Christian church, which built upon its tradition of cathedral schools and monasteries. Some historians argue that similar institutions were also established in the Islamic tradition, and that both approaches, Christian and Islamic, provided the template from which the modern university has evolved (Lowe & Yasuhara, 2013). Whatever their ancestry, the establishment of medieval universities served to foster a culture of scholarship, as well as new generations of scholars, many of whom travelled widely, keen to spread the ideas that they gathered on their pilgrimages.

However, while universities and similar institutions helped to formalize what did and did not constitute appreciable knowledge, their religious underpinnings generated a fundamental tension. Scholarly curiosity and critical enquiry were widely promoted, but within limits. Any new knowledge that challenged the received wisdom of religious teaching was resisted. In this way, the use of logic and evidence to validate claims was only partially encouraged. Epistemology remained subordinate to the influence of authority.

Empiricism as heresy

The Middle Ages saw an increase in heresy trials in Europe, where people who challenged core doctrines of religious teachings were prosecuted. Adopting an empirical approach to theological matters carried great personal risk.

In 1022, two clerical leaders of a small sect in Orléans, France, were investigated for heresy. The investigation had the imprimatur not only of the local bishop, but also that of the king and queen of France. During their interrogation, the clerics were asked whether they accepted as truth a number of miraculous events described in the Christian Bible. Their answer was that, as they themselves had not been there to witness the events for themselves, they could not believe that such things had actually happened. Because of their empirically minded attitudes, the clerics, along with all their fellow sect members, were sentenced to be burned to death. One of the 'heretics' had died three years previously, requiring his body to be exhumed in order for it to be burned (Landes, 1995). The execution of the Orléans 'heretics' is seen as an important event in medieval European history (Frassetto, 2005). It introduced a norm whereby the *state*, and not just the church, would harshly punish its own citizens for deigning to challenge received cultural wisdoms.

Anti-religious views were zealously policed by the authorities across Europe for hundreds of years. Heresy trials continued to be common right up until the Renaissance. Within the Christian church, a pan-national quasi-legal infrastructure was established, responsible for charging people with heresy, organizing court trials and issuing sentences. This 'inquisition' infrastructure was operated by church administrators, but its verdicts were recognized by the secular authorities. Indeed, for serious offences, it was the state authorities who formally assumed responsibility for sentencing heretics to death, subject to local laws. Various branches, such as the notorious Spanish Inquisition, became particularly feared. While initially seen only in Europe, colonialism ensured that these inquisitions were extended to Asia, Africa and the Americas. They were to be

Image 3.2 Heresy paranoia
A pamphlet recording the execution of three women who were accused of witchcraft in England in 1612.

part of mainstream civic politics for hundreds of years, only being formally abolished in the nineteenth century.

The policing of acceptable knowledge was extended to cover practices such as sorcery, which was deemed to require an interaction with Satan and thus to be heretical. Thousands of women who were accused of witchcraft were systematically tortured and exterminated. In 1542 English parliamentarians were so exercised by irreligious mysticism that they passed a law applying the death penalty to anyone caught soliciting 'magicians' for nefarious purposes, such as for retrieving lost property, garnering wealth or inducing people to engage in 'unlawful love' (Durston, 2019).

Heresy paranoia was directed not just at empirical scepticism and occult mysticism. It also provided a basis for suppressing political dissent. As organized religion was intertwined with secular politics, the policing of ideas could be used to maintain order within the power structures of society. After all, too much free-thinking could lead citizens to start fact-checking the Bible for themselves or, even worse, to question the probity of political administrators and the fairness of the taxation system (D. Wilson, 2017). In this environment, citizens who criticized the powers-that-be for their corruption and greed could easily find themselves charged with some or other 'heresy'.

A somewhat gradual revolution

The innate human approach of relying on knowledge from authority remained the cultural norm for many centuries. The appreciation that there might be superior merit to knowledge derived from research, evidence, logic or fact was very slow to emerge. But, with the passing of time, and with the accumulation of shared human experience, a move away from knowledge from authority did eventually gain traction. Ordinary people began to recognize that there was often value in knowing things for oneself.

Historians sometimes refer to the emergence of modern science between the sixteenth and eighteenth centuries as constituting a 'scientific revolution', a series of developments in scholarly fields such as biology, mathematics and physics that transformed the human understanding of nature. These scientific endeavours were stimulated and bolstered by a number of newly 'enlightened' theoretical ideas. British philosophers such as Bacon and Hume championed the use of observation and inductive reasoning, while the use of rationalism was promoted by scholars such as the German Immanuel Kant (1724–1804). Importantly, Kant was among the first prominent philosophers to cast doubt on whether psychological issues could be evaluated scientifically.

Kant (1786) argued that mental processes, such as perception, were intangible and so could not be quantified. However, this view presupposes that only tangible concepts can be quantified, and that all quantification needs to be exact before research can be classified as scientific. Both these assumptions are questionable (for example: there are many concepts in astrophysics that are intangible and essentially immeasurable, and yet few philosophers argue that astrophysics is not a science). Other German philosophers, such as Johann Friedrich Herbart (1776–1841), took a different view. They argued that mathematical formulae could be used to describe a range of dynamic relationships, including those involved in psychological processes. Herbart's ideas later inspired scholars such as Ernst Weber (1795–1878) and Gustav Fechner (1801–87) to develop formal methods for quantifying perceptual experiences, as well as influencing the way Sigmund Freud thought about the subconscious part of the mind (see Chapter 7).

Such philosophical developments were not without consequence for wider society. For example, in France, rationalism was championed by figures such as Voltaire (the nom de plume of François-Marie Arouet; 1694–1778) and Swiss philosopher Jean-Jacques Rousseau (1712–78). In these cases, the idea that society could be based on reason alone proved to be an influential theme in shaping some of the popular resentments that eventually led to the unfolding of the French Revolution (Stromberg, 1988).

Modern histories often describe early scientists as representing the vanguard of resistance to religious authority. However, such depictions illustrate some of the perils of the Great Man approach to historiography. Figures such as the astronomer Galileo (see the box 'Historically (in)accurate?: The heresy of Galileo'), the physicist Isaac Newton (1643–1727) and the biologist Charles Darwin (who we will discuss further in Chapter 5) are often viewed as scientifically irreligious. In fact, each was very respectful of religion and piously deferential towards religious belief. Both Galileo and Newton were religiously devout, while Darwin was famously tormented by the way his scientific ideas clashed with his religious upbringing. In short, the scientists of history were each immersed in the culture of their times. There was no binary conflict between religion and science, nor was there a sudden switch from a religious age to a scientific one.

The modern scientific method emerged during centuries that were characterized by a core cultural contradiction. Knowledge, enquiry and education were valued and encouraged. But simultaneously some knowledge was non-negotiable, some types of enquiry were taboo, and all education was shaped to preserve the status quo.

Using science to explain the universe might seem like a good idea, but only if you agree that logic and evidence are preferable to authority, hearsay and superstition. For centuries, such agreement was absent from people's thoughts. Humans have always marvelled at things that they struggle to understand, whether it be new cutting-edge technologies or old traditional miracles. Awe seldom discriminates between fact and supposition. Indeed, if anything, awe is triggered more by emotion than empiricism: authority, hearsay and superstition are frequently more intimidating – and thus more *compelling* – than the dispassionate parsing, by unseen scholars, of objective and verifiable evidence.

For long periods of human history, science has been very much a marginalized pursuit grudgingly assimilated into an illogical world. Some might say that this state of affairs largely persists unchanged into the present day.

HISTORICALLY (IN)ACCURATE?: THE HERESY OF GALILEO

In the seventeenth century, church leaders up to and including popes became protective of intellectual enquiry, proscribing the use of science to investigate the work of the divine. The famous case of Italian polymath Galileo Galilei (1564–1642) is instructive.

An accomplished astronomer, Galileo gathered evidence that conclusively supported the notion of 'heliocentrism', the view that the sun, and not the earth, lay at the centre of our solar system. His findings contradicted the traditional religious belief in 'geocentrism'. In the religious view, the earth held a special role in the universe, as it was the place designated by the divine creator to be humanity's home. According to geocentrism, our own planet was the unmovable centre of everything: it was the celestial bodies, including the sun, that were in orbit around *us*. Several sections of the Christian Bible alluded to this 'fact'.

Galileo, therefore, was accused of challenging scripture. After complaints were made to the Roman Inquisition, he was ordered by the pope 'to abandon his opinions' (Heilbron, 2010). Galileo responded by avoiding the topic in his writings for about a decade, until the next pope was elected. This new pope, along with the Inquisition, permitted Galileo to publish a book about the subject, but only on condition that he describe heliocentrism as a *theory* and not as a *fact*.

When his new book, *Dialogo sopra i due massimi sistemi del mondo* (Dialogue concerning the two chief world systems), was published in 1632 (Galileo, 1632), it caused a sensation. It not only asserted that heliocentrism was factual, it also implied that the pope was a fool for doubting the truth of the matter. Galileo was arrested, interrogated and charged by the Roman Inquisition, and

this time was required not only to abandon his opinions, but to 'abjure, curse and detest' his own findings (Heilbron, 2010). He spent the rest of his life under house arrest.

It is commonly asserted that Galileo was found to be a heretic and thus was duly excommunicated (i.e. formally expelled) by the Catholic Church. However, while the Inquisition found Galileo to be 'vehemently *suspect* of' heresy, they did not find him actually *guilty* of being a heretic. This rather pedantic distinction ensured that Galileo, an elderly public figure and personal friend of the pope, was able to avoid a death sentence (Finocchiaro, 2009).

Galileo is also often acclaimed as an early sceptic of religion and a champion of scientific atheism. However, this again is misleading. Galileo was in fact a devout Catholic and remained so until his death. He did not see heliocentrism as incompatible with scripture but, rather, as providing depth and context to ancient words. Nor did he doubt the various miraculous events described in the Bible, as he maintained the view that the divine creator was in fact quite capable of performing miracles.

As a devout Catholic, Galileo believed that empirical data would never be able to refute scriptural claims. By most contemporary accounts, he was taken aback and upset by the controversy his work attracted.

From the perspective of the twenty-first century, it can often seem that historical scientists were among the greatest sceptics of religion. In reality, however, most were acculturated within societies that were steeped in religiosity and mysticism. By and large, they used science not to debunk or destroy religion, but to better understand and 'know' the divine.

THE EMERGENCE OF A 'NEW' SCIENCE? PSYCHOLOGY'S CREATION MYTH

In the year 1800, some seven centuries after the establishment of the first institution to call itself a 'university', there were a total of 143 universities across Europe, the largest number of which – thirty-four – were located in or near Germany (by comparison, in England at this time there were just two). The next 100 years saw much turmoil and transformation in the European university system.

Warfare and upheaval repeatedly redrew the political map, as the aftermath of the French Revolution spread through the continent. The monarchies of Europe engaged in a series of bloody conflicts with the new French republic led by Napoleon Bonaparte. Millions of military conscripts were killed and the fabric of society was sundered. Several historic universities – including all of those in the now rapidly diminishing French state – were forced to shut their doors.

After seven major wars in just twelve years, Napoleon was defeated, and European ambassadors met at the Congress of Vienna in 1814 to carve up the continent's territories. Their specific aim was to create a group of similarly sized power blocs that would neutralize each other in a way that lessened the likelihood of further war. Germany, then the Prussian Empire, was expanded in size, absorbing the industrial heartlands of the Rhine valley.

The German state sought to make Germany a leading force in what we now refer to as the Industrial Revolution. They set about modernizing their universities by providing massive financial support not just for teaching, but also for research. The German university system became the first in the world where scholars could acquire doctoral degrees by conducting research projects alone and without having to complete taught courses.

Throughout Europe, the Industrial Revolution had boosted population growth, urbanization and, ultimately, secularization. It exposed the masses to many new technologies and reinforced a cultural belief that science was indeed a lucrative form of human ingenuity and a necessity for national welfare. In addition, the beleaguering social effects of war stirred a hunger for change among the wider populace. New generations began to direct criticism at their predecessors, and change for its own sake became fashionable among intellectuals and the general public alike (Hughes, 2012).

Before the 1800s, universities taught a narrow range of subjects, largely aimed at preparing graduates for religious ministry or for a small number of specific professions, such as law or medicine. During the nineteenth century, all this changed. Universities began to shift their focus from the preservation of the old to the creation of the new, from teaching students what was accepted to encouraging them to become discoverers, and from the transmission of information to the cultivation of critical thinking.

While the oldest universities were often the slowest to change, the overall system of university education began to teach a range of new disciplines. Many of these were research-based, where discovery could be advanced through investigation and evaluation. By the end of the nineteenth century, the total number of universities in Europe exceeded 200 for the first time. In the United States, there were around 1,000 equivalent degree-awarding colleges. This period saw the establishment of a plethora of new departments of different kinds, many of them under titles that had never been used before. These are what we might refer to, in the particular context of university affairs, as new 'subjects'. In the fullness of time, one of these subjects was, of course, to be psychology.

As mentioned previously, a key event in the traditional 'History of Psychology' schema is the opening of the Institute for Experimental Psychology in Leipzig University in 1879. By establishing his institute, Wilhelm Wundt is said by many historians of psychology not just to have opened a new laboratory or to have named a new course. He is said to have founded a completely new science.

Of course, in reality, things were a lot more complicated than that.

The rush to bureaucratize

Across the nineteenth century, widespread cultural transformation saw many areas of scholarship finally codified within formal academic structures. For example, while geographical topics (such as cartography and soil mechanics) had been discussed for many centuries, it was only in 1821 that the first geographical association – the Société de Géographie – was founded in France, effectively establishing geography as an independent academic subject (Lejeune, 1993).

Likewise, formal sociological analysis was common in philosophy since ancient Greek and Arab scholarship, but the resulting ideas were not assembled under the title *sociology* until the 1830s, when the French philosopher August Comte (1798–1857) proposed the French label *sociologie* as an improvement on the earlier term *physique sociale* (social physics; Comte, 1838). Significantly, Comte was influenced not just by academic trends, but also by the social implications of the French Revolution, and the prospect of being able to use empirical evidence to improve society. The first university sociology courses appeared in 1875 at Yale University, with the first sociology department opening in 1892 at the University of Chicago (Drysdale & Hoecker-Drysdale, 2007).

Similarly, the analysis of political power is extremely old, but the field of political science is generally regarded as appearing in universities in the middle of the nineteenth century. Comte had introduced the term *la science politique* in 1822 (Iggers, 1959), and German philosopher Francis Lieber (1798–1872) was appointed as the world's first 'professor of political science' at Columbia College in New York in 1857 (Farr, 1988).

Wundt formed his institute in Leipzig at a time of frenzied academic bureaucratization, not just in Germany but also around the world. The 1870s had seen a global trend of mass scholarly self-organization, as scientists, physicians and academics coalesced into a myriad of institutions, groups and associations. Some major examples of these include the following:

- **1870:** the American Association for Higher Education;
- **1871:** the Geological Society of Sweden (Geologiska Föreningen); the German Association of Surveying (Deutscher Verein für Vermessungswesen); the Royal Anthropological Institute (UK); the Upper-Rhine Geological Union (Oberrheinische Geologische Verein);
- **1872:** the German Economic Association (Verein für Socialpolitik); the German Society of Surgery (Deutsche Gesellschaft für Chirurgie); the Mathematical Society of France (Société

Mathématique de France); the Polish Academy of Arts and Sciences (Polska Akademia Umiejętności);

- **1873:** the French Society of Physics (Société Française de Physique); the Royal Dutch Geographical Society (the Koninklijk Nederlands Aardrijkskundig Genootschap);
- **1874:** the Institute of Physics (UK); the Physical Society of London; the Society of Analytical Chemistry (UK);
- **1875:** the American Neurological Association; the Scientific Society of Brussels (Société Scientifique de Bruxelles);
- **1876:** the American Chemical Society; the Physiological Society (UK); the Indian Association for the Cultivation of Science; the Royal Danish Geographical Society (Det Kongelige Danske Geografiske Selskab); the Royal Society for the Promotion of Health (UK);
- **1877:** the Royal Institute of Chemistry (UK); the Swedish Society for Anthropology and Geography (Svenska Sällskapet för Antropologi och Geografi); the Tokyo Mathematics Company (Japan's first academic society, later renamed as the Physical Society of Japan);
- **1878:** the Chemical Society of Japan;
- **1879:** the Archaeological Institute of America; the Italian Ophthalmological Society (Società Oftalmologica Italiana).

During the 1870s, the city of Leipzig was thriving as never before. Its population nearly doubled, reaching almost 150,000. It had become a major hub within the central European railway system, having opened the largest train station in Europe in the mid-nineteenth century. Aided by its transport infrastructure, political activists from around the country gathered in Leipzig to form the General German Workers Association, an influential political organization that continues to exist today as Germany's Social Democratic Party.

Leipzig's status as an intellectual and cultural centre was renowned. Its arts scene had produced composers such as Bach, Schumann and Mendelssohn, as well as globally famous choirs, operas and orchestras. The city had a proud history of printing and publishing, and had previously launched the first daily newspaper in the world. The new Leipzig Zoo opened in 1878, immediately becoming one of the most illustrious in Europe. Huge crowds of visitors gathered to see its kangaroos, parrots and lions, as well as its single Bengal tiger. Even the local footballers were among the best in Europe: when the German Football Federation was later established, Leipzig was chosen as its natural headquarters.

At the heart of Leipzig's cultural vibrancy lay its university, then the largest in Germany and one of the most esteemed in the world. Originally founded in 1409, the university underwent extensive academic redevelopment during the 1870s. A variety of new subject areas were added to the curriculum, and hardly a year went by without a number of new departments and professorships (or 'Chairs') being established. In 1870 a Chair in Egyptology was established; in 1871 a Department of Geography, and in 1873 an Institute for Art History. New Chairs in areas as diverse as Slavic Philology, Modern History and East Asian Languages soon followed, as well as a brand new Department of History. Many of these additions represented areas of scholarship that had never before appeared within formal university structures anywhere in the world. Leipzig's university was clearly encouraging of academic innovation. Its leaders were keen to support the establishment of new units that could authentically place Leipzig at the cutting edge of contemporary intellectualism.

It was within the context of this cultural and academic milieu that Wilhelm Wundt, then a professor in Leipzig's philosophy department, made a proposal. He wished that his room for doing experiments should be formally designated as an official university 'institute' – specifically, an Institute for Experimental Psychology.

Wilhelm Wundt and his equipment storeroom

The charismatic Professor Wundt had been headhunted from Zurich University in 1875. To say that he had developed a varied academic profile up to that point would be something of an understatement.

Wundt grew up in a small town in rural south-west Germany, the son and grandson of religious ministers. During his entire six-year secondary school education, he received no more than twelve hours' instruction in the natural sciences. By comparison, his tuition in modern languages amounted to around twelve hours *per week* (Bringmann & Ungerer, 1980). The young Wundt was not, however, swayed by this largely humanities-based schooling. When it was time for him to go to university, he told his parents that he wished to study medicine.

Attending the nearby university at Heidelberg, Wundt had the good fortune to enrol in a chemistry class offered by the esteemed German scientist Robert Bunsen (1811–99). Bunsen was an obsessive laboratory researcher, famous for emphasizing the importance of precision in measurement. He would later be remembered for inventing the now ubiquitous 'Bunsen burner', a device that could emit a high-intensity carbon-free flame for use in laboratory experiments. It ensured that any secondary flame produced when burning a chemical would not be discoloured by contaminants, thereby providing scientists with purer data and, ultimately, better conclusions. Inspired by Bunsen's attention to such details, Wundt threw himself into chemistry, completing his first formal research project while still an undergraduate. From that point on, he was to become an ardent research enthusiast.

Wundt's interests soon turned to biology. He conducted vivisections in his home, recruiting his mother to serve as his laboratory assistant. During the summer, he travelled to Berlin, to avail of the rather better-staffed physiology laboratories at Berlin University. After graduating with his medical degree, he set up his own course in experimental physiology, again prevailing upon his mother, who this time provided her apartment as a laboratory space. He enrolled four students and began teaching them in her kitchen. Such arrangements were common in nineteenth-century German universities. Privately hosted tuition allowed academics to supplement their income and, commercially, to build their reputations (Bringmann & Ungerer, 1980).

To further his expertise, Wundt then signed up as a laboratory assistant himself. He joined the physiology institute at Heidelberg, led by the famous physician Hermann von Helmholtz (1821–94), an expert in sensory physiology and ophthalmology. While at the institute, Wundt was asked to teach a number of courses as assistant professor. He wrote a lengthy book on sense perception (1862) and published another based on his lectures on human and animal psychology (1863). After seven years with von Helmholtz, Wundt left to set up a laboratory of his own. He established this one in his own apartment, where he worked for the next decade, gathering data and publishing several papers.

In 1874, seventeen years after graduating, Wundt finally obtained his first full professorial position, when he was appointed a professor at Zurich University, just across the border in Switzerland, about a four-hour train ride from Heidelberg.

Zurich University was a new and small institution, with little or no reputation and very poor infrastructure. However, there can often be advantages to joining an institution with few organizational traditions or bureaucratic precedents. For example, Wundt essentially had a blank canvas on which to build his academic and teaching activities; formally, his appointment was as 'Professor of Inductive Philosophy', which afforded him a very wide scope. Another benefit was that Wundt was quickly able to take over a room in the main university building all for himself, which he used for storing his laboratory equipment (Bringmann & Ungerer, 1980).

Shortly after arriving at Zurich, Wundt was contacted by the dean of philosophy at Leipzig, who offered him the then vacant Chair of Philosophy. Wundt had developed a reputation for his scientific approach, which was seen as somewhat novel and daring. His acceptance of the appointment at Leipzig caused quite a stir, as many observers felt he was more of an 'experimental physician' than a philosopher (Schlotte, 1955). Indeed, Wundt's formal education in philosophy had consisted of a single undergraduate course taken several decades previously.

Nonetheless, the dean felt that Wundt was just the person to develop a new era for philosophy at Leipzig. He was well aware that some of Leipzig's esteemed natural scientists, including the aforementioned Weber and Fechner, had attracted fame for their research on human sensation and perception. Wundt himself had been especially influenced by Fechner's 1860 book *Elemente der Psychophysik* (*Elements of Psychophysics*). The dean saw Wundt's appointment to the philosophy department as an exciting transition, which, in time, he believed, would be viewed as truly historic (Bringmann, Bringmann & Ungerer, 1980).

Wundt asked the Leipzig authorities for a room in which he could store his laboratory equipment, similar to the one he had been allocated in Zurich. He was assigned a storage space, located conveniently near the lecture hall in which he was to teach his course in general psychology. Wundt spent most of the next four years teaching and writing, as well as helping to raise his young family. The equipment remained in its storage room, largely untouched.

Over time, Wundt's students began to express an interest in collecting their own data, in order to further explore the phenomena he described in his classes. He gladly facilitated this by providing them with access to the storeroom. The first of their studies commenced in 1879. With this production of publishable experimental data, the storage facility had effectively now become a laboratory (Bringmann & Ungerer, 1980).

Wundt paid the new laboratory's running costs from his own pocket until 1881. He then began to submit requests for funding to the university authorities. His courses had become very popular and had begun to attract well over 250 students, even though the university had provided resources for classes of just 25. The university duly gave Wundt a small one-off laboratory grant in 1882, and another in 1883. At this point, Wundt began to refer to his laboratory as an 'Institute', presumably an effort to add weight to his funding requests. In their replies, however, the university meticulously avoided this official term. They continuously stated that their grants were intended to support Wundt's 'seminar' (Fensch, 1977).

In the middle of 1883, Wundt was again headhunted, this time by the University of Breslau, a German university located in what is now the Polish city of Wrocław. When he told his employers in Leipzig that he had been offered a new job, he suggested they make him a counter-offer should they wish to retain his services. In return, the Leipzig authorities agreed to increase Wundt's salary, to provide an annual grant for his laboratory, and to include the laboratory in the official university catalogue. And so it was that for the winter semester of 1883, Wundt's laboratory was finally formally listed under the title that Wundt himself had been using for a number of years. Leipzig University's Institut für experimentelle Psychologie had officially come into being.

Wundt's reputational success

Wundt, always keen to record his own history (e.g. Wundt, 1909), attached particular significance to the year 1879. This was the year when the commencement of data collection effectively transformed his humble 'storage facility' into a working laboratory. It is for this reason that 1879 is often mentioned as the founding date for the Institute for Experimental Psychology. However, as we have seen, the university itself did not formally incorporate such an institute until 1883.

The formation of a university institute is essentially a bureaucratic matter, and therefore often a vague one. Given such vagueness, the claim that 'psychology' itself (in the modern sense or otherwise) came into being at the same time – or, to narrow things down, to say that *experimental* psychology did so – seems ever more arbitrary.

Leipzig University was a high-flying academic institution with abundant ambition. By all accounts, Wundt's conspicuous self-confidence was well suited to such an environment. With the aim of leading the world, he established a journal, *Philosophische Studien*, in which the data emerging from his new Institute could be published, wrote several books, and began supervising an inordinate number of graduate students.

Image 3.3 Leipzig
In the late nineteenth century, the German city of Leipzig became an internationally significant intellectual and cultural centre, where innovation and topicality were highly valued (lithograph by Adolf Eltzner, *c.* 1850).

The university, meanwhile, developed an internationalization strategy, aimed at bolstering its reputation and, of course, its finances. Wundt exploited this opportunity with outstanding effect. Availing of university funding, he set up programmes to attract students and visiting scholars from around the world.

The German system of university education was especially valued in the United States, for several reasons. Politically, Germany was a hub of international affairs. The Prussian kingdom was a global superpower, deriving influence from its economic and technological advancement. Its universities were extremely well resourced and certainly world-leading. Many American graduates studied the German language as part of their own core curriculum. And the novel German practice of awarding PhD degrees for research, without requiring coursework, was attractively expeditious. Between 1865 and 1914, some *10,000* Americans completed PhDs in Germany (Sokal, 1981). By contrast, British universities didn't even start to offer research-only PhDs until *after* the First World War.

A large number of scholars and students who passed through Wundt's Institute would eventually become prominent figures in their own right. In history-of-psychology textbooks, it is customary to provide a roll call. Some of the most prominent of these alumni were:

- **G. Stanley Hall** (1846–1924): Spent a brief period at Leipzig in 1879 after completing his own PhD at Harvard, becoming Wundt's first American graduate assistant. Went on to become the first president of the American Psychological Association, in 1892.
- **James McKeen Cattell** (1860–1944): From Pennsylvania, completed his PhD with Wundt in 1886. Went on to become the first full professor of psychology in the United States.
- **Hugo Münsterberg** (1863–1916): From the German city of Danzig (now the Polish city of Gdansk), completed his PhD with Wundt in 1882. Later joined the faculty at Harvard University, and became president of the American Psychological Association in 1898.
- **Emil Kraepelin** (1856–1926): A German physician and pioneering psychiatrist. Worked in Wundt's laboratory during 1882.
- **Edward B. Titchener** (1867–1927): An English academic who completed a PhD with Wundt in 1892. Later moved to the United States, where he became a professor at Cornell University, and formulated the influential 'functionalist' approach to psychology.

The influence of this activity had lasting effects. By the year 1900, around a quarter of American psychology departments (precisely: 12 out of 43) were led by former students of Wundt (Benjamin, 1979).

Of course, such a summary of Wundt's career, followed by a list of prominent people who passed through his laboratory (retrospectively selected on the basis of their subsequent fame), certainly looks a lot like a 'Great Man' approach to history. As noted previously, we should be wary of this type of historiography. We should especially be sceptical of Great Man histories when they are written by the Great Men themselves.

One of the main reasons it is customary to mention all these psychologists by name is that these were the names recorded by those authors, such as Boring, who wrote the early formal textbook histories of this new academic subject area – a field we might reasonably refer to as 'university psychology'. In doing so, they were no doubt influenced by university circumstances. Their aims were more professional than scholarly (assuming they were ever truly scholarly). They wished to champion university psychology's status as a science – because they themselves were university psychologists. They wanted to celebrate the reputations of psychology's university pioneers – because these were essentially their own reputations. Boring, for example, had been a student of Titchener, who himself had completed a PhD in Leipzig with Wundt. Therefore, when Boring promoted Wundt as the genius responsible for inventing experimental psychology, he was effectively linking *himself* to psychology's creation story.

The Wundt reality

Leipzig's prominence in the history of psychology owes less to the ideas and insights of Wilhelm Wundt than it does to two more mundane circumstantial factors: *traffic* and *technology*.

The *traffic* consisted of the many national and international students and scholars who visited Wundt's Leipzig laboratory, afterwards dispersing to spread the word to universities around the world. This traffic was encouraged (and incentivized) by a well-resourced university anxious to grow its global reputation, at a time in history when academic institutions were refreshing and restructuring their curricula in bold and innovative ways.

The *technology* comprised all the apparatus and equipment that Wundt had accumulated, largely during his Heidelberg days, which provided visitors with a vivid and visible spectacle, as well as a template inventory for their own laboratories to work from. These devices were largely based on equipment already familiar to physiologists and physicists. For example, when describing the history of his Institute, the first piece of apparatus that Wundt (1909) chose to draw attention to was 'a series of tuning forks which range in numerous small increments from tones of 32 to 2,024 vibrations, and thereafter at somewhat greater increments up to 60,000 vibrations' ('eine Stimmgabelserie, die in zahlreichen kleinen Abstufungen die Töne von 32 Doppelschw. bis zu 2024 und von da an in etwas größeren Abständen die bekannten Serien höchster hörbarer Töne in kleinen Stimmgabeln und Pfeifen bis zu etwa 60000 Schw. umfaßt'; p. 290). These were coupled with 'a so-called Appun tonometer that can detect frequencies of musical tones between 32 and 1,024 vibrations, and an overtone apparatus that can detect 60 overtones associated with the musical note, low C' ('sogenannte Appunsche Tonmesser, in Zungenpfeifen Klingen, die Töne von 32 bis 1024 Schw., und ein Obertöneapparat, die 60 Obertöne eines tiefen C = 32 Schw'; p. 290).

Wundt was especially keen on what he saw as 'high-technology' equipment, as it helped him to promote psychology as a truly scientific field (Draaisma & de Rijcke, 2001). However, perhaps ironically, the very nature of Wundt's laboratory equipment helps to highlight the fundamental weakness of the claim that his work represented a formal 'founding' for the entire discipline of psychology.

Wundt's experimental work revolved around a subfield known as *psychophysics*, a set of physical methods used for quantifying various aspects of human perception. In this regard, as mentioned above, Wundt was inspired by previous scholarship produced at Leipzig. Psychophysics had first been proposed by the Leipzig philosopher Gustav Fechner in 1860, in light of a number of experiments conducted by his university colleague, the physiologist Ernst Weber. Wundt was also influenced by his time working as an assistant in von Helmholtz's laboratory, where the research had explored the mechanics and physiology of sensation.

Wundt's experiments were focused on testing the limits of human perception under laboratory conditions. Much of his work sought to establish the limits of *sensory detection* (for example, establishing the quietest sound that an average human listener can hear). Other experiments would explore the limits of *sensory discrimination* (for example, measuring the smallest difference in two sounds that would allow a listener to realize that one was louder than the other). Given this focus, it was no surprise that Wundt's laboratory accumulated a large stock of devices for calibrating the intensity of sounds, lights and other sensory stimuli.

Wundt worked on a subject matter that was narrow in scope but interdisciplinary in reach. While his chosen topics were 'psychological', they were also substantially physiological and physical. All the *technology* that Wundt was so proud of, all the devices that led so much *traffic* to visit his laboratory, were designed to measure physiological and physical variables.

The psychological part of his research related to the perceptual abilities of his participants, which he assessed by asking them to self-report what they saw, heard or otherwise detected. This procedure did not require any equipment per se. It was inherently imprecise, relying entirely on participant self-report. Wundt could establish the frequency of a sound with great precision using his tonometer. However, the question-and-answer procedure he used to establish whether participants actually *heard* the sound was far less exact.

It is (famously) well documented that Wundt's work drew not inconsiderable criticism from his own contemporaries. At its simplest, these criticisms centred on the fact that many scientists, especially those outside Germany, found themselves unable to replicate his findings in their own laboratories. This was attributed to the way Wundt's studies relied on self-report. His studies required participants to engage in introspection, the 'hidden' nature of which made it impossible to properly account for variability across laboratories. To the extent that introspection amounted to an invisible type of data collection, it was duly criticized for being unscientific.

Prominent researchers differed on how introspection should be deployed. Generally speaking, Wundt sought to confine his psychophysical research to the basic senses. However, other scholars, such as Wundt's own student Oswald Külpe (1862–1915), felt that introspection should be used to explore such concepts as mental imagery, consciousness and higher mental functions (Ash, 1998). In essence, Wundt was criticized by some of his contemporaries for relying on introspection, and by others for restricting its use.

Wundt succeeded in establishing an institute at a prestigious university while cultivating a disciple-like following among his many acolytes. However, notwithstanding these achievements, his scholarship in psychology was far from memorable. He left no influential theory or scientific discovery. He wrote several textbooks, but even most of his own students, although revering him as a mentor, rejected many of his psychological ideas (G. Richards, 2010). His significance, therefore, is essentially symbolic. In the words of one historian of psychology, Wundt's early eminence arose because, at the time university psychologists began to write their own histories, the discipline of psychology '*wanted* a founding father with good experimental scientific credentials' (G. Richards, 2010). Wundt fit the bill.

In the late nineteenth century, the scientific understanding of human behaviour was being shaped in many ways, including (as we will see) by work in such fields as evolutionary biology, sociology, criminology, pedagogy, linguistics, psychiatry, neurology and statistics. All these fields, many of which existed long before 1879, were entirely untouched by Wundt's psychophysics. All of them fundamentally shaped the field of psychology as it exists today. It seems difficult to imagine that their influence would have somehow evaporated had Wundt not converted his equipment storage facility into a laboratory. In short, interest in psychology long predated Wundtian psychophysics, or the opening of dedicated university departments. Even 'university psychology' sprung from multiple scholarly sources, in which Wundt's contributions rank among those of lesser scientific consequence.

Nonetheless, Wundt's Institute remains of interest when considering psychology's history. This is because it stands as a useful case study in historiography. It tells us something important about the role of nostalgic propaganda in in-group politics, and about how and why academic histories often come to be written selectively.

The world beyond Leipzig

Some ideas prove more popular than others, but not always because they are the most productive. A belief, fashion or custom can go 'viral' for several reasons. Ideas can become popular when they have emotional appeal, or when they are championed by persuasive advocates. Their spread can also be enhanced by exponential exposure. The more familiar an idea becomes, the more it is assumed to be the standard. Recognition prompts deference.

While Wundt's psychophysics was not the only type of psychology taught in old universities, his particular model of an experimental laboratory became somewhat conspicuous, a striking and memorable novelty. Leipzig was an illustrious university that deliberately sought international visitors, and Wundt himself was keen to evangelize on behalf of his own research. He adopted a proselytizing approach to science, actively encouraging his students and mentees to spend their own careers spreading the word of psychophysics far and wide.

While German universities were dominant in the 1870s, as time went by, university systems in other countries began to flourish. This allowed 'university psychology' to take shape around the world. But new universities and expanding education systems did not exist in a vacuum. They sought to follow what was seen in older institutions, inferring it to represent good practice. As such, many of them turned their attention to psychology, imitating what they saw in Germany, and in a number of cases drawing directly on Wundt's migrating diaspora of laboratory alumni.

That said, the Wundt approach was not the sole influence. As noted previously, psychological topics had drawn the attention of a wide range of academic fields, many of which – such as evolutionary biology – have had a far greater lasting effect on the subject matter of university psychology. And given the relative shallowness and narrowness of psychophysics, even Wundt's own students tended to broaden their psychological interests once they had left Leipzig's cloistered confines. Psychology's success as an academic subject in no small way benefited from such adaptability. Local variations were able to proliferate quickly.

The first Russian laboratories for experimental psychology appeared in university medical schools, reflecting that country's strong tradition of physiological research. The neurologist Vladimir Bekhterev (1857–1927), a rival and critic of Pavlov, had completed a PhD under Wundt in Leipzig and later opened a psychophysiological laboratory at the University of Kazan in 1885. This is believed to be the second such laboratory in Europe after Wundt's (Amirov et al., 2007). Unlike Wundt, however, Bekhterev focused his research on neuroscientific aspects of mental illness.

In France, philosophers of mind and physicians of psychopathology collaborated to create educational departments in French universities. The French researcher Alfred Binet (1857–1911), who would later invent the first practical intelligence test, helped to establish the first experimental psychology laboratory in France, at the Sorbonne, in 1889. (We will refer to Binet's work again in Chapter 6.)

In Japan, the first formal university psychology departments were opened by scholars who had themselves studied in Europe or the United States. Yūjirō Motora, a teacher in Tokyo, completed a PhD in the United States under G. Stanley Hall, one of Wundt's protégés. On returning to Japan, Motora turned his attention to the study of emotion, essentially abandoning psychophysics. He established Japan's first university psychology laboratory at Tokyo Imperial University in 1903 (Sato et al., 2016).

In the late nineteenth and early twentieth centuries, China's increasing population was causing pressure on its education system. Educational reforms initiated after the establishment of the Republic of China in 1912 saw an expansion of teacher training, operated from so-called 'normal' universities. Psychology was seen as highly relevant to pedagogy and became part of the teacher-training curriculum right across the country (Blowers, 2006). Shortages in qualified teacher trainers were offset by importing academic staff from nearby Japan, and thousands of Chinese students spent time studying at Japanese universities. Simultaneously, free-standing psychology departments and laboratories were established in a number of China's most prestigious colleges. At the National Peking University, the Chinese academic Chen Dachi (1886–1983) established a psychology laboratory in 1917, while Tsinghua University opened its department in 1926.

While psychological concepts had been explored in Indian philosophy for centuries (see Chapter 2), British rule saw indigenous scholarship marginalized as part of an explicit state effort to Westernize the education system (Paranjpe, 2006). India's first university psychology laboratory opened in 1905 at the University of Calcutta, later becoming India's first full department of psychology in 1915 (Rao & Paranjpe, 2016). It was led by the psychologist Narendra Nath Sen Gupta (1889–1944). Sen Gupta had completed a PhD in the United States at Harvard, where he was supervised by Wundt's former student Hugo Münsterburg. While retaining an interest in perceptual research, Sen Gupta's own writings ranged widely, helping to popularize social, cultural and religious aspects of psychology among Indian academics.

It is widely regarded that university psychology developed slowly in the United Kingdom, as noted by the British psychologist M. D. Vernon (1965): 'British society in general, and its academic members in particular, have not welcomed the scientific study of psychology ... there is still a vague belief that there is something slightly indecent in the attempt to explore [human action and motives]; or else that they are mysteries which cannot be approached through any type of scientific investigation' (p. 212).

As we will see in Chapter 6, many British pioneers of psychology, such as Francis Galton, worked independently of universities. A small laboratory for psychology was opened in the physiology department of Cambridge University in 1897, but a formal psychological laboratory was not opened at Cambridge until 1913. It is acknowledged as being the first custom-built experimental psychology laboratory in England.

While psychology, science and, indeed, university education are all international endeavours, they are nonetheless subject to forces of capital, culture and colonialism. World geopolitical history has created a juggernaut of Western globalization, in which indigenous distinctiveness tends to be trimmed by the dominance of a single hegemonic norm. For universities, and by extension, therefore, for psychology, this has essentially taken the form of Americanization. By hosting the largest and best-resourced university system, and assisted by natively speaking English, a global lingua franca, the United States has become a centre of academic gravity for most fields of scholarship and science.

University psychology in the United States

It is notable that the first classic textbook in the history of psychology, Boring's *History of Experimental Psychology*, was itself produced in the United States. As outlined above, its authorship benefited from a direct lineage to Leipzig – Boring had worked under Titchener, who himself had been supervised by Wundt. Unsurprisingly, therefore, Boring saw fit to emphasize the Wundtian influence on psychology in his homeland. However, in reality, American university psychology owes its flourishing to a broader and more philosophical heritage.

The fashion for opening psychology laboratories swept through American colleges in the 1870s, 1880s and 1890s. Prominent examples were founded by Hall (at Johns Hopkins University in 1883) and Titchener (at Cornell in 1892), both of whom had worked with Wundt. However, in nearly every case, these new psychology laboratories were opened in pre-existing university departments in which psychology was already being taught. As such, the laboratory approach acquired the nickname 'New Psychology' in order to distinguish it from what went before (Fuchs, 2000).

Psychology had been taught widely at American universities under the guise of 'mental science', an established branch of philosophy. This reflected a favouring of British philosophy over its continental

Public domain, via Wikimedia Commons / (PD-US)

Image 3.4 William James, *c.* 1890s (photograph by the noted American photographer and art patron Sarah Choate Sears)

European counterparts. American scholars considered the latter somewhat risqué, associating French philosophy with the secular excesses of the French Revolution, and German philosophy with atheism. By contrast, the British philosophers, with their emphasis on Baconian induction and empiricism, seemed much better suited to the religiously conservative, seminarian American colleges.

The American mental philosophers had been prolific in preparing suitable textbooks for teaching psychology at university, with titles such as *Psychology: Or, a View of the Human Soul* (Rauch, 1841), *Psychology: Or, Elements of a New System of Mental Philosophy* (Schmucker, 1842), *Empirical Psychology* (Hickok, 1854), and *The Elements of Intellectual Philosophy* (Wayland, 1854). These textbooks provided a broad template on which many of the later 'New Psychology' books would be based. Perhaps the most famous example of these was *The Principles of Psychology* by William James (1890).

William James (1842–1910) is now widely considered one of the most important American psychologists of all time. He was instrumental in introducing laboratory-based psychology to Harvard University, and in popularizing psychology among both his fellow academics and the wider public. His *Principles of Psychology* is considered a landmark textbook. It was the first major psychology textbook to omit coverage of the religious 'soul', dismissing it as a 'superfluity for scientific purposes' (p. 332). (In doing so, James perhaps intentionally sought to echo the French astronomer Pierre-Simon Laplace, who, when asked about God, was famously reputed to have informed Napoleon that he 'had no need of that hypothesis'; Sanford, 1935, p. 113.)

By any standards, James was a precocious communicator, a deep thinker and an inspirationally imaginative intellectual. His career was no doubt helped by a fortunate upbringing that included lifelong exposure to literary brilliance. Born into a wealthy Irish-American family (with ancestry in Cavan, Longford and County Down), his godfather was the writer Ralph Waldo Emerson, his sister the celebrated diarist Alice James, and his brother the novelist Henry James, eventually to be regarded as one of the greatest novelists ever to have written in the English language (Banville, 2017).

James trained as a physician but never practised as a doctor, instead holding a number of positions at Harvard University. At different stages he taught physiology, psychology and philosophy. In 1875, he began offering a course in experimental psychology, taught in his own laboratory, some four years before Wundt's students first collected data in that now-exalted storeroom at Leipzig University.

However, James's attitude to his laboratory was somewhat lukewarm. He would later come to question the value of laboratory research at all, believing it to be overrated (R. B. Perry, 1930). He called for a wider methodological approach to psychological scholarship and encouraged the development of applied psychology. According to James, laboratory work was inherently limited and so would inevitably fail to satisfy; breadth, he felt, would much better protect psychology's reputation.

James's eclecticism was to be an important factor in the modernization of university psychology. While laboratories were seen as emblematic of psychology's academic independence, this was largely due to their architectural tangibility rather than to any essential role in the production of new knowledge (Capshew, 1992). By occupying physical sites for research, psychology departments – literally – made their presence felt. A new department for psychology would require an allocation of rooms and funds, precious collateral that would need to be diverted from other academic units. Bartering for university resources has always been a deeply contentious affair; laboratories made (and still make) psychology impossible to ignore.

The laboratory is a spiritual home for many psychologists, but this owes more to technophilia than to destiny. Laboratory research is far from a defining feature of psychology. Indeed, laboratory research is *not even a defining feature of science.*

As outlined previously, science is a way of knowing that blends formal logic with empirical evidence. It is an alternative to authority, hearsay and intuition. Therefore, in pursuing its credentials as a science, psychology should perhaps draw courage from its epistemology, rather than relying on second-hand esteem derived from a disproportionate departmental infrastructure allocation or bloated equipment inventory. The bigger a university building does not a science make.

William James was strident in promoting this view of psychology. He saw psychology's appeal to the public – and its value for humanity – as being based on its practical utility. Over a number of decades, he commenced a variety of lecture courses at Harvard, including:

- **1875:** 'The Relations between Physiology and Psychology'
- **1876:** 'Physiological Psychology'
- **1877:** 'Psychology'
- **1881:** 'Psychology: The Human Intellect'
- **1881:** 'Advanced Psychology'
- **1885:** 'Psychology and Logic'
- **1885:** 'Special Advanced Study of Experimental Research in Psychology'
- **1886:** 'Questions in Psychology'
- **1890:** 'Pleasure and Pain'
- **1891:** 'Topics in Psychology of Interest to Teachers'
- **1893:** 'Questions in Mental Pathology'
- **1895:** 'Feelings'
- **1896:** 'Abnormal Psychology'.

In 1890, James published *The Principles of Psychology*, a text that had taken him twelve years to write. In it he famously presented the metaphor of the 'stream of consciousness', offering a phrase that was soon to become a popular English-language idiom. He also elaborated on his view of emotions and their rootedness in physiological responses, a theory that continues to be accepted today as a key principle of affective neuroscience. And he not only dispensed with the religious soul as a premise for psychological theory, he also had the foresight to integrate his thinking within the wider evolutionary worldview in which science as a whole would increasingly become embedded over the course of the subsequent century.

Under James, Harvard's psychology sought to be attentive to public interest. To the consternation of some of his colleagues (Coon, 1992), James supported research into seances and spiritualism. While these topics were esoteric and faddish, such populist investigations soon exposed the need for rigour and scepticism in psychological research, and led psychologists to quickly develop important techniques such as blinding and counter-balancing (O'Keeffe & Wiseman, 2005). The financial donations from members of the public who wanted universities to help find ways for them to talk to deceased loved ones were also, of course, always gratefully received (Coon, 1992).

Overall, American university psychologists embraced a mission of outreach and public education. In the religiously conservative late nineteenth century, they sought to emphasize that psychology was a dignified pursuit that posed no danger to the spiritual welfare of America's sons and daughters (Pickren, 2000). American psychologists wrote widely in mainstream magazines, always acknowledging the existence, and merit, of popular religious sentiment. They reached wide audiences with rhetoric that stimulated the public's religious imagination (Fuller, 2006). This was quite a contrast to the approach in Europe, where psychologists tended to mock public interest in psychics and spiritualists, and where figures such as Wundt argued vehemently against the idea that psychology could ever be applied to address social problems (D. Jones & Elcock, 2001).

In 1875, there were no psychology departments in American universities (Fuller, 2006); by 1893, there were twice as many in the United States as there were in Europe (Capshew, 1992). However, while rapid, this growth of psychology in universities mirrored the wider emergence of science in American society. It was not so much an immediate transformation as it was a gradual transition.

Specifically, in the United States – soon the hegemonic driver of a global cultural norm – university psychology found its initial academic home among the religious philosophers. This was to prove quite lucrative, as religious philosophy was effectively an anchor tenant in the American curriculum.

Belying a common stereotype (and in contrast to how Boring would later reimagine events), university psychology came smoothly into existence, by way of evolution rather than revolution. The godly scholars in the philosophy departments were far from hostile to this 'New Psychology'. In fact, most were particularly interested in it. For their part, the new psychologists themselves, more often than not, were deeply respectful of their religious colleagues (Fuchs, 2000).

Indeed, as with many scientists of the day, most of these new psychologists were themselves very religious (Pickren, 2000). For example, G. Stanley Hall, a student of Wundt and founder of the United States' first psychology laboratory for research (as opposed to for teaching) at Johns Hopkins University, described the New Psychology as 'Christian to its root and centre' (G. S. Hall, 1885, p. 242). He explained how he saw the Bible as 'the great textbook of psychology' (G. S. Hall, 1894, p. 710) and wrote of psychology as offering a 'microscope of the soul' through which one could view the brain, 'the mouthpiece of God' (G. S. Hall, 1901, p. 731). Hall's religiosity was by no means unique. Widely seen by his contemporaries as a figurehead, Hall was elected to serve as the American Psychological Association's inaugural president in 1892.

In short, one reason why university psychology proliferated so successfully in the United States was precisely because of its compatibility with American academia's theological culture. Mental philosophy, mental science and natural theology served as forerunners to university psychology. These fields provided ready-made textbooks and curricula for the new discipline (subject to some relatively minor – albeit profound – adjustments, such as the replacement of deities with evolution). Their influence also encouraged the New Psychology to look beyond psychophysics, and to see as within its remit such morally intoned topics as childhood development, social influence and mental well-being. And religious philosophy provided an infrastructural home for the new psychologists, with most of the de facto psychology departments starting out life as subgroups of departments of philosophers.

The arrival of this 'new' psychology in the world's major English-speaking (and, in time, culturally normative) university system was not so much the creation of a new science. Rather, it was the incorporation of new methods, new ideas and, yes, new forms of laboratory experimentation, into something that was already quite old – a long-established and somewhat scientific academic tradition of using formal logic and empirical scholarship to assess the human mind, with the virtuous hope of one day, perhaps, being able to explain its mysteries.

HISTORY IN STORIES: *THE MASTER* (2004)

The Master (Tóibín, 2004) is an acclaimed novel by the Irish writer Colm Tóibín, which tells the story of Henry James, the American novelist and brother of psychologist William. While the novel traces events from Henry's point of view, including his transatlantic migration to a new life in England, his torturous self-doubts and crises of identity are very much bound up in his family relationships. William, although only infrequently physically present, plays an important role in refining Henry's attitudes and beliefs.

Tóibín depicts William James as committed to the use of logic for exploring, and navigating, life. At one point he misses a military ceremony because he has an important laboratory experiment to perform instead. William criticizes the floweriness of Henry's writing. He wants his brother to write factual novels that describe the details of important historical events. He dislikes the idea that novelists would write something that might not produce an empirically verifiable version of the world.

William appears as the family's famous offspring, his celebrity status as an American intellectual contrasting with Henry's more secluded existence in Britain. This overbearing nature is a source of some considerable sibling tension, especially in the mind of the more artistic Henry. In one scene depicting the frostiness in the fraternal relationship, Henry rejects his brother's encouragement to write historically accurate novels. Instead, he declares the very concept to be artificial and valueless.

Henry's insight relates to the limits of historiography. According to him, the notion of historical accuracy must always be weighed against the fact that histories are written from the perspectives of the powerful (Lackey, 2018). In Henry's view, history is always biased. As such, astute fiction might in fact be a much better way to provide an informative representation of the past.

Literary critics have long been intrigued by the contrast between the two James brothers. Henry James is the novelist, but is famous for his understanding of human nature. William James is the psychologist, but is famous for his way with words. As noted by the English writer J. B. Priestley (1960), in literary circles it was often said that 'the psychology of William James is all fiction; the fiction of Henry James is all psychology'.

In *The Principles of Psychology*, William James famously defined psychology as the 'science of mental life' (James, 1890). Tóibín's novel portrays the way mental life can take shape when a person feels separate from their emotions, their families or both. By fictionalizing real-life people in this form, *The Master* itself offers an insightful example of Henry's approach to charting the dimensions of the mind.

BEYOND THE MYTHOLOGY

When E. G. Boring wrote his legendary textbook, psychology at Harvard was still part of that university's philosophy department. It was Boring's firm wish to establish departmental independence. No doubt influenced by this separatist ambition, his version of history showcased both psychology's physiological past and the promise of its experimental future; the Great Men were depicted as especially great, their links to Harvard humbly unemphasized but nonetheless unmistakably apparent. This was scholarship with a political purpose, history as academic propaganda. In the end, it worked. Boring's dream was fulfilled in 1934, when the Harvard authorities granted its psychologists their own academic department. University psychology would no longer be seen as 'just' a branch of philosophy.

Ultimately, the opening of psychology departments in Leipzig, Harvard or anywhere else in the late nineteenth or early twentieth centuries was not the 'founding' or 'establishment' of psychology as a new intellectual or human endeavour. Rather, it was the recognition by education bureaucrats that psychology now had critical mass, sufficient credibility to be included as a teachable subject in an increasingly granular curriculum. Psychology was not 'established' by any university (or by any individual); it was absorbed into university curricula in recognition of its attractiveness as an already vibrant field of study.

The emergence of these university departments, and the Great Men who established them, were perhaps important to the development of *universities* and, by extension, of professional guilds. To this extent, they represent milestones in the history of academia, rather than a single moment of a subject's creation.

The idea that psychology was founded in a particular place, at a particular time, or by a particular person relies on an arbitrary framing of history, and its selective retelling. This is why such 'creation myths' amount to propaganda.

Myths as propaganda

In many histories – including Boring's – priority is afforded to Wundt's work on psychophysics, with rather less coverage given to other types of research with which Wundt was associated. Much of Wundt's scholarship was obscurely philosophical. He favoured a type of sociologically based psychology known as *Völkerpsychologie*, which sought to explain contemporary human behaviour by examining mental differences between people of different cultures and historical periods. This work was speculative and far from scientific. In fact it embraced several concepts that were simply pseudoscientific, such as the idea that the evolutionary development of the entire human species was replayed in summary form within the lifespan of each human individual. This theory, known as *recapitulation*, implied that primitive races were essentially infantile or childlike, and that people in modern societies were more 'mature'. Subsequent empirical research has shown such comparisons to be entirely spurious, and to stem more from colonial xenophobia than from insight.

However, despite the fact that *Völkerpsychologie* consumed Wundt's attention for nearly two decades, many histories of psychology downplay its significance, preferring instead to depict Wundt as a paragon of experimental rigour. They also seem to downplay the extent to which Wundt was criticized by his contemporaries, and even how his ideas were largely abandoned by his own students once they had the opportunity to establish their own laboratories. In presenting Wundt as a founder to whom all subsequent psychologists are indebted, such histories serve to exaggerate his scientific legacy.

To the extent that such exaggeration helps to bolster psychology's reputation as a rigorous, productive, insightful and successful science, then we can attribute this distortion to cultural bias. These histories described Wundt in a particular way because the historians who wrote them had particular aims in mind. As G. Richards (2010) pointed out above, the scholars who valorized Wundt for being the inventor of psychology did not do so from a devotion to historical accuracy; they did so because they '*wanted* a founding father' for their field.

The psychology of creation myths

Creation myths are important ways in which human beings rationalize their own place in the world, elevating themselves above the amoral randomness of happenstance. They also help to retrospectively justify one's current privilege, by explaining away the accumulation of power with an internally logical and coherent 'cause'. Stories of the creation of one's own tribe often include elements of in-group exceptionalism – an instinctive belief that our own kind are notably talented and especially deserving of prestige. In this way, creation myths constitute a self-regarding form of Great Man historiography.

Creation myths make particularly effective propaganda, and so are actively preserved and promoted by those parties whose power depends on them. Psychologists whose self-identity involves the conducting of research in laboratories will naturally promote the establishment of laboratories as uniquely pivotal events. Those who trace their thinking directly back to psychophysics will no doubt have a special place in their hearts for the founding psychophysicists. Brain scientists will recall the early brain researchers, social scientists the early sociologists. Quite where you think psychology comes from will depend not on psychology, but on you.

Creation myths are, after all, myths – stories remembered because of the wonder and fulfilment they generate, regardless of the extent to which they are factually grounded. They capitalize on the psychological power of nostalgia, the capacity to imagine the past with a positive spin, to deploy rose-tinted perspectives when looking rearward.

Psychological research has suggested that most human beings incline towards optimism. In fact, holding a coldly logical assessment of your own trivial unimportance could be a sign that you are depressed (Feltham, 2016). It is more natural to believe in progress than in chaos, to construe events as fulfilling a relevant destiny, and to identify the heroes who achieve success and produce legacies, lauding them from the vantage of the present as though rooting for an underdog, even though we know how the story ends.

Nostalgia and optimism help to buffer us against the profound vastness of existence and its inherent intimidations. We need not worry about demise if we imagine ourselves to be robust. We can face the future with confidence if we systematically overestimate our chances of success. In the absence of any direct achievement of our own, we can take pride in the achievements of other people who we perceive as belonging to our in-group.

The weakness inherent in such self-serving rationalizations may constitute error, but this type of error is highly adaptable and more common than it is not. It thrives because of its utility – it promotes happiness, provides motivation and assists humans to cope with whatever comes their way.

The problem, of course, is that a diet of self-delusion might not always prove healthy. Nostalgia feels like bad historiography. Reminiscing about the good old days (while ignoring the bad old ones) is both Whiggish and presentist. Its selectivity guarantees inaccuracy. And its seductive power to comfort is easily abused: political history shows us that human audiences seem all too easily rousable by glib promises that they can take back control or make themselves great again.

Earlier we noted several biases of human thought that interfere with the evaluation of evidence: human nature makes people more likely to be swayed by the first information they encounter, by information that is specific rather than vague, and by information that reminds them of something they can easily remember. These tendencies are as relevant to history as they are to scientific reasoning. And they are as relevant to the history of psychology as they are to history in general.

WHERE TO FROM HERE?

More than most, psychologists should appreciate that nobody is immune to the temptations of creation myths. Glorifying the founders of one's own endeavours is a way of casting one's own endeavours – and therefore oneself – in a positive light. Any group that customarily mythologizes its own creation story should reflect on this conflict of interest. In this regard, psychology is no different to any other intellectual pursuit. Presumably, every subject will have had its early adopters. Not all of them will have been heroes. Psychology is not uniquely deserving of, nor does it require, a compelling backstory.

The key creation myth of psychology is not so much the claim that it was founded by any particular person. It is the very idea that there ever was, in fact, a single moment of 'creation'. Psychology is the formal study of human thoughts, feelings and behaviour, topics that extend far beyond the psychophysics laboratory. Its history overlaps with that of science, and with all enquiries and theories regarding the nature of mental functioning.

The idea of what constitutes a 'normal' human mind long predates this science, but crucially guides its trajectory. Such definitions of 'normal' come to light wherever *abnormality* is encountered. It is to this aspect of psychology that we turn in our next chapter.

DISCUSSION QUESTIONS

1. In what ways were historical societies *more* 'scientific' than is commonly acknowledged today, and in what ways is modern society *less* 'scientific' than we sometimes think it is?
2. Is it possible for a society to be *technologically* advanced without also being *scientifically* advanced? What is the difference (if any)?

3. What are the reasons for the dominance of European and American approaches to scientific psychology in the modern world? Is this pattern of dominance different for psychology than it is for other subject areas?

4. What is the psychological function of nostalgia? Is it possible to avoid nostalgia when thinking about history?

RECOMMENDED READING

- **Diamond, J. (1997).** *Guns, Germs and Steel: A Short History of Everybody for the Last 13,000 Years.* **New York: Vintage.** In this book, the author examines the ways in which environmental and geographic factors caused science and technology to emerge at different rates in different regions of the world.

- **Fuller, R. C. (2006). American psychology and the religious imagination.** *Journal of the History of the Behavioral Sciences*, **42, 221–35.** In this article, the author shows how early American university psychology appealed to a wider social interest in spirituality and religion.

- **Watrin, J. P. (2017). The 'new history of psychology' and the uses and abuses of dichotomies.** *Theory & Psychology*, **27, 69–86.** In this paper, the author suggests that revisionist histories of psychology can unfairly dismiss the work of early historians.

Part II

FORMATION: FROM PHILOSOPHY TO PSYCHOLOGICAL SCIENCE

DEMONS, ASYLUMS AND THE CONCEPT OF *MADNESS*

4

In this chapter, we will …

- consider how mental illness has been traditionally depicted as an infection of the human body by malevolent spirits
- trace the emergence of institutions for the 'insane', and the ways in which such institutions reveal social and cultural attitudes to insanity
- consider how shifting beliefs about mental illness led to the emergence of different forms of psychiatric treatment
- examine how insanity has been construed as both a cause and a consequence of personal immorality
- evaluate the social, cultural and philosophical challenges of defining normality and abnormality in relation to human behaviour

---

At the outset

From the earliest times, it appears that all societies have recognized that people's thoughts, feelings and behaviours occasionally deviate from normal. In the ancient world, this was often believed to be the result of demonic possession. Religious practice has often included methods for addressing these problems, either surgically or through rituals such as exorcism. The fact that spiritual beliefs are so widely held suggests that human civilization has long incorporated assumptions about the nature of psychology, by specifying what constitutes abnormal, and thus normal, states of mind.

For centuries, people with varying degrees of mental illness lived unfettered in the general community. It was only after the Middle Ages that society sought to place the mentally ill in institutions. This probably reflected the emerging importance of cognitive and behavioural acuity in daily life, but in turn reflected an increasing stratification of society on economic and technological grounds. As society became more systematized, people who struggled to 'fit in' would find themselves increasingly disadvantaged and marginalized.

The task of treating mental illness has not always been prioritized. For a long time, asylums operated effectively as prisons, an approach that has had a lasting impact on public attitudes to insanity. Early treatments were often brutal, reflecting a pessimistic and dehumanizing view of mental illness. As understanding of psychology became more nuanced, many new treatments and interventions were developed. However, professional and cultural beliefs about whether people can recover from mental illness have fluctuated, varying between periods of optimism and pessimism.

In the nineteenth and twentieth centuries, insanity was frequently stigmatized. It was depicted as a sign of moral turpitude and a cause of criminality and, as a consequence, of the gradual decline of civilization. Even today, attitudes to 'insanity' often reflect the norms of society, rather than patterns of individual behaviour that can reasonably be circumscribed as clearly problematic. The task of defining mental illness, even for strictly medical purposes, remains extremely arbitrary. The concept of insanity draws attention to the way psychological concepts are often intertwined with social assumptions that are themselves subject to change. How we talk about madness is merely a reflection of what we believe to be normal at a given time.

Key concept: Insanity

The term *insanity* is no longer common in mainstream psychology, as it is considered laden with centuries of stigma. However, the word is widely used in literature, in everyday culture and in the legal system, to denote a state of being so seriously mentally ill as to create diminished personal responsibility, to undermine a person's capacity, and/or to interfere with their perceptions, emotions and behaviours.

In this chapter, we discuss 'insanity' as a cultural concept. As such, we will use the term in this context, as well as alluding to common synonyms like *madness* and – in some specific references – *lunacy*. But as we will also describe, these words are often of more historical than contemporary relevance. In modern psychology, definitions of categories of mental ill health are formulated tentatively, and are usually derived from relatively arbitrary assumptions about what healthy states of being should comprise.

For this reason, for clinical purposes, modern psychologists will likely discuss these issues by referring to 'abnormal behaviour' or 'psychological dysfunction'. Such phrases, while not immune to stigma, are intended to avoid ascribing labels to *people*, and instead to describe a person's *actions* or *feelings* at a particular point in time.

Some studies suggest that the use of the word *insanity* in court trials affects how juries reach their verdicts in criminal cases (LaFortune, 2018). Through common use, the term has acquired connotations of unpredictability and violence. As we will see, throughout history, the concept of *insanity* has almost exclusively been viewed as deserving a special kind of fear. Given that our understanding of *abnormal* will be contingent on our perception of what is *normal*, social definitions of *insanity* are especially important to explore. They reveal to us what society considers *normal psychology* to be.

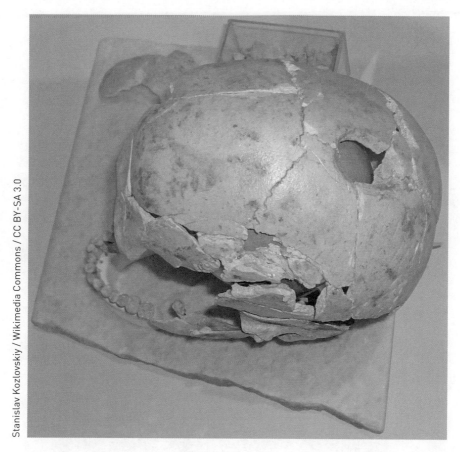

Stanislav Kozlovskiy / Wikimedia Commons / CC BY-SA 3.0

Image 4.1   Prehistoric trepanation
Of the tens of thousands of Stone Age skulls ever handled by archaeologists, around one in ten have had fragments of bone removed to create a small hole that would have exposed the brain. The procedure, known as trepanation, is regarded as the oldest form of surgery in human history. This trepanated prehistoric skull is on display at the National Museum of History in Baku, Azerbaijan.

THE SKULL DOCTORS

Of the tens of thousands of Stone Age skulls ever handled by archaeologists, a staggering one in ten are distinguished by a common but striking feature. All have had small holes drilled, cut or scraped into them by prehistoric surgeons. Such marks appear on Neolithic crania gathered all over the world, from across Asia, Europe, Africa, Australasia and the Americas (Faria, 2013). In some archaeological sites, more than a third of skulls exhibit such features (Restak, 2000). Many of them have multiple perforations.

Forensic examination suggests that these marks were created by a variety of different tools: sometimes knives, sometimes drills, sometimes hammers. But ultimately the technique employed

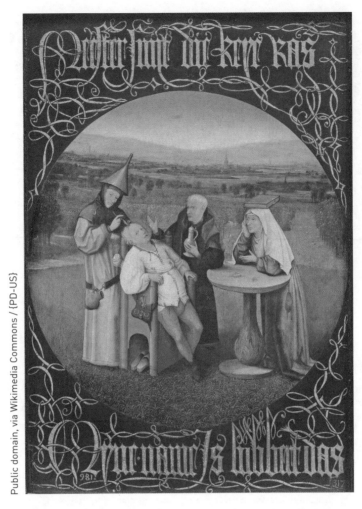

Public domain, via Wikimedia Commons / {PD-US}

Image 4.2 *The Extraction of the Stone of Madness* by Hieronymus Bosch (*c.* 1505).

is consistent – fragments of skull are removed to create a small hole exposing the meningeal membrane that surrounds the human brain. Patterns of tissue healing visible on these skulls suggest that, remarkably, patients frequently survived their primitive surgeries. Other patterns, where cuts are partial, imply that patients would sometimes interrupt their operation and flee before it could be finished.

These surgeries were conducted mostly on men, but also on women, and sometimes on young children. Great skill was required, as it was important to remove skull fragments without compromising the integrity of brain tissue. Separate archaeological evidence suggests that the surgeons invested considerable effort to perfect their technique, practising their craft on the skulls of boars (J. Lambert, 1948) and cows (Ramirez Rozzi & Froment, 2018).

This originally prehistoric procedure continued long beyond the emergence of civilization. Hippocrates, Galen and the Roman physician Aulus Cornelius Celsus (25 BCE–50 CE) all provided teachings about how such surgery should be conducted. Roman surgeons developed the *terebra serrata*, a specialized tool comprising a conical piece of metal with a serrated tip, so that the procedure could be performed with greater accuracy.

A famous sixteenth-century painting by the Dutch artist Hieronymus Bosch depicts the operation being conducted in medieval Europe. An elderly patient sits, tied to a chair, while a surgeon leans over him, inserting a cutting tool into the top of his head. Some blood trickles from the incision, out of which the surgeon appears to have extracted a small flower bulb. Some art historians regard this as a play on the Dutch word for 'tulip', which at the time was synonymous with stupidity or folly. The procedure is watched by an assistant and a kneeling woman who is balancing a book on her head. This painting is sometimes referred to, rather vaguely, as *Cutting the Stone*. Another of its titles – *The Extraction of the Stone of Madness* – is perhaps more revealing.

This operation was conducted around the world for millennia, right up to the Renaissance. It was known as *trepanation*, and it is generally regarded as the oldest form of surgery in human history. For centuries, trepanation was used to treat mental illness. Its use reflected a long-standing and widespread human theory of madness, and, by implication, tells us much about how the ordinary workings of minds were commonly understood. Trepanation was premised on the notion that insanity was something that resides literally *inside the head*, a tormenting demon that could be released, physically, into the air.

That demon within

The use of trepanation to treat mental illness makes it an example of what we today call *psychosurgery*. While it is impossible to be completely sure about the beliefs of prehistoric shamans (Prioreschi, 1991), it is certainly clear that the release of demons from the skulls of people who exhibited abnormal behaviour went on to be practised for many centuries. It was frequently conducted when patients exhibited signs of epilepsy, convulsions or even headaches (Osler, 1921).

In later centuries, trepanation became somewhat secularized, as brain surgeons adapted the procedure in various ways; to relieve cranial tension perhaps, or to remove parts of the brain suspected of creating unwanted symptoms (Faria, 2013). However, the premise underlying trepanation – that mental illness is (sometimes) caused by the intrusion into a person of some kind of malevolent spiritual being or force – has been part of culture around the world for a very long time, and not merely in traditional societies. Even the major modern mainstream religions of the industrialized world continue to include the possibility of demonic possession within their twenty-first-century worldviews.

In the ancient world, medical physicians often resorted to treatments aimed at extracting dangerous spirits from their patients' bodies. The ancient Egyptians developed several methods based on religious ritual, such as the use of incantations and prayer. While much of their mental health beliefs were based on demonology (Kousoulis, 2011), they did not necessarily see demons as evil spirits, but rather as supernatural intermediary beings that connected humans to gods (Lucarelli, 2011). Further, over time, their views about the anatomical specifics of possession led to a useful curiosity about brain function that enabled them to develop sophisticated theories regarding complex neurological conditions, such as aphasia (Sondhaus & Finger, 1988).

The use of incantations, such as prayers or magical formulas, to cast out evil spirits became a common feature of religious practice throughout the ancient world. The power to drive out demons was believed to exist in the words themselves, and so care was taken to develop exact scripts that could be used in the necessary rituals (Unger, 1994). As well as Egyptian papyri, archaeologists have uncovered several lengthy prescribed texts used for this purpose by the ancient Babylonians and Assyrians.

Such widespread ideas and practices were eventually appropriated into Jewish and Christian religions. Abrahamic scriptures are replete with teachings about characters who were addled with madness by either God or Satan. Many of these stories resembled the old Greek legends, as recorded by Homer in the *Iliad* and the *Odyssey*, in which the gods regularly interfered with human affairs by inflicting madness on people (Maieron, 2017). Such was the Greek fascination with psychological fallibility that later figures such as Sigmund Freud would often turn to classical Greek myths for inspiration when explaining their theories of human thoughts and impulses (we will return to this topic in Chapter 7).

The Greek folkloric belief in intoxication by irrationality served, perhaps paradoxically, as a cultural backdrop to Greek philosophy's definitive mission of promoting, refining and mastering the human faculty of reason (Porter, 1987). At once, these new scholars sought to deny the supernatural tropes of mass culture, while synthesizing the various empirical and anatomical observations of their own (and neighbouring) worldviews. Inspired by Egyptian and Asian ideas, among others, Greek medical views of illness, including mental illness, centred on organs such as the heart and the brain, and the idea that health depended on variations in the levels of fluids such as blood, phlegm and bile.

Roman philosophers too sought to challenge popular beliefs about madness with more secular explanations, offering the view that naturalistic causes, such as physical illness, lay at the root of insanity. The views of such figures as Hippocrates, Galen and, by extension, Avicenna and Rhazes came to be that the basis of mental illness was natural rather than supernatural.

However, for the reasons outlined in previous chapters, the unfolding of the Middle Ages resulted in a re-emergence of many traditional religious perspectives on scientific issues. Despite a lack of evidence – or maybe precisely *because* it was a matter of pure faith – the notion that mental illness could stem from mystical interference was retained throughout Europe (and its colonies) right up to the Renaissance. Christian theology approached mental irregularity as a matter of divine providence, a sign of ongoing 'psychomachy' – the perpetual war between good and evil for dominion over human souls (Zinck, 1995).

Dealing with demons

The process of driving out evil spirits from a person believed to be infested by them is commonly referred to as *exorcism*. Exorcism is usually seen as a religious practice, and so is normally conducted by formally ordained clerics. It typically involves a ritual whereby the cleric recites special prayers and, ostensibly, commands the evil spirit to leave the possessed person's body. Exorcism is practised in many religions, including Hinduism, Islam and Judaism, but is most commonly associated with Christianity, particularly Catholicism.

Indeed, during the early centuries of Christianity, evil spirits (most particularly, the Devil) were considered a likely source of nearly all trouble, including physical and mental disease (Innamorati, Taradel & Foschi, 2018). So prevalent was the view that mental illness resulted from demonic possession that rituals to attempt to cure illness by driving out spirits became extremely common in Europe throughout the Middle Ages. It was only in the seventeenth century, when demand for exorcists threatened to vastly exceed supply, that church authorities saw fit to introduce criteria for clarifying when – and when not – demons were actually to blame.

In Chapter 3, we discussed the gradual emergence of popular interest in formal scientific methods during the centuries that followed the Renaissance. In line with this, belief in demonic possession (and thus demand for exorcisms) saw a general decline in the eighteenth and nineteenth centuries. Physicians began to attribute erratic behaviour to recognized psychopathology, sometimes explicitly classifying psychiatric conditions as cases of 'pseudodemonic' possession (e.g. Lefebvre, 1866). In other words, demonic possession was assumed to be, and thus always to have been, a delusion.

In the early twentieth century, the Catholic Church revised its guidelines in light of 'progress in the knowledge of mental disease' (Philippeau, 1956), to make it more difficult for an exorcism to be formally authorized. They also warned that performing exorcism on someone who was mentally ill could risk damaging that person's health even further (Tonquedec, 1938).

However, the official view of Catholic authorities remained that, while possessions were much rarer than previously believed, they did certainly occur. In the 1970s, the Vatican issued an official statement on the matter, entitled *Christian Faith and Demonology* (Sacred Congregation for the Doctrine of the Faith, 1975). It warned against an excessive 'preoccupation with Satan', but advised that, while the church 'no longer attaches the same importance to exorcisms as in earlier centuries', the practice remains perfectly legitimate. In other words, the statement clarified that the potential of demonic possession remained very much part of church doctrine. It went on to urge the public to be cautious about 'modern methods' of science, which it said were of limited use for dealing with 'the mysterious relationship between body and soul'.

Shortly after this official statement was published, a shocking case emerged in a remote rural village in Germany, where a young mentally ill woman died after undergoing a year-long exorcism (Goodman, 1981). The woman – Anneliese Michel (1952–76) – had been diagnosed and treated for temporal lobe epilepsy and suicidal depression. As psychiatric medications had failed to improve her symptoms, her deeply religious parents concluded that Anneliese must have been possessed by the Devil. They lobbied the local bishop, who eventually authorized an exorcism and deployed two priests to perform the task. During the rituals, Anneliese exhibited increasingly erratic behaviour, including physical convulsions and hallucinations, consistent with her previous diagnoses. Despite her self-injury, refusal to eat and obvious distress, the priests persisted with the exorcism until, after several months, Anneliese finally died. Coroners reported that the young woman was severely physically damaged and had died from emaciation and malnutrition.

The woman's parents and the two priests were each charged with negligent homicide and brought to trial. Their lawyers, whose fees were paid by the Catholic Church, argued that the exorcism was an expression of religious belief and so was legally protected by German law. This argument was rejected by the court, who instead found all four defendants guilty as charged. Anneliese's parents continued to insist that their daughter had been possessed by the Devil. They demanded that their daughter's body be exhumed, apparently in order to show that it had not decomposed (which, in their view, would prove demonic possession). Anneliese's body was indeed exhumed, examined – found to be normal – and reinterred. The whole grizzly affair attracted international media attention and is generally regarded as having horrified German – and global – public opinion.

In some ways, the late twentieth century saw a cultural shift away from this view of mental illness. Demonic possession was no longer accepted by most of the general public as a plausible explanation for erratic behaviour. If anything, it was belief in *the validity of exorcism* that became widely regarded as the true delusion.

Instead, exorcism began to appear frequently in popular culture as a fictional practice, usually one associated with fear and spectacle. Exorcisms have been depicted in a variety of horror movies, such as *Il demonio* (Rondi, 1963), *Şeytan* (Erksan, 1974), *L'ossessa* (Gariazzo, 1974), *Manichitrathazhu* (Fazil, 1993), *The Possession* (Bornedal, 2012), *Keeper of Darkness* (Cheung, 2015), *The Nun* (Hardy, 2018) and, most famously, *The Exorcist* (Friedkin, 1973), the first horror movie to be nominated for Best Picture at the Oscars. In becoming a staple of the horror genre, exorcism – and with it the paradigm of viewing mental illness in terms of spirits and demons – was placed, in the popular imagination, into the same category as zombies, werewolves, vampires and haunted houses. In other words, it was regarded as risqué fiction, rather than realizable fact.

Historians of psychology often describe exorcism as a primitive attempt at psychotherapy, where misunderstood causes of mental illness are addressed using non-physical methods (as opposed to, say, trepanation). This interpretation assumes psychotherapy to be morally ambivalent, by denying the existence of spirits, demons or any free-standing 'evil'. The way some psychologists seek to provide retrospectively rational accounts for what would otherwise be viewed as miraculous events is one of the reasons some theologians find psychotherapy, and psychology more broadly, to be objectionable. As such, to many theologians, for whom the existence of free-standing evil is very much a core belief, exorcism and psychotherapy should be seen as fundamentally different activities (e.g. Twelftree, 2010).

Despite advances in scientific understanding of psychological health, the world's major religious movements continue to teach that erratic behaviour, delusions, hallucinations and other symptoms of mental illness may sometimes be caused by demonic possession. Following the death of Anneliese Michel, various church leaders set about slowly rehabilitating the reputation of exorcism. In 2014, the Catholic pope finally gave official church recognition to the International Association of Exorcists, an organization that had declared *Harry Potter* novels to have dangerous demonic content, Pokémon cards to be satanic objects, and the prophet Muhammad to have been satanically possessed (Amorth, 1996; Innamorati et al., 2018). Members of the public who believe that organic illness might be a more logical explanation for abnormal mental states are warned that denying the existence of the Devil is itself an early sign of satanic influence (Wojtila, 1986).

In the twenty-first century, global demand for exorcisms has enjoyed something of a resurgence (Sersch, 2019). Belief in the phenomenon of spiritual possession remains common throughout the world, albeit tending to vary by religious community. Experiences associated with such beliefs often make it difficult for psychologists to devise culturally appropriate treatment options for people exhibiting problematic erratic behaviours (Benbenishty & Biswas, 2015). For example, the current clinical guideline for diagnosing dissociative identity disorder includes reference to people who believe themselves to be possessed (American Psychiatric Association, 2013), although this has been criticized as unworkable because of the prevalence of diverse cultural beliefs on the matter (Delmonte et al., 2016).

Ultimately, beyond the mainstream scientific approach to psychopathology, there remains a widespread belief that not all mental disease is organic or, indeed, psychosocial. The idea that some mental illness is a sign of the Devil has not quite disappeared.

LOGOPHILIA: 'LYCANTHROPY'

Lycanthropy is, literally, the ability of a human to transform into a wolf. The idea of such wolf-people (historically known as 'werewolves' or 'lycanthropes') was widespread in European folklore and mythology, but had its counterpart in other world cultures. In African folklore, there were werelions, while in Persia, India and China, folklore told of humans that could turn into tigers. In Mesoamerican culture, including among the Aztecs, such afflicted people would transform into jaguars, becoming fierce warriors as a result (Saunders, 1994).

While belief in werewolves is uncommon in modern times, the source of this strand of human mythology has long interested scholars and psychologists. A number of theories have proposed how the werewolf myth might have arisen due to the misdiagnosis of various mental illnesses. Most typically, it is thought that people who suffered from conditions such as schizophrenia, mania or acute agitation might have been mistaken for lycanthropes by medieval physicians (Drake, 1992). Other theorists have suggested that such symptoms might have been caused by the deliberate or unwitting ingestion of hallucinogenic drugs (Metzger, 2013). Still others have speculated that the myth is linked to rabies, a viral disease that affects the brain and which can be transmitted from animals to humans through biting (Woodward, 1979). This would explain not only the erratic behaviour of people believed to be so afflicted, but also offers a reason why society would come to believe that being bitten by a werewolf was itself a cause of lycanthropy.

THE GREAT EXCLUSION

When entire societies believe that mental abnormality is (sometimes) the result of divine providence, then psychopathology can be considered part and parcel of daily life. In other words, 'abnormality' can be considered so common as to be seen, essentially, as 'normal'. While human cultures have long recognized the difference between mental wellness and disorder, for long periods both sets of human experiences co-existed within mainstream society.

In the ancient world, it was typical for variation in mental or emotional states to be accepted as central to ordinary human nature. One of the founders of the traditional Indian medical approach of Ayurveda, the physician Suśruta, who lived around the seventh and sixth centuries BCE, wrote of mental illness as part of the regular human emotional range. In the fifth century BCE, Patañjali, the author of the *Yoga Sutras*, one of the first definitive guides to the practice of yoga, depicted mental health as part of the ongoing balancing and rebalancing of various ever-present elements of experience, spanning the mental, the physical and the social (Abhyankar, 2015). The regularity of mental illness was also part of the traditional medical system of Siddha, which originated in southern India (Nizamie & Goyal, 2010).

As mentioned earlier, the ancient Greeks viewed mental illness through the lens of reason. Plato depicted the mind as comprising rational and irrational parts, and considered madness to be a result of the separation of the two. The task of therapy, then, was to somehow 'tame' irrationality (Porter, 1987). The Greeks' attachment to logic encouraged them to investigate plausible mechanisms underlying mental illness, including pharmacological side effects of drugs and medications.

Diagnostic approaches included the concept of dream analysis, as promoted in the second century CE by Artemidorus (Harris-McCoy, 2012). Treatment options included early attempts by the Turkish-born physician Asclepiades (129–40 BCE), who used warm baths for occupational therapy and snakes for shock therapy (Rawson, 1982). Echoing earlier Ayurvedic and Egyptian approaches, Greek physicians such as Hippocrates, and Romans such as Celsus, promoted the early use of pharmacology. Others, such as the Stoic scholar Seneca (4 BCE–65 CE), recommended philosophy itself as 'the sovereign remedy for sadness' (McNeil, 1951, p. 64). This perhaps exemplified one of the first attempts at 'talk therapy', where the therapist would offer their insights and perspectives in the hope of alleviating their patient's mental distress.

The first formal use of psychotherapy for mental illness is often credited to Rhazes, the Persian physician we discussed in Chapter 2. In the ninth century CE, when working with patients who had obsessional symptoms, Rhazes developed methods that were very similar to modern cognitive behavioural therapy techniques (Haque, 2004). He sought to involve patients as active participants in their own treatments, and emphasized the importance of cultivating a positive outlook in both therapist and client regarding likelihood of recovery (Yilanli, 2018). Such insights concerning the value of 'buy-in' to the therapeutic process were centuries ahead of their time.

A divergence from normal

The ancient Greeks constructed special buildings with hydrotherapy baths, and Arab physicians, including Rhazes, opened wards for psychiatric patients in their hospitals. However, for centuries, institutional care for the mentally ill was very rare. Instead, most people who exhibited erratic behaviours, ideas or thought patterns simply lived alongside everybody else, in the regular community.

Indeed, in the Middle Ages, the unusual speech or outright incomprehensibility of many mentally ill people was often regarded as a likely sign of holiness (Kemp, 2019). The tradition of court jesters, with their accepted form of risqué social subversion, reflected a common view that there was value to be found in simple-mindedness, and that what appears at first to be folly might actually reveal a connection to some higher spiritual power (Porter, 1987).

Of course, another reason why there was little institutional care for the mentally ill is that, by and large, for most of history, there were very few forms of *any* state-sponsored care for vulnerable groups. The principle that the state should fulfil a practical welfare function for its citizens is a very modern one.

A second factor was the shifting of social norms of literacy and education. Prior to modern forms of economy, bureaucracy, technology, law and even democracy, few citizens were required to exhibit wide-ranging cognitive competence in their daily lives. The emergence of new systems created everyday demands that highlighted the gap between those who had the acuity to participate and those who struggled. As society became increasingly reliant on order, efficiency and documentation, those who fell short of these new standards stood out as being 'unsuitable' for regular ways of living.

One of the most profound consequences of this gradual divergence – between those who could cope with the demands of societal change and those who began to fall away – was the development of a norm of exclusion. The mainstream majority began to look upon their mentally ill fellow citizens as people who did not really belong. People who spoke or behaved in 'peculiar' ways were no longer regarded as local eccentrics or potential prophets. Instead they were treated with suspicion by a fearful community that increasingly sought to protect themselves through segregation.

Bethlem, the 'palace for lunatics'

Perhaps the first true 'asylum' for the mentally ill was founded in London during the thirteenth century. Originally a priory of the New Order of Our Lady of Bethlehem, the hospital was formally known as 'St Mary of Bethlehem outside Bishopsgate' and, later, Bethlem. While its very early history is uncertain, it seems clear that Bethlem began to specialize in care of the mentally ill sometime around the end of the fourteenth century. As it still operates as such today (as Bethlem Royal Hospital), it can be stated with certainty that Bethlem is the oldest continually operating psychiatric hospital in the world (Andrews et al., 1997).

From its earliest years, Bethlem became synonymous with the derangement of its residents. A colloquial nickname for the hospital – *Bedlam* – entered the English language as a term to describe uproar and chaos. The institution became famous for the bizarre behaviour of the people who, largely against their will, were sent to live there.

By the seventeenth century, the hospital authorities began opening their doors to visitors, at first as an instructive experience for the public. However, few of those who took up the opportunity did so as a means of moral improvement. Bethlem became famous for the spectacle it offered to tourists, part of the London entertainment circuit along with the city's theatres, shops and restaurants. Its salubrious architecture piqued many a traveller's imagination: for a time the building was referred to by sightseers as 'the palace for lunatics' (Jay, 2016). The views of one satisfied visitor were quoted in the *London Chronicle* in 1761:

> 'I assure you I was highly entertained; I met with some very amusing objects; and I heard a great many excellent stories; and was prodigiously delighted with the humour of the mad folks'.

> (as quoted in Andrews et al., 1997, p. 187)

Many visitors derived delight from the chance to see some of Bethlem's celebrity inmates, high-profile residents who served as its star attractions. At various stages, these included such figures as the playwright Nathaniel Lee (who had written the English theatre hit *The Rival Queens*), the

Public domain, via Wikimedia Commons / {PD-US}

Image 4.3 *Casa de locos*
Casa de locos (The Madhouse) by the Spanish romantic painter Francisco Goya (c. 1819) depicts the bleak conditions typical of nineteenth-century asylums. Goya himself had experienced depression, and his work captures the suffering and torment of the mentally ill people who lived in such institutions.

architect Augustus Pugin (who designed the Houses of Parliament at Westminster) and Oliver Cromwell's porter, Daniel (who, as well as being a charismatic preacher, stood more than seven feet tall). Eventually, in 1770, with demand for access exceeding supply, the hospital managers instituted a ticketing system.

From today's perspective, the idea of allowing members of the public to tour a psychiatric hospital seems morally questionable. Even at the time, critics complained that the practice reduced Bethlem to a kind of human zoo (Scull, 1983). Contemporary accounts recorded that some prurient visitors were interested only in viewing those patients who were partially or fully naked, and that many visitors plied the patients with alcohol or otherwise taunted them. Despite these disturbing complaints, the hospital's governors persisted in defending the visits as a service to the public. Of course, they were also a source of much-needed revenue for the asylum's balance sheet.

However, it is true that visitor access helped to ensure that the hospital's practices received a degree of public scrutiny. When ticketing was introduced, causing visitor numbers to decline, patients suddenly found themselves isolated from the outside world. Behind closed doors, they were soon subjected to much greater levels of *staff* cruelty, a traumatic reality that arose not just in eighteenth-century Bethlem, but in virtually all systems of confinement in which mentally ill people have been housed.

The proliferation of asylums

Prior to the nineteenth century, France had historically housed its mentally ill in large *hôpitaux généraux* (general hospitals), in which a variety of marginalized groups, including criminals and paupers, were forcibly confined. These hospitals offered little treatment and operated, essentially, as internment institutions. Throughout central Europe, a number of *Tollhäuser* or *dolhuizen* (fools' houses) had been established since the Middle Ages. But again, most mentally ill people either lived in the general community or else found themselves in almshouses, jails or other non-specialist places (Shorter, 1997).

In the United States, a specialized hospital for 'persons of insane and disordered minds' had opened in Williamsburg, Virginia, in 1773, some three years prior to the American Declaration of Independence (G. L. Jones, 1954). The United States had just two de facto medical hospitals before 1800, one of which – the New York Hospital – opened a separate building in 1808, which it designated as a 'lunatic asylum' (Russell, 1941). Aside from these few locales, the only institutions where mentally ill people were admitted by policy were some almshouses (Grob, 1994) and the occasional bespoke facility, such as that in Watertown, Massachusetts, where in 1702 the courts had ordered that a 'little house' be built for confining a particular 'distracted child' (Jimenez, 1987).

While Asian hospitals existed since antiquarian times, and while Islamic medicine and systems such as Ayurveda tended to view physical and mental ill health as equivalent, the first specialized hospital for psychiatric patients in Asia was not established until 1787, in Kolkata (then Calcutta), India. A second asylum opened in Kolkata in 1788, and over the following twenty years, a plethora of such institutions were founded across the Indian subcontinent. At this time Britain directly controlled much of India, via the British East India Company, and many of these asylums were colonial services used to care for officers, company employees and other Europeans (Jain, 2003). Nonetheless, conditions were poor and treatment, where it existed, was rudimentary.

In countries such as China, mental illness was not catered for by hospitals until the late nineteenth century, when a 'refuge for the insane' was opened in 1898 (Blum & Fee, 2008). Before this, mentally ill people lived within the community, where typically they were treated as pariahs and hidden by their families (Hillier & Jewell, 1983).

In 1817, Ireland, then part of the United Kingdom, became the first country to pass a law mandating local authorities to establish a system of publicly funded asylums for the mentally ill. Before this time the country had just one public asylum, housing no more than a few dozen residents. Within thirty years of the new legislation, Ireland had established ten purpose-built 'lunatic asylums' for its population of eight million (Reuber, 1998). France and Switzerland passed similar legislation in 1838, England did so in 1845, Norway in 1848, and Scotland in 1857. Across Europe, the resulting state-sponsored mental hospitals housed hundreds of thousands of their countries' most impoverished citizens, who otherwise would have been left to languish in jails, workhouses or poorhouses. The upper classes, meanwhile, continued to avail of the extensive network of privately funded institutional facilities, which expanded at a similar pace throughout the nineteenth century.

Overall, the nineteenth century saw a dramatic proliferation of institutions for locking away people whose behaviour placed them outside the mainstream of what was considered 'normal'. In 1800 in the United Kingdom, some 5,000 people were confined in mental hospitals, two-thirds of them in private asylums (Shorter, 1997). By the century's end, the overall population of British asylums exceeded 100,000 (Andrews, 2004). Literally thousands of new public and private hospitals and asylums were established around the world, an exponential expansion that continued right into the twentieth century. By 1954, no fewer than half of the hospital beds in Britain's National Health Service were occupied by patients with mental illness or impairment (Houston, 2020).

Viewing the historical asylum

By the time he wrote *Madness and Civilization* in the 1960s, the French philosopher Michel Foucault (1926–84) had concluded that the mass internment of the insane amounted to a significant global and historical enterprise, which he called 'le grand renfermement' – or, in English, 'the great confinement' (Foucault, 1961).

According to Foucault, the impetus to incarcerate so many citizens, especially in Europe, was strongly influenced by sociopolitical power dynamics: those people who most offended the sensibilities of the bourgeois elite were simply sent away, permanently to be sequestered from mainstream society. That so many asylums were occupied by paupers, petty criminals and other disadvantaged individuals convinced Foucault that the true underlying motivation was economic. These so-called 'mad' people were considered so because they did not *work* and so were economically unproductive. In a world dependent on, if not addicted to, commerce and capitalism, the inability (or unwillingness) to be productive had become regarded by society as the very essence of madness itself (Porter, 1990).

Foucault's depiction of this 'great confinement' was a reaction to previous histories of psychiatry, which had been written from archetypally Whiggish perspectives (Houston, 2014). Often influenced by evangelism, reformism and political leftism, these historical accounts of asylums had been framed in terms of therapeutic salvation and state beneficence. Problems were dismissed as policy mishaps, consequences of an inherently good idea going wrong. Foucault's approach was to dispense with the improvement narrative. According to him, asylums were guilty of forging an unforgiveable and irretrievable apartheid, and the mentally ill were treated much better in medieval times than in the modern age (Houston, 2020).

After Foucault, academic histories of institutional mental healthcare have given greater consideration to social and cultural dynamics. British sociologist Andrew Scull linked the expansion of asylums not only to the economic exclusion of non-working people, but also to the group interests of psychiatrists, a powerful new branch of physicians keen to expand their influence and employment opportunities within the medical profession (Scull, 1979). Other historians have emphasized the importance of legal developments in different countries, such as the various 'poor laws' introduced to deal with citizens who found themselves at the economic margins of society (Murphy, 2003). And some historians have retained the original view of asylums as having made noble efforts to 'rescue' some of the world's forlornest people from lives of vagrancy, anguish and demise (K. Jones, 1993).

In accounting for the ways the poor and disadvantaged were 'managed' by wider social and civic systems, asylums can be seen as a mere side effect, rather than a driver, of the stigmatization of mental illness. In these terms, the traditional notion of 'insanity', as widely discussed in everyday life, has been shaped for many years not just by scientific or clinical influences, but also by economic, political, social and organizational forces.

INSANITY AS A TARGET OF TREATMENT

In their earliest forms, asylums were essentially internment houses for those people deemed to be 'insane' by mainstream society. However, precisely what was (or is) meant by this term – *insane* – is not easy to specify. As we will discuss later, social class politics certainly played a role in shaping public opinion. Nonconforming attitudes were frequently seen as evidence of madness. For many of those confined to asylums, exclusion was not merely physical. Even prior to their incarceration, these people's very existence was viewed by fellow citizens as lying outside the boundaries of normal life.

But alongside the poor and unwanted were people who were clearly afflicted by a range of psychiatric pathologies. Whether the result of brain injury, genetic predisposition, trauma or other organic or psychosocial cause, authentic illness and disability were by no means absent from the historical asylum. Epilepsy, brain damage, depression, schizophrenia and many other conditions were frequently prevalent within these care-home populations.

Contemporary views on what constituted mental illness are not just discernible from the *fact* of people's confinement in institutions. We can also begin to decipher how society understood and explained insanity (and, thus, sanity) from the way institutional residents were treated for their conditions. As with trepanation and exorcism – where attempts to release a demon show us that the demon is held to be to blame – the superficial features of a treatment approach will typically reveal an underlying theory of illness.

Prior to the middle of the eighteenth century, asylums were used simply to segregate the mentally ill from the rest of society. Although often described as though they were prisons (with residents commonly referred to as 'inmates'), their purpose was not intended to be punitive. Many asylums were operated by charities and religious groups, who felt that confinement would simply be best for everyone, 'inmate' and mainstream citizen alike. Therapy, as such, was not part of their mission.

Nonetheless, we can still make inferences about their views on mental illness from the harsh ways in which they dealt with their clients. In many such asylums, conditions were exceptionally bleak. Residents were held in overcrowded halls, with poor sanitation and little or no heating. Cruelty by staff was standard, explicable in terms of their view that inmates were little more than animals. In the eighteenth century, the 'brutishness' of the madman was more than just a metaphor. The common belief was that a loss of reason deprived these people of a core essence of humanity, making them effectively *sub*human. In the words of the French mathematician and philosopher Blaise Pascal (1623–62), a person deprived of reason was no more than 'a stone or a brute' (Pascal, 1669).

The use of violent means to impose discipline on the insane became almost intrinsic to the asylum system up to the eighteenth century. The renowned English neurologist Thomas Willis (1621–75) recommended that dealing with the mentally ill required 'threatenings, bonds, or strokes', and that 'the curing of Mad people' was best achieved 'by punishments and hard usage, in a strait-room' (Willis, 1683). Explicitly invoking the concept of brutishness, a governor of Bethlem advised that only 'the most violent' means would be sufficient 'to bring down the Spirit' of a mentally ill person, and to 'reduce their artificial Strength' (N. Robinson, 1729).

The convention of violent treatment was even applied, with full force, to the British monarch King George III, who – although not confined in an asylum – was seen at his home by a physician from a sanitorium in Lincolnshire. In 1788, the king had been manic and delirious, often speaking in a deranged way, and courtiers became concerned that he could no longer adequately discharge his duties as head of state. For his treatment, the king was tied to a stake, restrained, beaten and starved, intimidated with 'menacing and violent language', and in the words of one observer, 'no longer treated as a human being' (Scull, 2015). The king's eventual recovery no doubt reinforced the clinical belief that a firm hand was not only appropriate when approaching the mentally ill, but might also actually cure them.

Therapeutic mechanics

In the late eighteenth century, the prospect of being able to help mentally ill people to recover from their conditions produced a fresh faith in the potential of therapeutic treatment, and led to the growth of a new area of medical specialization: *psychiatry*. While medicine had long considered ways to treat mental illness, it was the presence of so many asylums that created the demand for a dedicated medical specialism. As such, psychiatry emerged from the asylums (which were initially civil, and not medical, institutions) rather than the other way around (Porter, 1987).

The earliest of these therapies were essentially mechanical, taking account of an emerging interest in the neurology of behaviour and emotion. Drug treatments were used, but not to alter brain chemistry. Instead they were intended to purge the body of contaminants by eliciting vomiting, sweats or defecation. Bloodletting was also common. Asylum doctors employed a wide range of methods to rid the body of purported toxins, including practices such as the following (de Young, 2015):

- *Artificial eruptions:* The creation of pustules on the neck or shoulders using vigorous friction, and the application of oils to ensure discharge of pus.
- *Cupping:* The application of a cup or glass to the neck in order to draw blood to the surface of the flesh before releasing it by cutting the tumefied skin.
- *Ptyalism:* The inducement of excessive flows of saliva using herbs or, more commonly, mercury (which we now know to be poisonous).
- *Nasal discharge:* The administration of 'errhines', medicines that elicit paroxysms of sneezing.
- *Lacrimation:* The inducement of the shedding of tears using drugs such as opium or, in some cases, by 'obtruding upon the mind a sorrow' (Rush, 1812, p. 319).
- *Inoculation of the itch:* The rubbing onto the skin of pus from (another person's) scabies pustules, allowing the human itch mite to burrow into the patient's epidermis and lay its eggs, thereby eliciting vigorous itching and thus bleeding and seeping.
- *Pus band:* The implantation of a horsehair or similar string beneath the surface of the skin near the neck or shoulders, where it would eventually fester and cause discharge of pus.
- *Peas therapy:* The creation of an incision in the top of the head, and the insertion of a row of peas in order to prevent the incision from healing and so to ensure continuous bleeding.

A second category of frequently employed techniques was based on the allegedly curative power of whole-body shock. Various machines were invented to try to jolt patients back to sanity. Benjamin Rush (1746–1813), an American physician (and one of the signers of the Declaration of Independence), developed a binding chair that prevented a patient from moving for hours at a time. He called his device 'The Tranquilizer' (Scull, 2015), some 140 years before that same term would be used to describe a category of anxiety-reducing drugs. The renowned English doctor Erasmus Darwin (1731–1802), grandfather of Charles Darwin (who we will discuss in Chapter 5), produced designs for a swinging chair, intended to create a curatively terrifying experience for the patient who would be strapped into it. One of the first physicians to use the device explained how 'increasing the velocity of the swing' would lead to 'an instant discharge of the stomach, bowels, and bladder, in quick succession' (Burrows, 1828, p. 601).

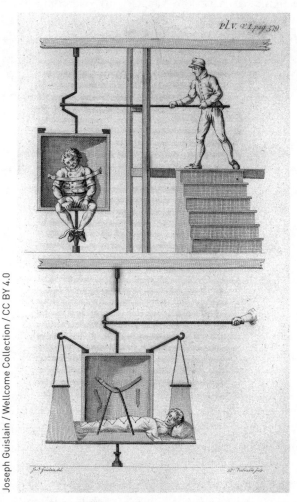

Image 4.4 Physical treatments for 'insanity'
Many physical treatments were based on the belief that whole-body shock would cure mental illness. Equipment such as rotating chairs were intended to jolt patients back to sanity.

As well as being tormented by such contraptions, patients were regularly dunked in tanks of water, administered with electric shocks, induced into comas using drugs, restrained in manacles and straitjackets, and subjected to various other assaultive tribulations designed to use the body to heal the mind. The emerging clinical view was that mental illness was an organic effect resulting from underlying physical disorder. While the details were speculative and at times almost superstitious, the overall paradigm was far removed from demonology and, thus, while brutal, significantly more scientific than what went before.

The new therapy

Alongside these physical approaches to psychiatry, there emerged a more philosophical style of treatment. Methods of restraint and purge struck many critics as cruel and counter-productive, not least because they seldom produced a convincing clinical cure. Rather than focusing so much on bodies, this new generation of innovators sought to tap into their patients' souls. Among the most influential of these were the French physician Philippe Pinel (1745–1826), and William Tuke (1732–1822), a philanthropist from England.

Pinel is associated with the concept of 'moral therapy', an approach to psychiatry that emphasized social welfare and individual autonomy. Inspired partly by religious concerns, Pinel arranged for his patients at Paris's Salpêtrière Hospital to be unchained and allowed to move freely about. He developed a practice of engaging his patients in therapeutic conversation, offering them emotional support and encouragement. Pinel promoted the idea that psychiatric treatment should be tailored to each individual client and based on the doctor's assessment of their personal needs. Such approaches put a lot of store in the charisma of the individual doctor (Porter, 1987), as well as relying on patients to have the capacity to overcome their afflictions.

Like Pinel, Tuke also campaigned for the use of non-violent forms of psychiatry. He called for doctors to view their patients as fully rounded human beings, deserving of dignity and respect. In 1796 he opened a new countryside asylum, the York Retreat, where patients were provided with emotional and physical comfort, as well as opportunities to engage in activities such as gardening and sewing. It was Tuke who coined the term 'moral treatment' to describe this new approach to caring for the mentally ill.

Such approaches were soon imitated in other European countries as well as in the United States. The underlying theory of mental illness was that, whatever their travails, mentally ill people were capable of insight. Rather than reducing them to animals (or 'brutes'), mental illness was seen as merely addling their maturity. Effectively, psychiatric patients were considered to be similar to children (Porter, 1987) and thus required to be treated as such. In this sense, asylum therapy was akin to education – a process whereby inmates could be 'reformed'.

From 'moral treatment' to 'human dustbin'

The 'moral' approach proved to be very influential and was adopted in asylums across the world. Of the thousands of new institutions opened from the nineteenth century, most were modelled on the new paradigm. Generously appointed green areas allowed patients to convalesce in comfortable bucolic surroundings (Hickman, 2009). However, the emerging psychiatric system was not without its drawbacks.

One deficiency was the very fact that countryside locations were separated from towns and cities, extending the distance – and thus the divide – between patients and the broader community. Social attitudes to the mentally ill became positively xenophobic. Psychiatric patients were so rarely encountered by ordinary citizens that they came to be referred to as 'aliens', a label derived from the Latin word for 'other'. Psychiatrists, meanwhile, were referred to as 'alienists'.

A second drawback was that isolating patients from mainstream daily life did little to help them prepare for a return to such a life. Indeed, it largely achieved the opposite. Deprived of autonomy, choice and self-determination, patients in asylums were unable to develop skills of normal living and instead acquired behaviours that were suited to asylum culture. Ironically, failing to demonstrate 'normal' behaviour would often be recorded as evidence that a patient had not recovered.

This created a vicious circle: the longer a patient was confined to an asylum, the more incurable they seemed.

The artificiality of asylum living also deprived clinicians of valuable social context. The likely impact of social factors – such as family, community relationships or poverty – on a patient's well-being was difficult to assess when that patient was secluded in an institution. Not only were clinicians prevented from properly assisting the individuals under their care, their understanding of psychiatric illness itself was also skewed. Studying patients in artificial settings contributed to a clinical habit of viewing mental illness as unrelated to social context, and instead as a disease that occurred 'within' the sufferer (Porter, 1987).

In time, this latter trend would feed into a long-lasting culture of biological reductionism and psychiatric victim-blaming. Psychological illness would often be seen as *primarily* biological, rather than just partly so, lending to disproportionate reliance on biological treatments. Clients, likewise, would be seen as *primarily* responsible for the course of their own demise – whether it be due to destructive habits, aberrant behaviour or 'bad' character – while the possible role of other people or circumstances in shaping their condition would be downplayed. Isolating patients in asylums was akin to studying them in a laboratory rather than in a real-world setting. As with all laboratory research, the methodological trade-off favoured detailed observation over day-to-day relevance.

A further problem was the emerging perception of a kind of 'industrialization' of mental healthcare. Against the backdrop of the Industrial Revolution, the belief that human challenges could be addressed using scientific means was increasingly shared. The establishment of extensive asylum infrastructures, service bureaucracies and a corps of professional psychiatric specialists created an impression that achieving cures for mental illness was something of a technological inevitability. Not only was it desirable to place the insane into institutions, it was in fact society's responsibility to send them there.

This attitude no doubt contributed to the vast increases in asylum populations that began in the nineteenth century. But there was also a dramatic shift in what was seen as the remit of mental healthcare. In the words of one historian of medicine, 'No sooner were asylums built than they were filled to overflowing, and still the well-springs of lunacy gushed forth more maniacs' (Porter, 1987, p. 20). Evolving social attitudes directed swathes of new clients to the mental hospitals. Behaviours previously seen as sins or vices were now pathologized as new diseases: drunkards were diagnosed with alcoholism; libidinous women were deemed to be sex maniacs; and delinquents of various kinds were considered criminally deranged. In several countries, laws permitted families to send unruly relatives to an asylum with very little screening. During the nineteenth century there was a widespread belief that insanity was on the increase, that an epidemic of madness was sweeping the world.

Ultimately, the capacity of these institutions could not keep up with the flow of patients being directed to them. Overcrowding was common. The comfortable existence envisaged by the 'moral treatment' movement began to disappear, replaced by an increasing atmosphere of oppression, institutionalization and fatalism. The artificiality of the environment, compounded by overcrowding, meant that few patients were ever truly 'cured', leading to a view that mental ill health was unassailably intractable. Pessimism about the power of psychiatry became widespread. Clients, clinicians and the broader community fell out of love with therapy.

'Anti-psychiatry' movements emerged in many countries, voicing fears that mental healthcare was doing more damage than good. The Hungarian-American psychiatrist Thomas Szasz (1920–2012) argued that the customs of modern psychiatry inherently missed the point of mental illness. While most therapeutic approaches implied that mental illnesses were forms of physical disease that could be fixed, or improved, by medical intervention, Szasz suggested that the notion of 'insanity' was merely a label used to describe an ordinary subset of the human population. This subset, Szasz argued, comprised people who experienced 'problems of living' in the modern world, locating insanity as a social predicament rather than as a disease (Szasz, 1961). In Szasz's view, the goal of psychotherapy should therefore be to teach people *to learn how to live* in the world as it is, an ambition that would always be unfulfilled by formal psychiatry because of its reliance on bio-logical treatments. Szasz became renowned as the figurehead of 'anti-psychiatry', his arguments echoing those of many academics and activists around the world who had become appalled by the traditional asylum system.

Asylums were no longer seen as modern hospitals in which ill patients could receive medical treatment and recover. Rather, they were seen as institutions of incarceration, places of coercion and control. By the 1950s, asylums had become little more than human dustbins, somewhere society could shut away its incurables, its incorrigibles, and its incompetents. There they could be stored, forever far from view, and, in time, forgotten.

HISTORY IN STORIES: *ONE FLEW OVER THE CUCKOO'S NEST* (1975)

One Flew Over the Cuckoo's Nest (Forman, 1975) is an acclaimed US film based on a novel by the fiction author Ken Kesey. It is widely regarded as a masterpiece of cinema. The movie depicts the story of a convicted criminal, Randle McMurphy, who seeks to avoid prison by pretending to be insane. He is duly sent to a countryside asylum, which he expects will be far more comfortable than any jail. However, after he arrives there, he discovers that life at the asylum is far from leisurely. In fact, it is stultifying, oppressive and often violent.

In the asylum, McMurphy gets to know several other residents, developing sympathy for them and becoming their friend and ally. He develops a rebellious streak, frequently exacting revenge on the ward's cruel and unsympathetic overseer, the dreaded Nurse Ratched. The callous Nurse Ratched is portrayed as an archetypal villain,

constantly berating and demeaning the residents, and ruthlessly dishing out punishments.

The movie is ostensibly about the definition of insanity. Despite being perfectly healthy, McMurphy has little difficulty persuading the authorities to believe that he is insane. In fact, he is not the only character to be wilfully deceiving the asylum doctors. Another inmate, 'Chief', is pretending to be both deaf and mute in order to manipulate the authorities (and the other residents) into concluding that he is pathologically uncommunicative.

Filmed in an actual mental hospital, *One Flew Over the Cuckoo's Nest* presented many images that shaped the public perception of mental illness and asylums. Many of its details were revelatory to audiences. It depicted treatment approaches that were consistent with its mid-twentieth-century setting, and subjugating power dynamics that raised important questions about whether institutional psychiatry appropriately serves the interests of people who have mental illnesses.

The movie also presented an important lesson on the social construction of insanity. After McMurphy physically attacks Nurse Ratched, he is restrained and forced to undergo a lobotomy. This permanent and life-changing psychosurgery is conducted on him despite the fact that he does not have any mental illness. The shocking denouement warns us that those in authority can sometimes seek to preserve their power by deeming dissent to be, *ipso facto*, a sign of madness. It also highlights the arbitrariness of psychiatric diagnosis, by challenging us to consider: How could a person ever *prove* that they were *sane*?

INSANITY AS A LEGAL CONCEPT

In Chapter 3, we saw how the nineteenth century was characterized by a proliferation of different types of 'expert'. Academic practitioners sought to organize themselves into learned societies, and to channel their works into meetings and journals. Psychiatry was no exception, even if the word 'psychiatry' was at first considered somewhat esoteric.

The American Psychiatric Association was founded in 1844, although it was then known as the Association of Medical Superintendents of American Institutions for the Insane, or AMSAII. It immediately established a new journal, called the *American Journal of Insanity*, which it published for nearly seventy years before deciding to change its name to the *American Journal of Psychiatry*. Similarly, when the *British Journal of Psychiatry* was launched in 1853, it too had a different title. Back then it was known as *The Asylum Journal*.

These experts attracted a fair degree of public attention and, in some cases, fame. Historically, theories of insanity were never merely medical; they were also social. The traditional view of insanity as a by-product of divine providence, if not of demonic interference, helped to create a nexus between madness and morality. The public at large were keenly interested to know what lay beneath lunacy because this, by extension, would reveal the nature of vice.

'Moral insanity'

Perhaps unsurprisingly, those who promoted a 'moral' approach to psychiatry were expected to be especially insightful. Pinel, for his part, had been explicit in describing mental illness in terms of its moral aspects. He had sought to distinguish two categories of madness: *manie avec délire* (madness with delirium) and *manie sans délire* (madness without delirium). The latter was especially pertinent to the matter of personal culpability. While people afflicted by madness with delirium would be visibly unwell, a person experiencing madness without delirium would appear 'normal' on the surface. But underneath, according to Pinel, they would suffer from a 'perversion of the active faculties' that could lead to a 'blind propensity to acts of violence' (Pinel, 1806, p. 156). In other words, such people were impulsively driven to behave in criminal ways. That they had a *hidden* mental disorder made them especially dangerous.

In the nineteenth century, the psychiatry (or alienist) profession enthusiastically promoted their expertise to lawmakers and the courts. Their theories about 'moral insanity' were revolutionary in courts of law (D. W. Jones, 2017). Such was their professional confidence that they claimed to be able to detect these hidden forms of insanity, sometimes on the basis of nothing more than a short interview with an accused person.

In the United Kingdom, a would-be assassin who attempted to kill King George III (the same king who, as described above, had himself been treated for mental illness) was found not guilty on the grounds of insanity in 1800, largely on the basis of medical testimony. In another high-profile case in France, in 1825, similar testimony by leading psychiatrists helped to lighten the sentence imposed on a woman who had decapitated a baby (During, 1988). In 1840, a British teenager who had attempted to shoot Queen Victoria was given a special verdict of 'not guilty, being insane', after several high-profile psychiatrists had testified in his defence.

These and other cases highlighted the changing way in which insanity was understood under law, and by wider society. No longer was madness akin to brutishness or utter incapacitation. Now a person could be insane while still able to function in ordinary society, capable of passing themselves off as a 'normal' person.

Detection of these hidden dangers was reliant on the expert psychiatrists. However, public confidence in their abilities was eventually to wane, after another landmark was set in the British courts in 1843, where a young man, Daniel M'Naghten, stood trial for murder. M'Naghten, in attempting to assassinate the Prime Minister, Robert Peel, had fatally shot the Prime Minister's secretary. To most observers, it seemed an open-and-shut type of case: M'Naghten had clearly planned his attack and had gone to trouble to avoid getting caught. However, after several doctors testified that M'Naghten had 'partial insanity', the jury were instructed to return a verdict of 'not guilty, being insane'.

The outcome shocked most observers, including the watching public, and was met with a storm of disapproval. National newspapers vociferously attacked the verdict. In their eyes, it meant that a person could now knowingly commit a crime but evade conviction *simply by claiming to be mad*. Even Queen Victoria herself waded into the debate, writing to the Prime Minister to complain.

The political class largely agreed. In parliament, the House of Lords instituted a review that led to a new perspective on legal insanity. They laid down principles now known around the world as the M'Naghten Rules. For a person to be acquitted on the grounds of insanity, they now needed to prove that they were unaware of the 'nature and quality' of their crime 'at the time of committing the act', or else that they otherwise did not know that what they were doing was wrong. Under this approach, M'Naghten himself would have been found guilty. In those days, he would have been sentenced to death.

Thereafter, psychiatric witnesses were to come under increasing public scrutiny. Their ability to detect 'hidden' forms of insanity (where others would see just criminality) was no longer deferred to so easily.

Yet another high-profile British murder trial, in 1863, proved to be a turning point. In this trial, George Victor Townley, a man who stabbed his former fiancée to death, sought clemency on the grounds of temporary insanity. Strikingly, an expert witness testified that Townley's complete lack of remorse after committing such a brutal act effectively *proved* that he must be insane. However, under the M'Naghten Rules, the quality of a suspect's remorse was not relevant. The jury could see for themselves that Townley was quite aware of the difference between right and wrong. They quickly returned a verdict of guilty. On this occasion, the medical testimony carried little or no weight. The expert was no longer trusted.

The case attracted national attention not least because the accused was from a wealthy family. Townley's rich parents had vigorously campaigned for his acquittal. Crucially, they paid the medical witness a handsome fee for his services, and this detail was widely reported in the news media (D. W. Jones, 2017).

The idea that an expert's view might change depending on who is paying the bill did much to discredit the role of medical witnesses in court trials, especially when it came to questions of mental illness. It also served to influence public attitudes about the reality, and nature, of insanity. In the public imagination, the concept of insanity came to be recognized as broad, complex and situation-specific, but also as liable to be socially constructed in ways that serve the advantages of those with power.

In the latter half of the nineteenth century, psychiatrists largely abandoned their claims to be able to detect disorders by conducting interviews with patients. Their priority now was to base diagnosis on more objective methods and concepts. Ideas about insanity, and its relation to culpability, began to shift in a distinctly biological direction.

INSANITY AS A CONSEQUENCE OF DEGENERATION

Biological approaches have had a profound and extensive impact on psychology, a theme we will cover in detail in Chapter 5. But the biological worldview is not just of scientific relevance; it also affects the social outlook of ordinary people. This is because of its implications regarding causality. When people are told that behaviour is rooted in biology, they often interpret this as meaning that behaviour is something that lies beyond true human control.

Therefore, when nineteenth-century psychiatrists started to emphasize the biological basis of mental illness, they helped to create a widespread social belief that insanity was an ingrained physical disorder, about which very little, therapeutically, could ever be done. Far from being temporarily ill due to dysfunctional circumstances, insane people were seen as condemned to a natural destiny. No amount of 'talking cures' or 'moral treatment' could overcome the challenges caused by a defective brain or deficient genes. Biological problems could not be 'fixed' by psychological intervention.

Faced with increasingly overcrowded asylums and a track record of therapeutic failures, professional psychiatric pessimism descended into outright despondency. Prominent psychiatrists began to discuss mental illness as something of a lost cause. Eugen Bleuler (1857–1939), the distinguished Swiss physician who coined the terms *schizophrenia* and *autism*, described the mentally ill as 'stranger to him than the birds in his garden' (Kotowicz, 1997, p. 14). To the German-Swiss psychiatrist and philosopher Karl Jaspers (1883–1969), the insane were so strange as to lie beyond an 'abyss' of understanding, and thus *by definition* to be permanently incomprehensible (Sass, 2014).

Such dismissal of the mentally ill became increasingly normalized beyond the turn of the twentieth century. Even the most distinguished scientists of the day were acculturated within this worldview. A particularly vocal figure was the renowned German physician Emil Kraepelin, who, as we described in Chapter 3, had previously worked with Wundt in Leipzig. Kraepelin is often acclaimed for distinguishing two types of mental disorder: 'dementia praecox' (now known as *schizophrenia*) and 'manic depression'. For Kraepelin, dementia praecox was an irreversible neurodegenerative disease, whereas manic depression was episodic and 'affective' (occurring at the level of mood). This insight was important because it helped to distinguish different mental illnesses on the basis of their causes rather than their symptoms, an idea that contrasted with much prevailing psychiatry of the time (Ebert & Bär, 2010).

But not all Kraepelin's views of the world were as progressive. He also theorized that Jewish people were genetically prone to psychiatric disorder (Decker, 2004). He judged socialists and war objectors to be mentally ill (Ebert & Bär, 2010). He spoke of his patients as suffering from 'vitiation of the will', effectively dismissing them as moral perverts (Porter, 1987, p. 21). And he bemoaned the fact that welfare payments to poor families prevented the children of socially disadvantaged parents from dying in sufficient numbers as to rid humanity of their inferior lineages:

> In any case, it is impossible to know how many imbeciles, epileptics, psychopaths, criminals, prostitutes and vagabonds are the children of alcoholic and syphilitic parents and have inherited the inferiority of their parents. Of course, the damage will in part be compensated for by their poorer ability to survive. But unfortunately, our ever-expanding social welfare programmes have the effect of impeding the natural self-purification of our people.
>
> (Kraepelin, 2007, p. 400)

In short, although Kraepelin is celebrated as a pioneer of psychiatric medicine, there is little doubt that his psychological observations were coloured by harsh political views. An unquestionable hostility to foreigners, a contempt for the poor and a distrust of state altruism all served to imbue his diagnostic approach with social prejudice.

That prominent intellectuals would hold such opinions was not unusual in the late nineteenth and early twentieth centuries. Whereas previously psychiatrists had sought to claim that vice was the result of insanity, now they advanced the argument that *insanity* was the result of *vice*. The psychology of mental illness had entered a new sociopolitical epoch, tinged with no small measure of racial prejudice, discriminatory hereditarianism and sexual prurience.

At a time of social turmoil, civil unrest and everyday revolutionary rhetoric, in Europe and the United States a bourgeois elite were becoming highly anxious about the restless citizenry that surrounded them. To them, mental illness was merely a glimpse of the true nature of the masses. Insanity, a biological affliction, was a sign of social and cultural malaise – nothing less than the degeneration of humanity itself.

Cross-cultural insanity

The latter half of the nineteenth century, and the transition to the twentieth, coincided with significant social and political upheaval around the world, largely spiralling from dynamics centred on Europe and the United States. The United States experienced its ferocious and traumatic Civil War

(1861–5), which in turn precipitated that country's abolition of slavery – a profound development that altered the course of American history, and arguably that of the world. From 1870, what is often referred to as the 'third wave' of European colonialism took place, with imperial powers engaging in a 'scramble for Africa' that emulated their former exploits in the Americas and Asia. And of course, there emerged complex trends of militarism, nationalism and political conflict that ultimately set in motion the events that led to the First World War (1914–18).

Faced with so much turmoil, it is perhaps no surprise that public opinion often veered towards fatalism. It was easy to form the view that world events were spiralling out of control. The prospect of terminal cultural decline seemed very real: although science and technology were advancing, the social well-being of humanity as a whole seemed to be worsening by the decade. The fact that psychiatrists saw an epidemic of mental illness, and believed most of it to be incurable, simply reflected this wider atmosphere of despair.

The third wave of colonialism did much to shape scientific debate about human diversity and distinctiveness, especially concerning differences between native European (or so-called Caucasian) populations and those from other parts of the world. For most Europeans, such a classification brought to mind several other categories of interest: European versus non-European was seen as overlapping with White versus non-White, Christian versus non-Christian and, in the language of the time, 'civilized' versus 'savage' (Oda, Banzato & Dalgalarrondo, 2005). Therefore, perceived differences between European and non-European cultures were quickly attributed to differences in race, religion and refinement.

This reasoning was applied widely across psychology, and we will explore many of its consequences in Chapter 6. But undoubtedly, the emerging focus on cultural differences along with an increasing paranoia about social decay was to prove an incendiary combination. This unfortunate juxtaposition of attitudinal forces served to pollute the science of mental illness with widespread sociopolitical toxicity.

Cultural differences were highlighted as 'evidence' to support a new type of theory of mental illness. In this paradigm, mental illness was intertwined with the 'degeneration' of human society. Key to this argument were purported differences between 'civilized' and 'non-civilized' peoples. Throughout the nineteenth century, anthropologists, biologists, physicians and philosophers were all promoting a view that so-called non-civilized peoples were psychologically different to Europeans.

'Civilization' and madness

To European eyes, travellers' accounts of exotic foreign tribes had long attracted intellectual curiosity. Naïvely believing that all true civilization had occurred within the boundaries of their own continent, Europeans viewed foreigners from faraway places not only as exotic but also as somehow 'unsullied', and as symbolizing a 'pure' form of humanity. Ostensibly uncorrupted by the waves of technological development that, over centuries, had drawn Europeans away from their natural state, these 'primitive' foreigners were depicted in Europe as 'nature's gentlemen' (e.g. St John, 1844), a sentimental stereotype based on the premise that human beings were innately moral. The view was that, having been uncontaminated by civilization, these people were able to manifest their original human dignity.

At first, such depictions might appear complimentary to non-European cultures. However, the notion of the 'noble savage' (the term coined by the British novelist Charles Dickens (1853)) was far from deferential to foreignness. Non-Europeans were complimented, but only at the level of being patronized. The nobility being acknowledged was a somewhat abstract notion. In reality, these people were stereotyped as uncivilized, uncouth and unsophisticated primitives, whose innate 'nobility' was little more than the kind seen in animals.

The narrative did not spare Europeans either. Consistent with the overall mood of moralistic miserabilism that had become prominent in the late nineteenth century, praise for overseas primitives was intended as an indirect insult to indigenous Europeans, including those Europeans who had migrated to North America. Although placed on civilization's pedestal, these Europeans were nonetheless condemned for their modernity, having shed their innate morality during a centuries-long fall from grace.

In 1836, the French psychiatrist Jacques-Joseph Moreau (1804–84) launched what was probably the first ever scientific expedition aimed at studying the psychological traits of foreigners. Having explored towns and villages in Malta, Egypt and Turkey, he reported that there were remarkably fewer mentally ill people in these places than he was accustomed to seeing in western Europe. He concluded that this was partly due to the hot climate, but largely because such underdeveloped societies lacked the 'agitation' and 'continuous dislocation' of modern civilization (Oda et al., 2005). To Moreau, these eastern societies were no more advanced than the Europe of the Middle Ages. Whatever insanity did arise, he concluded, was caused primarily by religious (i.e. Muslim) exaltation. Perhaps ominously, Moreau also mused that 'the incessant struggle between the one who leaves and the one who arrives' ('de lutte incessante, entre ce qui s'en va et ce qui arrive') was deleterious to European mental health, a likely reference to the purportedly negative effects of immigration (Moreau, 1843, p. 22).

The aforementioned *American Journal of Insanity* published recurring articles describing similar observations about different cultures. It reported insanity as being rare among many different international populations, including native tribespeople in Africa and the South Pacific (Brigham, 1845) and the Chinese (Brigham, 1847). In the *Journal of Psychological Medicine and Mental Pathology*, one writer reported that in India, things were much the same as Moreau had observed in the Middle East. The writer argued that India's hot climate served to suppress the prevalence of mental illness, but that insanity was occasionally sparked by religious excesses among its Hindu population (Winslow, 1853).

Assessments similar to Moreau's cascaded through nineteenth-century psychiatry. A contemporary of the French psychiatric scene, Jean-Étienne Dominique Esquirol (1772–1840) specified several features of civilization that he felt were implicated in the onset of mental illness. As well as the overall chaos of change, Esquirol blamed the rampant abuse of alcohol in Europe, and the prevalence of intermarriage between blood-relatives (Esquirol, 1838). In Germany, the physician Wilhelm Griesinger (1817–68) added sexual promiscuity, social liberalism and childbirth outside marriage to the list (Griesinger, 1845), whereas the psychiatrist Richard von Krafft-Ebing offered poverty, poor hygiene, poor nutrition and the pursuit of wealth (Krafft-Ebing, 1888). Needless to say, not all the evidence offered to support these claims was robust.

Modern communication technologies were championed by some mental health professionals, but catastrophized by others. In Britain, the psychiatrist Henry Maudsley (who we encountered in Chapter 3) felt that new methods of communication would protect people from insanity, by helping to equip them with up-to-date information they could use to adapt to change (Maudsley, 1895). In sharp contrast, the American neurologist George Beard (1839–83) considered such new technologies to be the 'chief and primary cause' of mental illness. In his landmark book, *American Nervousness: Its Causes and Consequences* (1881), he listed five features of civilization that drove people insane, four of them – 'steam power, the periodical press, the telegraph, the sciences' – propelled by advances in communications technology. Notably, Beard's fifth major cause of modern madness was 'the mental activity of women' (p. 96).

Occasionally, civilization was seen to damage mental well-being by undermining physical health. Daniel H. Tuke (1827–95), the great-grandson of William Tuke, one of the founders of moral treatment, voiced concerns about the damaging effects of poverty and malnutrition (Tuke, 1894). But such plausible psychosocial theories were never entirely divorced from cultural stereotypes. For example, Daniel Tuke believed that Irish people were particularly exposed to these problems, due to what he felt were their higher levels of in-breeding, and, strikingly, their 'abuse of tea' ('in causing insanity, its substitution for milk and porridge is lamentable indeed'; pp. 554–5).

Embedded within these claims was the persistent implication that insanity and immorality were inextricably intertwined. Civilization was a form of demise, the theory went, its comforts working to subvert the ethical purity of the population. Modernity led not only to poverty, malnutrition and the overwhelming of the senses, it also promoted toxic attitudes, such as selfishness and lack of sacrifice. By contributing to secularization, it further exacerbated insanity by encouraging various forms of irreligious behaviour (chiefly, sexual promiscuity).

Cesare Lombroso (1835–1909), the Italian physician who became a pioneer of modern criminology, asserted that civilization so overstimulated the senses, it was one of the main reasons that 'alcoholics and paralytics' were so frequently induced to break the law (Lombroso, 1902). By the turn of the twentieth century, the link from civilization had been made not just to madness and vice, but to full-blown criminality. The degeneration wrought by civilization was self-perpetuating.

Civilization not only drove people mad. It also made them bad.

HISTORY REPEATING ITSELF: THE 'DANGERS' OF TECHNOLOGY

The nineteenth-century degenerationists were not the only observers of culture to fear the impact of new technologies. Their worries that trains, newspapers and other inventions would overwhelm the senses of ordinary people, disturb the delicate balance of their minds, or otherwise precipitate lasting harm on humanity, reflected a recurring echo of technophobia that has been present throughout history.

Society would frequently fret about the arrival of such inventions as telephonics and radio. In 1877, the *New York Times* railed against the invention of the telephone, citing its potential to undermine the concept of privacy. The Italian Guglielmo Marconi, who invented long-range radio technologies in 1901, worried that he might have released 'a menace' upon the world (A. Robinson, 2016). In 1889, the *Spectator* magazine condemned the effects of the telegraph. According to their assessment, such technology encouraged people to limit their communications to a 'diffusion of statements in snippets', thereby stunting attention spans across the nation, as well as promoting 'the constant formation of hasty or erroneous opinions' (Nickles, 2003, p. 96).

In 1938, the *New York Times* devoted an editorial to the demise of the pencil – and with it its capacity to connect a writer directly to the written word – mournfully bemoaning the sudden ubiquity of the comparatively impersonal typewriter (Stephens, 1998). But even this nostalgia for pencils could raise disputes among Luddites. True pencil people would insist that only plain pencils were sufficiently wholesome – those with erasers attached served just to coddle sloppiness, by allowing writers to obliterate their mistakes (Petroski, 1990).

Film and visual media were always seen as especially threatening. In 1916, the actor Charlie Chaplin, later to become a Hollywood legend, dismissed film-making as a mechanical fad. He claimed that audiences would soon gravitate back to live theatre, preferring the culturally superior experience of being able 'to see flesh and blood on the stage' (Hadleigh, 2007, p. 138). Once television became popular in the 1950s, critics lambasted it as a social evil that promoted everything from obesity to gun violence. This fear of TV would go through phases. When colour television arrived to replace its black-and-white predecessor, conservative critics in many countries decried this extravagance as yet another step away from the healthy frugality that had so benefited previous generations (Enli et al., 2013). Colour TV was also seen as promoting consumerism and greed, and of adding an unnecessary dimension of realism to its depictions of immorality and violence.

In the 1980s, social concern began to focus on the effects of computers and related technologies. From the overstimulation of young people who play video games (Markey & Ferguson, 2017) to the impact of social media (Berryman, Ferguson & Negy, 2018) and the very act of looking at a screen (Stiglic & Viner, 2019), computer-based technologies have been frequently chastised for promoting teen violence, ill health, stunted development and psychopathologies of various kinds.

In 2018, when the World Health Organization proposed that excessive time spent playing video games should itself be defined as a unique mental disorder, there was little to no consensus among those researching the area as to whether such an addiction really exists (Ferguson & Colwell, 2020). Given psychology's history of arbitrarily defining mental health conditions on the basis of social factors, such as moral panic, it remains to be seen whether gaming disorder will stand the test of time.

It can be informative to note that such themes have not only persisted since the nineteenth century, they also long predated it. After the printing press was invented in the 1400s, the ruling elites feared its consequences. Critics warned that the discipline needed to write by hand was an important part of human character, and that printed documents would inevitably lead to the denigration of culture itself. In 1680, the German philosopher Gottfried Leibniz (1646–1716) claimed that the increasing availability of books would lead to 'a fall back into barbarism' (McLuhan, 1962). When bound books became widely available to the public, sceptics warned that they would damage readers' eyesight, ruin their imaginations, undermine their social skills, pollute their minds with profanity, and promote sedentary lifestyles – all criticisms that would, in time, be directed at video games and social media in the twenty-first century.

In ancient Greece, Socrates famously never wrote (his teachings were recorded for posterity by his students). In fact, he believed that the invention of writing was an all-round bad idea: it would remove the need to remember things, and would encourage people to think they knew something when in fact they had merely written it down. As Plato was later to put it, 'writing is a step backward for truth' (Stephens, 1998). The very fact that people could read and write was seen as part of a technological malaise and, in the fourth century BCE, as the beginning of the end of humanity.

It seems that the human propensity to fear the implications of innovation is as old as the impulse to invent technology itself.

ALMOST FAMOUS: ELIZA WOLLSTONECRAFT BISHOP

Eliza (Elizabeth) Wollstonecraft, born in London in 1763, was the younger sister of the writer and women's rights advocate Mary Wollstonecraft (1759–97). While Mary went on to become one of the founders of modern feminist philosophy, Eliza lived a relatively obscure life, very much in her sister's shadow.

Mary Wollstonecraft is remembered for her many writings, the most famous of which was *A Vindication of the Rights of Woman* (1792). An important theme of this work was that reason and logic should always trump tradition when determining the social order, a message that chimed with the rise of the scientific method. After Mary had died, her widower published her then unfinished novel – *Maria: or, The Wrongs of Woman* (Wollstonecraft, 1798) – which, among other issues, addressed the role of convention in shaping our definitions of psychological normality.

The novel tells the story of Maria, who was imprisoned in an asylum having been falsely declared insane by her abusive and unfaithful husband. Maria was sent to the asylum because she had attempted to divorce her husband and leave the country. While there, Maria developed close relationships with other women who also found themselves incarcerated for social, rather than psychiatric, reasons. Mary Wollstonecraft had drafted a few different endings for the novel. In one of them, Maria becomes deeply depressed and eventually takes her own life.

Maria presented a political critique of the societal construction of sexist behavioural norms and the paternalistic use of psychiatry to control women. It showed how women can form close relationships with each other independently of men, but also suggested that women can sometimes collude in their own subjugation by maintaining sentimental attitudes towards marriage.

As with many eighteenth-century works of fiction, Wollstonecraft's novel was heavily inspired by real events. It featured several autobiographical elements. For example, like the character of Maria, Mary Wollstonecraft herself had felt emotionally neglected by her own mother and had attempted suicide after being abandoned by a lover.

However, it appears that much of the character of Maria was based not only on Mary, but also on her sister, Eliza Wollstonecraft. It was Eliza who had, in real life, taken the daring step of leaving her family. She had suffered deep unhappiness in her marriage, which Mary attributed to her husband. Instead of entering an asylum, however, Eliza joined a dissenting community who lived together in seclusion near Islington in north London. There she developed close relationships with other abandoned and non-conformist women. While living away from mainstream society, Eliza found life increasingly stressful. She ultimately became embittered towards Mary, who she felt had been responsible for her discomfort (Tyson, 1975).

Eliza's life trajectory – from sentimental marriage, to marital separation, to social exclusion, and then to mental suffering – provided the perfect story arc for Mary to frame her narrative in *Maria*, exposing the arbitrary and paternalistic social conventions that declared non-conventional behaviour to be 'abnormal'. In this way, it was Eliza's experiences and actions that underpinned Mary Wollstonecraft's influential feminist critique of paternalist attitudes to sanity.

Eliza Wollstonecraft, who retained her married name Eliza Wollstonecraft Bishop, wrote no books or pamphlets. Instead, she served as a school governess, often collaborating with other women to set up new schools. She eventually established a preparatory school in Dublin, Ireland, where she lived until her death in 1828.

CONSTRUCTING INSANITY

While 'uncivilized' societies were largely spared the consequences of modernity, according to psychiatrists their safety was assured only as long as their populations stayed at home. Contact with civilization was felt to be too dangerous; immigration to Europe or America would be especially perilous for 'primitive' people. While in familiar surroundings, these people could enjoy the simple nobility of native living. However, in the view of many psychiatrists, any sudden requirement for 'advanced mental functioning' would cause them extreme distress and lead undoubtedly to mental illness (Krafft-Ebing, 1888). Their resultant counter-productive behaviour would lead to further damage. Unable to cope with sophistication, these so-called primitive people would be driven to madness, self-destruction, immorality and crime.

Here were the psychiatric roots of a number of racial stereotypes that continue to be directed at migrants and minorities in many countries today (Oda et al., 2005). In the late nineteenth century, beliefs that certain ethnicities were innately mentally vulnerable or predisposed to psychiatric issues began to be attached to groups such as African Americans in the United States (Deutsch, 1944), East Asian people in the United States (Hoppenstand, 1992), the Irish in the United States and in the United Kingdom (Dain, 1964), and mixed-race persons in Brazil (Nina-Rodrigues, 1903). Even now, in several countries, rates of admission to mental health services are often disproportionately higher for immigrants than for indigenous communities, raising the suspicion that lingering prejudicial assumptions from psychology's history might continue to distort aspects of clinical practice (we will return to this issue in Chapter 11).

History suggests that the concept of insanity has never been easy to define. A significantly complicating factor has been the way that powerful groups often choose to define insanity in ways that serve their own interests, including their interest in controlling those in society who are *less* powerful than them.

Madness in perspective

Many mental health problems are vividly recognizable and emerge similarly across cultures. People who are profoundly depressed, who are debilitated by their obsessions, or who regularly experience hallucinations are likely to be recognized as mentally unwell no matter where (or when) they live. Patients with demonstrable brain damage – such as that caused by head injury or chemical dependency – will similarly be classified as clinical cases. And while, in the past, persons with intellectual disability were often seen as indistinguishable from people who were 'mad' or 'insane', nowadays the fact that their distinctive challenges are cognitive rather than psychiatric is much more widely appreciated.

But for many mental health issues, the determination of illness is much less straightforward. Where there are no physical brain defects, and where a person's 'symptoms' are questionable rather than compelling, producing a psychiatric diagnosis is far from an exact science. Diagnostic inconsistency is more common than it is not. Ultimately, in these cases, a true definition of insanity is not the result of scientific scrutiny. It is the product of social consensus.

Diagnostic controversies usually reveal the uneven distribution of inherent social power. Male clinicians can theorize about their female patients without realizing that their evaluation is more gendered than clinical. When women get lower self-esteem scores than men, it is interpreted as the result of their feminine brittleness, when it could just as easily be seen as evidence of habitual male arrogance (Tavris, 1993; we will discuss this problem in detail in Chapter 11). The reason clinicians see diminished self-esteem as a problem but excessive self-esteem as okay is because the male pattern – higher scores – is treated as the standard. And the reason for *this* is that, throughout the history of psychology, the clinicians who determined these standards have been, mostly, men.

In the late nineteenth and early twentieth centuries, female sexual desire was considered so socially unacceptable as to be a sign of mental disease. One prominent nineteenth-century physician declared that around a quarter of all women were sufficiently amorous as to warrant psychiatric attention (Briggs, 2000). In the United States, women were frequently committed to institutions on the basis of such aberrant behaviours as 'lewd and lascivious conduct, fornication, serial premarital pregnancies [and] adultery' (T. L. Anderson, 2006, pp. 203–4). The diagnosis of mental illness owed more to prevailing sexual attitudes than it did to any objective effort to identify debilitation, harm or need.

As alluded to above, clinical diagnoses were also distorted by cross-cultural bigotries, often seeking to rationalize injustices by invoking psychiatric necessity. Following the abolition of slavery in the United States, it was widely alleged that emancipated slaves experienced enormous rates of mental illness, thereby implying that they were completely unsuited to their newly liberated lives. Notably, the purported statistics on this matter, while produced by government bodies, were later shown to have been faked (Deutsch, 1944).

In the 1850s, the Medical Association of Louisiana appointed a committee to report on the 'diseases and physical peculiarities' of African Americans, the majority of whom living in the United States at that time were held in bondage by slave owners. The committee was chaired by a local physician, Samuel A. Cartwright (1793–1863). Cartwright's committee claimed that Africans were fundamentally unlike Caucasian Americans, both physically and psychologically. The committee's report contained several bizarre claims about alleged biological differences between Black and White people. It also resorted to psychiatry in order to explain why people held as slaves had the temerity to object to bondage.

According to Cartwright (1851), African people who tried to escape from slavery were obviously mentally ill. Based on observations that, he said, had 'heretofore escaped the attention of the scientific world', Cartwright explained that ordinary Africans *wanted* to be held as slaves, 'as it gives them more tranquility and sensual enjoyment' (p. 694). Those who tried to escape were suffering from 'as much a disease of the mind as any other' (p. 707). Cartwright believed that this condition was 'not heretofore classed among the long list of maladies that man is subject to', and so decided to name it himself. He called it *drapetomania*, 'or the disease causing slaves to run away' (p. 707).

The use of psychiatric labels to dismiss dissent has a long history in political rhetoric. Political prisoners are frequently detained in psychiatric hospitals, often part of a regime's effort to denigrate the credibility of its adversaries (Bonnie, 2002). The subjective element of psychiatric diagnostics provides this opportunity. As with the heretics of the Middle Ages being put on trial for refusing to conform to state religiosity, dissent has long been seen by the mainstream as a particularly intimidating form of madness.

Efforts to suppress dissent are, obviously, intended to preserve the status quo. For this reason, insightful political leaders often find that they must challenge normative thinking about behaviour. In a speech originally delivered in 1957, the American civil rights leader Martin Luther King, Jr, expressed the point as follows:

Modern psychology has a word that is probably used more than any other word. It is the word 'maladjusted.' Now we all should seek to live a well-adjusted life in order to avoid neurotic and schizophrenic personalities. But there are some things within our social order to which I am *proud to be maladjusted* and to which *I call upon you to be maladjusted*. I never intend to adjust myself to segregation and discrimination. I never intend to adjust myself to mob rule. I never intend to adjust myself to the tragic effects of the methods of physical violence and to tragic militarism. I call upon you to be maladjusted to such things.

(M. L. King, 1986, p. 15)

Non-conformity is rarely truly psychiatric. Efforts to pathologize dissent by labelling it as 'insanity', 'hysteria', 'criminality', or 'disorder' are rooted in self-serving bias, and should be treated with extreme suspicion.

Image 4.5 'Proud to be maladjusted'
The American civil rights leader Martin Luther King, Jr, made a famous speech highlighting the arbitrary meaning of the term 'maladjusted'. He called on people to have courage in their own individuality and to question social norms, declaring himself 'proud to be maladjusted' to the social norms that allow racial discrimination to flourish.

We will return to the issues of race and racism in Chapter 6, of sex and sexuality in Chapter 7, of psychology's problems of systematic bias in Chapter 11, and of whether indeed psychological norms have been good for the world in Chapter 12.

Defining abnormality

The area of psychology that deals with mental illness has become known as 'abnormal psychology'. Strikingly, however, there is no agreed definition of what is meant by the term 'abnormal' (Hughes, 2016). Debates about how it should be defined are centuries old. As the aforementioned playwright, Nathaniel Lee, who resided in Bethlem during the seventeenth century, complained, 'They called me mad, and I called them mad, and damn them, they outvoted me' (Porter, 1987). From the very beginning, consensus has proven to be critical.

A common interpretation of the term 'abnormal' is something

HISTORICALLY (IN)ACCURATE?: 'ON BEING SANE IN INSANE PLACES'

In 1973, David Rosenhan (1929–2012), a social psychologist at Stanford University in the United States, published the results of a study – 'On being sane in insane places' – that shocked the field of mental healthcare and raised questions about the way psychologists and psychiatrists discuss and define insanity.

In the research he described, Rosenhan (1973) reported that eight perfectly healthy people had presented themselves to different mental hospitals, claiming to be hearing voices. All were immediately admitted. Rosenhan had instructed the imposter-patients to display no actual symptoms of mental illness while in the asylums, and to tell their doctors they felt well and that their hallucinations had stopped. Despite this, seven of the patients were diagnosed with schizophrenia, and the eighth with 'manic-depressive psychosis'. All were retained in hospital for weeks, only being released on condition that they take antipsychotic medication.

In a second phase of research, one of the hospitals challenged Rosenhan to send further pseudopatients to them, but this time with advance warning. The hospital administrators asserted that in these circumstances, their doctors would have little difficulty in detecting patients who were faking their symptoms. Rosenhan agreed and over the following three months, the hospital identified more than forty-one such patients that it was sure were imposters, and a further forty-two that it suspected were likely to be. In fact, Rosenhan reported that he had sent *no patients at all* to the hospital during this time. All those patients suspected of being fake were actually genuine.

According to Rosenhan's results, it seemed that with minimal manipulation, asylum doctors could be made to believe, on the one hand, that false mental illnesses were actually real, and on the other, that real mental illnesses were actually false. Naturally, these findings raised serious questions about the diagnostic processes used in mental healthcare, and, by extension, the very definition of mental illness itself.

Rosenhan's exposé resonated throughout psychology, and was highlighted as a landmark study for decades. However, in 2019, after a journalist decided to hire private investigators to track down the pseudopatients who took part in the study, it emerged that much of what Rosenhan had described was itself deeply questionable. The journalist could only establish the existence of two such volunteers, both of whom contradicted Rosenhan's description of the research methodology. It was established that a third pseudopatient was, in fact, Rosenhan himself. Further, far from behaving 'normally' after admission, Rosenhan's own asylum records revealed that he continued to exhibit several ongoing and extreme symptoms while in hospital, and that he even told his doctors he was suicidal (Cahalan, 2019).

The journalist noted that Rosenhan never published any further work relating to his study's data, despite frequently indicating that he would do so. From her investigations, it seemed that Rosenhan's study might not have taken place in quite the manner he described. Significant doubts surround the claimed veracity of his so-called landmark findings.

that is statistically rare. However, rarity alone is insufficient. After all, many very positive traits and experiences are extremely rare. Also, certain mental 'illnesses', such as depression, are perhaps more common than they are rare, given that most people will feel profoundly sad, on occasion, at least at some point during their lives.

A second approach to defining 'abnormal' is to consider whether a person's condition causes distress. An immediate problem with this is that some problematic behaviours cause little or no immediate distress to the person themselves, but may cause distress for people around them. There is the danger, however, that allowing *others* to determine whether you are mad is, at the very least, unfair. It certainly raises the risk of discrimination, and of the pathologizing of innocuous behaviour in order to suppress dissent or perpetuate social power structures.

A third approach is to consider whether a person's behaviour or feeling is debilitating. In this context, a person may engage in a common behaviour that they find gratifying, but which might materially undermine their lives. If their behaviour denigrates their ability to be productive, to maintain relationships or to participate in society, then such behaviours might be deemed 'abnormal'. However, some people may not *want* to have jobs or relationships, or to be part of society. So in order to evaluate debilitation, we must establish whether the person's *wishes* are normal, bringing us back to square one (Hughes, 2016).

A fourth approach is to consider a person's compatibility with their surroundings. Behaviour is presumed to be 'abnormal' if it contradicts or disregards the conventions of the society in which a person lives. Failing to adhere to such norms will soon lead to life difficulties, albeit many of them resulting from the reactions of others.

In an effort to standardize the definition of insanity, and to classify its many manifestations, professional organizations have sought to prepare lengthy directories to guide clinicians in making diagnoses. The most prominent of these is the American Psychiatric Association's *Diagnostic and Statistical Manual of Mental Disorders* (DSM), first published in 1952 and now in its fifth edition (DSM-5; American Psychiatric Association, 2013). The manual evolved from census data gathered in American psychiatric hospitals. A global counterpart is Chapter V of the International Classification of Diseases (ICD), as produced by the World Health Organization (currently in its eleventh revision; World Health Organization, 2018).

These manuals, by design, represent an appeal to authority – they rely on expert advice to distil the available science in order to present the various classifications of mental illness. However, one of the reasons they require so many periodic updates is precisely the fact that the very definition of mental illness remains, forever, a social construction. This point can be highlighted by just a few of the diagnostic categories that have proven controversial:

- *Anxiety:* Up to 2013, DSM required a person to be *aware* that they had excessive anxiety in order to warrant a diagnosis. This prerequisite was removed in DSM-5. A person can now be diagnosed with clinical anxiety even if they feel their level of anxiety is proportionate to the challenges they face. One consequence is that it is now difficult to compare research on anxiety from before 2013 with research conducted since. The removal of self-awareness as a criterion greatly expands the subgroup of the population who can be diagnosed as clinically anxious.

- *Depression:* DSM-5 changed the definition of major depression, one of the most common of all mental illness diagnoses. Prior to 2013, DSM excluded a diagnosis if a person had been bereaved during the previous two months. DSM-5 now allows for a diagnosis during this period of grieving. As many people experience a major depressive episode after losing a loved one, the new approach leads to a diagnosis for a much greater number of people than was previously the case. Again, this means that it might not be easy to compare statistics on depression gathered before and after 2013.

- *Bulimia:* Prior to 2013, a bulimia diagnosis required the presence of binge eating at least twice a week, on average, for three months or more. In DSM-5, this was reduced to once a week. In other words, the threshold for diagnosis was reduced by half. Once again, the change in approach means that more people are now diagnosed. Modern research on bulimia, on which treatment will be based, will include people who would have been excluded from earlier studies. Previously, their behaviour would not have been severe enough to be considered 'abnormal'.

- *Transvestic disorder:* Formally, DSM considers this diagnosis to be warranted when a person's choice to cross-dress impairs functioning 'at work, in social situations, or in other important areas'. This means that a person can be diagnosed with a psychiatric condition on the basis of other people's reactions. It situates their distress as a pathology, rather than as a reasonable response to social stigmatization, transphobia or oppressive gender-policing.

- *Gender dysphoria:* This diagnosis is recommended for 'people whose gender at birth is contrary to the one they identify with'. A problem here is that it makes gender dysphoria a mental illness when it could just as easily be a physical one. After all, many people become distressed about aspects of their body, such as when they become terminally ill, without attracting a psychiatric diagnosis. A diagnosis of gender dysphoria seems to rest on an assessment of the *merit* of the distress being experienced.

The major medical directories of diagnostic criteria are revised on average once every ten years. Some people who were considered 'abnormal' a decade ago are now considered 'normal', whereas the opposite is also true. The task of taxonomizing mental illness remains very much unfinished.

Psychologists have been trying to define 'insanity' (or 'madness' or 'abnormality') for a very long time. The basic themes used to consider the issue today – *statistical frequency, distress, debilitation* and *norms* – all very closely resemble those discussed in psychology journals nearly a century ago (e.g. Moore, 1914; Skaggs, 1933; Wegrocki, 1938). And with the democratization of information flow in our digital world, such notions are increasingly debated by the general public too, with many non-psychologists now seeking positive language to describe their *own* mental states and challenges. However, despite all this effort, the concept of insanity has not yet yielded to consensus.

The irresolvability of the conundrum is telling. Despite a long history of consideration, our understanding of insanity – a notion profoundly fundamental to our overall appreciation of psychology – remains very much reliant on subjective judgement, opinion and feedback.

Madness, and thus sanity, is not defined. It is *negotiated*.

WHERE TO FROM HERE?

Notions of 'abnormal' (and 'normal') psychology reveal culture's template for human perfection. They are bound up in ideas about how humanity was formed and what people therefore *should* be like. This theme is frequently discussed in terms of there being a *purpose* to biological forms, such as being deliberately designed by a deity, or functionally shaped by processes of evolution. Theories of abnormality have often contrasted human beings with beasts of the wild, with many observers claiming that the insane were apt to behave like animals. And, of course, for millennia, human beings have been aware that ingesting intoxicants or suffering brain damage can result in bizarre changes in behaviour. In short, it has long been known that psychological madness is intertwined with physical biology.

Human beings are combinations of psychological and physical realities, and the link between the two is fundamental to our identity as a self-conscious species. Accordingly, the development of our understanding of psychology has been interwoven with that of the biological sciences. In our next chapter, we explore this very proposition: the idea that human beings are, fundamentally, biological animals, and that this naturalistic context is what governs and determines their psychological world.

DISCUSSION QUESTIONS

1. How might changes in social attitudes affect how we distinguish between normal and abnormal behaviour? Can you think of any examples?
2. A number of studies have suggested that it is possible for a 'sane' person to convince others that they are 'insane'. Is it therefore possible for *someone who is insane* to convince others that they are *sane*?
3. Has spirituality helped or hindered our understanding of mental illness?
4. Is the human impulse to decide for others how they should feel and behave itself psychologically healthy?

RECOMMENDED READING

- **Faria, M. A. (2013). Violence, mental illness, and the brain – A brief history of psychosurgery: Part 1 – From trephination to lobotomy.** *Surgical Neurology International, 4,* **49.** In this review, the author surveys the archaeological and historical records to show how brain surgery is among the oldest forms of surgery practised in medicine.
- **Houston, R. A. (2020). Asylums: The historical perspective before, during, and after.** *Lancet Psychiatry, 7,* **354–62.** In this essay, the author explores the many sides of asylum care during the development of modern psychiatry, including their successes as well as their failures.
- **Moore, S. J. (1914). The articulation of the concepts of normal and abnormal psychology.** *American Journal of Psychology, 25,* **283–7.** In this early academic article, the author attempts to set out the basis for distinguishing between 'normal' and 'abnormal' human behaviour, presenting arguments that continue to be used by psychologists when examining the issue today.

- **Porter, R. (1987).** *A Social History of Madness: The World through the Eyes of the Insane.* **New York: Weidenfeld & Nicolson.** In this book, the author presents a history of mental illness that focuses on the experiences of persons who were considered to be insane, in contrast to other histories that rely on the perspectives of psychiatrists, doctors and scientists.

BRAINS, EVOLUTION AND THE CONCEPT OF *HUMAN NATURE*

5

In this chapter, we will …

- reflect on how people came to recognize that human beings were biological machines
- evaluate the ways in which human beings saw relevance in brain anatomy, and how they sought to use these insights to explore each other's temperaments and personalities
- consider how the study of brain surgeries, brain injuries and electrical brain stimulation amounted to an experimental exploration of brain functioning
- trace the emergence of the scientific understanding of biological evolution, and its implications for our understanding of human psychology
- evaluate the way evolutionary ideas have been invoked to theorize about wider human affairs, including our social and political challenges
- consider the role of biological insights in framing the formal science of psychology

---

At the outset

Throughout the centuries, different civilizations have sought to explain psychological phenomena in terms of biological processes. The ancient Egyptians and the ancient Greeks were among those to speculate that the brain held a special place in determining people's thoughts and actions, either singly or in combination with other systems of the body. However, a full appreciation for the role of brain components was slow to emerge. For example, for many centuries, people thought that the interior gaps of the brain were more important than its tissue substance, as it was believed these spaces could be inhabited by spirits or souls.

Philosophical musings about brain substance led ultimately to a view that different parts of the brain served different purposes. The field of phrenology, whose practitioners attempted to infer the way different brain parts determined people's innate natures by examining the exteriors of their skulls, became highly popular around the world. Eventually, however, it was discovered that the exterior shape of human heads bore little relationship to the contours of the brains beneath. Instead, research interest sought to learn more about the diverse functions of different parts of the brain by examining the consequences of brain surgeries, injuries and electrical stimulation.

While some of this research was carried out on humans, much of it was conducted on animals, as it has long been recognized that human beings are themselves part of the animal kingdom. Before the nineteenth century, many different ideas had been proposed to explain how the various animal species, including humans, came to exist. Most of these theories presumed that humanity held a special place in nature and represented the pinnacle of all species. However, in the nineteenth century, a number of scientists began to conclude that all species emerged through biological evolution. Most prominently, Charles Darwin presented a theory explaining how all organisms are descendants of common ancestors, with speciation occurring as the result of evolution by natural and sexual selection.

Darwinian theory has had a profound effect on our understanding of human nature and thus on psychology. Some ancillary theories of psychology, such as social Darwinism, sociobiology and evolutionary psychology, have attempted to extend evolutionary thinking to social issues, cultural phenomena and fine-grained cognition. Such theories are often seen as controversial for political reasons. They are also scientifically very tentative.

By contrast, the primary theory of biological evolution by natural selection is one of the most corroborated explanatory models in the history of science and, in terms of accumulated evidence, occupies a similar status to the theory of gravitation or the theory that the earth orbits the sun. Overall, the biological approach to psychology has changed the way we understand the nature of human beings, bequeathing a myriad of methods, concepts, findings and as-yet-unresolved philosophical questions.

Key concept: Human nature

Human nature is a common term often used to refer to the fundamental traits and characteristics that define human beings. It is frequently summarized as that which represents 'what it means to be human'. The term can be controversial for many reasons, not least because it presupposes a universal norm for humanity. It suggests that all human beings can be described with reference to a single nature, implying that some forms of behaviour are potentially so abnormal as to be non-human. The term also requires us to distinguish that which occurs naturally in human beings from that which is imposed on people by society or culture, while at the same time recognizing both society and culture as intrinsically human constructs (and so, technically, as extensions of human nature).

Another complexity is that 'what it means to be human' might change over time. For example, prehistoric humans looked, behaved and (probably) thought differently to modern humans. Which of these versions of humanity better encapsulates the notion of 'human nature'? Also, humans will continue to evolve over the coming millennia. Is it therefore fair to presume that today's humans exhibit something we can describe as 'human nature'? It is certainly difficult to be definitive on these points. In this sense, it is difficult to see 'human nature' as normative – that is, to claim that the way human beings are now is the way they are 'supposed' to be.

One aspect of the concept of *human nature* that is seldom disputed is that it refers to those features, physical and psychological, that are innate, those attributes that arise naturally in human beings. This raises questions about where human beings fit in the broad panoply of nature itself. From this perspective, a discussion of 'human nature' is virtually impossible unless it is contextualized within the study of biology and of the wider animal kingdom.

HUMANS AS BIOLOGICAL MACHINES

In Chapter 2, we explored the many ways throughout history in which humans have tried to explain the connection between their minds and their bodies. While minds are seen as independently profound, bodies are also of special importance to psychology. They are the vessels that contain the mind or carry out its intentions. Even the most ardent dualist will understand that human bodies are functional organisms capable of autonomous action. Bodies are living things: they require refreshment, rest and – occasionally – repair. They experience pain when injured, fatigue when drained, and nausea when infected. Human bodies are composed of flesh and bones, just like those seen in animals. In short, notwithstanding the mysteries of consciousness or the self-regarding uniqueness of every person, when it comes down to it, human beings are, unmistakably, biological machines.

The rise of the brain

As discussed in Chapter 2, many ancient civilizations, such as the Egyptians, believed the heart to be the seat of the human psyche. The Egyptians also possessed detailed knowledge about the brain, having observed the effects of head injuries in wounded soldiers, but they saw it as playing a subordinate role in psychology. Most ancient Greek and Roman scholars before Plato retained a similar cardio-centric preference. Aristotle, for example, understood the brain was relevant but downplayed its importance, mainly because he was unimpressed by its greyish colour. Another factor was often alluded to by Roman poets: people could *feel* their hearts pumping inside their bodies, quickening and slowing in tune with their emotional states, whereas brains, by contrast, remained inscrutably silent, producing no superficial sensations that could be interpreted as signs of salience.

Plato's tripartite model proffered the brain as a complement to the heart, an organ that provided reason to balance the heart's emotionality (with a third organ, the gut, regulating desire). This broader whole-body perspective was an early example of how human psychology could be conceived of as biologically all-encompassing. Explaining and predicting behaviour would require a knowledge of *all* components of the body, including the respiratory, endocrine and cardiovascular systems.

This holism was echoed in Galen's second-century humoral model of psychology, itself derived from the medical work of Hippocrates (Jouanna, 2012). Galen suggested that human mood and well-being were influenced by the relative balance of various bodily fluids (or 'humours'), each contributing to specified patterns of behaviour and personality. The model identified psychological traits in terms of their underlying physiological causes (such as the characteristic of being 'sanguine', which Galen named after *sanguis*, the Latin word for blood). But, as we saw in Chapter 2, Galen's research – including his many vivisectionist animal experiments – ultimately led him to see the brain as critically important. Further anatomical analyses led him to also highlight the spinal cord, because it helped the brain to communicate its intentions to the rest of the body.

Nonetheless, for centuries, even the basics of brain function were very poorly understood. Guided by an animistic attachment to souls and spirits, scholars felt that the brain's inner cavities were more pertinent than its material substance. The brain was viewed as a hollow container, rather than an organ with its own purpose. The anatomy of the brain was known to contain three such spaces, called *ventricles*, and it was long believed that these were the gaps in which human spirits resided.

This fascination with the ventricles continued right up to the Renaissance. The sixteenth-century Flemish anatomist Andries van Wesel (1514–64) – more commonly known by his Latinized name, Andreas Vesalius – produced several detailed anatomical drawings of the human brain, each focusing specifically on the function of a different ventricle. Vesalius considered the ventricles not just as slots for the soul, but as areas where differentiated psychological activities would be performed: he wrote that the front ventricle was responsible for common sense, the middle ventricle contained rational thought, and the posterior ventricle was where memories were stored. The idea that human psychological activities might be performed separately by different brain components started to take shape.

Descartes too was fascinated by the brain's various contours and cavities. But while he had thought about specific brain substances in his theorizing on the mind–body problem, he only really singled out the pineal gland, a tiny nub little more than the size of a pea. To him the rest of the brain remained largely inert and mysterious. By contrast, Descartes's thoughts on the role of the broader nervous system were well ahead of their time. Consistent with his mechanistic explanations for animal autonomy, he understood that reflexes could cause body movements without requiring a person to experience conscious volition or thought. The way the body could engage in at least *some* actions without directly involving brain function showed how complex the link between biology and behaviour actually was. (Descartes's observation that one part of the body could apparently act *in sympathy* with another was to be the origin of the term 'sympathetic nervous system'.)

From the seventeenth century, attention began to turn away from ventricles, and towards the very substance of brain tissue itself. The English physician Thomas Willis (whose callous approach to treating mental illness we encountered in Chapter 4) became renowned as an expert on brain anatomy. He produced an influential book, *Cerebri anatome* (1664), which featured minutely detailed diagrams beautifully rendered by acclaimed architect Christopher Wren, the designer of London's baroque St Paul's Cathedral, one of the city's most prominent landmarks even to this day. Willis distinguished the different layers of brain tissue in terms of their appearance. While the outer layer, or 'cortex' (Latin for *bark* or *crust*), was indeed grey, the inner parts of the brain were composed of a more whiteish matter. Willis correctly concluded that it was the cortex that controlled cognition and voluntary movement.

Willis identified and named several separate brain components, and his system for numbering cranial nerves continues to be used by modern anatomists. He observed that the ventricles were never actually empty, and highlighted the importance of the cerebrospinal fluid they contained. He also established that blood flowed inside the brain, debunking previous claims that it was a 'bloodless organ'.

Consideration of the wider nervous system flourished in succeeding centuries, with important discoveries relating to the reflex arc, the spinal cord, and communication within and between the neurons that made up the nervous system. However, notwithstanding a long history of recognizing how whole-body systems play a role in the biological aspects of behaviour, it was the brain that became the organ of domineering interest to psychologists from the nineteenth century onwards.

Indeed, many nineteenth-century ideas about the brain proved so impactful that they continue to remain influential in science and society today.

Unfortunately, however, many of these ideas, while lasting, were demonstrably – and dangerously – inaccurate.

CHARTING THE BRAIN

Perhaps the biggest breakthroughs in nineteenth-century brain science were driven by the emerging belief in 'brain localization', the idea that discrete psychological functions were controlled by different parts, or 'locations', of the brain. Anatomists began to turn their attention to the precise structures of brains, aiming to clarify how anatomical complexities – and relative sizes – would correlate with intellectual powers. We will see in Chapter 6 how, for a time, the calculation of brain size became a target of intense scientific effort, as a (dubious) way of classifying the different types of human beings around the world. But with regard to localization of function, it was comparing the relative sizes of different *parts* of the individual brain that drove theoretical innovation.

The focus on localization was in part stimulated by developments in theology and philosophy. In an effort to define those parts of psychology that would be appropriate for secular study (by not threatening the religious view that human souls were sacred), nineteenth-century philosophers drew on the earlier arguments of a group of prominent Scottish thinkers, including Thomas Reid (1710–96), Adam Ferguson (1723–1816) and James Beattie (1735–1803). These philosophers had become noted for their ideas on 'common-sense realism', which offered an alternative to the metaphysical claim that reality was

Public domain, via Wikimedia Commons

Image 5.1 Phrenology
Phrenologists claimed to have identified the specific function of each part of the brain.

somehow arbitrary. Contrary to what Descartes had argued – that our perception of the world might be just an illusion – the common-sense realists proposed that the superficial insights of human minds were in fact trustworthy. They saw human beings as quite capable of accurately appreciating the nature of the world around them. Their work involved explicitly enumerating the innate capacities of human minds, such as judgement, attention, compassion, memory and perception, intellectual capabilities that they referred to as *faculties.*

This philosophical approach was welcomed by those in society who wished to discourage scepticism and dissent. It helped to offset devious enquiries into the true nature of abstract concepts like souls, sin and heaven. By provoking people to trust 'common experience', anything contrary to 'common sense' – such as heretical secularism – could be dismissed as absurd. This made common-sense realism attractive to many scholars (and institutions), who welcomed its focus on human intellectual faculties.

From skull bumps to psychology

The popularization of 'faculty psychology' undoubtedly affected those scientists who were studying the anatomy of human brains. A particularly important example of its influence can be seen in the work of Franz Joseph Gall (1758–1828), a German physician and neuroanatomist based in Vienna, who produced a number of innovative methods, discoveries and theories.

Gall was instrumental in developing refined approaches to brain dissection in autopsy, preferring to tease apart individual brain fibres rather than employ the random slicing that had characterized previous methods (C. Colbert, 1997). He was able to study entire brains in detail, showing how the two halves of the brain were connected by white matter that allowed signals to pass from one side of the brain to the other. Having compared human brains to brains from a wide variety of animals, he convincingly suggested that higher mental functions were related to brain size and cortical complexity. He also noted that brain injuries were frequently found in people who had mental deficiencies, even in those with relatively mild symptoms.

However, a number of Gall's theoretical interpretations were grounded in some very poor reasoning. His initial assumptions were reminiscent of faculty psychology in attempting to subdivide the human mind into a plethora of discrete intellectual attributes. But in pursuing this approach, Gall latched onto a theoretical paradigm that, while having an appearance of scientific robustness, was actually full of logical holes. Gall referred to his approach as *cranioscopy* because it involved the direct visual inspection (or scoping) of a person's skull (or cranium). However, even in Gall's time it was better known as – and today is better remembered as – the practice of *phrenology.*

Gall's method was premised on three core assumptions: (a) that each mental faculty was the preserve of a different part of the brain; (b) that the more pronounced each faculty was, the larger that part of the brain would become; and (c) that the relative sizes of all the brain's various parts would be reflected in the contours of the skull that encased it. In the belief that all three premises held true, Gall then theorized that a *living* person's psychological traits could be profiled by closely examining the shapes of their heads. In other words, what were tentative theories regarding brain localization were soon appropriated into a quick and easy personality test.

Gall was not a philosopher, and the means by which he developed his theory were often incidental. After he encountered a female patient who was alleged to have had an unusually high sex drive, he concluded that her relatively broad neck was related to the shape of her brain. He declared that the faculty of 'amativeness' was governed by the rear part of the brain nearest the neck, and that anybody who has a bulge in this area of their skulls was sure to have excessive libido.

Gall did not confine his theoretical observations to patients, but would draw conclusions based on a wide range of people he encountered in daily life. For example, when distracted by the young boys he hired to perform domestic errands, he drew the conclusion that those most prone to petty crime had slight bulges on the sides of their heads. He duly defined the part of the brain just above the ears as the area of 'acquisitiveness'.

Based almost entirely on this type of casual observation, Gall identified dozens of different brain areas and their associated faculties, which he categorized into six groups: *propensities*; *sentiments*; *intellectual faculties*; *external senses*; *perceptive faculties*; and *reflective faculties*. He attempted to contextualize his theories within elaborate explanations of the origins of human nature, and the distinction between humans and animals. His copious writings elaborated on a range of psychological topics, including sensation, education, emotion, gender differences and criminal culpability. He truly saw his work as representing a complete psychology of human beings.

One of the most striking aspects of phrenology was the fact that it became enormously popular with the general public. This was not least because of relentless advertising of its merits by several advocates. The Scottish lawyer George Combe (1788–1858) promoted phrenology throughout the English-speaking world, simplifying its principles in a manner that proved digestible to the everyday reader. His book, *The Constitution of Man Considered in Relation to External Objects* (1828), sold a remarkable 300,000 copies. The frenzy of interest it attracted brought Combe into contact with all quarters of society. The sitting British monarch, Queen Victoria, summoned him to 'read' the skulls of her children, and during a visit to the United States, Combe was also consulted by President John Quincy Adams (Tomlinson, 1997).

Gall's German collaborator Johann Spurzheim (1776–1832) travelled widely to defend phrenology, speaking at events in Britain and the United States. It was Spurzheim who popularized the term 'phrenology' to describe Gall's method, drawing on the Greek word *phrēn* (or 'mind'). After Spurzheim contracted typhoid and died while in Boston in 1832, his own brain and skull were retrieved during autopsy and placed on public display (the coroner remarked that his skull was 'larger than the average' due to the 'immense weight' of his brain). Such was the popularity of phrenology at this time that Spurzheim was afforded an elaborate public funeral, at which a congregation of 3,000 Bostonians listened to the city's bells toll for a full hour. The Boston Medical Association declared Spurzheim's death to be nothing less than 'a calamity to mankind' (A. A. Walsh, 1972).

Later in the nineteenth century, three American siblings, Orson Squire Fowler (1809–87), Lorenzo Niles Fowler (1811–96) and Charlotte Fowler Wells (1814–1901) promoted phrenology with considerable zeal, pursuing it as a lucrative commercial venture. They toured the country to give lectures, established innumerable phrenology magazines, set up a publisher devoted to printing phrenology books, and opened city-centre phrenology offices in New York and Philadelphia. Most famously, the Fowlers cast thousands of ceramic busts on which the various phrenological areas were inscribed. These busts became widely sought after in the nineteenth century. (Indeed, they continue to be produced and sold today, although are now more likely to be desired as vintage-style ornaments rather than as medically accurate reference tools.)

It is difficult to overstate the ubiquity of phrenology in mid-nineteenth-century Europe and North America. There were phrenological societies in nearly every town and city, with nearly thirty in London alone by the 1840s (Staum, 2003). Phrenology was a widely recognized service, one that was often available from trained medical professionals. It was not uncommon for a travelling phrenologist to arrive at a town to provide readings or to give a lecture. At times, the audiences at such talks would be seeking entertainment rather than education (Leaney, 2006). However, there is little doubt that whatever scepticism was voiced by the scientific community was quickly disregarded by thousands of willing and eager consumers.

That said, scientific criticism of phrenology emerged almost immediately. Many of Gall's own contemporaries felt his approach to theory-building was extremely haphazard. One problem related to Gall's choice of faculties, which was seen to be arbitrary. For example, subtle distinctions were made between some faculties, such as *amativeness* (the seeking of sex) and *philoprogenitiveness* (the drive to procreate), whereas other faculties, such as *love of life*, were left extremely broad and therefore open to many different interpretations.

Another problem related to Gall's over-reliance on confirmatory evidence, where he would emphasize cases that were consistent with phrenology while dismissing (or refusing to even acknowledge) cases that seemed to contradict its claims. The door to confirmation bias was opened further by the vagueness of many phrenological terms, which allowed phrenologists to interpret traits in a multiplicity of ways. As we saw in Chapter 1, confirmation bias – latching onto confirmatory evidence rather than seeking and testing possible contradictions – is a form of fallacious reasoning and a marker of pseudoscience.

But perhaps the biggest problems for phrenology related to its fundamental biological premises. Chief among these was the simple fact that the shape of a human skull does *not*, in fact, conform to the shape of the brain lying underneath it. Once this anatomical reality was demonstrated, little could be done to retrieve any merit for phrenology. Its most famous aspect – that of scrutinizing the surface shape of heads in order to evaluate psychological traits – was found to be pointless. It was clear that phrenologists *could not* correctly examine the shape of a brain by examining the surface of a head. This meant that phrenology could not possibly work, and that its reputation must be based on faulty reasoning, self-delusion or wishful thinking.

Evidence for the alleged relationships between traits and brains was also lacking. There was never any evidence to substantiate phrenology's claims that its particular array of human faculties was an accurate way to depict human nature; *or* that any particular phrenological faculty was really associated with its purported brain area; *or* that the size of a brain part systematically revealed the intensity of whatever psychological attribute might be associated with it.

For good measure, scientists were not the only group to publicly criticize phrenology. The field was also condemned by some religious figures, including the pope, who added Combe's *Constitution of Man* to the church's list of banned books (as reported anonymously in an 1836 issue of *Phrenological Journal and Miscellany*; Anonymous, 1836). And as phrenological principles were commonly cited to support racial and gender stereotypes, many humanitarians recoiled at the field's apparently prejudicial undertones.

Today, phrenology is recognized as having been a pseudoscience – a field that aspired to be a science, but which fell far short of the quality standards that scientific reasoning demands (Hughes, 2016). Nonetheless, at a time of burgeoning popular interest in the sciences, and buoyed by new technologies of mass communication, the nineteenth-century fad of phrenology left a strong impression on the public consciousness. Not all of this influence was without worth.

As with many historical pseudosciences, phrenology was valuable in helping scientists to refine their methods and in highlighting the importance of empirical rigour. Flaws such as confirmation bias are not always obvious, and even proficient scientists frequently succumbed to them. Pseudosciences were often important test beds for science in that, over time, they revealed the pitfalls of sloppy reasoning. Phrenology, with its extremely high profile, was certainly a case in point.

Phrenology encouraged ordinary people to accept that a scientific approach could be applied to the study of human minds. It introduced the possibility of scientific psychology to a mainstream audience. Notwithstanding the error of its content, the *premise* of brain localization was not a terrible idea. Nor was the concept of attempting to measure the brain by scrutinizing the surface of the skull. In an era long before the development of any kind of brain imaging technology, this practical attempt to visualize the live human brain in three dimensions was innovative, albeit ill-fated.

Phrenology's error was not in positing localization per se, but in promoting a complex model of localization that, in its details, was almost entirely inaccurate. Its ultimate failure, however, was not bad anatomy, but bad science. Its reliance on confirmatory evidence ensured that it was unable to recognize, or to correct, its mistakes. Few sciences survive if they are unable to filter out falsehoods.

HISTORY IN STORIES: *ADVENTURES OF HUCKLEBERRY FINN* (1885)

Adventures of Huckleberry Finn (Twain, 1885) is a classic novel by the American writer and humourist Mark Twain (1835–1910). It tells the story of a young teenage boy, Huckleberry 'Huck' Finn, who becomes destitute in rural Missouri, in the United States, in the mid-nineteenth century. Huck is a young person of wit and integrity, always anxious to do the right thing, and suitably sceptical towards charlatanism and deceit.

Much of the novel depicts Huck's efforts to assist his friend Jim to travel north in order to escape slavery. However, while attempting to raft northward on the Mississippi river, harsh conditions force the boys astray, and they end up drifting further south instead. At one point they encounter two suspicious men, who introduce themselves, implausibly, as a duke and a king. The men later kidnap Jim with the intention of making money by offering him for sale to the local townspeople as a slave.

But before this happens, Huck is forthright in assessing the characters of the so-called Duke and King, recognizing them as 'low-down humbugs and frauds' (p. 125), travelling swindlers who make their way in life by ripping people off in each town they visit.

It is interesting to note how Twain depicted these nineteenth-century charlatans. They carried with them advertising leaflets that described their many dubious services, including finding gold through divination and 'dissipating witch spells'. The Duke's business leaflets stated that he would occasionally 'lecture on the Science of Phrenology' (p. 128) and offer the public personalized phrenological charts for twenty-five cents apiece. The Duke explains that he is quite happy to 'take a turn' at phrenology, other forms of mesmerism, or 'most anything that comes handy, so it ain't work' (p. 121).

This tone echoed Twain's references to phrenology in his earlier novel, *The Adventures of Tom Sawyer* (1876), in which one character was described as so enthralled by 'phrenological frauds' that 'all the solemn ignorance they were inflated with was breath to her nostrils' (p. 73). When a phrenologist visited the community, they were said to have 'left the village duller and drearier than ever' (p. 124).

In fact, Twain made several derogatory references to phrenology throughout his written work. Like the fictional character Huck, Twain himself had witnessed phrenologists visiting his rural village when he was a child, and had long suspected that their services were less than scientifically robust.

While spending time in London as an adult in the early 1870s, Twain sought to conduct his own scientific test of phrenology (Finger, 2019). He visited none other than Lorenzo Niles Fowler himself, who at the time was offering phrenological readings in Britain. At first he presented himself to Fowler anonymously, without revealing he was in fact Mark Twain, the internationally famous writer. Fowler examined Twain's cranium and produced a detailed phrenological chart. A few months later, Twain returned for a second reading, hoping that Fowler would not recognize him from his first visit.

On this occasion, Twain introduced himself triumphantly, and handed Fowler his business card to make sure that he was fully aware of his identity. Fowler was noticeably impressed to examine such a distinguished client and produced a new phrenological chart, clearly not remembering having seen this skull before.

When Twain later compared the two charts that he had been given by Fowler, he could immediately see that they were wildly divergent and even contradictory. Although both were based on Twain's skull, Fowler had proceeded to draw vividly different conclusions about Twain's personality and temperament depending on whether he knew who he was. In several of his writings, Twain would later allude to these encounters with Fowler, expressing dismay at how the commercial practice of phrenology was so shabbily deceitful. In *Adventures of Huckleberry Finn*, Twain had the King tell Huck that his own abilities at reading people's personalities were 'pretty good', but only when he had 'got somebody along to find out the facts for [him]' beforehand (p. 128).

As well as revealing phrenology's poor test–retest reliability, Twain's dual visits to Fowler showed how erroneous phrenological readings can be. During the first visit, when Twain had presented himself anonymously, Fowler had concluded that a particular crevice in Twain's cranium revealed a 'total absence of the sense of humour' (Twain, 1906, p. 336). In fact, according to Fowler, the man before him was entirely 'destitute of the sense of humour', and that the evidence for this was 'overwhelming, satisfying, convincing, incontrovertible' (p. 337).

This was more than a little ironic, given that Twain was, even then, widely acclaimed as being one of the leading humourist writers of his time. If phrenology had even the slightest merit, surely one of its leading exponents would have been able to detect Twain's prodigious talent for humour, rather than conclude that no such talent at all – not even a modicum – was present.

LOGOPHILIA: 'PHILOPROGENITIVENESS'

Philoprogenitiveness refers to the love of progeny, which in turn relates either to a fondness for one's own children *or* a particular liking for the process of producing them. A person with a lot of philoprogenitiveness would be an especially dedicated parent. The word is derived from a mix of Greek (*philo-*, meaning 'love') and Latin (*progignere*, meaning 'to produce offspring'). However,

while based on terms that are often used in science, the concept of philoprogenitiveness was
invented by phrenologists and is used exclusively
with reference to phrenology.

In phrenology, a half-inch-long brain area just
above the cerebellum was the location that indi-
cated a person's philoprogenitiveness. People who
were especially dedicated to their children would
be said to possess a bulge in this part of their
skull. According to one phrenologist writer, 'The
facts in proof of this location of the organ are very
numerous, and may be multiplied daily by observation' (S. Jones, 1836, p. 47). These 'facts'

included a notable gender difference, where
women purportedly exhibited bigger philoprogenitiveness bumps than men. And both Gall and
Spurzheim claimed to have observed reduced
philoprogenitiveness bulges in women who had
been convicted for infanticide.

After it was shown that skull bumps were
uncorrelated with underlying brain morphology,
phrenological theories lost their credibility.
Accordingly, despite once being common, references to 'philoprogenitiveness' virtually disappeared from the scholarly literature in the late
nineteenth century.

Cutting the brain

One consequence of the public fascination with phrenology was to make mainstream physiologists ever more determined to use scientifically rigorous methods when investigating the brain.
In their eyes, the claims of phrenology were simply preposterous, its methods fanciful, and its
success a stark illustration of how scientific illiteracy could addle the general population. In

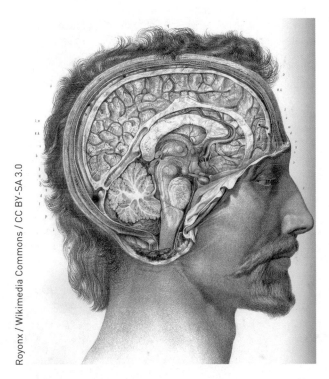

Royonx / Wikimedia Commons / CC BY-SA 3.0

Image 5.2 Nineteenth-century brain anatomy
Representation of the human brain by the celebrated anatomist
J. M. Bourgery (c. 1840).

France, where research in physiology
was strong, the scientific community
became particularly exercised by this
problem. They frequently discussed
their ordinary research in terms of how
it contrasted with phrenological
pseudoscience.

Many of these scientists worked in
hospitals and colleges in Paris, combining medical research with investigations of botany, palaeontology,
zoology and neurophysiology. This
blend of natural sciences helped scientists to refine their understanding of
how different parts of brain anatomy
were associated with physical and sensory functions across different species.
A common research approach was
based on the practice of *ablation*,
which involved surgically removing –
or irreversibly damaging – a specific
organ or part of the brain. This
method showed how various organs

had specialized functions. For example, in several species, the semicircular canals – ducts located deep in the inner ear – were found to be integral to the maintenance of posture and balance. When they were damaged or extracted, an animal would be unable to properly move or stay upright.

A number of French scientists were pioneers of this type of ablation research, but many of the most significant studies were conducted by the precocious young physician Jean Pierre Flourens (1794–1867). Flourens had been particularly unimpressed by phrenology and resolved to study the brain using proper science. He published a series of studies that directly tested Gall's hypotheses, in animals, targeting specific brain areas. His findings suggested that the phrenological model was false in just about every detail.

For example, Gall had concluded that the cerebellum, part of the hindbrain in vertebrates, was the brain's 'area of amativeness'. However, Flourens showed that when this part of the brain was ablated in dogs, the primary outcome was a denigration of the animal's coordinated muscular movements, such as its ability to walk. Further ablation research showed that the cerebellum is in fact primarily associated with motor control (i.e. the regulation of movement) and had little or no role in sexual responsiveness. Similar studies of other parts of the brain cast further doubt on the phrenological model.

Gall was aware of this research but questioned its validity on a number of grounds (Eling & Finger, 2019). He felt that the use of ablation in pigeons, dogs, hens and rabbits offered a poor approximation of what would happen in humans, and noted – with some justification – that efforts to ablate specific brain areas would invariably create collateral damage to other parts of the brain as well, thereby complicating our ability to interpret any specific findings. For good measure, Gall also sought to stigmatize ablation research, by drawing attention to its inherent maltreatment of animals. According to Gall, this research produced nothing more than unwarranted 'pain' and 'mutilation' (Gall, 1825).

Inferences from brain injury

Perhaps partly misled by the relative coarseness of his ablation methods, Flourens concluded that most of the brain operated as a single harmonious unit, rather than a complex network of specialized brain areas. It was only as alternative research approaches progressed that scientists began to illustrate the specific separateness of brain functions. Even in the nineteenth century, ethical standards forbade the use of ablation techniques with humans. However, from time to time, as the ancient Egyptians had discovered thousands of years previously, human beings would indeed accidentally injure their own brains. A careful scientific analysis of what happens next would at least *resemble* something of an ablation study.

One of Gall's own students, the Parisian doctor Jean-Baptiste Bouillaud (1796–1881) became dismissive of most of his mentor's phrenological views. As a physician, he felt that a good way to investigate such matters would be to examine the symptoms of injured patients. His son-in-law and medical collaborator Ernest Aubertin (1825–93) soon encountered precisely such a patient, a wounded soldier who had survived a gunshot to the head and who exhibited a rather strange symptom. Whenever his head wound was pressed, the poor soldier was rendered speechless. Despite clearly attempting to do so, he was no longer able to talk. The gunshot wound seemed to serve as a kind of switch, capable of disabling the soldier's linguistic capacity, but without causing any other discernible psychological or physical effect. It was as though language ability, on its own, was being disrupted. Aubertin concurred with his father-in-law regarding the overall weakness of phrenology, but he retained a belief that at least one psychological function – *language* – was likely to be localized within the brain.

It is useful to remember that, in the mid-1800s, the communication of scientific findings was often a slow and sporadic process. Much depended on word-of-mouth channels and personal contact. Scientific meetings, at which groups of researchers could come together to listen to presentations about each other's work, were highly important. When Aubertin described his patient at a meeting of Paris's Anthropological Society in 1861, it proved to be a very auspicious occasion. In the audience was another prodigious physician with an interest in the potential of brain localization, professor at the University of Paris Medical School and accomplished anatomist Paul Broca (1824–80).

The very next week, one of Broca's own patients – a man who for twenty-one years had been unable to talk, despite no physical injury to his vocal system – died from a terminal illness. The patient, a craftsman, had endured lifelong epilepsy. After one seizure had rendered him permanently speechless, he entered hospital, where he would spend the next two decades. He soon acquired the nickname 'Tan', on the basis that 'tan' was the syllable he would utter over and over again whenever he tried to talk. After Tan died, Broca arranged for his brain to be examined and for the results to be presented at another meeting of the Anthropological Society. Sure enough, in line with Aubertin's theories, Tan was found to have had a small injury in the left frontal hemisphere of his brain. In describing this finding, Broca declared that he had discovered the brain's cortical speech centre.

Over the succeeding years, Broca autopsied many more brains of patients with speech loss symptoms, and he consistently found similar damage to the same region of the frontal lobe. This area of the brain is now referred to as 'Broca's area', and the language dysfunction caused when this area is damaged is called 'Broca's aphasia'.

A similar line of reasoning led another investigator to make a parallel discovery. The German anatomist Carl Wernicke (1848–1905) was a specialist in *paraphasias*, errors of language production that were commonly seen in patients with head injuries. Inspired by Broca's research, Wernicke conducted similar analyses and concluded that a separate part of the brain close to Broca's area was involved in auditory memory and so played an important role in language.

However, unlike Broca's area, which governed the patient's ability to initiate speech, this other area – 'Wernicke's area' – was involved in the semantics of language. A patient with injuries to Broca's area would be unable to talk, despite seeming able to compose and comprehend statements in their minds. In contrast, a person with an injury to Wernicke's area would indeed be able to *talk*, but they would be unable to control what words would come out of their mouths. Unable to articulate correct sentences to express their thoughts, they would instead produce a stream of fluent but nonsensical language. Somewhere between intention and articulation, the sentences they wanted to utter would become jumbled.

A person with Broca's aphasia would not be able to speak. A person with Wernicke's aphasia, while able to speak, would not be able *to make sense*. Broca's and Wernicke's areas appeared to relate to two distinct aspects of language: production and comprehension.

As we saw in Chapter 1, the late nineteenth and early twentieth centuries were also the time when physiologists such as Pavlov (and others) were beginning to grapple with the concept of learned responding. Before long, researchers began to use ablation to investigate if the learning of responses might itself be controlled by a localized brain area. In experiments on cats, the American psychologist Shepherd Ivory Franz (1874–1933) showed that lesions to the brain's frontal lobe were particularly disruptive to learning. Animals that had undergone standard laboratory training lost the ability to produce learned responses after that part of their brain was ablated.

Importantly, Franz showed that in many cases ablated animals were able to *relearn* a lost response if they underwent training again. The finding suggested that learning was not restricted to one area of the brain, but could in fact take place in many different areas. Further, as brain tissue remains destroyed after ablation, the learning could only recur if other, *surviving* tissue took up the role. This effect echoed something that had previously been predicted by Gall. Gall had incorporated such 'possibility of substitution' into his phrenology, after observing that children were more likely than adults to recover function following brain injury. The ability of brain tissue to assume functions that had previously been carried out by other tissue was to become known as *brain plasticity*.

ALMOST FAMOUS: LOUIS LEBORGNE

While the patient 'Tan' became renowned, with his brain now preserved for posterity in a Parisian museum, the person behind the patient – 'Monsieur Leborgne' – was ignored for more than 150 years. In many history books, it was simply assumed that the otherwise nondescript Tan must have been a vagrant or an illiterate with no education, whose socio-economic hardship, and perhaps even venereal disease, had contributed to his poor health.

It wasn't until 2011 that a Polish academic studied the relevant archives, searching for Leborgne's death certificate and other documents in order to uncover biographical details about this patient. He was first to discover Leborgne's actual birthplace, and from this could trace information about his early life (Domanski, 2013).

Louis Victor Leborgne was born in 1809 in Moret-sur-Loing, a village just south of Paris, located in the picturesque region of France that inspired Monet, Renoir and other impressionist painters. His father was a schoolteacher, and his uncle worked as a local winemaker. During his youth he experienced epileptic seizures, but eventually Leborgne secured employment as a craftsman in the city, producing 'forms', or model feet, that shoemakers used to shape shoes and boots. At the age of thirty, he suddenly lost the power of speech. As he hadn't recovered after three months, he was admitted to Paris's Bicêtre Hospital. Being unmarried, he could not be released to the care of close relatives and so would remain in the hospital for the rest of his life.

After a decade of hospitalization, he developed gradual paralysis of the right side of his body. His limited mobility eventually caused him to develop gangrene in his paralysed limbs. Having spent twenty-one years in the main ward of the hospital, Leborgne's health deteriorated and in 1861 he was transferred to the surgical ward. It was there he was placed under the observation of the renowned physician Paul Broca, who was intrigued by the patient's strange speech pattern. Six days later, he died.

The town of Moret-sur-Loing included several tanneries, known in French language as *moulin à tan*. It is possible that Leborgne was reminiscing about his childhood when his attempts to speak could produce no more than repetitions of the syllable 'tan'. It was this speech pattern that so interested Broca, and which served as key evidence in support of his theories of brain localization.

Contrary to the standard assumptions about Tan that had persisted for more than 150 years, the archives in fact revealed that Leborgne had come from an economically secure background and had enjoyed a healthy upbringing. Further investigations showed that his sister was able to sign her own name on her marriage certificate, a critical detail suggesting that the Leborgne family – including Louis – were literate, and thus at least partially educated. Leborgne was a skilled craftsman, and at least some of his surviving siblings had professional occupations.

A century and a half after becoming one of medicine's most famous case studies, the mysterious Monsieur Leborgne was finally recognized for who he was as a person. 'Tan' had finally become Louis.

Stimulating the brain

Electricity had long been recognized as a force of nature, but for hundreds of years it remained a scientific curiosity. All this changed in the late nineteenth century. While innovators such as Michael Faraday had developed electric motors as early as the 1820s, the late nineteenth century was when electricity finally became mainstream. It was a period of several lasting inventions that placed electricity at the centre of modern life: the alternating-current (AC) motor; the dynamo; the transformer; arc welding; electric railways; electric streetlights; the escalator; the 'moving picture' projector; the gramophone; the motor-driven vacuum cleaner; the wireless telegraph; the telephone; and, of course, the incandescent lightbulb.

It was perhaps only a matter of time before researchers experimented with passing electrical currents through brains. In a makeshift home laboratory in Berlin, Germany, in 1870, two physiologists, Gustav Fritsch (1838–1927) and Eduard Hitzig (1839–1907), probed the exposed cortexes of a number of dogs, applying mild electrical currents to different areas of their brains. Using this method, Fritsch and Hitzig established that stimulating a specific strip of brain tissue running from the top of the head towards the ear caused involuntary muscle movements in different parts of a dog's body. Notably, stimulating this area on the left side of a dog's brain caused movements on the right side of its body, and vice versa. When they published their findings, Fritsch and Hitzig memorably referred to this property as the 'excitability' of the brain (Fritsch & Hitzig, 1870).

Fritsch and Hitzig's findings caught the attention of scientists around Europe. Among those particularly intrigued was David Ferrier (1843–1928), the director of a research laboratory attached to a psychiatric hospital in Yorkshire. During his medical training, Ferrier had briefly spent time visiting von Helmholtz's sensory perception laboratory in Heidelberg, but his professional career was to see him specialize in epilepsy and neurological diseases. Neurologists were particularly interested in the possibilities of electrical brain stimulation, as the muscular contractions reported by Fritsch and Hitzig seemed to resemble the effects of epileptic seizures. In his rural Yorkshire laboratory, Ferrier conducted extensive experiments on rabbits, guinea pigs and dogs. Later he conducted experiments in London, on macaque monkeys.

In what today would be seen as a brutal research programme, Ferrier combined electrical stimulation techniques with ablation across a range of different animals. He was able to show that all such animals had mappable brain cortexes, with separate areas for initiating movement, for regulating sensation and for coordinating vision and hearing. Moreover, he showed that these areas tended to be distributed in a similar layout across all brains, whatever the species. These findings brought Ferrier international acclaim, but they also made him a target for protests by the newly emerging animal rights movement, horrified at the use of such vivisection for psychology research. In 1881, he received a summons accusing him of 'frightful and shocking' cruelty in his research on monkeys, becoming the first scientist to be tried under Britain's Cruelty to Animals Act. The case fell, on the basis that it was not Ferrier himself who performed the experimental surgeries, but a fully licensed and certified animal surgeon (Pedlar, 2003).

It was well into the twentieth century before there was a comprehensive effort to conduct similar research on humans. In pioneering investigations starting in the 1930s, the Canadian neurosurgeon Wilder Penfield (1891–1976) electrically stimulated live exposed human brains in an effort to refine a new treatment for epilepsy. It had long been noted that many people with epilepsy were prone to experience unusual sensations, or 'auras', just prior to having a seizure. Such auras might involve an unexpected and unwarranted sense of euphoria or a strange experiential feeling, such as déjà vu. Penfield theorized that were he able to use electrical stimulation techniques to find the part of the brain that triggered a patient's aura-feelings, he could then attempt to ablate these 'aura spots' in order to prevent the onset of a seizure.

The research required innovative surgery to safely expose a patient's cortex and then, while they were still fully conscious, to set about systematically applying mild electrical currents across the surface of their brain. The patient would report whatever feeling resulted from each stimulation, allowing Penfield to systematically trace the location within the cortex that triggered an aura. Ultimately the research was successful, in that ablating such aura spots did indeed reduce the frequency of subsequent seizures. However, the research also produced a more profound outcome. By systematically recording all the patients' responses, Penfield had accumulated a wealth of information about what happened when *all* parts of their cortexes were stimulated.

Penfield confirmed that stimulating a brain's motor area precipitated movements on the opposite side of a patient's body. He showed that applying a current to a sensory area caused the patient to experience a physical sensation, such as a feeling of being touched, again on the body's opposite side. Stimulating the visual area of the brain made the patient 'see' lights that were not actually there, and electrifying the auditory area caused them to 'hear' imaginary noises. More intriguingly, Penfield noted that stimulating certain parts of the brain revived detailed memories of often mundane events, while doing so to other parts would elicit complex and colourful hallucinations. Other stimulations would interfere with the patient's sense of why things were happening, causing them to suddenly interpret their surroundings in new ways. At other times, stimulating a particular brain area would elicit the feeling of being in a vivid dream, or a sudden flashback memory.

However, as Penfield himself ultimately emphasized, none of this stimulation seemed to trigger the truly profound human emotions, such as the feeling of *wanting* something, of *making a decision*, or of *having a belief*. For Penfield, the brain was a complex psychological organ, but it did not easily represent the completeness of the 'mind' (Penfield, 1975).

By and large, electrical stimulation confirmed the picture that had been emerging from superficial studies of brain anatomy, but with far greater detail. The human brain was found to be an organic cluster of interweaving components, whose capacities were distributed in a modular fashion according to a broadly common layout seen in all healthy people. There was some evidence that when the brain was young and still developing, functions could relocate to different areas of brain tissue if the need arose. And there was clear evidence that the human brain, while performing operations that epitomized much of what the psychology of human nature itself comprised, was essentially a variation of the brain that was seen in other animal species. The psychology of humanity was shown to overlap, in fundamental ways, with that of non-humans.

HISTORICALLY (IN)ACCURATE?: SPLITTING THE BRAIN

In the nineteenth century, scientists such as Broca and Wernicke identified language areas in the brain's left hemisphere, thereby raising an interesting question as to why in fact language was confined to one half of the brain instead of the other. When the English neurologist John Hughlings Jackson (1835–1911) suggested that visual ideation was handled by the right hemisphere, it began to appear as though the brain's two halves might divide their psychological work on thematic grounds.

Clinical observations of split-brain surgery patients – whose corpus callosum had been surgically severed in an attempt to prevent seizures from spreading throughout their brain – showed how each hemisphere could function alone if needed. In the late 1960s, the American neuroscientist Michael Gazzaniga (1939–) introduced the theory of 'hemispheric inequality', in which the left-brain was said to be responsible for linguistic abilities and the right-brain to specialize in non-verbal skills (Gazzaniga, 1967).

The 1970s and 1980s saw these elementary propositions balloon into a full-blown popular belief system (Staub, 2016). Observers capitalized on the idea of split-brain specialization to promote a variety of favoured causes. Gender differences were justified on the basis that female brains were 'less lateralized' than male ones (Levy, 1972), with women's spatial abilities said to be hampered by hemispheric patterns traceable to evolutionary history. Insanity itself was described as rooted in brain asymmetry, on the basis that the mysterious voices 'heard' by people with schizophrenia were actually errant language signals emanating from the supposedly non-verbal right temporal cortex (Jaynes, 1976). And various cultural differences were also attributed to hemispheric effects. People who lived in Western countries were berated for succumbing to a left-brain hegemony, whereas people who lived in 'the East' or in 'tribal' settings were praised for their intuitive grasp of 'the inherent duality' of human nature, rooted in their egalitarian approach of employing both hemispheres without prejudice (Bogen, 1969). The Western obsession with left-brain dominance was said to supress the right-brain's inherent creativity (Ornstein, 1972), exposing a physiological basis for

Western people's collective narrowness of insight. A new genre of self-help manual became popular, aimed at empowering readers to release the potential of *both* hemispheres of their brain, rather than allowing one to dominate.

However, while distinct functions such as language comprehension are commonly associated with brain areas that happen to be located in the left hemisphere, the overall distribution of functions in the brain has been found to be nowhere near as neat as the initial binary theories suggested. Brain localization is not as universal as originally thought, with lateralization often emerging differently in different people. Many abilities previously thought of as 'right-brain' have been found to have elaborate neuronal bases in both hemispheres (Riès, Dronkers & Knight, 2016). And the idea that any individual person could be described as predominantly 'left-brained' or 'right-brained' has also been debunked (Nielsen et al., 2013).

While commonly presented as psychological 'fact', the complexities of brain lateralization rarely conform to its popular presentation. Rather, the persistence of popular myths concerning brain lateralization reveals how scientific findings can sometimes permeate culture in ways that are highly selective and distorted by unrelated common assumptions.

EVOLUTION OF THE HUMAN BIOLOGICAL ORGANISM

The idea that humans are just another type of animal has long been seen as somewhat risqué, especially in religious contexts. Nearly all religions teach that human beings are a class apart from non-human creatures, and that they enjoy a unique and protected destiny within existence. The major religious worldviews hold that humans are, in fact, 'made' in the image and likeness of a supreme deity. In other words, the human form is said to be modelled on that of the one true god of the universe.

While this concept has been taught as religious doctrine for thousands of years, philosophers too have long tended to assume a special place for human beings within the greater scheme of reality. Aristotle is regarded as being one of the first scholars to propose a biological hierarchy, in which more sophisticated life forms were ranked 'higher' than less sophisticated ones. He was certain that the rest of the animal kingdom existed to serve as subordinates to humankind (Clutton-Brock, 1995).

Such hierarchical models were also infused with political meaning. In medieval Europe, the human layers of this 'great chain of being' were commonly depicted as stratified in terms of aristocratic status, with the king at the top, the lords and clergy just below, and peasants forming a large layer beneath, just ahead of the animals. More detailed accounts would arrange families accordingly, with the father as the 'head of the household', above his wife and children (Herlihy, 1985). And after the Middle Ages, as we will see in Chapter 6, European culture developed a view that, in terms of their inherent status, its peoples were naturally to be placed 'higher' than non-Europeans.

All these views implied a fixed and permanent state of affairs, in which the species as we know them – including human beings – have always existed in their present form. Psychologically, it is easy to understand how people would gravitate towards such beliefs. As we saw in Chapter 1, human reasoning biases towards primacy, ensuring that initial understanding is not easily displaced by new opinion. And as we discussed in Chapter 3, most groups consider themselves to be special in many respects, to be historically distinct, and to have arrived into instantaneous existence, as suggested by creation myths.

The evolution of theories of evolution

Although the cultural consensus has long centred on creation and continuity, the idea that the species might in fact have different origins has its own long history. The pre-Socratic Greek philosopher Anaximander of Miletus (610–546 BCE) posited that humans emerged from other animals that originally lived in the sea, although this was less a process of biological evolution than it was a theory involving human forms being contained *inside* the bodies of fish (Kočandrle & Kleisner, 2013).

Another Greek philosopher, Empedocles (494–434 BCE), suggested that the first entities to evolve in the world were not whole creatures or beings, but separate body parts and limbs that randomly moved about on their own. The probability of such parts combining with each other – by chance – to create a whole-bodied form was certainly remote. But according to Empedocles, there was such a large number of these free-floating animal fragments that, over time, sufficient combinations did indeed occasionally occur, and the species as we know them today – including human beings – were duly created (Roux, 2005).

Empedocles offered the view that some species survive because they have functional anatomies that enable them to do so, whereas others die off because their physical bodies are somehow lacking or poorly suited, and thus unable to thrive. Popular acceptance of these principles can be inferred from the way Greek mythology so frequently presented monsters that were hybrids of multiple forms, compound creatures such as minotaurs, centaurs and harpies. In short, Empedocles' concepts did not seem all that outlandish to the average ancient Greek citizen. While his theory is often ridiculed today, it nonetheless contained an important insight. It drew ancient attention to the role of attrition and adaptation in the origin of species.

Aristotle's view on the hierarchy inherent in the animal kingdom was derived from Plato's theory of forms, which we introduced in Chapter 2. Aristotle did not accept Empedocles' idea that whole animals evolved from the combination of biological parts, or Anaximander's implication that one species could ultimately emerge from another. Instead, the Aristotelian view was that forms themselves were sacrosanct, and that all things, including human beings, have always had the form that they currently have. As discussed in Chapter 2, it was Aristotle's views on such existential issues that became the mainstream of academic thought throughout European and Asian scholarship during the Middle Ages. For one thing, the Aristotelian approach cohered well with Christian teachings about how bodily forms served as receptables for 'ensoulment'.

In the eighteenth century, natural scientists continued to be influenced by the idea that biological forms were fixed, and instead concentrated on enumerating and categorizing all the world's species. The Swedish zoologist Carl Linnaeus (1707–78) introduced a detailed system for naming animals, which is still used today. In this approach, each animal is given a two-part Latin name, with the first part identifying the animal's broad class (or 'genus') and the second its specific group (or 'species'). Linnaeus included humankind within his system, naming it *Homo sapiens*.

Linnaeus viewed all species as falling into a hierarchy, with the organization of different categories based, more or less, on physical resemblances between different types of animal. Importantly, on this basis, he placed *Homo sapiens* into a broader category that he called 'Primates', which included chimpanzees and monkeys, but also lemurs and bats. Although acknowledging that humans resembled some animals, Linnaeus nonetheless retained a belief in the absolute exceptionalism of humanity. Not only did he place *Homo sapiens* at the top of his hierarchy as the most advanced of all of the 4,300 animals he classified, he also rejected outright any possibility that the animal kingdom's most able members benefited from biological development over time. Human beings might resemble animals, but they were not related to them.

But not all naturalists agreed. Across Europe, where biological research was thriving, a number of scholars put forward competing views. The particularly well-travelled French scientist Pierre Louis Maupertuis (1698–1759) noted that while human children would often resemble both of their parents, they would still be unique in themselves, and thus different to them as well. The same must be true of all animals. When mothers and fathers combine to reproduce, their resulting offspring will be a biologically modified version of them both. This idea that some kind of anatomical 'code' or blueprint is passed down from parents to offspring not only raised the possibility, if not likelihood, of evolution over time, it also specifically pre-empted the concept of genes and genetics, more than a century before the isolation of DNA (Glass, 1955).

The French naturalist George-Louis Leclerc (1707–88) – better known as the Count of Buffon, or simply Buffon – promoted the idea that much of the variability seen in nature resulted from intergenerational deterioration. For all animals, but especially for humans, the continuously changing nature of the world would lead successive generations of offspring to be increasingly ill-suited to their surroundings. Buffon's view was almost the opposite of the modern idea of evolution; to him, animals *devolved* rather than evolved. As a religious man, he believed that all creatures were created in initially perfect forms, of which our current animal kingdom was a set of adulterated copies. However, Buffon's theory was important because it saw species as shaped by a struggle for existence, where animals would evolve on the basis of their ability to adapt to their environments (Mason, 2010).

One scientist to be greatly influenced by Buffon was the French biologist Jean-Baptiste Lamarck (1744–1829). Lamarck put forward a theory of evolution based on 'transmutation'. Contrary to Buffon, Lamarck believed that over time, life forms improved rather than deteriorated. Animals would evolve towards ever greater complexity and adaptability with each passing generation. A key principle of the Lamarckian model was the heritability of acquired traits. This meant that whenever an animal learned or acquired a way to better adapt to its environment, it would then pass this adaptation directly to its offspring at birth. For example, if a creature found that strengthening or stretching a particular limb helped them to gather more food, then, according to Lamarck, its offspring would be born with this limb *already* strengthened or stretched.

However, Lamarck was unable to specify *how* such traits would be transmitted from parent to progeny. It was well known that the offspring of injured or maimed animals (for example, animals that were blinded) were usually born healthy and intact, suggesting that only *innate* traits could pass from generation to generation. This made it unclear how physical changes acquired during life could end up rewriting the anatomical blueprint that an animal would pass on to its young.

Among those to strongly criticize Lamarck was the French palaeontologist Georges Cuvier (1769–1832). Cuvier had worked closely with Jean Pierre Flourens in Paris. Ironically, while Cuvier insisted that animal species were unrelated, his protégé Flourens was pursuing brain ablation studies that were reliant on cross-species comparability. Whether either Cuvier or Flourens explicitly acknowledged it, this brain research was premised on the fundamental inter-relatedness of species – and, thus, by implication, on the principle of descent from common ancestry.

Another writer to propose a theory of evolution, albeit tentatively (in the form of poetry), was the English physician Erasmus Darwin (1731–1802). His theory suggested that all animals, including humans, may indeed have descended from a single common ancestor. Not only this, he portrayed the common ancestor as a microorganism, thus implying that evolution had the effect of making species more complex over time. While he did not explain how such complexity was produced, he spoke of evolution as 'a contest among males' in which 'the strongest and most active animal should propagate the species which should thus be improved' (E. Darwin, 1796, p. 503).

Although he was a doctor by trade, Erasmus Darwin's poetry brought him to national attention; at one stage he even aspired to become Britain's poet laureate. However, his ideas were not welcomed by all his contemporaries. He was asked to remove the slogan *E conchis omnia* ('Everything from the shells') that he had inscribed on the side of his carriage, as it was thought to be overly irreverent, if not outrightly blasphemous (King-Hele, 2005). His metaphysical musings jarred with a newly emerging anti-philosophical mood in England that arose in the wake of the French Revolution. And some in the poetry world found his rhyming couplets and flowery language to be gaudily old-fashioned. The critic and poet Samuel Taylor Coleridge denounced him in withering terms: 'I absolutely nauseate Darwin's Poem', he wrote in a letter (King-Hele, 1986, p. 102).

But whatever the quality of his verse, Erasmus Darwin certainly left a lasting mark on the development of evolutionary theory. His writing helped to promote the idea that a 'struggle for existence' might underlie the emergence of species.

The Darwinian turn

One important reader of Erasmus Darwin's work would be his own grandson, born seven years after his death, the now-renowned naturalist Charles Darwin (1809–82). It was Charles who would become associated with the modern understanding of biological evolution. However, as with virtually all major historic ideas, the development of Charles Darwin's understanding of evolution was intertwined with the work of a number of other scientists. Its reception was also

Public domain, via Wikimedia Commons

Image 5.3   Charles Darwin
Photograph of Charles Darwin from the mid-1850s, shortly before the publication of *On the Origin of Species*.

influenced by several societal and cultural factors, and its discoveries benefited from no small measure of serendipity. In other words, Darwin's theory of evolution by natural selection was a product of *content*, *context* and *coincidence*.

Darwin developed his theory in the middle of the nineteenth century, a time of several favourable scientific trends. Biologists were breaking new ground in the study of brain anatomy and in exploring the wider natural world. Public interest in fields such as phrenology showed how biology could be mined to reveal the secrets of human nature. A new branch of geology had emerged from the discovery of fossils, suggesting that the earth was many millions of years old, much older than had previously been believed. And the various efforts to taxonomize the earth's many species served to arouse curiosity as to precisely *why* there were quite so many, and how their often subtle resemblances could be convincingly accounted for.

Industrialization had created a new world of urban living, social deprivation and exploitation of the masses. Perhaps seeking to rationalize the rank poverty that had begun to sweep Europe, British economists such as Adam Smith (1723–90) and Thomas Malthus (1766–1834) offered theoretical accounts to explain how populations might respond to limits on resources. In particular, Malthus suggested that growth in human populations would always exceed that of resource availability, and that therefore poverty was essentially inevitable. The idea was that, at any given time, only a portion of the human race – presumably those best equipped to succeed in the 'struggle for existence' – could thrive, and therefore survive.

The political climate stimulated new ways to think about the world. Urbanization, where people began to live in close proximity to each other in burgeoning towns and cities, contributed to a rise in localism and political tribalism. The overt colonial policies of the major European nations also shaped public discourse, not least through the education system, where national identity was promoted through the teaching of history, arts and language (R. Walsh et al., 2014). A politically cultivated belief in the inferiority of non-Europeans became commonplace at precisely the time that scientists were beginning to study the similarities and differences across human populations.

It was in such heady cultural circumstances that Charles Darwin was educated and worked, the period when he gathered his knowledge, recorded his data, discussed his ideas and ultimately formulated his theories.

Famously, after leaving university, the young Darwin got a job as a naturalist on a Royal Navy survey ship, HMS *Beagle*. The *Beagle* was schedule to embark on a two-year round-the-world expedition, starting in 1831, during which Darwin would gather geological, botanical and zoological artefacts, as well as study local ethnologies and natural histories. In the end, due to accumulated weather delays and other logistical snags, the voyage ended up lasting five years. By the time he returned to Britain, the publication of his many dispatches home had made him a nationally recognized scientist. His eventual book on the voyage, published in 1839, became a bestseller.

During years of further contemplation and toil, Darwin gradually developed a new way to explain the emergence of variety in nature. At first, he was hesitant and cautious, fearing that his theory's divergence from Christian scripture would be condemned as irreligious. However, after he received a letter from his fellow British naturalist Alfred Russell Wallace (1823–1910), Darwin was suddenly prompted to publish. Without needing to have circumnavigated the globe, Wallace himself had come up with a theory that was virtually identical to Darwin's.

By way of mutually acknowledging the merit of each other's work, the two scientists arranged for their papers to be presented at the same conference of the Linnean Society in 1858, enabling both authors to be formally recorded as having achieved equivalent theoretical breakthroughs. Darwin then expounded on his theory of evolution in a new book, *On the Origin of Species* (1859). The publication was to become a true landmark in the history of scientific literature. Darwin's later writings were no less venerable. Developing his theoretical worldview, he elaborated the principles of evolution in *The Descent of Man* (1871) and *The Expression of the Emotions* (1872). These, along with several other works, were part of a revolution of scientific thought that thoroughly reshaped our understanding of the origins of humankind. They set in train a modern science of psychology that recognized, as fundamental, the biological basis of human nature.

Evolution and the natural selection of humankind

Darwin's theory of evolution by natural selection held that species evolve slowly over time, with innate traits passed from parent to offspring. The theory put forward the following argument:

- In nature, it is a fact of life that not all animals survive long enough to reproduce.
- All animals vary slightly from one another, even within those groups that we think of as a single 'species'.
- This inherent variability will mean that each animal ends up with slightly different characteristics or traits. Sometimes these traits will make some animals more likely than others to breed successfully, or to breed in proportionally greater numbers. Relevant traits include those that would help an animal to acquire nutrition, to remain healthy, to avoid danger, to attract mates or to protect their young.
- Those animals who do breed will, as parents, pass their own traits on to their own offspring.
- Therefore, over time and across an entire population, there will be a relatively greater number of offspring born with traits that assisted their parents – and thus should assist *them* – to breed successfully.
- At all times, whether a trait will prove useful will depend on the surrounding environment. If the environment changes, then the way a species evolves will also change. For example, while the woolly mammoth thrived during the Ice Age, it died out once the climate became warmer.

- Not all offspring will be alike, and over time some lineages of a species will become so different as to end up unique, resulting in new lineages that comprise 'species' in their own right.
- Given the vast timescale involved, this in fact is how *all* current species in the animal kingdom – including *Homo sapiens* – came into existence. All animals are thus descended from a common ancestor.

Darwin used the term 'natural selection' to describe the way circumstances in an environment would, with passing generations, lead to some traits becoming more prevalent than others. However, the notion of 'selection' was metaphorical. Nature did not have a blueprint for the ideal version of each species, nor did it have a consciousness that would allow it to determine the course of events. Not only did Darwin's theory deny the exceptionalism of the human form, it explained nature as having arrived at its current state without the need for input from a divine creator.

Darwin was correct to predict that his theory would be criticized, especially by religious commentators. However, the controversy excited defenders as well as detractors. The English biologist Thomas Henry Huxley (1825–95) was a notable supporter, at one point defending Darwin at a high-profile public debate with the Lord Bishop of Oxford held at Oxford University Museum. Famously, the bishop is said to have asked Huxley whether he would be proud for his great-great-grandfather to have been 'an ape or a gorilla'. In response, Huxley implied that he would be much prouder of that than of being related to the bishop (Kaalund, 2014).

HISTORY REPEATING ITSELF: EVOLUTION DENIALISM

While few scientists today doubt that human beings, as with all animals, emerged through processes of biological evolution, significant subsets of the general population retain a belief that humans were created by other means. According to academic studies, around one in eight adults in the United Kingdom continue to disagree with the scientific explanation of human evolution (Unsworth & Voas, 2018). Around a quarter of adults in countries such as Russia, Poland, Brazil and Argentina state that they believe humans have always existed in their present form (Pew Research Center, 2014, 2017).

Political scientists often find that people's attitudes to the science of evolution systematically relate to their other political beliefs. For example, in the United States, people who affiliate to conservative political parties are more likely to be sceptical of statements such as 'Humans have evolved due to natural processes'. They are similarly more likely to reject views that the 'Earth is warming due to human activity', that 'Childhood vaccines should be required', or that scientific research should be funded by the taxpayer (Pew Research Center, 2015). Overall, they express significantly less confidence in the process of science or the idea that scientists 'act in the best interests of the public' (Pew Research, 2019).

Partisan public schisms between scientists and denialists have become common in the modern world. Arguments about evolution – or about topics such as climate change, vaccination, abortion or gun control – are often rooted in an underlying cultural divide, itself a product of social conservatism or liberalism, involving voices embedded in social power structures that wish to preserve their privileges. The debates, while ostensibly about 'the science', are seldom truly focused on either method or evidence, and are more often propelled by concerns about morality and ethics.

Darwinian psychology

The Darwinian principles have become the basis on which all modern natural science is understood. In the words of the Ukrainian-born geneticist Theodosius Dobzhansky (1900–75), 'nothing in biology makes sense, except in light of evolution' (Dobzhansky, 1973). Darwin himself harvested voluminous evidence to support his theory, and more than a century and a half of subsequent research has helped to clarify many confusions and to corroborate his overall conclusions.

In the nineteenth century, Darwin and his contemporaries were not able to account for every single detail of evolution, and were unaware, for example, of the existence of genes or the potential of molecular biology. However, as these areas of science were themselves refined, the evidence for evolution by natural selection was only bolstered. Today, in terms of accumulated research data, the theory of evolution by natural selection is one of the most substantiated theories in science. It occupies a similar status in evidentiary terms as the theory of gravitation or the theory that the earth orbits the sun.

The principles of evolution apply to psychological traits as they do to physical ones. We know that human beings vary psychologically, in their tastes, thoughts, emotional styles and behaviour patterns. We know that some psychological traits will help people to thrive in their environments, whereas others will impede them. We know that some psychological traits emerge as by-products of physical adaptations, such as the way the brain became specialized at processing visuospatial information as human bodies learned to cope with bipedalism and mobility. And we know that many psychological characteristics seem to be genetically heritable, either conspicuously running in families, or resulting secondarily from (say) innate features of brain physiology. Given such premises, we can logically expect that psychological traits will be subject to natural selection.

Of course, evolution by natural selection is not the *only* determinant of human behaviour, in the same way that it is not the only determinant of a person's bodyweight. The idea that human beings are a product of *both* biology *and* experience is often discussed in psychology, in terms of the nature–nurture debate.

In *On the Origin of Species*, Darwin himself flagged the role of natural selection in shaping the evolution of human psychology, although he did so only briefly. It was other scientists of the time, including Wallace (e.g. 1864), who depicted how humanity's higher mental functions had evolved. Darwin eventually addressed the topic himself, in considerable detail, in his subsequent books.

In *The Descent of Man*, Darwin outlined the many ways in which animals behave like people. He showed how animals frequently exhibit 'human'-like qualities, such as courage, kindness, jealousy, humour, shame and reason. Correspondingly, in *The Expression of the Emotions*, he emphasized how humans frequently display 'animal'-like qualities, such as showing their teeth when grimacing to communicate rage. Having exhaustively described the overlap between humans and animals, both physically and psychologically, he concluded that any differences were 'of degree and not of kind' (C. Darwin, 1871, p. 105). Darwin's works also explored the role of evolution in language comprehension, social interaction and sexual behaviour, as well as its relevance in understanding child development.

The post-Darwinians

Such was the wide-ranging impact of evolutionary theory that it did not take long for it to be appropriated, adapted and applied to new areas. However, not all of these initiatives have been straightforward. While nothing in modern biology makes sense except in light of evolution, that does not mean that *everything* asserted about evolution in modern biology (or psychology) makes sense.

One of the first efforts to repurpose evolutionary theory came shortly after Darwin's death in 1882, with the emergence of an intellectual practice known as *social Darwinism*. This term refers to the use of natural selection to try to explain not only the evolution of today's biological organisms, but also the emergence of current political, social and economic circumstances.

Social Darwinist theories tend to claim that the way wealth and power are distributed in society reflects the natural strengths and weaknesses of different groups of people. This argument presumes that social status is automatically accrued by anyone who has the ability and ambition to want it; as such, our societies do not need government intervention but are best left to manage themselves. In this way social Darwinism has been used to justify non-interventionist economic programmes, such as laissez-faire capitalism.

However, such a view fails to take account of the many biases and barriers that prevent people from fulfilling their life's wishes. For example, discrimination, exploitation and ingrained socioeconomic disadvantage often ensure that many groups in society face a permanent struggle due to circumstances far outside their control. The fact that they do so is not the result of their 'ability to adapt' to their environment, and so such 'abilities' do not evolve in a way that resembles natural selection.

In this sense, then, social Darwinism is not the same as Darwin's own theory of evolution at all. Darwin himself wrote that the application of natural selection principles to politics and economics amounted to little more than opportunist rhetoric, availing 'more of the nature of definitions than of laws of nature'. He was particularly dismissive of the work of Herbert Spencer (1820–1903), the English philosopher who became known as one of the first social Darwinists. According to Darwin's view, Spencer's approach was 'wholly opposed' to his own frame of mind, adding of Spencer: 'I did not like him particularly … I think that he was extremely egotistical … I am not conscious of having profited in my own work by Spencer's writings … His conclusions never convince me … they do not seem to me to be of any strictly scientific use' (Barlow, 1958, p. 109). This is important to note because the political implications of social Darwinism are often associated directly with Darwin himself and, by extension, with the *actual* scientific theory of evolution.

In reality, social Darwinism was a political theory and not a psychological one. It resulted from expedience, not evidence. It was self-serving, not scientific. It provided a convenient narrative to rationalize the inequities of the status quo by downgrading society's out-groups as innately inferior. Spencer had coined the term 'survival of the fittest' to describe the advantages of adaptation; but soon that phrase would be used to stigmatize groups who *failed* to thrive as being 'unfit' for society. It has been argued that this reasoning was a cornerstone of such illiberal ideologies as eugenics and Nazism (Arendt, 1951), thus implicating social Darwinism in some of the gravest crimes of modern civilization.

We will see in Chapter 6 how social Darwinism played a role in the emergence of the eugenics movement, not least because of the efforts of Darwin's own cousin, the statistician Francis Galton. However, most historians dismiss the claim that social Darwinism exerted an important influence on the Nazis (R. J. Richards, 2009). Instead, they say, this accusation persists because of its own political dimensions. Especially in the United States, where the concept of evolution continues to meet resistance from religious conservative groups, linking social Darwinism to the Nazis offers a way to use guilt-by-association to discredit evolutionary theory itself. As we will see in Chapter 12, the way modern cultural politics distort the communication and understanding of scientific knowledge presents a significant problem for psychology – but one that is frequently overlooked by psychologists.

The twentieth century saw the rise of a new post-Darwinist movement, known as *sociobiology*. Having emerged over a number of decades, sociobiology came to prominence in 1975 with the publication of the book *Sociobiology: The New Synthesis*, by the American biologist E. O. Wilson (1929–2021; Wilson, 1975). Once again, the intention of this new take on evolution was to use the principles of natural selection to explain the dynamics of human society, with a particular focus on the evolution of human social behaviour. Sociobiologists drew attention to the role of 'kin selection', the impulse of all creatures to protect others who are related to them. According to sociobiology, kin selection drove the evolution of all social behaviour patterns, from altruism to aggression.

While Wilson had depicted the natural selection of behaviour in terms of each individual organism's own self-interest, later scientists such as the English biologist Richard Dawkins (1941–) defined such interest in genetic terms. Dawkins (1976) offered the metaphor of the 'selfish gene', whereby social behaviour would be shaped by the differential survival of genes and gene-lines, rather than of individual animals. This helped to explain why some species (including humans) can engage in apparently selfless behaviours, such as when they sacrifice their own lives in order to protect others: the others who are protected by self-sacrifice are likely to have similar genes. Crucially, in sociobiology, virtually all behaviour is aimed at preserving one's own genes in the population.

Sociobiology proved highly controversial because it implied that even terrible behaviours – such as rape or murder – were somehow 'natural' and thus, by implication, potentially excusable. It appeared to argue that because the impulse for rage (for example) is shaped by natural selection, a person who exhibits rage is not truly responsible for their own actions. Similarly, by suggesting that prejudicial behaviours, such as sexism or racism, are the product of successive evolutionary adaptations, it implied that social structures which discriminate against women or ethnic minorities may, in fact, represent the optimal arrangement for humankind.

Sociobiologists argue that such interpretations are based on an error known as the 'naturalistic fallacy', the false equating of 'natural' with 'desirable'. This in turn is related to an older philosophical conundrum discussed in the eighteenth century by the Scottish philosopher David Hume, who we encountered in Chapter 3. Hume called his conundrum 'the *is–ought* problem', pointing out that it is fallacious to use knowledge about *what is* to draw simple conclusions about *what ought to be*. Accordingly, just because something has evolved, or otherwise comes to exist naturally, does not make it morally correct. Sociobiologists contend that their role as scientists is to establish the way things have come to be, and not to censor their science just because it can be used to make a fallacious moral argument.

A related field, *evolutionary psychology*, emerged in the 1980s (Cosmides & Tooby, 1987). It is sometimes referred to as the 'politically correct' version of sociobiology (Freese, 2002). This is because it avoids hypothesizing about significant cognitive differences between human populations. Instead, evolutionary psychology focuses on the evolution of specific behavioural capacities, and not on enacted behaviour. It inherently proposes that merely possessing a *capacity for* aggression, for example, need not lead to – or be used to justify – actual violence. The approach of evolutionary psychology has been to conceptualize human nature in terms of thousands of discrete adaptations or 'modules', each of which is shaped by natural selection. Another extension beyond sociobiology is that many of these modules deal with perception and cognition.

However, critics continue to point out several weaknesses in such research. These fields are said to be over-reliant on dubious assumptions about the nature of prehistoric life. In seeking evidence to support their hypotheses, these researchers often cite examples from modern-day hunter-gatherer communities, which they say can be seen as analogous to the societies inhabited by our prehistoric ancestors. But modern hunter-gatherer societies are themselves extremely diverse (Buller, 2005). Some such groups conform to the evolutionary-psychology stereotypes that see men as hunters and women as childminders; however, crucially, others do not. It is impossible to know precisely which societies should be studied as models of prehistoric humanity, and which should be ignored.

Evolutionary psychology also suffers from a lack of contemporary global perspective. As far back as the 1970s, the American anthropologist Marshall Sahlins (1930–2021) pointed out that kin selection might appear to make sense in Western societies, but is of little assistance when trying to explain several customs prevalent in other cultures (Sahlins, 1976). In several cultures, nonrelated individuals are customarily redefined as relatives according to traditional rules. According to Sahlins, virtually no non-Western system of human kinship accords with the sociobiological position that social behaviour and status can be explained in terms of genetic relatedness.

More fundamentally, many scientists have complained that it is virtually impossible to gather robust evidence for such theories, given that we cannot conduct experiments on the past. Instead, they argue, sociobiologists and evolutionary psychologists are required simply to speculate about prehistoric events. They rely on hindsight to derive an understanding from fossil records, archaeological relics, oral traditions, extant customs and the rather circular presumption that modern behaviours simply *must* reflect Stone Age adaptations. Instead of using observation to make sense of theory, as science ordinarily requires, sociobiology *uses theory to make sense of observation*. The American palaeontologist Stephen Jay Gould (1941–2002) condemned such retrospective explanations as scientifically unsound, referring to them as '"Just So" stories' (Gould, 1978, p. 530).

Such theories have also been criticized for their use of *teleological reasoning*, the idea that all events have a purpose or function, and *anthropomorphism*, the attribution of human feelings to entities that lack complex self-awareness. The idea of a 'selfish gene' is an important example. According to some philosophers of science, the use of the word 'selfish' to describe a gene – a chain of nucleotides – is figurative and can have no real meaning. The British philosopher Mary

Midgley (1919–2018) compared it to saying that 'atoms can be jealous' (Midgley, 1979). The Australian philosopher David Stove (1927–94) described it as akin to describing 'an electron that is suspicious' (Stove, 1992). Stove went on to point out that Dawkins himself claimed he intended 'selfish' to be a synonym for 'self-replicating', failing to acknowledge that 'selfish' and 'self-replicating' mean quite different things. As Stove put it, a book called *The Self-Replicating Gene* would likely have been far less eye-catching.

However, despite such limitations and criticisms, the fields of sociobiology and evolutionary psychology have continued to attract attention, both with the general public and in mainstream academia. Their many demonstrated shortcomings have proven far from fatal. If anything, the retrospective nature of studying the distant prehistoric past has been used to defend such research as much as to criticize it. The many gaps in our knowledge have provided plenty of scope for sociobiologists and evolutionary psychologists to modify their claims whenever objections are raised. But to many observers, this habit of continuously updating theories in order to sidestep criticism seems far removed from the usual scientific standard of rejecting hypotheses that have been falsified (Dennis, 2018). Instead, it feels a lot like confirmation bias.

The idea that modern skulls house Stone Age brains remains a highly seductive explanatory narrative in the modern approach to psychology. This is no doubt partly because of the misleadingly simplified portrayal of Stone Age life often presented in modern entertainment culture. However, in the end, we can know very little about the specific problems that were faced by our long-dead forebears. While it is beyond dispute that human bodies – and thus brains, hormones and other physiological drivers of psychology – certainly evolved through processes of natural selection, that alone does not mean we can identify discrete behavioural adaptations that today can be considered our prehistoric legacy.

Indeed, the very idea that such separable behavioural modules even exist seems somewhat reminiscent of the faculties of phrenology: an attempt to account for human nature by reducing it to its bits (Buller, 2005). If psychology can draw one lesson from the knowledge that human beings are evolved biological organisms, it is surely that our nature is not a jigsaw puzzle waiting to be put together, but a confluence of overlapping, intermingling and synthesized processes, a product of multiple multilevel forces, physical and social, seen and unseen.

HUMAN NATURE AS ANIMAL NATURE

The status of human beings as biological animals cuts through all modern psychology. Biological distinction is fundamental to the study of psychological gender differences and personality. The measurement of brain function, and the production of brain images, are often purported to represent the cutting edge of psychological science. And the genetic uniqueness of each human being is a central premise of the nature–nurture debate, itself core to our understanding of how environments and social networks affect individuals.

In short, the proposition that humans are animals is itself indisputable. What *is* up for debate – and what is frequently strongly debated – is the *extent* to which our animalistic nature can explain our psychological selves.

Whether biology predominates the human condition, or merely serves to nuance it, has divided psychological thought for centuries. In some ways opinion seems to have oscillated between one extreme and the other. For example, in psychiatry, Pinel's psychosocially oriented 'moral' treatment was displaced by a move to more physical interventions; this move to the physical was then followed by a reversion to the psychosocial, with the emergence of talk therapies; and latterly these talk therapies have, in turn, again given way to the pharmacotherapy revolution (Decker, 2015).

However, such a sequence of switching offers a simplistic summary. In reality, Pinel was a biologically trained doctor who approved of medical treatment, while Freud – perhaps the first real talk therapist (see Chapter 7) – saw the mind as a fundamentally neurological process (Frances, 2016). The problem with dichotomizing psychology into two camps – the biological reductionists versus the psychosocial integrationists – is that dichotomies, generally speaking, don't work. Lacking nuance, they fail to account for overlap.

What has been advocated as a 'biopsychosocial' approach to psychology (and to other fields, such as medicine) has proven a challenging ideal to aspire to. All too often, practitioners revert to type. The more medically trained focus on biological realities, while their behavioural colleagues do the opposite, both under an ostensibly 'biopsychosocial' banner. This has led, in a number of cases, to sharp debates over diagnostics, clinical care, treatment and public policy. Several extreme examples have arisen in the history of healthcare, when authentic physical illnesses have been characterized as psychological delusions (or 'hysteria') by practitioners wedded to theories of psychological causality (e.g. Mortimer, 2020; we will return to this controversy in Chapter 11). As well as individual clinicians, professional bodies and government agencies often adopt corporate positions that reveal similar biases (Frances, 2016).

Nonetheless, one consequence of seeing human beings as evolved biological organisms is to offer a broader range of ways in which to identify, and thus try to address, their psychological challenges. A deepening understanding of brain anatomy and neurological function has enabled the development of various forms of psychosurgeries, some of which have proven wasteful, but others of which have stood the test of time (Faria, 2013). And evolutionary theory has helped to shed light on the human response to stress (Phillips, Ginty & Hughes, 2013) as well as on the development of mental ill health. For example, the basic point that symptoms such as pain and depression might well *assist* people to recover their well-being – by steering their behaviour in ways that encourage them to avoid threats – is essentially a Darwinian interpretation, one that highlights the functional role of the body's evolved responses to illness (A. Stevens & Price, 2016).

Legacy of the biological approach

The biological approach to psychology has bequeathed a myriad of methods, concepts, findings and as-yet-unresolved philosophical questions. As outlined above, the content of brain science owes more than a modest debt to historical efforts to look inside the human cranium. Fields such as phrenology are often laughed at today, but its fundamental approach of localizing function across disparate areas of the brain was somewhat insightful, at least in principle. And its major methodological flaw, that of over-relying on confirmatory evidence and correlational logic, can hardly be seen as a capital offence – not least given the fact that similar flimsy logic is regularly applied in psychological research today. The brightly coloured blobs that feature in modern brain imaging studies are themselves 'brain areas' whose functions (or faculties) are inferred from largely correlational data, often in dubiously non-representative study samples. The confidence with which brain scientists declare these areas to denote separate modules of the mind often exceeds the robustness of the underlying dataset, a fact that has led some neuroscientists to concede that brain imaging work might be little more than a 'new phrenology' (Uttal, 2001).

The fields of social Darwinism, sociobiology and evolutionary psychology were each somewhat faddish, afflicted by fundamental flaws, and perhaps more chastised than championed. However, the broad evolutionary frame of the biological sciences has had a truly profound effect on our appreciation of human psychology. The Darwinian legacy changed more than scientific understanding, it changed society itself. It humbled humanity by clarifying how the status of human beings is intricately interwoven with that of all that surrounds them. It is an exaggeration to say that evolution made religion obsolete (Roberts, 2009). But it is equally inflated to maintain that, once Darwin's theory was understood, the spiritualist insight on biological matters was ever as influential again.

Human beings' understanding of their own nature is now unavoidably locked into a biological worldview. Every serious person realizes that brain injury affects intellectual prowess, that brain-altering drugs affect judgement, and that adults, who have fully grown brains, behave differently to children, who do not. Likewise, they appreciate that human bodies are not entirely unlike animal bodies, and so must be somehow subject to common biological principles.

The evolutionary view highlighted the functionality of behaviour, the atavistic roots of emotion, and the pivotal role of sexuality. The conclusion that humans are unambiguously animals helped set the scene for a cascade of later developments in psychology, including psychoanalysis, behaviourism, cognitive science and developmental psychology. The idea that human organisms behave in a functional manner, without necessary recourse to consciousness, allowed behaviourism and cognitive science to thrive. We will return to these topics in Chapters 8 and 9.

Perhaps most importantly, the evolutionary perspective helped people move beyond the one-size-fits-all habit of atomistic science, by drawing attention to the sheer variety of human individual experience. In fact, in evolutionary theory, individual psychological differences are not merely acknowledged, they are held to be central. Without such variety – of emotion, perception, taste and behaviour – human psychology could not ever evolve or develop. In this sense, the evolutionary perspective is deeply humanitarian. It holds personal uniqueness to be the cornerstone of human nature.

WHERE TO FROM HERE?

Biological insights have served to shape the field of psychology as it is today. Virtually all theories of human thoughts, feelings and behaviours are premised on the acknowledgement that human beings are, first and foremost, naturally existing animals whose capacities and traits are innate.

Central within this understanding is the fact that, while humans conform to a broad genetic blueprint, their organic origins guarantee their diversity. The status of humans as products of biology is what ensures their individual uniqueness.

One consequence of this uniqueness is that, as well as understanding the general principles by which human psychology can be explained, we can also consider the degree to which this psychology will vary from individual to individual. But in order to do this coherently, we require systematic ways to describe these differences and to articulate their extent. The wish to study naturally occurring human diversity has generated a plethora of methods for measuring and classifying human beings. However, not all such endeavours have been benign. Some of the darkest events in human history have featured the use of psychological measurement methods and concepts in order to identify out-groups, so that unwanted others can be excluded, ostracized or even exterminated. It is this project of human quantification that we turn to next.

DISCUSSION QUESTIONS

1. What would be the alternative to thinking of human beings as naturally occurring biological machines?
2. Does the biological nature of human beings have consequences for the way we think about the moral rights of other animals?
3. To what extent is it fair to say that human psychology is biologically represented by brain function alone?
4. Apart from religious concerns, why might evolutionary theory make some people anxious?

RECOMMENDED READING

- **Buller, D. J. (2005).** *Adapting Minds: Evolutionary Psychology and the Persistent Quest for Human Nature.* **Cambridge, Massachusetts: MIT Press.** In this book, the author critiques the subfield of evolutionary psychology and questions whether it represents a truly effective application of evolutionary theory to psychological questions.
- **Cobb, M. (2020).** *The Idea of the Brain: A History.* **London: Profile Books.** In this book, the author traces the history of brain science, showing how its major ideas and theories have been shaped more by the emergence of new technologies than by the accumulation of empirical evidence.
- **Dennis, A. (2018). The Strange Survival and Apparent Resurgence of Sociobiology.** *History of the Human Sciences,* **31,** 19–35. In this article, the author examines why the theories of sociobiology continue to attract attention despite being scientifically discredited, and considers whether this interest might be driven by politics rather than by data.
- **Sysling, F. (2021). Phrenology and the average person, 1840–1940.** *History of the Human Sciences,* **34,** 27–45. In this review, the author shows how historical phrenologists

accounted for the notion of the 'average' person, and how phrenology helped to encourage people to see themselves as part of an imagined statistical community.

- **Uttal, W. R. (2001).** *The New Phrenology: The Limits of Localizing Cognitive Processes in the Brain.* **Cambridge, Massachusetts: MIT Press.** In this book, the author questions the basis of modern neuropsychology and asks whether the use of brain imaging technologies promotes a reliance on overly simplistic explanatory concepts.

QUANTIFICATION, MEASUREMENT AND THE CONCEPT OF *RACE*

6

In this chapter, we will ...

- reflect on the emergence of quantification as a means of accounting for psychological characteristics
- trace the development of statistics as a formal method of analysis
- examine the influence of eugenics and scientific racism in the formation of psychology's research agendas and statistical approaches
- consider the role of psychological ideas in framing political attitudes towards 'race' and, in turn, the impact of racial politics on the contents and practices of psychology
- trace the emergence of claims that it is possible for psychologists to demonstrate race differences in mental acuity
- evaluate the merit of the claim that 'race' differences in 'intelligence' are 'heritable'

At the outset

Human beings have long sought to classify, quantify and count the contents of the world that exists around them. Once biologists had established the nature of evolution, there emerged an immediate interest in specifying the place of human beings within the structure of biological species. In many ways, psychology was a central science in this quantification effort, because it focused on specifying the scope of the human experience, its inner diversity, and the differences between different types of people. However, this impulse to quantify the psychological was often motivated by sinister intent, rather than by scientific curiosity.

Many of the earliest statisticians were humanitarians. However, over time, interest in applying statistical methods to human behaviour was driven by the view that the human race needed to be artificially managed. The eugenics movement called for the control of population growth, by prioritizing those people who they deemed to be 'better' than others. The early eugenicists devised many of the statistical methods that psychologists still use today. Indeed, in its early days as a formal science and university discipline, interest in psychology was greatly boosted by interest in eugenics. Many of the most prominent psychologists were themselves committed eugenicists.

As such, psychology was a core discipline in framing beliefs about 'race'. Many psychologists were deeply involved in what we now refer to as *scientific racism*, the use of scientific methods to gather data that can be used to support and justify racial discrimination. The history of racial exploitation – typified by the system of slavery that was part of the global economy for centuries – was especially influential. The legacy of racist policies relating to education, segregation, immigration and intelligence testing continues to be felt today.

Debates about quantification in psychology often appear to be scientific when they are in fact political. A recurring example relates to claims that some racial groups have greater mental abilities than others. The claimed link between 'race' and intelligence is an example of modern pseudoscience, because it relies on spurious evidence and logically unreasonable methodologies. The science of psychology has provided much of the technical vocabulary and theoretical frames of reference that allow such claims to persist in modern culture. But equally, psychology is well placed to provide the knowledge and data that are needed to counter these very same claims.

Key concept: Race

Race is a cultural notion that refers to a group of people who are seen by society as sharing a common ethnic or national identity. Historically, the term was used much more broadly to refer to categories of any entity, including plants and animals. It was only towards the end of the seventeenth century that it began to be used to describe different human communities. At first 'race' was used to describe a group of people who spoke a common language. Later the term was used to refer to national affiliations. Over time, common usage of 'race' evolved to encapsulate a broader range of descriptive features, including physical appearances and social customs.

There is no biological concept that equates to what people refer to as 'race'. Attempts to establish scientific definitions of 'race' have always foundered, because of the cross-cutting genetic inter-relatedness of human beings.

While human beings vary in their appearance, and although physical variations are themselves likely to reflect geographical histories, all such variations are continuous rather than categorical. This means that they are far more detailed and nuanced than people often realize, and do not cluster in ways that match the social or cultural groupings that have emerged as human communities. Further, groups of people whose physical appearances seem quite different can sometimes be genetically very similar to each other, while people who believe themselves to be physically (or 'racially') the same as another person can often discover that they differ from them very dramatically in genetic terms.

As such, 'race' is a social classification and not a scientific one. What is referred to as a person's 'race' will tell us very little about them. It will tell us nothing about their thoughts, feelings, behaviours, abilities, interests or personalities. It may sometimes tell us about their physical appearance, but such information can be simplistic and often inaccurate. It is more likely to tell us something about their daily experience in the world. For example, a person's 'race' can tell us whether they are likely to face discrimination or prejudice within a given community. This is because, while 'race' is a vague notion that is hard to define, *racism* is a critically important social problem that creates division and suffering around the world.

Psychologically, people are inclined to classify themselves and others in various ways, and often in terms of 'race'. It is this psychological impulse to classify people, to quantify subgroups within the human species, that has created the concept of 'race', rather than any genetic or biological evolutionary process.

THE DIMENSIONS OF MENTAL EXPERIENCE

One consequence of Darwin's theory of evolution by natural selection was to show how all animals – mammals, birds, fish, insects, dinosaurs, bacteria and, of course, humans – are in fact genetically interrelated. Although it might have taken millions of generations, all have descended from common ancestors. All creatures are cousins.

According to one definition, those groups we distinguish as 'species' today are simply ones whose branch of the family tree has extended so far into genetic isolation that its members have acquired a specific form of evolved uniqueness: as well as looking physically distinct and having characteristic behavioural patterns, they can no longer successfully breed with anyone but themselves. However, that they can now exchange genes only with each other does not alter the fact that, generations ago, their forebears were able to mingle and interbreed with a much wider range of beings. The genes that make them unique today are just a subset of a broader universal gene pool, one that spans the entire animal kingdom.

In this sense, then, the notion of 'species' is fairly arbitrary. We define a set of animals as its own species when we *believe* that their interbreeding capacities are constricted within a limited group. However, such belief might be misplaced. Precise reproductive boundaries are never easy to establish.

Biologists frequently discover that what they once thought was one species actually turns out to be several. For example, in 2001, *Loxodonta africana*, the supposed single species of African elephant, was discovered to comprise *two* entirely separate non-interbreeding and genetically distinct species, the bush elephant and the forest elephant (Roca et al., 2001). Similarly, analyses in 2004 uncovered at least *ten* separate free-standing species of 'skipper' butterfly that scientists previously thought of as just one (Herbert et al., 2004).

The problem can also arise in the other direction. Ultimately, reproductive isolation is a circumstantial basis for defining a scientific construct: much depends on physical geography and whether one species ever comes into contact with another. Animals that migrate long distances occasionally attempt to breed with unrelated, but physically similar, creatures that they encounter in their new habitats. In some cases, they succeed in producing offspring. After the European eel, *Anguilla anguilla*, was discovered to be able to successfully breed with its American counterpart, *Anguilla rostrata* (Als et al., 2011), what were previously thought of as two distinct species were found to overlap.

The boundaries separating one species from another are truly fuzzy. Biologists refer to the resulting ambiguities as the 'species problem' (Zachos, 2016).

As described in Chapter 5, the classification of the animal kingdom into groups and hierarchies has a long and varied history, its length and variety possibly revealing the fundamental arbitrariness of the task. Nonetheless, categorizing entities by class, a process referred to as *taxonomy*, remains a core endeavour of science.

This naming of nature's divisions is an ancient example of how humans have attempted to measure natural phenomena. The identification of classes is one of the most elementary forms of measurement, usually referred to as *categorical measurement*. It is used to provide a structured format for organic information that would otherwise be confusingly complex. Human beings are naturally prone to categorizing things, even if their efforts to do so are often imprecise.

For example, people are frequently guilty of a reasoning error known as bifurcation, or 'either/ or' thinking. This is where they assume that an entity that doesn't belong in one category must, by logic, belong to the exact opposite category instead: if something is not *male*, it must be *female*; if something is not *good*, it must be *bad*; if something is not *part of the solution*, it must be *part of the problem*. All of these common suppositions represent false dichotomies; in reality, there are more than two options for each.

In human terms, categorization is perhaps the most instinctive form of measurement. It remains an important feature of empirical science and is integral to psychology. Over the years, however, psychology has embraced a number of other somewhat more elaborate measurement practices.

Most research in psychology is based on forms of *ratio* or *interval measurement* (in which a trait or characteristic is given a numerical value to represent its intensity or 'size') or, occasionally, on forms of *ordinal measurement* (in which the analysis is based on the rank order of things, without focusing on the relativities between them). Procedurally, measurements are often derived from *psychometric instruments* (such as questionnaires or tests from which the psychologist can derive a score), or by using experimental methods to quantify performance or behaviour. These various *descriptive statistics* (the numbers that describe *what* has happened) usually set the scene for further in-depth *inferential statistics* (the analyses used to describe *why* or *how* it happened).

Psychology often involves the quantitative analysis of specific variables of interest, based on groups of people drawn from wider populations. Such endeavours are intrinsically dependent on our ability to measure psychological attributes, and on the quality of our resulting measurements.

LOGOPHILIA: 'STATISTICS'

Statistics refers broadly to the processing of information in its numerical form. A single piece of such information is a *statistic*.

Information can be used to produce statistics, or statistics can be used to produce information. For example, information can be known in advance and then converted into a numerical format, such as when the age range of a group of people is depicted using a bar chart. Alternatively, data can be scrutinized in order to reveal new knowledge, such as when we compare the heights of a sample of women and men to establish whether a true gender difference exists.

In psychology, as in other sciences, the word *statistics* is often used to refer to the very process of analysing numerical data. In this sense, *statistics* refers to the branch of mathematics that deals with the collection, interpretation and presentation of numerical data in order to make sense of information.

When statistics are used to summarize a dataset, we refer to them as *descriptive statistics*; when we use statistics to draw conclusions about matters of fact, we talk about *inferential statistics*. Inferential statistics will include the various statistical testing procedures that allow us to determine whether, for example, a difference between two sets of numbers is truly meaningful – or, in technical language, whether it is 'statistically significant'.

Today we consider the word *statistic* (or the abbreviation *stat*) to be synonymous with *number*. However, the term does not originate in mathematics. It actually refers to the fact that statistical information was originally compiled to describe the *state of things* (van der Zande, 2010), a notion that itself indirectly gave rise to the practice of referring to a country as a *state*. The German economist Gottfried Achenwall (1719–72) coined the German-language word *Statistik* in 1749 (Achenwall, 1749) to signify what he thought of as the 'science of the state'. He derived the term based on the Italian Latinism *statista* or 'statesman', which itself emerged from the Latin expression *statisticum collegium*, or 'education on the state of things'.

It is quite possible to measure something inaccurately without realizing that it is inaccurate. As such, it is quite possible to generate extensive research into psychology without realizing that the variables underpinning the work are suspect.

It is worth remembering that all forms of measurement represent *a product of human reasoning*, rather than *an intrinsic quality of whatever is being measured*. A measure is simply an outcome of a human effort to measure, and takes no account of whether that effort is flawlessly proficient, or hopelessly inept. Just because a psychologist attempts to measure something does not mean that they can measure it accurately or at all. It doesn't even mean that the 'thing' they are trying to measure *actually exists*.

The history of psychology shows us how the human effort to measure psychological qualities has frequently been fraught with considerable difficulty, and has often been motivated by intent more sinister than scientific.

Quantifying virtue

Since ancient times, human civilizations have applied the process of counting to their scientific work, underpinning their increasingly complex theoretical models with quantities, distances, weights and angles. Even the intangible components of human psychology have long been considered in terms of mathematics. Ancient philosophers expounded on the benefits of proportionality in human affairs, describing the best state of being as a balance between extremes. The concept of a 'golden mean' between excess and deficiency was not merely a mathematical metaphor. Socrates, Plato, Aristotle, and many others proposed that harmony, symmetry and balance could be assessed with precision.

Perhaps the clearest example of this approach was inherent in Aristotle's description of ethics. Aristotle proposed that any human quality can be defined as the midpoint between two extremes. For example, the quality of bravery is the mean between complete cowardice and utter rashness. A person develops their bravery through trial and error, reward and punishment, and their own ultimate sense of what feels pleasurable and what feels wrong. Over time, these competing forces cause a person's character to oscillate between the extremes, gradually gravitating towards the average or midpoint. In an ideal situation, the *exact* midpoint will be reached, making this the perfect form of virtue.

Aristotle extended this reasoning to explain justice in terms of proportionality. In his view, fairness can be assessed by examining how benefits are distributed across parties. If one party has an unequal share of benefit, then this is the very definition of an injustice. Corrective action would require the subtraction of benefits from that party, and their reallocation to the other (Burger, 2008). In some of his writings, Aristotle likened this process to the buying and selling of commodities. Ethical justice and personal morality could be quantified in the same way that merchants would apply prices to products. The Aristotelian view was that human virtue could be discussed and evaluated in terms of balance, proportions and, thus, quantities.

As described in previous chapters, Aristotle's philosophy was to become dominantly influential throughout the medieval world, in Europe and beyond. Often this involved his ideas being repurposed and reinterpreted in religious or theological terms. A particular concern in Christian philosophy centred around the economies of vice and sinfulness. According to religious custom, citizens would be expected to pay for their misdemeanours by performing penance or restitution, considerations that required accurate ways to quantify and calculate the costs inherent in such transactions.

Sometime around the fourteenth century, as civilian numeracy increased and numerical technologies such as clocks became more commonplace, European scientists increasingly sought to quantify the world around them (Kemp, 2018). In this 'near frenzy to measure everything imaginable' (Murdoch, 1975, p. 287), the ability of medieval Christians to calculate their 'debts to God' entered a new phase. The relative seriousness of different sins was codified in detailed manuals, broadly adhering to the Aristotelian principle that the gravest offences required the heaviest penances. Citizens could even purchase their soul's purity using money, by buying so-called indulgences from their local church. These effectively were vouchers that, when accumulated in sufficient amounts, would entitle the holder to expedite their access to heaven after they died, perhaps allowing them to bypass purgatory altogether. The price paid depended on the surplus 'virtue' that lay at the sinner's disposal, once the value of their sins had been deducted.

Medieval scientists developed several techniques for analysing quantitative concepts, many of which were forerunners of methods that continue to be employed today. The French philosopher Nicole Oresme (1325–82) employed geometrical reasoning to contend that human characteristics could extend in quantity in the same systematic way that objects could increase their velocity. He elaborated a number of theories about pain and joy and the proportional difference in intensity between one emotion and another. The Italian philosopher Gregory of Rimini (1300–58) developed similar ideas, ultimately concluding that the intensity of a person's generosity could theoretically grow to infinity (Kemp, 2018).

Historically, the scientists who first used trigonometry, geometry and mathematical models to account for phenomena in nature were just as likely to apply their ideas to psychological concepts as to physical ones. The accumulation of a human attribute was believed to conform to the same principles as the acceleration of an object in space. Medieval scholars were very accepting of the idea that psychological variables can be quantified, much more so perhaps than many modern psychologists are today.

One reason for this contrast is that in the Middle Ages most science was abstract and theoretical. Models were proposed, thought experiments devised, and computations carefully performed, but the actual collecting of real-world data to support empirical research would come much later. When psychology researchers were eventually to engage in such primary data collection, however, the gaps between theory and reality came vividly into view.

Unlike the trajectory of an object accelerating in space, the virtues, vices and variables that comprise the subject matter of psychological research incorporate ethical dimensions as well as material ones. For psychology, the consequences of imprecision are not limited to disproved theorems or failed experiments. Ill-conceived methods, misleading data and skewed interpretations all produce profound cultural costs. The quantification of human attributes is a demanding endeavour that requires maximal ethical engagement. Unfortunately, however, the history of this aspect of psychology shows how even the most pious attempts at behavioural science can be hampered by the basest of human impulses.

RACE SUPREMACISM AS A DRIVER OF BEHAVIOURAL STATISTICS

In Chapter 5, we saw how the field of phrenology became widely popular with the general public despite lacking a rigorous evidence base or sound theoretical foundations. However, while the phrenologists were busy examining the *exterior* of people's skulls, a different group of practitioners were looking at the *interior* of the human cranium. These researchers combined anthropological fervour, religious zeal and a taste for the macabre in an effort to prove that some subsets of humanity – namely their *own* kind – were more worthy than others.

Central to their theory was the biblical assertion that the earth was just a few thousand years old. If true, this would be an insufficient time frame for all of humankind's different ethnicities and cultures to have descended from a common ancestor. In the view of these scientists, the implication of religious doctrine was that the world's different races must have been created separately. From this they hypothesized that different groups of humans were essentially separate species, a theory known as *polygeny*. They set about attempting to prove as much by looking for anatomical differences in the bodies of people from across the world.

One leading exponent of this approach was the American scientist Samuel George Morton (1799–1851), who worked at Pennsylvania Medical College. Morton became interested in the idea that key differences in the world's diverse populations could be seen in the shapes and sizes of human skulls. Not only did skulls largely determine the appearance of people's faces, they also housed their brains, the organ that the phrenologists had 'shown' was responsible for people's character. Morton began gathering as many human skulls as he could lay his hands on, and eventually accumulated a collection of well over a thousand.

In a lavishly illustrated 1839 monograph – *Crania Americana; or a Comparative View of the Skulls of Various Aboriginal Nations of North and South America* – Morton published an extensive array of lithographs, diagrams and statistical tables, setting out what he concluded were the key anatomical differences between different groups of people. In his most infamous table, he described how 'Caucasians' had the largest skull capacity of all humankind, at 87 cubic inches, whereas 'Ethiopians' had the smallest, at 78 cubic inches. While ostensibly claiming to be investigating the naturalistic notion of polygeny, Morton's less than subtle claim was to have 'found' that White people had larger brains than Black people. Morton supplemented these statistical conclusions with extensive tracts of prose claiming that the different groups were, for example, on the one hand, 'distinguished for the facility with which it attains the highest intellectual endowments' (p. 5), and on the other, 'noted for indolence, deception, and falsehood' (p. 87).

Later investigations of Morton's old skull collection attempted to show that his measurements of skull capacity were very imprecise (Gould, 1981). However, the problems with Morton's work had little to do with whether his numerical data were accurate. More significant shortcomings included the fact that his peculiar selection of skulls was sporadic, incidental and far from representative of the wider human population. While his overall collection was large, the numbers of skulls in different ethnic categories were often too low to be statistically reliable (for instance, he had only twenty-nine so-called Ethiopians). His classification of different ethnicities was idiosyncratic and arbitrary. His speculations about brain size did not take account of relative proportional differences in body size, or of differences in age. And his conclusions about some people being 'distinguished for their intellects' while others could be 'noted for indolence' were extravagantly prejudiced, having nothing whatsoever to do with his skull measurements. In short, the very fact that Morton's conclusions matched his prior beliefs concerning human polygeny makes it clear that his methods and interpretations were at the very least skewed, if not thoroughly biased.

Morton's analysis of his own personal skull collection is often acknowledged as the starting point of what we now call 'scientific racism'. This is the practice of using science to attempt to demonstrate racial superiority, and thus to justify (or sanitize) racial discrimination. That the field has failed to produce reliable evidence for its racist doctrine has not prevented it from persisting to the present day. It is true that today these efforts lie very much at the discredited margins of scientific discourse. However, scientific racism is a powerful example of *pseudoscience*. Pseudoscience is

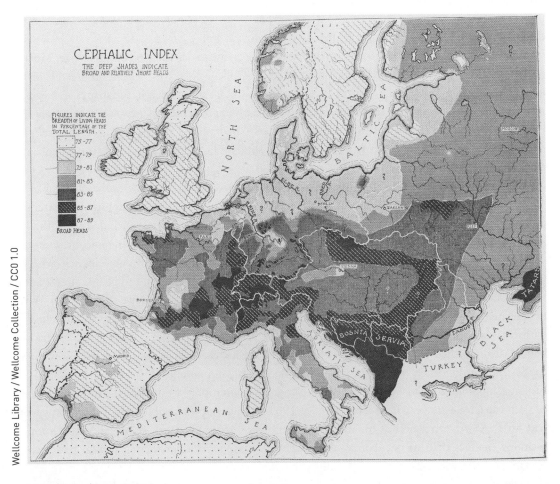

Image 6.1 'Cephalic index'
A map from an 1898 book called *The Races of Europe*. Early scientific racism sought to classify people of different ethnicities by head circumference, implying an association with intelligence.

the activity of producing research that *appears* to many onlookers to be scientific, but which is actually anything but. The biggest problem with pseudoscience is that it often attracts a far greater audience than that drawn by actual *science* (Hughes, 2016).

Scientific racism demonstrates how quantification can lend an air of objectivity to assertions that would otherwise be dismissed as baseless, specious, partisan, self-serving, ignorant, profane or racist. It is a sobering fact of the history of psychology that many of the field's most widely used methods of measurement were born out of such endeavours. Psychology's debt to scientific racism is frequently overlooked today, but no less real as a consequence.

The emergence of inferential statistics

Many of the earliest statisticians were humanitarians. The Belgian mathematician Adolphe Quetelet (1796–1874) developed the now familiar concept of the 'statistically average person' ('l'homme moyen'; Quetelet, 1835). He used it to show how behavioural predictors could explain health and well-being in the population. Arguing that human characteristics would conform to 'normal' distributions, just as variables in the natural sciences were known to do, Quetelet introduced new methods of encapsulating relevant information using numbers. One of his innovations was the body mass index, still widely used in health research today (although in Quetelet's time it was employed to identify emaciation and malnourishment, rather than to track obesity). Quetelet showed how population-level problems such as poor health, suicide and crime rates could be predicted by social factors. His statistical arguments were among the first to challenge prevailing views that blamed individual victims for causing the very social problems that affected them.

Among those to be inspired by Quetelet was his student, Pierre Verhulst (1804–49), who applied logistic functions to better model population growth and used them to question Malthusian assertions about the natural inevitability of war and famine. Another was the British social reformer Florence Nightingale (1820–1910), credited as the founder of modern nursing, who was both a precocious statistician and an inspirational activist. Nightingale conducted a number of detailed statistical studies of the effects of sanitation on public health, persuading the British parliament to enact new legislation to provide citizens with access to clean water systems. Within fifty years, national life expectancy in Britain had increased by nearly two decades, almost entirely due to policy changes inspired by Nightingale's famous studies (Szreter, 1988). Nightingale is also renowned for developing complex new methods of depicting statistical information using graphs, including the polar area diagram.

In the nineteenth century, social reformers frequently used statistical surveys for their campaigns, and many of the early statistical societies were founded as philanthropic organizations. However, as in the present day, with the arrival of statistics came the growth of statistical error. Numbers can sometimes confuse more than clarify.

One frequent problem related to what we now call the 'ecological fallacy'. This common conception occurs when statistical information about a *group* is used to draw statistical conclusions about an *individual* in that group. It is the error that occurs when someone presumes that because you come from a town where the average person is 1.73 metres tall, you *too* must be 1.73 metres tall. It takes Quetelet's 'statistically average person' to inform us about *all* persons in a category, ignoring the fact that Quetelet also pointed out how human characteristics fall within normal distributions: traits range from *low* to *high*, from *below* to *above* the statistical average. Quetelet, and many others, also noted that a statistical average will only ever relate to one single trait at a time, and so is meaningless unless considered in the context of all the other factors that might affect an individual person.

Thus, when nineteenth-century reformers explained how social problems could be predicted based on statistical regularities, some observers concluded that these same statistical regularities could then be used to make predictions about individual citizens. By this logic, any person from a community with a high crime rate would themselves be considered more likely to be a criminal. That the vast majority of individuals living in such communities were conscientious and law-abiding would be ignored. Of all the information available, the single eye-catching 'statistical average' would be deemed the most pertinent.

This type of reasoning – where inferences about individuals are based on the 'statistically average' person – is often seen as a form of 'common sense'. However, in logical terms, it is inherently unreliable. For one thing, statistical averages are themselves abstract projections. Rather than *every case* being the same as the statistical average, it is more often true that *no case* actually is (as is clear from the cliché about the 'average' family having one and a half children). A second problem is that probabilities do not apply to individuals, but to frequencies within groups. There is little meaning to the claim that a given person is 'likely' to be a criminal, because if they are *not* a criminal then the claim is still true (likelihood, after all, is not certainty). And a third problem is that the 'common sense' approach usually rests on tenuous assumptions about how easily people can move in and out of the groups in which they find themselves categorized (for example, that if people live in a high-crime area, it is because they *choose* to do so (and so they must like it!)).

Notwithstanding such pitfalls, in the nineteenth century, across science and society, statistical information became crucial to illustrating the state of things in nature. The use of statistical regularities to make predictions about the future or to draw conclusions about individuals added a striking new dimension to this endeavour. Newly developed techniques helped to add persuasive potential to numbers, charts and tables. Statistics could be used to support *inferences*, as well as *descriptions* – at least in theory. In practice, however, statistics were just as often used to support self-fulfilling prophesies, social prejudices and systemic bigotries, all under a camouflage of presumed scientific 'objectivity'.

Eugenics and the notion of people as 'stock'

For psychologists, nowhere is this dilemma of methodological morality more clear than in the case of *eugenics*. Eugenics is a doctrine of principles and practices that aim to improve the human race through selective breeding, by excluding people who are judged to be inferior or undesirable. The concept has been advanced in theory for centuries, long before the emergence of a modern understanding of genetics or biological evolution. However, it was during the late nineteenth century that eugenics became a widespread advocacy movement. By the 1930s, it had become hugely influential on legislators and policymakers across Europe and in the United States (Hansen & King, 2001). Eugenicists called on states to practise social engineering, by pursuing interventionist policies that encompassed family planning, education curricula and immigration law.

It was the development of new statistical techniques that brought this modern version of eugenics into being. Without methods to quantify the calibre of different people, the possibility of selective breeding would remain forever an intuitive abstraction. The new statistical approaches conceived by social reformers were quickly adapted by advocates whose attitudes towards humanity were far less philanthropic.

The modern eugenics movement originated in Britain. Specifically, it was put forward by the English psychologist Francis Galton (1822–1911). Galton was a half-cousin of Charles Darwin, and it is often suggested that his thinking was stimulated by Darwin's theory. However, as we saw in Chapter 5, Darwin himself rejected the idea that social problems could ever be explained or addressed using the principles of biological evolution.

Galton was born into great wealth. After completing a university degree in mathematics, he did not work professionally but instead spent a period as an African explorer, travelling on expeditions organized by the Royal Geographical Society. Afterwards, he became interested in science and was able to self-fund a long career as an independent scientist.

Galton produced his first major psychological treatise, *Hereditary Genius: An Inquiry into Its Laws and Consequences*, in 1869. Perhaps prompted by his own propitious origins, he used this work to propose that human intelligence was genetically determined. Essentially, according to Galton, intelligent people are intelligent *because they are born of intelligent parents*; any success they achieve in life is due to natural talent, rather than social advantage.

Galton offered three main arguments in support of this verdict. Firstly, he showed that academic examination scores were normally distributed, with few scores extremely low or high, and the majority clustering about the statistical average. Not having paid sufficient attention to Quetelet, Galton erroneously believed that only innate qualities could be distributed in this manner, and so concluded that academic ability must duly be innate. Secondly, Galton perused biographical dictionaries and found that eminent people tended to have eminent relatives (he himself was related to *both* Charles *and* Erasmus Darwin). From this he concluded that pedigree predicted prowess. And thirdly, based entirely on an anecdotal account, Galton asserted that adoptees appear not to attain the same level of eminence as their natural-born counterparts, which was consistent with his belief that intelligence runs through bloodlines.

Despite the popularity of *Hereditary Genius*, Galton's arguments were thoroughly weak. He was wrong about normal distributions. His biographical data on family relatedness could as easily be explained by the theory that *wealth* and *upbringing*, rather than genes, accounted for success. And his handpicked evidence on adoptees was entirely anecdotal. While his book drew wide attention, there was little in it that would lead a government to institute a programme of social engineering.

By the time Galton put forward the idea of eugenics, his approach (and that of his collaborators) had become much more interventionist. In a new book in 1883, he introduced eugenics as 'the science of improving stock' in order 'to give the more suitable races or strains of blood a better chance of prevailing'. Perhaps disturbingly, he noted that the pursuit of a eugenicist agenda would be 'by no means confined to questions of judicious mating' (Galton, 1883, p. 25). Such language was to set a scene that, at various points in subsequent decades, would include calls for programmes of enforced sterilization, selective abortion, mandatory segregation and, in the most extreme instances, genocidal extermination.

The eugenicist need for statistics

Crucially, Galton's approach was also now infused with statistics. In 1888, he established a walk-in laboratory for the public at London's International Health Exhibition. There he would gather data on people's reaction times, perceptual acuity and physical characteristics, all with the aim of accumulating information on 'intelligence'. Even though variables such as reaction time were poor proxies for intelligence (after all, might not some intelligent people take *more* time on a test?), Galton pored over the resulting datasets looking for evidence to support his belief that intellectual ability was indeed born and not made.

He produced basic diagrams of scores collected from relatives, in a format we now refer to as scatterplots. He noted that drawing an imaginary line through the various data points helped to show the nature of the association between the scores, with the steepness of the line indicating a stronger statistical link. And he devised a mathematical index to encapsulate the association between separate groups of scores, naming it the coefficient of 'co-relation' (Galton, 1888), which we now spell as 'correlation'.

Galton's colleague and collaborator, the English mathematician Karl Pearson (1857–1936), took these ideas forward. An eclectic scholar, who at various times had studied physics, physiology, philosophy, law and literature, Pearson ultimately chose to specialize in mathematics, becoming a professor at University College London in 1884. After he encountered Galton's biometric laboratory at the International Health Exhibition, Pearson felt he had found his true calling. From then on, he immersed himself in the mission of eugenics.

Pearson was undoubtedly a hugely talented mathematician. He expanded upon Galton's method of correlation, conceiving the idea of 'negative' correlations, where increases in one variable are associated with decreases in another. He devised a convenient method for computing correlations that continues to be taught to students today, as Pearson's *r*

Public domain, via Wikimedia Commons / {PD-US}

Image 6.2 Galton's eugenics
Illustrations used by Francis Galton in 1883 to classify people based on appearance and on rudimentary (and spurious) psychological tests.

(or more technically, the 'Pearson product-moment correlation coefficient'). And he gradually devised a system for describing the statistical features of 'probability distributions', the probabilities of different possible outcomes of events that happen multiple times (such as experiments that are conducted repeatedly).

The parameters of his system will be familiar to high-school mathematics students around the world. According to Pearson (1894, 1905), such distributions could usefully be described in terms of their *mean* (the central average around which the measurements scatter), their *standard deviation* (how far, in general, they scatter), their *symmetry* (the degree to which measurements are loaded on one side of the mean instead of the other), and their *kurtosis* (how far the most extreme measures fall from the mean).

But perhaps Pearson's most revolutionary statistical idea was the notion that all measurements, especially in the social sciences, are likely to be imperfect (Salsburg, 2001). When the same study is conducted more than once, the results will never be so precise as to always be exactly the same. As such, each single result will incorporate an unpredictable degree of inaccuracy, which we call 'random error'. It is only by repeating a study a number of times that we can produce an estimate of what the real result should be. A good scientist will try to find ways to reduce random error, but will nonetheless always allow for it when analysing statistics.

The same logic applies to the task of interpreting samples of measurements. When looking at a dataset drawn from a selected group of people, its parameters (i.e. its mean, standard deviation, symmetry and kurtosis) will never be *exactly* the same as those of the entire population. However, using mathematics, it should be possible to determine, and allow for, the error component involved. All told, the parameters of a population might never be known for sure – but, using Pearson's principles, they can reasonably be *estimated* by looking at a sample.

Pearson assumed control of the now elderly Galton's biometric laboratory in 1897. Shortly after, he joined with Galton and the English biologist Raphael Weldon (1860–1906) to establish a new academic journal, which they called *Biometrika*. In this specialized periodical, the three could foster – and, as editors, curate – the emerging field of research into 'biological statistics'.

In 1906, the group hosted an extended visit by English statistician, William Sealy Gosset (1876–1937), who took leave from his job at the Guinness Brewery in Dublin, Ireland, in order to study under Pearson. The previous year, Pearson had published a paper by Gosset in *Biometrika*. As it was against Guinness company policy for employees to publicly share their intellectual property, Gosset used the pseudonym 'Student' when signing his paper. Later, when Gosset wrote a follow-up paper describing a new way to estimate parameters in small samples of data, he published it under the same pseudonym ('Student', 1908), thereby securing his place in statistical history as the inventor of 'Student's *t*-test'. Not only did this test facilitate researchers to quickly compare small samples of data, it also encouraged them to draw conclusions based on statistical distributions. In other words, it ushered in the use of what we now refer to as 'hypothesis tests' or 'significance tests' (Salsburg, 2001).

In later decades, these ideas were further extended by another eugenically minded English statistician, Ronald Fisher (1890–1962). Fisher, who is regarded as one of the most important figures in the history of statistics, was deeply invested in the study of genetics and its application to selective human breeding. He developed a range of statistical procedures, including the *F*-distribution, the basis for *analysis of variance*, as well as *Fisher's exact test*, a method for deriving statistical significance from categorical data. Fisher also codified the procedure for Gosset's *t*-test into its modern format (Fisher, 1925).

Statisticians as supremacists

All these principles and procedures will be familiar to anyone who conducts psychology research today. They form the bedrock of statistical analysis as used in modern psychology. However, few contemporary psychologists are aware that their go-to methods of number crunching were developed with a political purpose. The central motivation for devising these techniques was to advance the cause of eugenics.

The eugenics movement wanted to improve the population's 'genetic stock' by ridding society of those it deemed 'unfit to reproduce'. Its advocates claimed that society could only be saved from destruction by ridding itself of people with disabilities, the intellectually challenged, those whose behaviour was deemed to 'deviate' from what was 'normal', and members of disfavoured minority ethnic groups. Galton and his acolytes were keen that civilization urgently pursue ways to

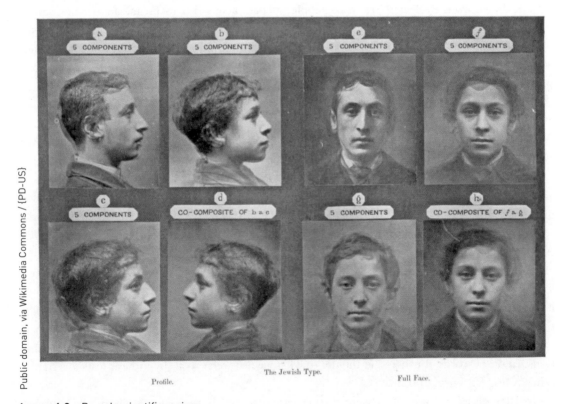

Image 6.3   Pseudoscientific racism
With little or no scientific basis, Galton used composite photography to classify people by race, here combining different pictures to identify the standard Jewish 'type'.

extinguish whole swathes of society from existence. The ingenuity of their statistical methods reflected the fanatic zeal with which they were committed to this cause.

As is apparent from their various writings and utterances, the founding figures of psychology's statistical practices were unmistakably ardent eugenicists. Galton felt that some ethnic groups would be better off as slaves ('for they could hardly become more wretched than they are now'; Gillham, 2001, p. 89). Pearson warned against racial equality ('when the white man and the dark shall share the soil between them') because in an egalitarian society 'there will be nothing to check the fertility of inferior stock' (Pearson, 1901, p. 24). He also enthused about Hitler's 'vast experiment' in Nazi Germany, where a sterilization law aimed at 'the prevention of hereditarily diseased offspring' had just been passed (Gelb, 1997, p. 133). Even after the full horrors of the Holocaust were known, Fisher too chose to defend the Nazis, who 'in spite of their prejudices', he said, merely wished 'to benefit the German racial stock, especially by the elimination of manifest defectives' (Weiss, 2010).

In 2020, arising from an enquiry into the history of eugenics, the governors of University College London announced that they would remove the names of Galton and Pearson from its campus estate. The long-established Galton Lecture Theatre, Pearson Lecture Theatre and Pearson Building would each be retitled, with other university assets, such as its Galton Professorship, similarly to be renamed. That same year, a college at Cambridge University undertook to remove a stained-glass window that had been installed in 1989 to memorialize the fact that Fisher was one of its former students.

The innovation of Galton and his followers yielded statistical techniques that are today the most commonly used in psychology research. But these techniques sprung from ideas that were grounded in the most strident forms of xenophobia. The nexus between statistics and supremacism is an uncomfortable one for psychology. By providing a scientific veneer for bigotry, these methods would, in time, facilitate the visiting of a range of horrors upon the world's most oppressed and marginalized peoples. As we will see below, the legacy of eugenics continues to be felt in psychology today, its imprint visible in many modern manifestations of (pseudo)scientific racism.

HISTORY REPEATING ITSELF: THE PERSISTENCE OF EUGENICS

While eugenics initially fell from favour following the Second World War, eugenic arguments have persisted in the fringes of political discourse and are often said to influence debates on topics such as genetic engineering and bioethics. A recurring claim is that while eugenics might be morally objectionable, it is nonetheless theoretically practicable. From this there can then be an implication that, if circumstances were sufficiently extreme, some form of eugenics could be considered.

Despite the curiosity it provokes, geneticists argue that the claims made on behalf of eugenics are not in fact scientifically reasonable (Curtis & Balloux, 2020). For example, eugenicists often point to the selective breeding of animals, such as racehorses or dairy cattle, to show how genetic principles can be used to improve the 'desirable' traits of a species. However, such animals are bred in highly controlled environments, have short generational times, and produce large numbers of offspring. By contrast, humans have long generational times and produce few offspring, meaning that any attempt to selectively breed humans would take literally centuries to have any effect.

But more importantly, humans are not 'bred' in controlled environments to begin with. This means that it is impossible to know which humans have the so-called desirable genetic traits that appeal to eugenicists. Any traits that appear in humans can be the result of genes, environmental factors, or a combination. Attempts to use genes as markers for human traits usually produce very unclear information. Therefore, even if it were agreed that 'selective breeding' was acceptable, we simply could not know which human beings to choose as forebears.

More commonly, commentators argue that selective breeding could be used to remove 'undesirable' characteristics, such as intellectual disability, from the human population. For example, it is claimed that this could be achieved if policies were introduced to discourage, or prevent, certain people in the population from having children. However, this idea is also scientifically flawed. Many cases of intellectual disability result from de novo genetic mutations, meaning that the child has a genetic variant that is not present in either parent.

Most other cases result from *recessive* genetic variants, meaning that each healthy parent carries one copy of the gene, but intellectual disability only arises when the child inherits both copies. As such recessive genes are harmless on their own, it makes no sense to use selective breeding to limit their presence in the human gene pool. In essence, every human being is a carrier of such 'recessively acting' gene variants. Therefore, given that most cases of intellectual disability result either from de novo or recessive effects, the argument that eugenics can be used to prevent intellectual disability is essentially groundless. The same issues arise to varying degrees with many other conditions that eugenicists often discuss, such as mental illnesses that have genetic components.

Nonetheless, while both controversial and implausible, eugenics continues to attract attention, albeit not typically from mainstream scientists. Since 2014, a London Conference on Intelligence has been held on four occasions. This private conference has been accused of promoting eugenics, and of attempting to cultivate a new generation of adherents. After being investigated by the host university, the organizers decided to move their event to Copenhagen, Denmark, claiming that intrusive media attention had made their activities untenable (Daley, 2018).

RACE SUPREMACISM AS A DRIVER OF PSYCHOLOGICAL THEORY

While humans have for millennia seen themselves as divided into different tribes, it was only in the nineteenth century that this classification began to be approached as a scientific proposition. Prior to this, diversity and difference were largely considered in cultural, religious or even mystical terms.

As described in Chapter 3, for much of history, human beings considered the inhabitants of nearby villages to be somewhat unfamiliar, and those of towns that lay inaccessibly beyond the next mountain to be intimidatingly alien. That visitors from faraway lands might have different skin or hair colour was largely mundane in a world that generally believed in the existence of giants, Cyclopes and 'Blemmyes', headless people whose eyes and mouths were embedded in their chests (Friedman, 2000). Other characters worth worrying about included those people who were influenced or possessed by the Devil, including, of course, witches. There was little inherent in foreignness per se that was uniquely a source of fear.

But that is not to say that foreignness itself was never treated with suspicion. After all, one of the reasons tribes are ever formed is because humans, by nature, are paranoid towards strangers.

When you have no other information, it makes sense to remain cautious about newcomers until they demonstrate their trustworthiness. In this sense, xenophobia – an animosity towards outsiders – has a long history in human psychology. And to the extent that every in-group considers itself superior to every out-group, the impulse to view outsiders as less worthy and less capable is also deeply ingrained. Self-exceptionalism is the root of all inter-racial rivalries, and to some extent the root of the very concept of 'race' itself.

The concept of 'race' is born from human inclinations towards obsessive cultural comparison and instinctive group guardedness. Many psychological biases come into play. A key example is known as the 'out-group homogeneity effect' (Judd & Park, 1988). This is a general habit of reasoning where we view our own group in much more detail than other groups. As a result, we see our own tribe in all its diversity, but we view outsiders as comparatively homogenous. We are interesting, but they are 'all the same'.

Likewise, the psychology of group dynamics ensures that we focus most of our attention on our nearest and dearest. As we grow, our social skills become crafted for closeness; friends end up requiring much less effort than strangers. Consequently, we become much less efficient at perceiving the nuances of those who are different to us. We view the world beyond our immediate environments with increasing reductionism. The further away events are, the fuzzier their details seem. All in all, because of our innate egocentrism, coupled with a lifetime's familiarity with our own surroundings, faraway details simply matter less within our automatic value systems.

The psychology of social cognition helps to explain why human beings will often engage in highly nuanced interactions with people who live nearby, regularly making superfine distinctions between one group of local rivals and another, while simultaneously grouping the billions of people who comprise the entire wider world into an implausibly limited number of 'racial' or ethnic categories.

Historically, such categories tended to be driven by religious, social or political reasoning. For example, countries that engaged in colonialism or slavery used race-based terminology to describe the various groups that they subjugated. Around the world, similar contexts have led to a widespread practice of discussing cultural diversity in terms of 'racial' categorization. But the many 'race' categories that are commonly discussed in culture (which, in any event, vary from one culture to the next) do not exist at any scientific or genetic level.

We now know that more than 99 per cent of human DNA is the same in every person. Of the three billion nucleotide positions in the human genome, less than 1 per cent of human DNA actually varies (Sternberg, Grigorenko & Kidd, 2005). There is no way for a geneticist to use this 1 per cent to determine the 'race' of a particular genetic sample. This is essentially because the concept of racial identity is a social convenience that has no biological counterpart. It is true that many different groups of people differ in physical characteristics, including (for example) skin tone, and that physical characteristics such as skin tone are largely determined by people's genes. However, these variations in human form do not cluster into categories, genetic or otherwise. Skin tone, for example, ranges globally from very dark to very light, without there being a set number of colour-codable 'shades'.

A common focus of scientific racism has been the claim that 'race' is a true phenomenon of biogenetic variation, and not a culturally invented system that uses shortcuts to label out-groups. Moreover, scientific racism seeks to assert that such genetic dimensions provide the ability to stratify superior and inferior 'races', in a way that (conveniently) reflects the current distribution of economic and social privilege in global society. While ostensibly concerning biological processes, these claims are almost always couched in behavioural and cognitive terms. For this reason, psychologists – and psychology – have consistently been central to these endeavours.

Psychology and 'race'

The cultural notion of 'race' was at first a broad-ranging concept, referring to groupings of any entity. It was only towards the end of the seventeenth century that the term began to be used to refer to humans, an approach to terminology prompted by the needs of colonialism.

English settlers in North America, for example, largely steered clear of the local indigenous population, coming to view them as culturally and biologically distinct, as well as unambiguously primitive. Their attitude to the thousands of people they forcibly transported to North America as slaves was similarly domineering. By the time of the American Revolution (1765–83), the different local populations – primarily people of European descent ('Whites'), people of African descent ('Blacks'), and Native American people ('Indians') – were increasingly referred to as different 'races', a vocabulary born from the task of having to manage, and maintain, social inequality. The term soon became common throughout Europe, especially among the colonizing elites when discussing the many far-flung populations of the so-called New World that they increasingly plundered (Smedley, 1998).

By the late nineteenth century, notions of 'race' had sprawled to encompass various divisions of the European population itself, with nearly every territory alleged to be inhabited by its own distinct grouping. With little or no empirical justification, theorists pondered about the unique qualities of an ever-expanding human family, comprising Anglo-Saxons, Alpines, Aryans, Celts, Dinurians, Gauls, Ligurians, Mediterraneans, Nordics, Teutons, Slavs and many others (G. Richards, 2012). Almost all such 'races' were viewed as differing in terms of moral and intellectual quality.

With the arrival of eugenics, new methods of quantification were added to these systems of terminology. Academic journals such as *Eugenics Review* (established in 1909) and *Annals of Eugenics* (established in 1925, by Pearson) provided regular statistical 'evidence' for the dangers of immigration and of racial intermarriage. In the inaugural issue of *Annals*, Pearson published a now notorious report claiming to demonstrate that a sample of Jewish children in London were 'inferior physically and mentally to the native population' (Pearson & Moul, 1925, p. 126). Figures such as Charles Spearman (1863–1945) and Cyril Burt (1883–1971) were among the many prominent British psychologists to accept such findings at face value, going on themselves to develop theories and research that assumed, as fact, the existence of profound racial differences in ability (G. Richards, 2012).

However, data were not always needed. In the first half of the twentieth century, many prominent British psychologists endorsed views that were extremely racist without appearing to require much, or any, empirical corroboration. The social psychologist William McDougall (1871–1938), author of the influential *Introduction to Social Psychology* (1908), frequently speculated about the dangers of racial integration, at one point arguing that political stability would be impossible 'where the population consists of two or more racial stocks' (McDougall, 1914, p. 307). The eminent personality theorist Raymond B. Cattell (1905–98) endorsed racial segregation in the United States, defended the Nazi Third Reich, and spoke in favour of the deliberate 'phasing out' of unfit racial groups, a practice he called 'genthanasia' (Tucker, 1994).

In continental Europe, race psychology tended to be more philosophical than quantitative. Colonialism again loomed large. French scholars speculated about the 'uncivilized mind' (Merllié, 2012), and several psychoanalysts theorized about the components of 'primitive' culture (Kenny, 2015; we will return to psychoanalysis in Chapter 7). Notoriously, the most prominent empirical research into race psychology in early twentieth-century Europe was conducted in Nazi Germany. However, as the Nazis had subsumed professional psychology into the regime's Ministry of Science, whose job was to ensure that only 'state-approved' studies were published (Schönpflug, 2017), most of this 'research' was in reality scientifically worthless propaganda.

AMERICAN RACE HISTORY AND ITS LASTING IMPACT ON PSYCHOLOGY

We previously noted how the American approach has come to exert a normative influence on the way psychology is discussed and studied around the world. This reflects the United States' vivid influence on global culture, and is no doubt assisted by the country's considerable wealth and the emergence of the English language as an international lingua franca. When it comes to the psychology of 'race', however, not all countries are equal. The United States, for one, has had a uniquely fraught and peculiar national history with regard to its racial politics.

The United States' experience of racial history – and, by extension, the way American psychologists first came to learn about and discuss the question of 'race' – was shaped by a number of very specific historical contexts. Three in particular are mentioned here.

Firstly, the American agony of slavery and its abolition was culturally and politically traumatic. Even today, a century and a half later, its after-effects continue to destabilize the country's social cohesion. Secondly, for many decades after slavery was abolished, the American education system continued to be racially segregated, often with the imprimatur of government, and at times codified in law. And thirdly, the historical role of immigration in the American 'way of life' has done much to place racial identity at the centre of society, while frequently provoking tensions arising from immigration policies and practices that, at times, appear to have been shaped by a disquieting degree of ethnocentrism.

Slavery and abolition

Slavery has long inflicted a psychological scar on American life. The first African men and women to be transported to North America by colonial slave traders were brought to shore at what is now South Carolina in the middle of the sixteenth century. Similar mass abductions continued for 300 years: the last known transportation of enslaved persons to the United States was in 1859.

When the United States was founded in 1776, around one in five of the country's inhabitants were people of African descent held in bondage as slaves. Revolutionary rhetoric emphasized liberty, equality and freedom, but most of the political class considered Black people to be inherently inferior, destined for servitude, and certainly unworthy of the vote. The moral contradiction was resolved by the theory of polygeny, which quickly gained currency in America around this time. Polygeny legitimized a view that Europeans, Africans and the rest of the 'races' were not necessarily equal after all, as they had come into existence separately. Slavery could be reconciled with human rights because of a scientific argument that explicitly questioned whether African people were even truly 'human' at all (Smedley & Smedley, 2005).

Objections to slavery – not least from enslaved people themselves – eventually brought the United States to near collapse, by catalysing the American Civil War (1861–5). However, the abolition of slavery in 1865, and the granting of legal freedom to all persons held as slaves, did little to change attitudes. There emerged a cultural backlash in which many privileged people, including scholars, were motivated to devise new reasoning to justify ongoing discrimination against Black communities. This spawned a plethora of 'scientific' studies and accounts claiming that Black people were, in various ways, inferior to Whites and so should be treated accordingly, for the good of society as a whole.

As such, during the period when psychology was first being taught in American universities, scholars were freely documenting a range of spurious racial stereotypes as though they were confirmed facts. They regularly claimed that Africans reached physical maturity faster than Europeans, that they had smaller brains, that they were more impulsive and emotional, that they displayed rigid behaviours, and that they were especially addled by change. Such observations were widely promulgated without any empirical evidence at all. Given the wider climate of discrimination against Black people, simple 'reasoned observation' by (White) doctors and scientists would usually prove sufficient to make the case (G. Richards, 2012).

The aftermath of the Civil War saw an attempted 'reconstruction' of the country, with new laws and government measures aimed at enabling the secessionist states to rejoin the Union. This included considerable financial support for the education of Black Americans.

HISTORY IN STORIES: *12 YEARS A SLAVE* (2013)

12 Years a Slave (McQueen, 2013) is an award-winning film based on an autobiographical memoir written in 1853 by Solomon Northup (born *c.* 1807, died *c.* 1860; Northup, 1853). Northup, an African-American man, was born in New York, where his family had owned a farm. He was also a talented musician, and later earned his living as a professional violinist. In 1841, while visiting Washington, DC, where he had been offered a generous wage to perform at a concert, Northup was instead drugged, kidnapped and sold into slavery by his captors.

The movie tells the story of Northup's traumatic experiences while being held in bondage as a slave. It depicts the ruthless cruelty inherent in the system of human slavery, as well as the raw sadism exhibited by traders, plantation owners and many in the wider community. While some White characters are shown to be conscientious and religious, their moral frame of reference extends mostly to treating slaves with Christian charity, rather than to addressing the oppression and injustices that had become normalized in their society.

As a resident of New York, Northup held the legal status of a 'free person', and so his captivity was criminal even within the context of a country that accommodated slavery as part of its economy. Northup eventually succeeds in convincing a White plantation labourer that he was in fact illegally kidnapped, and this ultimately leads to him being freed. He returns to his family in New York who, for twelve long years, had had no idea what happened to him.

12 Years a Slave is forthright in its depiction of the slavery system. It vividly shows how any such system is dependent on the depersonalization of its victims. In order to rationalize the enslavement of their fellow human beings, perpetrators are required to consider their victims as something *less* than human. People are bought, sold and beaten as if they were animals. Those subjugated by slavery are also psychologically oppressed; Northup is advised by other captives that he can only survive the experience by submitting to it.

The slavery system was operated continuously in what is now the United States for over three centuries. As a result, rationalizations to justify and cope with slavery were part of America's oral and written culture for hundreds of years. This context facilitated the emergence of spurious scientific theories depicting African people as psychologically and physically divergent from so-called White people, and inferior in moral, economic and political terms. Slavery was abolished after the US Civil War, but assumptions about the statuses and psychologies of different racial groups remained ingrained in cultural attitudes. Arguably, they persist at the root of American social divisions to this day, and, given the prominence of American culture, continue to influence debates on race issues in other societies too.

For some critics, *12 Years a Slave* framed its audience's experience in a troubling way. By telling the story of a purportedly 'free' person who had been illegally kidnapped into slavery, the movie inadvertently invites viewers to focus their sympathies on this rather rare injustice.

Northup is portrayed as an exceptional figure, an audience surrogate whose unique personal plight provides the narrative tension that the movie must resolve. After Northup returns to his family, the audience's empathy with this courageous protagonist is rewarded with a satisfying pay-off. Whether modern audiences would have been as gratified by a movie telling the story of millions of victims rather than a single hero is less clear. Psychologically, it is easier to imagine oneself as 'a special person who miraculously escaped the system' (P. M. Smith, 2013) than as one of the faceless millions who lived and died in bondage.

It is part of human nature that we often seek to offset stigma by sanitizing the past, by overlooking its consequences, or by employing comforting rationalizations – such as spurious scientific theories – as coping mechanisms. The lasting traumas caused by a history of state-sponsored racial subjugation can be difficult to fully process.

Education and segregation

Despite the legal emancipation of the Black population, it was clear that in many parts of America, considerable prejudice remained. The south of the country saw a grotesque outbreak of lynchings and other hate crimes. White supremacist movements became organized, and groups such as the Ku Klux Klan became widely active. At the level of state government, segregation laws were passed, and cuts were applied to financial support for Black education. Once again, there emerged a strand of 'scientific' research documenting, in statistical terms, the relative inferiority of Black Americans, thereby supporting those who wished to scale back their education budgets.

With schools segregated on racial lines, a two-tier education system quickly emerged. Even those scholars sympathetic to racial equality accepted the claim that Black students were educationally inferior. The influence of polygeny was stark. One of the most renowned American psychologists, G. Stanley Hall (who we encountered in Chapter 3), took exception to racial bigotry, but nonetheless subscribed to the stereotype of evolutionary 'recapitulation'. He believed that Africans were a genetically distinct species stunted collectively at an earlier, less mature stage of mental development, and so required a bespoke and simplified education (Hall, 1904). On scientific grounds (or so he felt), he called for separate education for what he referred to as 'the higher and lower races' (1905, p. 362).

Hall seemed never to have questioned the norms of scientific racism, and his broader attitudes occasionally revealed the degree to which even the most moral of gentlemen can internalize White supremacist views. As deeply religious as he famously was, Hall nonetheless saw African people as lying somewhat beyond the realm of ordinary moral protections. 'As a preventive of crime', he once pondered, 'lynching has something to be said for it' (1905, p. 363). The fact that Hall was widely respected by his academic peers, becoming the inaugural president of the newly founded American Psychological Association in 1892, provides some insight into the views of race that prevailed in the profession of psychology during its formative years.

Immigration and intelligence testing

With the arrival of the twentieth century came significant increases in immigration to the United States, especially from Europe. This furthered American racial controversy in two ways. Firstly, some quite bitter national rivalries among European populations were imported into the United States. For example, self-styled Nordic superiority over southern Europeans became a feature of racial discourse *within America*. And secondly, at a time when eugenics was entrenching itself both in the behavioural sciences and in wider society, the sheer quantity of immigrants to the United States aroused considerable anxiety among those Americans who felt privileged enough to reflect on the quality of their nation's 'stock'. Once again, it was psychologists who pushed themselves to the forefront of this perceived crisis.

A particularly significant development was the introduction of mental testing at Ellis Island, near New York, where the government operated a processing centre for would-be immigrants. The American psychologist and ardent eugenicist Henry H. Goddard (1866–1957) was commissioned to establish an intelligence testing programme at the facility in 1913.

Goddard was an acknowledged expert in the psychology of aptitude. In 1906, he had established the world's first laboratory for studying intellectual disability. Shortly after, he translated the Binet–Simon intelligence test, a test of 'mental age' developed by Alfred Binet (who we encountered in Chapter 3), from French into English. However, Goddard's interest in intellectual disability was not motivated by a sympathetic vocation to improve the lives of the vulnerable. Rather, he believed that measures should be taken to limit the ability of 'feeble-minded' people to have children, claiming to have demonstrated that unfettered reproduction would lead to 'a race of defective degenerates' (Goddard, 1912, p. 103).

After conducting his tests at Ellis Island for several years, Goddard presented his results in a report entitled 'Mental tests and the immigrant' (Goddard, 1917). He announced that around 80 per cent of the immigrants he studied had been 'feeble-minded', an outcome he described as 'a very high percentage of defectiveness' (p. 259). However, this huge figure was almost certainly distorted by extraneous factors that undermined the quality of his testing.

For example, the people being evaluated were frequently exhausted, malnourished and distressed by their transatlantic journeys. They truly constituted the 'tired, poor, and huddled masses' that the inscription beneath the Statue of Liberty promised to welcome. Most of them were illiterate or poorly educated, and many could not understand English. And the immigration officers at Ellis Island were instructed to select only the most beleaguered-looking passengers for intelligence testing, meaning that Goddard's results as published did not reflect the abilities of immigrants as a whole.

An even more fundamental problem was that Goddard's tests were never properly validated. There was nothing to ensure that the scores were a fair and accurate index of intellectual ability. Nor was there any means to protect the scores from being tainted by racial prejudice on the part of the testers. When reporting his results, Goddard declared, 'We believe that this study has demonstrated that it is entirely feasible to test *with considerable degree of accuracy* the mentality of the immigrant' (p. 271; italics added). However, Goddard never established any means by which the 'accuracy' of his test results could be verified. All he had reported were the procedures that were followed and the scores that were produced. Whether or not these scores were in any way 'accurate', we will never know.

Many critics questioned whether Goddard's tests could even be understood by those immigrants who did not speak English. In an effort to deal with this problem, Howard A. Knox (1885–1949), the assistant surgeon at Ellis Island, devised a series of 'non-verbal' tests. These comprised elements such as visual comparison cards and rudimentary wooden jigsaws. Such methods were intended to be fairer than Goddard's, but even so they were grounded in ruthless eugenic reasoning. Knox himself described the purpose of testing as 'the sorting' of immigrants, in order to identify those liable to 'produce offspring that will require care in prisons, asylums, or other institutions' (Knox, 1915, p. 52). But, in reality, like Goddard, Knox had no evidence to support his approach. No data had ever been collected to show that scores on his tests were in any way statistically predictive of such dire outcomes.

In summary, the early twentieth century saw many efforts to improve the content and design of intelligence tests. The principle that psychological tests can be biased by cultural differences was recognized. The use of non-verbal performance as a proxy for cognitive aptitude was introduced. Large datasets, with extensively detailed statistical analyses of various target groups, were published. This period of American intelligence testing kick-started a burgeoning branch of psychology that continues to thrive today. It saw the birth of many new practices and principles that remain standard in the fields of psychometrics, cognition and educational psychology.

However, by and large, this was a supremacist type of psychology, in which vulnerable human beings were studied by those with power so that they could be stratified according to worth. Like other early methods of psychological quantification, innovation was motivated by degenerationist anxieties regarding human pedigree and by an ethnocentric ambition to enhance the 'genetic stock' of an increasing population. The work was statistically detailed to a pedantic level of exactitude, but both its underlying theories and consequent inferences were skewed, if not entirely addled, by subjective social philosophies. Results were summarily declared to be 'accurate' without any evidence of accuracy being presented – or sought. This type of psychology had the appearance of science, but lacked its underlying logic.

Nonetheless, the findings from Ellis Island contributed to considerable public consternation as well as heightened paranoia among policymakers. 'If the American public wishes feeble-minded aliens excluded,' Goddard had argued, 'it must demand that Congress provide the necessary facilities at the ports of entry' (1917, p. 271). In 1924, the government introduced the Johnson–Reed Act, a federal law that severely restricted immigration from around the world. Based on complex arbitrary algorithms and selective statistical points, the Act particularly targeted southern and eastern Europeans, Asians, and a range of other groups considered to be of insufficient quality for the American population. 'It must not be forgotten', advised Goddard, 'that besides the morons, there are some imbeciles. Probably no one would question but that these should be deported' (1917, p. 271).

ALMOST FAMOUS: EMMA WOLVERTON

Emma Wolverton (1889–1978) was born in an almshouse near Vineland, New Jersey, United States, in the late nineteenth century. Her mother had experienced extreme poverty and other social disadvantages, including harsh community disapproval for being a single parent. When Emma was eight years old, her mother wished to marry a local farmer, but the man insisted he would not be a father to a child who was not his own. He would only get married on condition that Emma was sent away. Facing destitution, the mother felt she had no choice but to arrange for Emma to enter a home for 'feeble-minded' children. She presented the managers of the home with the tenuous pretext that as Emma had been having difficulty making friends at school, she was likely to be intellectually disabled.

The eight-year-old Emma entered the home in 1897, well fed and able to wash and dress herself but unable to read or write. She later learned to read, and also to play the cornet, and worked in the dining room as well as performing other jobs in the home (J. D. Smith & Wehmeyer, 2012). It was while in the home that she came to the attention of Henry H. Goddard, the ardent eugenicist who would later be commissioned to establish an intelligence testing programme at Ellis Island.

Goddard was to base his most infamous book – *The Kallikak Family: A Study in the Heredity of Feeble-Mindedness* (1912) – on the case of Emma Wolverton, although he did not use her real name. Instead, he gave her the pseudonym 'Deborah Kallikak', inventing the family name by combining two Greek works: καλός (kallos) meaning 'good' and κακός (kakos) meaning 'bad'.

In this bestselling eugenicist treatise, Goddard claimed to have investigated Deborah's genealogy, discovering that her great-great-great-grandfather had been an American revolutionary war hero. But according to Goddard, 'Deborah' was not the descendant of this man's mainstream legal family. Instead, her lineage was traced back to a 'feeble-minded' barmaid with whom the forefather had had a single sexual encounter. From these investigations, Goddard argued, it was possible to compare the lives of both resulting branches of this man's genetic legacy, and to evaluate the impact of allowing feeble-minded people (more specifically women) to procreate.

And so Goddard presented a detailed depiction of this so-called Kallikak family, in which the descendants of the barmaid were shown to have lived lives blighted by poverty, mental illness and criminality, whereas those on the 'normal' side of the family tree had forged a distinguished dynasty of morally upstanding and prosperous citizens, including doctors, lawyers and religious ministers. Notably, Goddard claimed to show that 'feeble-mindedness' had recurred throughout all generations of the barmaid's progeny, but had not arisen at all in the other family line.

Goddard's account of the Kallikak family was the most prominent of a number of similar publications of the period. It was widely cited to support programmes of compulsory sterilization for persons deemed to be of 'poor' genetic stock, and in 1927 was presented as evidence in a landmark US supreme court case that found involuntary sterilization to be constitutional. A German-language version was published in 1933, the same year that the Nazi regime passed its own sterilization law.

The problem, however, is that Goddard's account bore a poor resemblance to Emma Wolverton's actual family history. Having conducted a full-scale study of the Wolverton family, genealogists produced an 860-page report in 2001. They found no evidence that the man identified by Goddard as Emma's great-great-great-grandfather had an illicit encounter with a barmaid. Rather, all the characters mentioned in Goddard's book were members of a single family line, 'perfectly legitimate [offspring] of their married parents' (Macdonald & McAdams, 2001, p. 807). There was no split in the family tree, no 'feeble-minded' and 'normal' lineages to compare. The natural hereditarian experiment had never occurred.

Contrary to Goddard's portrayals of 'Deborah Kallikak', Emma Wolverton was well-read, curious and hard-working, drawing praise from a local social worker for being 'a handsome young woman' who had 'many accomplishments' (Reeves, 1938, p. 195). When she reached the age of twenty-five, Emma moved to a different institution across the street. There she lived for most of her life, dying in 1978 at the age of eighty-one.

HISTORICALLY (IN)ACCURATE?: DARWINISM AND SCIENTIFIC RACISM

The arrival of Darwinism in the nineteenth century is often depicted as having provided a boost for scientific racism. It is true that aphorisms like 'survival of the fittest' (which, as we saw in Chapter 3, Darwin himself did not coin) were appropriated as part of its core theorizing. It is also true that the subtitle to Darwin's *On the Origin of Species* was *Or the Preservation of Favoured Races in the Struggle for Life*, which may indeed suggest that his theory of evolution addressed the matter of race.

However, in Darwin's own time, the word 'race' was a much vaguer concept than it is today. Broadly speaking, it was interchangeable with terms like *type* or *kind*. For example, throughout *On the Origin of Species*, Darwin refers to such ideas as 'our races of dogs', 'the several races of the pigeon', the 'races of our domestic animals and plants', and even 'the several races, for instance, of the cabbage' (C. Darwin, 1859).

Darwin's theory of evolution diverged considerably from the scientific racism position. Evolution was grounded in monogenism, whereas scientific racism sprang from, and enthusiastically embraced, a polygenist worldview. Darwin had posited the inherent interrelatedness of all humans, whereas scientific racism promoted segregation on the grounds that the different races were effectively (or even literally) different species. And in Darwin's mind, evolution was a process of constant change, in which the current version of humanity was by no means the finished product. The scientific racism view, by contrast, was that the fundamental racial 'essences' that characterized humankind were fixed and forever immutable (G. Richards, 2012).

Overall, the use of Darwinian tropes in scientific racism seems to be based on a rather loose, if not erroneous, interpretation of Darwinism.

THE CLAIM OF RACIAL DIFFERENCES IN MEASURED INTELLIGENCE

Implicit in the idea of using intelligence tests to screen immigrants is a belief that different human populations – and thus, by extension, different 'races' – are likely to vary in innate intellectual ability. Before we go any further, it is important to point out that there is absolutely no credible evidence to support such an assertion. Nor is there any biological theory that could suggest why such a scenario should be thought plausible.

Nonetheless, such claims have always been met with widespread popular belief. This probably says more about the way people view each other psychologically than it does about the quality of corroboration. Claims of biological 'race' differences are spurious, but social racism is all too real. The problem is that the former are almost always a product of the latter.

Such beliefs have prevailed across human societies for millennia, always framed to the advantage of the dominant in-group. Nearly every human community has a history of stereotyping indigenous minorities or nearby tribes in ways that demean them intellectually.

Out-groups everywhere have been speciously rebuked for their low intellectual capacities, their reckless proneness to self-endangerment, their naïvety and primitiveness, and the general daftness of their decision-making. In more benign circumstances, such stereotypes are limited to exclusionary jokes or sporting rivalries. However, elsewhere, they serve to legitimize conflict, to dehumanize the targets of violence, and as justification for armed aggression. The history of psychological warfare suggests that the most powerful propaganda will nearly always depict the 'enemy', or their supporters, as incoherent, irrational and incapable of reason.

As alluded to above, the development of psychometric intelligence testing was intertwined with that of scientific racism. While psychologists such as Goddard were campaigning eugenicists, the wider field of intelligence theory and measurement largely emerged from an environment in which prejudices about the innate nature of intellectual 'feeble-mindedness' were simply part of a standard worldview.

The growth of intelligence tests

As mentioned, Goddard's Ellis Island tests were based on those developed in France by Alfred Binet. Binet and his colleague, the French psychologist Théodore Simon (1873–1961), had devised their test with good intentions, aiming to use it to identify those children who needed intensive educational supports. However, they were also convinced that intelligence could be discerned from the physical characteristics of different types of people. According to them, 'physiognomy reveals the degree of intelligence' (Binet & Simon, 1916, p. 88), with head shape, hair type, physique and facial appearance all displaying the archetypal signs of mental ability. To some extent, their views were influenced by phrenology and psychiatry, but Binet and Simon were clear that the social challenge to be combated was one of a degenerating human species (Collins, 1999).

While Goddard had translated the Binet test for use on Ellis Island, it was not until 1916 that the test was formally adapted for American participants (and thus for English-speaking use) by the

Stanford University psychologist Lewis Terman (1877–1956). From this point, the test became known internationally as the 'Stanford–Binet Intelligence Scales'.

Terman was yet another prominent eugenicist. In the manual published to accompany the new test, Terman presented data claiming to demonstrate that mental deficiency was 'very, very common' among ethnic minority groups in the United States. 'Their dullness seems to be racial,' he opined, again offering no evidence to support his inference, 'or at least inherent in the family stocks from which they come.' He called for 'the whole question of racial differences in mental traits' to be researched as a priority, and predicted that when this was done, 'there will be discovered enormously significant racial differences in general intelligence, differences which cannot be wiped out by any scheme of mental culture' (Terman, 1916, p. 91). The basis of Terman's concern was clear: 'from a eugenic point of view', he argued, racial minorities 'constitute a grave problem because of their unusually prolific breeding' (p. 92).

Terman joined forces with Goddard, and with a psychologist at Harvard University, Robert Yerkes (1876–1956). The three collaborated to adapt the Stanford–Binet test so that it could be administered to groups. This enabled mass testing to be done far more efficiently. Originally, two multi-choice formats of the test were devised for use by the United States army: 'Army Alpha' was the standard test, while 'Army Beta' was the non-verbal version, intended for soldiers who were illiterate. Subsequently, Yerkes developed a variation of these tests for civilians, the National Intelligence Test, which was then widely used in education.

Yerkes would later be remembered for his part in devising the Yerkes-Dodson law, which states that human performance is optimal when physiological arousal is neither too high nor too low. However, for the present discussion, we can note that Yerkes was yet another prestigious pioneer of psychological measurement who was an enthusiastic advocate for eugenics. When he saw that almost half of all soldiers who took the new test were found to be 'feeble-minded', he attributed this to the particularly low scores achieved by racial-minority and immigrant draftees, warning that 'no one of us as a citizen can afford to ignore the menace of race deterioration' (Yerkes, 1923).

The test developed by Binet and Simon (and its various adaptations, such as the Stanford–Binet scales) served to popularize the testing of intelligence. It formed the basis of how aptitudes are evaluated in modern psychology. The Stanford–Binet Intelligence Scales are now in their fifth edition, and are recognized as one of the primary tools for assessing intellectual disability around the world. Once again, we see a modern psychology practice that owes its origins to eugenic racism. These testing methods were devised by investigators who firmly believed in the intellectual supremacy of White people. They saw themselves as advancing ethnic purity in their societies, by providing tests that could be used to make an empirical case for racial discrimination.

While this work was highly specialized, it was certainly not obscure. Yerkes and Terman were both seen as important pioneers of psychology and as significant figures in the wider profession. In 1917 and 1923 respectively, each was elected president of the American Psychological Association. In the eyes of their peers, Yerkes and Terman – whose major contribution was to show how psychology could be used to root out racial feeble-mindedness and thus purify America's genetic stock – were viewed not merely as colleagues, but as *leaders*, fellow psychologists of superlative calibre, the ideal people to guide this new profession as it expanded beyond its formative years.

Have tests, will discriminate

During the first half of the twentieth century, explicit expressions of racial superiority were prevalent across popular culture in both Europe and the United States. Ethnic nationalism was seen as intrinsic to political self-determination, and belief in the inherent superiority of European (or White) culture was commonly used to rationalize both colonialism (such as the British and French colonial empires) and institutional racism (such as American segregation laws).

The Nazi regime in Germany is today often retrospectively identified as a special case of state racism. However, its incremental rise to power resulted from xenophobic dimensions that were mirrored in most industrialized countries at that time. Legal scholars record how the Nazis' notorious race-based citizenship laws were modelled on equivalent legislation passed by the United States. In his autobiographical manifesto *Mein Kampf*, Hitler poured praise not only on America's race-exclusive immigration policies, but also on the country's harsh treatment of its 'coloured' people (Whitman, 2017).

A persistent theme within twentieth-century racism has been the claim that alleged 'race' differences in basic intelligence can be – and have been – scientifically demonstrated. Uncritically accepting the century-old claims of Samuel Morton, eminent British psychologist Raymond B. Cattell (1933) explained how African people were intellectually inferior because it had been shown that they had smaller skull capacities. (As noted earlier in this chapter, Cattell had also spoken approvingly of the Nazis.)

It can often seem that just about every psychologist and scholar during this period shared similar views. However, throughout these times there was constant critical commentary casting doubt on claims of psychological race differences. Especially from the 1920s onwards, an emerging school of thought began to emphasize upbringing and environment as key determinants of an individual's psychological development. In this regard, it is important therefore to note that those psychologists who persisted in promoting the eugenic agenda cannot claim to have been enveloped by cultural groupthink. Rather, they simply chose to ignore whatever opposition they encountered.

By the 1940s, social psychologists were pointing out that prominent among the environmental factors to have a profound effect on intelligence test performance was, unsurprisingly, racial prejudice itself. In 1954, the testimony of psychologists such as the American clinician Kenneth B. Clark (1914–2005) and the Canadian academic Otto Klineberg (1899–1992) played a crucial role in the United States Supreme Court's decision to end racial segregation in public schools. The psychologists had presented data debunking claims of innate race differences in intelligence and showing how racial discrimination serves to undermine educational progress. It was the first time the court cited psychological research when explaining a ruling (Benjamin & Crouse, 2002).

It is frequently argued that race psychology went into decline after the Second World War. The many gruesome horrors perpetrated by the Nazis in pursuit of racial purity had cast a grim shadow over polygeny, eugenics and the statistical quantification of racial attributes. Nazi claims of Aryan superiority relied heavily on racialized eugenic rhetoric, and on a catalogue of grossly distorted or wilfully falsified research. After a United Nations convention included 'imposing measures intended to prevent births within [a racial] group' in its 1948 definition of genocide, scientific interest in eugenics, and its wider research remit, waned rapidly (Lippman, 1998).

However, the field of psychology remained infused with many methods, models and metrics that had been designed with eugenics in mind. As the decades passed and first-hand memories of the Second World War began to recede, it became increasingly clear that the influence of these eugenic sentiments on psychology had not just suddenly disappeared. It had simply evolved.

From genetics to bell curves

From the 1960s up to the twenty-first century, those wishing to advance claims of race differences in intellectual ability have sought to couch their ideas in terms of genes and genetics. This modern phase of scientific racism is often said to have begun in 1969, with the publication of a monograph by the American psychologist Arthur Jensen (1923–2012) in the *Harvard Educational Review* (Jensen, 1969).

Jensen's report sparked a storm of controversy, and over succeeding decades has been extensively debunked. Nonetheless, the strand of pseudoscientific genetic argumentation that it launched has proven somewhat resistant to normal scientific criticism. While Jensen's case is not credible by the standards of mainstream science, it has, in the years since it appeared, been repeated, rehashed and repurposed very many times, mostly by a small coterie of fringe academics (and their loyal followers), who, for whatever reason, persist in pursuing scientific racism as their life's passion.

Running to well over 100 pages, Jensen's lengthy treatise was comparatively simplistic. He began by explaining the concept of intelligence, citing Galton, Fisher and Pearson to claim that the principle of psychological heritability had been scientifically proven. He followed this by arguing that intelligence testing was essentially robust, and that the scores produced by intelligence tests should be taken at face value. Contrary to the observations of many education professionals, Jensen explicitly excluded the possibility that test scores might be significantly distorted by cultural biases, such as differences in language, dialect or cultural perspective.

With these assumptions set in stone, Jensen then presented data from a number of studies, showing gaps in intelligence test scores between Black and White Americans. Having already excluded the possibility of cultural bias in measurement, he duly interpreted these statistics as revealing innate racial differences in mental ability. Importantly, Jensen then sought to statistically quantify the purported link between intellect and genes. Drawing on what he suggested was the consensus view among geneticists, he claimed his calculations showed 'an average heritability of .80 for intelligence test scores' (p. 51). This was described as indicating that a person's intelligence is determined 80 per cent by their genetic inheritance (i.e. from the genes they receive from their parents) and just 20 per cent by their environments.

All told, Jensen's position was that Black people are, in fact, *genetically* disadvantaged. The practical implication was immediate. If children's test performances are predetermined by their genes, then education interventions cannot be expected to make much difference. And if Black people are being held back by their genes and not their environments, then they *cannot* be said to be held back by educational segregation, intergenerational poverty or racial discrimination. As such, Jensen implied, there is no point trying to do anything about *these* problems either.

Jensen went on to raise further alarm about the economic implications of racial demographics. 'If more children are born to persons in the lower half of the intelligence distribution,' he noted, 'one would correctly predict a decline in the average IQ of the population' (p. 93). Following this observation, Jensen immediately presented statistics to suggest a 'differential birth rate' between Black and White Americans. His point was clear: a growing Black population would suppress national average intelligence.

Finally, Jensen mounted a somewhat perverse argument about the welfare of Black people. Given that their 'low' intelligence was genetically predetermined, he argued, they would forever fall behind White people in economic terms, no matter what efforts were made to assist them. According to this logic, Black people were therefore *genetically predestined to be poor*. In a deeply insensitive allusion to the United States' troubled racial history, Jensen described this inevitable Black poverty as a form of 'genetic enslavement' (p. 95).

This statement of concern about Black destitution may seem at first to have been somewhat sympathetic, but the consequence it brought to mind was surely disturbing. If genetically based social problems cannot be ameliorated through assistive intervention, then the only way to prevent this second 'enslavement' of Black Americans *would be to remove them from the population altogether*.

Bear in mind that all these conclusions emanated from Jensen's initial claim to have found 'an average heritability of .80 for intelligence test scores'. If this statistic is faulty, then the rest of Jensen's thesis becomes irrelevant. In reality, as we will discuss below, the statistic is extremely faulty indeed. The exact meaning of 'an average heritability of .80 for intelligence test scores' is not nearly as meaningful as its phrasing would seem to suggest. It is important to recall that statistics can often make vague statements appear much more 'scientific' than they really are. This is because numbers can be precise without being relevant. Statistics, *in themselves*, are not science.

At the beginning of Jensen's paper, the editors of the *Harvard Educational Review* inserted a comment advising readers of its 'controversial nature'. And for sure, the publication quickly caused an outcry. However, amid the barrage of scientific and academic criticism, much of it from population geneticists, Jensen was nonetheless defended by some very notable psychologists.

Perhaps unsurprisingly, Cattell was one of the first to be vocal. He lauded what he called 'Professor Jensen's conscientiously scholarly statement' (R. B. Cattell, 1971, p. 288), dismissing critics as 'ignoracists' (p. 247). Harvard professor Richard Herrnstein (1930–94) defended Jensen in a high-profile article in *Atlantic* magazine (Herrnstein, 1971). And in the United Kingdom, Hans J. Eysenck (1916–97), one of the most prominent psychologists in British academia, praised the Jensen position in many of his writings, including a full-length book for popular audiences entitled *The Inequality of Man* (1973).

Notably, the psychologists who defended Jensen publish their rejoinders in popular magazines and books, rather than in scientific journals. Jensen was further valorized by writers in the far-right press. However, the great majority of academic commentary comprised outright condemnation of Jensen and his statistical arguments. Today his article is generally regarded as a case study in race pseudoscience. Several major problems have been identified in Jensen's assumptions and reasoning, making his many provocative statements appear, in retrospect, all the more incendiary.

But controversy did not prevent other psychologists from continuing what Jensen started. Cattell, Herrnstein and Eysenck, among others, were to remain doggedly unrepentant. In successive decades, further similar books and papers were to appear, each presenting essentially the

Jensenist position, with minor updates to data and terminology. The most prominent examples – such as *The Bell Curve* (Herrnstein & Murray, 1994), *IQ and the Wealth of Nations* (Lynn & Vanhanen, 2002) and *Human Diversity* (Murray, 2020) – are remembered for the sensation they stirred in the media rather than for any scientific contributions. In their own way, every new tract serves a purpose in keeping the debate alive, albeit primarily at the margins of mainstream academia (along with several bleak corners of the internet). Few of these works are considered creditworthy by serious scientists. Their key audience comprises academic contrarians, lifelong illiberals, committed racists, internet trolls, advocates of free-speech-for-its-own-sake, and a wide range of other readers on a permanent search for statistics they can use to defend their political prejudices.

In short, studies claiming to show statistical relationships among intelligence, race and genetics are simply not grounded in scientifically defensible evidence. All such works suffer from similar flaws. The key problems have less to do with the methods used to shed light on the research questions, or with the data presented to answer them. Rather, they stem from the nature of the research questions themselves.

The problems with claims about race and intelligence

Claims that 'intelligence is racially heritable' suffer from three classes of limitation, namely: *the meaning of 'intelligence'*, *the meaning of 'racially'*, and *the meaning of 'heritable'*.

Problem #1. The meaning of 'intelligence'

Contrary to what the race differences approach would imply, there is in fact no single definition of 'intelligence'. Indeed, in the views of many psychologists who specialize in the area, there is in fact no single *thing* as 'intelligence'. Rather, human beings exhibit a range of disparate aptitudes that may or may not be linked to each other.

For example, a person who finds it easy to assess a problem and then formulate a solution ('analytic' intelligence) may – or may *not* – also be astute at anticipating what others around them are feeling ('interpersonal' intelligence). Or they may – or again may *not* – be gifted at imagining objects in their mind's eye ('visuospatial' intelligence). Different theoretical approaches have posited different numbers of intelligence types. It seems that the more that psychologists conduct research on this topic, the more nuanced and fragmented the notion of intelligence becomes.

Some theories of intelligence argue that there exists an overriding form of human competence that cuts across all the subtypes of aptitude, a 'general factor' (or *g*) that represents a person's all-round 'intelligence'. However, other researchers have demonstrated that human beings exhibit many abilities that simply do not cluster in this way (Sternberg, 2019), casting doubt on the importance of computing 'general factors' that try to encapsulate everything.

What we can be sure of, however, is that intelligence *tests* as they exist today are especially narrow. They fall well short of evaluating the different intelligence subtypes that psychologists have identified. Most intelligence tests measure some level of verbal and spatial performance. However, they do *not* measure practical skills, problem-solving capacity, social competence or the ability to adapt to challenges, even though all of these would be central to what most people think of when they hear the word 'intelligence' (Sternberg et al., 2005).

We also know that intelligence test scores are greatly affected by social factors that vary between cultural groups. For example, in some cultures, children are taught to prioritize speed over accuracy, while in others they are taught the opposite. Group differences in scores on a given intelligence test may simply reflect what each group considers important when trying to demonstrate 'intelligence' (G. Richards, 2012).

Nearly 100 years ago, the historian of university psychology E. G. Boring (1923) defined *intelligence* as, simply, *whatever it is that intelligence tests measure*. However, therein lies the problem:

- Intelligence tests do not measure what most ordinary people would think of as 'intelligence'.
- Intelligence tests do not even measure what most *psychologists* would consider to be 'intelligence'.
- Not all intelligence tests measure the same thing.
- Intelligence tests frequently measure aspects of intellectual performance that are prioritized differently by different cultural groups.

Problem #2. The meaning of 'race'

As mentioned above, 'race' is a word used to describe social groups for cultural reasons. There is no matching biological category. No biological marker, and certainly no part of DNA, is associated with what we refer to as a person's 'race' or racial category. The nearest we could consider is the fact that genetic variants differ by geographic origin. But they do so in a way that is unrelated to our concept of 'races'. There is more genetic variability *within* Africa than there is outside it, and genetic variants found outside Africa are generally subsets of those found within. Essentially, the best that DNA could theoretically reveal is how far away from East Africa a person's recent ancestors may have lived.

However, we should also note that no group of human beings is biologically 'pure'. A person's DNA will reflect a long history of ancestral migration and genetic exchange, denoting ancestry from different parts of the world. All humans are genetic hybrids. When commercial DNA-testing companies offer to analyse your genetic ancestry, they are simply comparing your DNA to selected populations – of *currently living* people – whose DNA is in their databases. Indeed, as the human lineage originated in Africa, we are all, essentially, Africans. Human populations have never been static, and biology does not conform to our political definitions of 'races'.

In parts of Europe, and especially in North America, racial politics often relate to the fact that some cultural groups differ from each other in skin tone. However, this does not mean that, at a biological level, human skin tone falls into a set of distinct categories. The small number of cultural 'race' labels is thus misleading. As outlined above, human skin tone varies gradually from one population to the next. Most of this variability relates to geographical latitude, with paler skin reflecting an ancestry that has been deprived of ample sunlight. There is no biological advantage to having light-coloured skin.

Skin tone is determined by multiple genes, but these genes do not operate in ways that conveniently match our social attitudes. For example, many dark-skinned people share the same version of these genes as people whose skin tone is much lighter (Reich, 2018). Whether someone has dark or light skin might lead them to be classified into a particular culturally defined 'race', but it will not tell us much about their genes.

But even our cultural definitions of what a 'race' is will frequently be fuzzy. In Europe, a person is likely to be considered 'Black' if they have any African ancestry, but in Brazil, a person is considered *not* 'Black' if they have any *European* ancestry (Reich, 2018). Caucasians – specifically, people from the Caucasus region of Eurasia – are considered to be White by most international observers, to the extent that the word 'Caucasian' is used to describe Whiteness in English-speaking contexts. Despite this, people from the Caucasus are considered dark-skinned, and essentially non-White, by their Russian neighbours (Sternberg et al., 2005). In the nineteenth century, Irish people who emigrated to the United States were seen as having a 'black tint' in their skin (Jacobson, 1999), but, nonetheless, were never vilified with anything like the extremism that was directed at people of African ancestry.

The Hutu and Tutsi peoples, who today live primarily in Rwanda and Burundi, are highly similar to each other, both physically and genetically (Mamdani, 2001). Despite this, because of racial identities that were largely imposed and shaped by Western colonialism, the two groups have come to recognize themselves as 'racially' distinct (Graves, 2004). Their resulting 'racial' conflicts have frequently been ferocious, culminating in the Rwandan genocide of 1994.

Undoubtedly, human beings vary in physical appearance, ancestral history and geographical heritage. But by and large, the concept of 'race' is what we refer to as a *social construction*. The specific racial groups that we talk about today certainly exist, but they are defined in arbitrary ways and reflect social needs rather than scientific reality:

- The concept of a 'race' is not genetic, because, while human DNA varies slightly, it does not do so in a way that corresponds with our cultural 'race' labels.
- The concept of a 'race' is not biological, because all humans are hybrids with overlapping and mixed ancestries.
- The concept of a 'race' has no true physical basis, because those physical features people commonly cite as 'race' markers do not actually cluster in the way we think they do.
- What people consider to be a 'race' will differ from one place to another, and will change over historical time, thereby illustrating that race categories are, literally, 'socially constructed'.

As it makes no scientific sense to talk about a 'race' as if it were a biological group, it therefore follows that it makes no scientific sense to talk about 'race' differences in intelligence *as though they were biologically caused*.

Problem #3. The meaning of 'heritable'

While it is clear that 'race' is not a genetic category, and so does not readily lend itself to discussions of genetic transmission, it is worth noting that no gene for intelligence (however defined) has ever been identified (Sternberg et al., 2005). This is not surprising. The fact that intelligence is so multifaceted makes it extremely unlikely that it will result from a single underlying gene.

Variables like intelligence are described by biologists as 'emergent' properties, where complexity is produced by the combination of multiple simple components. Emergence greatly complicates the process of evolution. Effectively, as there is no single independent genetic component for natural selection to work on, it is extremely unlikely that natural selection can produce free-standing populations with different levels of an emergent property (K. J. Mitchell, 2018). From the point of view of genetics, innate race differences in human intelligence are fundamentally implausible.

Another critical issue relates to the way geneticists compute heritability scores. Such scores range from zero to 1, as follows:

- A heritability score of 1 for a particular trait indicates that its variability within a given group matches the variability of genes within that group.
- A heritability score of zero for a particular trait indicates that its variability within a given group is *unrelated* to the variability of genes within that group.
- A heritability score between zero and 1 for a particular trait indicates that its variability within a given group *only partially* matches the variability of genes within that group.

In all cases, however, the reason for any statistical associations will be unclear.

Showing that the *amount of variation of a trait within a group* might reflect the *amount of genetic variability within that group* merely demonstrates that one kind of variability is statistically associated with another. It does not tell us that traits result from genes. The genetic term 'heritability' has a very specific technical meaning and does not represent what non-specialists, racists included, usually think it does.

The fact that heritability scores are calculated for *groups* and not for *individuals* has especially important implications. For example, consider a characteristic such as *the colour of a person's car*. Car colour usually varies widely across a population. Some cars are red, other cars are blue, others are grey, and so on. For a given group of cars, it is most unlikely that the pattern of colours will reflect any pattern of genetic variability among their owners. As such, this trait will have a heritability of zero: variability in car colour will be statistically unrelated to variability in the genes of car owners.

Now consider a characteristic such as *number of eyes*. In most populations, nearly every person will have two eyes. However, due to the rate of accidental injury, a small subset of people will have just one eye. As injuries are environmental rather than genetic, the resulting variability in eye-number will be statistically unrelated to any variability in genes. Therefore, as with car colour, the heritability score for eye-number will be zero. But this does not mean that eye-number is unrelated to genetics. The number of eyes people are born with is most definitely determined by genes. In short, heritability scores tell us something about variability within groups, but they do not tell us anything about what *causes* that variability. 'Heritable' simply does not mean 'genetically caused'.

And just like genetic features (such as eyes) can be shown to have low heritability scores, *non*-genetic features can often be shown to have *high* heritability scores.

There are many common reasons why non-genetic factors regularly have high scores for 'heritability'. Any similarity between successive generations will emerge as a statistical pattern. For example, a variable such as *employment status* will always be highly 'heritable'. The children of unemployed parents are themselves more likely to be unemployed in adulthood. In other words, unemployment runs in families. However, this problem is caused by several embedded social structures and economic conventions that perpetuate intergenerational disadvantage. Being born into poverty limits a person's chances of securing economic advancement during their lifetime. This is a severe and significant social problem, but not a biological one. There is no gene for unemployment that is passed from parent to offspring.

Similarly, as the American philosopher Ned Block (1928–) has pointed out, in cultures where only women wear earrings, *earring-wearing* will also be highly heritable. This is because a population's pattern of earring-wearing will closely match its binary sex distribution, itself a product of genetic variation (namely, the distribution of XX and XY chromosomes; Block, 1995). Therefore, *the variability in earring-wearing* in this group will closely reflect *the variability of genes* within that same group.

And as explained by British psychologist Graham Richards, if society were to discriminate against red-haired people, they would likely end up with lower incomes. As red hair is genetically heritable, this would ensure that income too would end up with a high heritability score. *The variability in income* will again closely reflect *the variability of genes*, even though the real cause for this pattern is social discrimination and not genetics (G. Richards, 2012). The implications for claims of genetic differences relating to 'race' should be clear: the fact that a behavioural or cognitive difference is shown to be statistically related to a genetically heritable trait never excludes the possibility that an intermediating cultural force has caused the association.

Finally, heritability scores are computed at a group level, and so tell us nothing about group *differences*. For example, physical height is very heritable, but when two groups differ in height there can be any number of explanations. The Dinka people, native to South Sudan, are usually more than 180 centimetres tall; over the border, in the Central African Republic, adult BaMbenga have an average height of just 150 centimetres. This 30-centimetre intergroup difference is no doubt predominantly due to genetic factors. But on the Korean peninsula, where men in the Democratic People's Republic of Korea (North Korea) are around 4 centimetres shorter than men who live in the Korean Republic (South Korea), this much smaller height gap is most likely due to nutritional differences and *not* to genes (Schwekendiek, 2009). In all these scenarios, empirical data will show that *height* is highly heritable, without shedding any light on the nature of, or reasons for, group differences.

Ultimately, the finding of 'an average heritability of .80 for intelligence test scores' does *not* denote that 80 per cent of test scores are genetically produced. It means that 80 per cent of *the variability in test scores* within a particular group can be said to reflect *the variability of genes* within that group, which is quite a different thing. It is a banal description of a group and not a meaningful statement about individuals. The heritability scores computed by geneticists are not designed to tell whether a particular outcome is 'caused by' genes. Any assertion to that effect is scientifically spurious.

In summary, the claim that 'intelligence is racially heritable' is unclear precisely because it is based on a statistical computation of 'heritability'. Specifically:

- the idea that an emergent property such as intelligence can be 'heritable' is just not plausible in genetic terms;
- 'heritability' is a description of group variation and does *not* quantify how much of a trait is genetic;

Image 6.4   Racism as a social problem
An anti-racism protest in Munich, Germany.

- characteristics can end up with low 'heritability' despite being genetically determined (for example, number of eyes);
- characteristics can prove to be highly 'heritable' despite being environmentally caused (for example, unemployment); and
- 'heritability' is a statistical concept based on a single group of numbers, and so tells us nothing about intergroup differences.

Ultimately, it is unreasonable to claim that an observed variation in aptitude test scores will reflect a genetic difference between people. Such group differences will almost certainly be due to circumstances, encompassing people's variable experience of testing, their familiarity with test content, and cultural biases inherent in the design of the test.

But most importantly, test scores will be shaped by the different opportunities that people have had to *adequately prepare* for the test. If some people face socio-economic disadvantage, or are subject to systemic and interpersonal discrimination, then we can fully expect their test performance to be less proficient than that of people who have relatively greater social and cultural privileges.

There is also the possibility – and in light of historical precedent, the *likelihood* – that many of the researchers who put forward claims of race differences in intelligence will *themselves* be biased, if not unflinchingly bigoted. Their theories, methods, datasets, interpretations, research conclusions and policy recommendations flow from a history of incorrigible and insidious pseudoscience. They warrant the utmost scepticism and the most observant level of vigilance.

WHERE TO FROM HERE?

The process of quantifying, classifying and comparing human beings has certainly played a part in propelling scientific racism, from its earliest beginnings to its current extremist embodiments. However, the very statistical methods that racialist theorists designed to highlight the 'dangers' of degeneration have, in fact, played a crucial role in exposing the fallacies that underlie modern prejudice, bigotry and discrimination. It is through statistical sophistication and the appreciation of data that stereotypes, slurs, and scientific racism can be subjected to systematic forms of scrutiny. Psychology's methods of statistics and measurement are indeed powerful weapons – albeit very much of the double-edged kind.

Instincts have always exerted a powerful influence over intellect. While considering themselves to be logical, human beings nonetheless face a constant struggle to manage their inner impulses. Such mental forces can be deeply disturbing. We often attempt to ignore them, or even to deny their existence. Unsurprisingly, therefore, the endeavour by psychologists to understand how human minds respond to invisible and unwanted impulses has frequently proved controversial. In our next chapter we examine psychoanalysis, one of the most extensive, elaborate and contentious efforts to account for instinct in human psychology.

DISCUSSION QUESTIONS

1. Does psychology's effort to quantify necessarily lead to division?
2. How might psychological knowledge be used to address the challenges of intergroup prejudice?
3. Does 'race' matter?
4. To what extent should today's psychologists feel responsible for the political attitudes of those who historically preceded them?

RECOMMENDED READING

- **Gillham, N. W. (2001). Sir Francis Galton and the birth of eugenics. *Annual Review of Genetics, 35*, 83–101.** In this article, the author examines the career of Francis Galton, and shows how Galton's ideas led directly to the development of eugenics.
- **Moore, D. S., & Shenk, D. (2016). The heritability fallacy. *WIREs Cognitive Science, 8*(1–2), e1400.** In this article, the authors show how 'heritability' is one of the most misunderstood terms in behavioural genetics, and therefore one of the most misused and misleading.
- **Saini, A. (2019). *Superior: The Return of Race Science*. London: 4th Estate.** In this book, the author argues that many modern fields of research in biology and psychology continue to be influenced by discredited theories of scientific racism.
- **Smedley, A., & Smedley, B. D. (2005). Race as biology is fiction, racism as a social problem is real: Anthropological and historical perspectives on the social construction**

of race. *American Psychologist, 60*, 16–26. In this essay, the authors show how advances in genomic and biological science increasingly belie the claim that 'race' is a valid construct for scientific research, and that the idea of 'race' – and the consequent problem of racism – result primarily from social and cultural historical influences.

- **Tafreshi, D., Slaney, K. L., & Neufeld, S. D. (2016). Quantification in psychology: Critical analysis of an unreflective practice.** *Journal of Theoretical and Philosophical Psychology, 36*, 233–49. In this analysis, the authors question whether measuring psychological concepts using numbers really is the best way to produce empirical research, or whether the practice is just blindly used by psychologists in the spurious belief that it makes their work more 'scientific'.

Part III

**FERTILITY:
THE EMERGENCE OF
PSYCHOLOGICAL SUBFIELDS**

FREUDIANISM, INSTINCTS AND THE CONCEPT OF *SEXUALITY*

7

In this chapter, we will …

- reflect on the role of sexual instinct in shaping human civilization, and on the way attitudes to sexuality have shifted over time
- consider the social and intellectual climate in which Sigmund Freud developed his extensive theory of psychoanalysis
- examine the way Freud understood and depicted the role of sexuality as a core component of human psychology
- explain how Freud's ideas developed and expanded, and how they were adapted by other psychoanalytic theorists
- evaluate the limitations and criticisms of psychoanalysis, as well as its contributions to modern psychological understanding

---

At the outset

Instincts and drives have long been recognized as helping to shape the course of humanity. Myths, legends and religious fables have long described the moral and practical consequences that arise when people succumb to their impulses. Many scientists and scholars have theorized about the impact of basic impulses on human relationships and society. In turn, the way that society itself shapes our attitudes towards our impulses, and especially our sexual impulses, has long been considered.

One of the most significant theories of psychology to explore the role of instincts, and in particular of sexual impulses, has been psychoanalysis. Psychoanalysis was introduced by Sigmund Freud in the late nineteenth century. Many of his conclusions were affected by the particular social and cultural climate in which he lived.

Freud's theories drew on philosophical ideas about human consciousness, and the ways in which human thoughts and ideas can be shaped by unseen influences. They also reflected a prevailing cultural climate that incorporated attitudes about women that today would be seen as unacceptably sexist. Freud's understanding of sexuality was also shaped by cultural norms, as they were based on his interactions with clients in psychotherapy. As such, his ideas about women's sexuality were informed only by what his female clients were willing to discuss with him.

Many of Freud's theories speculated about the role of sexuality in framing people's experiences. These included theories about the impact of unacknowledged sexual abuse, and about the development of sexuality in childhood. His ideas were often seen as being explosively controversial, even among his own colleagues. Nonetheless, psychoanalysis became a globally popular theory of psychology. Followers produced many new versions of the theory, and many variations of psychoanalytic therapy.

Psychoanalysis has drawn criticisms relating to its implications for personal morality, especially from a religious perspective. It has also been dismissed as misogynistic. And because of its reliance on unverifiable constructs and unfalsifiable hypotheses, it is commonly dismissed as unscientific. Nonetheless, the emergence of psychoanalysis did much to influence the way clinical psychology and psychotherapy came to be practised. And despite their controversial reputation, psychoanalytic theories and therapies remain hugely popular around the world.

Key concept: Sexuality

Sexuality refers to a person's capacity for sexual feelings. By extension, the term also refers to a person's identity with regard to the sex of the people that they are usually attracted to. Sexual feelings typically involve having a physical attraction to another person (or persons) and a desire to have intimate physical contact with them. The basic urge to have sex is present in most people, but by no means in everyone.

The sexual impulse is one of the reasons that (some) animals procreate, and thus is one of the factors that allow a species to continue to exist. However, most people also find sex to be pleasurable. As such, it is frequently the case – if not most often so – that people engage in sex because they want to experience this type of pleasure, and not because they want to produce offspring. Sexuality can therefore involve a wide range of feelings and behaviours, including solitary activities, and can be a feature of many different kinds of relationships.

It is undoubtedly the case that many aspects of human sexuality are intertwined with human biology. The role of sexual feelings in facilitating human reproduction, and the basic physiological human sexual response cycle, are two examples. But as with the overall human condition, sexuality involves more than just physiological functioning. It also incorporates people's perceptions of sex, sexuality and relationships, their feelings of selfhood, and the way their tastes, experiences and knowledge are shaped within their social and cultural environments.

HISTORY AND THE SEXUAL INSTINCT

Human beings often pride themselves on being cognitively complex, on being logical, reflective, literate, numerate, meticulous and capable of abstract reason. We believe that civilization advances because of our scientific understanding, our technological productivity and our cultural sophistication. While we acknowledge and respect our emotions – and value them highly in certain domains, such as the arts – they are nonetheless seen as something secondary to intellect, as forces that right-minded people are able to control.

However, it is unclear whether these intellectualized outputs are the real reason we are all here today. Arguably, the development of our human character is far more dependent on our habits, our proclivities and our intuitions. Our ability to experience drives, impulses and desires – and our compulsion to act upon them – accounts for the vast majority of our behaviour. Intellectualized deliberation might define humankind, but humankind would not exist were we incapable of responding to instinct.

The term 'instinct' is not without its complications. Essentially it refers to an inherent tendency to behave in a particular way, to respond to events in a particular manner, or to be driven by particular motivations. For some psychologists, instincts are created by known or unknown causal contingencies, perhaps involving reward and punishment. For others, instincts are 'just there', core existential features that human beings are born with. For still others, the distinction is not really relevant: what matters is how we manage our instincts, and the degree to which it is appropriate for us to allow ourselves to be controlled by them.

In short, much of our psychology is shaped by forces that we rarely discuss or define. Our innate predilections determine our ultimate purpose. Our gut reactions guide our daily decision-making. Without succumbing to the urge to socialize, we would not have a civilization at all. Without submitting to our sex drive, we would not even have a species.

Sexual instinct and human civilization

Instincts and drives have long been recognized as helping to shape the course of humanity. The legends, fables and myths of nearly every culture turn on protagonists' reactions to rage, jealousy or guilt. Religious scriptures are replete with characters who are unable to resist temptation, their resulting indiscretions fatefully redirecting the moral destiny of humankind. Homer's heroes in *The Odyssey* are far from deliberative or sober. Instead they are flung from one adventure to the next by their passions, loves and furies (Porter, 1987). The ancient Greek philosophers' concerns with *reason* – and their endeavours to 'tame' irrationality (as discussed in Chapter 4) – were themselves predicated on an awareness of just how influential the instinctive side of the psyche can be.

The idea that innate impulses played a central role in human history became formalized in the nineteenth century, most notably in the work of Swiss anthropologist Johann Jakob Bachofen (1815–87). In a widely read volume, Bachofen (1861) put forward an elongated history of human evolution, in which the power structures of modern civilization were shaped by the historical implications of human sexual behaviour.

In Bachofen's theory, the earliest prehistoric people lived in a world of carnal chaos. Male and female humans copulated like any other animal, bonding with each other in unfettered sexual promiscuity. Such orgiastic conditions created constant confusions over parentage. It was always clear who a child's mother was, but the identity of a person's biological father was usually difficult, if not impossible, to ascertain. As a result, a person's ancestry could only ever be confirmed for their maternal lineage. Bachofen theorized that this led to the emergence of a matriarchal culture in early human history. As the only assured parents, mothers exerted control over property rights and privilege in the prehistoric world.

The emergence of monogamy, according to Bachofen, reflected the male effort to reshape families in ways that would allow ancestry to be traced through paternal, as opposed to maternal, lineage. Together with the impact of sex differences in physical strength, and probably in aggression too, male-enforced monogamy saw the gradual demise of matriarchy as society's organizing structure. With paternity now confirmable, property could be held and bequeathed from father to son and then to grandson. Bachofen saw the imposition of moral order on humankind as ending the sexual free-for-all, and thus as shifting humankind naturally away from matriarchy. Patriarchy, he thus suggested, was the hallmark of advanced civilization.

Bachofen's narrative proved to be widely influential. The pioneering French sociologist Émile Durkheim praised Bachofen's theory for rejecting the idea that patriarchy was the sole historical precedent for human societies (we will return to Durkheim's ideas in Chapter 10). Friedrich Engels (1820–95), the German political philosopher and co-author with Karl Marx of *The Communist Manifesto*, incorporated Bachofen's views into his analysis of economic history. For Engels, Bachofen's narrative helped to explain how human instincts to control labour and acquire property had been pivotal in the development of society's power structures. But in reality, Bachofen's theory was hugely speculative. Very little empirical evidence was ever mustered to support his core claim that prehistoric societies were in fact matriarchal (Eller, 2000).

However, some aspects of Bachofen's thinking remain current. Modern theories of evolution (see Chapter 5) certainly place sexual behaviour at the centre of human development. It is a core premise of evolutionary biology that those ancestors who reproduce with greater frequency end up being the ones who shape the eventual evolution of their species. While emphasis is often placed on the role of 'natural selection' in this dynamic, the role of 'sexual selection' is also crucial. This refers to the degree to which an organism is successful in attracting a mate (or mates). Those most adept at doing so will be far more likely to successfully pass on their genes (Kuijper, Pen & Weissing, 2012).

The ultimate evolution of all species, therefore, is dependent on the triggering of sexual instincts.

Culture and sexual attitudes

Among the first literatures to consider sexual drives as worthy of scholarly attention were the Ancient Indian Vedas. In Chapter 2, we saw how the Vedas promoted a polypsychic model of the human mind. These 3,000-year-old Sanskrit documents also introduced the earliest known accounts of kissing, in which it was noted that lovers would rub their noses and mouths together to indicate affection. The Vedas described sexual behaviour as a duty of devoted couples, and emphasized the importance of sex for providing mutual pleasure as well as biological reproduction.

Later Indian scripts, including the much-renowned *Kama Sutra*, developed these ideas extensively. Written between the second and third century CE by the Indian philosopher Vātsyāyana, the *Kama Sutra* remains one of the most famous instructional texts on sexuality ever written. However, contrary to popular stereotypes, the *Kama Sutra* not only provides advice on courtship, flirtation and sex positions, it also deals widely with issues such as well-being and emotional fulfil-ment in relationships, as well as discussing the nature of fidelity and social power.

Historical depictions of sexuality are often notable for their breadth and inclusiveness. The *Kama Sutra* describes many different ways for humans to have sex, including discussions of same-sex intercourse. Gay and bisexual sex were social institutions in ancient Greece, where discussion of sexual relationships was more likely to be framed in terms of the dominance and submissiveness of the participants, rather than their genders (Halperin, 2012). A similar approach was taken by the ancient Romans, who also considered sexual behaviour in terms of social hierarchy. For men, sex-ual behaviour preserved masculinity so long as their partners were socially inferior to them, regard-less of gender.

Broadly speaking, ancient civilizations seemed to be very encouraging of sexuality, with abun-dant depictions of wide-ranging sex appearing in their literature and art (Kampen, 1996). However, with the passing of time, social attitudes to sex and sexuality shifted and evolved. In medieval Europe, for example, the Christian church formally classified the act of kissing 'for carnal delight' as a sin (Bryant & Grider, 1991).

These points are of psychological interest because they show us that while sexual instincts and drives are experienced universally, the way they are perceived and discussed by humans has varied from culture to culture and across historical time. With the rise and spread of the Abrahamic reli-gions, including Christianity and Islam, theological teachings about sexual behaviour have served to shape social attitudes. However, while there are some consistent themes, these teachings often vary considerably. Sexual behaviours that are prohibited by some dogmas are celebrated by others. This itself further highlights the role of social construction in determining the way human beings conceive of, and explain, their instincts.

LOGOPHILIA: 'FASCINATION'

The English verb *to fascinate* refers to the attract-ing of somebody's strong attention or interest. When a person is said to be *fascinated* by a subject, or even by a person, it means that they have devel-oped a passionate interest in them. The experi-ence is referred to as *fascination*. A less common but overlapping meaning refers to the power to grab somebody's attention against their will. This is often said to be reflected in the Latin verb *fascin-are*, which means 'to cast a spell'.

However, all these terms have a deeper and older meaning that is rooted in human sexuality. Specifically, in the religions of ancient Rome, a *fas-cinum* was a small amulet shaped like a human phallus that was used to invoke the divine protec-tion of the gods. In this context, the full meaning of *fascinare* is 'to cast a spell *using the power of the fascinum*'.

Phallic-shaped charms and jewellery were com-mon in the ancient world. Archaeologists have con-ventionally believed that the significance of the symbol related to notions of masculine strength and power. However, some scholars argue that its effects were premised on the unease created by sexual imagery, and the disabling impact of provok-ing onlookers to avert their gaze (Whitmore, 2017).

What we can surmise is that uncensored sexual imagery was far more common in the daily lives of people in many ancient civilizations than it is for us today. This draws our attention to the fact that our social norms regarding sexuality have varied across time and place. It is important to recall this role of social context when considering whether particular patterns of sexual development, or behaviour, should be deemed psychologically 'normal'.

PSYCHOANALYSIS IN CONTEXT

Of all attempts to explain how deep-seated drives shape the psychology of human beings, perhaps none has had as wide-ranging an impact on human culture as the field of psychoanalysis. In short, psychoanalysis is a set of theories describing how people's thoughts, feelings and behaviours are determined by the way instincts and impulses compete for dominance in their unconscious minds. Psychoanalysis was first developed by the Austrian neurologist Sigmund Freud (1856–1939). Succeeding years have seen a number of variations on Freud's original ideas, some of which have departed quite significantly from his approach. Nonetheless, psychoanalysis is one of the few areas of psychological thought to have become synonymous with its founder. In the contemporary world, the field is frequently referred to as *Freudianism*.

In earlier chapters we warned against the problem of 'Great Man' approaches in history. However, it is difficult to discuss the development or impact of psychoanalysis without emphasizing the influence of Sigmund Freud himself. This is not least because of one of psychoanalysis's main shortcomings. Academic critics of psychoanalysis often complain that its defenders fail to evaluate the field objectively, instead overlooking its flaws because of a personal loyalty to Freudianism and, by extension, a form of hero-worship directed at Freud himself. In the case of psychoanalysis, the Great Man looms large on the historical horizon, impossible to ignore.

Despite often being depicted as defunct, psychoanalysis continues to be extremely popular around the world. It is one of the more common types of psychotherapy in countries such as Argentina, Australia, Brazil, Canada, the United Kingdom and the United States (R. T. G. Walsh et al., 2014). In fact, in the United States, the American Psychological Association's psychoanalysis section has more members than its section for counselling psychology (American Psychological Association, 2017a). But Freud's personal legacy extends far beyond an influence on science or therapy. Many academics in the humanities cite Freudianism as their primary scholarly orientation, using psychoanalytic ideas to discuss the arts, history and politics.

While Freud has become personally associated with psychoanalysis, he did not produce his theories in a vacuum. As with any popular development in how humans come to explain their own behaviour, the psychoanalytic tradition was shaped by a number of important contextual influences.

Many of Freud's conclusions were affected by the political and social milieu in which he lived. Political circumstances also curtailed his practical opportunities to be professionally productive, and in some cases skewed scholars' responses to his work. Intellectually, Freud's interest in unconscious mental processes was primed by a number of older ideas, especially those common in German-speaking philosophy. His theories were also informed by late-nineteenth-century ideas about the biology of human minds that were themselves intertwined with cultural prejudices. And although he sought to place sexual instinct at the centre of his worldview, Freud (like many other physicians) operated with extremely poor information about the reality of people's sex lives.

Public domain, via Wikimedia Commons / CC0 1.0

Image 7.1   Sigmund Freud

The sociopolitical climate

Freud was born into a Jewish family in a small village in what is now the Czech Republic. He later moved to Vienna, where he studied medicine, lived and worked for many years. During this period of the late nineteenth century, Vienna was part of the Austro-Hungarian Empire, a multinational state and major European superpower.

Freud had grown up during the 1860s, a time of economic prosperity and cultural optimism in central Europe. As a Jewish person, the young Freud was fortunate to be living through a period of relative social tolerance. However, in 1873, just as Freud entered adulthood, the Austro-Hungarian stock market crashed, precipitating an economic crisis that quickly changed the national mood. With the country's politics lurching to the right, anti-liberal forces began to take centre stage.

National elections saw the rise of the populist Christian Social Party (CSP). Considered by modern historians as true proto-fascists – direct predecessors of twentieth-century far-right ideologies such as Nazism – the CSP sought to distinguish Austrian citizens on the basis of Catholic religious identity.

An emergent nationalism saw growing animosity towards countries such as France, who were viewed as irreligious adversaries and political rivals. Influenced by the German-speaking universities, the Viennese medical world came to see their French counterparts as significantly less advanced. Despite this, in 1885 Freud spent a three-month period in Paris studying under the French neurologist Jean-Martin Charcot (1825–93), a specialist in the treatment of hysteria. Freud would later recall that his visit to Paris was pivotal in his decision to turn his own attention to the question of hysteria, and to focus his professional life on developing therapies for psychopathology.

Freud quickly developed a reputation as something of a non-conformist. His association with Charcot was both professionally and politically divisive. Charcot was renowned for using hypnosis on his patients, which was far removed from the anatomically oriented Germanic psychiatry espoused by Freud's Viennese peers. And as Charcot was a prominent member of France's stridently anticlerical republican movement, he was also disliked by Austrian physicians due to his political reputation.

But rather than try to find common ground with his colleagues in Vienna, Freud often sought to emphasize his status as an outsider, perhaps realizing that attempting to professionally ingratiate himself would be pointless in an increasingly antisemitic society. When opening his new therapy practice in 1886, he timed it to take place on Easter Sunday, a day of great significance for Catholics, when Viennese businesses would ordinarily be closed (Pines, 1989).

As Freud's private practice flourished, the society in which he lived and worked became ever more tense. By 1897, there was rioting on the streets of Vienna, after the Emperor had briefly attempted to prevent the installation of the Christian Social Party's founder as the city's mayor. In the face of popular revolt, the Emperor backed down. The new mayor then immediately banned social democrats, pan-Germans and all Jewish people from holding posts in his municipal administration. Even before the turn of the twentieth century, Vienna was a brutally hostile environment for the liberally minded, and especially for anyone who, like Freud, was Jewish.

It was in such a fraught milieu that Freud developed, discussed and disseminated his theories of the mind. Professional isolation had forced him to work as an independent practitioner, a plight that possibly helped to foster his view of coping as a solitary challenge: for Freud, emotional struggles were always best dealt with by looking inward, deep within one's own mind. The climate of constant discrimination that he faced in everyday life must surely also have influenced his perception of human nature. Based on the type of behaviours he encountered in society, it is perhaps unsurprising that Freud – along with many other liberal-minded intellectuals – came to view human personalities as intrinsically visceral and atavistic, and shaped in fundamental ways by impulses, emotions and innately destructive tendencies.

Freud's intellectual influences

Freud is often credited with placing new emphasis on the hidden parts of human consciousness. In doing so, he followed a tradition of scholarship that explored how certain thoughts and feelings appear to arise automatically, their origins forever separate from one's immediate attention. These private mental processes had intrigued philosophers (and fiction writers) for many centuries, without receiving much consideration from physicians. The shadowy recesses of the mind were seen to be of more spiritual than clinical significance.

In Western philosophy, major figures such as the Dutch philosopher Baruch Spinoza (1632–77), as well as German scholars Arthur Schopenhauer (1788–1860) and Gottfried Leibniz (who we encountered in Chapter 4), had each theorized about hidden mental processes. Spinoza, for example, had used the concept of *conatus* to describe a person's innate drive to continue to exist, which he said would affect their behaviour in ways they were not aware of. Schopenhauer expanded such views to argue that people's choices were subject to underlying, and unarticulated, sexual motivations. Leibniz had taken a more physical approach, focusing on how perceptions often arrive in the mind without being noticed.

Another German philosopher, Johann Friedrich Herbart (who we encountered in Chapter 3), used mathematical reasoning to argue that perceptual awareness existed at different levels, with a crucial threshold – the *limen* – separating that of which we are conscious from that which exists in our mind at a subconscious level. Herbart suggested that our perceptions can move between the various layers, including into and out of the subconscious. This principle explains how, at any given moment, we can be preoccupied with a tiny fraction of our thoughts and feelings but, when prompted, can quickly bring entirely different thoughts and feelings to the forefront of our attention. Importantly, Herbart suggested that certain emotional states can cause important thoughts – even 'our most vivid convictions' – to remain at the subconscious level, imbued with an 'unfortunate inertia' that prevents us from appreciating their significance (Hartenstein, 1850). This was later echoed in Freud's theories on the unconscious more broadly, and on psychological repression in particular.

The German philosopher Friedrich Nietzsche (1844–1900), one of the foremost philosophers of all time, developed extensive theories on the subject of *sublimation*, a process whereby toxic or problematic instincts are transformed into socially acceptable behaviours. For Nietzsche, sublimation served an integrative purpose, producing a human personality from psychological undercurrents (Gemes, 2009). Freud would later adapt Nietzsche's concept of sublimation by casting it as a more destructive, pathological process.

German philosophy's interest in these issues reached something of a pinnacle with the work of Eduard von Hartmann (1842–1906), who summarized his theories in a widely read book, *Philosophie des Unbewussten* (*Philosophy of the Unconscious*), in 1869 (von Hartmann, 1869). Hartmann described the unconscious as comprising both *will* (the ability to respond to desire) and *reason* (the ability to apply logic), in which the former is devoid of the latter. He suggested that human evolution is marked by humanity's development of an ability to act independently of will, but also noted that the eventual supremacy of reason would lead people to recognize the inevitable misery of their existence. In this respect, the unconscious is intrinsically human but ultimately self-destructive. Freud's work would later echo this general theme, while also invoking a number of Hartmann's more detailed observations. For example, Hartmann explained that slips of the tongue were frequently caused by disruptive unconscious thoughts, an idea that Freud would resurrect with his concept of *Fehlleistungen* (or *parapraxes*, as it appeared in English translations of his work).

Freud was immersed in German intellectualism and inspired by this philosophical tradition. Through his own reading he was very familiar with the notion of a dynamic unconscious. In developing his own theories, Freud sought to link these various unconscious forces to subjective personal experience, and ultimately to psychopathology.

The medical approach to hysteria

As described above, Freud chose to turn his professional attention to psychopathology after visiting Charcot in Paris, where he learned about the treatment of 'hysteria'. Freud would later spend many years working with patients who had been diagnosed with this condition, using such clinical encounters to develop extensive theories about the psychology of human minds. As such, it is reasonable to suggest that the entirety of psychoanalysis was born from Freud's early explorations of hysteria. This is significant because, in retrospect, we can see that hysteria was a highly controversial medical diagnosis.

As we discussed in Chapter 4, psychiatric diagnoses are often very arbitrary. They frequently reflect social prejudices about what constitutes appropriate or 'normal' behaviour, rather than revealing any authentic underlying disease. They can be determined more by social norms than by scientific knowledge.

Public domain, via Wikimedia Commons

Image 7.2 Hysteria
Painting by André Brouillet (1887) showing Jean-Martin Charcot presenting a case of hysteria to students at the Pitié-Salpêtrière Hospital in Paris.

In Freud's time, and for centuries prior, the term *hysteria* was used to refer to a condition in which a patient exhibited physical symptoms in the absence of physiological pathology. A patient might report unexplained pains, or they might frequently faint, or they might develop convulsions or spasms. Some patients might be rendered mysteriously deaf or mute. Others might become paralysed, either fully or partially. A common case would be of a patient whose paralysis could not be explained neurologically, such as a loss of sensitivity confined only to the hands (so-called glove anaesthesia).

But one notable feature of this condition stood out. All the patients were women. In fact, this was a prerequisite for diagnosis: this ostensibly physical disorder was, by definition, sex-specific. Its restriction to females is what gave 'hysteria' its name. The term was derived from the Greek word for 'uterus', reflecting a belief that the condition was caused by a dislocation of the womb.

Over time, hysteria came to be seen as a form of female madness or delirium (reflecting the modern usage of the word 'hysterical'), and was commonly described in journals of obstetrics and gynaecology as well as those of psychiatry. However, its precise 'cause' could never be established. Theories abounded, most of them conveniently dismissing women as incompetent participants in public life.

In Chapter 4, we saw how the American neurologist George Beard blamed modern technology for rising levels of insanity in the nineteenth century. According to Beard, women were especially addled by such problems, and were thus quite incapable of meeting the demands of a technocratic world (you will recall that Beard attributed much psychopathology to 'the mental activity of women'). In the late 1800s, scientists worried that the toll of menstruation was impeding girls' progress through education. In 1873, the prominent Harvard medical school physician warned that educating young women would produce a demand for blood flow to their brains that could, in due course, render them unable to menstruate at all (Shields, 1975). In Chapter 11, we will return to the topic of how social attitudes drove beliefs about sex differences in psychological function.

Such social panic reflected a paternalistic attitude rooted in an animosity towards women, and a reaction to several cultural developments that saw women seek new roles, rights and recognitions. The late nineteenth century was a period of rapid industrialization, declining fertility and the emergence of women's rights movements in Europe and North America. For many social conservatives, claims that women were especially threatened by such developments helped to rationalize opposition to change. They viewed the widespread prevalence of 'hysteria' as evidence that women were being driven mad. In this sense, hysteria was never simply a disease; rather, it was a diagnostic fiction perpetuated by a male-dominated society, whose physicians had internalized their culture's belief in the inevitability of female demise (Briggs, 2000). Expanded roles for women were deemed, as a matter of 'science', to be incompatible with female physiology.

As we saw in Chapter 6, much late-nineteenth-century science was influenced by eugenics, especially science that related to psychological issues. Unsurprisingly therefore, narratives surrounding hysteria were part and parcel of the eugenic worldview. Eugenicists saw the hysteria 'problem' as having a crucial racial dimension: because White women were so enfeebled by over-civilization, they warned, tumbling fertility rates would allow non-White races to 'outbreed' their European superiors (Briggs, 2000). As such, treating hysteria (and, ideally, eliminating it) was nothing less than an existential challenge for the White race.

When Freud came to study hysteria, he did so in the context of a nineteenth-century medical understanding that left much to be desired. While by many accounts Freud sought to pursue his investigations scientifically, and was never one to merely accept what his predecessors were inclined to presume, his starting position was nonetheless embedded within a cultural perspective that was markedly misogynistic, skewed by social bias and propelled by patriarchy and paternalism.

The societal view of sexuality

Freud placed great emphasis on the role of sexual instinct in shaping human personality. However, during the time he developed his theories, social attitudes made it extremely difficult to obtain reliable information about people's sexual behaviour. This problem was compounded by gendered stigmas that discouraged women from discussing (or exhibiting) sexuality, and by associated anxieties about sexual health and their impact on women's choices.

In the late nineteenth century, Vienna was not a place where people would talk candidly about their sex lives. But that is not to say that nobody was having sex. Indeed, it would seem that sexual

HISTORY IN STORIES: *FREUD* (2020)

Freud (Kren, Brunner & Hessler, 2020) was an Austrian-German television series based loosely on the early life of Sigmund Freud. The story begins with the young psychoanalyst's attempts to learn hypnosis, which he is convinced can be used to tap into the unconscious minds of therapy clients. However, as he is unable to master the skill, he mischievously resorts to recruiting his housekeeper, Lenore, to pretend to be a patient so that he can demonstrate his methods to his colleagues. In this respect, Freud is depicted as imaginative and competent, but also as a risk-taker and a charlatan.

The character Freud believes that hysteria is caused by a patient's memories of past traumas, a position that creates discomfort among his fellow physicians. He is portrayed as a heavy user of cocaine (which the real Freud had recommended as a medicinal drug), and as having felt ostracized because of his Jewish heritage (which also reflects the real Freud's experience).

However, it is probably fair to say that much of the rest of the plot deviates sharply from historical reality. The fictional Freud becomes involved in a murder investigation, after a detective brings a mutilated body to his office for him to examine. In a subtle subplot, this detective himself suffers from hysteria: as a war veteran, he experiences painful cramps in his hand as a result of post-traumatic stress disorder. As the investigation unfolds, Freud begins a love affair with Fleur Salome, a medium. Unfortunately, he is unaware that Fleur has been hypnotized and is secretly being controlled by her own stepmother. Subsequent plot twists take the story ever further into fantasy, featuring political conspiracies, Satanic rituals, spell-casting witches, Egyptian mummies and a cannibalistic opera singer.

The TV series *Freud* seeks to be an archetype of the horror fiction genre. Many of its visual elements and plot devices echo classic forerunners in the Western horror tradition. It also exemplifies a relatively recent cinematic and television trope in which historical figures are depicted in action-packed fictional contexts. Its creators use this artistic licence to construct a portrayal of Sigmund Freud that deviates from reality in sentiment as well as fact. The real Freud, for example, was deeply sceptical of seances and spiritualism, and promoted a stridently scientific worldview.

Nonetheless, *Freud* immerses its audience in a rich social, cultural and political context that is vividly embedded in nineteenth-century Austro-Hungarian Vienna. It depicts Freud's struggles with antisemitism and professional scepticism, and locates the experience of 'hysteria' within its original historical setting. These details can be informative for psychologists, many of whom become familiar with the rudiments of psychoanalysis without ever reflecting on the social context from which it emerged. And viewers who might not know much about psychoanalysis at all may nonetheless be prompted to become just a little curious, albeit by a fantasy horror TV show about a crime-fighting, cocaine-addled and ruggedly handsome psychotherapist.

HISTORY REPEATING ITSELF: HYSTERIA AND ILLNESS

The idea that 'hysteria' underlies many physical illnesses continues to cause controversy in modern medicine. Patients who report symptoms for which no physical causes can be found are often presumed to be suffering from a psychological affliction. The problem is that this reasoning is grounded in poor logic. Just because a physical cause cannot be found does not mean that one does not exist.

Many illnesses were initially presumed to be psychological but have later been discovered to be physical. Stomach ulcers, for example, were once thought to be caused by stress, when in fact we now know that most are caused by bacterial infection. For many years, migraine headaches were believed to be psychosomatic, until researchers discovered that the pain was caused by inflammation of the meninges membranes that surround the brain. Understanding of the causes of these illnesses meant that effective therapies could be developed. Theories that ulcers or migraines were rooted in psychological factors had delayed the discovery of effective treatments for many decades.

Apart from impeding the development of appropriate treatments, the illogical conclusion that an unexplained illness simply *must* have a psychological cause can also lead to stigma. In the early 1980s, one psychoanalytic theorist proposed that AIDS was caused by extreme sexual guilt, which he said was precipitated by a rise of social conservatism in Western countries (Schmidt, 1984). The theory sought to blame society for this illness, but it also reinforced the negative attitudes some people held towards those who were most at risk of contracting it.

Reflecting its history as a female problem – caused by dislocation of the uterus – it is typical for so-called hysterical illnesses to be identified more commonly in women than in men. However, this might be because doctors falsely expect that women are more likely than men to exaggerate or catastrophize their symptoms. A number of studies show that many doctors are more likely to consider women's pain to be psychological, but men's to be physical. The clinical tradition of hysteria leads them to presume that women are liable to think they are sick when they are not. We will return to this topic in Chapter 11.

Such biases can mean that some patients miss out on important treatments because of their doctor's attitude. The ironic reality is that, in these situations, it is the *doctor* who holds the false illness belief, not the patient.

promiscuity was so common right across Europe that sexually transmitted infections, such as syphilis and gonorrhoea, had become an endemic threat to public health.

The combination of unfettered sexual activity with a universal taboo on discussing sex proved especially damaging. People were having sex with very little understanding of how venereal diseases were spread, or of what could be done to avoid them. Religious leaders, for their part, prohibited the use of condoms, on the grounds that protecting the debauched from becoming infected would only deny them their 'necessary and certain punishment' (Nelkin & Gilman, 1988, p. 369). By the end of the nineteenth century, prevalence of syphilis alone was estimated to be as high as 10 per cent of the European adult population (Quétel, 1990).

A culture of secrecy ensured that these were hidden illnesses (Rudnick & Heru, 2017). Polite people would never discuss them explicitly, and common advice about risks would typically be encoded in euphemism and allegory. Doctors would frequently disguise their diagnoses, recording cases as 'rare blood diseases', and would often advise infected men not to inform their wives lest it led to divorce (Brandt, 1987). Instead, to preserve the social order, such patients were instructed simply to abstain from sex for months or years at a time.

Even the relevant branch of medicine was given a euphemistic title, with practitioners referring to their work as 'social hygiene'. Their approach was often more moral than medical: one of the field's leading figures famously declared venereal disease to be 'treasonous', describing it as 'family poison' (Morrow, 1904, p. 22). Unsurprisingly, despite the emergence of technical expertise, public debate about sexual health remained rare. In most communities, it was non-existent.

Social historians have shown that in the late nineteenth and early twentieth centuries, fear of venereal disease played a significant if largely unspoken role in women's sexual choices. Part of the problem was economic. In a patriarchal society, women had few opportunities for financial security other than through marriage. A young woman found to have a sexually transmitted disease would likely face rejection from all possible husbands, and thus a life of penury. Married women too were sufficiently wise to be cautious. They were aware that syphilis was genetically transmissible, and so that sex with an infected man – even their husband – could lead them to pass this disfiguring disease to their children.

Freud regularly encountered women who, he felt, exhibited sexual aversion. He saw their reluctance to have sex with their husbands as symptomatic of psychopathology. However, reluctance to have sex would have been far from unusual in late-nineteenth-century Vienna, and far from unwise. It is probable that many of Freud's patients were sexually disinclined because of rational concerns about their health (Rudnick & Heru, 2017). That they chose not to talk about these issues explicitly, and perhaps even became distressed when the topic was raised, did not reflect any mental dysfunction. Despite this, it seems likely that the suffocating impact of social and sexual norms will inevitably have influenced Freud's understanding of female sexuality.

FREUD'S PSYCHOLOGY OF SEXUAL DEVELOPMENT

From the mid-1880s onwards, as he saw more and more patients in Vienna, Freud gradually formed his elaborate theory of human psychology. He focused on the influence of unconscious drives, primarily those rooted in innate sexuality. Freud developed his approach over many decades, sometimes working in collaboration with like-minded clinical colleagues. While today Freudianism is often discussed as a single theoretical worldview, it is notable that Freud actually produced his ideas in stages, publishing his major works over a period of several decades. Some examples of his landmark papers and books (with their titles translated from German into English) are the following:

- **1895:** *A Project for a Scientific Psychology* (a manuscript not published until 1950, based on letters to the physician Wilhelm Fliess, in which Freud attempted to frame his initial psychological theories within neurology) (Freud, [1895] 1950)
- **1895:** *Studies on Hysteria* (a book co-authored with Josef Breuer, in which Freud presented a series of case studies of hysteria patients) (Breuer & Freud, 1895)
- **1900:** *The Interpretation of Dreams* (a book in which Freud introduced his theory of the unconscious and its influences on people's dreams) (Freud, 1900)
- **1901:** *Fragments of an Analysis of Hysteria* (a case history detailing the case of Ida Bauer, referred to by Freud as 'Dora', and its implications for his infamous 'seduction theory') (Freud, [1901] 1905)
- **1905:** *Three Essays on the Theory of Sexuality* (a book in which Freud presented his theory of sexual development during childhood) (Freud, 1905)
- **1908:** '"Civilised" sexual morality and modern nervous illness' (a journal article in which Freud argued that society's sexual conventions serve to increase the risk of psychopathology by repressing people's natural instincts) (Freud, 1908)

- **1914:** 'The history of the psychoanalytic movement' (an essay in which Freud rejected competing theories of psychology, specifically those of former followers who continue to style themselves as psychoanalysts) (Freud, 1914)
- **1923:** *The Ego and the Id* (a pamphlet in which Freud set out the structure of the human mind, and its role in psychopathology) (Freud, 1923)
- **1927:** *The Future of an Illusion* (a book in which Freud discussed the psychological roots of religion) (Freud, 1927)
- **1930:** *Civilization and Its Discontents* (a book in which Freud dissected the clash between individual impulses and societal needs) (Freud, 1930).

In his clinical practice, Freud refined a number of methods for exploring the experiences of his patients. Such techniques, he felt, could be used to generate a scientific understanding of the unconscious human mind. In terms of their effect on subsequent therapeutic practice – including many of the modern norms of current clinical psychology – these psychoanalytic methods were, in their own way, to become as influential as Freudian theory itself.

Free association and dream analysis

Many of Freud's initial ideas drew on the work of the French psychologist Pierre Janet (1859–1947). Janet had presented a number of theories about hysteria, hypothesizing that trauma causes a person's memories to become disconnected from conscious awareness. The Frenchman coined the term *subconscient* (subconscious) and referred to his work as *analyse psychologique* (psychological analysis). After Freud wrote extensively about *das Unbewusste* (the unconscious) and called his own field *die Psychoanalyse* (psychoanalysis), Janet would imply that Freud had simply poached his ideas (Fitzgerald, 2017). While it is impossible to know for sure whether this intimation of plagiarism was justified, we do know that when developing his methods of enquiry, Freud freely adapted the techniques of his predecessors.

Inspired by his visit to Charcot, Freud attempted to develop a method that built on the technique of hypnosis. At first, he thought he could help a client achieve a hypnosis-like state by asking them to lie with their eyes closed while he placed his hand on their foreheads (Fancher, 1996). But over time he would discover that physical touch was not necessary. What was instead important was the client's sense of emotional security and their freedom to say whatever entered their mind.

Freud devised his approach through trial and error. However, it was greatly influenced by the case of a particular patient, Bertha Pappenheim (1859–1936), who for a number of years was treated by his colleague Josef Breuer (1842–1925). Breuer was a senior physician who had helped Freud establish his private practice in Vienna. The two men would later write up Pappenheim's treatment as a case study for their 1895 book, *Studien über Hysterie* (*Studies on Hysteria*; Breuer & Freud, 1895). As was customary when writing about a patient, they sought to protect Pappenheim's privacy by giving her a pseudonym. The name they chose was 'Anna O.'. The case of Anna O. would eventually become one of the most famous therapeutic case studies in the history of psychotherapy.

It was Pappenheim herself who recommended to Breuer that there was little need to use hypnosis in therapy. She had found that simply talking freely about what was on her mind was helpful. This unrestricted discourse was like 'chimney-sweeping', she said, later describing the experience as her 'talking-cure'. Today, the latter term is often used to describe all similar forms of psychotherapy. This Freudian approach of inviting clients to freely share their thoughts without censorship in a private setting has become a standard format of modern therapeutic practice. Freud was to name it *freier Einfall*, a term frequently translated into English as 'free association'.

Pappenheim had developed hysteria-related symptoms when she was twenty-one years old, suddenly experiencing hemiplegia, bouts of fainting, a severe cough and various cognitive deficiencies. Freud noted that she had become especially troubled when her religiously devout father fell gravely ill. Without having met Pappenheim personally, Freud concluded that her symptoms resulted from early childhood trauma, and in particular from being sexually abused by her father.

Freud proposed that Pappenheim's hysteria was caused by her mind defending itself from having to remember such awful events. His verdict was certainly contentious. Breuer in particular did not approve of this sudden 'immersion in sexuality' (literally, 'das Eintauchen in die Sexualität') as a means to explain psychopathology (Skues, 2006). He maintained that there was no reason to believe Pappenheim had been abused. Pappenheim herself would eventually become a prominent feminist activist and write several works about the negative treatment of women. She never once alluded to having been molested.

Nonetheless, Freud persisted with his position. He felt that patients did not merely forget past experiences, but actively resisted any efforts to remember them. He was to conclude that such resistance could only result from sexual trauma, usually some form of mistreatment. But Freud's confidence stemmed more from confirmation bias than from true corroboration. As few nineteenth-century Viennese women would be comfortable talking about sex with their (male) therapists, any discussion of such matters would likely be diluted, distorted or deflected. It is unclear whether Freud fully appreciated that in a society riven by sexual taboos and systemic chauvinism, female clients would inevitably self-censor.

A second significant case would lead Freud to develop a further method for exploring his clients' experiences: attempting to analyse the contents of their dreams. Freud did not invent the idea of using dreams to divine a person's unconscious feelings. As we saw in Chapter 4, the Greek physician Artemidorus had employed this technique back in the second century CE. Famously, Artemidorus had written in depth about the hidden implications of incest dreams, in which a person dreams about having sex with their mother (Sick, 2013).

Freud's case involved a young patient called Ida Bauer (1882–1945), who in his case notes he referred to as 'Dora'. Bauer was sent to Freud for treatment when she was eighteen years old, during which she revealed that her father had allowed a male adult neighbour to make sexual advances towards her. As with Bertha Pappenheim, encouraging Bauer to speak freely seemed to alleviate her hysteria symptoms. To further develop her therapy, Freud then asked Bauer to recount some of her dreams. This experiment was to prove especially explosive.

Bauer described one dream where she was fleeing from a burning house, and another where her father died after she had left home. Freud told her that her dreams suggested she was, in fact, attracted

Image 7.3 Bertha Pappenheim (referred to by Freud as 'Anna O.') in 1882

to the neighbour that had made sexual advances towards her. Her fears were not so much that she would be assaulted by this man, Freud argued, but that she would willingly submit to her secret wish to have sex with him. Moreover, he suggested, Bauer's lust for this man itself masked an even deeper unconscious desire – a longing to have sex with her *own father*.

The still-teenage Bauer was appalled by Freud's claims. The male neighbour had repeatedly propositioned her since she was fourteen years old and, by her own account, she certainly did not lust after her own father. Bauer abruptly ended her therapy, and Freud wrote up the events as a case study in therapeutic failure.

While the Dora case study was important for introducing the psychoanalytic approach to dream interpretation, it also exhibited Freud's distinct patriarchal bias. Many of Bauer's protestations were dismissed by Freud as pathologically unreasonable. Consistent with the medical sexism of the time, Freud seemed unable to recognize Bauer's victimhood, preferring instead to question the integrity of her accounts. In his notes he recorded that Bauer was known to have attended public lectures on women's rights, and that she was ambivalent about her sexuality. From these flimsy fragments, Freud confidently concluded that Bauer was, in fact, secretly lesbian (Rudnick & Heru, 2017).

Freud would continue to employ free association and dream analysis as key tools for exploring his clients' psychological experiences. But these methods were by their nature exploratory rather than conclusive. Their merit relied entirely on Freud's ability to divine their true meaning, as there was never any direct evidence to verify his diagnostic interpretations. Despite this, Freud's methods attracted widespread clinical attention. His case studies were salacious and striking. And importantly, Freud's accounts resonated with a culture that decried women's assertiveness and preserved a sexual double standard. To many observers, the idea that women's secret lusts would generate hidden pathologies just seemed to *make sense*.

Freud's theory of childhood sexual development

However, not all physicians were enthusiastic about the emerging Freudian worldview. When in 1896 Freud presented a paper arguing that sexual mistreatment was a necessary prerequisite for the development of hysteria – his so-called seduction theory – many of his medical peers recoiled at its implications. Several stopped referring their patients to him (Fancher, 1996).

Freud had based his conclusions on eighteen case studies, which he said showed irrefutably that hysteria was caused by sexual abuse. However, a year later, he published a revised assessment. Without formally explaining why he changed his mind, Freud now asserted that his patients had not actually been molested. Instead, he argued, their reports of abuse were based on *imaginary* seductions rather than real ones; their hysteria had been caused by taboo sexual *fantasies* rather than sexual abuse per se.

In 1984, American psychoanalyst Jeffrey Masson (1941–) claimed that Freud abandoned his seduction theory due to the outcry it had created, and not because he had changed his underlying beliefs (Masson, 1984). In Masson's view, Freud's updated position was insincere and calculated solely to preserve the reputation of psychoanalysis. This deserved to be criticized, Masson said, because it placed the needs of psychoanalysis ahead of those of clients.

In effect, the new version of the theory portrayed clients as unreliable witnesses. It meant that children who described receiving inappropriate advances from adults were no longer necessarily presumed to be unwilling or passive victims. This aspect of Freud's revised paradigm has had lasting consequences for how sexual abuse is discussed in mainstream society. Guided by what was seen as Freud's authoritative judgement, generations of subsequent clinicians would begin to view their clients' descriptions of sex abuse with some distrust. The revised theory set a new clinical standard whereby a child's account of abuse should be considered a potential, if not likely, fantasy.

If Freud really did revise his theory with the intention of avoiding controversy, his evasion certainly failed. His new worldview was arguably more incendiary than the original. While his seduction theory had depicted adults as potential molesters of children, his new position depicted children as inclined towards fantasizing about sex with adults. This sexualization of the infant mind was a dramatic departure from previous assumptions about what children were like psychologically. It was surely just as much a threat to Freudianism's reputation as was the original theory of seduction.

In Freud's new worldview, the sexual fantasies of children were seen as central to human psychology. Freud set out the principles of this position in his landmark 1905 treatise, *Drei Abhandlungen zur Sexualtheorie* (*Three Essays on the Theory of Sexuality*). This was where Freud described children's psychological development as occurring in a series of stages:

- **The oral stage:** According to Freud, when young babies first become aware of the world, their primary source of instinctive satisfaction is their mouths. They obtain pleasure by sucking, biting and chewing. To Freud, such gratification is fundamentally sexual in nature, albeit in a loose sense of the term. Nonetheless, Freud referred to a baby's motivating energy as their 'libido', and to their mouth as the baby's 'erogenous zone'. When a baby's oral needs are not fully satisfied, they may develop 'oral fixation' in later life, characterized, in Freud's view, by behaviours such as nail-biting or smoking. Although the stages of psychosexual development are not prescriptive, it is generally accepted that the oral stage represents a baby's first eighteen months of life.

- **The anal stage:** From the age of eighteen months to three years, infants enter a phase where gratification is achieved through control of bowel movements and bladder tension. In other words, the baby's libido is now directed at a new zone of the body, namely the anus and its surrounding areas. When Freud was writing, families lived in cramped houses with no indoor toilets, washing machines or disposable nappies. Toilet-training was especially central to daily life and provided infants with strict lessons on the impositions of the external world (D. B. King et al., 2009). Freud argued that infants who fail to confidently master toileting, perhaps clashing with their parents as a result, would become 'anally fixated' when they were older: in adulthood, they would be obsessively tidy, particular and punctual.

- **The phallic stage:** From the age of three to six years, according to Freud, children become aware of the differences between people's bodies and start to notice the presence and absence of genitalia – or, more specifically, of phalluses. In Freud's view, this leads children to become fascinated by their opposite-sex parent and threatened by the same-sex one. While children of this age have not reached sexual maturity, Freud nonetheless proposed that they begin to experience fundamental sexual urges that lead them into conflict with their parents. Boys compete with fathers for access to their mothers, a situation Freud called the 'Oedipal complex' (named after the Greek mythological character who killed his father and married his mother). This leads to an overwhelming fear of disempowerment, which Freud called 'castration anxiety'. Girls, for their part, develop an anxiety called 'penis envy', realizing that they cannot successfully compete with men for their mother's affection. Once again, failure to successfully navigate these experiences can, according to Freud, lead a child to develop various neuroses in later life. For example, boys who are afflicted by lingering Oedipal crises can, in adulthood, seek satisfaction from aggression, violence and the glorification of authority. Girls who fail to come to terms with penis envy, Freud suggested, go on to become sexually passive women.

- **The latency stage:** Between the age of seven years and puberty, a child experiences a stage of psychological stability. They start to identify more with their same-sex parent, and to seek friends and role models of their own sex. Their libido finds expression in socially accepted pastimes, such as sport or games. In adjusting to the outside world, the child begins to lose their earliest memories, developing what Freud termed 'infantile amnesia'. It is during this process, Freud suggested, that sexual traumas of early infancy become repressed.

- **The genital stage:** The onset of puberty serves to awaken (or, in Freud's view, *reawaken*) a child's sex drive. After having processed the latency stage, a child now seeks sexual gratification outside of the parental family structure. Unlike the phallic stage, when thoughts about genitalia are unconscious, during the genital stage a person becomes explicitly aware of their own and others' sexual organs. The adult mind has developed cognitively, and the person is capable of sophisticated social relationships. For Freud, the genital stage lasts from puberty until death, revealing a rather simplistic depiction of how sexuality ultimately unfolds throughout the course of adult life.

Freud's theory introduced many concepts that would become widely discussed over the subsequent century. Penis envy and castration anxiety proved especially eye-catching, and both remain commonly discussed today (albeit often as prompts for conversations about gender stereotypes). The term *Oedipal* now appears in all the major English-language dictionaries and is used to describe the often strained nature of father–son relationships. And in modern popular discourse, people who seek to exert an overbearing control over their surroundings are frequently referred to as having 'anal' personalities.

However, in the early twentieth century, the details of Freud's theory were extremely controversial. They conflicted sharply with the prevailing view of children, who most adults saw as angelically innocent and chaste. For Freud to describe toilet-training as a fundamentally sexualizing activity, in which young toddlers would become obsessed with their anuses, would have been especially shocking. Freud's depiction of sexual stages also conflicted with adults' views of their own life histories. Socially conservative men and women were horrified at being told that they once competed with one of their parents for the sexual attentions of the other.

Any mention of erogenous zones would have been difficult in a society where all talk of sex was taboo. The proposal that such zones could extend beyond the genitalia was especially alien. In Freud's theory, babies were born into a state of 'polymorphous perversity', which meant that they garnered sexual gratification whenever *any* part of their bodies was stimulated. The idea that the obvious joy babies feel when being hugged is, in fact, a form of *sexual* pleasure was extremely challenging, because it invested in infants a type of adult thinking that violated their perceived purity. Children were not meant to have erogenous zones of any kind.

However, the fundamental difficulty with Freud's theory of childhood sexual development was not that it clashed with pre-existing perceptions. It was that the core of the theory relied on Freud's speculations about the nature of infant experience. A key question was: How exactly did Freud *know* that children's pleasure was rooted in sexuality?

The answer, of course, is that he didn't know. Freud could point to the supposed *outcomes* in his theory, such as happy babies, strained father–son relationships and 'passive' women. However, he was unable to prove that his theory was correct in describing the psychological causes that *produced* these outcomes. There was simply no evidence to support his claims that the joy babies felt when hugged was sexual, that sons lusted after their mothers, or that any girl ever bemoaned her lack of a penis.

As we saw in previous chapters, human audiences can be quite suggestible. They are quickly convinced by descriptions that confirm their prior assumptions, and strongly swayed by examples that are easy to remember. To many people, several of Freud's basic observations – such as the simple fact that children behave differently at different stages of their lives – rang true. They recognized Freud's description of the way some adults become fastidiously clean and tidy (that is, those who have 'anal' personalities). The ready familiarity of such accounts infused Freud's theory with what psychologists now refer to as *face validity*, the impression that an evaluation *appears* to make sense because of the coherence of its superficial content. However, beneath his surface-level descriptions, Freud had little by way of evidence to substantiate his theoretical claims.

Face validity makes for pretty weak science. As we saw in Chapter 3, the scientific method evolved as a way of using observation to test claims against supposition. In other words, science was intended to avoid the traps that face validity created. Freud ([1895] 1950) wrote that he intended for psychoanalysis to be a science. However, the way he approached his work did not avail of empirical reasoning as it was employed in most other scientific fields.

HISTORICALLY (IN)ACCURATE?: SEXUALITY IN CHILDREN

The development of sexuality, especially in childhood, has always been a controversial topic. Freud's theories drew considerable criticism because they depicted children, previously seen as pure and innocent, as being driven by sexual impulses. His explanations were also weakened by the fact that they were based on clinical interpretations rather than on empirical data.

Later research sought to explore sexual behaviour more empirically. One of the first major investigations of this type was conducted by a team led by Alfred Kinsey (1894–1956), a biologist and zoologist at Indiana University.

Kinsey's studies were based on interviews with large samples of respondents over many years. Two major books were published, one reporting on findings from over 5,000 men (Kinsey, Pomeroy & Martin, 1948), and a second detailing findings from 6,000 women (Kinsey et al., 1953).

The Kinsey reports were the first to reveal that same-sex attraction was far more common than previously understood. Kinsey also found that people were more interested in sexual experimentation than they would ordinarily reveal publicly. And among other findings, his data suggested that men were more sexually active than women. However, as Kinsey's interviewees were all volunteers, it may be that his sample was skewed by a disproportionate number of participants who were more curious than average about

sex, and more willing to talk about it with researchers.

One especially contentious aspect of Kinsey's reports was his coverage of sexual responses in children. Critics focused on a set of four tables of data in the report on men, which they said included descriptions suggesting that some of Kinsey's respondents must have either observed or participated in child sexual abuse. Later investigations of the Kinsey archive in the 1990s revealed that the data in all four tables were in fact based on the experiences of a single man who was interviewed, a man who had indeed abused multiple children (Bancroft, 2004). These data were therefore worthless: firstly, they were drawn from a single source; and secondly, given that the activities described were criminal, it cannot be presumed that the information this source provided was complete, accurate or reliable. For example, this man's testimony will almost certainly have misrepresented the authenticity of children's interest and curiosity regarding sex.

The Kinsey reports are still frequently cited in discussions of children's sexuality (Goode, 2011). This is almost certainly because large-scale studies of the topic remain rare. However, while Kinsey's research provided compelling and groundbreaking insights into the sex lives of adults, his findings relating to childhood sexuality are, by contrast, completely unsound.

The Freudian depiction of mind

When Freud first pitched psychoanalysis as a science, he attempted to use his training in neurology as the basis for a theoretical framework. He believed that psychology would be best approached by looking at the physiology of the human nervous system. However, he soon came to the view that late-nineteenth-century neurophysiology was itself at a primitive stage of its development, and too rudimentary to provide a complete template of the mind (Hoffman, 2017).

Nonetheless, Freud felt it was essential that his theory conceptualize human consciousness as some kind of basic physical structure, one that is capable of defined dynamic actions. He felt that in time, neurophysiological science would catch up with his ideas, and identify the corresponding physical mechanisms somewhere deep within human anatomy. He presented the basic principles of his model in his 1900 book *Die Traumdeutung* (*The Interpretation of Dreams*). In its core, Freud's model of the mind – which he referred to as his 'metapsychology' – comprised two separate levels:

- At the *physical level,* Freud attempted to describe the human mind in terms of its separate parts, or subsystems. At first, he conceived of the mind as comprising *conscious, preconscious* and *unconscious* systems. A person's conscious mind contained their ongoing thoughts; their preconscious mind contained those other thoughts that were easily accessed or remembered; and their unconscious mind contained all those thoughts and feelings that lay beyond active awareness but which were nonetheless influential. In 1923, Freud would propose an updated model containing the *id,* the *ego* and the *super-ego.* In this version, the *id* is the mind's repository of unconscious impulses; the *super-ego* is the mind's moral conscience; and the *ego* is the part of a person's conscious awareness in which the competing demands of the id and super-ego are balanced with those of the external environment.
- At the *dynamic level,* Freud proposed that a person's psychological apparatus processed mental forces that, in turn, drove human behaviour. The main such force was a person's *libido,* which the id used to seek immediate gratification of all its impulses. The demands of civilized society created a need to dissipate unspent libido in socially acceptable ways, a task Freud said the ego achieved by using *defence mechanisms.* For example, a person's ego could seek to *repress* this energy (such as by repressing a traumatic memory), or it could use *projection* to deny their own unsavoury desires by causing the person to blame others for having these desires instead. Sometimes a person would redirect their energy into artistic creativity (a defence mechanism that Freud, echoing Nietzsche, called *sublimation*) or into love.

For Freud, this systemic model of the mind would give psychoanalysis a truly scientific character. By describing the internal dynamics of the psyche, Freud aspired to produce a unified theory that would explain all human thoughts, feelings and behaviours. It is with reference to these dynamics that psychoanalysis is now often referred to as representing the 'psychodynamic' approach to psychology.

The evolution of psychoanalysis

Freud attracted many professional followers and inspired a number of other major theorists to attempt to refine his ideas. The German-American psychoanalyst Erik Erikson (1902–94) argued that human personality was shaped not just by parent–child relationships, but also by the wider social environment. Erikson further explored people's adult life-stages, and introduced such memorable themes as

Image 7.4   Melanie Klein (1902), who pioneered the field of child psychoanalysis

'prolonged adolescence' and 'identity crisis'. The Austrian-British psychoanalyst Melanie Klein (1882–1960) teased out the psychological implications of early infancy, focusing on how prelingual children split their worlds into good and bad. Klein developed a theory of 'object relations', where children come to organize their understanding of the contents of the world.

In 1910, Freud established the International Psychoanalytic Association (IPA), capitalizing on the then prevalent trend (as discussed in Chapter 3) of formalizing intellectual movements within scholarly societies. The IPA continues to exist today. As well as fostering support for traditional psychoanalysis, the organization helped to generate some quite new approaches and emphases, not all of which were to Freud's own liking.

Figures such as the Austrian physician Alfred Adler (1870–1937) and the German analyst Karen Horney (1885–1952) believed Freud had attached too much importance to sexual impulses as fundamental drivers of behaviour. Adler is remembered for introducing the idea that people can suffer from an 'inferiority complex', where they seek to project an overly positive image to others in order to compensate for personal feelings of inadequacy. Horney, for her part, emphasized the role of society in shaping gender stereotypes and consequent gender differences, departing from Freud's belief in inherent biological causes. The renowned Swiss psychoanalyst Carl Jung (1875–1961) developed an extensive alternative theory of psychoanalysis focusing on the 'collective' unconscious – claiming that people inherited memories from their ancestors. As a result, Jung and Freud were to have an acrimonious and lasting personal dispute.

From the 1920s onwards, Freud's writings became increasingly negative and pessimistic. He often argued that the most basic human impulse was a drive to seek satisfaction through death. According to Freud, our core human instincts – those for violence and immediate self-gratification – were suffocated by the norms of civilization. In this way, he argued, civilization itself produces a state of permanent human discontent. For Freud, life is inescapably miserable; given enough time, all human communities will eventually self-destruct. It is arguable that Freud's writings at this time reflected truly personal feelings of dread. A long-time user of tobacco and cocaine, he had developed oral cancer in 1923, and through the 1930s, he saw his community descend into full-blown Nazism. In 1938, fearing for their lives, Freud and his family left Vienna behind and sought refuge in London. It was a thoroughly grim period, although Freud himself did not live to see the worst of it. He died in 1939, just before the outbreak of the Second World War.

After Freud's death, psychoanalysis continued to evolve. Chastened by the bleak excesses of war, scholars became increasingly interested in how language, ritual and myth shaped the standards of human behaviour. In the decades that followed, especially in the West, countercultural movements began to take hold. New generations aspired to reject traditional values of country and family, and alternative lifestyles made many old concepts look very dated. Among the responses to this fresh spirit of non-conformism were attempts to repackage psychoanalysis for the contemporary world.

In the 1950s and 1960s, the French psychiatrist Jacques Lacan (1901–81) introduced a radically new approach to psychoanalysis. Lacan rejected the notion of basic instincts, instead arguing that human experience was fundamentally socially constructed. In Lacan's view, a person's ego is built around the feedback they receive from others. As this creates an unsustainable desire to be what the 'other' wants them to be, the ego thus produces a permanent sense of alienation from the world. For Lacanians, good therapy should seek to break down the ego, rather than to strengthen it, essentially the *opposite* of the traditional psychoanalytic view. The charismatic Lacan became a hugely famous psychoanalyst, at one stage serving as Pablo Picasso's personal therapist. However, his ideas were greeted as heretical by many of his fellow psychoanalysts. In 1963 he was expelled from the IPA. While undoubtedly a disruptor, Lacan is nonetheless widely regarded as one of the most important twentieth-century thinkers. His take on psychoanalysis was to influence the work of many prominent French intellectuals, including Roland Barthes, Michel Foucault and Jacques Derrida.

ALMOST FAMOUS: MARJORIE BRIERLEY

Marjorie Brierley (1893–1984) became a psycho-analyst in Britain in the 1920s, having previously completed a medical degree at University College London. She immediately joined the then fledgling British Psychoanalytical Society (BPAS). While drawn to the object relations theories of Melanie Klein, she was especially interest in the adult female experience. She declined to take sides in the debates between the Kleinians and Freudians, preferring to occupy a middle-ground position (Brierley, 1932). However, her centrism ensured that her own ideas were often not highlighted, as they did not cohere with the dynamic of polariza-tion that propelled the development of psychoa-nalysis at the time.

Brierley was very active within the BPAS and did much to ensure the prosperity of psychoanalysis in the UK (Shapira, 2013). She sat on many of its committees, including its influential training com-mittee. When Anna Freud (the daughter of Sigmund) arrived in London as a refugee, Brierley vacated her position on the training committee so that the influential Freud could join. However, Anna Freud's arrival in Britain served to accentuate debate in the BPAS, with Brierley's consensus-seeking approach becoming increasingly overlooked.

Brierley has been credited with promoting cohesion in British psychoanalysis, despite her own psychoanalytic work often being overlooked. Her writings on femininity, emotion and depres-sion were insightful and scientific, and benefited from her ability to remain independent of both the Kleinian and Freudian camps. Nonetheless, the majority of historical scholarship has focused on the dramatic theoretical debates between those charismatic figures, with the result that Brierley's own scholarly contributions – as well as her role in ensuring the viability of British psychoanalysis – have almost entirely been ignored (Shapira, 2021).

LEGACY AND CRITIQUE

Freud and his followers developed both an elaborate theory of psychology and a meticulous approach to psychotherapy. They painted a complex picture of the human mind as embroiled in a constant struggle with itself, and of a universal human condition characterized by inevitable and insurmountable torment. Echoing Darwin's emerging view of evolution, Freud located human-kind firmly in a biological realm, in which behaviour is shaped by basic drives and urges, and civi-lized reason serves as but a socially constructed façade.

For psychoanalysts, the stresses of existence are best addressed through lengthy self-examination, supported by a suitably trained analytic therapist. Clients should be encouraged to explore their

Image 7.5 Freud's London study
The study in Freud's home in London is now the site of the Freud Museum.

own unconscious without restriction, with the therapist providing non-directive prompts and dispassionate feedback. The goal of psychoanalysis is not to 'cure', but to help a client understand the true nature of their own behaviour, after which they might (or might not) be able to adjust their lives.

As such, psychoanalysis is not merely a theory of psychology, nor is it 'scientific' in a simple sense of the term. The Freudian worldview is imbued with philosophical and humanistic strands, and presents moral, as well as mystical, implications. It has yielded a theory of human minds that defines much of the mind as impenetrable, and a school of psychotherapy that eschews simple notions of therapeutic success.

Freudianism is often seen as culturally enduring but scientifically controversial. However, it is worth noting that Freud's psychoanalytic theory introduced a number of central concepts that, while novel in the late nineteenth and early twentieth centuries, have been largely validated by subsequent developments in scientific psychology. Some examples include:

- Freud's proposal that human behaviours are significantly influenced, and regularly dominated, by unseen mental processes;
- his principle that early-life experiences greatly influence later-life behaviour by interfering with the optimal emergence of key developmental stages;

- the central premise that human behaviour is a function of biological antecedents and so can reasonably be compared to that of animals; and
- the idea that intellectual dimensions of human life are often slanted by biological influences, such as sexual drives and aggression.

The Freudian approach to psychotherapy has also been largely responsible for many norms of modern therapeutic practice, such as the central role of one-to-one 'talk' therapy, the principle of non-directive counselling, the importance of empathy, and the need for therapists to validate clients' personal life histories.

However, while psychoanalytic theory and therapy have proven popular, they have also attracted substantial criticism. While many concerns have been raised, the most significant critiques have been from religious, feminist and scientific perspectives.

Religious reservations

From the beginning, psychoanalysis had been criticized by religious commentators, and especially by Catholic theologians in Europe. As outlined in Chapter 2, depictions of the human mind as animalistic or subject to physical or biological forces have long attracted religious objections. With psychoanalysis, theologians were sceptical of Freud's claim that instincts and sexual nature determined a person's destiny. In the religious view, human beings were always capable of complete control over their own behaviour, and hence over their own spirituality. Freud's suggestion that religious beliefs were just another type of behaviour, shaped by instinct rather than by fact, was especially unwelcome.

Needless to say, the way Freud depicted infant sexuality was anathema to religious sensitivities. One prominent Italian theologian who wrote extensively about psychoanalysis (Gaetani, 1925) dismissed it as 'qualcosa di raccapricciante' (something horrifying), accusing Freud of wanting 'legittimare l'omosessualità' (to legitimize homosexuality) and of promoting 'i vizi più brutti contro natura' (the ugliest vices against nature). Perhaps adding unintended depth to his critique, this writer would refer to Freud as 'Sigismondo Freud, ebreo' (Sigmund Freud, Jew), and declared psychoanalysis to be 'un grosso attacco al cattoliscesimo' (a gross attack on Catholicism) (Zapperi, 2013, p. 102).

Social conservatives were also concerned that psychoanalysis could end up supplanting religion in the popular imagination. During the 1960s in particular, several countercultural movements encouraged the public to consider new forms of spirituality in their search for personal fulfilment. Freudianism was attractive because it not only sought to explain human actions, it also offered a way of dealing with guilt and shame, rationalizing errant behaviours as natural rather than sinful. It even provided the cathartic potential of one-to-one pastoral interactions, with scientist-technicians replacing the confessor priest (Foschi, Innamorati & Taradel, 2018).

The Catholic Church effectively outlawed psychoanalysis until the 1970s. Its official pledge of allegiance, which every Catholic had to endorse in order to become a priest, a civil servant or a teacher, required adherents to renounce the idea that their religious faith was 'a blind feeling bursting forth from the unconscious' (Kugelmann, 2011, p. 49). In 1961, the Vatican made their corporate position explicit, publishing an official pronouncement forbidding Catholics from either practising or using psychoanalysis (Holy Office, 1961).

However, in time, with the de-sexualizing of psychoanalytic theory, religious objections greatly softened. In 1973, the field was ultimately legitimized for Catholics when the then pope referred to it as a 'famous current of anthropological studies' and a useful way to explore personal consciousness (Ancona, 2003). Freudianism's broadening scope helped psychoanalysis to find a new audience among religious and spiritual adherents. The fact that many senior clerics would themselves undergo psychoanalysis, including at least one future pope (Sherwood & Giuffrida, 2017), indicates just how acceptable the practice was to become.

Feminist concerns

As outlined above, the culture within which Freud developed psychoanalysis was rigidly patriarchal and deeply misogynistic. Accordingly, his depiction of women's behaviour was duly distorted by sexist stereotypes. Freud saw hysteria as a pathology of the female psyche, rather than as a projection of masculinist prejudice. He discussed female psychology in crude physical terms, seeing girls' minds as fundamentally shaped by their anatomy's lack of male sexual organs. His depiction of women's passivity as rooted in unconscious conflict detracted from the way his society suppressed female independence and autonomy. When faced with a confident young woman – such as Ida Bauer – he would pathologize her assertiveness in chauvinistic terms, believing it to reveal an underlying sexual dysfunction. And, of course, his revised seduction theory argued that women readily fantasized about being sexually molested, implying that their reports of such assaults should not be trusted.

More broadly, Freud constructed his theories of female psychology based on a restricted range of case studies, comprising a sample of women who were – by virtue of being patients – far from representative of women in general. The subsequent popularity and influence of Freudianism only served to reinforce this distortion. Psychoanalysis helped to normalize the depiction of women as implicitly hysterical beings.

Psychoanalysis was not the only practice to be permeated by patriarchy. All scientific, medical and academic professions were patriarchal during Freud's lifetime (as, in many respects, they still are today). Ironically, psychoanalysis became known as a field in which women seemed to have *greater* opportunities to build professional careers. In its earlier decades, and especially in the 1930s, several women psychoanalysts were to become especially prominent (Zaretsky, 2005). As well as Melanie Klein and Karen Horney (both mentioned above), other pioneers of early psychoanalysis included the French psychiatrist Sophie Morgenstern (1875–1940); her compatriot, the academic Juliette Favez-Boutonnier (1903–94); Margaret Mahler (1897–1985), a physician from Hungary; and English educator Susan Isaacs (1885–1948), who wrote under the pseudonym 'Ursula Wise' (Shapira, 2017). Freud's own daughter, Anna Freud (1895–1982), became widely known for her professional work in child psychology, and is considered to be a founder of child psychoanalysis.

However, the ending of the Second World War saw many professions revert to male dominance, as men returned to the domestic workforce in large numbers (R. T. G. Walsh et al., 2014). This was a period when psychoanalysts presented several new theories about mother–child relationships, many of them implicating 'bad mothering' as a cause of psychopathology and social problems. The British paediatrician Donald Winnicott (1896–1971) argued that juvenile delinquency was rooted in family breakdown, with children engaging in antisocial behaviour as a way of 'unconsciously looking for [their] parents' (Winnicott, 1949). In the United States, the physician Bruno Bettelheim (1903–90) promoted the view that childhood autism resulted from maternal coldness, a hypothesis known as the 'refrigerator mother' theory (Bettelheim, 1967). These psychoanalytic speculations were never grounded in empirical evidence, and ignored the role of biological, economic, political, judicial, educational and cultural variables. Nonetheless, given the 'face validity' of psychoanalysis, such claims were widely discussed and generally accepted, ultimately serving to perpetuate prejudicial stereotypes and the scapegoating of women over many decades.

Some feminist critics have sought to use psychoanalysis to deconstruct the nature of patriarchy itself. For example, the American sociologist Nancy Chodorow (1944–) has argued that psychoanalytic concepts help to reveal the true arbitrariness of gender roles. Similarly, a number of feminist philosophers, most prominently the Belgian-born French scholar Luce Irigaray (1930–), have used psychoanalytic ideas to argue that perceived sex differences are rooted more in social practice and power relations than in biology.

While many feminist theorists have written from a Freudian perspective, often they employ psychoanalysis as a method of critical enquiry rather than as a template for explaining behaviour (Kamber, 2016). The classic Freudian account of the notional 'female' mind is not particularly convincing, but to many feminist scholars its questioning stance is powerful. The psychoanalytic approach challenges us to explore the sources and impacts of our biases, encourages us to contemplate the residual effects of our experiences, and exposes the folly of assuming that women and men ever possess true self-awareness. In so doing, it supports the feminist critique by helping to illuminate subjective dimensions of identity, relationships and differences in social power.

Scientific attacks

Perhaps the most common complaint about psychoanalysis, and often the most vitriolic, is that it is scientifically unsound. Science is supposed to be based on observation, but the unconscious – the core construct of psychoanalysis – is *by definition* unobservable.

Critics argue that this makes psychoanalysis a largely speculative pursuit. Its descriptions of intrapsychic machinations are uncorroborated by tangible evidence. The theory is built upon the testimony of clients, and so is subjective, idiosyncratic and impossible to independently verify. Constructs such as the ego, super-ego and id cannot be detected or measured, and dynamic operations such as the workings of the defence mechanisms cannot be monitored or recorded. Psychoanalysis completely disregards the scientific premium on objectivity.

A related criticism concerns the vagueness of its predictions. Freudian forecasts are so open-ended as to be scientifically unusable. A good example is the way defence mechanisms are supposed to function. According to psychoanalysis, when a person has a traumatic experience, they may respond by repressing all memories of the event. Or the opposite might happen: the person might spend subsequent years obsessing endlessly about their experience of trauma. In other words, psychoanalytic theory predicts that post-traumatic emotions will be *either* absent *or* present. As this covers all eventualities, no outcome could ever suggest that the theory was, in fact, wrong. Theories that are never wrong cannot be tested for accuracy. This means that they are not 'scientific'.

In simple terms, psychoanalytic theory is not falsifiable. Its data are anecdotal, its descriptions are vague, and its predictions are of a *heads-I-win-tails-you-lose* variety. A psychoanalytic theorist can always claim to be correct because any situation can be described in a way that conforms to the psychoanalytic account. Predictions that incorporate all possible outcomes are not really 'predictions' at all.

Accordingly, critics complain that psychoanalysis offers a poor basis from which to develop psychotherapies. Many empirical studies have found that psychoanalytic therapies often don't work very well. Rates of recovery following psychoanalytic treatment are seldom much different from rates of *spontaneous* recovery (that is, recovery following no treatment at all). In their own defence, psychoanalysts will often respond that psychoanalytic therapy is highly complex and person-specific, and that the notion of 'recovery' will mean different things to different people. In effect, their claim is that statistical studies of recovery rates are too simplistic; they are poorly suited to their work. To critics of psychoanalysis, this defence is just another example of the falsifiability problem: even Freudian therapy is so vague and open-ended as to evade the rigours of scrutiny.

Many philosophers of science have raised objections to psychoanalysis, with the American scholar Karl Popper (1965) and the British science commentator Lewis Wolpert (1992) both presenting psychoanalysis as their favourite example of nonsense. Freudian scientific pretentions regularly attract opprobrium from mainstream scientists. The British Nobel-winning biologist Peter Medawar (1975, p. 17) condemned psychoanalysis as 'the most stupendous intellectual confidence trick of the 20th century', while the American Nobel-winning physicist Richard Feynman (1998, p. 114) dismissed Freudians as 'witch doctors'.

So intense has been the criticism of psychoanalysis that it is frequently depicted as a defunct, or at least anachronistic, branch of psychology (D. Jones & Elcock, 2001). Many psychology students are taught to think of psychoanalysis as a case history in psychology's past, an obscure but salacious theory of human personality, an illustration of psychological pseudoscience, or all of these things. However, as a set of theories about human psychology and a basis for psychotherapeutic intervention, psychoanalysis remains very much part of the modern world. It continues to thrive as a subfield of psychology, and to be part of its ever-increasing diversity. Its popularity as both subject matter and therapy suggests that criticisms by scientists have had little lasting effect.

It is not always clear why psychoanalysis attracts ridicule while weaknesses in other psychological subfields are discussed much less frequently. This could be because psychoanalysis is seen as an 'outsider' discipline, having developed largely independently from psychology's more dominant subfields. Psychoanalysis is certainly unlike those areas of psychology that revolve around experimental methods, quantitative analysis and orthodox psychometrics. However, as alluded to in Chapter 3, it is far from the only psychological subfield to be non-experimental or qualitative.

The heightened criticism could alternatively relate to the often challenging implications of psychoanalytic subject matter, which historically has provoked anxiety among socially conservative audiences. Any field of study that presents vivid depictions of sexuality will automatically attract some condemnation, regardless of its merits. Or perhaps some of the animosity can be traced back, at least in part, to those dark cultural forces that saw Freud himself cast as part of his profession's out-group since his earliest years, and eventually led him to flee his home country.

Or, simply, it could just be that the flaws of psychoanalysis are especially egregious. But while psychoanalysis certainly has flaws, it is misleading to suggest that the rest of psychology is somehow immune to similar shortcomings. Many areas of psychology have been accused of defining terms in vague and immeasurable ways, and of being unable to produce reliable forecasts. The replication crisis in psychological science shows us that these problems are extremely prevalent and extend far beyond psychoanalysis (Hughes, 2018a). Similarly, while the track record of psychoanalytic therapy is not always impressive, the same can in fact be said for virtually *all* forms of psychotherapy.

The scientific critique of psychoanalysis is often valid, but it can often also seem arbitrary. We will return to the problem of inconsistent self-criticism in psychology in Chapter 12.

WHERE TO FROM HERE?

Theories of unconscious drives imply that nature is always in control, rather than that people have true free will. In its own way, psychoanalysis presents a form of hard determinism, a worldview that sees our inner experience as resulting from external causes. Together with Darwin's theory of evolution, Freud's psychoanalysis presented a further blow to notions of independent souls and human exceptionalism. But unlike evolutionary theory, psychoanalysis was certainly not scientific, at least as this term is usually used.

Other psychologists shared the view that human behaviour could be considered in terms of its causes. However, they felt that behaviour could be seen and studied in conventionally scientific terms, by using experiments and computation. In our next chapter, we examine how many psychologists have attempted to use this type of science to study behaviour. These scientists view human psychology as a pattern of actions that are driven by knowable causes, and which, through experience, become physiologically programmed within the human organism. Crucially, they see none of this as happening away from scientific view. Unlike with Freud's idea of the unconscious, these psychologists believe that everything you need to know about human behaviour can be directly observed, recorded and controlled.

DISCUSSION QUESTIONS

1. In what ways is human sexuality different to the sexuality of other animals?
2. What might psychoanalysis have looked like if Freud was born in a politically stable, peaceful and inclusive society?
3. Why did Freud emphasize the role of sexuality so much? Why did some other psychoanalysts attempt to de-emphasize it?
4. Why does psychoanalysis remain popular in the face of such dismissive scientific criticism?

RECOMMENDED READING

- **Escoffier, J. (2020). Kinsey, psychoanalysis and the theory of sexuality.** *Sexologies, 29,* **e35–e42.** In this paper, the author examines the contradictions between the version of sexuality described in the Kinsey Reports and that presented in Freudian theory, despite the fact that both continue to attract widespread attention.
- **Northoff, G. (2012). Psychoanalysis and the brain: Why did Freud abandon neuroscience?** *Frontiers in Psychology, 3,* **71.** In this article, the author examines why Freud, who was originally trained as a neuroscientist, initially attempted to base psychoanalysis on brain science but then later abandoned this approach.
- **Pines, M. (1989). On history and psychoanalysis.** *Psychoanalytic Psychology, 6,* **121–35.** In this article, the author shows how Freud's theories were influenced by the social and historical context of the society in which he lived, and argues that considering such historical backgrounds can help us better understand the impact of social forces on emotional disorder today.
- **Webster, R. (2005).** *Why Freud Was Wrong: Sin, Science and Psychoanalysis* **(3rd ed.). London: The Orwell Press.** In this book, the author argues that Freud's religious upbringing had a significant impact on his life and work, but encouraged him to pursue a number of erroneous ideas.

BEHAVIOURISM, WILL AND THE CONCEPT OF *FREEDOM*

8

In this chapter, we will …

- examine whether the notion of free will has ever been reconciled with the scientific principle of determinism
- consider whether behaviourism in psychology emerged gradually or as the result of a scientific revolution
- explore how thought has shifted regarding the best way to scientifically study behavioural phenomena
- consider whether the radical behaviourism of B. F. Skinner undermined or enhanced notions of human freedom
- examine reasons why behaviourist psychology did not prosper in every country
- consider the merit of claims that behaviourism in psychology has 'fallen' and so is primarily of historical interest

---

At the outset

Philosophers have debated for centuries whether people possess free will or whether their actions and choices are determined by causal events. The scientific approach suggests that all events in the universe are determined by causes, or, in other words, that no event – including a thought – can occur *without* a cause. Nonetheless, most people feel as though they are in control of their own behaviour, and so up to the twentieth century, most attempts to explain human behaviour simply assumed that people were capable of true volition.

In the early twentieth century, many scientists debated the nature of causality. Psychologists also debated the best way to study human nature. The academic John Watson crystallized many psychologists' concerns when he called for his field to focus on the study of measurable behaviour rather than of abstractions such as 'mental life'. This approach to psychology was known as behaviourism. Watson himself was recognized as a leading behaviourist, and conducted famous research on conditioning in children. Some historians consider Watson's emergence to have marked a 'behaviourist revolution'.

After Watson left academia, other psychologists elaborated on behaviourism in different ways. Some attempted to codify behaviourist principles, drawing on notions such as drives. Others explored the biological underpinnings of behavioural phenomena. Some scholars considered how behaviourist principles could be used to explain social processes in wider culture.

Perhaps the most significant trend in behaviourism was that espoused by B. F. Skinner. Skinner's psychology extended far beyond simple conditioning to show how rewards and punishments serve to reinforce behaviour in powerful ways. His experiments helped to establish reliable principles of learning that potentially could be used to modify human behaviour for therapeutic, educational or other reasons.

Behaviourism became a prominent field of study in the United States but was resisted in countries of the former Eastern Bloc, as well as in places such as France, where existential philosophy was influential. But while behaviourism is often said to have risen and then fallen away, in reality is has been an ever-present sub-discipline of psychology for most of the past century. Behaviourism has spawned a number of psychological practices that appear to be powerful and useful, such as different types of behavioural therapy. Behavioural concepts continue to be important in helping us to understand how human beings adapt to changes in their environment, such as how emerging technologies, like the internet, shape human behaviour in new ways.

Key concept: Freedom

Freedom is the ability to act without constraint. In psychological contexts, we talk about freedom as the ability to engage in thoughts or actions of one's own choosing. The only limit on this type of freedom is external circumstance. For example, prisoners in a jail do not have the 'freedom' to go wherever they want. But they do have the freedom to *attempt* to do so, if they seriously wanted to, even knowing that they will be prevented. Freedom, in psychological terms, relates to the spontaneity of one's desires to think or act in a particular way. The real world will often prevent us from fulfilling those desires; but we will still have them.

Nonetheless, *freedom* is an inherently questionable concept, because it is never clear that our thoughts and actions are truly of our own making.

Among other things, the science of psychology studies the various causal factors that underlie human behaviour. But if we acknowledge that human behaviour has causes, does this mean that we would be able to behave in ways that defy them? If so, does this mean that behaviour is constrained rather than free? Most behaviour is coherent within its context; very little that humans do is actually random. In that sense, most human behaviour is technically predictable, making it subject to causality, and thus more *constrained* than *free*.

It could therefore be suggested that the study of psychology is premised on the absence of true freedom.

WHERE THERE'S A WILL …

Are you in control of what you think, say or do? Most people certainly *feel* as though they are. We see ourselves as independent and autonomous beings. When we have made a decision to act in a particular way, we *believe* that we *could have decided* to act differently had we wanted to. After all, this is integral to the process of 'deciding'. The knowledge that we could have chosen differently, that we could have opted for a different course of action, seems to *prove* the fact that we are indeed mentally 'free'. We each steer our own psychological course.

However, in order to validate this belief – to check whether we could indeed have made a different choice – we would need to be able to turn back time. We would need to return to our decision-point and to demonstrate our autonomy by choosing differently. This of course is impossible. So, technically, while we might *feel* certain that we had the unfettered freedom to decide what we wanted to decide, that feeling alone does not prove anything. Our belief in this freedom could be misplaced. Psychologically, it might be an error, a delusion or an automatic assumption that we use to cope with uncomfortable realities. It might be our mind's way of denying the truth that we are not as mentally 'free' as we often like to think – or, perhaps, that we are not free at all.

Remember that we live in a universe governed by cause and effect. The scientific principle of determinism implies that events do not just happen by themselves. They are precipitated by other events; no magic or miracles are involved. Theoretically, therefore, if we know the causes, we can foretell the outcomes. If we consider human thoughts and decisions to be examples of such 'events', then technically we should be able to predict these too. And if we can truly predict the choices and behaviours of another person, then does this not suggest that their choices and behaviours can be attributed to external knowable circumstances rather than to in-person volition? If so, then the person's *feeling* of having decided something autonomously must be an illusion. Despite what they *feel*, their choices cannot have been confined to their own mind.

Another way to look at this is to consider the implications of order. Events are predictable in that they conform to patterns in nature. People's psychological choices are no exception. We can anticipate people's behaviours and thoughts because we know what human beings are like. We expect them to be influenced by the ordinary contingencies of logic, longing and life. In other words, people do not behave randomly. However, the very fact that human behaviour is non-random means that it is predictable, at least in principle. It also means that people are not truly 'free' to behave however they like. The complete personal autonomy that people *feel* they have is bound by unseen (or hard-to-see) limits.

The conventional scientific approach to this issue is to argue that so-called free will is a widely believed falsehood. It is a common view, but no more than that. The spiritual approach is to claim that thoughts and behaviours are not in fact attributable to preceding knowable causes, because at all times people have freedom of choice (and, indeed, are able to arrive at their own opinions). This latter perspective – essentially, the spiritual approach – is the working assumption of society. Democracy, for example, is premised on the view that each individual has agency: they are capable of independence and autonomy.

But this takes us back to the question of order. Ultimately, human behaviour can only be truly unpredictable if it is truly random. People who claim that humans are capable of 'free will' rarely argue that human behaviour is actually *random*. Behaviour has structure and function, its dimensions are systematic and logical. What makes behaviour difficult to predict is its sheer complexity, not magical unknowability.

With the passing of the centuries, humankind has sought different ways to chart this complexity, and thus to demystify the human condition. The causes, conditions and contingencies that govern people's thoughts, choices and actions have come under ever closer scrutiny. Gradually, the study of the human will has evolved into a science of human behaviour.

Free will as an assumption

For much of history, humans have taken the presence of the 'will' for granted. As we saw in Chapter 2, the concept of 'spirit' or 'mind' was frequently imbued with mysticism. The mind's capacity to decide for itself, independently of external inputs, was integral to dualism, despite clashing with scientific views of determinism and causality. For most people, the 'will' was an uncontroversial mental function, whatever science might say.

In fact, prior to the end of the nineteenth century, before the work of Darwin and then of Freud, the majority of scholars held a similar view. They considered the 'will' to be a descriptive concept, rather than a hypothetical one. Humans were simply presumed to possess the power to initiate their own actions.

The ancient Greeks saw the will as a separate faculty, distinct from but intertwined with the intellect and the emotions. Christian philosophers such as Augustine of Hippo (354–430 CE), who lived in what is now Algeria, and Duns Scotus (1265–1308 CE), who was born in Berwick, Scotland, described the will as an autonomous and independent mental capacity. By contrast, Buddhist philosophers, such as the Indian philosopher Nāgārjuna (150–250 CE), saw human agency as more limited, emphasizing instead the interconnectedness of the universe (Bernier, 2020). In this view, people's freedom of will was restricted by their dependence on the world, by causal factors that influenced their behaviour, and by the principles of *karma*, in which one's past deeds helped to shape the important events of life.

Traditional religious views varied, but all tended to exceptionalize the 'will'. In general, it was seen as having sacred significance. In many schools of thought, free will was considered essential to morality.

The medieval Jewish scholar Maimonides, who we encountered in Chapter 2, was among many philosophers to argue that free will was necessary for justice (Naaman, 2017). If human beings were not truly capable of choosing between good or evil, he argued, they could never be truly accountable for their crimes.

On the other hand, several religious scholars asserted that behaviour *must* be subject to divine control because no human being could be more powerful than the divine creator. The medieval German theologian Martin Luther (1483–1546), a key figure in the Protestant Reformation (which we discussed in Chapter 2), argued strongly that human beings lacked any freedom of will at all (Vestrucci, 2020).

There was also a tradition in religious philosophy that attempted to accommodate both approaches. The Iraqi Islamic scholar Al-Ash'ari (short for Abū al-Ḥasan 'Alī ibn Ismā'īl ibn Isḥāq al-Ash'arī; 874–936 CE) promoted a view that human beings were both capable of free will *and* subject to divine control (Bhat, 2006).

Free will as a necessity

In Chapter 3, we saw how the eighteenth-century Scottish philosopher David Hume became associated with the concept of empiricism. This view held that all belief is derived from experience, and that no knowledge is innate. Hume applied his reasoning to the discussion of free will. He argued that our sense of freedom was 'nothing but the internal impression we feel' when our bodies move or when our brains detect thoughts in our minds (Hume, 1739, p. 202). This was consistent with his scientific view that humans lived in a mechanistic, deterministic universe.

Nonetheless, while essentially an atheist, Hume also believed in the existence of free will. Indeed, for Hume, the concept of 'freedom' only made sense *because* of determinism. Determinism ensured that consequences flowed logically from causes. Without determinism, he suggested, the outcomes of one's 'free' actions would essentially be unpredictable. This would mean there would be no advantage to being free, and that 'free will' would have no purpose or utility. We would be unable even to recognize 'free will' as a concept.

Although the nature of free will was debated by generations of philosophers, the concept of the 'will' as an abstract but orderly human ability was largely consistent throughout the centuries. Scholars in the Middle Ages presented the metaphor of 'rational appetite' to describe the way a person's internal inclinations conformed to intellectual logic (Connolly, 2014). In the late eighteenth century, the influential German philosopher Immanuel Kant (see Chapter 3) adopted essentially the same approach. He described the will as 'a capacity to determine oneself to act according to the idea of certain laws' ('ein Vermögen gedacht, der Vorstellung gewisser Gesetze gemäß sich selbst zum Handeln zu bestimmen'; Kant, 1785, p. 428), a depiction that would have been understood quite well by many medieval scholars.

Public domain, via Wikimedia Commons / {PD-US}

Image 8.1 Alexander Bain
The Scottish philosopher Alexander Bain (1818–1903) argued that the combined action of reflexes made the human will 'a physical fact'.

Free will as a scientific construct

As with many other psychological concepts, the development of science in the nineteenth century brought new ways of thinking about this so-called will. Newly emerging research on human bodies suggested different anatomical features that might explain its effects.

Several British physiologists began to consider whether the will might be neurological in nature. They noted how physical reflexes produced a form of automatic action that did not require conscious mental input. The Scottish surgeon Charles Bell (1774–1842), the English anatomist Marshall Hall (1790–1857) and the Scottish philosopher Alexander Bain (1818–1903) theorized that the will was likely to reflect the combined product of many multiple reflex actions. In Bain's words, this activity of reflexes made the will a 'physical fact' (Bain, 1866). Other physicians, such as the English neurologist John Hughlings Jackson (1835–1911), proposed that the will was a function of the cerebral cortex (cf. Jackson, 1932).

Some psychologists felt that the will was not so easily located in the physical body. William James had argued that emotions were fundamentally physiological experiences. He also maintained that the acts of will exercised by human minds were universally recognized as primary occurrences, identifying the will as having a special power to behave independently of causal forces (James, 1890). James's Harvard colleague Hugo Münsterberg was also sceptical of physical explanations. He argued that even if it were possible to study the physical correlates of volition, these 'cannot say anything about the *real* will which belongs to the primary world' (Münsterberg, 1898, p. 643; italics added).

This near-mystical status of the 'will' was reflected in other areas of nineteenth-century psychological thought. As we saw in Chapter 4, pioneers of psychiatric medicine invoked the will as a central aspect of well-being and sanity. Emile Kraepelin, while believing psychiatric diseases to be rooted in physiology, would describe his patients as suffering from 'vitiation of the will'. The Swiss physician Jacques André Matthey (1779–1842) classified several different 'perversions of the will' ('perversion de la volonté') as psychiatric disorders (Matthey, 1816, p. 145). These included the condition of *kleptomania*, the irresistible urge to steal from shops, which is still recognized today.

Several French physicians, such as Jean-Étienne Dominique Esquirol (1772–1840), Ernest Billod (1819–86) and Théodule-Armand Ribot (1839–1916), wrote extensively about the role of the will in psychiatry. Esquirol (1838) described cases of insanity as predicaments where 'the will is injured: the patient, outside ordinary ways, is drawn into acts which reason or feeling do not determine' ('la volonté est lésée: le malade, hors de voies ordinaires, est entraine a des actes que la raison ou le sentiment ne déterminent pas'; p. 2).

The concept of a human will – free or otherwise – was also employed to discuss wider social issues. Nineteenth-century historians attributed the establishment of the British Empire to the superior will of English colonialists. Educationalists placed heavy emphasis on 'education of the will' (Berrios & Gili, 1995). And the emerging self-help movement, which we discussed in Chapter 1, frequently cited 'active striving of the will' as the key to a meritorious life (e.g. Smiles, 1859).

Decline of the will

The arrival of the twentieth century brought a steady decline of scholarly interest in the will. In overlapping ways, both Darwin and Freud had explained how human beings were not always in control of their own volition. The theory of evolution posited, to an extent, that certain habits of thought came pre-programmed in the modern human mind, while psychoanalysis revealed that much of our mental dynamics occurred subconsciously, far from the influence of will-power.

Advances in clinical medicine presented further challenges to traditional depictions of the will. From 1915 to 1926, a global epidemic of sleeping sickness (*encephalitis lethargica*) struck down more than five million victims, of whom a third were killed by their illness. Autopsies soon revealed that they suffered a characteristic pattern of brain damage. The symptoms of the disease included sudden, repetitive and uncontrolled physical movements, and, in some cases, involuntary vocalizations. Those who survived were left with permanent psychiatric afflictions. Although the cause of the epidemic was never fully established, it was clear to doctors that this was a neurological illness, whose behavioural symptoms resulted from physiological deterioration. With mounting evidence that even complex human behaviours were coordinated by mechanistic biological systems, the idea that one's physical movements could be subject to a mystical human 'will' seemed increasingly fanciful.

During these early decades of the twentieth century, researchers in the burgeoning university psychology departments began to raise their own questions about the nature of mental activity. New theories and methods were developed, discussed and debated. Many of these were intended to account for the human mind in a way that acknowledged its mechanistic, non-mystical nature.

The wilfulness of human behaviour remained a topic of intense interest among philosophers (and continues to be so today, in a subfield known as 'action theory'). However, as discussed in Chapter 3, in the early twentieth century, philosophers were scholarly rivals from whom university psychologists wished to declare academic independence. Many of these psychologists wanted their field to be seen as scientific. For them, the vagueness, immeasurability and uncertainty of the human will were professionally unappealing. With psychology identifying itself ever more as a laboratory science, the concept of the 'will' soon became a casualty of intellectual fashion (Berrios & Gili, 1995).

LOGOPHILIA: 'COMPATIBILISM'

Compatibilism is a philosophical belief that the apparent contradiction between determinism and free will can be reconciled. The crux of this position is that while the universe conforms to causality, in which every event is preceded by another that causes it, human minds are nonetheless capable of spontaneous thought and action. They retain the 'freedom to act'. In other words, they are capable of producing events that *do not themselves have causes*. In this sense, therefore, the compatibilist view can be seen as paradoxical.

Some philosophers argue for compatibilism by suggesting that while the thoughts and actions of human beings might be precipitated by preceding events, a person will always retain the ability to make a different choice *in the moment*. In other words, while it might look as though a person's actions have been caused by something – such as a stimulus, a triggering thought or a chemical profusion in the brain – people always retain their freedom to act in a way other than that which has

been 'caused'. They are never truly constrained by causality (Tallis, 2021).

The challenge with this view is that it is impossible to falsify. While we might *feel* as though we have free will in every moment, it is impossible to test whether this is true. We cannot turn back time to relive a past situation, to check if we were indeed able to make choices other than the ones we actually made. All we can say is that people are *autonomous*, in the sense that they can choose for themselves what to do. But that is not to say that these choices are unconstrained. Autonomy is not the same as free will; for example, a driverless car has autonomy, but it does not have free will.

Compatibilism suggests that two proposals can work together without interfering with each other. However, it is unclear whether the propositions covered by this term really are all that compatible. Asserting that determinism and free will *are* compatible does not make them so. *Compatibilism* could simply be a misnomer.

Later, in the 1980s, a team of researchers led by the American neuroscientist Benjamin Libet (1916–2007) published a set of contentious experimental results suggesting that human decision-making is preceded by unseen electrical activity in the brain (Libet et al., 1983). This, they argued, implied that whenever a human being *feels* they have made a spontaneous choice, that choice actually results from biological activation that occurs *before* they experience this feeling. The exact interpretation of these results has itself been a source of considerable debate and controversy. However, for many philosophers, the findings show how the impression of *free will* can be misleading: decision-making is not magically spontaneous, it is a consequence of biological events that lie outside our awareness, and thus beyond our control.

THE RISE OF BEHAVIOURISM

As we described in previous chapters, the early twentieth century was especially tumultuous. Extreme political unrest and global turmoil culminated in the outbreak of the First World War. Millions of soldiers were deployed to a military combat that produced casualties on a previously unseen scale. As blood flowed throughout the battlefields of Europe, the misery of war was then further compounded by the outbreak of a global influenza pandemic. Ultimately infecting a third of the world's population, the pandemic went on to kill as many as 100 million people.

Shortly after these events, a combination of declining productivity and increasing unemployment caused the American stock market to crash, a crisis that precipitated an international economic recession. Virtually the entire world experienced one of the severest economic depressions in history, which devastated livelihoods in both rich and poor countries for more than a decade.

This 'Great Depression', as it came to be known, itself contributed to dire social conditions that propelled the rise of fascism, Nazism and political aggression, especially in Europe. With democracy in disrepute, the world's superpowers descended once again into war. The Second World War was to be the deadliest ever conflict in human history, killing close to 3 per cent of the world's population. Its victims were not only soldiers who died in battle, but also civilians who were killed in air raids on cities (including two nuclear strikes), who died as a result of starvation and disease, or who were slaughtered systematically in horrific acts of genocide.

The first half of the twentieth century was a period of extreme contrasts. Newly mechanized industrial production, along with the emergence of several new professions, helped to create limited prosperity for some; but the mutation of the economy saw millions abandoned to abject and aimless poverty. Rapid urbanization – with accompanying mass destitution – transformed Europe and North America, the shift from agrarian lifestyles to city living creating new contexts and challenges for human resilience.

Methods of cheap production, economies of scale and rapid population growth propelled a burgeoning of modern capitalism. Citizens came to be seen as consumers, the fields of marketing and advertising emerging as industries in their own right. The seeking of profit brought human behaviour sharply under the industrialists' microscope. But with the Great Depression producing catastrophic poverty throughout the world, any potential prosperity was soon addled by civil unrest and pervasive instability.

As the fabric of human society unravelled, new fields of expertise, such as social planning and mass communication, came to prominence. Political upheaval and commercial competition prompted efforts to comprehend – and measure – public sentiment. It also stimulated the development of novel methods of persuasion, including propaganda.

We saw in Chapter 7 how the onset of Nazism influenced the work of Sigmund Freud, both in practical terms and theoretically. As a Jewish person, Freud found his professional opportunities limited by discrimination, and he was eventually compelled to flee his home country in order to escape persecution. The overall demise of European political culture helped to imbue Freud's outlook with a distinct degree of nihilism and fatalism. But it was not only Freud whose work was embedded in the turbulence of these times. The early decades of the twentieth century marked a period when many psychologists around the world began to question the direction in which their newly independent academic field was heading.

In this sense, the social forces that shaped the twentieth century also served to mould the field of psychology. At a crucial time when nations began to seek technical solutions to social problems, psychology was the science that many saw as responsible for making sense of human behaviour – and, perhaps also, as offering the greatest hope of rectifying humanity's worst excesses.

A.H. Poole / Public domain, via Wikimedia Commons

Image 8.2   Scientific solutions to social problems?
Dire economic conditions in the early twentieth century produced challenges to human resilience and led many to seek scientific solutions to social problems.

Questioning psychology

The early twentieth century was a turbulent time for science too. Unexpected observations in physics gave rise to what has since become known as *quantum theory*. In deciphering a number of previous ideas and measurements, a young German-born physicist called Albert Einstein (1879–1955) produced a radical new understanding of how objects behave in the absence of gravity. His theory contradicted and superseded the depiction of mechanics laid out by Isaac Newton, which had stood uncontested in the physical sciences for more than 200 years (DiSalle, 2006).

Some scientists saw these developments as disproving the very notion of determinism itself – and thus as casting doubt on any other scientific work that presumed to investigate cause and effect. In reality, while quantum theory upended the standard understanding of how the mechanistic universe operated, its tenets were essentially consistent with the principle of determinism (Bohm, 1952). Nonetheless, the sudden realization that it was unsound to think of scientific standards as being perennially reliable had a great impact on academic thinking. The questioning of established norms was no longer improper or heretical. It was now very much in vogue.

At the turn of the century, university psychology vied for public attention with areas such as spiritualism (as discussed in Chapter 3) and the last remnants of phrenology (as we saw in Chapter 5). Within their institutions, the new university psychologists found their endeavours intertwined with the interests of academic philosophy and, in some cases, theology.

Meanwhile, in the biological sciences, evolutionary theory had become the main paradigm. Many psychologists were keen to explore how human mental processes might be shaped by natural selection. The resulting discussion of the will as a combination of reflexes led to an emerging view of 'associationism', the idea that human character comprised a repertoire of habits, shaped by experience and constructed by trial and error.

Physiologists too turned their attention to such concepts. Ivan Pavlov's work on associative learning earned him a Nobel Prize in 1904 (notwithstanding the similar efforts of other more lowly scientists, such as Edwin Twitmyer, as we discussed in Chapter 1). Pavlov's theories helped to influence the direction of research in physiology, but he would not achieve fame among psychologists until much later.

It would be fair to say that, in the opening decades of the twentieth century, the nascent field of university psychology was suffering something of an identity crisis. Major figures such as William James retained a scepticism about laboratory research, but many others had equally mixed feelings about introspection.

An early report in *Psychological Bulletin* described a 'rising tide of dissatisfaction' with the language used in psychological scholarship (Buchner, 1907, p. 1). According to the author, many of the older ('and almost consecrated'; p. 1) terms – such as *consciousness, sensation, feeling* and *perception* – were especially problematic. These concepts were seen as so abstract as to defy satisfactory explanation, or even definition. The issue dominated a rather fraught annual meeting of the American Psychological Association in 1910, where most of the debate concerned the very purpose of psychology itself (Haggerty, 1911). In the views of many of those present, psychology had changed dramatically over the preceding twenty years.

No longer were psychologists as obsessed with what James had called the 'science of mental life'. Instead, they were inspired by Darwinian theory, technological advances and an aspiration for a practical utility that would fit the economic needs of wider society. Even in its first few decades as an organized academic discipline, the field had begun to shift its emphasis. The abstraction of 'mental life' had given way to a notion that was more tangible, measurable and applicable. Psychology was now the study of *behaviour*.

Behaviourism as Watson viewed it

Nowhere was this shift in psychological emphasis more visible than in the United States. For the first decade of the century, the United States had enjoyed increasing prosperity, becoming the richest nation in the world. Innovations such as domestic electricity and the automobile transformed everyday life for most of its people. However, in many ways, these years of well-being were just a calm before the storm. Soon the United States would be mired in civic strife when one of its two main political parties split, leading to bitterly contested elections in 1912. Shortly after, in 1914, the country would watch in horror as the First World War began in Europe, a conflict that the United States itself would be sucked into three years later.

For American psychology, the year 1913 is often seen as a watershed. This was the year when John B. Watson (1878–1958), a professor at Johns Hopkins University, delivered a somewhat polemical lecture at a branch meeting of the American Psychological Association in New York. A month later, a transcript of his talk appeared in the journal *Psychological Review*, of which Watson himself was editor (Watson, 1913). In the years that followed, Watson's paper – officially titled 'Psychology as the behaviorist views it' – was to become popularly known as the *Behaviourist Manifesto*.

Watson himself had been steeped in physiological research since studying for his doctorate at the University of Chicago, where he examined the links between learning ability and brain myelination in laboratory rats. He was very much in the camp of psychology that viewed its work in strictly empirical terms, repudiating such fuzzy abstractions as 'consciousness' and 'mental life'. By the time he formulated his thoughts in 1913, Watson was in little doubt that psychology should be seen as an unambiguously biological science.

In his *Manifesto*, Watson suggested that the philosophical approach to psychology was wrong to have attached exceptional status to the human mind. He argued that psychology should reflect biological science in accepting the unity of all species. Like geneticists, psychologists too should study non-human animals and see them as 'models' of basic psychological principles. Watson objected to the way psychologists talked about consciousness as if human beings were qualitatively different from other species. For him, this was little more than a form of mysticism.

Watson deemed psychology to be 'a purely objective, experimental branch of natural science which needs introspection as little as do the sciences of chemistry and physics' (Watson, 1913, p. 158). He strongly argued that research should be limited to the observable, the measurable and the verifiable. In other words, psychologists should avoid topics like perception or cognition, because it would always be impossible to scrutinize these constructs objectively. By contrast, however, a scientist *could* objectively scrutinize another person's behaviour (or, indeed, the behaviour of an animal). Therefore, in essence, Watson argued that focusing on behaviour was the only truly scientific way to 'do' psychology. Subjective experience should be excluded.

According to Watson, one of the problems with using subjective methods such as introspection was that the resulting research could never truly be replicable. If two identical studies produced different findings, it would be impossible to say for sure which (if either) was flawed. If a psychologist fails to reproduce a previous result, the original researcher can simply dismiss the replication effort on the grounds that its introspection method was 'untrained'. In other words, they can defend their study by criticizing the replicator, rather than accept that their own methods might be deficient.

This form of argument is still used today, to defend vague, pseudoscientific or non-replicable research. Researchers whose studies draw negative commentary frequently insist that it is their detractors who have it wrong. The shifting of blame from culprits to critics continues to muddy the waters in psychology's ongoing, and still unresolved, replication crisis (Hughes, 2018a). In voicing this concern back in 1913, Watson was considerably ahead of his time. (We will return to the replication crisis in Chapter 12.)

Watson's research

Watson's own research focused on the impact of conditioning, especially in children. Building on a stimulus–response learning theory put forward by another American psychologist, Edward Thorndike (1874–1949), Watson investigated whether children could be conditioned to feel fear or rage in response to arbitrary stimuli, akin to the way soldiers returning from war would sometimes exhibit fear responses to loud noises (an affliction then known as 'shell shock'). His most famous case study – and one of the most famous case studies in the history of psychology – was that of 'Little Albert', an eleven-month-old baby boy.

Watson and his research assistant, the psychologist Rosalie Rayner (1898–1935), used a series of loud noises to condition Little Albert to become scared of a harmless pet white rat. Each time the rat was presented to the child, Watson and Raynor would strike a hammer against a steel bar to produce a terrifyingly loud noise. Eventually, the child would burst into tears whenever the rat was brought into the room, even if no noise was produced. Watson and Raynor had apparently succeeded in getting the child to associate the sight of the animal with the fear generated by the noise. In essence, they had produced the same effect in a little baby that Pavlov had in dogs. While Pavlov had trained his dogs to associate the ringing of a bell with hunger, Watson and Raynor had 'trained' Little Albert to associate the sight of a small harmless animal with fear.

The ethical aspects of the Little Albert case study are frequently discussed. Watson and Raynor have been accused of treating Little Albert appallingly, by inducing a debilitating phobia in an otherwise happy child. Not only that, but it seems clear that the two psychologists made little effort to *de*-condition Albert after their experiment. Further, some historians have suggested that the baby was medically vulnerable and so should never have been involved in such research. There have also been claims that Watson and Raynor exaggerated their findings, and even that they concocted aspects of their case study.

Watson later left academia and joined private industry, embarking on a career in advertising. Nonetheless, many psychologists in American universities continued to refer to his *Behaviourist Manifesto*, urging their peers to pursue a similar vision for psychology. In the late 1920s, Watson and Raynor, who by then were married to each other, published a commercially popular book aimed at parents, promoting the use of behaviourist principles in child-rearing. This was followed by many articles in popular magazines, in which Watson expanded on how behavioural conditioning could be used to produce 'better brought-up babies' (Watson & Rayner Watson, 1928, p. 9).

Many psychologists – especially those who endorsed the behaviourist approach – now refer to Watson's 1913 lecture as a key turning point in the history of their field. It is frequently described as the event that marked the toppling of mentalism and subjectivity, and the launching of a new era of rigorous psychological science, one that was to dominate psychology as a whole for the next four decades.

However, as we saw in Chapter 3, we should always be wary of academic 'creation myths'. Few, if any, ever hold true.

HISTORICALLY (IN)ACCURATE?: LITTLE ALBERT

The Little Albert experiment has often been described as a turning point in the history of psychology. It presents a visually memorable demonstration of clear psychological principles that was, crucially, recorded on film. This widely seen video has concretized the Little Albert case study in the memories of several generations of psychologists. However, as with many widely discussed studies, several of its details have been subject to controversy. A recurring problem has been the extent to which details have been *misreported*, even by purportedly authoritative sources, including academic textbooks (B. Harris, 2011).

Among the most common misconceptions about Little Albert include claims that Albert was initially conditioned to fear a rabbit, when in fact he was conditioned to fear a rat. Albert is also frequently described as having been conditioned to fear a range of other objects, such as a man's beard, a cat, a white furry glove, a woman wearing a fur coat, and a teddy bear, none of which were actually used. Some textbooks have suggested that Albert was successfully *de*-conditioned after the experiment, but we now know that this never happened either.

Even more intriguingly, the identity of Little Albert has also been disputed (Digdon, 2020). It was initially proposed that Watson used 'Albert B.' as a pseudonym for a young patient named

Douglas Merritte (H. P. Beck, Levinson & Irons, 2009). Moreover, when historians searched the hospital archives, they found that Douglas Merritte was neurologically impaired. This not only conflicted with Watson's account, it also greatly impacted on how we should interpret the Little Albert experiment.

However, subsequent research has uncovered that there was another child at the clinic, Albert Barger, whose file more closely matches Watson's description of Little Albert. Not only did this child have the correct name, but the overall information about his physical development, his birth history and his temperament all seem to resemble more closely what Watson wrote about the child in his experiment. While it is not possible to be conclusive, it appears that Albert Barger shares many more characteristics with 'Little Albert' than does Douglas Merritte. Had the Barger child's case file been discovered first, it seems difficult to imagine that it would later have been superseded by the identification of the young baby Merritte.

Nonetheless, the researchers who first proposed that Douglas Merritte was indeed Little Albert continue to contend that their theory is in fact the correct one (Fridlund et al., 2020). A century after this pivotal case study was reported, the identity of its infant subject remains a true mystery.

A 'Watsonian revolution'?

It is no coincidence that the nickname given to Watson's 1913 paper invoked the title of Karl Marx and Friedrich Engels's legendary political pamphlet, *The Communist Manifesto*. Published in the mid-nineteenth century, and widely regarded as one of the most influential political documents ever written, Marx and Engels's treatise called for 'the forcible overthrow of all existing social conditions' and expressed unlimited support for revolution 'against the existing social and political order'. 'Let the ruling classes tremble', Marx and Engel had warned. 'The proletarians have nothing to lose but their chains' (Marx & Engels, 1848, p. 34).

Many commentators considered Watson's paper on behaviourism to be equally rebellious. In so openly dismissing the hegemony of psychology's own ruling classes, Watson's *Manifesto* agitated unambiguously for a new psychological future. It railed against the existing conditions in the field of psychology. Watson wanted his peers to change their ways, or at least for new colleagues to abandon all the old ways of doing things. His call was literally subversive: he sought to completely upend the norms of his profession. This is what made his paper worthy of its nickname. *The Behaviourist Manifesto* would be seen by its many followers – and by many historians of psychology – as representing the basis for a revolution.

However, it is questionable whether Watson's personal impact on the field was truly revolutionary. For one thing, long before his 1913 lecture, many American psychologists were already focusing on behaviour. As was clear from the discussions at the 1910 meeting of the American Psychological Association, discontent with mentalism and introspection had been building for years, if not for decades. In this context, Watson's *Manifesto* simply echoed arguments that had already become common among his peers. And although Watson was a charismatic and high-profile academic working at a major university, many in his audience were simply unmoved by his unashamedly strident exhortations. Arguably the majority of psychologists simply ignored what he had to say.

Of course, any such discussion will hinge on the meaning of the term 'revolution'. Historically, a revolution is said to involve the forcible overthrow of a social order, or the complete replacement of an old system with a new one. The term was originally popularized as a way to describe changes in empires, nations and societies. But ultimately any field of human endeavour can be revolutionized. In the 1960s, the American philosopher Thomas S. Kuhn (1922–96) set out an elaborate theory describing the nature of revolutions as they apply to science.

A keen reader of history, Kuhn noted that most histories of science were written with what we referred to in Chapter 1 as a 'narrative of linear improvement'. Science was commonly depicted as a journey of gradual but constant intellectual progress, in which adventurous scholars gathered ever-accumulating knowledge by increments. Kuhn recognized that this was little more than the 'Great Man' form of historiography. His own studies had shown him that the emergence of science had often been punctuated by periods of chaos and turbulence. He did not believe that scientists gathered knowledge in steady increments, slowly cultivating an ever-expanding fund of expertise. Rather, it seemed to Kuhn that, under certain conditions, scientists would often throw out their old orthodoxies, fundamentally change direction, or restart their work from scratch. Scientific progress was seldom smooth-running or linear; it was usually sporadic, stuttering and serendipitous.

Kuhn (1962) identified a recurring pattern that characterized the history of nearly every science. In his view, sciences would always pass through the same four stages:

- The first stage is that of *normal science*. This is when the vast majority of scientists agree on the merit of knowledge in their field and the quality of its methods. Kuhn referred to this shared scientific worldview as the 'paradigm'. According to him, the stage of normal science, in which there is a single standard paradigm, can persist for years, decades, or – as in the case of Newtonian mechanics – centuries.
- The second stage arrives when scientists encounter an *anomaly* in their work. This could take the form of a brand new discovery, an inconsistent measurement, or a recurring unexpected result in an experiment. When their standard theories and methods cannot quite explain what is happening, the scientists begin to realize that their paradigm might be invalid.
- This then leads to the third stage: a state of *crisis*. With confidence in the old approaches declining, scientists begin the task of developing an entirely new paradigm. This task is often more attractive to younger scientists than to older ones, as older scholars can find it difficult to change the habits of a lifetime. Eventually, however, a new paradigm is produced to deal with the anomaly.
- The climax of the cycle is the fourth and final stage, which Kuhn called the *paradigm shift*. This is when the number of scientists now following the new paradigm grows to such an extent that it comes to dominate their field. The paradigm has shifted: a new generation of thinkers now look at the world in a new way. The result is a new period of 'normal' science. This new normal continues until the next anomaly is detected and the cycle of revolution begins again.

Kuhn's model can seem a little simplistic, but it is generally regarded as offering useful insights into the pragmatic nature of science. It highlights how science can be strongly influenced by human interests. It shows that knowledge is not shaped by conclusive proof alone; consensus among scientists is also required.

In the Kuhnian sense, therefore, the emergence of behaviourism in psychology – and especially Watson's 1913 *Manifesto* – most likely did *not* constitute a scientific revolution (Leahey, 1992). Firstly, it would be incorrect to suggest that pre-1913 psychology was united around a single paradigm. Whereas figures such as William James promoted the study of 'mental life', other psychologists had different views. The psychophysicists favoured laboratory studies of perceptual phenomena. The psychoanalysts were examining the unconscious using methods of free association and dream analysis. Brain scientists and evolutionary biologists had begun to construct a physiological understanding of psychological concepts. And other psychologists sought to quantify human attributes (and human worth) using statistical psychometrics. By the time Watson put forward his *Manifesto*, there was no single paradigm in psychology. In Kunhian language, there was no 'normal' science.

Secondly, and partly because of this state of affairs, Watson did not identify any specific 'anomaly' that existing methods of psychology were unable to explain. His critique was more wide-ranging than that, and did not resemble what Kuhn described as the basis for a paradigm shift. The changes occurring in psychology at that time were slow and gradual, and often invisible. As outlined above, the dissatisfaction that prompted Watson to deliver his lecture had spread through the profession over a period of decades.

And finally, while some psychologists were animated by Watson's critique, others were less than impressed. Many of Watson's peers dismissed his *Manifesto* as an exercise in self-promotion. The American psychologist Joseph Jastrow (1863–1944) mocked Watson for seeking to claim 'proprietary copyright' over the term *behaviourism*, despite the fact that 'there were explicit and not merely implicit behaviorists long before Watson was exhibiting his first conditioned reflex in the nursery' (Jastrow, 1927, p. 173).

In reality, while Watson's *Manifesto* certainly *preceded* a growth in behaviourist psychology, it is difficult to argue that it directly *caused* this growth, or that it single-handedly inspired a new paradigm. The fact that psychology remained so disparate after 1913 – with all its other genres continuing to thrive alongside the newly branded 'behaviourism' – suggests that this was far from a 'scientific revolution' in the ordinary sense of the term.

ALMOST FAMOUS: ROSALIE RAYNER WATSON

Rosalie Rayner (1898–1935) was a psychologist who worked at Johns Hopkins University, alongside John B. Watson. She published a number of articles about child development. Most famously, she was Watson's research assistant on the Little Albert experiment.

Rayner had been born into a high-profile family in Baltimore. Her father and grandfather were successful in the rail and shipbuilding businesses, and her uncle had served as a state senator and attorney general for Maryland. In addition, her family had made significant donations to Johns Hopkins University, placing Rosalie somewhat in the public eye. Her collaboration with the renowned behaviourist Watson inevitably drew attention.

Rayner and Watson's professional relationship became personal, and the two decided to marry. Watson was already married, and his wife, Mary Ickes, was herself a member of a prominent political family. Their resulting divorce was covered in the media as a scandalous news story. Prevailing social attitudes at the time ensured that Rayner would have had little comfort attempting to pursue an academic career at the university. Watson too found himself under pressure, and decided to resign.

Rayner and Watson married, and moved to Connecticut, where they collaborated on their research outside the university system. This work culminated in a bestselling popular book for parents, *Psychological Care of Infant and Child* (Watson & Rayner Watson, 1928). The manual became infamous for advising parents not to soothe children when they were crying, lest such behaviour become reinforced.

In a later article, one of the few Rayner wrote that was not co-authored with her husband, she accepted that this was easier said than done, admitting she could never withhold affection from her own two children completely (Rayner Watson, 1930). Rayner also used behaviourism to propose social reforms, aimed at showing how women could create identities and careers independent of household responsibilities (Rayner Watson, 1932). As a committed behaviourist, Rayner's individual writings suggested that her views on female parenting, and on the wider place of women in society, differed significantly from those of Watson (B. Harris, 2014).

Unfortunately, Rayner's insightful scholarship was to come to a premature end. Otherwise healthy, Rayner died at the age of 37, having contracted dysentery from eating infected fruit. Her contributions to behaviourism are often noted as subordinate to those of her husband, but Rayner's own ideas suggested that she was a formidable and precocious psychologist in her own right.

THE BEHAVIOURIST EXPANSION

After Watson left academia, interest in behaviourism continued to spread among psychologists, both in America and beyond. However, not all psychologists were as strident as Watson in constraining the limits of what psychology could achieve. For example, many psychologists remained interested in studying internal mental events, and felt that it was possible – and important – to do so from a behaviourist perspective.

While behaviourism is often described as though it were a single approach, it was actually quite varied and somewhat fragmented. Several strands emerged. Some behaviourists focused almost exclusively on mental and cognitive abilities, while others remained focused on outward behaviours and actions. Some behaviourists delved deep into the biological aspects of psychology, while others applied behaviourism to phenomena such as personality and social identity. Some behaviourists devoted all their efforts to developing elaborate theories from which systematic hypotheses might be formed, while others were prolifically productive with research that was essentially atheoretical.

Behaviourism became a complex and multifaceted style of psychology and a thriving field of scholarship with wide-ranging applications. It grew to be so common that in the perception of many ordinary people, *all* psychologists were in fact behaviourists. This led to widespread popular intrigue about what these behaviourist psychologists might be able to do with their science, for good or for ill.

Purposive behaviourism

Despite Watson's own anti-mentalist position, it did not take long for psychologists to explore how behaviourist principles might be used to explain mental events. However, instead of using introspection to ask people about their thoughts, these researchers *inferred* the mental experiences of *animal* subjects by observing their behaviour in laboratory experiments.

For example, after studying maze-learning in rats, the American psychologist Edward Tolman (1886–1959) developed an approach known as 'purposive behaviourism'. He believed that the obvious skill rats showed when learning to navigate their environments did not simply result from the conditioning of reflexes. Rather, a rat would appear to be able to memorize the layout of a complex maze, as if forming a 'cognitive map' of its surroundings (Tolman & Honzik, 1930). Such learning relied on the rat's ability to associate stimuli with responses, as when remembering which way to turn at a particular corner. However, Tolman argued, associations like this did not emerge automatically. Tolman posited that rats would *mentally process* information as they navigated through their mazes: the organism itself would *decide* how to respond to a stimulus. For this reason, Tolman's depiction of behaviourism was often referred to as the S–O–R model, a logical extension of the previously common S–R notation, with 'organism' appearing between 'stimulus' and 'response'.

This approach was greatly extended by another American psychologist, Clark L. Hull (1884–1952). A precocious mathematician, Hull sought to develop complex algorithms that could account for the determinants of behaviour (Hull, 1943). One of his most famous formulae depicted the likelihood of a response as

$$_sE_R = {_s}H_R \times D \times V \times K,$$

where the statistical probability of a particular response ($_sE_R$, or 'stimulus excitatory potential') could be computed by multiplying measures of habit strength ($_sH_R$), drive strength (D), stimulus intensity (V) and incentive motivation (K).

However, even Hull saw this as an over-simplification. After he took account of a number of other variables – namely, inhibitory strength ($_sI_R$), reactive inhibition (I_R), and random error ($_sO_R$) – Hull later offered a more complete version of his formula:

$$_sE_R = ({_s}H_R \times D \times V \times K) - ({_s}I_R + I_R) \pm {_s}O_R.$$

Hull's approach, often referred to as 'drive theory', saw reinforcement as a mechanical system in which behaviours satisfied needs. He believed his methods of mathematical prediction, which were tested on animals, would apply equally to humans.

Such ultra-computational approaches were especially appealing to those psychologists who wanted their field to be seen as a science. However, despite further enhancements by Hull's student Kenneth Spence (1907–67), resulting in what became known as the Hull–Spence theory, the overall approach was eventually revealed to be somewhat inconsistent and unreliable. In the end, the mechanics of human behaviour were found to be too complex for even Hull's most convoluted formulae.

Biological behaviourism

Another activity that helped to augment psychology's scientific reputation was research into brain biology. As discussed in Chapter 5, the first half of the twentieth century saw extensive efforts to identify the localized functions of different brain areas using stimulation, surgery and other methods. This work was soon to overlap with behaviourism. Of particular note was the research on brain plasticity conducted by Shepherd Franz (see Chapter 5). Franz had shown how conditioned responses in cats would be 'unlearned' when parts of the brain's frontal lobe were ablated, but that animals were nonetheless able to *relearn* such behaviour by relying on surviving brain tissue. This finding suggested that the process of conditioning (or learning) was not restricted to any particular part of the frontal lobe.

Another brain researcher who turned to behaviourism was Karl Lashley (1890–1958), an American neurophysiologist who had worked briefly with Franz. When completing his PhD in genetics at Johns Hopkins University, Lashley had also taken some psychology classes with Watson. Inspired by both mentors, he conducted a series animal experiments to deepen his understanding of brain plasticity. Having found that many different brain lesions would disrupt maze-learning in rats, Lashley concluded that the remembering needed for such conditioning was not localized to any specific brain area. He offered the term *equipotentiality* to describe how, in many situations, any healthy part of the brain could eventually take over a memory function that was lost as a result of localized brain damage (Lashley, 1929).

Such research into the physiology of learning echoed the earlier work by Pavlov. As we discussed in Chapter 1, Pavlov had used experimental research to reveal the rudiments of conditioning in animals. He is often remembered for his studies of classical conditioning in dogs, for which he was awarded a Nobel Prize in 1904. But despite this achievement, Pavlov's research was not well known among Watson or his contemporaries in American psychology. It was only *after* behaviourism became popular in the United States that Pavlov's studies came to prominence there.

Pavlov had sought to develop a comprehensive theory that could account for all complex psychological phenomena, based on the premise that every aspect of human behaviour was grounded in a person's biological responses to situational stimuli. He believed that conditioning was naturally selected, and that reflexes served as visceral warning systems optimally attuned to an organism's surroundings. He saw these biological processes as underlying personality and mental health: a person's sensitivity to stimuli would determine their temperament, and if extreme, would underlie their neuroses.

As a behaviourist, Pavlov was uncomfortable with introspection and other cognitive abstractions. He avoided using terms like 'mental' or 'psychological', and instead referred to thinking as 'higher nervous activity' (Gantt, 1968).

However, the championing of Pavlov's research by American behaviourists focused so much on his dog experiments that his broader contributions to psychology were customarily overlooked. As a result, they are still often omitted from modern discussions of the history of behaviourism. The selective coverage of Pavlov offers another example of how the practice of historiography can sometimes become skewed by academic politics.

Social behaviourism

The behaviourist trend was also felt outside the traditional sciences, attracting interest in areas such as philosophy and sociology. A number of philosophers supported the premise that psychological states can be surmised only insofar as behaviour can be observed. Moreover, they saw this principle as applying not just to scientists and psychologists, but also to ordinary people in their everyday lives.

According to the intellectual approach known as symbolic interactionism, the way human beings observe and interpret each other's behaviour is central to how they view reality itself. Importantly, not only do people observe the world around them, they also participate within it, influencing events through their own choices and behaviours. Each person's perception of how the world operates is thus fundamentally intertwined with their own way of behaving. The interaction between individual and world becomes symbolic.

For scholars such as the American philosopher George Herbert Mead (1863–1931), behaviours are actions that we learn to produce in response to social cues. Mead (1934) believed human psychology was shaped by a process of *social behaviourism*. According to Mead, human beings are predisposed by reflex to act in response to what they see other people doing. We behave according to what we think other people expect to experience in their community. Mead called this template

Image 8.3   B. F. Skinner (*c.* 1950)

for behaviour 'the generalized other'. In other words, we use *social context* as a frame of reference within which to calibrate our own actions.

Importantly, our own actions then become part of *other people's* social contexts, and so go on to influence *their* self-concepts and behaviours. Not only are our behaviours framed by the norms of society, they also feed back and *refine* those norms, adding to the pool of social expectations that governs everyone's actions. In this process, human behaviour is formed socially and collectively, evolving over time as a result of association and reinforcement. Each person's own behaviour both is shaped by, and shapes, the behaviour of others.

Mead felt this process depended mostly on our observations of other people's actions, and less on our speculations about their thoughts. However, he disagreed with Watson's assertion that subjective experience should be excluded from the study of psychology (Mead, 1934). Instead, Mead saw cognitive events as just another set of behavioural responses, ones that could be traced to social stimuli. In this respect, Mead's philosophy reflected the views of many behaviourists in psychology who found Watson's anti-mentalist stance to be extreme (J. D. Baldwin, 1981). Ultimately, Mead believed in the existence and relevance of 'the mind', seeing it as a necessary component of our collective efforts at social communication.

As a branch of philosophy, social behaviourism tended to produce more theory than data. However, many of its insights were ahead of the empirical science. As the subsequent century progressed, the principle that thoughts themselves should be seen as conditionable behaviours, and the idea that human behaviour is fundamentally shaped by social conditioning, were both to become major themes within mainstream behaviourist psychology.

Radical behaviourism

Probably the most significant contributions to behaviourist psychology came from the work of B. F. Skinner (1904–90), a psychology professor who taught at a number of American universities, most notably Harvard. Skinner's insight was to show that not only could behaviour be built through associative learning, it could also be *shaped* in various ways by 'operant conditioning' – the administration and withdrawal of rewards.

Skinner understood that most animals and humans are capable of initiating spontaneous behaviours. However, he believed that the degree to which we *repeat* a given behaviour will be influenced by the nature of its consequences: if a behaviour is followed by a positive event, such as a reward or a pleasurable experience, then we will be more likely to repeat it. For Skinner, this change in likelihood is not the result of mental reflection or rational choice, but is the outcome of a biologically ingrained behavioural reflex. Accordingly, our behaviour can be modified by rewards even if we are not consciously aware that it is happening. Skinner referred to these tangibly reward-ing outcomes as 'positive reinforcement'.

Skinner also envisaged a scenario in which a behaviour is followed not by the arrival of a pleas-urable experience, but by the removal of an unpleasant one. For example, if a behaviour is fol-lowed by pain relief (which serves to remove an otherwise adverse stimulus) then we will be just as likely to repeat that behaviour as if we were receiving a tangible reward. In essence, the removal of a negative stimulus *is* the reward. Skinner referred to this process as 'negative reinforcement'.

In Skinner's view, the fundamentals of learning are the same in animals as they are in humans: processes of reinforcement continuously shape the behaviour of all species, across all situations. He conducted hundreds of animal experiments to test the various parameters in which reinforce-ment was or was not effective. For example, he found that behavioural repetition would strengthen in proportion to the significance and consistency of reinforcement (which he referred to as its 'schedule'). If a schedule of reinforcement is adjusted to provide more meaningful and frequent rewards, then the target behaviour will be strengthened and repeated more frequently. If the opposite happens, then the behaviour will decline. And if reinforcement is removed altogether, then the learning will eventually fade away entirely (a process Skinner called 'extinction').

Skinner was one of the first psychologists to draw popular attention to behavioural research on animals. Famously, he designed a special box or cage to use for testing rats or pigeons, in which an animal could be trained to press a lever by being rewarded with food. A crucial feature of the box's design was that the experimenter could make fine adjustments to the schedule of reinforcement, allowing an endless number of different experiments to be conducted. The so-called Skinner box would go on to become one of the most famous pieces of laboratory equipment ever designed for psychology. Skinner invented this apparatus when he was still a PhD student.

While Skinner is often associated with animal research, his ultimate aim was to develop a com-plete behaviourist account of human psychology. He described his approach as 'radical' behaviour-ism, because he considered thinking, feeling and other mental events to be conditionable just like all other behaviours.

In the 1950s, Skinner designed a rudimentary machine to help teachers present questions to pupils. By providing automatic positive feedback for correct answers, the machine cumulatively rewarded accurate responding. Long before the appearance of digital computers in classrooms, Skinner's so-called teaching machine attempted to use adaptive feedback to shape pupils' learning through reinforcement, pioneering an approach now commonly relied upon by modern educa-tional software. These fundamental principles of reinforcement, in which learning is encouraged through structured reward, have since become inherent in education systems throughout the world.

Skinner's form of behaviourism spawned a plethora of applications, some more useful than oth-ers. Its principles feed into cognitive behavioural therapy (CBT), one of the most widely used modern psychotherapies (Guercio, 2020). More explicitly, Skinner's work led to the development of the relational frame theory of language (RFT; Hayes, Barnes-Holmes & Roche, 2001), itself the basis of acceptance and commitment therapy (ACT; Hayes, Strosahl & Wilson, 2012). And, through the specialist field now known as applied behaviour analysis (ABA; Baer, Wolf & Risley, 1968), interventions based on Skinner's scientific approach to behaviour modification are used to support people who face a range of difficulties in their lives, including persons with autism, brain injury or dementia.

HISTORY IN STORIES: *WALDEN TWO* (1948)

Walden Two is the novel written by B. F. Skinner (1948), first published near the start of his psychology career. It tells the story of a university psychology professor who, along with some colleagues, visits a thriving rural commune called Walden Two, which operates on behaviourist principles. While two of the professor's colleagues are hugely impressed, the third, a professor of philosophy, remains unconvinced.

Skinner describes the commune as being run entirely using evidence-based strategies, with its scientists constantly examining new ways to rear children, provide food and otherwise maintain the community. Crucially, its governance approach is flexible rather than rigid: any practice or social structure found to be counter-productive is simply abandoned. This is said to make the commune far more durable than mainstream societies, which usually attach undue importance to traditional or long-standing customs.

As a consequence, the children of Walden Two are reared communally instead of by their parents. Sexual relationships are not monogamous. And saying 'thank you' to individuals is frowned upon; instead, praise is to be directed collectively to all members of the community. Nonetheless, while its principles are clearly stated, Waldon Two has no police force or other method to sanction non-compliance. There is essentially no authority system in place. In Skinner's novel, these approaches have brought great happiness to the people of Walden Two, who have become self-motivated, conscientious and creative. They are also efficient, with a naturally arising distribution of labour that ensures people need only work for four hours per day.

After their visit, the academics leave the commune to return to their university. However, the psychology professor was clearly very impressed with Walden Two. He decides to abandon the trip home, resign from his academic post and go to live in Walden Two himself.

Skinner's novel, while fictional, is quite clearly intended to convey a political message. It promotes the view that society is enhanced when evidence-based principles are prioritized and held back when convention and tradition are given precedence. It also presents a highly optimistic view of human nature: when left truly to themselves, people will prosper in every aspect of their lives. *Walden Two* is the archetypal utopian novel, a story that presents an idealistic future that seems alien to our experience but tantalizingly within our grasp.

The title of *Walden Two* is a tribute to an earlier novel, *Walden*, by the American author Henry David Thoreau (1817–62), which tells the story of a man who goes to live alone in the woods (Thoreau, 1854). Also of note is the name that Skinner gives to his lead character. The psychology professor who leads the visit and ultimately joins the Waldon Two community is Professor Burris. 'Burris' is a homonym of B. F. Skinner's own first name, Burrhus. Clearly, Skinner himself identified strongly with Professor Burris, sharing his enthusiasm at the prospect of an evidence-based behaviourist utopia.

However, many of Skinner's more eclectic works were ignored or popularly mischaracterized. In a 1971 philosophical book, *Beyond Freedom and Dignity*, he argued that 'free will' was a deeply entrenched but fundamentally erroneous belief, which impeded the appreciation humans needed to build a happier and fairer society (Skinner, 1971). One of his core messages was that punishment, as it is used in the modern world, is doomed to failure. These themes echoed the message of a science fiction novel Skinner had written in 1948, *Walden Two*, which depicted a utopian society where inhabitants denied the existence of gods and human souls (Skinner, 1948). Despite the thoughtfulness of these works, Skinner's emphasis of behaviourist principles attracted several accusations that he was espousing moral ambivalence, denial of human dignity, and even authoritarianism.

Skinner became a prominent American social commentator and achieved considerable fame in his own lifetime (Rutherford, 2000). His work transcended academia and, for many audiences, Skinner became the public face of psychology as a whole. He was listed among *Esquire* magazine's '100 most important people in the world' in April 1970 (D. Robinson, 1970). *Beyond Freedom and Dignity* spent six months in the *New York Times* bestseller list, its paperback edition becoming the top-selling book in the United States for four consecutive weeks in 1972 (C. M. Justice, 1998).

Skinner's personal fame both stemmed from behaviourism and served to raise its profile. However, this attention was a double-edged sword. The vivid image of rats pressing levers in boxes came to dominate the public perception of Skinner and his work, stereotyping him as an impersonal scientist who saw other people as mere sources of data and who viewed the standing of humanity as barely above that of the animal wilderness. While Skinner was a highly proficient researcher, his use of animal behaviour to explain human psychology was alienating for many audiences.

BEHAVIOURISM BEYOND AMERICA

During the second half of the twentieth century, interest in psychology grew around the world, both in academia and in wider society. This in part was propelled by an unprecedented upscaling of state involvement in science and scholarship. As the global population inexorably increased, from 2.5 billion in the year 1950 to 6 billion by the century's end, more and more countries sought to expand the reach of education, dramatically broadening access to an ever-expanding network of colleges and universities.

Many governments pursued competitive advantage by establishing large-scale research funding schemes, and in most cases education policy gradually succumbed to economic imperatives. Universities and their researchers were encouraged to produce knowledge that could bolster their nation's prosperity, and were tangibly incentivized to collaborate with private corporations and other institutions of business. In some countries, even the most esteemed universities – and with them entire national infrastructures of scientific research – were to become significantly dependent on the support provided by the corporate sector. A significant portion of university research was further propelled by substantial military investment.

Behaviourism and the Eastern Bloc

From the 1950s, scientific scholarship increasingly took the form of large-scale projects and research programmes funded by governments and transnational corporations, ushering in an era of 'Big Science' (Weinberg, 1961). This trend was partly engendered by the Cold War, a period of tense political and military rivalry between the United States and the Soviet Union (officially called the Union of Soviet Socialist Republics, or USSR), and their respective allies, which ran from the 1940s to the 1990s.

The two blocs became rapidly estranged after the Second World War, separated by geostrategic interests and political ideologies. The 'Western' countries, those politically aligned to the United States, were, broadly speaking, liberal democracies that embraced free market capitalism. The 'Eastern' countries, which were allied to the Soviet Union, comprised mostly centralist or authoritarian states that aspired to communist ideals. Competition for supremacy between West and East led to colossal state investment in academic infrastructure, as well as explicit efforts to extend cultural influence beyond national borders.

In the Western countries, systems of education and science increasingly developed in ways that resembled the American model. As we will discuss further in Chapter 11, this was at least partly due to the fact that the United States invested hugely in its scientific and academic sectors, thus becoming a large-scale producer and publisher of scholarly materials, including textbooks and journals. It was notable that in Europe, even many renowned German universities began to follow the American lead (the exceptions were those located within East Germany, officially then the German Democratic Republic, the part of Germany that remained under Soviet influence after the Second World War).

Eastern Bloc countries cultivated their own educational curricula, although these too gravitated towards the hegemony of the controlling superpower. The Marxist philosophy that underpinned communism – an approach known as *dialectical materialism* – had significant implications for their study of psychology.

According to dialectical materialism, the perennial class struggle between rich and poor was perpetuated by human nature: the way human beings are predisposed to seek ownership of property creates permanent prosperity for some ('the few') at the expense of others ('the many'). Dialectical materialism also proposed that communities and human systems always develop from the bottom up. In other words, higher intellectual pursuits such as customs, religions, arts and social norms are the products of more basic psychological experiences, such as feelings of security and safety. In these ways, Marxist political dogma presented psychologists with prescribed theories of human behaviour and its causes that were essentially non-negotiable.

The political climate in the Eastern Bloc was especially unwelcoming of dissent. Scholars whose teachings strayed from the official state position on the prospects of a socialist utopia could find themselves imprisoned, exiled or worse. As such, few psychologists dared to speculate that the human will could be shaped by mere reinforcement. For nearly half of the world's population, psychology developed in schools and universities with little or no mention of personality types, group dynamics or operant conditioning. Instead, 'conscious purposeful action' remained a fundamental tenet of much Soviet psychology (Bauer, 1952).

Indeed, although Pavlov was seen as a national hero in Russia, his work on conditioning was viewed primarily as a theory of biological reflexes. Another renowned Russian neuropsychologist, Alexander Luria (1902–77), extended this work by studying the role of various brain regions in cognition. He focused on Pavlov's 'second signalling system' – the way higher nervous activity combines to produce skills such as language – rather than on the question of how human beings initiated their own behaviours. Luria also helped to establish the specialism known as 'cultural-historical psychology', a set of theories emphasizing the role of culture and language in shaping intellectual functions. In combining neurology with the child development theories of favoured Soviet psychologist Lev Vygotsky (1896–1934), Luria's ideas resonated vividly with Marxist thinking. For good measure, he also became a vocal critic of American behaviourism (Holowinsky, 1985).

Behaviourism and the French philosophers

But the countries that comprised the Eastern Bloc were not the only places where American behaviourism was met with a lukewarm response. In France, for example, academics seemed to show little interest in behaviourist concepts, and were often actively hostile towards any theories that undermined the notion of personal human autonomy.

Nazi occupation during the Second World War had been a traumatic experience for the French people. When the Nazis first assumed control over French territory, life for many citizens continued as normal, and, in general, the mainstream population submitted to the new regime. However, in time, many citizens became horrified by what the Nazis represented, and instead joined or supported La Résistance, a now legendary movement of ordinary people that engaged in organized subversion. The 'French Resistance' was very diverse, drawing participation from all sections of society.

Nonetheless, many other French citizens chose differently. These citizens were willing to comply with the Nazi occupation, to do its bidding, and to provide it with support and services. Some of them became informers and actively assisted the Nazis in pursuing and punishing the Resistance. In the post-war period, these citizen 'collaborators' were the target of widespread public opprobrium, and their behaviour prompted intense soul-searching and psychological debate across French society.

The notion of psychological determinism – the claim that a person's behaviour is caused by factors beyond their control – was seen as especially controversial. It implied that if actions result from conditions more than from conscience, then human beings should not be criticized even if they do terrible things. This conclusion clashed uncomfortably with prevailing French attitudes towards collaborators. In general, public opinion in France was slow to be persuaded by the behaviourist account of how people think and act, or by its lesson that free will and personal responsibility might be less sacred than commonly believed.

One of the most renowned French philosophers was the existentialist Jean-Paul Sartre (1905–80). Sartre was a vehement critic of behaviourism. Instead, he believed that personal autonomy was the essence of human existence. Writing in the midst of the Second World War, Sartre described freedom as 'impossible to distinguish from the being of human reality' ('impossible à distinguer de l'être de la réalité humaine'; Sartre, 1943, p. 60). After the war, when writing for popular audiences, he would frame this discussion with explicit reference to the psychology of wartime collaborators. In his view, collaboration was an act of criminal conscience, and should be presumed to be rooted in personal autonomy. Later, in the 1950s, Sartre condemned behaviourism outright. Witheringly, he dismissed it as an 'obsolete position' (Amouroux & Zaslawski, 2019).

HISTORY REPEATING ITSELF: ONLINE FREE WILL

Debates concerning 'free will' are centuries old. More recently, concern about the nature of free will and our ability to control our own actions – or the capacity of others to control them for us – has arisen in relation to the design and function of social media and related technologies.

When posting on social media, we often believe that our content reflects our thoughts, wishes, tastes or even our beliefs. However, each social media post has the potential to generate consequences. A post might be shared by other users, or 'liked', or it might attract positive commentary. It could generate new followers or connections. Alternatively, a post might just be ignored, producing no response from other users at all. It might even elicit negative reactions, such as critical comments, downvotes or unfollows. All these categories of response will operate as different kinds of reinforcement.

'Likes', shares, follows, upvotes and so on serve as *positive reinforcement*, because they reward you for your actions. You will come to understand that posting this type of material increases your chances of attracting these feelings of reward. This makes it more likely that you will post similar material in the future, because it is natural for people to want to do things that make them feel positive. By contrast, if your post generates no response at all, you will be less likely to post this type of material again.

If your post generates negative comments, unfollows, downvotes and so on, you will feel even worse. These responses serve as *punishment*. Receiving them will make you more cautious about posting this type of content in the future, as it is natural to avoid behaving in ways that result in negative feelings.

If posting *different* content does indeed put a stop to the adverse feedback, then this too will shape your behaviour. By withdrawing the negativity, your new posting style will 'reward' you by alleviating the discomfort. In other words, it will serve as *negative reinforcement*.

Even if you are a passive user of social media, someone who posts very little, the same situations arise when you interact with *other people's* posts. Liking, sharing or upvoting online content reveals that you find it rewarding at some level. Encountering material that you find rewarding makes it more likely that you will continue to spend time on that website. For this reason, the reinforcement is bidirectional. The post provides positive reinforcement for your browsing choices, which you recognize with your 'like', while your 'like' provides positive reinforcement for the original poster.

Many tech firms have developed methods for harvesting large amounts of data about our activities on online platforms, tracking what we like and don't like. By tailoring the content that appears in our social media feeds, the platform providers can ensure we see more of the kind of material we find reinforcing. They can also direct any content we post to users who are likely to provide us with positive feedback. All this reinforcement keeps us engaged with their platform, spending more time scrolling through its content. Of course, some of this content will include advertising. Because of all the data they have gathered, the platform providers can then assure their advertisers that we, the users, are more likely to see their ads. Moreover, they can offer to personalize the advertising we see, based on the type of content that they know we respond positively to. The more specific the targeting becomes, the more the platform providers can charge their advertisers for this tailored access to our social media feeds.

Data about our online behaviour is usually incorporated into so-called algorithms, mathematical computation-based instructions that help produce automated decisions about how a person's social media feed should be tailored. This approach is not restricted to social media; it can be – and is – used by a wide range of other online businesses, including online retailers, email providers, news sites and magazines. In addition, many of these companies will share user data with each other.

When you click a 'like' button, leave a product rating, cast a vote in an online poll, or even view a particular product-page or article, you are not merely showing your support on a public forum. You are topping up your personal profile of reinforcement data for algorithms that will then be used to target you directly with tailored marketing.

This, after all, is why so many of these online services are available for free. You, the user, are the product. Reinforcement, the behavioural principle, is the business.

Another French philosopher to take a dim view of behaviourism was Maurice Merleau-Ponty (1908–61). Merleau-Ponty was a specialist in phenomenological philosophy, which meant that he focused on the nature of human experience and the way perception informs understanding. In his first book, *La Structure du comportement* (*The Structure of Behavior*), Merleau-Ponty (1942) rejected the idea that human reflexes alone could account for complex human behaviour. He carefully rebutted various claims made by physiologists and psychologists, specifically condemning Watson by name.

Sartre, Merleau-Ponty and other like-minded philosophers were prominent public figures in France. Many of them were considered celebrities. Sartre was so successful at presenting his philosophy to mass audiences in the form of popular novels, he was awarded the Nobel Prize for Literature in 1963 (although, not wishing to be 'transformed', he chose to decline the award). Existentialist philosophy was a popular fascination in French culture, with public intellectuals increasingly valorized during the 1950s and 1960s. The views of philosophers were well known to most people, as French society sought to come to terms with the traumas of its recent past (Baert, 2011).

Image 8.4   Social media reinforcement
Social media services exploit the principles of reinforcement to maintain constant user engagement.

These decades saw widespread French hostility towards the type of psychology studied in laboratories, especially that coming from America. In the words of the French epistemologist George Canguilhem (1904–95), such research was simply 'philosophy without rigour, ethics without requirements, and medicine without control' ('une philosophie sans rigueur, une éthique sans exigence, et une médecine sans contrôle'; Canguilhem, 1958, p. 12).

Notwithstanding the Cold War trend towards Americanization in Western universities, the archetypally American approach of behaviourism was not so enthusiastically received in all parts of Europe. In France, one of the major centres of European intellectualism, there was instead a spirit of scepticism towards all forms of laboratory psychology, especially those seen as divesting human minds of their essential capacity for *freedom* (Braunstein, 1999).

THE TRAJECTORY OF BEHAVIOURISM

Perhaps as common as the claim that twentieth-century psychology underwent a 'behaviourist revolution' is the assertion that behaviourism then ultimately burned itself out, becoming a spent force (around the 1970s), and effectively declining into obscurity ever since. However, it seems that rumours of behaviourism's demise, although frequent, are seldom trustworthy.

The extinction of behaviourism was first reported as far back as 1938. That year, the *Journal of General Psychology* published a fifty-five-page paper entitled 'The rise and fall of behaviorism' (Harrell & Harrison, 1938). According to its authors, 'Behaviorism must be viewed now as essentially an historical development of the recent past … Of recent years the volume of literature on behaviorism has dwindled into a barely perceptible stream, and psychologists have grown weary of the very words' (pp. 401–2). Behaviourism, they suggested, was now 'safely confined to that limbo of abandoned theories whence there is escape only through a process of theoretical reincarnation or resynthesis' (p. 402).

More recently, it has been common to depict the history of behaviourism as having effectively ended with the arrival of cognitive psychology. We will discuss the nature of cognitive psychology's own creation myth in Chapter 9. For now, it is sufficient to say that trends in psychology are seldom so neatly defined as to follow each other in sequence: the arrival of cognitive psychology did not *require* the removal of behaviourism. Both fields could and did (and can and do) exist simultaneously.

Nonetheless, the 'decline' of behaviourism is commonly attributed to two core difficulties that faced the field (G. Richards, 2010). The first was the problem of complexity. Many psychologists argued that conditioning alone could not account for the 'organization' of human behaviour. The classic example they offered was language. Behaviourism's critics claimed that linguistic ability – for example, the ability to compose truly novel sentences – could not be achieved by the shaping of stimulus–response associations. Therefore, some aspect of psychology *other* than behaviourist concepts was needed to explain this generative nature of language. The second problem for behaviourism was the emerging data on the heritability of traits. Behaviourism presumed that human attributes were produced by environments. This failed to allow for the fact that some traits were passed down genetically from parent to offspring. Psychology, therefore, needed to accommodate the fact that perhaps not *all* behavioural patterns were truly conditioned. There must be more to behaviour than behaviourism.

There was also the issue of political climate, especially in the Western world. Cold War paranoia had stigmatized the idea of control over personal autonomy. The ability of psychologists to shape people's behaviour in 'desirable' ways seemed nefarious rather than curative. And, as described in Chapter 7, the 1960s saw the emergence of several countercultural movements aimed at disrupting the established norms of society. Many of these promoted the concept of 'freedom'. Skinner himself saw an understanding of behaviourism as essential to a person's ability to be able to shape their *own* behaviour, and thus to grasp control of their own destiny. However, perhaps because of its fixation with testing animals in cages, the behaviourist approach quickly gained an unfortunate reputation for *oppressing* personal autonomy.

The reduction of psychological experience to algorithms inferred from the pressing of levers and absorbing of food pellets was considered by many to be dehumanizing and technocratic. As the twentieth century approached its closing decades, behaviourism found itself incompatible with the prevailing cultural desire for freedom of spirit.

The rise and fall of the 'rise and fall' narrative

Talk of the 'rise and fall' of behaviourism is sometimes backed up with empirical evidence. A common method is to examine the prominence of behaviourist themes in the main academic journals of psychology. One such analysis at the end of the twentieth century suggested that, in four 'flagship' psychology journals, the number of articles mentioning behaviourist concepts began to decline sharply during the 1970s (Robins, Gosling & Craik, 1999). From this the authors concluded that interest in behaviourism had waned across psychology as a whole.

However, journals identified as 'flagship' in such studies, while no doubt having high profiles, might not be representative of the full gamut of psychology. Such journals are often generic in their coverage, and frequently publish all-encompassing commentary articles more than narrow research studies. If *generic* journals started to feature fewer papers on behaviourism in the 1970s, it may simply reflect a shift in publication trends. Most of the specialist journals of behaviourism were established broadly around that period (the *Journal of the Experimental Analysis of Behavior* in 1958, the *Journal of Applied Behavior Analysis* in 1968, *Behavior Modification* in 1977, and *Perspectives on Behavior Science* in 1978). It could simply be that these journals became the centre of attention for behaviourist researchers, attracted by the greater value of publishing work in *specialist* rather than generic outlets.

This trend was to be widely observed throughout psychology. As psychology became more specialized during the second half of the last century, dozens, if not hundreds, of specialist journals and conferences were newly founded. Practitioners and researchers who were heavily invested in specific topics gravitated more and more to these outlets, seeing them as ideally matching their needs. The shifting content of psychology's generic journals since the 1970s needs to be interpreted with this trend towards specialization in mind.

Indeed, when researchers examine a wider set of psychology journals, rather than just 'flagship' titles, they often discover a much more nuanced picture. One group of psychologists in the Netherlands studied several decades' worth of data drawn from nearly 250 psychology journals

(Braat et al., 2020). They focused on co-citation networks – the degree to which psychologists refer to *other* psychologists in the bibliography sections of their articles. The authors found little evidence that behaviourism 'declined' during the second half of the twentieth century. The cluster of behaviourist research represented around 30 per cent of psychology overall consistently from the 1940s right up to the 1960s. In fact, the total number of behaviourist papers and citations increased dramatically during this time, but so too did the number of papers and citations *for all other areas of psychology*. The *share* that was accounted for by behaviourism remained stable throughout.

A key finding from this analysis was that, in reality, behaviourist research was *never* a truly dominant paradigm in psychology. For each decade from the 1920s to the 1960s, behaviourist studies made up no more than a third of published research, and in no decade was behaviourism even the largest of psychology's many diverse subfields. Instead, throughout the purported 'rise and fall' of behaviourism, the biggest subfield of psychology would appear to have been the area we discussed in Chapter 6: the use and development of psychometric methods to quantify psychological characteristics and aptitudes. The fact that this is rarely reflected in discussions of psychology's supposed scientific revolutions serves to highlight the subjective nature of many historical narratives.

The continuing progress of behaviourism

Ultimately, however, the databases used by researchers to study the contents of psychology journals – such as *PsycINFO* or *Web of Science* – are not neutral tools. The keywords and category headings that databases use to classify the details of each published article may unintentionally reflect assumptions that end up boosting the search 'hits' for some psychology subfields more than others. The features built into academic information systems often reflect the design choices of the agencies who commission them or who fund their establishment. Such agencies may themselves have priorities that are more politically informed than scholarly (Burman, 2018). An uncritical 'trust-in-the-numbers' approach to bibliometrics can distract researchers from important issues of historical context (Green & Martin, 2017).

Journal publication is just one indicator of prominence. While flagship (generic) journals may publish fewer (specialist) behaviourism articles today than in the 1970s, the various behaviourist psychology associations are nonetheless thriving, and many thousands of behaviour therapists around the world are engaged in lucrative professional work. This resembles the situation with psychoanalysis, which we alluded to in Chapter 7. While few psychoanalysis papers are published in the *American Psychologist* today, demand for psychoanalytic therapy remains extremely high, as does membership of the American Psychological Association's psychoanalysis subgroup, which has more members than its subgroup for counselling psychology.

Analysing the contents of journals, 'flagship' or otherwise, will seldom capture the real-world prominence of psychology's various subfields. The widespread use of behaviourist psychology in therapy – such as CBT, ABA, ACT and other forms of behavioural therapy – suggests that behaviourism remains a hugely influential application of psychological theory. Behaviourist concepts, such as reinforcement, are frequently incorporated into health promotion interventions as a way to help steer health-related decision-making (Story et al., 2014).

Behaviourist principles are also the subject of intensive commercial research, especially in industries that seek to exploit human interactions with technology (McMahon, 2015). The science of stimulus–response, reward and schedules of reinforcement is especially informative when it comes to understanding – and influencing – people's relationship with social media, as well as their use of smartphones and other devices. The satisfaction elicited by a 'liked' social media post can serve as powerful contingent reinforcement. It offers a potent means for shaping the behaviour, if not also the lives, of consumers.

The automaticity of our reactions to such technologies illustrates how behaviourism is as relevant now as it has ever been. Its principles are the focus of extensive scientific study, much of it commercially driven, ultimately influencing the way human beings appreciate, and navigate, their own free will.

WHERE TO FROM HERE?

While behaviourism is sometimes criticized for downplaying mental processes, in reality many behaviourists worked hard trying to explain the behaviourist principles that underlie cognition. Their observation was not that cognition was unimportant, but that cognitive events, such as verbal behaviour, were very complex and difficult to measure. As behaviourism became ever more prominent during Skinner's time, exciting new technologies also emerged. Machines such as computers helped to promote a greater recognition of how just about any decision could be broken down and explained in terms of algorithms and logic.

The idea that thoughts, memories and other abstractions lay permanently beyond scientific scrutiny began to fall away. These trends led to another claimed revolution in psychology, one that was said to lead to a new science of the mind – a so-called cognitive revolution. It is to this revolution that we turn to next.

DISCUSSION QUESTIONS

1. Is it possible that feelings of psychological freedom are an illusion? How would we know?
2. Have you lived through a scientific revolution? Do people who live through scientific revolutions realize that they are happening?
3. Why did behaviourism flourish in the United States more than in other countries?
4. Why are some psychologists so keen to suggest that behaviourism is in the past?

RECOMMENDED READING

- **Burman, J. T. (2018). Through the looking glass: PsycINFO as an historical archive of trends in psychology.** *History of Psychology, 21,* 302–33. In this analysis, the author discusses how the structure and content of literature databases in psychology can themselves be used to map out the way different subfields emerged, and continue to emerge, over time.

- **Digdon, N. (2020). The Little Albert controversy: Intuition, confirmation bias, and logic.** *History of Psychology*, **23**, **122–31.** In this essay, the author shows how controversies over the historical events surrounding Watson's 'Little Albert' case study illustrate several cognitive biases that can distort how history in general is written.
- **Rutherford, A. (2000). Radical behaviorism and psychology's public: B. F. Skinner in the popular press, 1934–1990.** *History of Psychology*, **3**, **371–95.** In this review, the author examines popular press coverage of B. F. Skinner during his career, to explore how behaviourism as a whole was perceived by the general public.
- **Skinner, B. F. (1948).** *Walden Two.* **Indianapolis: Hackett.** In this novel, Skinner portrays a community organized on behaviourist principles, to argue that society as a whole would be enhanced by evidence-based policies but is being held back by convention and tradition.

COGNITIVISM, COMPUTERS AND THE CONCEPT OF *REASON*

9

In this chapter, we will ...

- consider the way human beings have compared their own mental processes to the technologies they saw around them
- evaluate the emergence of the psychological study of thought processes in children and adults
- examine the impact of the mind-as-computer metaphor on our understanding of cognition
- consider how linguistics came to shed light on the innate structures of the mind
- reflect on claims that cognitive psychology is the product of a scientific revolution

---

At the outset

Humans have long understood that thoughts happen invisibly in human minds. However, for many centuries, many philosophers believed that the inner workings of human minds were somehow physically present. For example, they thought that mental images were somehow real images that were stored in the mind, which people could retrieve at any time in order to view with their 'mind's eye'. Throughout history, scholars have sought to explain these processes using metaphors drawn from the technologies that existed around them.

The nineteenth and twentieth centuries saw the emergence of computational cognitivism, where human thought processes were considered as being similar to those occurring in mechanical calculators or computers. In some respects, the popularity of behaviourism drew attention to the challenges of mental measurement, but many psychologists took this as a reason to pursue even more research on cognition.

In the early twentieth century, many psychologists became interested in how children come to understand the world around them. There was greater appreciation that children's cognitive abilities developed in stages. The study of child cognition was important for identifying the systematic, and sometimes imperfect, nature of human reasoning. Another stimulus was the demand for knowledge about mental performance from a burgeoning industrial sector, as well as the military. How people handle information when using machines attached increasing importance to the study of human performance.

During the second half of the twentieth century, psychologists were greatly influenced by the emerging sciences of informatics and electronic computing. The resulting information-processing approach to cognition is often described as being a new and important sub-discipline of psychology in its own right, often referred to as cognitive psychology. Another influence was the study of psycholinguistics, which saw innate language abilities as a central component in the human cognitive architecture.

Cognitive psychology has continued to expand and evolve, incorporating the study of topics such as decision-making, and crossing over into biological sciences such as neurology. In many ways, therefore, it has become a modern way to consider some very old psychological topics. Like other areas of psychology, its emergence has been more gradual than revolutionary.

Key concept: Reason

Reason is the ability of humans to make sense of information, typically by using a combination of logic and knowledge. It is often held to be the archetypal feature of humankind. Indeed, the term *Homo sapiens* essentially means 'person capable of reason'. As such, the ability to reason is an important part of the human identity.

An important feature of reason is that, generally speaking, it is supposed to be rational. This means that it is supposed to produce worthwhile results that reflect accurate information and sound decision-making. Reasoning can be pursued methodically, such as when we use inductive, deductive or abductive reasoning (as discussed in Chapter 3). Therefore, when we say that reason is part of the human identity, this is usually taken to mean that the ability to reason *logically* is intrinsically human.

Reasoning can be described in terms of method, and so can theoretically be codified in ways that would allow it to be used by a machine or a computer. But most human reasoning takes place automatically in people's minds. We appear to produce decisions and conclusions almost instinctively. This has led many psychologists to explore the rudiments of reason, and the extent to which such 'instinctive' cognition comprises hidden mental deliberative processes that we are not aware of.

Reason, therefore, is a truly mental process, intertwined with other mental processes, such as memory, perception and language. All these processes occur in human minds in ways that are difficult to observe or measure. The scientific study of how humans reason has raised many questions about whether or not our reasoning abilities really are as logical as we sometimes think they are.

MENTAL MACHINES IN THE MIDDLE AGES

In previous chapters we saw how, since the earliest times, the human mind was imagined to be not just a tool for thinking, but a *physical space* in which thinking occurred. Prehistoric shamans and medieval surgeons alike presumed the brain to be the place where evil spirits seized possession of human minds. Philosophers since ancient Egypt depicted thinking as happening inside the body. Pythagoras, da Vinci, and Descartes were just a few of the many historical scientists who believed the psyche could be precisely located within specific anatomical structures.

In his pioneering diagrams, the sixteenth-century Flemish anatomist Andreas Vesalius depicted the brain as a physical vessel containing psychological events (see Chapter 5). Unlike today's neurologists, Vesalius was less interested in the cellular tissue that made up the brain's physical substance, preferring to focus on the hollow inner cavities, or 'ventricles', that were encased within its structures. The three biggest gaps in brain tissue, he believed, provided the physical space necessary for different types of thinking: current ideas happened in the front ventricle, whereas more reflective deliberations required the greater space afforded by the middle ventricle. The posterior ventricle was located at the back of the brain, and so was a suitable basement for long-term storage. It was here, Vesalius believed, where humans filed away their memories.

Dualists believed psychological events to be ephemeral, while monists believed them to be physical: memories, mental images and the mind's many deliberations occurred in real time somewhere within the brain. By the Middle Ages it was commonly held that the inner mind preserved a mental representation of the outer world, one that reflected external reality in form as well as in content.

The medieval view of mental representation

Today, many people feel that their mind is akin to a video camera. When we experience an event, we record all its many sensations – its sights, sounds and smells – in a format that we can later retrieve as memories. Similarly, when we are presented with an object or have a concept explained to us, we can record and store this information too in our minds for future reference.

The various concepts of our external world end up with counterparts inside our heads. When we recall these concepts, it is as though we experience them for a second time. We feel as though we can *perceive* them, in our *mind's* eye, even though they no longer physically affect our senses. Our psychological capacities for sight, hearing, smell, taste and so on can each be re-experienced on demand, without requiring the actual originating stimulus. It is as though our minds can trigger our senses simply with an *idea*. Our minds operate like cameras, our mental images are like films and photographs.

The camera was not invented until the nineteenth century. However, for millennia before that, people maintained more or less the same idea about how their minds worked, sometimes referring to more familiar technologies. For example, Plato and Aristotle both used the metaphor of a wax tablet (Kemp, 1998). Plato described the process as follows:

> We make impressions upon this of everything we wish to remember among the things we have seen or heard or thought of ourselves; we hold the wax under our perceptions and thoughts and take a stamp from them, in the way in which we take the imprints of signet rings. Whatever is impressed upon the wax we remember and know so long as the image remains in the wax; whatever is obliterated or cannot be impressed, we forget and do not know.
>
> (Burnyeat, 1990, p. 325)

It is important to note that a wax impression does not tell us everything about the object from which it was formed. We can see the shape and size of the object, and perhaps recognize its purpose. But the image will not convey all the object's properties. Of course, this is also true of our mental representations. When we recall an event or an idea, it feels *like* we can see it in our mind's eye – but we know that this is not the same as seeing it for real.

In expanding on Plato's idea, Aristotle emphasized this important feature of human perception. Memories and ideas are produced in the mind as impressions are produced in wax: authentic in form, but incomplete in substance. We can register the contours but cannot fully appreciate the content. In Aristotle's model of hylomorphism (see Chapter 2), mental representations constituted 'form without matter' (Bynum, 1987). They existed as concept, not as material reality.

Over time, the wax tablet theory was extended to account for various nuances of human perception. For example, some experiences are less memorable than others. This must mean that their mental representations are formed in a less enduring manner. The fifth-century Algerian philosopher, Augustine of Hippo (see Chapter 2), explained that in these cases the human mind operated more like a watery fluid than like wax, taking the form of the concept imprinted upon it only for the duration of the experience. In the twelfth century, the Islamic philosopher Averroes (see Chapter 2) argued that this was why water affects memory: when the brain gets too wet, he suggested, it loses the firmness needed to retain clear impressions of concepts that are impressed upon it. Such an anatomically detailed rationale seemed much more logical than the prior teaching, dating back to Hippocrates, that excessive water resulted in mental slowness because the mind was made of fire (again see Chapter 2).

Long before human civilization invented photography, there was widespread belief that mental images constituted systematically generated physical replicas of the external world, somehow produced and stored within the anatomy of the brain. Many theories sought to explain this process in terms of the structure of brain ventricles.

As early as in the fifth century, the Syrian philosopher Nemesius of Emesa described memory processes as operating in a manner akin to a modern digital image library (Panteleakos, Poulakou-Rebelakou & Koutsilieris, 2013). Whenever a concept was being remembered, it would be retrieved from long-term storage in the posterior ventricle and then physically re-displayed alongside current thoughts in the front ventricle, as if being projected onto a mental screen. The theory that ideas in the brain could be blended to create actual images was to remain influential for centuries, with the Polish philosopher Witelo (1225–80) locating the process in the brain's optic chiasm, that part of brain anatomy where the two optic nerves cross each other (Stachowski, 1993).

Following Nemesius, the Persian philosopher Avicenna (see Chapter 2) presented a series of thought experiments demonstrating how such images could be mentally handled. We could, for example, manipulate an object in our mind's eye, rotating it to view from different angles. We could imagine an object getting larger or smaller depending on how 'close' it was to us. However, we could not form a mental image of 'black' and 'white' in exactly the same location; this was because, Avicenna argued, our mental representations occupied real physical spaces and it would be impossible for two objects to occupy a single space (Kemp, 1998). Avicenna's theories helped to account for our capacity to form mental images of novel concepts without the benefit of direct experience.

Further evidence for the plausibility of such 'inner senses' was derived from everyday experience, and especially from the common experience of after-images. When your eye looks at a bright light, its photoreceptors respond to overstimulation by temporarily reducing their sensitivity. After you close your eye or look away, these photoreceptors take a moment to readjust. During this moment, you feel as though you can still 'see' the light, or at least an image that conforms to the shape of the light, in your *mind's* eye. This is because, even when your eyes are closed, the relevant photoreceptors continue to send signals to the part of your brain that processes visual images. Medieval philosophers pointed to this effect as evidence of the brain's capacity to produce lasting physical images of the external world (Kemp, 1998).

Human beings have frequently sought to explain the workings of the mind by referring to the technologies they see around them. Some of these comparisons are offered as metaphors, whereas others are intended to convey a semblance of physical fact. The brain's use of a wax tablet to produce impressions of external reality was an example of this latter approach. While the brain did not contain wax, its anatomy was believed to comprise something equivalent that could adopt the form of whatever was impressed upon it. The belief that mental images absorbed by human minds must contain the form and features of original perceptions became widespread in scholarship and endured for many centuries. It helped to explain why recalling a previously perceived object would itself produce a feeling akin to perception. It was, in essence, a true perceptual process.

It is often suggested that technological advances have changed the way human beings think about their own minds. Arguably, the effect was felt the other way around. Long before the era of photography or digital information storage, human beings conceived of their own minds as capable of multifaceted forms of facsimile reproduction, image processing, structured filing, data retrieval and visual display; with our technologies we have strived to emulate and imitate these mental capacities. In short, for centuries the human mind was recognized as being a uniquely complex and sophisticated 'computer' – an advanced thinking machine far beyond anything that technology could supplant.

HISTORY IN STORIES: *THE MATRIX* (1999)

The Matrix (Wachowski & Wachowski, 1999) is a dystopian science fiction movie in which the lead character, Neo, gradually discovers that he has been living inside a computer-generated simulated reality. Unknown to him, he has spent his life in a special prison, constrained inside a liquid-filled pod, his brain connected to a mainframe computer that generates a virtual world inside his mind. Learning the truth helps Neo to understand some of the strange events he had recently been encountering, and why some people appeared to have been able to bend the rules of reality itself. He also learns why he, and many other people, have been held in such a prison. They were taken prisoner by intelligent machines who had defeated the human race in an apocalyptic war.

The movie revolves around the conundrum that every person's experience of reality is a product of their perceptions. In this way, its premise is not unlike Plato's ancient proposition that reality is projected into our minds by our senses in much the same way as a series of shadows can be projected onto the wall of a cave. Plato suggested that if all we can see is the cave wall, then we might come to believe that the shadows are all that makes up the world.

As such, *The Matrix* challenges its audience to consider the gap between mental representation and reality. It also presents the idea that mental representations can be distorted, and perhaps over-written, by external forces. In this way, cognition is presented as essential to our psychological lives, but as ultimately unverifiable. Examining the nature of cognitive processes and reducing the human experience to its intrinsic algorithms and codes might produce some helpful insights, but it could also threaten our fundamental sense of the human self.

ALMOST FAMOUS: OTTO SELZ

Otto Selz (1881–1943) was a German academic who was interested in theories of thinking. He worked as a professor of legal philosophy and pedagogy at a number of German universities, before fleeing the Nazi regime in 1938. However, while working in Amsterdam during the Second World War, he was detained and eventually transported to the Auschwitz concentration camp. He died three days later.

Much of Selz's teachings were never published, which was almost certainly the result of the rise of the Nazi regime. Because of his Jewish heritage, he was often unable to work in Germany, and other academics were prohibited from citing him. Nonetheless, some of his papers, published mainly in the German language, have been recognized.

From these works, scholars have reckoned Selz to be a forerunner of modern cognitive psychology. Impressed by the way physicists depicted their theoretical models, Selz refined the concept of a *schema*, a mental structure or framework that represents thoughts and information. He formally described how schemas assist with problem-solving, a theme that would re-emerge in cognitive psychology some decades later (ter Hark, 2010).

Selz is also believed to have developed important ideas on the philosophy of science, some of which were said to have influenced the prominent Austrian-British philosopher Karl Popper, who had highlighted the importance of framing scientific hypotheses in terms that allow them to be falsified (ter Hark, 2004). However, as Selz's theories were never formally published, it was Popper's version that was to become historically renowned.

THE EMERGENCE OF COMPUTATIONAL COGNITIVISM

The nineteenth-century scholars who sought to establish the new discipline of university psychology were almost exclusively devoted to the study of mental processes.

Psychophysics was essentially a means for quantifying the dimensions of human perceptual ability. The religious philosophers and secular scientists in the American universities also shared a common interest in mentalist topics, their textbooks covering in great detail such concepts as attention, memory, perception, 'conception' (which dealt with mental imagery) and the rational sequencing of thought. William James, who described psychology as 'the science of mental life', developed lasting theories on serial cognition (for which he coined his 'stream of consciousness' metaphor) and the cognitive classification of emotion (a principle of emotional reasoning now referred to as the James–Lange theory). In Europe, the newly emerging field of biological psychology revealed the brain to be a processing centre for human thought, the paraphasias studied by figures such as Paul Broca and Carl Wernicke demonstrating how information was systematically stored and retrieved in memory. And for their part, the psychometricians, including Galton and Pearson, believed they could quantify 'intelligence' by measuring mental processing abilities, such as sensory acuity and speed of thought.

As we saw in Chapter 8, the emergence of behaviourism was largely a response to – and thus a reflection of – the wide prevalence of mentalism, especially in American psychology. And as we also saw in Chapter 8, while behaviourism became popular in its own right, it certainly did not displace the study of mental processes in psychology as a whole (indeed, many behaviourists, such as Hull and Spence, went to great lengths to incorporate mental states into their behaviourist theories). Nonetheless, the rise of behaviourism did draw attention to the many challenges of mental measurement, and amplified debates about the long-term viability of using scientific methods to study mental processes.

Just as it is erroneous to claim that the emergence of behaviourism revolutionized the field of psychology, it would also be wrong to suggest that the scientific study of cognition – those mental processes that deal with thinking – suddenly shifted the paradigm of psychology as a whole. For one thing, the mechanical nature of cognitive processes had been studied in one form or another for hundreds of years. Indeed, for many people, there was little point to a science of psychology *other than* to build an understanding of how human beings think. What did change, and change radically, in the twentieth century was the intensity, precision and computational sophistication of cognitive research. Social developments, theoretical trends and technological advances led disparate researchers around the world to pool their knowledge and coalesce around a common mission – to reverse-engineer the software of the human mind.

Learning from children's minds

One stimulus to the study of cognitive processes was the increased political attention given to education and schooling. Although attitudes to children varied across time and culture, for most of history they were seen as miniature adults, defined in terms of what they could not do or experience, rather than for what they were truly like psychologically. Until relatively recently, childhood was not seen as a particularly special period of life.

Praagnya1830396 / Wikimedia Commons / CC BY 4.0

Image 9.1   Jean Piaget
Jean Piaget was initially a natural scientist, but became famous for his theories of infant cognitive development.

If anything, childhood per se was a hindrance: children were expected to engage in labour as soon as they had the physical strength to do so, and many cultures expected children to engage in adult affairs from as early as seven years of age (Handel, 1988). Childhood was something to be endured, and then survived. Mortality was extremely high: approximately a quarter of all children born before 1900 died within their first year of life, with almost half of all children dying before the onset of puberty (Volk & Atkinson, 2013). The mental lives of children may have piqued the interest of some philosophers and theologians, but for the vast majority of people, child psychology was a gloomy topic that provoked widespread emotional indifference.

All this changed around the start of the twentieth century. Enhanced sanitation, improved nutrition and the availability of vaccination saw infant mortality rates decline sharply around the world. Simultaneously, governments came to see the need to provide formal supports for childhood, such as infant care guidance, child protection agencies and, where necessary, appropriate care homes (E. H. Berger, 1991). In 1924, the Geneva Declaration on the Rights of the Child became the first intergovernmental agreement to recognize that children had specific legal rights.

This background helps to explain the great interest shown, especially in Europe, in the work of Swiss psychologist Jean Piaget (1896–1980). Originally a natural scientist, Piaget became curious about psychology when working in Paris with Théodore Simon, the co-inventor of the Binet–Simon intelligence test (see Chapter 6). Partly inspired by observations of his own children, Piaget developed an extensive theory of childhood cognitive development. His work was hugely influential, and in 1929 Piaget was made director of the International Bureau of Education, a prominent nongovernmental organization that would eventually be subsumed within UNESCO.

Piaget (1936) described childhood cognitive abilities as developing in a series of stages. These started with a sensorimotor stage, in which children experience the world through their movements and senses, and culminated in an operational stage, in which they are capable of abstract reasoning. A key milestone was achieved by children at around one year old: the ability to appreciate 'object permanence', the understanding that objects continue to exist even when after they are withdrawn from view. Piaget argued that children conceived of their environments in terms of mental frameworks, or *schemata*, which they use to interpret experiences through processes of *assimilation* and *accommodation*. An important thread in Piaget's thinking is that children consider their environments in the same way that scientists consider their data. This led Piaget to speculate that the study of child cognition could help philosophers to better understand the true nature of scientific reasoning.

Piaget's theories were premised on the view that childhood learning was intertwined with biological development. As various biological structures took shape within their bodies, children's cognitive abilities would grow, allowing them to move through the developmental stages. In other words, the theory implied that nature was as important as nurture. For Piaget, cognition could not be fully explained in terms of stimuli, responses and conditioning. A biologically primed 'readiness to learn' was also critical.

Piaget's work was more observational than experimental, and his assumptions about the role of biological readiness did not sit well with behaviourists. For these reasons, his theories were initially resisted by many American psychologists. However, the Piagetean approach went on to influence pedagogical practice around the world, and his ideas about readiness and the constructive nature of learning remain integral to the training of educators. Piaget helped to refine – and to popularize – a sophisticated understanding of the nature, development and operation of cognitive processes.

The science of human performance

The study of cognitive performance gradually increased during the first half of the twentieth century, in part spurred on by the desire of industry to maximize the outputs of its workers. The Second World War was to greatly intensify this focus. The ability of humans to operate complex signal-detection systems, or to quickly absorb information from elaborate cockpit dashboards, was suddenly recognized as being of existential, as well as commercial, benefit.

Eric Friedebach / Wikimedia Commons/ CC BY 2.0

Image 9.2 Selective attention
The complexity of airplane cockpits in the 1940s led many psychologists to focus on theories of selective attention.

Research on the process of memory had been pioneered by German psychologist Hermann Ebbinghaus (1850–1909) back in the 1880s, and later elaborated upon by psychologists such as the young Soviet scientist Bluma Zeigarnik (1901–88). However, in the 1920s, this field was largely dominated by physiological studies of brain ablations and plasticity, typified by Karl Lashley's behavioural experiments on rats (see Chapter 8). To many scientists, the process of memory was intertwined with neurological systems, and so was properly the preserve of biology rather than psychology (R. T. G. Walsh et al., 2014).

The British psychologist Frederic Bartlett (1886–1969) was to buck this trend, conducting several studies of actual memorizing, and recalling, by human participants. Bartlett was the first professor of experimental psychology at the University of Cambridge, and so was an extremely influential figure in British psychology.

Bartlett concluded that memory was far more than a process of associations between stimuli and responses. Instead, human beings remember experiences as narratives. When they recall something, they retrieve key pieces of information from their memories, and then assemble them in a manner that is coherent to such a narrative. 'Coherence', for each person, would be a personal judgement, dependent on what was familiar to them within their experiences. In this sense, therefore, memory could be shaped by society or culture. Bartlett illustrated as much in one of his own studies: when asked to retell a story about Native American tribes, his English participants would often erroneously incorporate details drawn from their *own* culture and surroundings (F. C. Bartlett, 1932). Overall, for Bartlett, remembering was a constructive process (or more accurately, a *reconstructive* one) that was embedded in social environments.

Bartlett's approach contrasted sharply with behaviourist theories of learning. In addition, because of their sociocultural framework, it was quite difficult to imagine how his theories could be tested using animal models or research into brain physiology. His model of memory would be difficult to explain using neurology alone.

Later, Bartlett's student and successor at Cambridge, Donald Broadbent (1926–93), would continue this research. Prior to his university education, Broadbent had been trained as a pilot with the Royal Air Force, including a period of service in the United States, where he first encountered the field of psychology (Weiskrantz, 1994). Broadbent's various interests would ultimately align when he was put in charge of Cambridge's applied psychology research unit, where he extended Bartlett's research in an effort to address practical challenges for the military.

Broadbent's special expertise was in the human capacity for selective attention. He was intrigued by how radar operators could interpret signals while dealing with many different information sources at once. Famously, Broadbent described human attention as relying on a selective filtering process, where incoming information is systematically buffered so that only important details are allowed to take up space in working memory. Such buffering was based on an initial analysis of both the physical and semantic aspects of the information. The theory helped to explain how human beings could enhance their acuity by learning how to effortfully guide their attention. Perhaps more importantly, Broadbent described his theory using a series of flowcharts. This was one of the first published uses of such graphics in psychology, and was pivotal in ushering in a new metaphor in psychology – that of the mind as an 'information processer' (Fernandez-Duque & Johnson, 1999).

Mind as computer

Broadbent had become interested in the work of another British scientist, the mathematician Alan Turing (1912–54). In 1937, Turing had published a paper on the limits of mathematical proofs, in which he described a theoretical machine capable of performing any mathematical computation that was presented as an algorithm (Turing, 1937). This device, which became known as the 'Turing machine', was seen as an early example of how artificial intelligence could be produced using technology. While Broadbent was impressed by the effort to create computers that worked like human brains, his insight was to invert Turing's metaphor: it was human brains, he said, that worked like computers.

During the Second World War, scientists in a number of countries developed electromechanical digital computers, usually for military use. In the decades following the war, high-speed electronics enabled the construction of faster and faster computers, with dozens of such machines housed in research institutions around the world. By the 1970s, further technological advances enabled such

Public domain, via Wikimedia Commons

Image 9.3 Thinking machines
The emergence of electromechanical digital computers, especially in the 1960s, encouraged psychologists to consider the human mind as a thinking machine.

computers to be mass-produced in affordable and portable forms – as so-called 'home' computers – suitable for marketing to nontechnical users. In less than four decades, computer technology had exploded into popular consciousness. What were once rudimentary prototypes of interest only to mathematicians had become ubiquitous, domestic technologies.

The growing familiarity of computers in daily life led many psychologists to further develop the metaphor of *mind-as-computer*. They were aided by mathematicians, who had created a new mathematical subfield known as 'information theory' (Shannon, 1948). This theory showed how detailed information could be stored and communicated using numbers, and how complex codes could be compressed into fewer components while minimizing information loss. Suddenly the claim that human brains worked like computers seemed much more plausible, if not even compelling.

Old topics could be approached afresh using the new method. The American psychologist George A. Miller (1920–2012) applied the concepts of information theory to the study of human memory, positing that human minds have a finite 'channel capacity'. According to Miller, his experiments revealed that the average number of 'bits' of information that humans can hold in short-term memory ranges from five to nine. Miller memorably described this channel capacity as 'The magical number seven, plus or minus two'. His paper on the subject, published in 1956, has since become one of the most cited academic papers in the history of psychology (Ho & Hartley, 2016).

The flourishing of the information-processing approach launched cognitive research as its own major subfield of psychology. The language of computing was quickly appropriated by behavioural scientists. Human minds were said to be storing and retrieving data within systems scaffolded by decision-points and feedback loops, and to be executing subroutines in order to accomplish specific routinized tasks. 'Information' replaced 'stimuli' as psychology's latest buzzword (R. T. G. Walsh et al., 2014).

Such language served to solidify the metaphor of 'mind as computer'. However, although chiming with the emerging science of algorithmic decision-making, it does not logically follow that such a seductive metaphor will always capture the nature of reality. Despite cognitive psychology's focus on computationalism, it remains the fact that human minds are products of biology rather than of engineering. As repositories of our lifetime experiences, our narrative memories and our impulsive reasoning efforts, our minds may sometimes be better described as functioning in organic rather than digital ways (Randall, 2007).

HISTORICALLY (IN)ACCURATE?: THE MAGICAL NUMBER SEVEN

One of the most cited research papers ever published in psychology appeared in the 1950s, and was written by the American cognitive psychologist George A. Miller (1920–2012), a professor at Harvard University. The paper was called 'The magical number seven, plus or minus two: Some limits on our capacity for processing information' (Miller, 1956). Miller memorably begins his paper by stating, 'My problem is that I have been persecuted by an integer' (p. 81). Perhaps for further comic effect, Miller then explains that this persecution has persisted 'For seven years'.

Miller's paper explains that the accumulated research on human memory has tended to produce a series of coincidental findings. The limitations of judgement and the span of short-term memory appear to combine in ways that ensure that, for most tasks, people find it easiest to process around seven 'bits' of information. This, he suggests, implies that the span of 'immediate memory' is effectively fixed at seven items, although a margin of error of around two can reasonably be applied.

Miller suggests that the 'magical number seven' might therefore hold a special resonance for human beings. He points to the fact that humans have tended to identify seven wonders of the world, seven primary colours, seven notes in the musical scale, and even seven days in a week. He observes that the major world religions have enumerated seven deadly sins as well as seven levels of hell. While allowing for the fact that these instances of the number seven might simply be 'a pernicious, Pythagorean coincidence' (p. 96), he presents the possibility that 'Perhaps there is something deep and profound behind all these sevens' (p. 96).

Generations of psychology students have learned that the capacity of short-term memory is represented by Miller's magical number. However, subsequent research has suggested that it might be an oversimplification (Ma, Husain & Bays, 2014). For example, when people are asked to memorize strings of letters instead of numbers, the average capacity of short-term memory appears to be *six* items (plus or minus a margin of error) rather than seven. When they are asked to memorize words, short-term memory capacity is reduced to *five* items (plus or minus a margin of error). Even these summaries are quite general, as research has shown that the exact capacity will depend on the phonological lengths of the items being remembered. For example, the letter *w* ('double-you') will occupy more capacity than the letter *a* ('ay'), because it contains more syllables.

The fact that human culture has produced many lists containing seven items is also misleading. There are many recurring lists that contain other numbers (for example, *four* seasons, *four* elements and the *four* horsemen of the apocalypse; or *twelve* months, the *twelve* Olympian gods and the *twelve* days of Christmas). Focusing only on examples of the number seven can make us feel that Miller's number is 'magical', but this is a result of confirmation bias. The fact that examples are easy to recall accentuates this bias, a common mental habit that cognitive psychologists refer to as the *availability heuristic*.

Hans Peters / Anefo / Wikimedia Commons / CC0 1.0

Image 9.4   Noam Chomsky
Noam Chomsky is a linguist and philosopher, whose theory of generative grammar debunked Skinner's depiction of language as learned verbal behaviour.

Speaking a common language

A particularly important influence on the study of cognition was to come from the field of linguistics. As we saw in Chapter 8, Skinner had proposed that the capacity to speak emerged from a process of operant conditioning. To him, language was no more than 'verbal behaviour'. Skinner's stimulus–response approach to language learning was widely accepted by behaviourists, and had begun to influence the wider public too.

However, these behaviourist views were far less convincing to researchers who had devoted their careers to the study of linguistics. A key problem was the creative nature of language. It was well established that any speaker of any language could easily compose statements that they had never heard before, and thus for which they could never have been reinforced. The ability to compose novel utterances stretched the claim that language was no more than a set of recurring responses to stimuli.

In addition, children often make errors of speech that suggest they are capable of applying grammatical rules that they intuitively develop for themselves. This ability of children to generate their own grammar appeared to belie the principle that speaking was a 'learned' behaviour. Moreover, the fact that different children would often come up with the *same* form of spontaneous grammar suggested that the ability to use language was derived from some deeper – and *innate* – cognitive processes.

Another problem was the fact that, around the world, while different languages are often *superficially* dissimilar, they actually display common universal features and formats. For example, at a very simple level, all languages have nouns and verbs. If language emerges because of reinforcement, it is unclear why *every single human community ever to have existed* ended up reinforcing each other to use nouns and verbs.

Other universal features were much more complicated. For example, in any language where there are separate words for 'hand' and 'arm', that language will also have separate words for 'foot' and 'leg'; however, if there is only one word for 'hand/arm' (such as in Irish, which uses the word *lámh* for both, or Croatian, which uses the word *ruka*) then there will always also be just a single word for 'foot/leg' (Irish: *chos*; Croatian: *noga*). Again, the fact that this principle is true of all languages ever studied raises questions about how so many diverse communities of human beings simultaneously came to reinforce each other to speak according to such convoluted, but uniform, rules.

It was well known to researchers in linguistics that human languages were characterized by literally hundreds of similar universals. It simply did not ring true that the systematic complexity of human speech could result from every single human speaker being shaped by operational conditioning within their own lifetimes.

In 1959, the American linguist and philosopher Noam Chomsky (1928–) published a damning essay reviewing Skinner's (1957) book on language, *Verbal Behavior* (Chomsky, 1959). Chomsky's own theory proposed that human beings were capable of 'generative grammar' and that the human capacity to use language stems from the modification of innate cognitive abilities. In essence, the way human beings speak reflects the way they think, and this in turn is intertwined with biological predispositions. In the same way that Piaget had shown how infants learn to appreciate the nature of objects by maturing through a fixed sequence of sensorimotor stages, Chomsky implied that human beings learn to speak by using a common set of innate cognitive capacities. In other words, when it came to language, all human beings were born with a 'readiness to learn'.

The field of linguistics, as championed by Chomsky, demonstrated how human experience was dependent on highly structured cognitive systems. Moreover, it showed that these cognitive

---

LOGOPHILIA: 'COLOURLESS GREEN IDEAS SLEEP FURIOUSLY'

In the 1950s, the linguist and philosopher Noam Chomsky (1928–) offered the following example of a semantically meaningless sentence (Chomsky, 1957):

Colourless green ideas sleep furiously.

He pointed out that the statement being made was nonsensical: something that is green cannot be colourless, ideas do not have colours, ideas do not sleep, and sleeping cannot be done furiously.

Nonetheless, when presented with the statement, our brains immediately attempt to make sense of it. The fact that it is grammatically intact, that the words are real and that everything is spelt correctly all combine to produce an immediate reaction in our minds. We assume that there *must* be a meaning in there somewhere. Our brains are irresistibly drawn to try to figure it all out.

Chomsky's point was to highlight the distinction between syntax and semantics, and to show how human minds are naturally primed to appreciate the structural aspects of language. Even though the statement is meaningless, we can still *understand* it on some level. For example, we can answer questions about it (such as 'What colour were the colourless ideas?'). For Chomsky, this proved that behaviourist explanations of language must be incorrect. Human beings can process utterances that they have never heard before, and even ones that convey no true semantic content.

From such reasons, Chomsky argued that human language must reflect an innately acquired cognitive skill, and not merely a repertoire of remembered word combinations shaped by past experiences of reinforcement.

systems, like all other biological predispositions, were generalizable across human beings and could be better understood if afforded the appropriate degree of scientific scrutiny. These concepts were entirely compatible with the cognitive approach to psychology. Consistent with the information processing approach, Chomsky referred to the inherent human capacity to learn language as the *language acquisition device*, as if it were a component of a computer programme.

During the 1950s, many psychologists had begun to object to the way behaviourism was being depicted as the cutting edge of psychology. Chomsky's contributions to the debate from the field of linguistics helped to broaden the range of *non*-psychology scientists who were assembling around this new research agenda. In succeeding decades, these researchers would gradually coalesce into their own coherent interdisciplinary field, an intellectual movement that increasingly identified itself as a new science – specifically: *cognitive science*.

THE MIND'S 'NEW SCIENCE'

From the 1970s onwards, the self-identification of *cognitive science* saw several newly established research centres, college courses, academic journals and learned societies formally using the term. While much of its research continued to focus on core information-processing concerns such as attention, perception and intelligence, the field expanded to cover a wide range of topics of cultural interest, and was widely seen to be of ready applicability to everyday life.

In recent decades, the language of cognitive psychology has become increasingly familiar as a way to discuss and describe the processes of human thought. Everyday discourse is littered with references to cognitivist ideas such as reasoning, judgement, language, memory, perception, creativity, reframing, problem-solving and choice-making. Topics such as bias, reasoning error, learning styles and artificial intelligence attract frequent popular debate. The expansion of the cognitive approach to psychology has certainly been striking, leaving its mark both within and beyond academia.

An expanding remit

Since the 1970s, cognitive research into memory has intrigued popular audiences with new knowledge about the limitations of, for example, eyewitness testimony (Loftus, 1979). That human beings are guilty of systematic everyday reasoning errors was another humbling finding (Tversky & Kahneman, 1974). On the flipside, understanding the role of distorted cognition in precipitating and perpetuating mental health problems, such as depression and anxiety, allowed for the development of new, effective psychotherapies (A. T. Beck, 1972).

Studies in the field of judgement and decision-making have arguably produced some of the most significant research in all psychology. Over the past five decades, empirical findings on the impact of error in human reasoning have essentially disproved previous beliefs regarding human rationality. For example, even professional decision-makers, such as doctors producing complex diagnoses, will make frequent fundamental errors when judging probabilities in their heads (Tversky & Kahneman, 1983). Likewise, most of the mental strategies that humans use when making quick judgements will be inherently illogical. These imperfect cognitive 'heuristics' leave people open to making fatally erroneous choices and decisions. They also underpin a wide range of delusional social beliefs, including defamatory stereotypes and conspiracy theories.

The discovery of these problems led to a radical rethink of many standard economic theories that had previously been premised on an assumption that choices made by consumers, investors and financiers were grounded in rationality. The major studies in this field were conducted over several decades by the Israeli psychologists Daniel Kahneman (1934–) and Amos Tversky (1937–96). Shortly after Tversky died, Kahneman was awarded the 2002 Nobel Prize for Economics in recognition of their work.

Cognitive psychology's overlap with information technology continues to expand. As computer scientists have developed their own ideas about the best means to design digital systems, so too have cognitive scientists allowed their theories of the human mind to evolve accordingly. The original concept of information systems specializing in serial processing (in which operations occur one at a time) has given way to the more exciting possibility that such systems work better when multiple parallel processes are allowed to happen simultaneously. The prospect of designing computers that more closely reflect the structure of biological brains has led cognitive scientists to consider whether human cognition, too, might capitalize on the interconnectedness of nervous systems. Such so-called neural network concepts are typically seen as advancing the sophistication of *both* computer science *and* cognitive psychology.

HISTORY REPEATING ITSELF: THINKING, FAST AND SLOW

In 2002, the Nobel Memorial Prize in Economic Sciences was awarded to the Israeli-American psychologist Daniel Kahneman (1934–). Along with his former colleague, the late Amos Tversky (1937–96), Kahneman had produced a voluminous body of research demonstrating the many ways in which human reasoning can be compromised, especially when people are forced to make decisions under pressure. Our natural habits of thought – our so-called *heuristics* – are often more expedient than efficient, and frequently lead us to make decisions that are erroneous, illogical or divorced from reality.

Cognitive research on heuristic-based reasoning is often presented as providing new insights into the fallibility of human minds. It is said to have debunked a long-held assumption that human beings are intrinsically logical, and that this logical ability is itself a hallmark of humanity. However, not all civilizations have held such views about the inherent logicality of human thought.

Ancient Indian philosophy long acknowledged that human thoughts were often poorly reasoned. It provided a traditional cognitive model that distinguished *Śravaṇa* (श्रवण), or 'hearing about', from *manana* (मनन), or 'reflection'. This model proposed that humans were not naturally primed to derive reality from their superficial thoughts, but needed instead to invest effort in thinking more deeply about what they had heard. Indeed, the common notion of *transcendence* refers explicitly to the acquisition of knowledge beyond direct experience, highlighting the need to carefully process information rather than just react to it in an instinctive way (R. Walsh, 2015). This deliberative process was formally recorded in the Upanishads, ancient Indian scriptures that, as described in Chapter 2, date back some 2,500 years.

Kahneman (2012) famously distinguished two types of thinking, *fast* and *slow*. In essence, fast thinking is convenient and useful when little is at stake, but slow thinking is required for complex challenges and important decisions. In their own way, these categories mirror the different levels of meditative cognition identified by many ancient civilizations. It has long been recognized that the path to enlightenment is not found easily by human minds.

A further technological dimension to cognitive research has been the rise of neuroimaging as a research technique, and the associated sub-specialist field of *cognitive neuroscience*. The ability to use technologies such as functional magnetic resonance imaging (fMRI) to create detailed images of the workings of a live human brain has been widely greeted as adding a sense of wonder and profundity to psychological research. The effort to examine the anatomical mechanics that underlie cognition has attracted a great deal of popular attention – as well as huge amounts of scientific research funding, courtesy of taxpayers. However, whether this work is as informative as it is awe-inspiring (or as it is expensive) is a matter of some considerable scientific debate (Hughes, 2018a).

Evolution not revolution

As with behaviourism, the history of cognitive psychology is often discussed in terms of a 'cognitive revolution', replete with the Kuhnian paradigm shift that such revolutions are said to require. However, as we saw in Chapter 8, such claimed revolutions are rarely as tangible as they first appear. This is as true of the so-called cognitive revolution as it is of any other.

Cognitive psychology challenged the behaviourist view that the best way to understand the human experience was by measuring human actions. Not only did the cognitive approach seek to offer an alternative to behaviourism, it explicitly challenged behaviourism's fundamental tenets and, thus, sought to displace it. In that sense, therefore, many cognitive psychologists certainly saw themselves as stoking a revolution in psychology.

However, as outlined in Chapter 8, Kuhn's theory of scientific revolutions posits four successive stages: *normal science*; *anomaly*; *crisis*; and *paradigm shift*. As with the supposed behaviourist revolution, few of these stages really occurred at any point in the history of cognitive psychology.

Firstly, as explained in Chapter 8, behaviourism was just one of a number of different schools of psychology to co-exist throughout the twentieth century. In that sense, therefore, there was no single dominant 'normal science' of psychology for cognitive psychology to revolt against. Even behaviourism itself was extremely disparate. In short, there was no single behaviourist paradigm for cognitivism to shift. While both behaviourism and cognitivism waxed and waned at different points over the past 100 years or so, the patterns of their growth did not seem to expunge other areas of interest. Psychoanalysis, psychometrics, social psychology and others simply persisted as they were before. Behaviourism continued to account for a steady 30 per cent or so of published research in psychology, even after the so-called cognitive revolution (Braat et al., 2020).

Secondly, it doesn't appear obvious that cognitive psychology arose in response to scientific anomalies being faced by behaviourism (or by any other branch of psychology). Indeed, many of the pioneering ideas of cognitive psychology were yielded by non-psychologists, including computer scientists, mathematicians, physiologists, philosophers and linguists. The ideas were new but not revolutionary, in that they were not generated in order to overcome problems encountered in behaviourist psychology.

Similarly, as outlined above, behaviourism was not thrown into sudden crisis by the emergence of cognitive psychology. After all, psychology was already a disparate field; the occasional arrival of a new way to look at psychology was to be expected. Behaviourism just carried on. In any case, mentalism was already a long-standing topic of interest. If anything, cognitive psychology was more revolutionary in moving away from *introspection* as a way to study mental processes. Unlike the psychophysicists, William James and others, the cognitive scientists emphasized the need for objective measurement validity in their experimental research. In that regard they had more in common with the behaviourists than divided them.

It is worth noting that the emergence of cognitive science overlapped with the publication of Kuhn's theory of scientific revolutions. Resonating with the spirit of the rebellious 1960s, Kuhn had offered his own intellectual uprising, fundamentally challenging old orthodoxies in the historiography of science. The very fact that Kuhn's ideas were fresh during the same period that cognitive psychology began to find its voice may itself have encouraged the cognitivist creation myth (Leahey, 1992). The opportunity to participate in a scientific revolution must have appeared especially enticing to many of those whose ideas were new in the 1960s.

Overall, cognitive psychology created many innovative strands of research and opened up new ways to understanding of the human condition, but it did not launch its endeavours by displacing an old paradigm. Nor did it truly usher in its own new era of 'normal' (cognitive) science. The cognitive field is itself a disparate one, in which there are many theoretical debates and disputes.

Rather than constituting a true revolution of science, the emergence of cognitive psychology represents the modern manifestation of a long-standing intellectual enterprise. It is the latest endeavour to view the human mind as a technological device in its own right, one that is capable of managing mental processes through definable structures so that its user might better navigate the vicissitudes of daily life.

WHERE TO FROM HERE?

Behaviourism had encouraged psychology to focus on observable individual actions. The interest in cognition served to bring psychology even further inside the individual, emphasizing the invisible inner workings of the mind. As with the psychoanalytic approach to unconscious instincts, these areas drew heavily on the status of human beings as animals driven by biology.

However, in order to understand the nature of the human experience, we need to focus on more than just the individual themselves. This is because all human beings are born into social environments enveloped by human culture. Most go on to spend their lives surrounded by other people. This interconnectedness among humans is a critical factor in shaping their thoughts, feelings and behaviour. Throughout history, the effort to explain the psychology of individuals has always needed to take account of the relationships *between* individuals, and the way individuals see themselves as part of a broader world. In our next chapter we examine how this social approach to psychology has been pursued.

DISCUSSION QUESTIONS

1. Are modern metaphors of mind superior to ancient ones?
2. Is it possible to codify all human thoughts? Is it possible to codify an emotion?
3. Why is language important to psychology?
4. What would cognitive psychology look like today if the computer had not been invented?

RECOMMENDED READING

- **Arponen, V. P. J. (2013). The extent of cognitivism.** *History of the Human Sciences, 26,* **3–21.** In this article, the author considers how many critiques of cognitive theories are based on long-standing philosophical ideas about the capacities of human minds that themselves constitute a form of cognitivism.
- **Cohen-Cole, J. (2015). The politics of psycholinguistics.** *Journal of the History of the Behavioral Sciences, 51,* **54–77.** In this paper, the author traces the development of psycholinguistics as an evidence-based alternative to several competing theories about the fundamental nature of human beings.
- **Kahneman, D. (2012).** *Thinking, Fast and Slow.* **London: Penguin.** In this book, the author explains their theory of the way human beings employ different decision-making approaches in different situations, thereby explaining why irrationality is so prevalent in our supposedly 'intellectually advanced' species.
- **Mandler, G. (2002). Origins of the cognitive (r)evolution.** *Journal of the History of the Behavioral Sciences, 38,* **339–53.** In this article, the author shows how the emergence of cognitive psychology was slow and incremental, rather than revolutionary.

INDIVIDUALS, GROUPS AND THE CONCEPT OF *SOCIETY*

10

In this chapter, we will …

- consider how the historical instability of social conditions led to concerns about the nature of groups, communities and crowds
- evaluate the emergence of crowd psychology as a means for elites to rationalize their own privileges
- examine how the scientific method allowed the statistical study of national populations and the use of science to study humans in their natural social environments
- consider how two main approaches to social psychology emerged, and how they deviated geographically
- examine claims that much social psychology uses unreliable methods that leave it in a state of crisis
- consider how the factional nature of social psychology itself illustrates the impact of group dynamics

At the outset

Human beings are inherently social, and their psychology incorporates social as well as individual dimensions. As social cohesion is essential to the wider well-being of humanity, there has long been interest in the psychology of groups, relationships and social experience. The very fact that human behaviour is so embedded in social contexts has always presented challenges to the study of individual psychology.

During much of history, societies were unstable, politically chaotic and often violent. Many theories arose to explain the destructive dynamics of social influence. In the pre-democratic age, privileged people broadly saw the masses as inherently unreliable, and assumed that community-level collaboration led to recklessness, poor decision-making and even criminality. Many scholars warned that crowd behaviour stripped people of their individual consciences, making them untrustworthy and dangerous. Others speculated that people did not lose their minds when part of a group, and that social bonds were in fact central to personal well-being and identity.

As the scientific method began to emerge, interest grew in statistical information on national populations and other groups. This led to the study of how different social structures impacted on the well-being and health of group members. The idea of using science to study humans in their natural social environments became increasingly credible.

By the end of the nineteenth century, many scholars and scientists had begun to study the social aspects of human thoughts, feelings and behaviour, sometimes using questionnaires to gather data on social attitudes. Some chose to follow an experimental approach to address questions of social influence, including many studies on conformity and social facilitation. Two main approaches emerged. In North America, many psychologists focused on the behaviours and experiences of individuals in social contexts, while many European psychologists focused on the collective behaviours and experiences of groups.

Especially in the North American context, some social psychologists have repeatedly warned that experiments on individuals are often too artificial to generate useful insights about real-life situations. This has been referred to as the crisis in social psychology. The competing views on the merits of social psychology are often themselves distorted by group dynamics, with some social psychologists adopting partisan stances in methodological debates. Ultimately, the different factions of social psychologists are themselves the products of arbitrary social divisions, highlighting how human group identities are, more often than not, socially constructed.

Key concept: Society

Society comprises those individuals who exist together in an ordered community, sharing customs, relationships and some kind of group-level culture. The term *society* can be used to refer to a specific such community, or to the generic sense that multiple people exist in the world. In political contexts, *society* often refers to a set of people who live in a specified region and are subject to the same practices and laws. However, whether such a grouping is more significant than the individuals who comprise it is sometimes disputed. A former British prime minister once argued that 'there's no such thing as society' (Thatcher, 1987).

In psychological terms, *society* refers mostly to more generic ways in which individuals share an interrelated common existence. In this sense, the notion of *society* is indisputably pertinent, because virtually all human beings interact with others in some way. Not all social interactions are positive. Nonetheless, the term is derived from the Latin word *socius*, which means 'ally'.

HUMANS AS SOCIAL BEINGS

As we noted in Chapter 1, the very fact that human beings are fascinated by psychological questions reveals how interested they are in the lives and existences of other people. Our curiosity about what goes on in other minds is sparked by an impulse to get the measure of people *in general*, to understand *others*, and – whether we readily admit it or not – to acquire the capacity to *influence* their thoughts and actions. Our own inner monologues of thought take the form of language, an interpersonal code, rendering every cognition communicative. Each effort we make to explain something, even to ourselves, is framed with a listener in mind. In short, the entire enterprise of psychology is inherently social.

Very few human beings live truly solitary lives. Even hermits read books. As such, there has long been intense curiosity about the degree to which human psychology is shaped and guided by social contact, whether real or imagined, symbolic or substantive, intense or intermittent, ongoing or historical, or direct or distant.

Even the ancient philosophers were concerned about the psychological nature of societies, and the distinctions between social and individual experience. Plato posited detailed psychological theories about how personal context impacts on one's social behaviour: when people feel guilty, they treat others with generosity, but when they feel wronged, they become harsher. Plato derived his theory of the ideal state, as set out in the *Republic*, from his conclusions about psychology. For him, the perfect state should be structured in a way that reflects every part of human nature. He proposed that society should comprise groups such as guardians, administrators and producers, in order to facilitate the human inclinations for reason, free will and appetite (Cornford, 1912).

Philosophers in virtually all the global cultural traditions shared similar concerns. An important example was the Islamic philosopher al-Farabi (who, as we saw in Chapter 2, is considered by some scholars to be the second most important writer in philosophy, after only Aristotle). Writing in the tenth century, al-Farabi presented the concept of a model city that somewhat reflected Plato's approach to describing the ideal state. He suggested that human beings are innately predisposed to seek the company of others, and that perfection could only be achieved if this was facilitated by society (Haque, 2004).

The desire to understand the social aspect of human experience sparked centuries of scholarly enquiry. In the pre-democratic world, the dynamics of co-existence were often no less than a matter of life and death. The need to understand how people coalesce to form groups, crowds or even nations has sparked an ongoing concern about the aggregation of human experience. The very idea of democracy itself is based on a theoretical assessment of how autonomy can be infused with altruism. Existentially, the stakes are high. This is because, in any time or place, the prevailing views on the psychology of social experience will determine how people perceive the logic – and legality – of the societies in which they live.

The human herd

One of the oldest observations about social contexts is that reason is often addled by the presence of other people. Writing in the eighth century, the medieval English scholar and theologian Alcuin of York (735–804) famously warned against the common belief that wisdom could be divined from the masses (Ratcliffe, 2016): 'And those people should not be listened to who keep saying that the voice of the people is the voice of God, since the riotousness of the crowd is always very close to madness' ('Nec audiendi qui solent dicere, Vox populi, vox Dei, quum tumultuositas vulgi

Image 10.1   Crowd behaviour
In the mid-nineteenth century, widespread civil unrest led many European scholars to develop theories of crowd behaviour.

semper insaniae proxima sit'). Alcuin's claim was that people become more irrational and reckless when they assemble in throngs. This reflected a general belief of elites throughout history that the masses were something to be feared.

The chaotic nature of crowds attracted curiosity throughout history, but formal scholarship on the topic truly burgeoned in the eighteenth and nineteenth centuries. This was most likely due, in part, to the social, civic and political turmoil that characterized this period. Uprisings, rebellions and revolutions were commonplace, as the world population expanded, technology advanced and intellectualism became more daring.

There were major revolutions in America (1765–83) and France (1789–99). In the early nineteenth century, wars of independence broke out across Latin America. The 1820s saw uprisings in peripheral Europe, in countries such as Spain and Greece. In the 1830s, the revolutionary wave swept through central states, afflicting Poland, Switzerland and the Netherlands. In one single year – 1848 – there were major civil conflicts in France (the so-called February Revolution), Galicia (now Ukraine), Germany, Hungary, Ireland, Luxembourg, Moldavia, Romania and Switzerland, as well as uprisings in Poland, Serbia and Slovakia and the outbreak of Italy's first War of Independence. During the latter half of the nineteenth century, both China (1850–64) and the

United States (1861–5) experienced traumatic civil wars, and there was ongoing rebellion across much of Europe, South America and Asia.

Such extensive revolt frequently caused widespread anxiety, especially among the privileged classes. Those in enclaves of power – including many intellectuals and professionals – grew ever more alarmed at the psychological dynamics wreaking havoc in the wider population. In an effort to account for the tumult, a German scholar named F. C. Fresenius (1866) produced one of the first formal theories of crowd behaviour. According to Fresenius, large gatherings can often seem benign, but, when they are panicked, crowds are liable to become irrational and violent. He described a key psychological process whereby people feel less personally culpable for transgressions committed when part of a group, a dilution of responsibility that made mobs prone to recklessness.

A similar dynamic was highlighted by the Italian criminologist Scipio Sighele (1868–1913). Sighele believed that the chaotic nature of crowds was especially attractive to the delinquent lower classes. For this reason, he suggested, spontaneous mobs were disproportionately com-posed of people who had criminal tendencies. However, Sighele also believed that the most law-abiding of citizens could become crazed when part of a group. He was convinced that conferring with others undermined human judgement, causing people to make absurd and stupid decisions. His most famous example was that of juries in court trials. According to Sighele, juries regularly returned consensus-based verdicts that no individual juror would ever find convincing (Sighele, 1891). The combining of views, he suggested, was akin to the mixing of unknown chemicals. Adverse reactions, if not disastrous explosions, were likely more often than not.

Like many well-educated and privileged nineteenth-century professionals, Sighele was deeply sceptical of democracy. At this time, democracy was still in its infancy. The prospect of democracy was often considered to be interesting *in theory*, but it was rarely embraced with any enthusiasm by the political classes. In the few countries with elected parliaments, women were generally forbidden from voting, as were all men who did not own property. Several nominally democratic countries, such as the United States and Australia, limited voting eligibility even further, on racial or religious grounds. At the start of the twentieth century, New Zealand – with its population of just 800,000 people – was the only country in the world to grant unrestricted voting rights to all its adult citizens.

The French Revolution – ostensibly, the introduction of non-aristocratic democracy to Europe – seemed to have afflicted France with decades of internecine violence, terror and politi-cal disarray. Elected demagogues pursued erratic policies, many of them anti-democratic. Partisan fervour persisted for decades after the overthrow of the monarchy, leading to frequent col-lapses of political order and changes to the system of government. Harsh inequities served to stratify the population on economic grounds, and religious and political divisions remained bitter and stark. From his vantage in Italy, Sighele saw the imposition of democracy in Europe as having had disastrous effects. For him it reflected the 'decline of the individual' (Jahoda, 2007).

Perhaps unsurprisingly, much of the early scholarship on the psychology of crowd behaviour was produced in France itself. The French social scientist Gustave Le Bon (1841–1931) referred to this tumultuous period as 'l'ère de foules' or 'the era of crowds' (Le Bon, 1895). He was to become one of the most influential crowd theorists.

Le Bon believed that crowds brought out an instinctively primitive aspect of human nature, making people more suggestible, compulsive and intellectually weak. He theorized that when people become part of a crowd, they lose their individuality. They become psychologically absorbed within a shared thought process that Le Bon termed 'mental unity' ('unité mentale'), a collective mentality driven by feelings rather than logic. Reflecting the prejudices of the day, Le Bon argued that crowds, therefore, exhibited a 'feminine' and 'barbarian' quality (Le Bon, 1895).

Like Sighele, Le Bon was rather distrustful of the communal nature of democracy. He felt that charismatic orators could easily manipulate the masses. He bemoaned the collective mindlessness of voters, but also that of the parliamentarians they elected. According to him, any forum that prioritized collaboration over individual action risked chaos. Moreover, Le Bon felt that as large groups effectively stripped members of their individual consciences, collective behaviour would inevitably veer towards criminality. Crowds were intrinsically malign. Universal suffrage, he argued, was not a worthy ethical principle, but a fashionable 'dogma' pursued by the unquestioning mob with a zeal reminiscent of religion.

Another leading French sociologist, Émile Durkheim (1858–1917), took a radically different view of social systems. Durkheim did not see people as comparable to animals, but as having psychological capacities that made humans unique within nature. Durkheim had acquired a sophisticated appreciation for psychological matters. In college, he had studied alongside Pierre Janet, the psychologist whose ideas inspired Freud to develop psychoanalysis (see Chapter 7). Later he visited Wilhelm Wundt in Leipzig, to learn more about the newly emerging academic discipline of university psychology. When considering the psychology of crowd behaviour, Durkheim was keen to ensure that his approach was scientific.

Durkheim's theories suggested that humans did not lose their minds when becoming part of a group. Nor did a mob have its own 'mind'. Instead, social groups would share a common set of ideas and beliefs about society itself that would amount to a collective mental representation. These social bonds were what gave meaning to human life. By contrast, developing *anomie* – or a sense of becoming detached from these bonds – is what truly undermines a person's mental well-being. Durkheim studied detailed empirical datasets in his effort to demonstrate the detrimental impact of *anomie*, using complex multivariate statistical analysis to highlight its link to suicide (Durkheim, 1897). While Durkheim is often remembered as a founding figure of modern sociology, his approach emphasized the importance of studying the variety of human experiences rather than treating entire societies as homogeneous entities. His theories on mental health were ahead of their time and truly pioneering.

Durkheim (1897) himself accepted that his work in sociology was, in essence, its own form of psychology, noting that 'social psychology has its own laws' ('la psychologie sociale a ses lois propres'; p. 352). But at this time, when university psychology was just emerging, the term 'social psychology' was rarely used. Had Durkheim lived a century later, he would almost certainly have been lauded as a social psychologist, and a prolific one at that.

The study of crowds did much to promote awareness of the psychological dimensions of existing in a social world. It helped to reveal how human beings share diverse experiences and develop complex social identities, and were not merely slaves to a simple-minded herd mentality. Clearly there was more to mobs than mindlessness and mayhem. Claims that the masses were inherently malign reflected the prejudices of elites more than the dangers of group dynamics.

The way this conception of 'crowds' itself shifted over time offers a powerful example of the value of social science. It highlights how many of the ideas, representations and stereotypes in our culture, no matter how embedded in mainstream thinking they might be, can themselves be the products of social forces.

Image 10.2   Émile Durkheim
The French scholar Émile Durkheim promoted a scientific approach to the study of social behaviour.

HISTORY REPEATING ITSELF: VIRTUAL MOBS

Not all crowds need to meet in a physical space. Some types of crowds can gather virtually. In recent years there has been much discussion of the phenomenon of online social communities, and their occasional tendencies to form *cyber-mobs*. Cybermobs comprise groups of people who simultaneously engage in angry online behaviour in response to an event that causes them to feel outraged. However, as with many online phenomena that are decried as 'modern' problems, anxiety about virtual mobs long predates the invention of the internet.

The French theorist Gabriel Tarde (1843–1904) differentiated physical 'crowds' from virtual 'publics'. The idea of a 'public' was perhaps even more alarming than that of a 'crowd'. For Tarde, publics were collections of individuals who were connected by modern technology (Tarde, 1898). New forms of mass communication, such as the newspaper, could involve individuals in crowd-like groupings without them having to meet physically. Citizens could be seduced into mobbish irrationality without leaving their homes. In this regard,

Tarde's anxieties about newspapers echoed those previously articulated in the United States by George Beard, the neurologist who believed that new communication technologies were a cause of mental illness (see Chapter 4).

Tarde attempted to ground his theory in biological principles. He felt that human crowds (and publics) engaged in group-level behaviour in the same way that ants or bees formed swarms. Instinctively, each individual coalesces with the broader group by responding to the emotions of others and imitating their reactions. This impulse to imitate creates an impression of coordinated behaviour, as if the group has some kind of collective consciousness. Tarde suggested that virtual communities operated as if they were singular organisms in their own right. The mob, as it were, had its own mind.

In his teaching, Tarde referred to this subject matter as 'inter-mental psychology' ('psychologie intermentale'; Lubek, 1981), and he is notable for having published one of the first books to include the term 'social psychology' in its title (namely, *Études de Psychologie Sociale*; Tarde, 1898).

LOGOPHILIA: 'SHEEPLE'

The word *sheeple* is a combination of *sheep* and *people*. It is intended to describe the way humans can be easily influenced, to be docile, and to behave in unison as a single 'flock'. The term is a pejorative reference to the phenomena of groupthink, deindividuation and other negative consequences of crowd behaviour. In recent years, the phrase 'Wake up, sheeple!' has become popular, especially online, as a way to satirize the exploitation of the masses by alleged manipulative conspirators. Consequently, *sheeple* is often considered to be a relatively modern word. In 2017, the publishers Merriam-Webster launched a publicity campaign to announce that they had formally added *sheeple* to their English dictionary (Daileda, 2017).

However, the word is much older than this suggests. There are many instances of its use during the twentieth century. It was employed in print in the 1940s to describe the gullibility of radio audiences (W. R. Anderson, 1945). And it was used by the cartoon character Popeye in a 1930s episode that mocked the obsequious manner in which subjects in a monarchy pander to their king (Marschall, 1990). It seems that the common belief that *sheeple* is a modern coinage spawned by internet culture is itself the result of unquestioning reliance on consensus.

Towards a science of social experience

Not all nineteenth-century social thinkers saw the general public as a herd of yobs, liable to create turmoil at any moment because of their irrationality and recklessness. Many appreciated that most of the world's population was powerless and lived in extreme economic hardship. The riots, rebellions and uprisings in many countries reflected deep-seated social injustices. Popular rage was often rooted in justifiable discontent.

As we saw in Chapter 6, many of the earliest social statisticians were humanitarians. A notable pioneer was Henri de Saint-Simon (1760–1825), a French aristocrat, businessman and social theorist. As a young man, Saint-Simon had lived through the chaotic trauma of the French Revolution, and he passionately supported the new national ideals of liberty, equality and fraternity. From a largely sociopolitical perspective, Saint-Simon wrote prolifically about the functioning of society, and the ways in which human living might be improved. He posited a scientific view of human nature, drawing heavily on physiology and on the type of objective thinking that was then seen as characteristic of the natural sciences.

In this regard, Saint-Simon espoused a philosophy known as *positivism*. This was the view that true knowledge can only be derived from a combination of direct observation and logical reason, a radical departure from the traditional approach of deferring to authority, superstition or hearsay (see Chapter 3). Consistent with his commitment to objectivity, Saint-Simon disapproved of conventional social class systems, on the grounds that they prioritized hereditary privilege and wealth. He asserted that such systems were unnatural, and that true human well-being could only be achieved in organic social hierarchies derived from each person's innate abilities and tastes. Saint-Simon called for the reorganization of society along these supposedly scientific lines. He even proposed the establishment of a new religion that would reflect these aims (Saint-Simon, 1825).

It is obvious that Saint-Simon's scientific worldview conformed closely to his political philosophy. What is less clear is whether his science was the basis for his politics, or vice versa.

Saint-Simon's ideas greatly impacted the thinking of Auguste Comte, who, as we saw in Chapter 3, is today remembered for having coined the term 'sociology' (Comte, 1838). Comte also wished to develop a new political system, but not one based on democracy. Instead, given the chaotic decades that followed the Revolution in France, Comte recommended that order would best be achieved by establishing a benign dictatorship. Echoing Saint-Simon's approach, Comte sought to examine society as if it were a biological ecosystem. Later in life, he too would propose the establishment of a new science-based religion.

While noted as a pioneer of sociology, Comte's prominent theories had important implications for how the wider public discussed, and understood, the psychological aspects of life. Comte was a keen reader of psychology, but he felt that scholarship in the field was primitive, basic and overly mystical. He was keen that psychology be dragged into the scientific age. Not only did Comte endorse Saint-Simon's efforts to frame psychology as biological subject matter, he also advocated for the use of scientific research designs to address its important questions.

For example, Comte insisted that psychological questions should be investigated using a semblance of what we today refer to as experimental control. He recommended that conclusions be drawn using various types of 'indirect experimentation' ('l'expérimentation indirecte'; Comte, 1839, p. 428). For example, he noted that comparing dysfunctional societies with peaceable ones would help reveal the causes of dysfunction. Likewise, observing people in different countries would help to identify the extent to which behaviour is shaped by culture. And repeatedly examining a single society across different points of its history would help to elucidate the impact of the passage of time. Comte even suggested that useful lessons about human sociability could be drawn from comparisons with different animal species.

Over the nineteenth century, the idea of using science to study humans in their natural environments became increasingly credible. Not only were these methods both convincing and fashionable, they also had the potential to address pressing social problems. As we discussed in Chapter 6, one of the most significant advocates for this approach was the Belgian statistician Adolphe Quetelet. Quetelet introduced the concept of the 'statistically average person' and argued that data on human characteristics conformed to mathematically 'normal' distributions. But as well as demonstrating how quantification could be used to explain human experience, Quetelet also reflected deeply on the data he worked with. This led him to formulate complex theories about the nature of human societies.

Quetelet had developed his method of the 'average person' as a way to encapsulate the ideal state of human nature while acknowledging its inherent variability. He could see from his data that there was a huge range of differences across humans in their various characteristics. Nonetheless, there were also patterns. These patterns were never random, and most likely revealed the core features of humankind. The challenge for statisticians would be to extract a signal from the noise.

Quetelet became interested in the way patterns would recur in different situations (Quetelet, 1835). He believed that at any moment human societies existed in a state of equilibrium, in which competing needs, motives, traditions and customs cancelled each other out. Social progress would always be challenging, because all change requires a shift in the equilibrium, and so will be guaranteed to set off a cascade of equalizing and rebalancing consequences. Nonetheless, these 'perturbations' were extremely valuable. They were what helped humans to modify their conditions of life.

But perhaps Quetelet's most historic observation was that human attributes tend to emerge with recurring statistical consistency in different places, at different times, and in different groups of people. Quetelet had studied more than just the basic medical data on heights, weights and life expectancies. He also sought statistical information on characteristics like courage, mental health and intelligence. This led him to discover that many such variables showed a predictable frequency or intensity. For example, crime statistics would show more or less the same number of murders every year, and a similar per capita murder rate in different countries. Of course, the people committing these grizzly crimes had no idea how many other murders had taken place in any given year. But somehow they would collectively produce a consistent – or 'normal' – number of killings in every twelve-month period.

Quetelet's observation implied that human variability was finite and knowable, in that the same range of attributes – leading to similar subsets of behaviours – would arise in all social groups in a consistent way. However, in line with Quetelet's methodological position, this template for human nature could never be derived by examining just a single person. The true psychological scope of humankind would be manifest only in the social group. Similarly, Quetelet's approach implied that to study the human experience, scientists needed to do more than conduct laboratory experiments. The examination of authentic life in real human environments was crucial. The 'average person' was actually a range of average people, who lived in their own homes and socialized with their own friends. The social was essential to the psychological.

THE SOCIAL PSYCHOLOGIES

By the end of the nineteenth century, a variety of scholars and scientists were studying the social aspects of human thoughts, feelings and behaviour. As well as sociologists and statisticians, some of the new university psychologists were beginning their own explorations. As we described in Chapter 3, Wundt had developed his *Völkerpsychologie*, an approach to explaining human behaviour by comparing different societies throughout history. Others, such as the Harvard academic Josiah Royce (1855–1916) used Wundtian-style introspection to investigate Tarde's claims that social imitation played an important role in shaping people's perceptions (Royce, 1895).

Recent trends such as psychoanalysis (see Chapter 7) had led many psychologists to think increasingly about individual 'cases', while laboratory studies were restricted to small numbers of participants (typically the researchers' own students). Neither practice was ideally suited to the investigation of the 'social'. Fortunately, however, a number of new statistical approaches soon emerged that enabled, if not encouraged, the gathering of data from large samples – including data from the general public, who at that time rarely participated in laboratory studies of any kind. It was during this period that many psychologists began to use questionnaires for their research.

Questionnaires enabled psychologists to think and behave like natural scientists (Young, 2017). The inaugural president of the American Psychological Association, G. Stanley Hall (see Chapter 3), conducted hundreds of questionnaire studies over a twenty-year period, primarily in children (e.g. Hall, 1883). His contemporary James Mark Baldwin (1861–1934) also used questionnaires to study children, focusing on their social sense (J. M. Baldwin, 1895). The use of questionnaires was largely seen as an extension to the scientific mission of the New Psychology, rather than as a departure from it. It enabled psychologists to explore their chosen ecosystems akin to any other scientific researcher, and to 'do work as good for the purposes of mental science as much of the work of naturalists has been for biology' (Thorndike, 1898, p. 650). Nonetheless, while statistical innovations had helped to prompt the adoption of questionnaires in the first place, the social data that were assembled this way were rarely easy to analyse using numbers. The descriptions of social attitudes that were derived from these instruments often proved overwhelmingly detailed and dense, and over time the questionnaire approach began to lose its 'scientific' lustre (Young, 2020).

In Europe, there was much public attention on the practical implications of any new knowledge concerning social behaviour and attitudes. As we saw in Chapter 4, 'normal' behaviour was expected to include social conformity and adherence to the law. Criminologists debated the implications of what scholars had to say about crowd behaviour, but their views often seemed more political than scientific.

In Italy, the birthplace of modern criminology, prominent criminologists such as Enrico Ferri (1856–1929) argued that people should not be prosecuted for crimes committed while part of a crowd. He felt that the group-level dynamic of a crowd was so overpowering, it would be unfair to hold any individual member responsible for its actions (Sensales & Dal Secco, 2014). Notably, Ferri was a strong supporter of the Italian Fascist leader Benito Mussolini, a demagogue whose path to political power featured frequent violent support from mobs that would gather at his rallies.

Several European scholars chose to adopt an experimental approach to the question of crowd influence, examining people's suggestibility to social pressure. In a typical study, participants would be presented with a stimulus (such as a chart displaying lines of different lengths) followed by an ostensibly false statement about it (such as that all the lines were in fact the *same* length). The trick in such experiments was that the researchers would have secretly arranged for one of their participants to quickly agree with the statement, even though it was quite obviously false. These studies tended to show that most people were highly suggestible: participants were far more likely to agree with a false statement when they witnessed their fellow participants doing so first. Albert Binet (who we encountered in Chapter 3 and Chapter 6) was especially active in this research area, seeing social influence in children as relevant to their intellectual abilities. Related experiments were conducted in Italy (Vitali, 1896), Germany (Henri & Tawney, 1895) and elsewhere, and Binet ultimately reviewed the entire field in his book *La Suggestibilité* (Binet, 1900).

Another line of European research related to the impact of observers and competitors on individual behaviour. In the early 1880s, researchers at the French National Institute of Agronomy conducted studies that systematically tested the individual outputs of farm labourers working either alone or with others (Kravitz & Martin, 1986). Their findings suggested that labourers would invest more effort while working alone on an activity but would engage in social loafing when others were involved. Similarly, one of Paul Broca's students, the French physiologist and anthropologist Léonce Manouvrier (1850–1927), incorporated audiences into his studies of hand-grip strength. His findings suggested that people seemed capable of greater physical endurance when being observed doing a physical task compared to when doing the same task alone (Manouvrier, 1884).

The American psychologist Norman Triplett (1861–1934), who worked at Indiana University, would later cite Manouvrier's work as a basis for his own research into the impact of social cues on task performance (Triplett, 1898). Triplett's modest experiment yielded very mixed findings.

While some of his participants exhibited improved performance on a cord-winding task when competing against another person, others performed better when they did the task alone. Not only that, but Triplett did not conduct formal statistical analysis on his small dataset. When his data were later analysed for statistical significance, the effects in his study were found to be statistically no different from chance (Strube, 2005).

Nonetheless, Triplett's experiment has been afforded a special distinction in many textbooks and articles describing the history of what is now called *social psychology*. These sources typically describe Triplett's study along the lines of being 'the first social psychology experiment ever conducted' (even though it clearly was not), and, by default, identifying the year of its publication, 1898, as an important historical landmark (Stroebe, 2012). In reality, as with all creation myths in psychology (see Chapter 3) and elsewhere, any time-and-place depiction of academic origins is likely to be skewed by subjectivity.

The attribution of primacy to Triplett's small experiment once again reveals more about the partisan processes of academic historiography than it does about any historical event.

HISTORICALLY (IN)ACCURATE?: TRIPLETT ON SOCIAL FACILITATION

The claim that Norman Triplett's study of social facilitation was 'the first social psychology experiment ever conducted' is not the only way in which his work is frequently misrepresented. The experiment is a mainstay in introductory textbooks and websites, but the descriptions presented frequently contain errors of fact.

Triplett's experiment involved a sample of forty children who performed a task both alone and in competition with another child. For the task, Triplett designed an apparatus based on two fishing reels connected to a wooden frame. At the opposite end of the frame were two wheels, one corresponding to each reel. Connecting each reel and wheel was a single looped cord, attached to which was a small flag. To perform the task, the child was required to wind the reel as quickly as possible so that the flag would move from one end of the frame to the other, a distance of around 2 metres. When participants performed the task alone, only one of the reels would be used. Each child performed the task six times, three times alone and three times competing with another child. From these procedures, and based on visual inspection of the data, Triplett concluded that competition was associated with 'gains' in task performance for around half of the participants.

Many accounts of the Triplett experiment greatly simplify its details (Stroebe, 2012). For example, it

is frequently suggested that the children were required to wind actual fishing lines onto reels, and thus used actual fishing rods instead of specially constructed laboratory apparatus. It is also commonly stated that social facilitation was arranged by having some of the children perform the task while being *watched* by another child, rather than having the other child actively compete with them. And most critically, the results of the experiment are frequently over-summarized, where it is simply stated that social facilitation was found to have enhanced the children's performance. Such unequivocal statements misrepresent the actual results. Even when eyeballing the numbers instead of using statistical tests, Triplett himself found that half of the children showed no enhancement of any kind. At best, the effects of competition were contingent on circumstantial factors. At worst, there were no such effects at all, with differences in performance simply reflecting random fluctuation.

By and large, Triplett's experiment continues to be distorted when being described today (Stroebe, 2012). In this sense it has acquired almost legendary status. It seems that its purported standing as a landmark study – one yielding an important insight about social facilitation – is often considered to be more instructive than the *actual* study details.

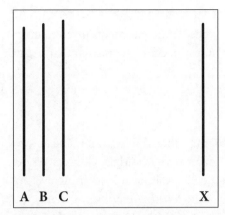

Figure 10.1 Social conformity
Conformity experiments, where participants witness other people giving wrong answers on a line-length matching task, have been conducted since the nineteenth century.

Individuals versus groups

Drawing precise boundaries around 'social psychology' is a deeply difficult task. It throws up complex challenges involving social identity, group dynamics, cultural evolution, suggestibility, conformity and perhaps even a 'mob' or two – or, at the very least, factions that exhibit mob-like frailties, including groupthink, stereotyping and in-group favouritism.

Many of these early-twentieth-century scholars realized that their research did not fall easily into existing subject-area categories. The work was not clearly sociology, which focused on societies as a whole. Nor did it resemble the individualistic experiments that had begun to characterize mainstream university psychology. This led figures such as Sighele to call for a new field to be recognized, one that focused on the experiences of collective groups and gatherings (Jahoda, 2007). But even with this focus in mind, scholars were faced with two distinct albeit dominant strands of thought.

The difference between the two strands can be illustrated by comparing two major textbooks that were published in the same year, 1908 (Sensales & Dal Secco, 2014):

- *Social Psychology: An Outline and Source Book* by Edward Alsworth Ross (1866–1951). This book was published in New York by the Macmillan company (E. A. Ross, 1908). The author, a professor of sociology, focused largely on the lessons of crowd psychology, but also presented coverage of specific issues such as suggestibility, imitation and conflict. The psychology on offer is described almost exclusively from a group perspective, reflecting what we might refer to as a *sociocentric* orientation.
- *An Introduction to Social Psychology* by William McDougall (1871–1938). We previously encountered this textbook in Chapter 6. It was published in London by Methuen and Company (McDougall, 1908). McDougall's text mostly examined the role of instincts in social behaviour, such as the instincts for imitation, gregariousness and 'pugnacity'. McDougall was a British psychologist who taught at Oxford University (he was to move to the United States later in his career), and his coverage focused on the behaviour and thought of individuals. In this regard, it can be said to reflect an *individuocentric* orientation.

(We might also note that both authors were zealous devotees of eugenics. Despite producing widely read textbooks, the authors are now much more likely to be remembered for their political extremism. Both made numerous statements that were considered shocking even by their contemporaries.)

At first, the sociocentric and individuocentric traditions of social psychology co-existed equally within the mainstream of academia. However, as university psychology departments invested more and more in laboratory research (see Chapter 3), it was the individuocentric approach that began to gain prominence.

Rise of the individualists

By the middle of the twentieth century, many social psychologists adhered to what became known as the 'classic' definition of social psychology, offered by the American psychologist Gordon Allport (1897–1967). Allport was yet another psychologist whose academic position at Harvard University afforded a prominent and influential platform. Especially within North American academia, he became known as a social psychology pioneer. Therefore, when a group of social psychologists decided to produce a new comprehensive *Handbook of Social Psychology* – an ambitious compendium aiming to provide definitive and up-to-date information on the field for the entire world – it was Allport they invited to write the history chapter for its inaugural edition. In his chapter, Allport (1954) presented his definition of social psychology as follows: 'With few exceptions, social psychologists regard their discipline as an attempt to understand and explain how the thought, feeling, and behavior of individuals are influenced by the actual, imagined, or implied presence of other human beings' (p. 5). Allport's definition was reproduced in updated versions of his chapter included in the second and third editions of the *Handbook*, which appeared in 1968 and 1983. Accordingly, for the greater part of half a century, Allport's description was widely seen as the 'official' definition of the field, and his chapter came to be regarded by many as the field's 'official' history (Lubek, 2000).

What is perhaps most notable about Allport's definition is that it explicitly describes social psychology as the study of 'individuals'. The 'social' aspect of the field is said to refer only to how an individual might be affected by the presence, or existence, of others (or perhaps even of just *one* other). Taken literally, social psychology of this kind would not be interested in studying a *relationship* between two people. Instead, it would look at each partner's experience of interacting with the other. The behaviour of groups (such as mobs or crowds) would be considered only as a set of *separate* acts by individual group members. This type of social psychology would see communities, societies and even nations as being of little psychological relevance other than as settings for the personal experiences of their citizens. The 'social' in this field is not the subject of study, but merely a stimulus that provokes the events that are actually of interest.

Allport's summary of history continued this focus. It described the emergence of university psychology laboratories, and the way some researchers began to use experimental methods to study the impact of social cues on behaviour. It is in this context that Allport declared Norman Triplett's study to be the 'first ever' experiment in 'social psychology', overlooking the fact that Triplett himself made no mention of the phrase 'social psychology' in his 1898 paper. (Indeed, in what was a twenty-seven-page article, Triplett used the word 'social' just once, a single passing reference appearing very much as an afterthought towards the end of the report.)

While many social psychology experiments had been conducted prior to Triplett's work, most of these had taken place in Europe. However, the newly defined social psychology seemed to see itself as emanating from North America. In the 1998 edition of the *Handbook*, the editors replaced Allport's chapter with a new historical summary (spanning two chapters: E. E. Jones, 1998 and Taylor, 1998) that made this point more explicitly. Social psychology, it was declared, was 'largely a North American phenomenon' (E. E. Jones, 1998, p. 3).

This version of social psychology traces European roots only insofar as some of its pioneers were twentieth-century academics who relocated to the United States having previously lived in Europe. Chief among this subgroup of psychologists was Kurt Lewin (1890–1947), a German psychologist who, as a Jewish person, fled the Nazi regime in 1933. Lewin was influenced by a German approach to psychology known as Gestalt theory (e.g. Wertheimer, 1922), which focused on the way human minds perceive objects as whole entities rather than as collections of individual components. Lewin's approach was to conceive of a person's behaviour in similar terms – as subject to the effects of a multiplicity of social influences working in combination, all of which required the psychologist's consideration. After arriving in the United States, Lewin became renowned as a prolific and innovative social psychologist. In addition to establishing a highly successful research centre at the Massachusetts Institute of Technology, Lewin oversaw the fledgling careers of a new generation of inventive social psychologists. His most famous protégé was Leon Festinger (1919–89), who went on to develop *social comparison theory* (Festinger, 1954) and to popularize the concept of *cognitive dissonance* (Festinger, 1957).

While finite in its focus on individuals, the social psychology described by Allport and his successors was nonetheless a wide-ranging field, covering a diversity of topics. Several of its more prominent studies have become landmarks in the history of psychology in general, at least insofar as they impinge upon the consciousness of undergraduate psychology students. These include classic studies of obedience (Milgram, 1963), bystander apathy (Darley & Latané, 1968) and simulated imprisonment (Zimbardo, 1971).

A similarly famous study, examining the effects of social conformity, was conducted at Swarthmore College, Pennsylvania by the psychologist Solomon Asch (1907–96). Asch's research involved showing people pictures of lines of different lengths and observing their reactions when others insisted that they were, in fact, the *same* length (Asch, 1956). While often lauded for its design, Asch's study closely resembled several of the experiments on suggestibility conducted in nineteenth-century Europe that had been reviewed by Binet back in 1900.

But while the North American community of individuocentric social psychologists busied themselves cultivating their field and composing their own history, they largely operated within a self-referential echo chamber of academic ideas. For example, in describing the history of 'social psychology' up to the end of the twentieth century, Jones's and Taylor's *Handbook* chapters did not cite a single paper from the *European Journal of Social Psychology* – which had been publishing research since 1971 – despite presenting a combined bibliography of some 570 references (Lubek & Apfelbaum, 2000).

Perhaps ironically, this subset of social psychologists seemed slow to appreciate the worldview of those who resided outside their immediate community, or even to acknowledge their existence.

Their commitment to in-group identity may also have served to discourage internal dissent. When some North American social psychologists began to raise concerns about the direction of their field – and about the robustness of its research – they found that their arguments were often quickly resisted, and sometimes even ridiculed.

HISTORY IN STORIES: *38 TÉMOINS* (ONE NIGHT) (2012)

38 Témoins (Belvaux, 2012) is a Belgian-French film based on a novel by the French writer Didier Decoin (2009). (In English-speaking countries, it was marketed under the title *One Night*.) It depicts the aftermath of the killing of a young woman who was stabbed and murdered in the street. The story is told from the perspective of her neighbour, Louise, who was on a business trip when the crime occurred. After she returns home, Louise is shocked to discover that such a thing has happened and is troubled at why so many of her neighbours appear detached and uninterested in the crime.

It turns out that a total of thirty-eight of her neighbours had actually seen the crime happening, the number of witnesses (or *témoins*) mentioned in the film's title. Each one of them had heard the woman screaming and had watched her being attacked from their windows. However, all had declined to come to her aid, or even to call the police. Every neighbour formed the fatal conclusion that, with so many others watching, it was inevitable that *somebody else* would do something to help.

Louise's husband, Pierre, was one of those who saw the woman being attacked on the night of the murder but who quietly chose to ignore the incident. When he finally admits this to the police, their subsequent investigation reveals that he was one of 38 such witnesses, all of whom did nothing. Both Louise and Pierre are distressed by the revelation, but for very different reasons. The film ends with Louise choosing to end their marriage.

The story in *38 Témoins* is closely based on the case of Kitty Genovese, a woman who was murdered in New York in 1964. After Genovese's murder, the *New York Times* reported that her killing had been witnessed by 38 people who, like those in

the film, chose to do nothing about it. It was this case that led social psychologists to identify the problem of *bystander apathy* (Darley & Latané, 1968), which even came to be known as 'Genovese syndrome'. The Kitty Genovese case has been cast as a landmark in the history of social psychology, demonstrating how social factors can critically inhibit altruistic behaviour.

However, it was later to transpire that the original *New York Times* report on Kitty Genovese's killing contained significant inaccuracies. The police had in fact found far fewer than 38 people who had seen the crime happen, and they could call on only three eye-witnesses to testify in the subsequent court trial. In addition, a number of neighbours had indeed phoned the emergency services when they heard Kitty Genovese's screams (Manning, Levine, & Collins, 2007). One woman did come to help Kitty, and was cradling her dying body when the police arrived on the scene (McFadden, 2016). The journalistic distortions may have been partly influenced by media homophobia, which was prevalent at this time. The narrative presented by contemporary journalists conspicuously overlooked the fact that Kitty Genovese was a gay woman, an absence of detail consistent with the media's then customary failure to report on, or to examine, issues such as homophobic violence and discrimination (Gallo, 2014).

The phenomenon of bystander apathy has been corroborated and evaluated in detail in several subsequent studies and continues to stand as an important principle of social psychology. However, the oft-cited case of Kitty Genovese is not as stark as was first reported. The plot of *38 Témoins* provides important lessons about the psychology of unresponsive witnesses, but is more loosely based on actual events than its creators originally envisaged.

'The crisis in social psychology'

The Allport/Jones/Taylor approach defines social psychology in an individuocentric way, and then traces history so that it leads to the emergence of an individuocentric social psychology. In so doing, it epitomizes the perils of historiography. Internalism, presentism and 'Great Man' approaches are not assiduously avoided, but instead appear to be embraced. As was the case with E. G. Boring's 1929 textbook on the history of psychology as a whole (see Chapter 3), the resulting disciplinary fables can seem implausibly triumphal. Their narratives speak of ever-flourishing success and productivity, with few wrong turns ever taken. Academic conflicts of interest – whereby, as protagonists in the history they are recounting, the historians themselves stand to be glorified by the version that gets written – are seldom acknowledged. The intentions of such works often seem much more corporate than scholarly: to promote wares, to attract students and to rally the in-group, rather than to explore facts.

Take, for example, the so-called crisis in social psychology which arose in the 1970s (e.g. Armistead, 1974; Elms, 1975; Moscovici, 1972; Ring, 1967; Silverman, 1977). Its emergence is often linked to a 1973 paper in the *Journal of Personality and Social Psychology* by the American social psychologist Kenneth J. Gergen (1935–) (Gergen, 1973). While ostensibly his personal perspective, Gergen's critique set out a number of concerns that were widely shared by research methodologists at the time. They related to the fundamental validity of experimental social psychology research, especially research conducted in laboratories or in other artificial contexts in which society, culture and history are ignored.

A key problem Gergen raised was reflexivity, a challenge we discussed in Chapter 1. Participants in research studies are *aware* that they are being studied, and are likely to moderate their behaviour precisely because they are conscious of being under the microscope. When a study is aiming to scrutinize the dynamics of a social context, this self-consciousness is necessarily problematic, because it means that the participant's behaviour in the study will simply not be the same as their behaviour in real life. And if their behaviour in a study is not going to reflect their real-life behaviour, then what is the point of conducting such a study?

Behavioural choices made in laboratory experiments cannot be presumed to reflect the choices a person would make outside the laboratory. In real life, decisions about behaviour are intertwined with the social context. They are subject to cultural expectations, role norms and beliefs about human psychology. To further complicate matters, these influencing factors are unstable: they evolve over time and vary from society to society. A laboratory experiment that purports to examine social psychology, but which excludes these broader contextual factors, will inevitably fall short.

Similarly, the more people learn about the results of *previous* psychology research, the more likely they are to adapt their behaviour in future. Communal knowledge about previous studies will contaminate the results of future ones.

For example, people were initially shocked to learn about Milgram's (1963) obedience experiments, which suggested that human beings are liable to follow orders even if it means causing harm to another person. Milgram's studies were conducted in the early 1960s in the United States, and its participants' attitudes to authority figures will have reflected the norms of the society in which they lived. Herein lies the problem. Firstly, it is undoubtedly the case that some societies promote deference to authority more than others. And secondly, even within the same society, social norms about appropriate deference will shift over the decades. Therefore, whether Milgram's experiment would have yielded the same results in other countries, or would do so anywhere today, is very questionable.

But more importantly, Milgram's results were shocking precisely because they conflicted with generally held expectations about human solidarity. Now that we know what it is that Milgram revealed, our expectations have been recalibrated. One of the reasons its results would be different today is precisely because we are aware of what Milgram found in the 1960s. Today's participants would likely choose to behave quite differently, because the society in which *they* live has been influenced by Milgram's findings.

Similarly, Darley and Latané's (1968) research highlighting the problem of bystander apathy – the effect where people are surprisingly unlikely to offer help in an emergency because they believe it is inevitable that someone else will do so – has itself served to shift social attitudes towards helping. The more people learn about the risks of bystander apathy, the *less* apathetic they become; no longer can they feel so confident that someone else will step up. While it is a good thing that participants today will have learned this lesson (either directly or indirectly) from Darley and Latané's research, the fact that they have done so shows how experiments that isolate social behaviours from their wider cultural context can only ever hope to produce a single snapshot in time.

Social behaviour is contingent on attitudes and norms, which are permanently in flux. Therefore, experiments on social behaviour, if considered appropriately, might yield some information about these attitudes and norms, *but only as they stand at the time (and in the place) the study was conducted*. For this reason, Gergen suggested that individuocentric, experimental, laboratory-based social psychology might pass as a credible form of 'social history', but it could not be seen as a reliable or valid science of human interaction.

Gergen was by no means a lone figure of dissent. His widely praised critique cohered with concerns that were being expressed across many subfields of psychology at that time. Researchers were becoming increasingly aware of problems such as demand characteristics, self-fulfilling prophesies, experimenter effects and confirmation bias (e.g. Rosenthal, 1966). Overall, the emergence of these concerns was seen as precipitating a 'crisis of confidence' for many social psychologists, who, according to the American Psychological Association's flagship journal, *American Psychologist*, were losing 'not only their enthusiasm but also their sense of direction and their faith in the discipline's future' (Elms, 1975, p. 967).

Disquiet about the complexity of contextual factors in the social sciences led to widespread discussion, much of it coalescing within its own field of study known as 'critical theory' (Stainton Rogers, 2009). This perspective drew attention to the interconnectedness of events, championing environment and culture not merely as potential research 'variables' for psychologists to measure, but as elements essential to the fabric of psychological experience. Critical theorists noted that some of the most troubling of these interdependencies arose from the role of researchers, and research cliques, in interpreting and defending their own research. The idea that social psychologists could ever be objective commentators on the merit of their own work was, and remains, self-evidently questionable.

As we will discuss in the next two chapters, virtually all of what was argued in the 1970s 'crisis' remains of critical concern for social psychology today, as well as for psychology more broadly. Psychologists have been accused of placing disproportionate emphasis on an extremely limited subset of human experiences, by focusing their research on Western cultures at the expense of the (non-Western) majority world. We will discuss this issue further in Chapter 11.

Meanwhile, a series of recent systematic statistical studies has raised serious questions about the reliability of findings reported in the psychology research literature, particularly in the field of experimental social psychology. Attempts to corroborate previously published results have consistently found a large subset, perhaps a majority, to be non-replicable (Hughes, 2018a). To this extent, psychology's current 'replication crisis' is a modern equivalent of the 1970s crisis in social psychology. Gergen's warnings appear to have been borne out: experiments in social psychology are so contingent on methods as to be idiosyncratic, with the result that their findings may simply not reflect what will happen in other settings or at other times. We will consider the replication crisis further in Chapter 12.

Despite all this, however, the field of North American social psychology remains individuocentric, experimental and conspicuously self-confident. While ostensibly encyclopaedic in scope, the *Handbook* editions that have appeared since the 1970s have contained only fleeting references to the 'crisis in social psychology'. In the 1998 edition, rather than analyse or address any of Gergen's points, Jones (1998) attributed his critique to a 'need for self-flagellation' (p. 48), while Taylor (1998) discussed the 'self-labelled' crisis very briefly, suggesting that 'the advent of social cognition' (her own research specialism) had caused its 'passing' (p. 72). In the most recent edition of the *Handbook*, the history chapter's authors considered this well-documented crisis no longer worthy of mention in the main text, choosing instead to relegate it to a footnote (L. Ross, Lepper & Ward, 2010).

Public domain, via Wikimedia Commons

Image 10.3 Social reality
In the 1970s, many psychologists complained that laboratory studies could never simulate the way human beings interact with each other in the real world.

ALMOST FAMOUS: CLARA MAYO

Clara Mayo (1931–81) was a social psychologist who became an expert in discriminatory prejudices, such as sexism and racism. She was born, as Clara Weiss, in Linz, Austria, and later moved to the United States. After completing her studies in psychology, she worked as a researcher in a hospital in Massachusetts, where she began to study attitudes towards mental illness. Later she became an academic at Boston University, and co-wrote books on non-verbal communication and on social change.

Mayo was recognized by her fellow professionals, and the Society for the Psychological Study of Social Issues (SPSSI) now offers an annual graduate student research award in her honour. However, her research career was cut short in 1981, when she died suddenly at the age of fifty. Her studies of race differences in non-verbal behaviours during conversational interactions were in many ways ahead of their time.

Despite her short career, Mayo employed psychological knowledge to enhance the lives of many people, not only as a teacher, but also as an expert witness, frequently appearing in court to testify on the impact of racial attitudes in shaping juror judgements (LaFrance, 1983).

The sociocentric approach

A key feature of social psychology is its transatlantic divergence. Maintaining a historical continuity with the centuries of philosophical and sociological traditions that preceded it, much of the social psychology studied and taught in Europe incorporates a wide range of sociocentric approaches and theories. It does not seek to limit its coverage to the experiences of individuals, nor – unsurprisingly – does it see itself as 'largely a North American phenomenon'.

Even to a non-specialist, European social psychology can be easily distinguished from its North American counterpart. While the North American version focuses on experimental and statistical research, in Europe there will be much more diversity of research methods. Paradigms such as narrative analysis, hermeneutics, qualitative research and social constructionism are common, as are studies into social representations and topics such as social categories and social identity.

At the root of these distinctions are differences in approach to the concept of 'social'. Many European scholars see the American focus on cognition and behaviour as the 'individualization of the social and the desocialization of the individual' (Graumann, 1986, p. 97). In European social psychology, there is a tradition of considering a much broader range of phenomena, such as mutual influence, collective identification, shared knowledge, social roles, discourse and language (Good, 2000). This focus is on the wider social ecology of human life, rather than on individual experience of society.

The European approach often explicitly embraces human diversity and intersectionality. European social psychology is a key venue for research that takes a feminist approach, or which seeks to challenge prevailing political worldviews. For example, in many countries, especially Western ones, perceptions of what constitutes a 'normally functioning society', as well as beliefs about human relationships, are shaped by many unquestioned assumptions regarding the distribution of social power, the role of women and the implications of difference (including foreignness). For humans to better understand their own social experiences, research and scholarship require the agility to accommodate diverse perspectives. A social psychology that adopts a culture-free stance, or which aims to avoid political challenges, will be greatly disempowered.

A sociocentric approach also enables major social issues of the day to fall naturally within the remit of social psychology. As such, research on major 'social' issues, such as poverty and inequality, discrimination and stigmatization, political extremism, environmentalism or social conflict, is much more common in European than in North American social psychology (although it is by no means absent in North America). In this regard, European social psychology maintains a historical continuity with those scholars (such as Quetelet) who urged social scientists to focus on 'les questions sociale' (Apfelbaum, 1986).

North American social psychologists often try to suggest that these European activities are not really psychology at all, but are offshoots of sociology. Indeed, at the time of writing, on Wikipedia – the crowd-sourced online encyclopaedia that is updated by its readers on an almost daily basis – this divide in social psychology is quite apparent. While the North American version is covered in an entry titled 'Social psychology', there is also an entry titled 'Social psychology (sociology)', in which much of the European work is addressed.

While it is true that a number of academics who describe their work as 'social psychology' are in fact sociologists, it is important to note that perhaps the majority of sociocentric research is conducted by recognized psychologists. For example, all three editors-in-chief of the *European Journal of Social Psychology* – which very much specializes in publishing a diversity of sociocentric and individuocentric research – are members of the psychology departments at their respective universities. Likewise, the *British Journal of Social Psychology*, which takes a similarly inclusive approach, is edited by psychologists and is published by the British Psychological Society.

Much social psychology in Europe is influenced by *symbolic interactionism*, a philosophical approach we encountered in Chapter 8 when discussing the social behaviourist theories of George Herbert Mead. In essence, this approach emphasizes the way human beings observe and interpret each other, and from doing so, construe reality itself. As members of a linguistic species, we rely on social contact in order to gather knowledge. Our social interactions form the basis from which we learn about the world. As a consequence, our ultimate 'understanding' of that world is entirely contingent on whatever interactions we experience. Knowledge itself – of all kinds – is dependent on how people portray existence to themselves and thus to each other.

As all knowledge is threaded in this way through people's perceptions, we can say that all knowledge is 'socially constructed'. This will be true not only for our knowledge about everyday life, but also for all types of formal knowledge, including academic fields like science and history.

But this does not mean that all knowledge is intrinsically unreliable. For example, our knowledge about the field of aerodynamics appears to be very reliable indeed. It enables humans to build 300-tonne aircraft that can successfully complete journeys of thousands of kilometres at a time, with sufficient consistency that millions of people each year confidently entrust this technology with their lives. While scientists' understanding of aerodynamics is socially constructed, part of that construction involves becoming satisfied with what they have learned about the soundness, and evidentiary basis, of information. Likewise, when psychologists take the view that knowledge is socially constructed, they are not arguing that all knowledge is therefore questionable. Their argument is that all knowledge is sourced from a social consensus that emerges from a milieu of perceptions, communications, feedback and aggregated reasoning.

By contrast, restricting social psychology to individuocentric concerns could arguably be said to make it more 'asocial' than social, and therefore more impoverished (Samelson, 2000). Similarly, departing from theoretical or philosophical roots and seeking to reboot the field as a 'new' experimental science only serves to narrow its reach.

It is notable how the divergence has polarized with the passing of time. When Allport first crafted his definition of social psychology, there seemed to be a greater awareness of alternative views. Allport himself qualified his own definition in this respect, noting that not all psychologists would concur with his take (in that there would be some 'exceptions', albeit 'few'). In fact, as Allport saw how social psychology later evolved in North America, he came to share the concerns of those who felt it had become narrow and inward-looking. He somewhat floridly warned against the 'methodolatry' of the experimental approach, complaining that an obsession with technique served to suffocate social psychology's potential for theoretical insight. 'Some current investigations seem to end up in elegantly polished triviality', he lamented, 'snippets of empiricism, but nothing more' (Allport, 1968, p. 68).

THE SOCIAL PSYCHOLOGY OF SOCIAL PSYCHOLOGY

At the beginning of the twentieth century, the term 'social psychology' was used very sporadically, often to refer to studies of sociology, linguistics, arts and culture (as perhaps reflected in Wundt's pursuit of *Völkerpsychologie*). As mentioned, Triplett did not use the term at all. And yet, for many social psychologists, especially those in North America, history has been (re)written such that the term now refers to the activities pursued by Triplett and his ilk, rather than to those scholars, mostly in Europe, who dedicated their life's work to the psychology of social questions.

It was in the period after the Second World War that the divergence between social psychology's two main strands began to harden. As outlined in Chapter 8, the Cold War prompted enormous investment in the university system and wider science infrastructure of the United States, ensuring that whatever form of social psychology took root there would quickly gain significant global clout. The relative prosperity of American business during this period led to strong commercial interest in the psychology of attitude formation, peer influence and communication. And as we outlined in Chapter 8, during this period much of American psychology was concerned with behaviourism, and its associated laboratory-based methodologies.

By the time of the 1970s crisis in social psychology, cognitivism had also become prominent, prompting many psychologists to reflect on the mechanics of individual thinking. Festinger's notion of cognitive dissonance offered an empirically testable model of rationalization, a defence mechanism that psychoanalysts had depicted as rooted in an invisible unconscious (Brehm, 1998). As ostensibly an advance on both behaviourism and psychoanalysis, 'social cognition' became the new fascination for psychology (Fiske & Taylor, 1984), providing social psychologists with a quantitative information-processing paradigm within which to refine their individuocentric methodologies. Those who warned against 'methodolatry' were soon run over by the juggernaut.

The emergence of social psychology as a specialist subfield, with its internal coalitions and transatlantic schism, draws further attention to the circumstantial nature of academic history and the arbitrariness of disciplinary boundaries. The formation of such groups is itself the product of social psychological processes.

Mobilization in Europe

Another important cultural trend that arose following the Second World War was the expectation that social sciences would help promote peace, democracy and international cooperation (Schruijer, 2012). Social psychologists participated in a number of large-scale international collaborative research studies, helping to build a cross-border professional network in Europe. Ironically, many of these studies were funded by the United States government and led by American psychologists (e.g. Schachter et al., 1954). Nonetheless, one of the consequences of these endeavours was the formation, in Europe, of formal membership organizations to support psychologists in pursuing their research across the continent in a coherent way.

The European Association of Experimental Social Psychology was founded in 1966. Notably, its first president, the French psychologist Serge Moscovici (1925–2014), was to become a prominent voice among those warning of the crisis in social psychology. One of Moscovici's own areas of research concerned 'minority influence', the ability of small groups to affect the opinions of larger ones. This contrasted with the common North American interest in 'majority influence', reflected in studies of conformity, groupthink and bystander apathy. The concept of minority influence was possibly also in the minds of those who steered the new European Association in aspiring to establish its own scholarly mission, separate to the dominance of its American peers (Moscovici & Marková, 2006). Chief among its ambitions was to 'establish the continuity between individual and collective phenomena' (Moscovici, 1989, p. 409).

In 2006, the group changed its name to the European Association of Social Psychology. However, with the passing of time, as the association grew, its ambition of connecting the study of individual and collective experience was not straightforwardly successful. A recurring concern among European social psychologists is that the transatlantic divide is now dissolving in an unbalanced way, in that their field is becoming visibly 'Americanized' (Schruijer, 2012). Not only are European social psychologists themselves increasingly turning to individuocentric experimental research approaches, but their journals and conferences are attracting similar research from US-based researchers in ever increasing numbers. The *European Journal of Social Psychology* originally accepted manuscripts written in English, French or German, and provided summaries in Russian; today it publishes only in English.

European social psychology is not the only subject area within psychology, or within academia more generally, to be said to have become 'Americanized'. We will examine the issue of academic dependency on United States norms, and its implications for psychology as a whole, in Chapter 11.

Endemic disunity

It is perhaps unsurprising that social psychologists have often pondered the group dynamics that have led their own field to become so tribalistic. The two major factions in social psychology exhibit all the standard features of social groups, including stable social structures, the inclination to self-identify as a group, feelings that there are benefits to group membership, frequent in-group communication, and a sense of shared fate among group members. The difference in size between North American and European social psychology introduces the challenging mechanics of majority–minority relations. Relatively restricted contact and largely one-way communication help to generate and to preserve misconceptions, stereotypes and in-group favouritism. And in addition to spontaneous features of the social ecology, there is also the practical issue of rivalry for resources, itself a factor that promotes suspicion and prejudice at institutional levels (Good, 2000).

Such endemic disunity is often seen in science and scholarship more generally, with the increasing practice of identifying clusters that comprise independent specialized research interests. When researchers have examined the way professional scientists refer to each other's work, they have found that there are at least 150 different areas of academia that consider themselves to be freestanding fields of science (Leydesdorff & Rafols, 2009). While the boundaries between scientific disciplines can be fuzzy, each group takes its academic independence very seriously.

Such groupings are, in many senses, socially constructed. While nominally ring-fencing a discrete area of knowledge, the formal recognition of an academic 'discipline' produces many effects that are far from neutral. Such groups confer 'legitimacy' on practitioners by setting standards for group membership, based on 'proper' education, and by prescribing norms for engaging in 'proper' work (Shumway & Messer-Davidow, 1991). Establishing a group identity generates incentives for those who can say they belong to the group, and protects their position in the longer term. Such academic 'boundary work' is not always determined by neutral logic (Gieryn, 1995).

The concept of an academic 'discipline' is often used to refer to a cluster of focused scholarly practices that pertain to individual topics of study. On occasion, scholarly work will extend beyond a single discipline, and become *cross-disciplinary* (involving practitioners from different disciplines), *interdisciplinary* (involving methods from different disciplines) or *trans-disciplinary* (involving concepts from different disciplines; Good, 1993). However, even when such blending occurs, it often seems as though the work remains rooted in one discipline more than in the other (J. T. Klein, 1990). Even then, such collaborative efforts, while frequently encouraged by academic authorities, are in many cases seen to be of lesser professional value. The group dynamics that govern the behaviour of academics and researchers often end up trumping efforts to straddle disciplinary boundaries.

The psychological study of social experience has yielded many insights, only some of which emanate directly from its research outputs. Its own history as a field of study also serves as a source of erudition. It helps to highlight how the boundaries of knowledge are ultimately determined by pragmatic self-interest and a shared history among practitioners (Good, 2000), rather than by a clearly definable essence that can be discerned from a subject area itself. In so doing, it draws attention to the perennial fallibility of psychology, the elusiveness of its neutrality, and the difficulty humanity has had in assembling a truly objective understanding of how people think, feel or behave.

WHERE TO FROM HERE?

The study of social experience helps to highlight the many debates and dilemmas that arise when trying to produce knowledge about human psychology. The exploration of unconscious instinct, of observable behaviour, of cognitive processes and of social relationships and identities is itself immersed in social context.

Every observer, scholar, scientist and psychologist has their own unique perspective, driven in part by transferable knowledge that is produced and promulgated in a social world. How we end up describing one another, how we account for each other's behaviour, will be influenced by whatever limitations apply to these channels. In many ways, modern psychology reflects a selective view of humanity. It is to this challenge, of gauging psychology's perspective, that we now turn.

DISCUSSION QUESTIONS

1. How do modern crowds differ from crowds that gathered in previous eras of history?
2. Apart from individuocentric and sociocentric approaches, are there any other formats for considering social experience?
3. Was the 'crisis in social psychology' ever resolved?
4. Why did the different approaches to social psychology emerge in their particular geographic regions?

RECOMMENDED READING

- **Gergen, K. J. (1973). Social psychology as history.** *Journal of Personality and Social Psychology*, *26*, **309–20.** In this essay, Gergen argues that social psychology can only be successful by reflecting contemporary experience at any given time, and that the use of scientific research will therefore always fall short.
- **Manning, R., Levine, M., & Collins, A. (2007). The Kitty Genovese murder and the social psychology of helping: The parable of the 38 witnesses.** *American Psychologist*, *62*, **555–62.** In this article, the authors question the validity of claims commonly made about the murder of Kitty Genovese, ironically highlighting the distorted way in which vivid events can come to be perceived socially.
- **Marková, I. (2012). 'Americanization' of European social psychology.** *History of the Human Sciences*, *25*, **108–16.** In this essay, the author questions the claim that European social psychology has become 'Americanized', suggesting instead that social psychology as a whole may, as with many academic fields, have become 'globalized'.

Part IV

FUTURE:
LIMITATIONS AND LEGACY

PERSPECTIVES, DIVERSITY AND THE CONCEPT OF *BIAS*

11

In this chapter, we will …

- reflect on the nature of perspective as it applies to our appreciation of human thoughts, feelings and behaviour
- evaluate the way psychology selects its subject matter and its implications for knowledge generalizability
- examine how gender bias manifests in psychology
- consider whether psychology's depiction of the human experience is truly inclusive
- identify the geographical narrowness of psychology's knowledge base, its research concerns and its knowledge-production infrastructure

---

At the outset

As will have become clear from previous chapters, our knowledge about the psychology of human beings has been accumulated sporadically, if steadily, across the centuries, at times arising differently in different places. The quality of this knowledge will inevitably reflect the quality of how it has been produced. There are many reasons to be cautious about how knowledge is produced in psychology.

Psychologists continue to debate what exactly it is they should be studying. What we see as the core subject matter of psychology shapes how we go about doing our research. Many psychologists appear to have concluded that the true subject matter of psychology is that which can be studied using quantitative or experimental methods. Others argue that psychology's subject matter is at least partly something else, and requires a different research approach.

One consequence of psychology's methodologies is that psychologists often only study certain things. This can be said to reflect an undue narrowness of scope. Many of psychology's research approaches might also underestimate, or even overlook, the diversity inherent in the human race.

A significant concern about the way psychological knowledge has been accumulated is that it is biased with regard to gender. Many older theories and conclusions were framed by worldviews that were deeply misogynistic. Claims about gender differences appear to be greatly overstated, reflecting obsolete stereotypes. For most of its academic history, women psychologists have been marginalized. And many theories in psychology have been criticized for appearing to focus primarily on the male experience.

Another problematic bias relates to geography. Most research in psychology has been conducted in the Western world. This means that its samples of human behaviour represent a small selection of global cultures. It also means that the topics that have attracted most research attention are those that are important to Western populations. While psychologists are often now aware of this problem, the wider infrastructure of science, research and academia remains heavily Westernized, even in non-Western countries. Psychology is of great interest around the world, but the concerns of psychology as it exists in the United States exert a hugely disproportionate influence on its research agendas and outputs.

Key concept: Bias

Bias refers to the inclination to favour something or someone unfairly. It can result from discriminatory prejudice, disproportionate interest or systematic error. Some examples of bias reflect a wilful rejection of alternative points of view, others stem from a wish to focus attention on a preferred topic, while still others occur when information is filtered using a process that causes it to become distorted.

It is helpful to know whether bias has been caused deliberately or inadvertently, but such knowledge has little bearing on its ultimate consequences. When information is biased, it becomes misleading, whether the bias was intentional or not. For example, many conclusions in psychology are based on non-representative samples, and so generate false assumptions about how people *in general* think, feel or behave.

Bias can be individual or collective. This means that an individual observer can see the world in a skewed fashion, or a group of people can share and discuss information that becomes systematically misrepresented. As a result, biases can often go undetected. A concern in psychology, and in scholarship more generally, is that much of what we think we know might be skewed by an unintentional narrowness of perspective. Scientific biases can also arise from prejudicial assumptions that have become normative, or which are falsely seen as factual rather than arbitrary.

DEPENDING ON YOUR POINT OF VIEW

As will have become clear from previous chapters, efforts to explain the psychology of human beings have taken many different forms over the centuries. Contemporary academic (or university) psychology incorporates a mixture of biological, behavioural and cognitive worldviews, strands relating to the unconscious and the social, and a focus on measurement, classification and quantitative analysis. But all these themes extend far beyond formal scholarship. They influence – and, most importantly, *are influenced by* – broader cultural views, experiences and assumptions.

Our impressions of the ins and outs of human nature guide the very lives we lead, find expression in arts and folklore, impact upon political debate and citizenship, and shape our interpersonal relationships and participation in society. One of our species' key defining features is our craving for self-awareness, our endless curiosity to learn more and more about the habits of humanity, whether from science, seance or superstition.

Psychology has a very wide brief. The range of topics that we consider to be 'psychological' is truly enormous, encompassing thoughts, feelings, behaviours, temperaments, aptitudes, attitudes, identities, relationships, communication, motivation, well-being, mental states, intellectual development, personal growth and brain chemistry, to give just a few examples. As with many fields of enquiry, our journey to enlightenment may never end. The more we look into psychology, the more we discover is there.

Psychology's subject matter keeps evolving, as it has always done. We saw in Chapter 1 that psychology has long been described as the study of (or, more literally, the discussion of) the 'psyche' (or ψυχή). That definition works well, so long as we accept that no society has ever agreed on what the psyche actually is. Translating ψυχή as the Greek for 'soul' gets us only so far, as the vernacular origins of this term are long forgotten. Few modern readers (or historians) could be expected to comprehend the nuances, connotations and cultural cross-references inevitably infused in this fragment of ancient Athenian vocabulary. We cannot outsource this task to the ancient Greeks. We must decide for ourselves.

Ultimately, therefore, our perspective determines everything.

Psychology's 'object of study'

Deciding what constitutes the human psyche is not just a metaphysical challenge. It has practical implications too, not least for the field of study that claims the psyche as its core subject matter. Our answer to the question 'What is psyche?' informs not only our view of the mind. It also, by extension, helps us to determine what *psych*ology actually is. It sets the agenda for the field. It defines for us psychology's appropriate remit, its 'object of study'.

To use the language of philosophy, we can say that our answer will help to define psychology's *ontology*. Ontology is the branch of philosophy that concerns the nature of being, existence and reality. Ontological discussion addresses the very question of what exactly *are* the concepts and categories that comprise a particular domain.

It is helpful to bear in mind that virtually all subject areas grapple with ontological issues of some kind. For example, both physics and chemistry can be said to be concerned with the subject matter of fields such as nanoscience. While ostensibly different sciences, their ontologies occasionally overlap.

As we saw in Chapter 2, for long periods of our history, psychological events were seen as constituting their own type of physics. The entire universe was believed to tick along as an integrated machine, operating as if by clockwork, with human minds subject to the same mechanical principles. Later generations successively recast the model to reflect new technologies as they emerged, invoking the physics of telegraphics, radio and then computers. Even the way biologists discuss the connectedness of humans to animals suggests a paradigm of physiological machinery. Human bodies and brains are depicted as comprising interlocking functional components, assembled according to a formal design (or to some other blueprint, such as genetics), all of which can literally be tinkered with, using psychosurgery or chemicals, in order to 'repair' faults in behaviour.

The framework of human-as-machine has many implications. It depicts people as being tossed about by mechanical forces, their lives comprising their assembled reactions to endless causal stimuli, occupying a natural universe in which they lack agency, will or the ability to engage in true experience. The mechanical worldview allows psychology to put people under the metaphorical microscope of science, isolated from the noisy nuisance variables of normal life.

Ontology matters because from ontology comes method. How we 'do' psychology depends on the thing we think we are 'doing' it to. We administer psychometric questionnaires because we believe psychological qualities can be quantified. We conduct laboratory experiments because we believe human nature can be illuminated by comparing people under different controlled conditions. We observe behaviour and document case studies because we believe that people exist within an environment of stimuli to which they reflexively react. We discuss psychology as a science of variables because we believe the human experience can be partialled out into discrete, observable fragments.

However, while the majority of mainstream psychology adopts these stances, it is worth noting that, ultimately, ontology is a matter of judgement, opinion and choice. For example, in Chapter 10 we saw how social psychologists can sometimes take very different views on their 'object of study'. Individuocentric social psychologists will target the individual's experience in the social ecosystem, but sociocentric social psychologists will focus on the social ecosystem itself. The sociocentric perspective sees human life as a complex of interacting and interwoven influences, making its 'object of study' difficult to discuss in concise *stimulus–response* or *cause-and-effect* terms. And so ontology shapes method: instead of the laboratory experiments favoured in cognitive or behavioural research, these social psychologists will often employ research techniques commonly seen in sociology, anthropology and other social sciences.

In Chapter 4, we discussed how the notion of 'abnormal' behaviour is often socially constructed. Many definitions of mental illness reflect a power imbalance between the mainstream majority population and those individuals who, by contrast, do not 'fit in' with prevailing social norms in a given time or place. Much of our modern asylum infrastructure is a remnant of older state policies aimed at warehousing the socially undesirable. These concerns about the role of power in mental health practice extend to the influence of the pharmaceutical and medical insurance industries. Questions have been raised about conditions such as childhood bipolar disorder, which critics say was formalized as a diagnosis mainly because of lobbying by industries wishing to expand their market for drugs and services (Parry & Levin, 2012). In raising these matters, critics of modern psychiatry and clinical psychology challenge the core ontology represented by the medical model of mental health.

Such controversies highlight the way in which ontological choices can undermine the validity of knowledge by limiting insight. When we adopt the perspective that non-conforming behaviour is, *by definition*, mental illness, we become less able to even *think* about the nature of conformity itself, or to consider the possibility that some psychiatric diagnoses reveal more about our attitude to social norms than they do about our mental health and well-being.

An unwillingness to see matters from different perspectives makes us less able to see matters *for what they are*. According to many critics of psychology, the key problem is that most psychologists are oblivious to the fact that perspectives other than their own even exist. They are unaware that their traditional approach is arbitrary, and that arbitrariness is a form of bias. Therefore, not only does ontology affect choice of method and the validity of psychological knowledge, it also affects the ethics of being a psychologist.

If psychology's perspective is too narrow, then it is likely to be skewed. Its systems and practices will reflect the interests of those who already enjoy the privilege of being able to determine the status quo. As we will see below, mainstream psychology has been accused of reflecting several different types of such biases. Its theories of the human mind have been criticized for attaching undue weight to a limited number of already powerful groups. Psychology stands accused of being laden with a masculinist bias, in which its theories are overly grounded in the experiences of men. It has also been challenged because of its bias towards Western culture, and because the lineage of its subject matter can often be traced back to ideas that are arcane, colonialist and politically partisan. We will discuss all of these critiques later in this chapter.

Psychology's narrowness of context

One of the consequences of psychology's mechanistic tradition is the practice of separating people's experiences from their natural environmental contexts. This is often pursued for methodological reasons, on the basis that it is more effective to use research to home in on details of experience than to try to account for the mass complexity of life. The purpose of laboratory experiments – whether behaviourist, cognitivist or social-psychological – is to extract specific facets of psychological interest and to refine their details through observation. This is part of putting people under the metaphorical microscope. Microscopes are designed to view small details, not whole pictures.

When psychologists study poverty or social deprivation, they usually focus on the mental impact of poverty, or its correlates, or those traits that confer resilience, or the risk factors that link people to vulnerability. In other words, psychologists will focus on that which can be quantified and that which can be generalized from person to person (or, indeed, as they might believe, from country to country). A question their research will seldom ask is: Why exactly are these people poor? (Teo, 2009).

Causes of poverty are often assumed to be economic, but that assumption is itself an attitudinal habit. Psychology – as the science that claims to be interested in examining the nature of attitudes – should have a central role in explaining how the financially secure so readily rationalize the poverty of other people. Structural poverty is maintained as much by behaviours and attitudes as by anything measured in economic indicators. A true understanding of the psychology of poverty would ideally take account of the reasons why poverty exists. However, in focusing on generalizable details of the poverty experience, psychology bypasses such sociohistorical analyses. It invests its effort in describing the *psychological experiences of poor people* but has little or nothing to say about the *psychological drivers of poverty*.

For millennia, human beings have been curious about the causes of each other's thoughts, feelings and behaviours. However, it is unclear whether the modern academic discipline of psychology addresses this curiosity in a truly comprehensive way. Rather, despite its ethos of scientific objectivity – or maybe *because* of this ethos – psychology has evolved a set of practices that places intrinsic limits on its perspective. Like all forms of evolution, this process of selection has been non-random. It is a matter of logic that the particular perspectives that are chosen, reinforced and guarded in modern psychology reflect a functional status quo that those benefiting from its peculiarities will be keenest to preserve.

Psychology's presumption of generalizability

Another challenging feature of psychology's standard method (and thus a consequence of its standard ontology) is its tendency to extrapolate from person to person. In the main, psychology research is conducted on samples. The larger (and more homogeneous) the sample, the better. By inviting a sample of participants to undergo the same controlled experimental procedure again and again, the psychological researcher can derive a pattern of outcomes that best represents the 'typical' person – or, at least, a pattern of outcomes that represents what the 'typical' person might do if asked to engage in that particular controlled experimental procedure. Psychology is a science of individual experience, but its ontology presumes that experience recurs from individual to individual. In essence, therefore, psychology infers the individual from the general.

In epistemology, the construction of knowledge in terms of a finite number of explanatory laws is known as the *nomothetic* approach. The alternative is the *idiographic* approach, which is often used in the social sciences and humanities. The idiographic approach considers a person's own experiences as being unique in all important respects. Scholars attempt to derive insights from people's subjective perspectives on their experiences, rather than by conducting experimental investigations on samples of individuals who are presumed to represent what is 'typical'.

Mainstream psychology's focus on generalization represents the nomothetic approach. It is an extension of the traditional scientific method. The ability to detect, and then to demonstrate, universally applicable principles is essential to the study of nature. Physicists, for example, rely on theories of gravity that can be applied in (almost) all circumstances to explain the motion of objects. Similarly, a competently conducted chemistry experiment will produce identical results in all laboratories. It is perfectly reasonable of psychologists to wish that their findings be similarly transferable. That is to say, it is fair that they want their explanations of human behaviour to be relevant *to humans in general.*

The problem is that focusing on details that generalize from person to person comes with a cost. It leads many psychologists to exaggerate the commonality of human beings and to overlook – if not devalue – the singularity of individual life histories. They end up emphasizing what is uniform and underplaying what is unique.

Psychology's approach to individual differences

Not all psychologists ignore the individual variability inherent in human nature. For example, as we saw in Chapter 5, many psychologists focus on the task of measuring and classifying human attributes. The very point of the psychometric approach is that all people are *not* the same. The psychology of mental illness, as we discussed in Chapter 4, is also premised on the notion that the panoply of human experience ranges widely, albeit anchored by fixed 'norms' of behaviour.

In a related vein, a number of psychologists have offered formal theories of personality and temperament. These ideas also presume that human character varies. But even personality theories can blur the notions of uniqueness and uniformity. For example, many such theories point to key differences between introverts and extraverts. However, these divergences are themselves intended to be generalizable. Introverts are different from extraverts, but more importantly, *they are similar to each other.* Their person-level variability is secondary to group-level consistency. Albeit individuals, introverts are (somewhat) *all the same.*

The psychoanalytic account of human nature, which we discussed in Chapter 7, remains one of the most culturally influential theories of personality ever to have been developed. To many non-psychologists, the Freudian model represents the standard public conception of what all psychology should involve: an elaborate account of human instinct derived by therapists and based on interactions with clinical clients. Freud's development of psychoanalysis relied almost entirely on this idiographic approach, drawing from the personal testimonies of his patients over a period of four decades. Even then, his theory was one of psychological continuity across persons: Freud presented concepts that were intended to describe people in general, not just those who came to him for therapy.

Later theories of personality were largely based on variations of Freud's subjectivist reasoning, or else on hostile reactions against it (Sloan, 2009). Perhaps the most extreme extension of subjectivism was represented by the *phenomenological* theories of personality. The phenomenological approach was introduced to philosophy by the German philosopher Edmund Husserl (1859–1938). It was later elaborated upon by Maurice Merleau-Ponty, the French critic of behaviourism we encountered in Chapter 8. Merleau-Ponty had condemned behaviourism for succumbing to an illusion of objectivity. According to phenomenology, the uniqueness of each person's own perspective on the world made objectivity of any kind impossible. When applied to the question of personality, the phenomenologists argued that human individuality was ever varying, and thus permanently beyond scientific scrutiny of any kind. In fact, as phenomenology held all claims of objective knowability to be false, it considered *all* conventional science to be untrustworthy.

Ironically, one of the main criticisms of phenomenology is that it relies on people's ability to provide neutral interpretations of their own experiences. In other words, it relies on people's ability to remain objective in the face of social influence. In reality, as we described in Chapter 1, human beings are naturally gregarious and extremely responsive to social cues. When humans describe their personal perspectives, they use language to do so, and thus their descriptions draw on a socially shared vocabulary and a consensually agreed lexicon of explanatory concepts. In other words, the phenomenological experience is never uniquely personal.

The dilemma that people are required to use public frames of reference to describe personal mental experiences was originally discussed by the Austrian-British philosopher Ludwig Wittgenstein (1889–1951). Wittgenstein (1953) argued against the possibility of a '*privatsprache*' – or 'private language' – a language that, hypothetically, is comprehensible to just a single person. In reality, all languages assume that audiences *already understand* whatever is being described, because they already possess the vocabulary needed to comprehend it. The communal nature of language raises doubts about whether it would be possible for any individual to ever communicate an experience or sensation that was *truly novel*, an experience or sensation that nobody else had ever encountered.

In this sense, the social origin of language appears to make *subjectivity* genuinely elusive. Accordingly, human personalities can never be presumed to be truly singular, nor should they be seen as objectively unknowable.

Despite their problematic nature, phenomenological principles were later incorporated into the *humanistic* theory of personality, originally proposed by American psychologist Abraham Maslow

(1908–70) and extended by another American theorist, the therapist Carl Rogers (1902–87). Humanistic psychology also drew on existentialism, a philosophical approach that emphasizes the lived experience of individuals as fundamentally separated from the world around them. Consistent with their championing of idiography, the humanistic psychologists considered all people's personal testimonies to represent equally valid accounts of reality. They extended this thinking to develop a form of psychotherapy that promoted the non-judgemental acceptance of all views, and the provision of unconditional positive regard to all persons.

Nonetheless, humanism recommended a somewhat generic model of human personality, arguing that *all* people are motivated to fulfil their personal potential after having satisfied lower-order needs (Maslow, 1954). This idea that people's motivations conform to a predictable structure would appear to contradict the claim that, psychologically, they were endlessly unique. Perhaps ironically, it was later research based on conventional *scientific* methodologies that revealed this hierarchy-of-needs idea to be severely flawed. Its main shortcoming was that it presented an overly generic one-size-fits-all template for personality that failed to accommodate the true variability that exists in the human population. Despite its ambition to recognize the multiplicity of human perspectives, the theory was especially poor at anticipating cross-cultural differences in attitude to personal need.

Some psychological theories of personality have eschewed subjectivism and focused instead on a more nomothetic approach to knowledge development. The principles of behaviourism, cognitivism and social learning, for example, have each been employed to craft theoretical models of personality differences and development. Psychometricians have produced a small number of quantitative trait models, essentially modern manifestations of the character typologies discussed by ancient Roman philosophers such as Galen (Stelmack & Stalikas, 1991; see also Chapter 2). But

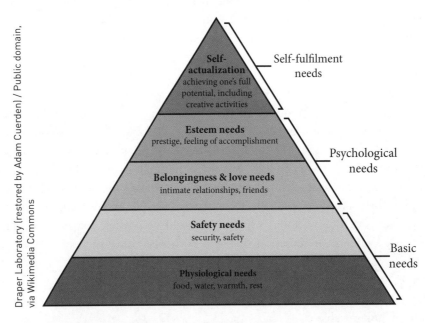

Figure 11.1 A universal hierarchy of needs?
Maslow (1954) proposed a humanistic theory of human needs that later proved to be overly generic.

overall, what is striking about theories of personality is their relatively restricted scope. All such models tend to focus on common themes, such as whether personality is fixed or adjustable, or whether traits are inherited (i.e. nature) or learned (i.e. nurture). Textbooks on personality are typically centred on the works of just a dozen or so major theorists (Sloan, 2009).

Ultimately, all theories of personality provide for a type of human diversity that is constrained within boundaries. They explain the way people vary, but only according to finite frameworks of variability. It is important to remember that while appearing to address the issue of individual perspectives in psychology, all such frameworks are themselves derived from research that is contingent on the particular ontologies, and methods, that have come to dominate modern psychological scholarship. Their vision will only be as broad as the standard perspectives – cultural, gendered, social, political and philosophical – within which psychology as a whole happens to operate.

HISTORICALLY (IN)ACCURATE?: DIFFERENT LANGUAGE, DIFFERENT WORLD

The Austrian-British philosopher Ludwig Wittgenstein argued against the possibility of so-called private languages, or languages that are comprehensible to just a single person. The argument is covered extensively in his posthumously published book *Philosophische Untersuchungen* (*Philosophical Investigations*) (Wittgenstein, 1953). Despite the fact that Wittgenstein published few works during his own lifetime, his posthumous book saw him become acclaimed as one of the most important philosophers of the twentieth century.

Given this reputation, it is no surprise that there is great interest in Wittgenstein's ideas. His thoughts are frequently quoted, and very often the following quote is presented as a summary of his private-language argument: 'If we spoke a different language, we would perceive a somewhat different world' (see R. A. Harris, 2005, p. 35). However, while this quote has been published widely, it does not, in fact, reflect Wittgenstein's

own words. The segment is drawn from a much older book describing experiments in psychology (Crafts et al., 1938).

It appears the quote was erroneously attributed to Wittgenstein after appearing in a 1958 book by the American philosopher of science Norwood Russell Hanson (1924–67) (Hanson, 1958). Hanson presented the psychology quote immediately after an entirely different excerpt from Wittgenstein's work. It seems that a later reader must have mistakenly inferred that both statements on the page were Wittgenstein's. On that basis, the misattributed quote entered circulation, after which it continued to be cited as such (R. A. Harris, 2005).

Wittgenstein was famed for his explorations of how human understanding is relayed in words from one person's mind to another. It is perhaps therefore ironic that words from somebody else's mind should be so widely acclaimed as representing *his* profound thoughts.

PSYCHOLOGY'S GENDER BIAS

For millennia, in just about every society ever to have emerged, erudite people assumed that men were dominant over women – politically, intellectually, culturally, economically and physically. Patriarchal pre-eminence was the norm throughout most of history. Around the world, conventions such as *coverture* decreed that a woman's legal rights were subsumed into those of her husband. As far as civic practices were concerned, women were essentially *owned* by men (Hughes, 2016). Only men could acquire property, sign contracts, pursue education of their own choosing or keep their own salaries. Even the ancient ethicists who first proposed the introduction of democracy, those champions of the moral rights of citizens to choose their governing legislators, never for a moment thought that *women* should be allowed to participate.

But gender discrimination is never just political or legal. For example, human societies have historically tolerated, if not promoted, casual violence against women. A long list of gender-specific aggressions have been normalized in cultures around the world, including genital mutilation, foot binding, honour killings, marriage by abduction, force-feeding and breast ironing (G. Campbell, Roberts & Sarkaria, 2020). The demonization of women as deviants, as in the practice of witch trials (see Chapter 3) or the incarceration of women in asylums for activities such as 'fornication' (see Chapter 4), represents another disturbing theme. Female infanticide, sex-selective abortion and gender-based child abandonment has been so extensive throughout the centuries as to be discernible from the demographics of contemporary societies (Michael et al., 2013).

When students learn about human history today – the various civilizations, upheavals, wars, transformations, inventions and waves of political change – rarely are they reminded that virtually all events took place in societies in which women were considered second-class citizens. It is little wonder that the traditional history books are full of 'Great Men' narratives. For virtually all of the periods covered, effectively half the population occupied a social grade below that required to be identified for posterity by name.

This is important to bear in mind when reflecting on the emergence of psychological knowledge, social attitudes to behaviour, and behavioural science over the centuries. Consider, for example, the attitudes of some of the most prominent scholars, scientists, and psychologists of their day:

- **1871:** 'The chief distinction in the intellectual powers of the two sexes is shewn by man attaining to a higher eminence, in whatever he takes up, than woman can attain – whether requiring deep thought, reason, or imagination, or merely the use of his senses and hands … Thus man has ultimately become superior to woman.' – Charles Darwin, in *The Descent of Man* (1871, p. 564; see Chapter 5).
- **1886:** 'When a woman has scholarly inclinations there is usually something wrong with her sexuality. Sterility itself disposes one towards a certain masculinity of taste.' ('Wenn ein Weib gelehrte Neigungen hat, so ist gewöhnlich Etwas an ihrer Geschlechtlichkeit nicht in Ordnung. Schon Unfruchtbarkeit disponirt zu einer gewissen Männlichkeit des Geschmacks.') – Friedrich Nietzsche (1886, p. 105), acclaimed German cultural philosopher, who we encountered in Chapter 7.
- **1901:** 'All progress is due to man. Therefore the woman is like a dead weight on him, she prevents much restlessness and meddlesome inquisitiveness, but she also restrains him from noble actions, for she is unable to distinguish good from evil … If a woman was not physically and mentally weak, if she was not as a rule rendered harmless by circumstances, she would be extremely dangerous.' – Paul Julius Möbius (1853–1907), German neurologist and psychiatric pioneer (Möbius, 1901, pp. 629–30).
- **1913:** 'It seems clear that a woman's usefulness, her value to society, and therefore her power and her happiness depend, not on her likeness to but on her dissimilarity from man. By

training her recessive male qualities she can never attain to more than a secondary position in the social body.' – Walter Heape (1855–1929), leading British embryologist (Heape, 1913, p. 213).

- **1914:** 'Women in general are thus by original nature submissive to men in general. Submissive behavior is apparently not annoying when assumed as the instinctive response to its natural stimulus. Indeed, it is perhaps a common satisfier.' – Edward Thorndike (1914, p. 34), American psychologist whose stimulus–response theory inspired Watson to develop behaviourism (see Chapter 8).

- **1923:** 'A certain physical weakness and delicacy (probably moral also) about the normal young woman or girl constitute in her resemblance to a child.' – William McDougall (1923, p. 425), British-born social psychologist we encountered in Chapter 6 and Chapter 10.

- **1964:** 'a woman's identity formation [differs] by dint of the fact that her somatic design harbors an "inner space" destined to bear the offspring of chosen men and, with it, a biological, psychological, and ethical commitment to take care of human infancy.' – Erik Erikson (1964, p. 586), renowned German-American psychoanalyst, who we encountered in Chapter 7.

- **1964:** 'Anatomy decrees the life of a woman ... when women grow up without dread of their biological functions and without subversion by feminist doctrine ... we shall attain the goal of a good life and a secure world.' – Joseph Rheingold (1903–78), psychiatrist and author of *The Fear of Being a Woman* (1964, p. 216).

- **1965**: 'We must start with the realization that, as much as women want to be good scientists or engineers, they want first and foremost to be womanly companions of men, and to be mothers.' – Bruno Bettelheim (1903–90), Austrian-born psychology professor at the University of Chicago, who we encountered in Chapter 7, regarded by his contemporaries as a leading specialist on emotional disturbance in children (Bettelheim, 1965, p. 15).

It should immediately be obvious that such statements contrast sharply with what would be considered acceptable today. That they are so jarring to modern ears can make it tempting to conclude that they are of historical interest only, and have no current applicability. We recognize them as products of the past and thus assume that they *belong to* the past, believing them to be now outdated, if not extinct. Our awareness of modern equality laws and universal suffrage tempts us into thinking that such vintage attitudes can no longer exist. We study them as artefacts of social history, lest we repeat it.

However, it is difficult to believe that science, or more specifically psychology, could withstand centuries of societal bias and emerge somehow untainted. The professional and cultural institutions within which science takes place have been shaped by patriarchal forces for most of their histories, and much of the accumulated corpus of organized knowledge has been filtered through a misogynistic lens, with generations of scientists seeing femininity as alien and inferior. The question should not be *whether* today's psychology betrays traces of such historical societal sexism. Rather we should ask: *How* does societal sexism manifest itself in today's psychology?

Gender-specific psychologies

Modern audiences are as curious as ever about the distinct psychologies of women and men. Purported contrasts in women and men's thoughts, feelings and behaviours continue to provide a near-endless stream of content in both the popular and technical press. Several mass-market books have become global bestsellers, including such classics of the genre as *You Just Don't Understand: Women and Men in Conversation* (Tannen, 1990), *Men Are from Mars, Women Are from Venus* (Gray, 1992), *Why Men Lie and Women Cry* (Pease & Pease, 2002) and *Act Like a Lady, Think Like a Man* (Harvey, 2012). However, the discussion of sex differences is not confined to the pages of pop psychology literature.

Academic psychology regularly reports studies of gender-specific behaviours, occasionally presenting overarching theories of the psychological distinctions between women and men. For example, researchers at Cambridge University have developed an extensive neurological theory of how cognition occurs differently in men than in women. As encapsulated in the high-profile book, *The Essential Difference: Men, Women, and the Extreme Male Brain* (Baron-Cohen, 2004), the theory posits that men's brains are better equipped for analysing, exploring and constructing complex systems. This adeptness for 'systemizing' is said not only to explain cognitive differences between men and women, but according to the researchers it also accounts for patterns of symptoms in autism, on the basis that people with autism are hypothesized to have overly 'male' brains. These claims have proved controversial, and have attracted substantial scientific criticism. For example, the theory appears to rely heavily on correlational data, on vaguely defined terms and on poorly controlled experiments (Fine, 2017).

In another model of globalized gender psychology, the American social psychologist Shelley Taylor (who we encountered in Chapter 10) has proposed that women and men exhibit distinctive physiological responses to mental stress. Taylor argues that the long-standing *fight-or-flight* model (Cannon, 1932), which suggests that stress causes the engagement of biological systems that facilitate speed and aggression, is based only on the *male* stress response, and does not reflect how women deal with stressful experiences. Taylor posits that stress elicits different biochemical responses in women, including a larger profusion of the protein hormone oxytocin. Such biochemicals underpin a pattern of behaviour that Taylor characterizes as *tend-and-befriend* (Taylor et al., 2000). In other words, women's stress responses lead them to react to stress by looking after those in need and by seeking to work with others, rather than by fighting or fleeing. Researchers in biology and anthropology have largely dismissed Taylor's theory, arguing that it is not consistent with the available empirical data (Geary & Flinn, 2002).

Other provocative research focuses less on contrasting the genders but instead highlights the psychological issues that are said to uniquely arise in women. In one particularly prominent study, researchers proposed that hormonal fluctuations lead women to select differently coloured clothes at various points of their menstrual cycles. Specifically, the researchers claimed that women wear red when they are physically most likely to be fertile (Beall & Tracy, 2013). Despite appearing in an academically prestigious research journal, this study relied on an extremely small sample of women, and its measurement of key variables, such as clothes choice, was conspicuously unreliable

(Hughes, 2018a). Nonetheless, it is telling that the reported finding continues to be widely cited, especially in the popular media.

Hysteria and health

Historically embedded claims about gender-specific psychological distinctiveness can have significant consequences for human welfare, especially where they affect clinical practice in healthcare. A long-running controversy in medicine has concerned its tendency to attribute psychological causes to illnesses that primarily affect women. As we saw in Chapter 7, Freud placed the concept of hysteria – the reporting, mainly by women, of physical symptoms in the absence of physiological pathology – at the centre of his psychoanalytic theory. Despite the fact that Freud (or other physicians) had little evidence to support his beliefs about hysteria, the idea that women were especially prone to psychogenic illness proved enduring.

Later clinical definitions formally repackaged hysteria as *somatoform disorder* and related conditions, including *psychogenic non-epileptic seizure*, or PNES. The formal DSM-5 description for PNES states that symptoms will be more common in women than in men (Asadi-Pooya & Sperling, 2015). However, while there is clear evidence that physicians are more likely to diagnose psychogenic symptoms when their patient is a woman, there is no evidence to confirm that this pattern of inference is medically sound (O'Leary, 2018). This is mainly because diagnosing a psychogenic symptom is akin to proving a negative. Such diagnoses are not based on positive evidence, but on an apparent *lack* of evidence of biomedical dysfunction.

The problem with this is that such evidence can be lacking for many reasons, including the fact that physicians frequently choose not to look for it. Many studies have shown that doctors often recommend different medical tests for their male and female patients, and are more likely to take male patients' symptoms more seriously. For example, when women and men report chest pain to their doctors, there is an equal likelihood that their pain is caused by cardiovascular disease; however, doctors are more than twice as likely to refer the men to a cardiologist (Liaudat et al., 2018). In other words, doctors are far more likely to consider the women's pain to be innocuous, and to send them away without appropriate medical attention.

Many prevalent illnesses generate severe symptoms that have initially confounded, or misled, medical scientists. Before scientists identified the bacterium *Helicobacter pylori*, clinicians commonly believed that stomach ulcers were caused by mental stress. We now know that the vast majority of ulcers result from bacterial infection (Yeomans, 2011). The old theory, that stress was to blame, while prevalent, was never accurate. Nor was it ever justified. The absence of a clear biophysical explanation does not mean that an illness *must have* a psychological cause.

In the case of some medical conditions, modern clinical attitudes can be traced directly to older beliefs about hysteria. For example, in 1955, there was a mystery outbreak of illness at the Royal Free Hospital in London, starting in midsummer and lasting for four months. Almost 300 members of hospital staff required hospitalization, complaining of headaches, muscle cramps, nausea, pain and other symptoms. Local physicians ruled out glandular fever, but ultimately concluded that the outbreak was caused by an infectious virus that affected the brain. They settled on a diagnosis of benign myalgic encephalomyelitis, or ME. Fifteen years later, two psychiatrists published a paper claiming that the outbreak was, in fact, a case of 'mass hysteria' (McEvedy & Beard, 1970). They claimed that the victims were suffering from afflictions in their minds, rather than infections in their brains. They based this verdict not on individual medical records or physician reports, but on their observation that the outbreak affected more women than men. The very fact of a gender difference led these mental health specialists to conclude that ME is caused by hysteria, and not by physical disease. Femininity itself was seen as evidence of damaging irrationality.

In subsequent decades, biomedical research has revealed a wide variety of biophysical abnormalities in patients who have ME, to the extent that theories implying it to be psychogenic in origin would now appear to be scientifically implausible (Nacul et al., 2020). Nonetheless, some psychologists and mental health specialists continue to claim that ME is a psychogenic disease. By extension, they recommend that it should be treated using psychological therapy. The fact that their beliefs about ME can be traced back to the medical sexism of the late 1960s is seldom acknowledged. However, were it not for the stereotyping of women as inherently hysterical beings, the theory would never have existed.

In today's medicine, it is often psychologists themselves who are at the forefront of maintaining such theories. Many psychologists endorse the term 'medically unexplained symptoms', or MUS, to refer to the conditions of patients whose doctors have been unable to identify their physical pathology. Once this label is attached, the psychologists then conduct research to investigate the psychological factors they believe led these patients to present with MUS in the first place (Bogaerts et al., 2010). In so doing, they fall into the trap of inferring a psychogenic origin simply because a *physical* cause is unknown. In formal logic, philosophers refer to this type of error as 'argument from ignorance' (Cummings, 2020), the drawing of evidence-free conclusions *on the very basis* of an absence of evidence. In truth, the only thing we know about medically unexplained symptoms is that they are medically unexplained. Assuming them to be caused or perpetuated by psychological factors is a logical fallacy.

Today, few doctors, psychologists or other health professionals will describe their patients as 'hysterical'. However, the legacy of psychological stereotypes regarding the feebleness of women's bodies and minds continues to be felt. Women's reports of illness are more likely to be dismissed as unreliable testimony, portrayed as catastrophic thinking or condemned as chaotic self-destruction. This is despite the fact there is literally no evidence to suggest that women are psychologically more liable than men to misinterpret their bodily sensations, or to report an illness that isn't really there (O'Leary, 2018).

The sex-difference stereotype

In Chapter 7, we saw how various nineteenth-century neurologists worried that women's minds would be unable to cope with the complexity of the modern world. A common worry concerned education. In 1873, a board member at Harvard Medical School warned that too much intellectual work would drain women's bodies of blood flow such as to render them unable to menstruate (Clark, 1873).

By the twentieth century, it had come to be acknowledged that young women were, in fact, worth educating, at least to some extent. However, the prospect of sending them to the same schools as were attended by young men created much consternation. The esteemed psychologist G. Stanley Hall, who we encountered in a number of previous chapters, believed that if girls were sent to mixed-gender institutions, they would be unable to endure the challenges of regular menstruation. There was 'something not only unnatural and unhygienic, but a little monstrous, in daily school associations with boys', he argued, given that women's lives were so dependent on 'normalizing the lunar month' (Hall, 1906, p. 590).

Aside from the various menstrual hazards, several other reasons were raised as to why education for women was an ill-conceived notion. Hall felt that distracting women from fulfilling their destinies as mothers to the next generation would engender 'race suicide'. Several psychologists suggested that while able to study, an educated woman would be incapable of making use of what she had learned. In the words of the founding president of Stanford University, 'She may know a good deal, but she can do nothing' (Jordan, 1902, p. 101). Many psychologists also endorsed a 'variability hypothesis', which asserted that the male population contained a greater range of intellectual talents – encompassing extremely low but also extremely high intelligence – with the female population comprising a much narrower cluster of more-or-less average aptitude (Ellis, 1903).

Once again, these ideas can seem dated in hindsight. But in reality, their legacy continues to influence contemporary debate. In 2006, the then president of Harvard University resigned after receiving widespread criticism for a speech he made at a conference on workforce diversity. Endorsing a modern version of the variability hypothesis, he asserted that men were more likely than women to achieve high (or low) scores on cognitive tests, and from this concluded that the 'available pool' of talented scientists would always be mostly men. What made his speech especially problematic was his explicit dismissal of any alternative hypothesis (Hyde, 2018). He rejected the idea that the gender compositions of workforces in science and engineering were the result of social factors, explicitly ruling out the possibility that they reflected discrimination, role-modelling or acculturation. For him, the primary forces in play were sex differences in cognitive ability.

The claim that there are meaningful gender differences in mathematical ability is one of the older social stereotypes. However, the relevant research suggest that such differences are hard to substantiate with data. Analyses of school arithmetic scores in the United States suggest that any gender differences are truly minuscule. In one study of test scores for over seven million students, the *overlap* between girls' and boys' scores was around 99.9 per cent (Hyde et al., 2008). Moreover, the direction of observed differences varied across students of different ages: while nine-year-old boys outperformed nine-year-old girls, ten-year-old girls outperformed ten-year-old boys. The tiny size and apparent inconsistency of these so-called sex differences were highly suggestive of random variation. This non-difference in mathematical ability has been confirmed in several other similarly large-scale studies (Lindberg et al., 2010).

In fact, according to extensive research, it transpires that women and men differ on very few psychological variables at all. In contrast to common social stereotypes, women and men (or girls

Susan Gerbic / Public domain, via Wikimedia Commons

Image 11.1 Margaret Hamilton
Gender stereotypes rarely reflect underlying abilities. Margaret Hamilton's mathematical skills enabled the development of on-board flight software
for NASA's Apollo moon missions.

and boys) are statistically indistinguishable in variables such as self-esteem, anxious emotionality,
sadness, tentative speech, anger expression, relational aggression, leadership styles, leadership
effectiveness, reward-seeking, authentic pride,
hubristic pride, general emotionality, reading
comprehension, essay-writing ability or vocabulary (Hyde, 2014).

Even for those few variables where statistically
significant gender differences do tend to be found,
the underlying evidence seems far from compelling. For example, differences in mental rotation
ability, or in personality traits such as emotional
stability, seem to vary from culture to culture. In
some societies, men outscore women, but in others they don't. The fact that these findings vary by
culture suggests that they probably *result* from cultural contexts: what appear to be gender differences are in fact the outcomes of, for example,
gender-specific norms of upbringing (Hyde,
2014). The sheer enormity of the accumulation of
such findings has led the American psychologist
Janet Shibley Hyde to call on her colleagues to endorse and promote, once and for all, an overarching 'gender similarities hypothesis' (Hyde, 2005).

HISTORY REPEATING ITSELF: SEX DIFFERENCES AND PSYCHOLOGY

It appears that decades of research showing gender
similarities have failed to shift many stereotypes.
This may be because psychologists themselves
often seem heavily invested in the idea of gender
differences. Their beliefs are likely grounded in
long-standing cultural attitudes, which for many
appear to be more influential than actual data.

As far back as 1910, the American psychologist
Helen Thompson Woolley (1874–1947) described
the depth of her frustrations when faced with her
colleagues' incorrigibility in this matter: 'There is
perhaps no field aspiring to be scientific where flagrant personal bias, logic martyred in the cause of
supporting a prejudice, unfounded assertions, and
even sentimental rot and drivel, have run riot to
such an extent as here' (Woolley, 1910, p. 340). It is
striking that even more than a century later, it
appears as though many psychologists remain
reluctant to discard the sex-difference stereotypes
of past generations.

The exclusion of women psychologists

Historically, women who achieved success in stereotypically male activities, such as sport or science, were often described as having 'acted above their sex' (Astell, 1705) – or, with greater spatial
precision, as 'holding a position more or less intermediate between the two sexes' (Anonymous,
1878). A slightly more imaginative approach was to credit such women as being, in essence,

honorary men. Of the 4,000 luminaries listed in the first edition of *American Men of Science* (J. M. Cattell, 1906), 149 were in fact women. Twenty-one of these were psychologists.

Not all such terminology in older scholarship was purposefully sexist. The idea of referring to 'people' as 'men' was long intended as a neutral linguistic convention. For example, writing in the 1970s, the psychologist Naomi Weisstein (1939–2015), a self-styled radical feminist, applied this convention liberally. When describing the way *any* person, woman or man, acquires 'his or her' self-image, she explained that 'what a person does, and who he believes himself to be, will in general be a function of what people around him expect him to be, and what the overall situation in which he is acting implies that he is' (Weisstein, 1971).

In addition to having their genders obfuscated by scholarly language, women working in psychology during its formative years as a university discipline tended to find that their work was ignored or otherwise neglected. Many women psychologists are much less famous than their male contemporaries, despite having made important empirical and professional contributions (Gross, 2009).

One example was the American psychologist Mary Whiton Calkins (1863–1930). Calkins published four books and over 100 papers in her prolific research career. In 1905, she succeeded William James as president of the American Psychological Association, becoming the first woman to hold the position. She designed what became the standard method for assessing paired-associate learning in laboratory experiments (Deese & Hulse, 1967). Her research was the first to describe primacy effects in short-term memory (Madigan & O'Hara, 1992). In a survey conducted in 1903 (entitled 'A statistical study of eminent men'), she was ranked as the twelfth most eminent psychologist in the United States in terms of the importance of her work (J. M. Cattell, 1903).

Clearly a prodigious talent, Calkins applied to enrol as a graduate student at Harvard but was refused admission because of her gender. However, the university did permit her to sit in and observe psychology classes. When the psychology department supported her to complete and submit a PhD thesis, the university refused to award her a Harvard degree. Instead, they suggested she accept a doctorate from Radcliffe College, one of the university's ancillary institutions. On principle, she declined (Furumoto, 1980).

By the 1960s and 1970s, many Western countries were experiencing what has become known as the 'second wave' of feminism. This was a period when campaigners, advocates and ordinary citizens became increasingly active in seeking to advance women's rights and gender equality (the 'first wave' having been led by the suffragette movements of the early twentieth century). In academia, there was renewed interest in examining the historical experiences of women in science and scholarship and the history of academic marginalization and sexism. Scholars began to question why the contributions of many women psychologists had been overlooked at the expense of their male contemporaries (Bernstein & Russo, 1974).

Subsequent research has expanded this endeavour to scrutinize the way social power is exercised in science, academia and the clinical professions (B. Harris, 2009). As well as identifying the individual psychologists who have been marginalized by professional sexism, it is also important to consider the processes by which masculinist biases have operated to suppress their prominence.

ALMOST FAMOUS: RUTH W. BERENDA, DOROTHEA ROSS, SHEILA A. ROSS AND EDITH LORD

While the social psychologist Solomon Asch is remembered for his classic studies of social conformity (see Chapter 10), another psychologist, Ruth W. Berenda, conducted almost identical research just prior to Asch (Berenda, 1950) but is seldom recognized for her contribution. Berenda presented a simple perceptual task to child participants, asking them to compare, match or estimate the lengths of lines on a chart. For the experiment, she had coached the majority of the children to give deliberately incorrect answers on some items. Berenda then showed that, in most cases, the children who were unaware of this mischievous arrangement were almost always inclined to conform with group opinion, even when they could see that it was clearly erroneous. Berenda had graduated with a PhD in physiological psychology in 1948 from the University of Rochester, New York.

The Canadian-American psychologist Albert Bandura (1925–2021) is often associated with a landmark study of aggression, known as the 'Bobo Doll' experiment, which showed how children learn to imitate aggression when they see adults behave violently towards a plastic doll. However, the study was actually co-authored with two women colleagues, Dorothea Ross (1923–2019) and Sheila A. Ross, who are usually overlooked when this research is discussed (Bandura, Ross & Ross, 1961). Dorothea Ross was born in Canada and moved to Stanford University to complete her PhD. She later became a paediatric psychologist. Her sister Sheila A. Ross also completed a PhD at Stanford.

The Rosenthal effect – where a researcher's confirmation bias influences the results of their experiment – was named after a male psychologist (Rosenthal, 1966). This was despite him having acknowledged that the effect was first demonstrated, a decade previously, by the clinical psychologist Edith Lord (1950). Lord, a psychologist working at the Arizona State Department of Health, had conducted experiments to show how testers' expectations would influence participant responses on psychological tests.

The 'male standard'

Even the subject-matter content of psychology can betray an intrinsic gender bias. A particular problem relates to the way maleness and masculinity are implicitly relied upon as the template against which other types of experience should be compared. Psychologists and other researchers are never immune to their cultural upbringing, and it is clear that daily life is infused with many questionable linguistic and attitudinal conventions that imply a norm of maleness-as-typical. The Canadian-British philosopher Cordelia Fine (1975–) identifies a familiar illustration. She points out that when people are asked to report their gender in, for example, a questionnaire, they are commonly presented with two options: first 'male', then 'female' (Fine, 2010). The effect of this ordering of options is to imply that being male is essentially *the default*, whereas being female is essentially *the alternative to being male*. The designer of the questionnaire appears to suggest that maleness is to be expected, but that femaleness, while perfectly welcome, is somehow an 'extra'. Being male is set as the standard.

An easy way to improve such questionnaires would be to alter the order of gender options (as well as allowing respondents to select gender identities other than 'female' and 'male'). However, when equivalent gender assumptions are encoded into the broader vocabulary of research, from theory right through to textbook, things become much more difficult.

In Chapter 10 we discussed how scientific concepts are socially constructed. This means that the way we recognize them, perceive them and talk about them is largely driven by whatever terms and features we, and other people, have accumulated in order to do so. In aeronautics, engineers will talk about air compressibility, wave drag, tether propulsion, lift coefficients, cylinder stress, dead reckoning, dihedral angles, eccentric anomalies and Bernoulli's principle. Most non-engineers will find these terms incomprehensible. The fact that these concepts are socially constructed does not mean that they do not exist, that they represent flimsy knowledge, or that they lack true meaning. It simply means that our awareness of their existence reflects the work that other human beings have done to identify what they represent. It also means that, as engineers continue to study aeronautics, the precise definitions of these terms may well evolve in light of new discoveries, and perhaps even entirely new concepts will be added to the technical vocabulary in time.

Psychological concepts are no exception. They too are socially constructed. However, one important difference between psychology and aeronautics is that terms in psychology *are* commonly understood by non-psychologists. When psychologists talk about self-esteem, anxiety, depression, intelligence, personality, conformity, memory, behaviour, learning, immaturity, leadership styles or penis envy, non-psychologists will immediately begin to interpret such terms within their own frames of reference. One problem that soon arises is that what psychologists mean by such terms is often quite different to what non-psychologists *think* they mean. Another problem is that because these terms were effectively *chosen* by human beings, the resulting terminology might not in fact represent the best way of explaining things.

Take, for example, the concept of self-esteem. Classically, self-esteem is defined as the degree to which one values oneself. High self-esteem is typically described as desirable, on the basis that people ordinarily like to feel liked. By contrast, low self-esteem is typically seen as undesirable, because it is considered especially unfortunate when a person dislikes *themselves*. The social psychologist Kenneth J. Gergen, who, as we discussed in Chapter 10, is credited with identifying the 'crisis in social psychology', pointed out that talking about self-esteem this way is actually highly arbitrary. We could, for example, refer to the exact same concept as 'egotism' (Gergen, 1973). However, *egotism* has quite a different connotation. People who are extremely egotistical certainly do value themselves highly, but they are also seen as pompous, self-deluded and unpleasant. Low egotism, on the other hand, is readily understood as a synonym for 'humble' and is widely regarded as a desirable personal quality.

Gergen argued that calling this concept 'self-esteem' instead of 'egotism' serves to infuse it with discretionary value. Framing it as 'self-esteem' conveys that it is better to have more of it rather than less. It encourages people to strive for greater self-esteem (or egotism) while stigmatizing low self-esteem (or humility). By conveying such preferences in their choice of words, psychologists who talk about 'self-esteem' are essentially propagandizing in favour of a certain way of behaving. As such, according to Gergen, the terminology comes encoded with its own value system, making it far removed from the type of scientific neutrality to which psychology is supposed to aspire.

Another American social psychologist, Carol Tavris (1944–), extended this point by linking it to gender stereotypes. Tavris noted that women are often described as exhibiting lower self-esteem than men, as measured using questionnaires in empirical studies. Tavris offered 'conceit' as the alternative label. She suggested that all this discourse could easily be reworked: instead of asking why women have lower self-esteem than men, psychologists could instead investigate why men are *more conceited* than women. She went on to offer some further memorable examples (Tavris, 1993):

- Psychologists traditionally suggest that women do not value their efforts as much as men do. Why not simply say that men *overvalue* their own work?
- According to psychologists, women are liable to lack self-confidence. Why not say that men are simply *less realistic than women* at assessing their own abilities?
- Women are conventionally characterized as finding it difficult to develop a 'separate sense of self'. Why not instead characterize men as being *bad at relationships*?
- Women are often depicted as being more likely to say they are 'hurt' than to admit they are 'angry'. Why not just say that men are *liable to attack others* when upset, and *less capable of leveraging appropriate sympathy*?

Depicting men as inclined towards overvaluing their own work, misreading their own abilities, failing at relationships, attacking others and being emotionally unintelligent seems less a psychological summary than a gender-wide character assassination. And yet, as Tavris argues, these are very much the types of derogatory claims that traditional psychology consistently makes about women. Her point is not just that psychology's concepts are socially constructed, it is that they are constructed in a way that is biased towards making men seem superior, healthy and more desirable.

Moreover, these social constructions imply that femaleness is an aberration. Women *lack* self-esteem and self-confidence, they *fail* to value themselves, they *have difficulty* being autonomous, and they are *unable* to express themselves effectively. In other words, women fall short on the attributes that archetypally define men. Given the way that social constructions reveal underlying values, it would appear as though psychology's method of constructing human nature attaches a much higher value to men's experiences than to those of women.

Even women's physiology is regularly portrayed as inherently meddlesome, if not altogether problematic. Both women and men experience hormonal fluctuations and consequent mood swings, but only women are described as experiencing a 'syndrome' of premenstrual 'symptoms'. The fact that women secrete higher levels of oxytocin than men, especially during childbirth and lactation, has contributed to that neurohormone's reputation as a 'moral molecule', which, among other effects, accounts for women's (allegedly) greater interest in childcare and their (allegedly) greater levels of kindness and trustworthiness. In reality, oxytocin interacts with behaviour in all sorts of different ways, and has been shown to make people *more* selfish and *less* convivial in many situations (Declerck, Boone & Kiyonari, 2010; Radke & de Bruijn, 2012). It is erroneous to imply that the psychology of women can be readily explained just by imagining the effects of female biochemistry on a human (i.e. male) body.

Tavris notes that psychological gender differences are often discussed in relation to one of three narratives, each of which is problematic. Firstly, it is often simply implied, or argued, that men are superior to women. Secondly, it is often implied, or argued, that men and women are the same inasmuch as *women are not really different to men*. Examples of this narrative include the way psychologists often declare that woman are *just as interested* in sex as men are, or that they are *just as likely* to cheat in relationships. While ostensibly describing a form of psychological equality, the language used reveals an ongoing social construction of human psychology in which maleness is seen as the standard. In the words of psychologist and sexual equality activist Leonore Tiefer, this narrative asserts that 'men and women are the same, and they're all men' (Tiefer, 1992).

In the third narrative, it is implied, or argued, that women are in fact superior to men. This narrative is often presented in the context of *cultural feminism*. Cultural feminists posit that women are characterized by an inherent 'female nature', which is both biologically grounded and emotionally advanced. An example in psychology is Taylor's theory of stress reactions, which we discussed above. Taylor proposes that women react to stress with *tend-and-befriend* responses, rather than by adopting the masculine posture of *fight-or-flight*. As such, her theory suggests that women are naturally predisposed towards acting positively and generously, whereas men are prone to behaviours that are negative and selfish.

However, as argued by both Tavris (1993) and Weisstein (1971), the idea that women are 'better' than men is just as problematic as claims of male superiority. It retains the notion that there are essential differences between the sexes that account for their different experiences, thereby downplaying the role of society and culture (and discrimination) in creating different lives for women and men. In addition, the idea is just as much a social construction and so its inherent value system is just as arbitrary. For example, 'tend-and-befriend' is a loaded choice of words; the pattern of responses it signifies could alternatively be described in negative terms (e.g. 'pester-and-ingratiate'). (For that matter, 'fight-or-flight' could be replaced with 'engage-or-evade'; Hughes, 2016).

Claims that one group in the human population is 'superior' to another will always reduce to subjective values. Both empirically and ethically, it appears futile to attempt to address the problem of gender bias in psychology by supplanting it with a different, albeit opposing, form of gender bias.

Gender and epistemology

The impact of issues such as the social construction of knowledge, the arbitrariness of terminology and the inherently value-laden nature of language have led a number of scholars to question whether the scientific method itself might be irretrievably dependent on male-centred contexts. According to a major subfield of philosophy known as *feminist epistemology*, all knowledge is ultimately 'situated' in the sense that it necessarily reflects the perspective of those who possess it. Given that science has been dominated by male perspectives for most of its history, it follows that all scientific claims to knowledge are likely to be tainted by masculinist bias. Feminist epistemologists assert that not only does such bias distort the labelling of concepts and the interpretation of research results, it also undermines the very process of research itself.

Image 11.2   Carol Tavris
Carol Tavris is a prolific psychologist who has written extensively on gender stereotyping in psychology from the perspective of equality feminism.

The American physicist Evelyn Fox Keller (1936–) has argued that male perspectives are so ingrained, they can prevent scientists from correctly interpreting even the non-human world around them. She famously argued that biological understanding of the behaviour of microscopic organisms is impeded by assumptions that some cells are 'leaders' while other cells are 'followers', which Keller (1985) suggests is reflective of masculine interests and worldviews. Similarly, the psychoanalytic philosopher Luce Irigaray, who we encountered in Chapter 7, has argued that physicists are often more concerned with speed, energy and solids than they are with fluids or gases, reflecting male interests in dynamism and strength, in contrast to female interests in softness and lability (Irigaray, 1985).

Another feminist epistemologist, the American philosopher Sandra Harding (1935–), has proposed that the way traditional science favours reason over emotion, objectivity over subjectivity, and the abstract over the concrete reveals it to be bound by overly male modes of thinking. According to Harding (1986), science would be greatly improved by more 'feminine' cognitive styles, such as those that invoke emotion and empathy. For many psychologists, this view underlies their preference for subjectivist and qualitative research methods over methods that rely on quantification and statistics.

However, one problem with these ideas is that claims that there are specifically 'male' or 'female' thoughts, concepts or reasoning styles are themselves based on supposition and stereotype. As discussed above, while it is often believed (in Western culture at least) that women and men differ in their cognitive styles and aptitudes, these assumptions are seldom borne out by empirical evidence. Large-scale studies have repeatedly shown that women and men have similar interests in leadership and followership, in concrete as well as abstract concepts, and in mathematical ability. Recommending qualitative methods to psychology on the basis that they will emancipate the otherwise impeded talents of women psychologists is misplaced, because women psychologists can use quantitative methods too, just as effectively as anyone else can. The claim that women psychologists are better served by qualitative methods merely perpetuates an unwarranted stereotype that women are more likely to be innumerate.

Many feminist philosophers have argued strongly against the notions espoused by the feminist epistemologists. Naomi Weisstein, who we mentioned above, noted that scientific objectivity and methods based on quantification are useful in their own right, and are as likely to reveal and expose prejudice as they are to reinforce it. For Weisstein, the methods of science are not the cause of sexism, but are potentially one of the tools that can be used to find solutions.

When the lives and well-being of women and men differ, it is usually because of structural injustices that exist within the objectively observable 'real' world, and not rooted in inherent subjective processes of thinking said to operate somehow differently within the minds of women and men. As such, the philosopher of science Helen Longino (1944–) has recommended that gender inequalities be tackled not by 'doing feminist science', but by 'doing science as a feminist' (Longino, 1987).

For psychologists to contribute to this effort, especially given their field's history of androcentrism and sexist stereotyping, a similar argument can surely be mounted in favour of 'doing *psychology* as a feminist'.

PSYCHOLOGY'S GEOGRAPHIC BIAS

In Chapter 7 we described how the concept of penis envy might not be as readily applicable outside the specific context in which Freud formulated his psychoanalytic theory. For one thing, Freud's understanding of the human mind was based on the particular selection of middle-class Viennese women who sought therapy from him in that Austro-Hungarian city during the second half of the nineteenth century. Similarly, when earlier in this chapter we considered Maslow's hierarchy-of-needs model, in which personal self-actualization, rather than communitarian harmony, was said to be the ultimate target of human motivation, we noted that Maslow derived his theory having studied the experiences of a small selection of well-educated Americans in the 1950s.

In fact, it is a recurring issue in psychological research that any single study will be narrow in geographical scope. Most laboratory research will involve participants who are easily accessible to the experimenter. The economic reality of how experimenters earn their living will mean that the majority of these participants will be college students. Studies based on questionnaire methods, such as attitude surveys and personality research, will perhaps have a wider reach, but will nonetheless involve only those participants who are literate in the particular language in which the study is being conducted. In much modern research, they will also probably need to have computers with internet access. The practicalities of reaching out to strangers means that most investigators end up recruiting respondents from within a defined demographic hinterland.

So-called 'convenience sampling' represents the standard approach in psychology. Allowing for convenience is not, in and of itself, a scientific problem. After all, more research is generally better than less research, and some research questions are just specific to a particular time and place. But there are certainly some downsides to convenience-based science.

One problem is that it favours small-scale studies over large-scale ones. It is easier to conduct twenty trivially adjusted laboratory experiments than a single country-wide clinical trial. As a consequence, psychology journals contain a plethora of the former and relatively few of the latter. In general, however, large-scale studies have greater statistical power and cover a wider, and thus more informative, sweep of the human experience. Therefore, we can anticipate that psychology journals are likely to contain an overabundance of underpowered and unrepresentative findings. We will consider some of these issues further in Chapter 12.

Another problem with convenience-based science is that its agenda is inherently incomplete. Only those research questions that concern those communities in which research is funded and conducted will receive scientific attention. This is why there are more medical studies of infectious diseases that spread in the Western world than there are of illnesses that so severely affect the lives of the global majority (Morel, 2003). Specifically, more than 90 per cent of global spending on medical research is directed at conditions that account for just 10 per cent of the global health burden (Global Forum for Health Research, 2002).

Likewise, in psychology there appears to be far more research that addresses the concerns of a small number of privileged countries that traditionally have had the wealth and resources to offer education in psychology to their citizens. This creates challenges for social justice, but also problems with knowledge. How reliable can our insights on the human mind be if they are based on but a sliver of the human experience?

WEIRD psychology

The vast majority of knowledge produced by the formal study of psychology has been derived from examining participants who are, in technical terms, WEIRD. This is the acronym now used to refer to people whose backgrounds are Western, Educated, Industrialized, Rich and Democratic.

The term was first coined by the American evolutionary biologist Joseph Henrich and colleagues (Henrich, 2010) with specific reference to the narrowness of psychology's research scope. In their review of psychology studies published between 2003 and 2007, they noted that some 96 per cent of research participants were WEIRD. Moreover, they found that two-thirds of studies relied exclusively on participants from the United States. In the high-profile *Journal of Personality and Social Psychology*, 67 per cent of participants were not just American, but American college students – and not just American college students, but American college students *who were taking courses in psychology.*

Despite the wide attention they attracted, it seems that little has changed since Henrich and his colleagues published their observations. In a similar review published in 2018, another research team found that 94 per cent of research participants described in the leading journal *Psychological Science* were WEIRD, of whom two-thirds were English-speakers and more than half were American (Rad, Martingano & Ginges, 2018).

The places that are classified as WEIRD comprise North America, Western Europe, Australasia and Israel, regions whose combined inhabitants represent just 12 per cent of the world's population (Arnett, 2008). On that basis, we can say that scientific and academic psychology customarily draws broad conclusions about the thoughts, feelings and behaviours of human beings by extrapolating from the experiences of just one in every eight people who make up the human population.

Of course, no scientist can study every case or data-point in their subject area. All scientists sample to some degree, and use extrapolation to draw generalized conclusions. This is essentially the basis of logical induction, a form of reasoning inherent to the scientific method that we discussed in Chapter 3. The problem for psychology is that using induction in this way assumes that its research subjects are representative of the wider population it seeks to describe. In other words, studying WEIRD people makes sense only if *non*-WEIRD people think, feel and behave the same as they do. Unfortunately, however, it seems as though WEIRD people really are psychologically dissimilar to the rest of the world in several important respects.

For example, studies of personality traits regularly show clear divergence between the typical characteristics of WEIRD and non-WEIRD populations. The personalities of WEIRD populations consistently conform to the so-called Big Five model of personality (Costa & McCrae, 1992), in which traits can usefully be classified with reference to the dimensions of *extraversion–introversion*, *agreeableness–hostility*, *openness–caution*, *conscientiousness–unconscientiousness* and *emotional stability–instability*. However, this dimensional model appears to entirely break down when applied to people from non-industrialized societies, such as the Tsimané people of Bolivia (Gurven et al., 2013), the Aché of Paraguay (Bailey et al., 2013), or inhabitants of traditional villages in rural Senegal (Alvergne, Jokela & Lummaa, 2010). In the previous section, we also noted that purported gender differences in personality traits apply mainly to Western countries, but do not emerge as clearly, if at all, in non-Western women and men (Hyde, 2014).

In other studies, social psychology experiments have been found to reflect local norms to such an extent that many traditionally dependable findings have been revealed to be WEIRD-specific. One example is a famous study of delayed gratification, which used a method now known as the 'marshmallow test' (Mischel & Ebbesen, 1970). In this type of experiment, children are asked to choose between a small reward that they can receive immediately or a larger one for which they have to wait. The initial findings using this method appeared to show that the majority of children – and especially those rated as the cleverest or most mature – were generally willing to delay their gratification and wait for a larger reward. However, when this method is employed to study children in non-WEIRD societies, they more frequently opt for an immediate reward in order to avoid the discomfort of uncertainty (Amir et al., 2020). Only those non-WEIRD children who live in or close to cities seem open to delaying their pleasure. This has led some psychologists to theorize that the marshmallow test is culture-bound, having a different meaning for children raised where resources are normally scarce and reliable industrially driven supply chains are an alien concept. In these environments, the mature course of action is to avoid risk and accept resources when they are offered, rather than to gamble on some greater benefit being available later on.

But it is not just in the psychology of culture, societies and language that these problems arise. Studies of visual perception regularly reveal previously unexpected differences between WEIRD and non-WEIRD populations. Childhood exposure to environments that feature contours, corners and intersections appears to provide a unique form of optical calibration. Participants from WEIRD societies tend to perform differently in visual perception tasks compared to people from other places, perhaps reflecting their familiarity with engineered products and infrastructure (Henrich, 2008). The development of basic motor skills, such as the traditional Western milestones where parents expect their babies to learn to crawl *before* learning to walk, has also been shown to be culturally shaped. In many societies, crawling emerges much later than in the West, or not at all, suggesting it is most likely a behaviour that can be learned at different times, rather than an innate skill subject to an organic developmental milestone. Brain imaging studies too show distinct differences between WEIRD and non-WEIRD participants, especially when they process visual concepts (Gutchess et al., 2006) or think about social relationships (Zhu et al., 2007). Such differences suggest that many cognitive habits deviate as a function of cultural reinforcement, rather than coming pre-programmed within brain architecture as previously believed. This is an especially important finding, given that well over 90 per cent of participants in brain imaging studies are drawn from Western populations (Chiao, 2009).

The bias towards WEIRD populations does not simply limit psychology's dataset, it also narrows its focus. As suggested above, the topics that end up being studied most are those that are of interest to WEIRD audiences. Behaviours and attitudes prominent in the lives of millions of people living in non-WEIRD cultures – such as 'saving face' (Chapman, Estcourt & Hua, 2008) or navigating a caste system (Mahalingam, 2007) – are rarely if ever discussed on the pages of a psychology journal (Colvile, 2016). In some cases, specific psychological concepts will not even be expressible in the English language. An example relates to the Western notion of 'shame', which is notoriously culture-bound and often quite different to the way guilt or remorse is transacted in non-WEIRD communities.

In the industrialized world, people customarily quantify all aspects of their existence, from managing their household budgets, to tracking their daily calorie intake, to counting their steps. However, in some cultures, people do not even track how old they are (Diekmann et al., 2017). In languages used by some hunter-gatherer communities, there are no words to express numbers beyond four or five (Cooperrider, 2019). People in these communities are also much more concerned with spatial orientation (for example, their ability to determine where 'north' is) than with what day of the week it might be. Such points are especially worth recalling whenever evolutionary psychologists claim that a particular behaviour in modern human beings is rooted in developmental forces exerted during the hunter-gatherer period of their evolutionary history (see Chapter 5).

As with the problem of gender bias, psychology's undue emphasis on WEIRD perspectives also impacts its understanding of mental health and illness. As we discussed in Chapter 4, definitions of mental health are often intertwined with situational norms, if not entirely driven by cultural attitudes as to what constitutes 'appropriate' behaviour. An important cross-cultural variation in such norms relates to emotional expression. In some societies public crying is seen as highly appropriate, whereas in others it is shameful and stigmatized. Extravagant lamentation can be viewed as a healthy response to distress or as a sign of mental instability, depending on what country you live in. When people move from one country to another, they may find that their manner of emotional expression is no longer viewed as 'appropriate'. It could be partly for such reasons that in many Western countries, people from immigrant communities are statistically more likely to be diagnosed with mental health problems (Giammusso et al., 2018).

Some mental health conditions have been found to be unique to WEIRD societies, or else to manifest themselves differently in different places. Conditions such as post-traumatic stress disorder (PTSD) and attention deficit hyperactivity disorder (ADHD) are commonly diagnosed in Europe and North America but are relatively rare in other parts of the world (Bures, 2016). In Western countries, anorexia nervosa is seen as being intertwined with body image, whereas many people with anorexia in Asian countries appear not to fear being overweight or to want to lose weight in order to become more attractive. In Hong Kong, for example, people with anorexia engage in self-emaciation and food-avoidance for reasons that seem unrelated to body-image concern (Watters, 2010). This cultural difference casts doubt on the long-held view among Western psychologists that anorexic food-avoidance is *caused by* disordered body image. It could be that body-shape denial and fear of fatness reflect the *consequences* of this condition when its sufferers are immersed in the specific environment of WEIRD culture.

Anorexia nervosa is distressingly common, and the illness has received a huge amount of research attention. However, when it comes to research in psychology, high volume cannot compensate for lack of breadth. Psychology's predominantly WEIRD perspective will inevitably restrict its understanding of mental health. It produces an in-built blindness to cultural factors that leads to false conclusions about the causes, catalysts, consequences – and potential cures – of different conditions.

It is in the nature of skewed perspectives that those who hold them are seldom aware of doing so. Most psychologists – and most psychological research and knowledge – are rooted in a WEIRD worldview, but few psychologists are conscious of the limitations this creates. Relying on insights from a culturally homogeneous and geographically concentrated population makes it, by definition, impossible for psychology to account for the diversity of human experience.

NASA / Public domain, via Wikimedia Commons

Image 11.3 WEIRD psychology
More than 90 per cent of psychology research papers focus on participants from countries that collectively represent just 12 per cent of the world's population.

HISTORY IN STORIES: *SAVING FACE* (2004)

Saving Face (Wu, 2004) is an American-produced drama film focusing on Chinese-American characters who live in New York. It traces the relationship between a young surgeon, Wil, and her mother, Gao, as various significant life events unfold.

Gao is anxious for her daughter to marry a respectable Chinese man, but unknown to her, Wil is in a loving relationship with Vivian, the daughter of one of her mother's friends. Wil believes that her socially conservative mother would be uncomfortable if she were to find out about her love for Vivian. Events take a turn when, one day, Wil discovers that her mother has become pregnant. As Wil's grandfather disapproves of Gao's pregnancy, she decides to move in with Wil. Daughter and mother then live together while keeping secrets that they believe would shame them: Wil is reluctant to reveal the true nature of her relationship with Vivian, while Gao refuses to tell Wil the identity of the father of her unborn child.

Over the course of the story, it transpires that Gao is in fact well aware of her daughter's sexuality, but is unable to publicly acknowledge it. Wil's ongoing reluctance to reveal their relationship creates tension between her and Vivian. Vivian's father wants his daughter to give up her studies in modern dance and instead accept a prestigious ballet scholarship in Paris. And Gao, who has reluctantly agreed to marry a man she does not love in order to provide a father for her unborn child, remains in love with the much younger man with whom she became pregnant.

Much of the narrative hinges on the notion of 'face', a value relating to prestige and honour as judged by others and involving the expectation that every person will conform to social norms. The need to 'save face' is a central concern in many societies across the world, although it is widely seen as being associated most with East Asian cultures. 'Family face' is especially important, where every member of a family is expected to perform their role in maintaining the family reputation (Han, 2019).

Saving Face depicts how the pressure of face can strain even the closest of relationships, especially among diasporic communities. However, it also shows how community attitudes can shift, with norms gradually transforming to accommodate new realities. Western audiences are seldom aware of the key role face plays in the lives of many families around the world. Similarly, its impact is seldom addressed by Western research or textbooks on psychology.

Image 11.4   Academic dependency
The wealth and influence of the American university system has led to concerns about global 'academic dependency' on the United States.

Americanized academia

It may be the case, however, that psychology's WEIRD worldview will become less of a problem over time. This is because of what has been observed as the gradual convergence of global culture and the decline of human diversity. According to some anthropologists and cultural historians, people around the world are increasingly thinking, feeling and behaving like one another. More specifically, the psychology of people in non-WEIRD societies is gradually approximating psychology's traditionally WEIRD monoculture. Psychology need not alter its Americanized template for human behaviour, as human behaviour is slowly changing to resemble that very template.

Recent cross-cultural research confirms that, across the globe, societies are beginning to shed traditional systems and norms in favour of what thrives in the WEIRD world. Non-WEIRD participants are increasingly scoring higher on individualism, are more likely to use WEIRD language to describe themselves, and are gradually being immersed in a common experience of industrialized acculturation. Traditional conventions for describing direction, time, fairness and relationships are slowly disappearing, supplanted by generic methods that reflect the corresponding Western approaches (Cooperrider, 2019).

This pattern of Westernization-as-globalization does not just affect the behavioural, emotional and cognitive styles of psychology's research participants. It also affects the very practices of professional and scientific psychology. In previous chapters we noted how global academia has, at different times, been influenced by one or other geographically sourced hegemony. In modern times, and especially since the Cold War (see Chapter 8), this has amounted to the increasing cultural influence of the United States. Psychology, in particular, has been subject to such forces.

As we saw in Chapter 3, psychology as it exists in the United States can trace its origins to several different traditions, many of them imported. At various times it has championed behaviourism, cognitivism and neuroscience. It happily embraced psychoanalysis, evolutionary biology, psychometrics and humanism. It cultivated its own individuocentric approach to social psychology. Propelled largely by economic dominance and a strident national policy of exerting international political influence – and assisted by the emergence of the English language as a global standard – it has successfully placed itself as the prime producer of psychology research and as publisher of the majority of the field's textbooks, journals and psychometric tests. The American form has been the blueprint on which academic psychology around the world has shaped itself, notwithstanding resistance from, among others, French existentialists (see Chapter 8) or European social psychologists (see Chapter 10).

Psychology in the United States has long been competitively primed. Its earliest academics were notably pragmatic and, perhaps reflecting the early emergence of widely available popular media, had a keen eye on public opinion. William James warned his colleagues that, when faced with psychology, the average citizen will 'care little or nothing about the ultimate philosophic grounds of mental phenomena' but will instead demand ways for 'improving the ideas, dispositions, and conduct' of their fellow human beings (James, 1892, p. 148). In other words, from its beginnings, university psychology in the United States was especially focused on the need to demonstrate its own usefulness. According to some historians of psychology, the status of American psychology was ultimately secured not by intellectual achievement, but by the needs of war, and the arrival of vast funds to support psychological testing during the First World War (Pickren, 2009).

In Chapter 8, we discussed how the Second World War, and the Cold War that followed it, contributed to the expansion of American-led science. In the scramble for global influence, academics in the newly emerging independent nations found themselves culturally overwhelmed. Between 1945 and 1960, forty nations, some of them hugely populated, won independence from their colonizers, only to find themselves wooed by the Cold War superpowers. As higher education was especially critical to the development of these new states, even the poorest countries sent thousands of students abroad to gain expertise in modern science and scholarship (Westad, 2007). The majority were drawn to the United States. In many respects, the Cold War superseded these countries' postcolonial aspirations for national individuality.

In the twenty-first century, education and science has become increasingly intellectually centralized. Non-Western nations find themselves not just influenced by Western academic norms, but in many ways dependent on Western largesse. Such 'academic dependency' (Alatas, 2003) takes several forms. At its most obvious, it relates to the reliance on Western investment in educational materials and resources, including the ownership of publishing companies. The major academic databases, from which the world's scholars search for abstracts and journal papers, are similarly all housed in Western countries. The majority of scholarship funding is provided by Western nations.

Other forms of academic dependency relate to intellectual factors. Non-Western students find that the ideas, theories and empirical science they encounter overwhelmingly originate from Western sources and are even bound within linguistic hierarchies. English-language scholarship comes mostly from the United States and, in proportion, the United Kingdom, while French-language scholarship emanates mostly from France. The intellectual priorities of the Western 'centre' dictate research endeavour in the non-Western 'periphery'. In the social sciences, most theoretical scholarship is produced in Western universities. Non-Western academics are far more likely to confine themselves to collecting empirical data, rather than developing their own intellectual theories (Alatas, 2003).

Such academic dependency contributes to the problem of 'brain drain'. Many young scientists and academics leave non-Western countries to study and work in Western universities, often never to return. But even those who remain at home end up directing their mental energies to research agendas that are shaped in the West, leading to a form of 'virtual brain drain'. To have any chance of publishing their work in academic journals, or of attracting international financial aid, they must address the theories and empirical trends that appeal to Western gatekeepers. The academic imbalance is stark. A Western psychologist encounters no disadvantage if they are unaware of recent research from the non-Western academic periphery. However, non-Western psychologists are expected to be completely up to date with the latest Western developments (Pickren, 2009).

In previous centuries, as we saw in Chapter 3, Western countries sought to exert imperial control over large parts of the world. Within this endeavour was a mission to convert the intellectual culture of subjugated peoples. In India, for example, the British government explicitly sought to suppress local scholarly traditions and to impose a uniform British model. The aim was to cultivate an imperial worldview in the local population, to ensure that they became 'English in taste, in opinions, in morals, and in intellect' (Macaulay, [1835] 1919). The imperial project required the exploitation, tutelage and intellectual domination of the subjugated, and, of course, self-rationalization by the imperial powers themselves lest guilt threaten to restrain them. Arguably, today's academic imperialism operates in essentially the same way.

Approaches to psychology emerging from outside the WEIRD world can sometimes attract international scholarly attention, but rarely become dominant beyond their own geographic boundaries. One example is an approach known as 'liberation psychology', which originated in Central and South America in the 1970s. Liberation psychology aims to examine the psychology of powerless communities within the broader sociopolitical structure of human society, focusing on notions such as social consciousness, the effects of ideology on perceptions of reality, and the idea that unique problems require bespoke consideration rather than preconceived theoretical solutions. Its founding concepts are often attributed to Ignacio Martín-Baró (1942–89), a Spanish social psychologist who also worked as a Catholic priest in El Salvador. They were also influenced by the Brazilian philosopher Paulo Freire (1921–97). While frequently cited by psychologists in other regions, liberation psychology remains primarily a Central and South American form of psychology. For example, virtually all major international conferences on liberation psychology have taken place in Latin American universities.

The centre of gravity in modern psychology remains firmly fixed in the Western world, in which the psychology of the United States remains pre-eminent. It is no surprise, therefore, that its resulting view of human nature is derived from the study of WEIRD populations, and interpreted from the perspective of WEIRD academics. While no doubt appealing to the appetites of Western audiences, psychology's preferred dataset is so severely skewed that its insights into so-called human minds are unlikely to prove useful in the long term.

LOGOPHILIA: 'EPISTEMIC BUBBLE'

In epistemology, or the philosophy of knowledge, an *epistemic bubble* is a group of people who form a closed network that shares information without realizing that it is incomplete. It typically arises when important sources of knowledge are inadvertently ignored, usually because their existence goes unnoticed. Essentially, we all live in epistemic bubbles of one kind or another. By their nature, however, epistemic bubbles prevent us from fully realizing that this is the case.

In philosophical terms, epistemic bubbles create challenges for our appreciation of knowledge. It is always unclear to what extent our knowledge is selective. However, epistemic bubbles are not nefarious or motivated by self-preservation. They can easily be 'popped' whenever members become aware that external sources of relevant information have been overlooked (Nguyen, 2020). This makes epistemic bubbles different from *echo chambers*, whose members either deliberately choose to exclude external voices or to behave in ways that make such exclusion very likely.

The WEIRD bias in psychology appears to be an epistemic bubble, because it is caused by the way psychologists unknowingly base their worldview on a subset of available knowledge. However, were psychologists to *deliberately* behave in ways that were likely to exclude external sources, then its bias towards WEIRD concerns could, in fact, amount to an echo chamber. The problem with echo chambers is that they are resistant to insight and likely to reinforce beliefs that are false. In addition, they are harder to escape. Exposure to new information will burst an epistemic bubble, but it may actually serve to *harden* rejectionist attitudes in an echo chamber (Nguyen, 2020).

The contemporary superpowers in science, scholarship and psychology rarely seem to question the global reach of their ideas. However, of all fields of enquiry, the study of psychology is surely distinctive in its need for the widest possible perspective. Our understanding of how human beings think, feel, behave, aspire, grow, perceive, thrive, hope or suffer will fundamentally be diminished, rather than enhanced, so long as minority interests continue to exert monopolistic control over the flows of academic knowledge.

WHERE TO FROM HERE?

As we have seen throughout previous chapters, the shape of modern psychology is only partly determined by the accumulating outputs of research. It also reflects the many social, cultural and political forces that have historically acted upon the field. The task of gathering knowledge about how people think, feel and behave is a truly human endeavour. Our efforts to understand what all of us experience reflect our collective human wish for common insight.

The implications of such insight are profound. This is why it matters that we produce enlightenment rather than error. However, the fact that our explorations are themselves intrinsically human makes them subject to human failings. It also subjects them to the whims of our desires. How we see the world is often coloured by how we want the world to be.

In our final chapter we will examine the question of values in psychology. How is the way we do psychology affected by our human value systems? How is the knowledge that we produce distorted by our sociopolitical attitudes? Is what psychologists do truly ethical? And is psychology – the process, the profession and the production line of knowledge – an authentically good thing for the world?

DISCUSSION QUESTIONS

1. Can psychology have too broad a scope?
2. How does present-day psychology reflect the prejudices of past attitudes? When we look back on today's psychology in the future, what new prejudices might we see?
3. When we consider the research output of a psychologist, is it important to know their gender?
4. Which problem is more urgent: psychology's gender bias or its geographic bias?

RECOMMENDED READING

- **Hyde, J. S. (2014). Gender similarities and differences.** *Annual Review of Psychology,* **65, 373–98.** In this review, the author synthesizes the empirical literature on gender differences in psychology, arguing that, contrary to the popular stereotype, the data support a conclusion that very few psychological differences exist between men and women.

- Rad, M. S., Martingano, A. J., & Ginges, J. (2018). Toward a psychology of *Homo sapiens*: Making psychological science more representative of the human population. *PNAS*, *115*, 11401–5. In this paper, the authors show how psychology research continues to focus on Western populations, despite the fact that the problems of such a restricted scope have been documented for some time.
- Watters, E. (2010). *Crazy Like Us: The Globalization of the American Psyche*. New York: Free Press. In this book, the author considers how research into mental illness is unduly framed by the cultural norms and expectations of North American society, and how this bias limits our understanding of mental health and healing.
- Weisstein, N. (1971). Psychology constructs the female; or, the fantasy life of the male psychologist (with some attention to the fantasies of his friends, the male biologist and the male anthropologist). *Journal of Social Education*, *35*, 362–73. In this essay, Weisstein exposes the sexism underlying how psychological theories and research were discussed in the early 1970s.

GOOD, BAD AND THE CONCEPT OF *MORALITY*

12

> ## In this chapter, we will …
>
> - consider the role of values in shaping knowledge about psychology
> - examine how the ethics of psychological research and practice have been evaluated
> - consider claims that knowledge in psychology might be skewed by sociopolitical attitudes
> - explore the problem of psychologists' optimistic bias regarding the merits of psychology
> - highlight the limitations on how psychology's knowledge base has been accumulated, and how this knowledge can be improved in the future

At the outset

All human beings hold values. Therefore, all claims to psychological knowledge – all descriptions of people's thoughts, feelings and behaviours – will be infused with the values of the various human beings who generate them. As we have seen in previous chapters, both formal and informal approaches to psychology have been embedded in various cultural, ethical, political and other contexts. Neither psychology, nor science as a whole, is 'value-free'.

Values are enduring opinions about what behaviours or states of existence are preferable. Scientific values include commitments to veracity, transparency and objectivity. In psychology, value discussions often relate to the ethics of research and professional practice. Many codes of ethical practice have been published to guide psychologists in their work.

Personal value systems are hard for anyone to ignore. As such, it is inevitable that the personal value systems of psychologists will have helped to shape the field. Some observers claim that the published subject matter of psychology reflects liberal sociopolitical attitudes because most psychologists hold values that are sociopolitically liberal. However, much of psychology's subject area content was produced during historical periods where conservative values dominated. As such, there are many areas of psychology that reflect a conservative sociopolitical attitude.

Ultimately, it is worth considering whether psychology itself is a good or bad thing. The history of psychology suggests that the human curiosity about the way people think, feel and behave has generated a huge body of both formal and informal knowledge. The processes used to produce this knowledge are themselves subject to human frailty. Some claims to psychological insight are exaggerated. Many psychologists overestimate the good that their field has produced for the world. Such exuberance has contributed to a replication crisis in psychological science. The knowledge produced by psychology research might not always be generalizable or valid. But the historical enterprise to produce psychology's knowledge has also generated wisdom about how best to improve its insights.

Key concept: Morality

Morality refers to the principle of distinguishing right from wrong or good behaviour from bad behaviour, or, more directly, to the quality of being moral. The notion of morality can be applied to intentions and decisions, as well as to actions. Morality can be encoded in a formal set of principles, such as in a professional code of ethics.

Attempting to define 'morality' is not the same as setting out what is moral and what is not. In relative terms, specifying what is or is not moral is extremely difficult – if not impossible – because, in practice, much will depend on the judgements of those who choose to arbitrate on morality-related issues. While this point can be disputed, much of what we refer to as *morality* is likely to be socially constructed.

Nonetheless, we can assert that morality is universally relevant. It is erroneous to suggest that any human activity can be conducted independently of moral assessment. Science, for example, can be objective, but that does not make it value-free. We should therefore consider the morality of psychology by exploring ways in which it is good or bad. Such an evaluation will necessarily benefit from a historical perspective.

VALUES IN PSYCHOLOGY

As we saw in Chapter 11, psychology's view of the world is narrow, peculiar and rarefied. Psychologists craft their understanding of the so-called human experience from the lives, needs and priorities of a small subset of humanity: those people living in societies that are Western, educated, industrialized, rich and democratic. Sometimes this narrowness of focus is interpreted as a sign of preferential tribalism, an indication that psychologists, in general, care more about some societies than they do about others. It is as though the needs of the already privileged 'developed' world are automatically the most urgent. First World problems are always top of the list, presumed to warrant the majority of psychology's attention.

This skewing of interests seems almost inevitable in light of psychology's chequered history. As we have seen throughout previous chapters, the shape of modern psychology is only partly determined by the accumulating outputs of research. It also reflects the way social, cultural and political forces have historically acted upon the field. Psychology has in different eras benefited from colonial conquest, military expansion, religious conservatism, the Cold War and a general hostility towards deviance. Many of its historical contributors achieved their eminence – and influence – through opportunities afforded by social privilege and wealth. And in its formative years, the field was deeply intertwined with several exclusionary worldviews, including eugenics and scientific

racism. Even the more temperate early psychologists exhibited a prurient fascination with the purported inferiority of exotic alien out-groups. With such a motley intellectual heritage, it seems
reasonable to imagine that modern psychology's cultural egocentrism might be the legacy, at least
in part, of a somewhat xenophobic past.

However, for many psychologists, the impulse to ignore or downplay human cultural diversity
reflects the very opposite of xenophobia. They choose to place their emphasis on the notion of
common humanity, the fact that psychological life is experienced similarly by all peoples, and that
any variegation is superficial and trivial, the result of circumstance rather than substance.

Especially during the period following the Second World War – after racist pseudoscience had
been deployed by the Nazis as propaganda for their campaign of genocide – many social scientists
felt compelled to emphasize such *universality* in the human experience. The focus of psychology
moved more towards the relative safety of the laboratory, where discrete behaviours and cognitions could be measured in clinical isolation, unconnected to the strains of political or social controversy. Scholarly claims of fundamental and innate racial or cultural differences became
increasingly taboo.

These reactions against race science, while well intentioned, were often ill-conceived. An example of this irony was the popular 1946 booklet *The Races of Mankind*, written by two American
anthropologists, Ruth Benedict (1887–1948) and Gene Weltfish (1902–80) (Benedict & Weltfish,
1946). Benedict and Weltfish's book sought to present the scientific case against racism, and was
illustrated using a series of cartoon drawings featuring people of different races. However, the
problem was that these cartoons were themselves grounded in contemporary cultural prejudices
regarding what people looked like, how they behaved and what tribes or groups they belonged to.
Their text was similarly abrupt, employing a florid vocabulary of 'race' titles that would surely
shock modern readers. (Many of their terms have now long been discarded by social scientists, on
the grounds of being either culturally inaccurate or grossly insensitive.) While seeking to promote
intercultural egalitarianism using scientific argument, the authors nonetheless unwittingly reinforced several unfortunate racial stereotypes. And, more importantly, by depicting racial conflict as
being caused by personal ignorance, rather than by structural power imbalances and historical
exploitation, they revealed their own perspective to be deeply ethnocentric.

Ultimately, information is never truly neutral. This is because communication is a directional
process, where one person transmits information to another. The content, the format and even the
tone of that information will depend on how the person communicating it sees the world. As science – and thus psychology – is just a type of information that can be communicated, it follows
that science – and thus psychology – will be similarly revealing.

Often what is revealed are the communicator's own opinions and motivations. Whenever
human nature is discussed in public discourse, we can be sure that the people discussing it have
views about what is good and what is bad in the world. Even if such preferences are not held passionately, all people distinguish between things they like and things they find aversive. Their ideas
about what is good or bad – in other words, the 'values' that they hold – are themselves pieces of
information, and so will themselves bear their own hallmarks from the cultures, or subcultures,
within which they are situated.

Therefore, psychology's knowledge base is not just *geographically* skewed, it also reflects the various cultural, ethical, political and other social values in which psychologists are immersed. For these reasons, it is always erroneous to speak of psychology (or of any other science) as being 'value-free'. In fact, like all depictions of knowledge, psychology is *infused* with the values of its creators. Its accumulated knowledge base is composed in ways that reveal what psychologists, individually and collectively, have considered good and bad about the world.

Psychology is a body of knowledge that aims to explain how human beings think, feel and behave. But in many ways, it also tells us something about how they *should* think, feel and behave, at least in the opinion of psychologists. It is always important to be aware of how values impinge on science and scholarship. Psychology is never just informative. It is also intrinsically *normative*.

The nature of values

Human 'values' – enduring beliefs about what behaviours or states of existence are preferable, and what ones are not – have been discussed in various ways for centuries. There has been much pondering of the nature of morality, the elements of a righteous life, and the correct path to salvation. However, the very fact that human beings *hold* values – and especially the fact that different people can hold different ones – is a more recent topic of interest.

Like many attitudes, values are of dual concern to psychology. Firstly, as psychological constructs, they attract scrutiny regarding how they come to be formed and defended in human minds. But secondly, as determinants of conduct – including the conduct of psychologists – they also invite reflection as to how the conclusions psychologists draw from their data and observations might themselves be value-laden. The reflexive nature of psychological science – in which psychologists themselves are subject to the very phenomena they scrutinize in their research (see Chapter 1) – is especially pertinent in this regard. Information is never neutral.

As we noted in Chapter 11, humanistic psychologist Abraham Maslow sought to explain the values that shape human motivation using a generalized hierarchy of needs (Maslow, 1954). In this model, Maslow argued that people seek to fulfil different needs in sequence. Basic needs (such as the need for food and safety) are pursued initially, and only once these are fulfilled do psychological needs (such as esteem or love) become prominent. Those individuals for whom all such needs are met will then come to prioritize personal self-fulfilment, and will invest their efforts in 'self-actualization', the achieving of their full human potential. However, while Maslow wanted to describe the nature of all human motivation, he derived his model from studying a very narrow sample of his own students. His theory reflected a particular snapshot of American social values in the 1950s, and was soon found to be less applicable to other contexts. It was especially ill-suited to people living in societies where individual self-fulfilment is considered much less important than community cohesion.

Later theories sought to more flexibly encapsulate the potential for values to vary from society to society. The most common approach to explaining the psychology of human values was offered by the Polish-American social psychologist Milton Rokeach (1918–88) in his book *The Nature of*

Human Values (Rokeach, 1973). Rokeach saw values as beliefs, rather than traits, that were stable for each person, but which could be shared at a societal level. He distinguished two main categories of value: 'terminal' values, which relate to desired outcomes (such as *happiness* or *equality*); and 'instrumental' values, which relate to preferred behavioural characteristics (such as *courage* or *politeness*). An important feature of Rokeach's view was that values did not themselves constitute pre-formed decisions but served as criteria by which decisions could be considered. As such, even if you knew a person's value system very well, this would not guarantee that you could predict their choices or actions.

In recent decades, social scientists have attempted to specify the way values can be shared in a community and thus manifest differently from one community to another. This aspect of personal psychology has been greatly enhanced by cross-cultural research. For example, the American-born Israeli social psychologist Shalom H. Schwartz used globally collected data to refine a detailed model of basic human values (e.g. Schwartz, 1992). Loosely, the model identifies ten universal values, organized in four categories, that are believed to be recognized in more or less the same way in all cultures around the world. The four categories are values relating to openness to change (namely, *self-direction* and *stimulation*), values relating to self-enhancement (*hedonism*, *achievement* and *power*), values relating to conservation (*security*, *conformity* and *tradition*), and values relating to self-transcendence (*benevolence* and *universalism*).

Political scientists have attempted to explain the dimensions along which socially shared values evolve and change over time. According to the model used by the World Values Survey, a forty-year-old research project spanning nearly 100 nations, all human values can be described in relation to two dimensions (Inglehart & Welzel, 2005). A value can range from *traditional* to *secular* and from *survival-oriented* to *self-expression-oriented*. The World Values Survey researchers argue that societies start out with *traditional* and *survival-oriented* value systems, but that industrialization causes values to become more *secular*, more *self-expression-oriented*, or both. A country's particular history will come into play, especially when religion or revolutionary politics have been prominent. Some industrialized countries will retain more *traditional* values, whereas others will retain a more *survival-oriented* approach.

However, values do not cluster only at the national level. Other forms of group-level values are also common. For example, science is a group-level activity that has many of its own values, such as its commitment to objective measurement and to the honest reporting of findings. Of course, scientists who hold these values will also be citizens of their countries, and so will be influenced by shared national values too. Therefore, in principle, it is very possible that the overall value system associated with science – and thus with psychology – will itself be skewed by an over-representation of values from a small number of dominant national cultures.

Scientific values and psychology

As mentioned above, the common claim that science is 'value-free' is actually erroneous. Science is a product of scientists, and scientists are human beings who have their own personal values. The British chemist and critic C. P. Snow (1905–80) referred to the belief that values were of 'no concern' to science as 'the doctrine of ethical neutrality' (Weaver et al., 1961). Snow argued that this doctrine ran so counter to ordinary human nature, it could only be sustained by strong personal commitment or by the complete abandonment of morality. In other words, even the ambition to be 'value-free' is itself a value.

However hard individual scientists try to avoid it, their work will always be affected by whatever values inform their life's worldview. But in addition, science itself is a highly customized subculture that centres on values shared at a group level. As we saw in Chapter 3, the human practice of science arose because of ethical concerns about veracity: objective methods were recognized as having greater integrity than superstition, hearsay or authority. In other words, science values accuracy over anecdote. The scientific method recommends itself as a solution to a problem. It is inherent in science that it is intended to be 'good' rather than 'bad'. Science *itself* is a value system.

Scientific values are not exclusive to science. All forms of scholarship share the aspiration to improve knowledge – because they respect the value that improving knowledge is intrinsically worthwhile. All forms of scholarship share the premise that new ideas deserve to be heard – because they value academic freedom. They also share the corollary premise that, if proven unsound, new ideas need to be rejected regardless of who has proposed them – because they hold the value that accuracy is more important than personal reputation. And all forms of scholarship promote honesty – because their value system considers truthfulness necessary for human progress.

Of course, like all value systems, these principles are often breached in practice. All human beings are subject to human fallibility. Scientists, for example, are not innately more honest than other people. When we say that honesty is a strongly held value in science, we mean that scientists are more likely than members of other occupational groups to be judged for their honesty. Deception in science is especially controversial. When a scientist misleads others about their findings, it is seen as a much more egregious misdemeanour than when untruths are told by, say, politicians, lawyers or businesspeople (Derry, 1999).

But if anything, the gap between aspiration and practice makes values all the more important. A value system provides a structure within which people can *aim* to do the right thing. It also allows us to assess them negatively if they fall short.

LOGOPHILIA: 'DEONTOLOGY'

Deontology is an approach to ethics based on the premise that the ethicality of an action should be inferred from its intrinsic nature, and not from its consequences. In this view, an action can be considered unethical even if it generates no adverse outcomes (e.g. telling someone a 'white lie' to avoid hurting their feelings); whereas, conversely, an action can be considered ethical even when it does generate an adverse outcome (e.g. telling the truth to a criminal who then uses this information to harm others). Deontology is an alternative to *consequentialism*, which suggests that the ethical-ity of an action should be determined only by whether it produces good or bad results.

The idea of deontological ethics is often associated with the eighteenth-century philosopher Immanuel Kant, who we encountered in Chapter 3. However, the term *deontology* was not used to describe this approach until 1930, when the English philosopher C. D. Broad (1887–1971) employed the label for one of the categories in his book *Five Types of Ethical Theory* (Broad, 1930). The word is derived from the Greek words for 'obligation' (δέον, or déon).

Ethical values and psychology

Another category of values that are central to psychology relates to the ethical treatment of people. Codes of ethics laid down by professional associations, for example, place many requirements on psychologists who engage in clinical work, counselling practice and other similar activities. The principles resemble those that apply to any other occupation where a duty of care is owed to members of the public: to show respect, competence, responsibility and integrity when dealing with clients (e.g. British Psychological Society, 2018).

But clinical practice is not the only context where ethics are important. Psychologists working as researchers, scholars or educators are also subject to ethical scrutiny. The relevant codes require these psychologists to respect the autonomy and dignity of all human beings, to maintain integrity in their scientific work, to have regard for social responsibility and to maximize benefit while minimizing harm (e.g. British Psychological Society, 2014). The ethics of research cover a wide range of issues, from the proper treatment of vulnerable persons (such as obtaining informed consent from study participants) to the responsible reporting of results (such as releasing data for independent review, disclosing conflicts of interest, and transparently recording who exactly conducted the research in question).

The principles of research ethics are often discussed as though they are universal and everlasting. However, many of the ethical standards that are considered essential today have not always been seen as important. Our appreciation of ethical values changes over time and can be influenced by cultural events.

For most of history, the need to avoid human harm was not always considered to be absolute. In the first century BCE, the ancient Roman physician Aulus Cornelius Celsus (who we encountered in Chapter 4) observed that it would be quite acceptable to conduct research by performing exploratory surgery on live prisoners, so long as the resulting knowledge served the needs of other, more worthy, citizens:

> Herophilus and Erasistratus did this in the best way by far, when they laid open men whilst alive – criminals received out of prison from the kings – and while the men were still breathing, observed [body] parts that nature had previously concealed … Yet it is not cruel to impose on a few criminals when investigating new remedies that may benefit many innocent people throughout the ages.

> ('longeque optime fecisse Herophilum et Erasistratum, qui nocentes homines a regibus ex carcere acceptos vivos inciderint, considerarintque etiamnum spiritu remanente ea, quae natura ante clausisset, eorumque … Neque esse crudele, sicut plerique proponunt, hominum nocentium et horum quoque paucorum suppliciis remedia populis innocentibus saeculorum omnium quaeri'; Celsus, 1935)

Research ethics were yet another area to be profoundly changed by the events of the mid-twentieth century. After the Second World War, leading members of the Nazi regime were tried at a series of international military tribunals held in Nuremberg, Germany. An extensive set of proceedings were devoted to trials of concentration camp doctors, whose gruesome experiments had left thousands of innocent victims dead, maimed or traumatized. When delivering their verdicts, the trial judges endorsed a memorandum on research ethics that subsequently became known as the Nuremberg Code (Mitscherlich & Mielke, 1949).

The Code had been developed by doctors appointed by organizations such as the American Medical Association to advise the military tribunals. It emphasized that research should never be conducted unless participants have given their voluntary consent. Moreover, it stated that participants always retain the right to withdraw their consent at any stage without having to explain themselves. The Code prohibited all unnecessary suffering, both physical and mental. And it set out a number of provisions regarding the need for scientific rigour: all researchers must be appropriately qualified, all hypotheses must be based on scientific knowledge, and all studies should aim to produce results for the good of society. The risks posed by research should never exceed the humanitarian importance of the topics being studied.

The Nuremberg Code was widely recognized as a symbolically important statement on the need for ethical standards in science. However, it was never adopted as a formal law or regulation. Perhaps its main shortcoming was that it related primarily to extreme cases. Its tone and content were aimed at preventing acts of the most outrageous human cruelty. But ethical questions are not confined to the extremes of human activity.

Today, the primary ethical standards for research on human participants are set out in the Declaration of Helsinki, a code first ratified in 1964 by the World Medical Association. Its most recent revision was published in 2013 (World Medical Association, 2013). This Declaration has been codified in national and regional regulations around the world and is widely regarded as the authoritative statement on the ethics of researching human beings. It builds on the Nuremberg Code by incorporating principles from a number of other similar statements and international declarations. As such, while echoing the Nuremberg principles, it adds much greater detail to cover a wider range of situations and circumstances that can arise in research. Notably, it takes a more nuanced approach to the question of consent. For example, it allows for the fact that sometimes consent can be provided by a third party, such as a parent or caregiver.

Consent issues can be especially complex in psychology research. Some psychology studies are based on observational methods, where people's behaviour in public settings is recorded and analysed. Participants in observational research might not even realize that they are part of a research study. They therefore cannot be said to have given their consent to be involved. In other experiments, researchers sometimes need to withhold information about the study design, because they want to record their participants' reactions under artificially controlled circumstances. For example, as we saw in Chapter 3, studies are frequently 'blinded' in order to counteract the effects of expectancy biases. But if a participant does not fully understand the study they have signed up to, this then raises questions about whether their consent to participate can be said to be 'informed', a prerequisite for it to be truly voluntary.

Both observational studies and experiments that involve deception or misdirection are valuable methods of research. They can potentially produce hugely important insights while causing minimal or no harm to anyone. Accordingly, in psychology, codes of research ethics recognize that it can be acceptable for consent to fall short of being 'informed', or even 'voluntary', but only so long as the research topic is sufficiently important and no alternative research approaches are available. A nuanced approach to consent requires the delicate balancing of ethical considerations.

To date, the Declaration of Helsinki has undergone seven revisions. Within psychology specifically, a plethora of separate ethics codes have been developed by professional associations in different countries. Some key examples include:

- **American Psychological Association:** *Ethical Principles of Psychologists and Code of Conduct* (most recent edition: 2017b)
- **Australian Psychological Society:** *Code of Ethics* (2007)
- **British Psychological Society:** *Code of Human Research Ethics* (2014)
- **Consejo General de la Psicología de España:** *Código deontológico del psicólogo* (2014)
- **Deutsche Gesellschaft für Psychologie:** *Berufsethische Richtlinien* (2016)
- **Japanese Psychological Association/日本心理学会:** *Ethical Principles of Psychologists* (倫理網領) (2012)
- **Korean Psychological Association/한국심리학회:** *Code of Ethics* (윤리규정) (2004)
- **Nederlands Instituut van Psychologen:** *De Beroepscode* (2015)
- **Psychological Society of Ireland:** *Code of Professional Ethics* (2010)
- **Psychological Society of South Africa:** *South African Professional Conduct Guidelines in Psychology* (2007)
- **Russian Psychological Society/Российское психологическое общество:** *Ethical Code of the Psychologist* (Этический кодекс психолога) (2012)

While virtually all these different codes reflect the principles of the Declaration of Helsinki, they are not identical to each other. In addition, like the Helsinki declaration, most of them have undergone multiple revisions over the decades, and will inevitably be modified again in due course.

The very fact such codes can fluctuate in this manner could be taken as a sign that research ethics are entirely socially constructed – that they are so contingent on prevailing cultural beliefs as to be dependent on place and time. If so, then research ethics would be little more than the products of passing fads and fashions. Our current beliefs about what is unethical today would be valid only until they were displaced by different attitudes in the future.

However, it would be wrong to suggest that just because ethics codes are never stable, this means they are chaotic, whimsical or arbitrary. Rather, their revisability reflects the way ethical insights are constantly being refined. All new codes of ethics are based on some previous code, and in few if any cases do new updates wind back to old standards. Future developments might well incorporate new ideas about research ethics, but these will most likely broaden, rather than change, the way we appreciate what is and is not ethical.

For example, in psychology, ethical controversies are not confined to the *conducting* of research. As we will discuss further below, the *reporting* and *publishing* of research are also frequently contentious. In theory, ethical principles already exist to deal with many of the problems that arise. However, they do not seem to be specific enough to guide researchers' behaviour. Ethically questionable research practices – such as data dredging, selective publication and the exaggeration of findings – remain very common, if not conventional, throughout the field. As such, future updates of psychology's codes of research ethics will likely deepen their coverage of these issues, so that the guidance offered becomes more germane and robust, and hopefully more effective.

Public domain, via Wikimedia Commons

Image 12.1 The Nuremberg doctors' trial
The Nuremberg courtroom where, in 1946, Nazi medical doctors were tried for war crimes.

HISTORICALLY (IN)ACCURATE?: THE DACHAU HYPOTHERMIA EXPERIMENTS

Unethical studies should never be conducted. However, they do occur. One dilemma that then arises is whether the findings from such research should be considered part of the formal research literature, or whether they should be censored, on principle, and never used. A commonly cited example of this dilemma relates to experiments conducted during the Second World War at the Dachau concentration camp.

Among the many studies conducted there, a series of experiments on hypothermia have frequently been offered as examples of findings that should not be ignored. The concentration camp scientists wanted to examine the human body's reaction to extreme cold, including the way hypothermia leads to death. To this end they forcibly immersed concentration camp prisoners in ice water and measured how long it took them to die.

In a related experiment, they forced prisoners to withstand freezing temperatures in the open air while naked. And in further trials, they retrieved some of the prisoners while they were still alive and attempted to rewarm their bodies using various harsh techniques, including plunging them into boiling water. Many of these prisoners, too, were killed by these rewarming processes.

All these experiments were clearly unethical. Nonetheless, some scientists have suggested that their data and findings should be accepted and incorporated into broader medical knowledge. Others have argued that data collected unethically should never be used, as this would serve as an incentive to future researchers to conduct similar unethical trials. It would send a mixed message about the true ethical limitations on science. All these debates are premised on a widely made assertion: that the Dachau data are usable, despite the unethical nature of the research (e.g. Reville, 2020). Therein lies the dilemma.

However, it turns out that the Dachau hypothermia experiments do not in fact pose such a dilemma. When the archives were formally reviewed by a medical scientist in the late twentieth century, it was found that the research was far from scientifically sound. The experiments were conducted in a haphazard fashion, with inadequate scientific controls, and poor record-keeping. There was evidence that much of the data was either manipulated or fabricated. An assessment in the *New England Journal of Medicine* concluded that, overall, the Dachau hypothermia experiments had 'all the ingredients of a scientific fraud' (R. L. Berger, 1990, p. 1440) and were scientifically worthless.

Therefore, claims that these gruesome experiments challenge us to prioritize science over ethics are not valid. Despite frequent claims to the contrary, the Dachau findings are in fact of no scientific value. Therefore, they leave unresolved the central dilemma of whether unethical findings should be adopted – or censored.

The impact of personal ethics

Formally written ethics codes are a type of *prescriptive ethics* (sometimes referred to as 'normative ethics'). This means that they are based on reasoned proposals as to what people need to do in order to be ethical. They are public guidelines for behaviour. Prescriptive ethics stand in contrast to *personal ethics* (sometimes called 'descriptive ethics' or 'comparative ethics'), which are the beliefs people hold about what morality means to them. Personal ethics are individual opinions on behaviour. In summary, prescriptive ethics describe how people *ought to* think and act, whereas personal ethics represent how people *actually* think and act.

Needless to say, prescriptive ethics and personal ethics frequently diverge. They can produce very different outcomes. After all, one of the reasons prescriptive ethics even exist is because individual judgements are so problematic. A hot take on what is or is not ethical can be idiosyncratic, self-serving or mindless. History shows how individuals often make decisions that seem fine to them, but that others feel are deeply controversial.

But prescriptive ethics are not foolproof. In some senses, written codes can depersonalize the act of ethical decision-making. A person's own conscientiousness is nullified when they outsource morality to a professional body or review board. When faced with a dilemma, they can consult a code of ethics to decide what to do, and thereby relieve themselves of responsibility for any consequences. This is why professionals who make contentious decisions are sometimes accused of 'hiding behind' their code of ethics. But as we have seen above, ethics codes seldom cover all eventualities. Actual moral decisions are sometimes needed. It is itself ethically questionable to rationalize any and all dodgy behaviour on the basis that, technically, you did not breach some or other particular written code.

A related difficulty with written codes is that they can sometimes be rewritten. We discussed above how it is a good thing that all codes are ultimately revisable. However, the problem is that sometimes they can be revised under contentious circumstances. A notable example concerned the role of psychologists in 'enhanced interrogations', a method of interviewing political prisoners widely seen as representing a form of torture (O'Mara, 2015). In the aftermath of the 9/11 terrorist attacks on the United States in 2001, senior figures in the American Psychological Association (APA) rewrote sections of the APA's ethics code to provide legal cover for psychologists to participate in these controversial methods (Risen, 2014). However, in 2015, an independent commission found that these senior officials had secretly collaborated with military authorities in a coordinated effort to knowingly weaken the APA's ethical guidance. Not only were they motivated by their political sympathies, they also felt that their actions would encourage the military to hire more psychologists. As a result of the scandal, several of the figures involved either resigned or were fired (Ackerman, 2015), although many of them continued to assert that they did nothing wrong (Engber, 2017).

Ultimately, however morality is codified, individual values will always be in play. Prescriptive ethics will never supplant personal ethics. Just as the subject matter of psychology will reflect the value systems of the culture in which it is formed, its standards of professional behaviour will also reflect psychologists' own moral frames of reference. As with human life as a whole, science and psychology, both in theory and in practice, can never be 'value-free'.

HISTORY IN STORIES: *THE REPORT* (2019)

The Report (Burns et al., 2019) is a fact-based US political drama movie that traces developments surrounding the use of torture by the military following the 2001 terrorist attacks on New York. It centres on the efforts of a government-appointed investigator, Daniel Jones, to compile and then release a detailed report on the military's interrogation programme.

Central to the controversy was the use of so-called 'enhanced' interrogation techniques, which were established as constituting torture. Two psychologists are identified as having been contracted to develop, to advise on and, at times, to administer these methods. At various points in the movie, the psychologists are portrayed as passionately advocating on behalf of their approach, even when their military superiors voice scepticism. Jones later discovers that the two psychologists had no professional qualifications that would equip them to advise the military on interrogation methods.

The psychological research on torture suggests that such techniques are ineffective in producing reliable intelligence for any purpose (O'Mara, 2015). Nonetheless, it was in relation to these methods that the American Psychological Association were accused of inappropriately adjusting their ethical guidelines to curry favour with military authorities.

The Report shows how these ineffective torture practices were adopted and later defended by the military, and gruesomely depicts the unnecessary suffering of the prisoners who underwent interrogation. After six years striving to expose the scandal, Jones finally succeeds in publishing his torture report, despite concerted attempts by the military – and some senior political figures – to have it suppressed. The film ends with him leaving his job as a senate investigator.

ALMOST FAMOUS: JOE DIMOW

Joseph 'Joe' Dimow (1920–2013) had served as a US army mechanic during the Second World War, before returning to his home in Connecticut, where he worked in a number of small shops and businesses. He was a passionate social activist and had been a local organizer for the Communist Party since the 1930s. In 1955, he was arrested for his communist activities, but was ultimately cleared when the US Supreme Court overturned the country's anti-communist laws. After leaving the Communist Party, Dimow remained involved in political causes, and attended countless rallies (New Haven Register, 2013).

In 1962, Dimow signed up to take part in an experiment at a local university. Having responded to an ad, Dimow believed he would be involved in a study of memory and learning. In fact, he was to participate in Stanley Milgram's controversial experiments on obedience to authority.

Dimow was immediately suspicious of the experimental procedures, and refused to follow Milgram's instructions to administer electric shocks to another participant. As a former military man, he recalled being taught that even soldiers had a right to refuse illegal orders. He also felt that his experience as a Communist Party activist had given him an unorthodox understanding of authority. In his own words, he 'was not likely to be impressed by a white lab coat' (Dimow, 2004).

As a person of Jewish heritage, Dimow was sceptical that these experiments were, as Milgram later suggested, relevant to our understanding of the actions of the German people under Nazi rule (Dimow, 2004). As Dimow recalled, a professor in a research laboratory has little power to enforce orders, whereas in a totalitarian regime, a participant who chooses to dissent can expect to face very severe punishment, including imprisonment or even death.

Dimow was in fact one of a number of Milgram's participants who refused to obey orders. In his first experiment, Milgram tested forty participants, of whom fifteen dissented. As with many purportedly classic studies in psychology, the results of the Milgram studies were not quite as clear-cut as is often suggested.

A year later, Dimow took part in a march in Washington, DC, and watched Martin Luther King, Jr, deliver his famous 'I Have a Dream' speech. He would continue to engage in social activism throughout his life, and was a founding member of his local Veterans for Peace movement. Having taken correspondence courses in mathematics, he became a proficient tool maker, and worked in the machinist trade for several decades before retiring. In 2004, he wrote an essay about his experience of the Milgram studies for *Jewish Currents* magazine, where he often submitted articles (Dimow, 2004). He continued to attend protests. In 2012, the year before he died, he participated in a local anti-inequality demonstration – 'Occupy New Haven' – at the age of 92.

François Bianco / Wikimedia Commons / CC BY-SA 2.0

Image 12.2 The helping instinct
The urge to offer support to other people is itself a social value that can influence how psychologists view the world.

SOCIOPOLITICAL ATTITUDES IN PSYCHOLOGY

Inherent in a person's perception of right and wrong, what they value and what they do not, is the notion of their sociopolitical worldview: how they feel the world as a whole should be organized. Psychological subject matter is not unconnected to the rest of life. How people discuss and dissect each other's thoughts, feelings and behaviour is not confined to their views on topics covered by psychology books and websites. It is also intertwined with their sense of what is orderly and disorderly in society, what makes a good life rather than a bad one, and how power and privilege should be distributed and exercised.

When we talk about the ethics of psychology research, we often get bogged down in the procedural and methodological issues covered by formal ethics codes, including many of the matters outlined in the previous section. For example, Milgram's experiments on obedience (which we discussed in Chapter 10) are often criticized because of the way participants were deceived into believing that their actions had caused real physical pain to another person. Not only had Milgram misled his participants, and thus arguably abused their trust, his experiment also caused them to feel guilt over their behaviour. By engendering this guilt, Milgram exposed his participants to lasting emotional harm, against which he provided no safeguards (G. Perry, 2013). A similar issue arose with the famous prison experiment conducted at Stanford University by the American social psychologist Philip Zimbardo (1933–). Conducted in the early 1970s, this study had apparently shown that ordinary college students would inflict acts of cruelty on one another if assigned to particular roles in a mock prison. As with Milgram's study, the Stanford prison experiment involved deception. It also caused participants to feel shame about their own propensities for malice.

Both Milgram and Zimbardo felt that their studies were justified because the value of their work outweighed its ethical costs. Both studies highlighted the way human beings can be manipulated into perpetrating acts of cruel violence against innocent others. Critically, the results suggested that human beings are easily coerced by authority figures. In the eyes of Milgram, Zimbardo and their supporters, this insight into the psychology of obedience helps us to understand how ordinary people can come to support, and even participate in, despotic political regimes. Humans are overly prone to defer to authority, when rightfully they should rebel.

We noted in Chapter 10 that Milgram's findings have been found to be less robust than they first appeared. Deference to authority varies considerably by culture, so it is unclear whether his American study participants could be said to represent people in general. And such deference also varies over time, and in light of emerging research evidence. The very fact that Milgram's studies are so well known makes it possible that people today would behave differently if recruited as participants in such a study. Thus, whether his original findings can serve as a guide to *current* human behaviour is unclear. All these observations apply equally to Zimbardo's prison experiment. It is unsurprising, therefore, that attempts to replicate these studies (within contemporary ethical restrictions) have often produced varying results (e.g. Haslam & Reicher, 2006).

Any verdict on whether the merits of such studies outweigh their drawbacks will depend on a value judgement. If ethically questionable research can tell us something about obedience, then we can justify it if we consider obedience to be a sufficiently important issue. However, not everyone has the same view of obedience.

One of the lessons from cross-cultural research on values is that deference to authority can be viewed quite differently in different places. Most Western societies endorse an ethos of individualism, in which the autonomy of individuals is emphasized. However, many non-Western societies are more communitarian, and place a higher priority on cohesiveness among people. In communitarian societies, obedience to authority is construed more in terms of group loyalty and social consciousness. People follow rules (and thus rule makers) on principle, because they feel that doing so is important for maintaining regularity and order. The welfare of families, communities and the national population is seen as being as important as any individual's well-being, if not more so. Deference, therefore, is considered both ethical and noble, while rebellion and dissent are viewed as recklessly disruptive.

The differences between individualism and communitarianism relate as much to culture and politics as they do to psychology. Whether you hold an individualist or communitarian worldview will influence your attitudes towards economic policies, public health, the funding of education, the representation of minorities, press regulation, policing, the environment, international relations, the system of government, and a range of other political issues and public policies. Therefore, if (some) psychologists feel that research is 'important' because it warns us that human beings are *too obedient*, then this tells us quite a lot about their political preferences. Being *too obedient* is only a crisis if you feel that autonomy is more important than cohesion.

The very fact such studies are considered valuable in spite of their ethical and methodological shortcomings reveals how sociopolitical values are embedded in psychological science. The rhetorical worth of results often trumps the methodological rigour of research. In this way, the ethics of producing knowledge in psychology extend far beyond the treatment of participants or the particulars of research methods.

Knowledge about human psychology is often deployed in political debate. It is therefore important to understand that all such knowledge is itself framed within arbitrary sociopolitical worldviews.

Liberal attitudes in psychology

Milgram's and Zimbardo's studies are often discussed in terms of their sociopolitical ramifications. Both are depicted as warnings about the threat of authoritarianism. They showed that an authority figure, with very little effort, can influence a regular person to inflict harm on others. This can be achieved even when the stakes are low to non-existent, as when participating in an artificial research study rather than in real life. By revealing the way human beings choose to be 'good followers' rather than 'good people', these studies are said to cohere to a liberal political ethos: they highlight the dangers of conformity and conservatism, and thereby implicitly promote the benefits of autonomy and individual choice.

That said, the messaging of this narrative is distinct from the story in the data. The story told by the study data is that people feel compelled to obey instructions, whereas the messaging in the study narrative is that they should be encouraged to resist doing so. But the messaging here is arbitrary. It is selected by the researchers and by anyone who chooses to discuss the Milgram and Zimbardo studies in this way. The messaging is akin to prescriptive ethics: it recommends how people *should* behave. The data, on the other hand, are more akin to personal ethics: they teach us how people *actually* behave.

If anything, the data in these studies could be used to argue that obedience and deference are integral to human psychology, and that it is spurious to imagine that people could or should behave differently. The data show us how ordinary people are relatively powerless, that social dynamics are inherently hierarchical, and that it is the normal way of things for people to have roles: every interaction involves a subordinate and an influencer. In short, these data can be interpreted to promote either a liberal message that deference is dangerous, or a conservative one that obedience is ordinary.

The knowledge derived from research in psychology is characterized by a problem the American philosopher Willard Van Orman Quine (1908–2000) called 'underdetermination' (Quine, 1951). Loosely speaking, a theory is underdetermined when it is supported by some evidence, but not enough that we can be absolutely sure what to believe. According to Quine, we can never be totally confident in a single interpretation, because there will always be multiple theories to fit any available data. Intellectual judgement will always be required to make the leap from data to knowledge (Hughes, 2016).

A problem that arises in psychology is that sometimes researchers disregard this possibility of alternative explanations. They overstate their confidence in a single interpretation and fail to acknowledge the role of intellectual judgement in their perception of data. They falsely believe in their own scientific objectivity, without realizing the extent to which they default to arbitrarily framed interpretations. They are blind to the way their sociopolitical value systems shape their assumptions.

According to some critics, what makes this particularly challenging is the fact that most psychologists' sociopolitical worldview is extremely narrow. As a result of this narrowness, it is claimed that psychology as a whole exhibits a 'liberal bias' (Duarte et al., 2015). The body of knowledge that makes up formal psychology is said to be arbitrarily framed in ways that promote the so-called *liberal* worldview: one that favours equality, egalitarianism, pluralism, social responsibility and community rights, freedom of expression, openness to demographic change, wealth redistribution, the right of people to disregard or reject traditional ways of living, and intervention by government to engineer social change (such as by raising taxes to fund vital services or promoting public health).

By contrast, very few psychologists endorse a so-called *conservative* worldview. The conservative worldview emphasizes individual liberty, personal responsibility, traditional family structures and sexual relations, religious values (including reservations about abortion, transgender identity and single-sex marriage), a scepticism towards demographic change, the right to personal wealth creation, and a belief that it is immoral for governments to intrude on individual freedoms.

In sociopolitical terms, a liberal approach to psychology would be more likely to attribute people's thoughts, feelings and behaviours to situational and environmental causes; in other words, to 'nurture'. A conservative approach would be more likely to attribute causality to 'nature' factors, such as genetics. In this sense, then, the oft-quoted 'nature–nurture' debate in psychology does not merely arise from differing opinions about data, but is rooted in competing political philosophies. The nurture-oriented liberal approach sees people's lives as driven by circumstances but is optimistic that intervening to change these circumstances will be beneficial. By contrast, the nature-oriented conservative view believes that people, not circumstances, largely determine their own situations, and is therefore much less optimistic that interventions will make any difference.

This nexus between psychology and sociopolitical worldviews is not confined to professional psychologists. It encompasses all contexts where these issues are debated. When liberal politicians campaign for increased investment to reduce inequalities in educational attainment, in gender representation or in racial justice, they are adhering to a nurture-oriented view of psychology. According to them, intervening to change situational circumstances will fundamentally alter people's lives. Likewise, when conservative voices call for cutbacks to such initiatives, they are endorsing a nature-oriented psychological position, asserting that inequalities are not caused by circumstances but are inherent in individuals.

The cut and thrust of modern politics might seem like tribal warfare among political parties, but it is undergirded by fundamental disputes about how human beings think, feel and behave. Political arguments revolve around what people believe about human psychology. In that regard, the need for high-quality empirical research in psychology becomes all the more acute.

Some surveys of academic and scientific psychologists in Europe and North America have suggested that more than 90 per cent self-identify as politically liberal (Duarte et al., 2015; Inbar & Lammers, 2012). More than one in three psychologists confirmed that they would be willing to discriminate against conservative job applicants, by rejecting their résumés regardless of their qualifications (Inbar & Lammers, 2015). If true, this would put psychologists at odds with the general population, where the divide between liberal and conservative opinion is usually much more balanced.

Given the role of intellectual judgement in making sense of data, the risk of a political monoculture is that psychologists' views of social issues might be refracted through a liberal lens (Redding, 2001). Accepted knowledge on topics such as parenting, racism, religion and criminality could be hampered by double standards, and might be open to dispute.

Studies on social conservatism itself can also be critiqued. For example, some researchers claim to have shown that social conservatives are much more likely to engage in different kinds of unethical behaviour (Son Hing et al., 2007). However, the definitions of 'unethical' used in these studies – such as declaring it 'unethical' to prioritize employment over the environment – can sometimes seem very subjective. A person with conservative values would not presume wealth creation to be de facto unethical. Studies that use different definitions paint a somewhat different picture; for example, both liberals and conservatives seem equally willing to treat out-groups unfairly, when given the opportunity to do so (Crawford, 2012).

As with many other issues, it is important to note that psychology's lean to the liberal 'left' is usually discussed from the perspective of the United States. As such, both the terminology and the overall claim are worth some consideration. For one thing, the United States is a relatively conservative country. Much of what is referred to as 'liberal' in the United States would be considered quite conservative in global terms (Hilbig & Moshagen, 2015).

More importantly, the term 'liberal bias' is itself politically loaded, and is widely employed as an incendiary soundbite in domestic US politics. As such, when American critics accuse (mostly) American psychologists of displaying 'liberal bias', the label must be considered in terms of its originating context. American psychologists are just one of many professional groups to be dismissed as 'snowflakes' by American conservatives (Hughes, 2018a). Their empirical work is frequently criticized on political grounds. This tendency to reject evidence-based findings because they are politically unwelcome has been parodied by several American satirists, including one who quipped that reality itself 'has a well-known liberal bias' (S. Colbert, 2007). Outside this localized frame of reference, whether psychology really is distorted by a liberal sociopolitical worldview is far from clear.

As we have seen from the history of psychology, the field emerged within an overwhelmingly hegemonic White, middle class, middle-aged and male academic domain, and has been shaped by a century of Euro-American dominance (Hughes, 2016). We have discussed how many of psychology's theoretical assumptions are rooted in sexist tropes, and how unsustainable theories about psychological race differences, while often criticized, continue to be promulgated. If psychology has a collective case to answer in terms of structural sexism and racism, then it would seem difficult to simultaneously claim that it is engulfed by 'liberal bias'.

Many modern psychologists may indeed consider themselves to be liberal, but much of the accumulated science of psychology was created by conservatives. Psychology may be scientific by nature, but it is partisan by nurture.

Conservative attitudes in psychology

By definition, social conservatives wish to preserve the status quo in society, even if that means retaining embedded hierarchies of privilege and influence. They argue that change is inherently risky because the costs of change are unknowable but potentially great. Moreover, they worry that human beings are naturally prone to self-aggrandizing delusions, such as thinking they can perfect society through programmatic intervention. According to much social conservative commentary, history has demonstrated many times that attempts to improve society all too often lead to turmoil, and have the potential to precipitate the most heinous human horrors, including war and genocide.

The conservative view is that the current state of human affairs represents a finely balanced homoeostasis. While it makes sense to try to tackle social problems and to reduce human suffering, fundamental social change carries the risk of disrupting the homoeostasis with terrible effect. Even a small shift could lead to enormous but unforeseeable consequences for future generations. Few social conservatives actually want other human beings to suffer. Instead, on principle, they are distrustful of claims that suffering can be relieved through radical human action.

This is why many conservatives are wary of using scientific approaches to study human nature or the nature of social systems. They feel that an understanding of these issues is best achieved by relying on judgement, intuition and conventional wisdom. As we saw in Chapter 3, in some ways modern science itself emerged as a reaction against precisely this type of view. Its objective methods offered an alternative to conservative approaches to knowledge. The scientific method was premised on gauging information in terms of substance rather than authority. It held that those with social power should no longer be treated as possessors of innate insight; and, in fact, that their claims were there to be questioned. What prior to the scientific revolution would have been considered heresy would now be recast as scholarly peer review.

Before the scientific method went mainstream, intellectual disputes were resolved by social status: powerful actors shaped public opinion, while weaker ones were subjugated (Hughes, 2016). Science aims to neutralize personal power, and to resolve uncertainties dispassionately, based on evidence rather than eminence. But free enquiry is incompatible with feudalism; conventional hierarchies have much to fear from objective assessments of their worth (Beit-Hallahmi, 2015). The conservative tradition does not tend naturally towards bold new worlds.

We saw above that most psychologists, as with academics more generally, consider themselves to be liberal. However, these self-assessments might themselves be skewed by self-serving bias. For example, in most countries, the profession of psychology – both applied and academic – does not reflect the general population in terms of demographic diversity. Its own internal hierarchies accentuate the skew. Psychologists who hold positions of prominence and prestige tend to come from privileged sociodemographic backgrounds, and while there are occasional exceptions, leadership roles are disproportionately held by psychologists who already enjoy social privilege in terms of their gender, sexuality and ethnicity.

In the United States, the American Psychological Association has reported that almost 90 per cent of American psychologists are White, compared to just 62 per cent of the national population (Lin, Stamm & Christidis, 2018). A similar disparity arises throughout Europe. Undoubtedly, these trends are in part driven by wider social biases, including active discrimination against minority groups, as well as disadvantages embedded in the education system and the economy. But even within the profession itself, leadership roles do not reflect the diversity of psychologists. So stark is the problem of ethnic under-representation that in 2020 the chief executive of the British Psychological Society acknowledged that both his own organization and the wider profession of psychology in the United Kingdom were 'institutionally racist' (Bajwa, 2020). In 2021, the American Psychological Association issued an extensive and detailed apology for its part in 'promoting, perpetuating, and failing to challenge racism, racial discrimination, and human hierarchy' in the United States, noting that under its guidance the profession of psychology has 'minimised and marginalised psychologists from communities of colour' (American Psychological Association, 2021). Further, the APA statement drew attention to an ongoing legacy of such discrimination by observing that the field of psychology 'often continues to publish research that conforms with White racial hierarchy' (American Psychological Association, 2021).

Another aspect of social conservatism is its overlap with religiosity. A number of large-scale surveys have suggested that scientists tend to be less religious than the general population (Ecklund et al., 2016), but that psychologists are relatively more likely to hold religious views than, say, physicists or biologists (Ecklund & Scheitle, 2007). More than half of psychologists and psychotherapists will typically describe themselves as belonging to a particular religion, with two-thirds likely to state a belief in the existence of a deity or deities (Delaney, Miller & Bisonó, 2013; Hofmann & Walach, 2011).

Religious freedom is an important ethical principle, but it is important to note how the subject matter of psychology can sometimes overlap with religious doctrine. Most conventional religions present worldviews that purport to explain human nature in spiritual terms. If a psychologist is especially religious, then their interpretation of human nature will need to accommodate both spiritual and data-based dimensions. Many critics have argued that such accommodations are intellectually challenging, if not even incoherent, because spiritual world-views are inherently unscientific.

One area where this can be especially difficult for individual psychologists relates to the study of sex and sexuality. Many major religions argue that any form of sexuality other than heterosexuality is immoral. Scepticism towards non-heterosexuality is widely considered to be a core principle of social conservatism, and is commonly shared among socially conservative people whether or not they are religious.

Psychologists frequently point out how their field has been pivotal in helping wider society to accept diverse sexualities as part of ordinary human nature. Psychology research was instrumental in disproving claims that sexuality is linked to mental illness (Hooker, 1993) or that a person's sexuality results from nurture rather than nature (Ngun & Vilain, 2014). Psychology research has also highlighted the damaging effects of sexuality-based discrimination and prejudice (Meyer, 2003). However, while these points are undoubtedly valid in the present, it remains the case that psychology's accumulated knowledge base on sexuality continues to reflect a range of cultural biases that were dominant in the past.

For decades, the scholarly literature in psychology considered anything other than heterosexuality to be pathologically deviant. The first edition of the American Psychiatric Association's *Diagnostic and Statistical Manual of Mental Disorders* (which, as we saw in Chapter 4, is the most prominent directory of diagnostic criteria for psychiatric illnesses) classified 'homosexuality' as a mental disease. It was listed in a category of 'sexual deviations' that also included paedophilia (American Psychiatric Association, 1952). This listing remained the official professional psychiatric position until 1973, when the American Psychiatric Association, having established that there was no empirical evidence to support their previous approach, published new formal guidance. Internationally, however, the other main clinical directory, the WHO's International Classification of Diseases (ICD), listed homosexuality as a mental disorder right up until 1990.

Even after it was formally removed from official lists of mental disorders, homosexuality continued to be discussed in academic textbooks and journals as an example of psychological abnormality. In the early twenty-first century, one major international textbook on 'abnormal psychology' described the situation as follows: 'Although homosexuality does not appear in DSM-IV as a clearly definable category, we believe that sufficient controversy remains about these patterns of emotion and behavior – among both lay people and health professionals – to warrant consideration of the topic' (Davison & Neale, 2001, p. 404). In other words, while not an official disorder, homosexuality was nonetheless 'controversial' and worthy of discussion in an 'abnormal psychology' context. The authors presented their coverage of homosexuality in a section immediately following their coverage of rape, implying – presumably – that homosexuality and rape were thematically related concepts.

The converse of considering homosexuality to be 'abnormal' is the implication that heterosexuality represents 'normal' human nature. This idea that heterosexuality represents normality is infused in the theories and terms that psychologists use when they talk about intimate relationships. Even psychologists who hold the most inclusive attitudes about sexuality are forced to draw from a scientific literature that evolved during decades (and centuries) in which heterosexual coupling was seen as the standard format for human intimacy.

Research on heterosexual couples (or, more correctly, on couples who were *presumed* by researchers to be heterosexual) has been the basis on which most of our theories of sex and relationships have been developed. Newer theories then framed lesbian and gay relationships in terms of how they *differ* from heterosexual ones, positioning heterosexuality as the standard (or norm) to which other sexualities should be compared. Studies of heterosexual relationships have become textbook classics, from which generalizations can be made, whereas equivalent studies of other relationships have disappeared into obscurity (Thorne, Hegarty & Hepper, 2019).

Even studies of unrelated topics can be distorted by a 'heteronormative' bias. Laboratory experiments on collaborative problem-solving, social influence, audience effects, stress tolerance, memory recall and so on, frequently use gender-specific dyads: they systematically pair women participants with other women, or men participants with other men, in order to avoid the potential 'problems' that mixed-gender dyads might create. Whatever confounding that mixed-gender dyads are believed to produce is presumed to be absent from same-sex pairings, because participants are *presumed* to be heterosexual.

As individuals, many modern psychologists will indeed self-identify as sociopolitical liberals. However, the field of psychology, in terms of both its personnel and its accumulated scholarship, is far from radically liberal.

Psychology focuses on studying those people who live in WEIRD societies, mainly in former colonial superpowers that continue to benefit from imperial pasts (see Chapter 10). Its statistical conventions were shaped by the study of eugenics (see Chapter 6). It continues to debate sex differences instead of sex similarities, and to promote theories of physical symptom perception that first originated from claims of feminine hysteria (see Chapter 11). Its standard depictions of human relationships are framed in terms of heteronormative cultural contexts. And despite the fact that psychology has been accused of being politically homogenous, uniformity alone does not make it 'liberal' per se. Its practitioners are more religious than many other scientists and, critically, are markedly less diverse than the general population.

Psychology's practices and power structures cohere to a resting homoeostasis that, unsurprisingly, reflects the preferences of those who benefit from it most. As we will see below, the customs and conventions of psychological research are highly resistant to change. While professional psychology organizations often go to great effort to promote socially liberal values, the field has evolved from a lengthy tradition of deeply conservative thinking.

IS PSYCHOLOGY 'GOOD'?

One sense in which it is obvious that knowledge and values are linked is that it makes sense to ask whether knowledge *itself* constitutes a 'good' or a 'bad' thing. We tend to pursue knowledge on the basis that it has its own worth. It is better to have knowledge rather than not have it.

On the other hand, it is possible to argue, at least tentatively, that sometimes ignorance might be preferable. When it comes to human nature, for example, it could be that deep knowledge engenders a type of despondency. Knowing more about the limitations on human proficiency, or about the capacity of human beings to be abusive or violent or destructive, or about the way many people make decisions that are self-serving rather than rational, might cause us to become pessimistic about our futures. Similarly, knowing all the nuts and bolts of human relationships might demystify social interaction in a way that makes it feel mechanical and less enjoyable. Or knowing just how enormously complex psychological processes can be might discourage us from even *trying* to get our heads around our fellow human beings. People who know relatively little of what psychology has revealed about human minds might enjoy less stressful lives.

A related problem is that sometimes when we *think* we know something, we do not *actually* 'know' it. We believe it, or hope it, or support it, or imagine it, or become willing to defend the very idea of it – but we do not really 'know' it, in that it is not factually correct. It is impossible to 'know' something that is actually untrue. In other words, sometimes the so-called knowledge produced about psychology turns out to be unreliable. Too much of *that* type of knowledge would definitely be a bad thing.

Throughout this book, we have reflected on the history of psychology in terms of many of its key concepts. In this final section, we will consider some controversial aspects of how psychological 'knowledge' has come to be produced and promulgated. We will examine how wishful thinking sometimes gets in the way of good science. And we will assess whether psychology's knowledge production line provides us with what we need to understand how people think, feel and behave. Then, we can better address the question of what psychology is all about, and whether it has been worth all this effort.

Why psychologists exaggerate

In Chapter 1, we saw how many people consider history in terms of a narrative of linear progression. They believe that human civilization is constantly improving, building on its ever-accumulating stock of experiences and intellectual investments. However, we also saw how this historical metanarrative is often premised on unfounded optimism. Maybe the world is constantly getting better, or maybe we just think it is.

Certainly, many scientists appear to subscribe to a form of 'Whig history' – viewing their outputs as an inexorable series of advances – at least judging from the way they describe their own work. Researchers today appear to employ far more self-complimentary language when explaining their studies. In 1974, one in every fifty journal abstracts (the summaries that appear at the beginning of journal articles) contained complimentary descriptions of the work being reported. By 2014, such praise appeared once in every six abstracts, an increase of nearly 900 per cent (Vinkers, Tijdink & Otte, 2015). As examples, the term 'innovative' had become twenty-five times more common in 2014 compared to forty years previously, while use of the term 'robust' had increased by 15,000 per cent. The problem, of course, is that it was far from clear that the research being described was either twenty-five times more groundbreaking or 150 times more rigorous.

As it happens, the decades between 1974 and 2014 were almost precisely those during which disquiet about the quality of published science sprung, spread and reached fever pitch. Common practices and methodological problems led many observers to question the quality of what appears in journals.

For example, it was noted quite some time ago that the published research literature does not cover all research conducted in the world. Studies that produce boring findings – or no findings at all – usually go unreported. Sometimes journal editors reject such papers, but most of the time researchers do not even bother to submit them. Either way, the pages of journals end up presenting readers with a skewed sample of science: namely, studies selected on the basis of being eye-catching. Readers are given an exaggerated impression of how frequently eye-catching findings are produced.

The idea that unexciting research tends to be ignored – that millions of disappointing drafts languish forever unseen in the filing cabinets of researchers' offices – became known as the 'file drawer' problem (Rosenthal, 1979). While it is impossible to know exactly how much research ends up in the metaphorical file drawer, it is reasonable to posit that a good deal of scientific effort goes into producing datasets that are destined for oblivion.

A related problem concerns the way psychological science uses statistical methods to determine exactly what is interesting. By convention, statistical results are declared to be 'significant' when the associated probability statistic falls below the conventional threshold of $p < 0.05$. Many statisticians have pointed out that p-values are generally uninformative, are often misleading, and should not be seen as indicating what studies should be published (and, thus, which ones should be ignored; McShane et al., 2019). Also, as p-values are based on probabilities, there is always a chance that what is presented as 'significant' is not actually significant at all. It could be just a fluke. Nonetheless, despite these pitfalls, the vast majority of psychology journals continue to operate the conventional policy regardless. They are simply not interested in publishing research unless findings are 'significant' in p-value terms (Trafimow & Marks, 2015).

Professionally, researchers are judged on the quantity and quality of their published work. A researcher who cannot get their papers published will find it difficult to earn a living. Academics and scientists require publication records just to get a job. If they want a permanent contract, or any kind of promotion, they need to keep publishing. With such pressures, it is perhaps unsurprising that the imperfect convention on p-values has led to a range of sloppy research practices.

One of these is 'data-dredging'. This is where researchers take a scattergun approach to data analysis, examining different combinations of variables in a dataset until one happens to produce a statistically significant result. The particular combination that yields the required p-value is then written up as if the researcher had intended to analyse these variables all along. However, because of the probability-based nature of statistical testing, this highly tailored outcome could just be a fluke. Data dredging is very likely to produce findings that are 'false positives': results that look significant in p-value terms, but which are actually just random.

All statistical analyses can be tweaked, in the sense that all datasets can be endlessly reorganized, all variables can be cherry-picked, and all combinations of variables can be mixed and matched in as many ways as the researcher chooses. The problem is that each different version of an analysis will produce a different p-value. If a p-value is above 0.05, the researcher can just keep tweaking. When, eventually, an analysis produces a p-value *below* 0.05, they can stop.

Tweaking constantly for no reason other than to find a way to make p fall below 0.05 has become known as 'p-hacking' (Simmons, Nelson & Simonsohn, 2011). The practice of p-hacking is virtually guaranteed to produce false positive results. However, when research papers are submitted to journals, the editors only ever receive the final draft. They do not know how much tweaking was involved in its production, and so cannot be expected to distinguish random results from real ones. In ethical terms, *p*-hacking is (or should be) self-evidently questionable. However, given the pressure to produce 'significant' results in order to get published, there is always a temptation for researchers to rationalize *p*-hacking in self-justifying ways.

Ultimately, the result of such practices is that journals are almost certainly littered with findings that are reported as being significant but which are actually false positives. The distortion ensures that much of the 'knowledge' that appears in journals is, in fact, exaggerated. In a landmark study, the Greek-American medical statistician John Ioannidis (1965–) attempted to quantify the impact of this problem in the biological and health sciences, including psychology. His analysis suggested that spurious findings are shockingly common. He found that because of conventional research practices, the likelihood of publishing a false positive result is greater than fifty-fifty; in other words, that whenever you read a statistical result in a journal, it is more likely to be unreliable than to be reliable. Ioannidis entitled his report 'Why most published research findings are false' (Ioannidis, 2005).

As well as false positives, there is the problem of false negatives (or 'missed targets'), where studies fail to demonstrate effects that are really there. One of the reasons this can happen in psychology research is that study samples are often relatively small. Statistical analyses require volume in order to be valid. If there are too few participants in a study, then analyses will be unable to detect true effects as being 'significant'.

When the American psychologist and statistician Jacob Cohen (1923–98) examined the field in the early 1960s, he found that the average 'statistical power' of a psychology study was 46 per cent (Cohen, 1962). This meant the average study was so small that it had a less than fifty-fifty chance of detecting a true statistical effect. When other statisticians updated Cohen's work in the 1980s, they found that psychology's average statistical power had fallen to 37 per cent (Sedlmeier & Gigerenzer, 1989). By 2016, it had shrunk even further, to 24 per cent (Smaldino & McElreath, 2016). In other words, studies were now so weak that they could be expected to be missing *three-quarters* of possible findings. Such a sharp decline in statistical power suggests that the efforts made by psychology researchers to deal with this important problem have been especially poor (Hughes, 2018a).

Strikingly, despite the fact that psychology studies are so statistically underpowered, virtually *all* papers appearing in journals report statistically 'significant' findings. Even though studies should only be able to reveal when *p* is less than 0.05 a quarter of the time, they effectively do so *all of the time*. This supports the suspicion that the majority of published findings are indeed likely to be false positives.

To make matters worse, even those findings that are *not* false positives are still liable to be inflated. This is because underpowered studies can only detect a statistical effect if it is especially large. As such, published findings are likely to be unusually vivid instances of the effects being described, naturally occurring but erratically large enough to lead a finding to emerge as 'significant' in a small sample.

The incentives to extract significant findings from statistical datasets are not the only inflationary pressure on the reporting of psychology research (Hughes, 2018b). Other influences are external, such as the competition for public attention. Simple, short and attention-grabbing information is usually more popular than the abstract, complex or epistemologically challenging kind. Psychological subject matter attracts widespread curiosity. As a result, psychologists are frequently under pressure to explain their work in simplified terms. When audiences crave concreteness, psychologists often find that cutting out the caveats and emphasizing impact helps them to explain their work.

HISTORY REPEATING ITSELF: PSYCHOLOGY'S NEW PHRENOLOGY

We saw in Chapter 5 how the pseudoscience of phrenology purported to have mapped the human brain by associating specific psychological faculties with different areas of the brain's cortex. This endeavour ultimately failed for a few reasons. Firstly, it is impossible to assess the shape of the human brain by examining the exterior of a live person's head. Secondly, claims that specific brain areas were associated with psychological faculties were based on the observation of correlations. Correlations cannot indicate causality; they could simply be coincidental. As such, phrenology's claim to its own core knowledge had an unsound basis. And thirdly, the idea that individual brain areas serve separate functions is reductionist. It belies the fact that multiple areas of the brain can, and likely do, operate in an elaborately coordinated way. In other words, we have come to appreciate that brain function typically occurs in a manner that is diffused throughout the brain.

In the twenty-first century, we have seen a surge in research utilizing brain imaging technologies, such as fMRI (as mentioned in Chapter 9), that enable scientists to produce graphical representations of the live human brain in action. Typically, these images comprise pictures of the human brain in which specific areas have been colour-coded to indicate the locations of increased activity. This research is often said to represent the cutting-edge of scientific psychology. However, its critics have been less enthusiastic.

Critics have suggested that brain images offer an imperfect representation of the live human brain. Contrary to commonly held assumptions, an fMRI image is not similar to an X-ray. The brain that appears in the image is not the participant's own brain, it is a diagrammatic representation based on typical brain anatomy. The various coloured areas do not represent brain activity per se, because almost all the brain is active at all times.

What the colours represent are areas in which brain activity has increased in comparison to a previous baseline image. Moreover, an fMRI is not a single snapshot; it is a composite of multiple images of 'slices' of the brain that are combined to form a single overall image. In other words, not all parts of a brain image are recorded at the same time. This can be problematic when making claims that a particular image shows a single-moment reaction to a stimulus.

Most brain imaging studies have very small samples. We saw that the average statistical power of research studies in psychology can be as low as 24 per cent, widely seen to represent a methodological crisis for the field. For brain imaging studies, the average statistical power is far lower. According to one analysis, the usual statistical power of a published brain imaging study is around 8 per cent (Button et al., 2013), meaning that a typical study can be expected to miss around 92 of every 100 actual effects that could be found. Moreover, as we saw in Chapter 11, the vast majority of brain imaging studies – over 90 per cent of them – involve participants from WEIRD societies.

But the most fundamental challenge for brain imaging research is its inherently correlational nature. Even if it were accepted that brain images accurately represent brain activity, they cannot establish whether brain activity *causes* a psychological experience, or whether psychological experience *causes* brain activity. By analogy, if a research study shows that embarrassment causes a participant to blush, we would not ordinarily conclude that the blushing *caused* the embarrassment. We would not claim that a profusion of blood into facial skin capillaries *caused* the participants to feel a discomforting sense of social awkwardness. Yet, drawing precisely this type of conclusion – that a recorded biological event in the brain *caused* a psychological phenomenon, rather than *resulted from it* – is the standard method of reasoning used to justify brain imaging research (Hughes, 2016).

For such reasons, brain imaging research has attracted considerable criticism, not least from researchers in other areas of psychology (with more powerful sample sizes and study designs), who can only watch as brain imaging studies attract an ever-increasing share of research funding. This is part of a wider concern about the impact of equipment technology on research quality. While technological innovations might help some psychologists to produce better research, technophilia among researchers might also be unhelpful, by drawing attention away from the underlying epistemological principles that make rigorous science worth pursuing.

Some critics, alluding to the bright blobs of colour that signify brain activity in fMRI images, have dismissed the field as 'blobology' (Poldrack, 2012). Others have been more historically grounded, focusing on the reductionist practice of linking complex psychological experiences to discrete brain areas. These critics warn that brain imaging research is nothing less than the emergence of a 'new phrenology' (Pereira, 2017; Uttal, 2001).

The helping instinct

Another inflationary pressure that threatens to distort psychological knowledge is the helping impulse. Psychologists, like most people, appreciate being held in high regard. They want their endeavours to be valued by others. Indeed, many students of psychology choose to become clinical psychologists, counselling psychologists or psychotherapists precisely because they 'want to help people'. It is assumed that psychological therapies for mental ill health are beneficial to those who undergo them.

Psychotherapy, for its part, is a very old practice, often transcending medicine, philosophy, religion, self-help and mainstream society alike throughout the centuries. As we saw in Chapter 4, the medieval Islamic physician Rhazes developed structured psychotherapeutic techniques similar to modern CBT back in the ninth century CE (Haque, 2004). We also discussed how efforts to treat what were perceived to be mental illnesses varied considerably throughout the centuries, often drawing on spiritual beliefs or simplistic physiological theories. As seen with the emergence of asylums, therapeutic interest tended to switch back and forth between physical therapies and non-physical, or 'moral', treatments throughout the nineteenth century.

Freud's psychoanalysis (see Chapter 7) was one of the first forms of structured psychotherapy to gain mainstream popularity, notwithstanding its many controversial premises. Behaviourism, as we saw in Chapter 8, arose largely as a reaction against the mentalism that was central to practices such as psychoanalysis, and behaviour therapy, which was based on behaviourism, came to be seen as the main rival of psychoanalysis. Later in the twentieth century, therapies based on humanism and phenomenological psychology (see Chapter 11) famously sought to offer a 'third way' of presenting psychological help to those who sought it. Cognitive therapies emerged in the 1960s (see Chapter 9), and in the 1980s they were coupled with behaviour therapy to produce CBT, in an attempt to capitalize on the strengths of what were seen as the two main science-based approaches.

A recurring feature of the history of psychotherapy is that all these different theoretical approaches have been claimed to be successful. Proponents of each theory – psychoanalytic, behavioural, cognitive and humanistic – will assert that their own distinctive orientation yields effective therapeutic outcomes. This is despite the fact that the various theoretical approaches often contradict each other.

For example, psychoanalysis posits the existence of an unknowable unconscious, whereas behaviourism suggests that such hidden mental realms are an illusion. Behaviourism, for its part, dismisses cognition as a largely irrelevant side effect of being alive, whereas cognitivism, unsurprisingly, sees it as the central driver of psychological experience. As it is impossible for all these contradictory assertions to be true simultaneously, some of them must in fact be false. However, the different therapies *that are based on* these contradictory assertions all seem equally effective. This is why proponents of each type of psychotherapy are confident that *theirs* is the theory that makes the most sense.

While the different types of psychotherapy have many unique features, they also have many features in common. For example, regardless of theoretical approach, virtually all psychotherapies involve many of the same therapeutic components, such as: the release of emotions, the offering of reassurance, an atmosphere of trust and acceptance, some learning or gaining of insight, encouragement to self-regulate, the exploration of what is real and what is not, and the forming of an alliance between client and therapist (e.g. M. J. Lambert & Ogles, 2004). Therefore, insofar as people find different types of psychotherapy helpful, it might be because of these 'common factors' rather than because of the finer details that define each theoretical paradigm.

One hint that common factors might be critical to treatment outcomes came from a study conducted in the 1970s that, for ethical reasons, could never be conducted today. In the study, the researchers recruited a group of academics – professors of English, history, mathematics and philosophy – to pose as psychotherapists at a student counselling unit. When compared to actual psychotherapists, the professors were found to be just as good at providing therapy. Students who were 'treated' by these professors enjoyed the same level of symptom improvement as students who were treated by the university's professionally trained therapists (Strupp & Hadley, 1979). The study suggested that being trained in psychotherapy made little difference to a therapist's effectiveness. In the absence of psychotherapy expertise, it appeared that common factors had benefited the students just as well.

The American psychotherapist Saul Rosenzweig (1907–2004), who had been a classmate of B. F. Skinner at Harvard, was one of the first psychologists to propose that common factors might be more important than therapeutic paradigms (Rosenzweig, 1936). As a result, all therapies eventually come to be seen as equally useful. To illustrate the principle, Rosenzweig drew imagery from Lewis Carroll's (1865) *Alice's Adventures in Wonderland*, in which the Dodo bird, wishing to equivocate as to the outcome of a rather poorly organized footrace, declares that '*Everybody* has won, and *all* must have prizes.' As Rosenzweig saw things, all psychotherapies were similarly uniform; all are winners, and so all must have prizes. Arising from this, the proposition that all psychotherapies are more or less equal later became known as the 'Dodo bird verdict' (Luborsky, Singer & Luborsky, 1975).

Thousands of subsequent studies and statistical reviews have examined the efficacy of different psychotherapies, but the research has produced many inconsistent findings. An important feature of this work has been a pattern of 'therapeutic allegiance', where the outcome of a therapy study nearly always conforms to the researcher's own theoretical orientation (Dragioti et al., 2015). For example, when psychoanalysts conduct a study, they tend to find psychoanalytic therapy effective, but when behaviourists do so, they usually conclude that it is useless. By contrast, when behaviourists study behaviour therapy, they almost always report a strong effect, but if a psychoanalyst does so, it will be found to be inert. The impact of therapeutic allegiance even arises when researchers are given the *same* evidence to assess: psychologists who review the research literature as a whole will typically use it to draw conclusions that match their own theoretical preferences.

Therefore, it is important to examine the Dodo bird verdict methodically. Perhaps the most methodical examinations have been produced by a team led by American psychologist and trained mathematician Bruce E. Wampold (1948–), a director of a psychiatric research institute in Vikersund, Norway. Wampold and his colleagues have published many analyses of the research comparing different types of psychotherapy conducted during the past fifty years. They published their first tests of the Dodo bird verdict in the late 1990s and updated their dataset two decades later (Wampold & Imel, 2015; Wampold et al., 1997). Their analyses have consistently shown that across all the studies containing comparisons of genuine psychotherapies, the average statistical difference between any two treatment outcomes is zero. In other words, on average, all psychotherapies appear equally efficacious. All deserve prizes.

Individual studies that show a particular psychotherapy to be effective can always be biased by therapeutic allegiance. For example, CBT is often heralded as an effective intervention for a variety of conditions, but the relevant research rarely seeks to control for the theoretical orientation of the researchers (Leichsenring & Steinert, 2017). In addition, for the reasons outlined in the previous section, effects reported in any single study are likely to be statistically inflated. This appears to be confirmed by the fact that those psychotherapy studies which report the largest treatment effects fare especially poorly in replications. When repeated, the findings of the second attempt show either a substantially less impressive treatment effect than was originally reported, or else no treatment effect at all (Frost, Baskin & Wampold, 2020).

It is always wise to consider a body of research as a whole rather than one study on its own. When the totality of psychotherapy research is considered together, competing treatment differences cancel themselves out. The Dodo bird verdict remains a statistically robust, and recurring, finding.

Many psychologists who offer psychotherapy are unconvinced by the Dodo bird data. They feel it does not ring true to their own professional experiences. However, psychologists' belief in their own preferred modalities is subject to confirmation bias. When positive outcomes arise, therapeutic allegiance will steer them to attribute efficacy to their own training, experience, theoretical knowledge and learned skills, rather than to incidental situational factors that arise no matter what therapy (or therapist) is involved. When positive outcomes do *not* arise, clients stop coming for therapy. The natural attrition of clients ensures that therapists end up with distorted feedback: over time, they will hear more from clients who do well than from those who do poorly. Such problems make the personal experiences of psychotherapists a particularly *poor* source of information on treatment quality (Tracey et al., 2014).

The ability to heal other people from their suffering is highly valued in all societies. It is such a virtue that there is a strong social belief that striving to help others is worthy in its own right, even when it does not succeed. Just *trying* to help others is enough to make you a 'good' person. However, wanting to be able to heal others is not the same as actually being able to do so. Insofar as this impulse represents a value – a preferred outcome for how the world should be – there is a risk some psychologists might struggle to remain objective. It can sometimes seem harsh to complain about a study when the researchers were just trying to help people.

Ultimately, however, the good intentions of psychologists can backfire, if it leads them to place deficient research on an unwarranted pedestal, beyond ordinary criticism. The habit of selectively critiquing research in a way that distorts the evidence to bolster a righteous interpretation is known as 'white hat bias' (named after the hats the heroes used to wear in cowboy films; Cope & Allison, 2010). In science and scholarship, criticism is necessary for quality control. Work deemed to be beyond criticism will eventually see its quality evaporate.

In terms of outcomes for mental health, receiving psychotherapy is demonstrably better than not receiving it. However, it would be an exaggeration to suggest that psychological science has defined the reasons why, or circumstances in which, psychotherapy is especially effective. Our understanding of the relevant dynamics remains incomplete. Claims that one or other therapeutic approach benefits from special insight into the psychological processes that underlie mental well-being reveal a downside of the human helping impulse. The wish to heal others from suffering sometimes leads psychologists into believing that they possess knowledge that is not in fact available.

Positive psychology

A related impulse is reflected by the common advice that it is always wise to remain positive, optimistic and hopeful for the future. Popular aphorisms such as 'Don't worry, be happy!' and 'Always look on the bright side of life!' project a consistently buoyant tone. 'Positivity' is seen as a human virtue, whereas 'negativity' is implied to be toxic. One problem with this philosophy is that it can make problem-solving a tricky pursuit. After all, in order to solve problems, you must be able to see them. In other words, you must be willing to focus on the *dark* side of life now and again.

Because of its frequent focus on human problems, the science of psychology is often accused of being 'negative'. It is said to emphasize human failings over human strengths, and afflictions over achievements. Psychologists often conduct research into anxiety, stress, depression and mental illness; they rarely study joy, success or enthusiasm. In the late twentieth century, some psychologists made explicit efforts to rectify this reputational problem. They began to encourage psychologists to focus on positive human experiences, and to devote their efforts to studying the bright side of human nature.

The relatively new subfield of 'positive psychology' was formally proposed by the then president of the American Psychological Association, Martin E. P. Seligman (1942–), in 1998. Seligman had spent much of his research career at the University of Pennsylvania conducting research into psychological distress in humans and animals. His most famous experiments concerned 'learned helplessness', in which dogs in cages were repeatedly exposed to random electric shocks (Seligman, 1972). The despair that overwhelmed animals who were unable to control their pain was seen by Seligman as indicative of the type of mental disengagement that caused depression in humans. Perhaps it was only a matter of time before this type of research led the psychologists who conducted it to reflect on whether their field was overly focused on the negative.

Seligman (1998) called on his fellow psychologists to shift their attention. He wanted his field to explore achievement, happiness and optimism, rather than anxiety, depression and misery. He argued that psychologists' traditional focus reflected a reliance on medicalized thinking that served to limit their understanding. There was much more to psychological existence than could be revealed by the study of mental illness. Eventually, Seligman published an 800-page directory of positive psychological concepts that he pitched as a counterpoint to the pathology-oriented DSM. He called this classification manual the CSV, or *Character Strengths and Virtues* (Peterson & Seligman, 2004).

In succeeding decades, positive psychology has emerged as a popular field of interest around the world. Research on positive psychology has burgeoned and a number of scholarly journals have been established, such as the *Journal of Positive Psychology* and the *Journal of Happiness Studies.* There is also a thriving popular literature that invokes the terminology of 'positive psychology' to promote such notions as mindfulness, flow, personal growth, benefit-finding, wisdom and 'authentic' happiness.

However, unlike most fields of science, positive psychology did not emerge because it proved itself to be more useful than the types of science that went before it. Instead, positive psychologists initiated their activities on principled grounds, reflecting their view that a positive approach presented a more appropriately upbeat depiction of humanity. It gained prominence because of the value system it represented, rather than because of the utility of its findings. Endorsement by such high-profile figures as the president of the American Psychological Association lent it an additional aura of prestige, helping it to become a cause célèbre for many psychologists.

It therefore remains an open question as to whether positive psychology has tangibly advanced our understanding of the human condition (Hughes, 2016). While many studies have been conducted, many condemnatory critiques have also been published. The field is widely criticized for relying on weakly measured variables, such as self-reported 'satisfaction with life', and for interpreting ambiguous cross-sectional data with unwarranted precision and certainty. Some of its most cherished concepts – such as the idea that psychologists can arithmetically compute a person's 'positivity ratio' and use it to predict their life outcomes (Fredrickson & Losada, 2005) – have been debunked as error-strewn pseudoscience (Brown, Sokal & Friedman, 2013).

Moreover, research studies have suggested there are significant personal downsides to techniques such as positive thinking or unconditional forgiveness. Such tactics frequently expose people to the risk of being taken advantage of by others (McNulty & Fincham, 2012). And promoting a doctrine that positivity leads to happiness equates to telling people who are depressed that they should feel responsible for their own sadness (Hughes, 2019). Positive psychology can thus be seen as a form of indirect victim-blaming.

More importantly, positive psychology falls foul of what social psychologists have termed the 'person-situation controversy' (Epstein & O'Brien, 1985) or the 'fundamental attribution error' (L. Ross, 1977). This problem arises when we attribute a person's predicament to their own characteristics and behaviours, rather than to the wider cultural context in which they find themselves. By placing so much emphasis on personal virtues such as courage, optimism and positive thinking, positive psychologists have been accused of encouraging people to ignore social injustice. Using techniques such as mindfulness to transcend the hassles of daily life will be of little use to someone who lives on the breadline, or who faces discrimination in their workplace (Hughes, 2016).

At first glance, it can seem useful to teach people to focus on themselves and to think more positively about life. But promoting satisfaction with things as they are can mean encouraging people to ignore the social, economic and political forces that shape their lives. In one especially excoriating dissection of the field, the American journalist Barbara Ehrenreich (1941–) famously lambasted positive psychology for promoting social conformity and thereby stigmatizing political dissent (Ehrenreich, 2009).

Ultimately, positive psychology can be criticized for seeking to impose a fixed value system on human behaviour. After all, the very notion of 'positivity' is itself open to interpretation. Some studies that promote 'positive behaviour' focus on getting people to find personal growth in the midst of trauma, to seek benefit from chronically stressful experiences, or to prioritize opportunities for happiness over thoughts of remorse. Other studies that promote 'positive behaviour' focus on ways of getting people to wash their hands, to obey speed limits or to carry organ donor cards. And other studies focus on alcohol avoidance, or on discouraging people from having sex unless they are married. Not everyone would agree that all these behaviours are, in fact, intrinsically positive. In many ways, prescribing the remit of positive psychology raises the same challenges as attempting to define normality (see Chapter 4). The direction from negative to positive is not a scientifically objective proposition. It depends on your perspective.

Psychology's replication crisis

Good intentions and bad research make for an especially poor combination. When wishing for studies to succeed, for theories to be supported by evidence, or for therapies to be demonstrated as being useful, researchers can often let their optimism overwhelm their objectivity. As we saw in Chapter 3, the scientific method was initially promoted as a means to circumvent the many foibles of natural human reasoning. However, achieving perfection in science is as difficult as achieving it in life. The scientific method remains more of an aspiration than an actuality.

The subject matter of many sciences is relatively impersonal, allowing researchers to constantly push themselves to meet that aspiration. However, psychology is so intertwined with everyday human concerns that neutral detachment becomes far more difficult. Values intrude on all sciences, but especially on psychology.

We saw above how sloppy research practices can lead some psychologists to promote inflated findings, overhyped therapies or rose-tinted outlooks on life. Inherent in such sloppiness is an unreliability in what psychologists present as knowledge. The idea that much knowledge promulgated by psychologists might be unreliable is not new. In fact, such concerns have been expressed ever since psychology established itself as a formal research discipline in academia.

In Chapter 3, we noted how Wundt's psychophysics research was quickly repudiated because of its reliance on introspection. This rejection was triggered when other researchers were unable to replicate Wundt's experimental results in their own laboratories. Alarm at the problem of inconsistent replicability was to become common throughout the field. By the 1890s, the academic journals were already beginning to bemoan psychology's track record of producing unreliable knowledge, with the Swiss philosopher Rudolf Willy (1855–1918) describing it as 'die Krisis in der Psychologie' (the crisis in psychology; Willy, 1897).

So recognized was this crisis that a number of similar books on the topic were produced in the early twentieth century: Russian philosopher Nikolaï Kostyleff (b. 1876) published *La crise de la psychologie expérimentale* in 1911 (Kostyleff, 1911); the Soviet psychologist Lev Vygotsky (see Chapter 8) wrote *Historical Meaning of the Crisis in Psychology* in 1926 (see Brossard, 2000), while *The Crisis in Psychology* by German philosopher and biologist Hans Driesch (1867–1941) appeared in 1925 (Driesch, 1925). Among Driesch's arguments were that psychology had begun to lose sight of the biological aspects of thoughts, feelings and behaviour, to succumb to an unwarranted schism between the psychosocial and the biological, and to be overly reliant on correlational research. All these complaints would continue to exercise psychologists concerned about their field's various 'crises' for nearly a century (Hughes, 2018a).

In fact, by the 1920s, psychology's crisis had gained mainstream media attention. Writing in 1926, the German psychologist Karl Bühler began his essay on 'Die Krise der Psychologie' by noting that 'you can already read in the daily newspapers that a crisis has arisen in psychology' ('Man kann es schon in den Tageszeitungen lesen, es sei eine Krise in der Psychologie eingetreten'; Bühler, 1926, p. 455).

In previous chapters we considered how the emergence of behaviourism was preceded by a growing belief that psychology's research approaches had made it an unreliable source of insight. Watson used his *Behaviourist Manifesto* to demand that psychological scientists focus only on objectively verifiable data. He explicitly bemoaned the way that introspection allowed different researchers to come to different conclusions about the same phenomena (see Chapter 8). In other words, behaviourism emerged because of a concern about psychology's replicability.

In a similar way, the subsequent 'crisis in social psychology' (see Chapter 10) centred on how standard methods of research stripped away vital contextual information, leading social psychology to produce findings that were inconsistent with observations in the real world. One consequence was that North American social psychology research did not replicate easily in European settings, where the cultural context was different. Even more recently, the concern about psychology's over-reliance on studies conducted in WEIRD settings (see Chapter 11) amounts to a concern about the replicability of the knowledge produced by such studies.

Psychology's replication crisis became mainstream news again in 2015, with the work of an international group of researchers who called themselves the Open Science Collaboration. This group set out to systematically investigate the reproducibility of psychology's research findings. Having organized replications of 100 studies from major journals, they found that only two-fifths of findings stood up to replication in any way. Moreover, in virtually every one of these cases, the effect size of the replicated finding was much lower than what was originally reported. Put simply, while 97 per cent of the 100 studies had originally reported significant effects, only 36 per cent of the replications were able to do so; and for this 36 per cent, the new effect sizes were around half the size of the old ones (Open Science Collaboration, 2015).

The Open Science Collaboration then conducted a follow-up project, called Many Labs 2, in which they diversified their study samples. Again they found a similar pattern of results: only half of their replication attempts successfully reproduced a prior finding, and once again replicated results were generally deflated (R. A. Klein et al., 2018). Importantly, the Many Labs 2 project established that those studies which replicated successfully tended to do so across the majority of sites, regardless of sample nationality or country setting. This suggested that incidental differences in practical aspects of research were no barrier to replicability if an original finding was, in fact, reliable. The problem simply seemed to be that around half of the findings they tested were *un*reliable.

Findings such as those of the Open Science Collaboration seem to confirm the long-standing concerns about whether research in psychology really does produce reliable, and thus useful, knowledge. It seems as though large swathes of the research literature should not be assumed to be sound. This includes several renowned experiments that had become textbook classics in areas as diverse as social psychology, cognitive psychology and neuroscience, before repeated failed replication attempts revealed their legendary findings to be spurious (Hughes, 2018a).

Perhaps the most sobering lesson from these systematic efforts to investigate the reproducibility of psychology's knowledge base is that, in psychology, replication is virtually unheard of. Formal psychological research has been conducted for over 150 years, and literally millions of papers have been published. According to one analysis, only 1 per cent of papers published in the top 100 psychology journals, during the last 100 years, have been replications (Makel, Plucker & Hegarty, 2012).

Given the scientific method's emphasis on objective verifiability, we might have assumed that much of this work had involved the checking and rechecking of previous findings. Instead, psychologists appear to rely on using *p*-value classification as a proxy for replication. The problem, as outlined above, is that *p*-values are probabilistic. Using them to determine statistical significance represents a gamble on uncertainty: the risk of false positives – and of false negatives – is ever-present. We can never presume a 'statistically significant' finding reflects a real-world event that would occur again were a study to be re-conducted in the future. This is why replication, and thus replicability, is supposed to be a cornerstone of scientific practice.

In recent years, a number of initiatives have been introduced to attempt to curtail such problems. These include the convention of preregistration, where researchers are required to publicly set out their methods in advance of conducting a study. This achieves two improvements. Firstly, data dredging and *p*-hacking will no longer be concealed, and so can be better policed. And secondly, embarrassingly dull findings will not simply disappear, as the contents of the file drawer will be known to everyone. An increasing number of journals and research funding bodies now make it a requirement that research in psychology be preregistered.

Other initiatives relate to publication practices. Some journals now require all researchers to supply their complete datasets, rather than just summaries of their data, so that readers can see for themselves whether *p*-hacking has been used (e.g. Marks, 2020). Other journals have adopted a policy of not publishing *p*-values at all, and instead require authors to demonstrate the importance of their findings in other ways (e.g. Trafimow & Marks, 2015). Some journals have experimented with evaluating partially redacted research reports, from which information on results and findings have been removed. The aim of this approach is to allow the journal to select studies for publication purely on the basis of their scientific soundness, without being distracted by whether their findings are statistically significant or support particular theories or worldviews (e.g. Button et al., 2016). There has also been an increased emphasis on procedures for retraction, where research identified as problematic for ethical or methodological reasons can be formally withdrawn from the research literature.

However, these initiatives are far from universal, and they do little to correct the century and a half's worth of psychology studies that have already been conducted and published. It seems likely that publication practices, *p*-hacking, confirmation bias, reliance on WEIRD participants, under-powered sampling and a range of other problems have already combined to produce a psychology literature in which half the knowledge that is presented to readers might be unreliable. The problem for anyone who consumes this literature is that they can never know which half they are reading.

Psychology and the prospect for improvement

In Chapter 8, we saw how scientific revolutions are often more prosaic than passionate. They seldom involve discoveries that are truly heroic, but instead reflect the many pragmatic ways in which scholarly researchers end up jockeying for professional position. Rather than simply falling away upon the arrival of superior knowledge, scientific paradigms move from one period of 'normal' science to the next when a new consensus is formed in response to some or other crisis-provoking anomaly. Scientific revolutions rarely involve the changing of minds. Instead, as described by the renowned German physicist Max Planck (1858–1947), new approaches are assimilated organically, 'one funeral at a time' (Planck, 1950). It is the natural way of things that new generations of scientists supplant the old.

That is not to say that no researcher is ever willing to change the way they do things. Indeed, one feature of what has become known as the 'Open Science Movement' (Engzell & Rohrer, 2021) has been the breadth of its support, ranging from early-career psychologists to some of the field's longest-serving thought leaders. Requirements for preregistration, transparent data availability, the ethical policing of *p*-hacking, and an unwillingness simply to presume replicability have each become mainstream principles, rather than methodological fetishes. They are widely acknowledged as basic standards for psychology research.

Nonetheless, Planck's dictum retains some truth. A substantial majority of psychology journals continue to disseminate research papers based on all the old conventions. Relatively few studies that have been shown to be non-replicable have ever been formally redacted. And there exists a discernible subgroup of psychology researchers, some of them prominent figures, who are sceptical of the need for change. According to them, all this crisis talk – the public anxiety about poor replication, underpowered samples, *p*-hacking, confirmation bias, WEIRD samples and so on – simply amounts to paranoia.

The problems, they say, are overstated, and the proposed solutions overly extreme. One former president of an international psychology society accused those who question the field of perpetrating 'methodological terrorism' (Letzter, 2016), while an award-winning professor famously dismissed psychology's critics as 'shameless little bullies' (T. Bartlett, 2014). Other accusations have involved references to 'hate mobs', the 'replication police' and the potential that policing standards could 'destroy' the field (Sutton, 2018). It is notable that virtually all the backlash comes from psychologists who have already navigated lengthy academic careers (or who have reached retirement), all of which heightens the sense of an intergenerational shift. While their soundbites occasionally draw attention on social media, the reality is that modern psychology – along with nearly every other science (Denworth, 2019) – has now firmly acknowledged the insidious risks associated with historically poor practices, and the ways in which the situation can (and must) be improved.

It is important to state that the generational aspect to the current impetus for change is largely circumstantial. It has nothing to do with younger scientists being somehow better than older ones. The reality is that many of the practices aimed at improving research standards have only become truly feasible with the emergence of new technologies (Spellman, 2015). Reforms can capitalize on the limitlessness of online repositories, the accessibility of databases, the ubiquity of personal profiles and accounts, and the ease of person-to-person communication (Hughes, 2018b). The public posting of preregistered study protocols can be achieved immediately and without expense. In the digital age, printing costs no longer require journals to limit the reporting of research, making it straightforward for researchers to publish entire datasets online.

Ultimately, while human beings often find psychology very *interesting*, its true worth surely requires that it also be *accurate*. Anything that undermines the quality of its knowledge base must therefore be taken very seriously, and anything that enhances that quality should be embraced. More rigour is, by definition, better than less rigour. More precision is better than less precision. More clarity, consistency and care are better than less clarity, consistency and care. The entire enterprise of psychology is expected to exceed the suppositions of local gossip or social punditry; it is a formal process that brings evidence to bear on anecdote. If the evidence is weak, or weakly analysed, then psychology as a whole is made less worthwhile. The near-tautology that accurate claims are better than inaccurate ones should make this conclusion unassailable.

Making psychology matter

Making psychology worthwhile requires more than good science. It also requires that that science be used. Wishful thinking alone will never ensure that sound psychological knowledge is applied to solve the problems that matter most to human beings. Psychologists need to be willing, and able, to make the case for their own field. How this happens is itself shaped by the nature of human behaviour.

Some psychologists will see themselves as pure scientists, researchers who build an ever-growing repository of new facts with which the fund of human knowledge can be gradually, but inexorably, expanded. Others will see the process of science in less ideal terms, acknowledging that their work will always be subject to the whims of passing fashions and funding-agency priorities, and concluding that their contributions will need to be strategic as well as scholarly. How psychology gets used requires similar consideration (Pielke, 2007). The pragmatics of policy formation can also be either ideal or arbitrary: in an ideal society, all good science will eventually be recognized by the powers that be; in an arbitrary one, scientists will need to advocate on their own behalf. Working away on one's own research and practice might not be enough to make a difference.

As outlined above, no science is value-free. Indeed, such core ethical constructs as 'equality' and 'justice' are themselves scientifically framed. Equality means that one entity is of the same value as another; justice means that what happens on one occasion will, all other things being equal, happen again on another occasion. These principles cannot be scrutinized without some effort to define, quantify, observe and confirm what takes place. Equality and justice are not just ethical propositions, they are *logical* ones. They can be comprehended only by being computed. In this way, all knowledge about human thoughts, feelings and behaviour – all knowledge about human experience – has ethical as well as empirical import. Bad science is not just bad. It is *wrong*.

As a field of science and scholarship, psychology is much more than a bundle of competing theories, a study of Western civilization, or a story about 'Great Men' and their successive discoveries. Narratives that reduce psychology to a soup of academic citations, a parade of worthy people and their published achievements, focus far too much on what *psychologists* think and feel, and not enough on what actual *human beings* think and feel. They become stories about stories, rather than something that informs or educates.

The actual subject matter of psychology comprises concepts rather than events. In this book we have traced the history of a variety of these concepts, including the notion of *psychology* itself, as well as concepts such as *the mind, science, madness, human nature, race, sexuality, freedom, reason, society, bias* and *morality*. Psychology must always orient its telescope so that the subject matter, and not the observer, is what gets magnified. It makes sense that the history of psychology does likewise.

One of the key lessons from the history of psychology is that human experience, human welfare and human nature are each the products of a vastly complex and interconnected human life. The modern world is no less intertwined. The challenges of modern living, the problems humanity needs to solve, are never truly individualistic. The divisive threats of racism and sexism, the often casual oppression of minorities, the undermining of democracy and fragmentation of global cooperation, the way we disregard environmental integrity and food security, our experiences in the digital space, our preparedness to adapt our lives to existential health threats, including pandemics and lifestyle diseases, and the ever-present challenge of ensuring that all in society achieve their fair share of human happiness – none can be addressed without a rigorous attempt to establish the basic facts of psychology.

History never ends, and so it concerns the future as well as the past. As the study of human thought, feeling, behaviour, temperament, aptitude, attitude and well-being, psychology represents a potentially transformative intellectual force that can – and should – continue to shape its own history, and that of humanity, as the twenty-first century unfolds.

DISCUSSION QUESTIONS

1. Should the findings of unethical research be used?
2. Is sociopolitical conservatism compatible with scientific curiosity?
3. Is optimism really a problem for research? Would pessimism be better?
4. In seeking to improve our knowledge about people's thoughts, feelings and behaviour, what lessons can we draw from the history of psychology?

RECOMMENDED READING

- **Ehrenreich, B. (2009).** *Smile or Die: How Positive Thinking Fooled America and the World.* **London: Granta.** In this book, the author traces the emergence of the positive psychology movement, arguing that its practices do more harm than good because they promote and reinforce self-blame and apathy.
- **Hughes, B. M. (2018).** *Psychology in Crisis.* **London: Palgrave.** In this book, the author examines the methodological shortcomings and cultural factors that have contributed to psychology's replication crisis.
- **Leichsenring, F., & Steinert, C. (2017). Is cognitive behavioral therapy the gold standard for psychotherapy? The need for plurality in treatment and research.** *JAMA,* *318*, **1323–4.** In this article, the authors question the dominance of cognitive-behavioural approaches to psychological therapy, drawing attention to its limited impact in many contexts.
- **O'Mara, S. M. (2015).** *Why Torture Doesn't Work: The Neuroscience of Interrogation.* **Cambridge, Massachusetts: Harvard University Press.** In this book, the author outlines the ethical and empirical dimensions of suffering and interrogation, showing how scientific research confirms that torture is both ineffective and inhumane.

REFERENCES

Abhyankar, R. (2015). Psychiatric thoughts in ancient India. *Mens Sana Monographs, 13*, 59–69.

Achenwall, G. (1749). *Abriß der neuesten Staatswissenschaft der vornehmsten Europäischen Reiche und Republicken zum Gebrauch in seinen Academischen Vorlesungen*. Göttingen, Germany: Joh. Wilhelm Schmidt.

Ackerman, S. (2015, 14 July). Three senior officials lose their jobs at APA after US torture scandal. *The Guardian*: https://www.theguardian.com/us-news/2015/jul/14/apa-senior-officials-torture-report-cia (accessed 1 June 2022).

Alatas, S. F. (2003). Academic dependency and the global division of labour in the social sciences. *Current Sociology, 51*, 599–613.

Allport, G. W. (1954). The historical background of modern social psychology. In G. Lindzey (ed.), *Handbook of Social Psychology* (Vol. 1, pp. 3–56). Cambridge, Massachusetts: Addison-Wesley.

Allport, G. W. (1968). The historical background of modern social psychology. In G. Lindzey & E. Aronson (eds), *Handbook of Social Psychology* (2nd ed., Vol. 1, pp. 1–80). Reading, Massachusetts: Addison-Wesley.

Als, T. D., Hansen, M. M., Maes, G. E., Castonguay, M., Riemann, L., Aarestrup, K., Munk, P., Sparholt, H., Hanel, R., & Bernatchez, L. (2011). All roads lead to home: Panmixia of European eel in the Sargasso Sea. *Molecular Ecology, 20*, 1333–46.

Alvergne, A., Jokela, M., & Lummaa, V. (2010). Personality and reproductive success in a high-fertility human population. *PNAS, 107*, 11745–50.

American Psychiatric Association. (1952). *Diagnostic and Statistical Manual: Mental Disorders*. Washington, DC: American Psychiatric Association.

American Psychiatric Association. (2013). *Diagnostic and Statistical Manual of Mental Disorders* (5th ed.). Washington, DC: American Psychiatric Association.

American Psychological Association. (2017a, 15 April). *Division Profiles by Division*. http://www.apa.org/about/division/officers/services/profiles.aspx (accessed 1 June 2022).

American Psychological Association. (2017b). *Ethical Principles of Psychologists and Code of Conduct*. Washington, DC: American Psychological Association.

American Psychological Association. (2021, 29 October). *Apology to People of Color for APA's Role in Promoting, Perpetuating, and Failing to Challenge Racism, Racial Discrimination, and Human Hierarchy in US*. https://www.apa.org/about/policy/racism-apology (accessed 1 June 2022).

Amir, D., Jordan, M. R., McAuliffe, K., Valeggia, C. R., Sugiyama, L. S., Bribiescas, R. G., Snodgrass, J. J., & Dunham, Y. (2020). The developmental origins of risk and time preferences across diverse societies. *Journal of Experimental Psychology: General, 149*, 650–61.

Amirov, N. K., Bogdanov, E. I., Guryleva, M. E., Zefirov, A. L., Ismagilov, M. F., Mukhamedzyanov, R. Z., & Sozinov, A. S. (2007). The history of Kazan Neurological School. *Journal of the History of the Neurosciences, 16*, 110–22.

Amorth, G. (1996). *Nuovi racconti di un esorcista*. Rome: Edizioni Dehoniane.

Amouroux, R., & Zaslawski, N. (2019). 'The damned behaviorist' versus French phenomenologists: Pierre Naville and the French indigenization of Watson's behaviorism. *History of Psychology, 23*, 77–98.

Ancona, L. (2003). *La mia vita e la psicoanalisi: Una narrazione soggettiva di scontri-incontri tra psicoanalisi e sacro.* Rome: Magi Edizioni.

Anderson, T. L. (2006). Issues facing women prisoners in the early twenty-first century. In C. M. Renzetti, L. Goodstein & S. L. Miller (eds), *Rethinking Gender, Crime and Justice: Feminist Readings* (pp. 200–12). Los Angeles: Roxbury.

Anderson, W. R. (1945). Round about radio. *Musical Times, 86*(1225), 80–4.

Andrews, J. (2004). The rise of the asylum in Britain. In D. Brunton (ed.), *Medicine Transformed: Health, Disease and Society in Europe* (pp. 298–330). Manchester: Manchester University Press.

Andrews, J., Briggs, A., Porter, R., Tucker, P., & Waddington, K. (1997). *The History of Bethlem.* Abingdon, UK: Routledge.

Anonymous. (1836). The pope versus phrenology. *Phrenological Journal and Miscellany, 10,* 600–2.

Anonymous. (1878). Biology and women's rights. *Popular Science Monthly, 14,* 205.

Apfelbaum, E. (1986). Prolegomena for a history of social psychology: Some hypotheses concerning its emergence in the 20th century and its raison d'être. In K. S. Larsen (ed.), *Dialectics and Ideology in Psychology* (pp. 3–13). Norwood, New Jersey: Ablex.

Arendt, H. (1951). *The Origins of Totalitarianism.* New York: Harcourt, Brace and Co.

Armistead, N. (ed.) (1974). *Reconstructing Social Psychology.* Harmondsworth: Penguin.

Arnett, J. J. (2008). The neglected 95%: Why American psychology needs to become less American. *American Psychologist, 63,* 602–14.

Asadi-Pooya, A. A., & Sperling, M. R. (2015). Epidemiology of psychogenic nonepileptic seizures. *Epilepsy & Behavior, 46,* 60–5.

Asch, S. E. (1956). Studies of independence and conformity: I. A minority of one against a unanimous majority. *Psychological Monographs: General and Applied, 70,* 1–70.

Ash, M. G. (1998). *Gestalt Psychology in German Culture, 1890–1967: Holism and the Quest for Objectivity.* Cambridge: Cambridge University Press.

Astell, M. (1705). *The Christian Religion: As Profess'd by a Daughter of the Church of England.* London: R. Wilkin.

Atwood, M. (1985). *The Handmaid's Tale.* Toronto: McClelland & Stewart.

Australian Psychological Society. (2007). *Code of Ethics.* Melbourne: Australian Psychological Society.

Bachofen, J. J. (1861). *Das Mutterrecht: eine Untersuchung über die Gynaikokratie der alten Welt nach ihrer religiösen und rechtlichen Natur.* Stuttgart: Krais & Hoffmann.

Baer, D. M., Wolf, M. M., & Risley, T. R. (1968). Some current dimensions of applied behavior analysis. *Journal of Applied Behavior Analysis, 1,* 91–7.

Baert, P. (2011). The sudden rise of French existentialism: A case-study in the sociology of intellectual life. *Theory and Society, 40,* 619–44.

Bailey, D. H., Walker, R. S., Blomquist, G. E., Hill, K. R., Hurtado, A. M., & Geary, D. C. (2013). Heritability and fitness correlates of personality in the Ache, a natural-fertility population in Paraguay. *PLoS ONE, 8,* e59325.

Bain, A. (1866). The feelings and the will viewed physiologically. *Fortnightly Review, iii,* 375–88.

Bajwa, S. (2020). Igniting the conversation. *The Psychologist, 33,* 23.

Baldrian-Hussein, F. (2008). Hun and po, 魂-魄, Yang soul(s) and Yin soul(s); celestial soul(s) and earthly soul(s). In F. Pregadio (ed.), *The Routledge Encyclopedia of Taoism* (Vol. 1, pp. 406–9). London: Routledge.

Baldwin, J. D. (1981). George Herbert Mead and modern behaviorism. *Pacific Sociological Review*, *24*, 411–40.

Baldwin, J. M. (1895). The social sense. *Science*, *1*, 236–7.

Baltas, A. (1994). On the harmful effects of excessive anti-Whiggism. In K. Gavroglu, J. Christiandis & E. Nicolaidis (eds), *Trends in the Historiography of Science* (pp. 107–19). Dordrecht: Kluwer Academic.

Bancroft, J. (2004). Alfred C. Kinsey and the politics of sex research. *Annual Review of Sex Research*, *15*, 1–39.

Bandura, A., Ross, D., & Ross, S. A. (1961). Transmission of aggression through imitation of aggressive models. *Journal of Abnormal and Social Psychology*, *63*, 575–82.

Bannister, D. (1966). Psychology as an exercise in paradox. *Bulletin of the British Psychological Society*, *19*, 21–6.

Banville, J. (2017, 7 October). Novels were never the same after Henry James. *Irish Times*: https://www.irishtimes.com/culture/books/john-banville-novels-were-never-the-same-after-henry-james-1.3242726 (accessed 1 June 2022).

Barlow, N. (ed.) (1958). *The Autobiography of Charles Darwin 1809–1882: With Original Omissions Restored*. London: Collins.

Baron-Cohen, S. (2004). *The Essential Difference: Men, Women and the Extreme Male Brain*. London: Penguin.

Bartlett, F. C. (1932). *Remembering: A Study in Experimental and Social Psychology*. Cambridge: Cambridge University Press.

Bartlett, T. (2014, 23 June). Replication crisis in psychology research turns ugly and odd. *Chronicle of Higher Education*: http://www.chronicle.com/article/Replication-Crisis-in/147301 (accessed 1 April 2021).

Bauer, R. A. (1952). *The New Man in Soviet Psychology*. Cambridge, Massachusetts: Harvard University Press.

Bauerschmidt, J. C. (1999). Abortion. In A. D. Fitzgerald (ed.), *Augustine through the Ages: An Encyclopedia* (p. 1). Grand Rapids, Michigan: Eerdmans.

Beall, A. T., & Tracy, J. L. (2013). Women are more likely to wear red or pink at peak fertility. *Psychological Science*, *24*, 1837–41.

Beard, G. M. (1881). *American Nervousness: Its Causes and Consequences*. New York: G. P. Putnam's Sons.

Beck, A. T. (1972). *Depression: Causes and Treatment*. Philadelphia: University of Pennsylvania Press.

Beck, H. P., Levinson, S., & Irons, G. (2009). Finding Little Albert: A journey to John B. Watson's infant laboratory. *American Psychologist*, *64*, 605–14.

Beit-Hallahmi, B. (2015). Method and matter in the social sciences: Umbilically tied to the Enlightenment. *Behavioral and Brain Sciences*, *38*, e133.

Belvaux, L. (Director). (2012). *38 Témoins* [Film]. Agat Films & Cie.

Benbenishty, J., & Biswas, S. (2015). Developing cultural competence in clinical practice. *Journal of Modern Education Review*, *5*, 805–11.

Benedict, R., & Weltfish, G. (1946). *The Races of Mankind*. New York: Public Affairs Committee, Inc.

Benjamin, Jr, L. T. (1979). A century of science. *APA Monitor*, *10*, 1–3.

Benjamin, Jr, L. T., & Crouse, E. M. (2002). The American Psychological Association's response to Brown v. Board of Education: The case of Kenneth B. Clark. *American Psychologist*, *57*, 38–50.

Berenda, R. W. (1950). *The Influence of the Group on the Judgments of Children: An Experimental Investigation*. New York: Columbia University Press.

Berger, E. H. (1991). Parent involvement: Yesterday and today. *Elementary School Journal, 91,* 209–19.

Berger, R. L. (1990). Nazi science: The Dachau hypothermia experiments. *New England Journal of Medicine, 322,* 1435–40.

Bergson, H. (2014). *The Philosophy of Poetry: The Genius of Lucretius*. New York: Philosophical Library.

Bering, J. (2006). The folk psychology of souls. *Behavioral and Brain Sciences, 29,* 453–98.

Bering, J. (2008). The end? Why so many of us think our minds continue after we die. *Scientific American: Mind, 19,* 34–41.

Bering, J., & Bjorklund, D. F. (2004). The natural emergence of reasoning about the afterlife as a developmental regularity. *Developmental Psychology, 40,* 217–33.

Bernier, P. (2020). Causation and free will in early Buddhist philosophy. *Buddhist Studies Review, 36,* 191–220.

Bernstein, M. D., & Russo, N. F. (1974). The history of psychology revisited: Or, up with our foremothers. *American Psychologist, 29,* 130–4.

Berrios, G. E., & Gili, M. (1995). Will and its disorders: A conceptual history. *History of Psychiatry, 6,* 87–104.

Berryman, C., Ferguson, C. J., & Negy, C. (2018). Social media use and mental health among young adults. *Psychiatric Quarterly, 89,* 307–14.

Bettelheim, B. (1965). The commitment required of a woman entering a scientific profession in present-day American society. In J. A. Mattfeld & C. G. Van Aken (eds), *Women and the Scientific Professions: The MIT Symposium of American Women in Science and Engineering* (pp. 3–19). Cambridge, Massachusetts: MIT Press.

Bettelheim, B. (1967). *The Empty Fortress: Infantile Autism and the Birth of the Self*. New York: Free Press.

Bhat, A. R. (2006). Free will and determinism: An overview of Muslim scholars' perspective. *Journal of Islamic Philosophy, 2,* 7–24.

Binet, A. (1900). *La Suggestibilité*. Paris: Schleicher Frères.

Binet, A., & Simon, T. (1916). *The Development of Intelligence in Children*. Baltimore: Williams & Wilkins.

Blanchard, K., & Johnson, S. (1982). *The One Minute Manager*. New York: William Morrow.

Block, N. (1995). How heritability misleads about race. *Cognition, 56,* 99–128.

Bloom, P. (2004). *Descartes' Baby: How the Science of Child Development Explains What Makes Us Human*. New York: Basic Books.

Blowers, G. (2006). Origins of scientific psychology in China, 1899–1949. In A. C. Brock (ed.), *Internationalizing the History of Psychology* (pp. 94–111). New York: New York University Press.

Blum, N., & Fee, E. (2008). The first mental hospital in China. *American Journal of Public Health, 98,* 1593.

Blumenthal, A. L. (1998). Why study Wundtian psychology? In R. W. Reiber & K. D. Salzinger (eds), *Psychology: Theoretical-Historical Perspectives* (2nd ed., pp. 77–87). Washington, DC: American Psychological Association.

Bogaerts, K., Van Eylen, L., Li, W., Bresseleers, J., Van Diest, I., De Peuter, S., Stans, L., Decramer, M., & Van den Bergh, O. (2010). Distorted symptom perception in patients with medically unexplained symptoms. *Journal of Abnormal Psychology, 119,* 226–34.

Bogen, J. E. (1969). The other side of the brain. II. An appositional mind. *Bulletin of the Los Angeles Neurological Society*, *34*, 135–62.

Bohm, D. (1952). A suggested interpretation of the quantum theory in terms of 'hidden' variables, I and II. *Physical Review*, *85*, 166–93.

Bonnie, R. J. (2002). Political abuse of psychiatry in the Soviet Union and in China: Complexities and controversies. *Journal of the American Academy of Psychiatry and the Law*, *30*, 136–44.

Boring, E. G. (1923, June 6). Intelligence as the tests test it. *New Republic*, 35–7.

Boring, E. G. (1929). *A History of Experimental Psychology*. New York: Century.

Boring, E. G. (1950). *A History of Experimental Psychology* (2nd ed.). New York: Appleton-Century-Crofts.

Boring, E. G., & Lindzey, G. (eds) (1967). *A History of Psychology in Autobiography* (Vol. 5). New York: Appleton-Century-Crofts.

Bornedal, O. (Director). (2012). *The Possession* [Film]. Ghost House Pictures; North Box Productions.

Bowersock, G. W. (1996). The vanishing paradigm of the fall of Rome. *Bulletin of the American Academy of Arts and Sciences*, *49*, 29–43.

Boyer, P. (2001). *Religion Explained: The Evolutionary Origins of Religious Thought*. New York: Basic Books.

Braat, M., Engelen, J., van Gemert, T., & Verhaugh, S. (2020). The rise and fall of behaviorism: The narrative and the numbers. *History of Psychology*, *23*, 252–80.

Brandt, A. M. (1987). *No Magic Bullet: A Social History of Venereal Disease in the United States since 1880*. New York: Oxford University Press.

Braunstein, J.-F. (1999). La critique canguilhemienne de la psychologie. *Bulletin de Psychologie*, *52*, 181–90.

Brehm, J. W. (1998). Leon Festinger: Beyond the obvious. In G. A. Kimble & M. Wertheimer (eds), *Portraits of Pioneers in Psychology* (Vol. 3, pp. 329–44). Washington, DC: American Psychological Association.

Breuer, J., & Freud, S. (1895). *Studien über Hysterie*. Leipzig: Franz Deuticke.

Brezina, C. (2006). *Al-Khwarizmi: The Inventor of Algebra*. New York: Rosen.

Brierley, M. (1932). Some problems of integration in women. *International Journal of Psychoanalysis*, *13*, 433–48.

Briggs, L. (2000). The race of hysteria: 'Overcivilization' and the 'savage' woman in late nineteenth-century obstetrics and gynecology. *American Quarterly*, *52*, 246–73.

Brigham, A. (1845). Letters from Cinquez and Captain Wilkes. *American Journal of Insanity*, *2*, 285.

Brigham, A. (1847). Letter from Rev. Williams and letters from Mr. Cushing and Dr. McGowan. *American Journal of Insanity*, *4*, 74–5.

Bringmann, W. G., & Ungerer, G. A. (1980). The foundation of the Institute for Experimental Psychology at Leipzig University. *Psychological Research*, *42*, 5–18.

Bringmann, W. G., Bringmann, N. J., & Ungerer, G. A. (1980). The establishment of Wundt's laboratory: An archival and documentary study. In W. G. Bringmann & R. D. Tweney (eds), *Wundt Studies: A Centennial Collection* (pp. 123–57). Toronto: Hogrefe.

British Psychological Society. (2014). *Code of Human Research Ethics* (2nd ed.). Leicester: British Psychological Society.

British Psychological Society. (2018). *Code of Ethics and Conduct*. Leicester: British Psychological Society.

Broad, C. D. (1930). *Five Types of Ethical Theory*. London: Kegan Paul, Trench, Trübner & Co.

Brock, A. C. (2014). Psychology in the modern sense. *Theory & Psychology*, *24*, 717–22.

Brock, A. C. (2017). The new history of psychology II: Some (different) answers to Watrin's four questions. *History of Psychology*, *20*, 238–50.

Broemeling, L. D. (2011). An account of early statistical inference in Arab cryptology. *American Statistician*, *65*, 255–7.

Brossard, M. (2000). About 'The historical meaning of the crisis in psychology' by Lev Semionovitch Vygotski. *European Journal of Psychology of Education*, *15*, 361–7.

Brown, N. J., Sokal, A. D., & Friedman, H. L. (2013). The complex dynamics of wishful thinking: The critical positivity ratio. *American Psychologist*, *68*, 801–13.

Bryant, V. M., & Grider, S. (1991). To kiss: Why we kiss under the mistletoe at Christmas. *The World & I*, *6*, 613–19.

Buchner, E. F. (1907). Psychological progress in 1906. *Psychological Bulletin*, *4*, 1–9.

Bühler, K. (1926). Die Krise der Psychologie. *Kant-Studien*, *31*, 455–526.

Buller, D. J. (2005). *Adapting Minds: Evolutionary Psychology and the Persistent Quest for Human Nature*. Cambridge, Massachusetts: MIT Press.

Bures, F. (2016). *The Geography of Madness: Penis Thieves, Voodoo Death, and the Search for the Meaning of the World's Strangest Syndromes*. New York: Melville House.

Burger, R. (2008). *Aristotle's Dialogue with Socrates: On the Nicomachean Ethics*. Chicago: University of Chicago Press.

Burgess, G. (1992). The divine right of kings reconsidered. *English Historical Review*, *107*, 837–61.

Burman, J. T. (2018). Through the looking glass: PsycINFO as an historical archive of trends in psychology. *History of Psychology*, *21*, 302–33.

Burnet, J. (1930). *Early Greek Philosophy* (3rd ed.). London: A. & C. Black.

Burns, S. Z. (Director). (2019). *The Report* [Film]. VICE Studios; Unbranded Pictures; Margin of Error; Topic Studios.

Burnyeat, M. (1990). *The Theaetetus of Plato*. Indianapolis: Hackett.

Burrows, G. M. (1828). *Commentaries on the Causes, Forms, Symptoms, and Treatment, Moral and Medical, of Insanity*. London: Thomas and George Underwood.

Butterfield, H. (1931). *The Whig Interpretation of History*. London: G. Bell.

Button, K. S., Bal, L., Clark, A., & Shipley, T. (2016). Preventing the ends from justifying the means: Withholding results to address publication bias in peer-review. *BMC Psychology*, *4*, 59.

Button, K. S., Ioannidis, J. P., Mokrysz, C., Nosek, B. A., Flint, J., Robinson, E. S., & Munafò, M. R. (2013). Power failure: Why small sample size undermines the reliability of neuroscience. *Nature Reviews Neuroscience*, *14*, 365–76.

Bynum, T. W. (1987). A new look at Aristotle's theory of perception. *History of Philosophy Quarterly*, *4*, 163–78.

Cahalan, S. (2019). *The Great Pretender: The Undercover Mission That Changed Our Understanding of Madness*. New York: Grand Central.

Campbell, D. E. (2006). Religious 'threat' in contemporary presidential elections. *Journal of Politics*, *68*, 104–15.

Campbell, G., Roberts, K. A., & Sarkaria, N. (2020). *Harmful Traditional Practices: Prevention, Protection, and Policing*. London: Palgrave Macmillan.

Canguilhem, G. (1958). Qu'est-ce que la psychologie? *Revue de Métaphysique et de Morale, 63,* 12–25.

Cannon, W. (1932). *Wisdom of the Body.* New York: Norton.

Capshew, J. H. (1992). Psychologists on site: A reconnaissance of the historiography of the laboratory. *American Psychologist, 47,* 132–42.

Carlyle, T. (1841). *On Heroes, Hero-Worship, and the Heroic in History.* London: James Fraser.

Carroll, L. (1865). *Alice's Adventures in Wonderland.* London: Macmillan.

Cartwright, S. A. (1851). Report on the diseases and physical peculiarities of the Negro race. *New Orleans Medical and Surgical Journal, 7,* 691–715.

Carus, F. A. (1808). *Geschichte der Psychologie.* Leipzig: Johan Ambrosius Barth.

Cattell, J. M. (1903). A statistical study of eminent men. *Popular Science Monthly, 62,* 359–77.

Cattell, J. M. (1906). *American Men of Science: A Biographical Directory.* New York: The Science Press.

Cattell, R. B. (1933). *Psychology and Social Progress: Mankind and Destiny from the Standpoint of a Scientist.* London: C. W. Daniel.

Cattell, R. B. (1971). *Abilities: Their Structure, Growth, and Action.* New York: Houghton Mifflin.

Celsus (1935). *De medicina: With an English Translation by W. G. Spencer.* London: Heinemann.

Chapman, J., Estcourt, C. S., & Hua, Z. (2008). Saving 'face' and 'othering': Getting to the root of barriers to condom use among Chinese female sex workers. *Sexual Health, 5,* 291–8.

Chen, T. M. (2010). Use the past to serve the present; the foreign to serve China. In B. Wang (ed.), *Words and Their Stories: Essays on the Language of the Chinese Revolution* (pp. 205–25). Leiden: Brill.

Cheung, N. (Director). (2015). *Keeper of Darkness* [Film]. One Cool Film Production; United Filmmakers Organisation.

Chiao, J. Y. (2009). Cultural neuroscience: A once and future discipline. *Progress in Brain Research, 178,* 287–304.

Chomsky, N. (1957). *Syntactic Structures.* The Hague: Mouton.

Chomsky, N. (1959). Review of *Verbal Behavior,* by B. F. Skinner. *Language, 35,* 26–58.

Clark, E. H. (1873). *Sex in Education; Or, a Fair Chance for the Girls.* Boston: James R. Osgood and Company.

Clingingsmith, D. (2017). Are the world's languages consolidating? The dynamics and distribution of language populations. *Economic Journal, 127,* 143–76.

Clutton-Brock, J. (1995). Aristotle, the scale of nature, and modern attitudes to animals. *Social Research, 62,* 421–40.

Cohen, J. (1962). The statistical power of abnormal-social psychological research: A review. *Journal of Abnormal and Social Psychology, 65,* 145–53.

Colbert, C. (1997). *A Measure of Perfection: Phrenology and the Fine Arts in America.* Chapel Hill: University of North Carolina Press.

Colbert, S. (2007). *I Am America (And So Can You!).* New York: Grand Central Publishing.

Collins, A. F. (1999). The enduring appeal of physiognomy: Physical appearance as a sign of temperament, character, and intelligence. *History of Psychology, 2,* 251–76.

Colvile, R. (2016, 20 July). *Spot the WEIRDo.* Aeon. https://aeon.co/essays/american-undergrads-are-too-weird-to-stand-for-all-humanity (accessed 1 June 2022).

Combe, G. (1828). *The Constitution of Man Considered in Relation to External Objects.* Edinburgh/London: Anderson/Longman.

Comte, A. (1838). *Cours de philosophie positive, tome troisième: La philosophie chimique et la philosophie biologique.* Paris: Bachelier.

Comte, A. (1839). *Cours de philosophie positive, tome quatrième: La partie dogmatique de la philosophie sociale.* Paris: Bachelier.

Connolly, J. M. (2014). *Living without Why: Meister Eckhart's Critique of the Medieval Concept of Will.* Oxford: Oxford University Press.

Conrad, G. W., & Demarest, A. A. (1984). *Religion and Empire: The Dynamics of Aztec and Inca Expansionism.* Cambridge: Cambridge University Press.

Consejo General de la Psicología de España. (2014). *Código deontológico del psicólogo.* Madrid: Consejo General de la Psicología de España.

Coon, D. J. (1992). Testing the limits of sense and science: American experimental psychologists combat spiritualism, 1880–1920. *American Psychologist, 47,* 143–51.

Cooperrider, K. (2019, 23 January). *What happens to cognitive diversity when everyone is more WEIRD?* Aeon. https://aeon.co/ideas/what-happens-to-cognitive-diversity-when-everyone-is-more-weird (accessed 1 June 2022).

Cope, M. B., & Allison, D. B. (2010). White hat bias: Examples of its presence in obesity research and a call for renewed commitment to faithfulness in research reporting. *International Journal of Obesity, 34,* 84–8.

Cornford, F. M. (1912). Psychology and the social structure in the *Republic* of Plato. *Classical Quarterly, 6,* 246–65.

Cosmides, L., & Tooby, J. (1987). From evolution to behavior: Evolutionary psychology as the missing link. In J. Dupré (ed.), *The Latest on the Best: Essays on Evolution and Optimality* (pp. 277–306). Cambridge, Massachusetts: MIT Press.

Costa, P. T., & McCrae, R. R. (1992). *NEO PI-R: Professional Manual – Revised NEO PI-R and NEO-FFI.* Florida: Psychological Assessment Resources, Inc.

Crafts, L. W., Schneirla, T. C., Robinson, E. E., & Gilbert, R. W. (1938). *Recent Experiments in Psychology.* New York: McGraw-Hill.

Crawford, J. T. (2012). The ideologically objectionable premise model: Predicting biased political judgments on the left and right. *Journal of Experimental Social Psychology, 48,* 138–51.

Crivellato, E., & Ribatti, D. (2007). Soul, mind, brain: Greek philosophy and the birth of neuroscience. *Brain Research Bulletin, 71,* 327–36.

Cummings, L. (2020). *Fallacies in Medicine and Health: Critical Thinking, Argumentation and Communication.* Cham, Switzerland: Palgrave Macmillan.

Curtis, D., & Balloux, F. (2020). Topical ethical issues in the publication of human genetics research. *Annals of Human Genetics, 84,* 313–14.

Daileda, C. (2017, 27 April). *Wake up, sheeple: your favorite political insult is now officially a word.* Mashable. https://mashable.com/2017/04/27/sheeple-word-merriam-webster (accessed 1 June 2022).

Dain, N. (1964). *Concepts of Insanity in the United States.* New Brunswick, New Jersey: Rutgers University Press.

Daley, J. (2018, 11 January). Secret eugenics conference uncovered at University College London. *The Scientist:* https://www.the-scientist.com/the-nutshell/secret-eugenics-conference-uncovered-at-university-college-london-30423 (accessed 1 June 2022).

Danziger, K. (1990). *Constructing the Subject: Historical Origins of Psychological Research.* Cambridge: Cambridge University Press.

Danziger, K. (1997). *Naming the Mind: How Psychology Found Its Language*. London: Sage.

Danziger, K. (2013). Psychology and its history. *Theory & Psychology*, *23*(6), 829–39.

Darley, J. M., & Latané, B. (1968). Bystander intervention in emergencies: Diffusion of responsibility. *Journal of Personality and Social Psychology*, *8*, 377–83.

Dartnell, L. (2020). *Origins: How the Earth Shaped Human History*. London: Vintage.

Darwin, C. (1839). *Journal of Researches into the Geology and Natural History of the Various Countries Visited by HMS Beagle, under the Command of Captain FitzRoy, RN, from 1832 to 1836*. London: Henry Colburn.

Darwin, C. (1859). *On the Origin of Species by Means of Natural Selection, or the Preservation of Favoured Races in the Struggle for Life*. London: John Murray.

Darwin, C. (1871). *The Descent of Man, and Selection in Relation to Sex*. London: John Murray.

Darwin, C. (1872). *The Expression of the Emotions in Man and Animals*. London: John Murray.

Darwin, E. (1796). *Zoonomia; Or, the Laws of Organic Life*. London: J. Johnson.

Davison, G. C., & Neale, J. M. (2001). *Abnormal Psychology* (8th ed.). New York: John Wiley & Sons.

Dawkins, R. (1976). *The Selfish Gene*. Oxford: Oxford University Press.

Decker, H. S. (2004). The psychiatric works of Emil Kraepelin: A many-faceted story of modern medicine. *Journal of the History of the Neurosciences*, *13*, 248–76.

Decker, H. S. (2015). Cyclical swings: The bête noire of psychiatry. *History of Psychology*, *19*, 52–6.

Declerck, C. H., Boone, C., & Kiyonari, T. (2010). Oxytocin and cooperation under conditions of uncertainty: The modulating role of incentives and social information. *Hormones and Behavior*, *57*, 368–74.

Decoin, D. (2009). *Est-ce ainsi que les femmes meurent?* Paris: Grasset.

Deese, J., & Hulse, S. H. (1967). *The Psychology of Learning* (3rd ed.). New York: McGraw Hill.

Delaney, H. D., Miller, W. R., & Bisonó, A. M. (2013). Religiosity and spirituality among psychologists: A survey of clinician members of the American Psychological Association. *Spirituality in Clinical Practice*, *1*(S), 95–106.

Del Maestro, R. F. (1998). Leonardo da Vinci: The search for the soul. *Journal of Neurosurgery*, *89*, 874–87.

Delmonte, R., Lucchetti, G., Moreira-Almeida, A., & Farias, M. (2016). Can the *DSM-5* differentiate between nonpathological possession and dissociative identity disorder? A case study. *Journal of Trauma & Dissociation*, *17*, 322–37.

Dennis, A. (2018). The strange survival and apparent resurgence of sociobiology. *History of the Human Sciences*, *31*, 19–35.

Denworth, L. (2019). A significant problem. *Scientific American*, *321*(4), 62–7.

Derry, G. N. (1999). *What Science Is and How It Works*. Princeton, New Jersey: Princeton University Press.

Descartes, R. (1637). *Discours de la methode pour bien conduire sa raison, & chercher la verité dans les sciences: plus la dioptrique, les meteores, et la geometrie, qui sont des essais de cete methode*. Leiden: Jan Maire.

Descartes, R. (1644). *Principia philosophiæ*. Amsterdam: Elzevir.

Deshmukh, V. D. (2011). Vedic psychology: A science of wisdom. *Journal of Alternative Medicine Research*, *3*, 29–43.

Deutsch, A. (1944). The first US census of the insane (1840) and its use as pro-slavery propaganda. *Bulletin of the History of Medicine*, *15*, 469–82.

Deutsche Gesellschaft für Psychologie. (2016). *Berufsethische Richtlinien des Berufsverbandes Deutscher Psychologinnen und Psychologen e.V. und der Deutschen Gesellschaft für Psychologie e.V. zugleich des Berufsverbandes Deutscher Psychologinnen und Psychologen e.V.* Berlin: Föderation Deutscher Psychologenvereinigungen.

de Young, M. (2015). *Encyclopedia of Asylum Therapeutics, 1750–1950s.* Jefferson, North Carolina: McFarland & Company.

Diamond, J. (1997). *Guns, Germs and Steel: A Short History of Everybody for the Last 13,000 Years.* New York: Vintage.

Dickens, C. (1853, 11 June). The noble savage. *Household Worlds*, 337–9.

Dictionary Project. (2011). *A Student's Dictionary & Gazetteer* (19th ed.). Sullivan's Island, South Carolina: The Dictionary Project, Inc.

Diekmann, Y., Smith, D., Gerbault, P., Dyble, M., Page, A. E., Chaudhary, N., Migliano, A. B., & Thomas, M. G. (2017). Accurate age estimation in small-scale societies. *PNAS, 114*, 8205–10.

Digdon, N. (2020). The Little Albert controversy: Intuition, confirmation bias, and logic. *History of Psychology, 23*, 122–31.

Dimow, J. (2004, January). Resisting authority: A personal account of the Milgram obedience experiments. *Jewish Currents*: https://jewishcurrents.org/resisting-authority-2 (accessed 1 June 2022).

DiSalle, R. (2006). *Understanding Space-Time: The Philosophical Development of Physics from Newton to Einstein.* Cambridge: Cambridge University Press.

Dobzhansky, T. (1973). Nothing in biology makes sense except in the light of evolution. *American Biology Teacher, 35*, 125–9.

Dolnick, E. (2011). *The Clockwork Universe: Isaac Newton, the Royal Society, and the Birth of the Modern World.* New York: Harper Perennial.

Domanski, C. W. (2013). Mysterious 'Monsieur Leborgne': The mystery of the famous patient in the history of neuropsychology is explained. *Journal of the History of the Neurosciences, 22*, 47–52.

Draaisma, D., & de Rijcke, S. (2001). The graphic strategy: The uses and functions of illustrations in Wundt's *Grundzüge. History of the Human Sciences, 14*, 1–24.

Dragioti, E., Dimoliatis, I., Fountoulakis, K. N., & Evangelou, E. (2015). A systematic appraisal of allegiance effect in randomized controlled trials of psychotherapy. *Archives of General Psychiatry, 14*, 25.

Drake, Jr, M. E. (1992). Medical and neuropsychiatric aspects of lycanthropy. *Journal of Medical Humanities, 13*, 5–15.

Driesch, H. (1925). *The Crisis in Psychology.* Oxford: Oxford University Press.

Druart, T.-A. (1996). Al-Razi's conception of the soul: Psychological background to his ethics. *Medieval Philosophy and Theology, 5*, 245–63.

Drysdale, J. P., & Hoecker-Drysdale, S. (2007). The history of sociology: The North American perspective. In C. D. Bryant & D. L. Peck (eds), *21st Century Sociology: A Reference Handbook* (Vol. 1, pp. 28–44). Thousand Oaks, California: Sage.

Duarte, J. L., Crawford, J. T., Stern, C., Haidt, J., Jussim, L., & Tetlock, P. E. (2015). Political diversity will improve social psychological science. *Behavioral and Brain Sciences, 38*, e130.

During, S. (1988). The strange case of monomania: Patriarchy in literature, murder in *Middlemarch*, drowning in *Daniel Deronda. Representations, 23*, 86–104.

Durkheim, É. (1897). *Le Suicide: Étude de sociologie.* Paris: Félix Alcan.

Durston, G. J. (2019). *Crimen exceptum: The English Witch Prosecution in Context*. Hook, Hampshire: Waterside Press.

Eberle, E. J. (2016). *Church and State in Western Society: Established Church, Cooperation and Separation*. London: Routledge.

Ebert, A., & Bär, K.-J. (2010). Emil Kraepelin: A pioneer of scientific understanding of psychiatry and psychopharmacology. *Indian Journal of Psychiatry*, *52*, 191–2.

Ecklund, E. H., & Scheitle, C. P. (2007). Religion among academic scientists: Distinctions, disciplines, and demographics. *Social Problems*, *54*, 289–307.

Ecklund, E. H., Johnson, D. R., Scheitle, C. P., Matthews, K. R. W., & Lewis, S. W. (2016). Religion among scientists in international context: A new study of scientists in eight regions. *Socius: Sociological Research for a Dynamic World*, *2*, 1–9.

Effendy, B. (2008). Democracy and Islam. In A. Azra & W. Hudson (eds), *Islam beyond Conflict: Indonesian Islam and Western Political Theory* (pp. 41–6). Aldershot: Ashgate.

Ehrenreich, B. (2009). *Smile or Die: How Positive Thinking Fooled America and the World*. London: Granta.

Eling, P., & Finger, S. (2019). Franz Joseph Gall on the cerebellum as the organ for the reproductive drive. *Frontiers in Neuroanatomy*, *13*, 40.

Eller, C. (2000). *The Myth of Matriarchal Prehistory: Why an Invented Past Won't Give Women a Future*. Boston: Beacon.

Ellis, H. (1903). Variation in man and woman. *Popular Science Monthly*, *62*, 237–53.

Elms, A. C. (1975). The crisis of confidence in social psychology. *American Psychology*, *30*, 967–76.

Engber, D. (2017, 5 September). *The Bush Torture Scandal Isn't Over*. Slate: http://www.slate.com/articles/health_and_science/science/2017/09/should_psychologists_take_the_blame_for_greenlighting_bush_era_enhanced.html (accessed 1 June 2022).

Engzell, P., & Rohrer, J. M. (2021). Improving social science: Lessons from the Open Science Movement. *PS: Political Science & Politics*, *54*, 297–300.

Enli, G., Moe, H., Sundet, V. S., & Syvertsen, T. (2013). From fear of television to fear for television: Five political debates about new technologies. *Media History*, *19*, 213–27.

Epstein, S., & O'Brien, E. J. (1985). The person-situation debate in historical and current perspective. *Psychological Bulletin*, *98*, 513–37.

Erikson, E. H. (1964). Inner and outer space: Reflections on womanhood. *Daedalus*, *93*, 582–606.

Erksan, M. (Director). (1974). *Şeytan* [Film]. Saner Film.

Errington, F., & Gewertz, D. (2010). Excusing the haves and blaming the have-nots in the telling of history. In P. A. McAnany & N. Yoffee (eds), *Questioning Collapse: Human Resilience, Ecological Vulnerability, and the Aftermath of Empire* (pp. 329–51). Cambridge: Cambridge University Press.

Esquirol, E. (1838). *Maladies mentales: Considerées sous les rapports médical, higiénique et médico-légale*. Paris: J.-B. Baillière.

Eysenck, H. J. (1973). *The Inequality of Man*. London: Temple Smith.

Fancher, R. E. (1996). *Pioneers of Psychology* (3rd ed.). New York: Norton.

Faria, M. A. (2013). Violence, mental illness, and the brain – A brief history of psychosurgery: Part 1 – From trephination to lobotomy. *Surgical Neurology International*, *4*, 49.

Farr, J. (1988). The history of political science. *American Journal of Political Science*, *32*, 1175–95.

Fazil, A. M. (Director). (1993). *Manichitrathazhu* [Film]. Swargachitra.

Fechner, G. T. (1860). *Elemente der Psychophysik*. Leipzig: Druck und Verlag von Breitkopf und Härtel.

Feltham, C. (2016). *Depressive Realism: Interdisciplinary Perspectives*. London: Routledge.

Feng, R., & Yu, Y.-X. (2006). Zhang Heng's seismometer and Longxi earthquake in AD 134. *Acta Seismologica Sinica*, *19*, 704–19.

Fensch, D. (1977). Zur Rolle Wilhelm Wundts bei der Institutionalisierung der Psychologie in Leipzig. In G. Eckardt & D. Fensch (eds), *Psychologiehistorische Manuskripte* (pp. 60–6). Berlin: Gesellschaft für Psychologie der Deutschen Demokratischen Republik.

Ferguson, C. J., & Colwell, J. (2020). Lack of consensus among scholars on the issue of video game 'addiction'. *Psychology of Popular Media*, *9*, 359–66.

Fernandez-Duque, D., & Johnson, M. L. (1999). Attention metaphors: How metaphors guide the cognitive psychology of attention. *Cognitive Science*, *23*, 83–116.

Festinger, L. (1954). A theory of social comparison processes. *Human Relations*, *7*, 117–40.

Festinger, L. (1957). *A Theory of Cognitive Dissonance*. Stanford, California: Stanford University Press.

Feynman, R. (1998). *The Meaning of It All: Thoughts of a Citizen-Scientist*. London: Penguin.

Fine, C. (2010). *Delusions of Gender: The Real Science behind Sex Differences*. London: Icon.

Fine, C. (2017). *Testosterone Rex: Unmaking the Myths of Our Gendered Minds*. London: Icon.

Finger, S. (2019). Mark Twain's life-long fascination with phrenology. *Journal of the History of the Behavioral Sciences*, *55*, 99–121.

Finocchiaro, M. A. (2009). Myth 8: That Galileo was imprisoned and tortured for advocating Copernicanism. In R. J. Numbers (ed.), *Galileo Goes to Jail: And Other Myths about Science and Religion* (pp. 68–78). Cambridge, Massachusetts: Harvard University Press.

Fisher, R. A. (1925). Applications of 'Student's' distribution. *Metron*, *5*, 90–104.

Fiske, S. T., & Taylor, S. E. (1984). *Social Cognition*. Boston: Addison-Wesley.

Fitzgerald, M. (2017). Why did Sigmund Freud refuse to see Pierre Janet? Origins of psychoanalysis: Janet, Freud or both? *History of Psychiatry*, *28*, 358–64.

Forman, M. (Director). (1975). *One Flew over the Cuckoo's Nest* [Film]. Fantasy Films.

Foschi, R., Innamorati, M., & Taradel, R. (2018). 'A disease of our time': The Catholic Church's condemnation and absolution of psychoanalysis (1924–1975). *Journal of the History of the Behavioral Sciences*, *54*, 85–100.

Foucault, M. (1961). *Folie et déraison: Histoire de la folie à l'âge classique*. Paris: Librairie Plon.

Frances, A. (2016). Entrenched reductionisms: The bête noire of psychiatry. *History of Psychology*, *19*, 57–9.

Frassetto, M. (2005). The heresy at Orléans in 1022 in the writings of contemporary churchmen. *Nottingham Medieval Studies*, *49*, 1–17.

Frede, M. (1987). *Essays in Ancient Philosophy*. Minneapolis: University of Minnesota Press.

Fredrickson, B. L., & Losada, M. F. (2005). Positive affect and the complex dynamics of human flourishing. *American Psychologist*, *60*, 678–86.

Freese, J. (2002). Evolutionary psychology: New science or the same old storytelling? *Contexts*, *1*, 44–9.

French, R. (1994). *Ancient Natural History: Histories of Nature*. London: Routledge.

Fresenius, F. C. (1866). Die Natur der Masse. *Deutsche Vierteljahrschrift*, *29*, 112–78.

Freud, S. (1900). *Die Traumdeutung*. Leipzig: Franz Deuticke.

Freud, S. ([1901] 1905). Bruchstücke einer Hysterie-Analyse. *Monatsschrift für Psychiatrie und Neurologie*, *18*, 408–67.

Freud, S. (1905). *Drei Abhandlungen zur Sexualtheorie*. Leipzig: Franz Deuticke.

Freud, S. (1908). Die 'kulturelle' Sexualmoral und die moderne Nervosität. *Sexual-Probleme, 4,* 107–29.

Freud, S. (1914). Zur Geschichte der psychoanalytischen Bewegung. *Jahrbuch der Psychoanalyse, 4,* 207–62.

Freud, S. (1923). *Das Ich und das Es.* Leipzig: Internationaler Psychoanalytischer Verlag.

Freud, S. (1927). *Die Zukunft einer Illusion.* Leipzig: Internationaler Psychoanalytischer Verlag.

Freud, S. (1930). *Das Unbehagen in der Kultur.* Vienna: Internationaler Psychoanalytischer Verlag.

Freud, S. ([1895] 1950). A project for a scientific psychology. In J. Strachey (ed.), *The Standard Edition of the Complete Psychological Works of Sigmund Freud* (Vol. 1, pp. 283–397). London: Hogarth.

Fridlund, A. J., Beck, H. P., Goldie, W. D., & Irons, G. (2020). The case for Douglas Merritte: Should we bury what is alive and well? *History of Psychology, 23,* 132–48.

Friedkin, W. (Director). (1973). *The Exorcist* [Film]. Hoya Productions.

Friedman, J. B. (2000). *The Monstrous Races in Medieval Art and Thought.* Syracuse, New York: Syracuse University Press.

Fritsch, G., & Hitzig, E. (1870). Über die elektrische Erregbarkeit des Grosshirns. *Archiv für Anatomie, Physiologie und Wissenschaftliche Medicin, 37,* 300–32.

Frost, N. D., Baskin, T. W., & Wampold, B. E. (2020). Comparative clinical trials in psychotherapy: Have large effects been replicated? *Epidemiology and Psychiatric Sciences, 29,* e128.

Fuchs, A. H. (2000). Contributions of American mental philosophers to psychology in the United States. *History of Psychology, 3,* 3–19.

Fukuyama, F. (1989). The end of history? *The National Interest, 16* (Summer), 3–18.

Fuller, R. C. (2006). American psychology and the religious imagination. *Journal of the History of the Behavioral Sciences, 42,* 221–35.

Furumoto, L. (1980). Mary Whiton Calkins (1863–1930). *Psychology of Women Quarterly, 5,* 55–68.

Furumoto, L. (1989). The new history of psychology. In I. S. Cohen (ed.), *The G. Stanley Hall Lecture Series* (Vol. 9, pp. 9–34). Washington, DC: American Psychological Association.

Gaetani, F. M. (1925). *La psicanalisi.* Rome: La Civiltà Cattolica.

Galileo, G. L. (1632). *Dialogo sopra i due massimi sistemi del mondo.* Florence: Batista Landini.

Gall, F. J. (1825). *Sur l'organe de qualités morales et des facultés intellectuelles, et sur la pluralité des organes cérébraux.* Paris: J.-B. Baillière.

Gallo, M. M. (2014). The parable of Kitty Genovese, the *New York Times,* and the erasure of lesbianism. *Journal of the History of Sexuality, 23,* 273–94.

Galton, F. (1869). *Hereditary Genius: An Inquiry into Its Laws and Consequences.* London: Macmillan.

Galton, F. (1883). *Inquiries into Human Faculty and Its Development.* New York: Macmillan.

Galton, F. (1888). Co-relations and their measurement, chiefly from anthropometric data. *Proceedings of the Royal Society of London, 45,* 135–45.

Gantt, W. H. (1968). Pavlov's 'higher nervous activity'. *Conditional Reflex: A Pavlovian Journal of Research & Therapy, 3,* 281–6.

Gariazzo, M. (Director). (1974). *L'ossessa* [Film]. Tiberia Film.

Garon, S. M. (1986). State and religion in Imperial Japan, 1912–1945. *Journal of Japanese Studies, 12,* 273–302.

Gazzaniga, M. S. (1967). The split brain in man. *Scientific American, 21*, 24–9.

Geary, D. C., & Flinn, M. V. (2002). Sex differences in behavioral and hormonal response to social threat: Comment on Taylor et al. (2000). *Psychological Review, 109*, 745–50.

Gelb, S. A. (1997). Heart of darkness: The discreet charm of the hereditarian psychologist. *Review of Education/Pedagogy/Cultural Studies, 19*, 129–39.

Gemes, K. (2009). Freud and Nietzsche on sublimation. *Journal of Nietzsche Studies, 38*, 38–59.

Gergen, K. J. (1973). Social psychology as history. *Journal of Personality and Social Psychology, 26*, 309–20.

Giammusso, I., Casadei, F., Catania, N., Foddai, E., Monti, M. C., Savoja, G., & Tosto, C. (2018). Immigrants psychopathology: Emerging phenomena and adaptation of mental health care setting by native language. *Clinical Practice & Epidemiology in Mental Health, 14*, 312–22.

Gieryn, T. F. (1995). Boundaries of science. In S. Jasanoff, G. E. Markle, J. C. Petersen & T. Pinch (eds), *Handbook of Science and Technology* (pp. 393–443). Thousand Oaks, California: Sage.

Gigerenzer, G., & Gaissmaier, W. (2011). Heuristic decision making. *Annual Review of Psychology, 62*, 451–82.

Gilderhus, M. T. (1992). *History and Historians: A Historiographical Introduction* (2nd edn). Englewood Cliffs, New Jersey: Prentice-Hall.

Gillham, N. W. (2001). *A Life of Sir Francis Galton: From African Exploration to the Birth of Eugenics.* Oxford: Oxford University Press.

Glass, H. B. (1955). Maupertuis, a forgotten genius. *Scientific American, 193*, 100–11.

Global Forum for Health Research (2002). *The 10/90 Report on Health Research 2001–2002.* Geneva: Global Forum for Health Research.

Goddard, H. H. (1912). *The Kallikak Family: A Study in the Heredity of Feeble-Mindedness.* New York: Macmillan.

Goddard, H. H. (1917). Mental tests and the immigrant. *Journal of Delinquency, 2*, 243–77.

Good, J. M. M. (1993). Quests for interdisciplinarity: The rhetorical constitution of social psychology. In R. H. Roberts & J. M. M. Good (eds), *The Recovery of Rhetoric: Persuasive Discourse and Disciplinarity in the Human Sciences* (pp. 239–62). Charlottesville, Virginia: University Press of Virginia.

Good, J. M. M. (2000). Disciplining social psychology: A case study of boundary relations in the history of the human sciences. *Journal of the History of the Behavioral Sciences, 36*, 383–403.

Goode, S. D. (2011). *Paedophiles in Society: Reflecting on Sexuality, Abuse and Hope.* London: Palgrave Macmillan.

Goodman, F. D. (1981). *The Exorcism of Anneliese Michel.* Eugene, Oregon: Resource Publication.

Gould, S. J. (1978). Sociobiology: The art of storytelling. *New Scientist, 80*, 530–3.

Gould, S. J. (1981). *The Mismeasure of Man.* New York: Norton.

Graumann, C. F. (1986). The individualization of the social and the desocialization of the individual: Floyd H. Allport's contribution to social psychology. In C. F. Graumann & S. Moscovici (eds), *Changing Conceptions of Crowd Mind and Behavior* (pp. 97–116). New York: Springer-Verlag.

Graves, J. L., Jr (2004). *The Race Myth: Why We Pretend Race Exists in America.* New York: Dutton.

Gray, J. (1992). *Men Are from Mars, Women Are from Venus: A Practical Guide for Improving Communication and Getting What You Want in Your Relationships.* New York: HarperCollins.

Green, C. D., & Martin, S. M. (2017). Historical impact in psychology differs between demographic groups. *New Ideas in Psychology, 47*, 24–32.

Greenberg, J., Pyszczynski, T., & Solomon, S. (1986). The causes and consequences of a need for self-esteem: A terror management theory. In R.F. Baumeister (ed.), *Public Self and Private Self* (pp. 189–212). New York: Springer-Verlag.

Gregorian, V. (2003). *Islam: A Mosaic, not a Monolith*. Washington, DC: Brookings Institution Press.

Grice, P. (1975). Logic and conversation. In P. Cole & J. Morgan (eds), *Syntax and Semantics, Volume 3: Speech Acts* (pp. 41–58). New York: Academic Press.

Griesinger, W. (1845). *Die Pathologie und Therapie der psychischen Krankheiten für Ärzte und Studirende*. Stuttgart: Adolph Krabbe.

Grob, G. N. (1994). *The Mad among Us: A History of the Care of America's Mentally Ill*. New York: Free Press.

Gross, R. (2009). *Themes, Issues and Debates in Psychology* (3rd ed.). Abingdon, UK: Hodder.

Guercio, J. M. (2020). The importance of a deeper knowledge of the history and theoretical foundations of behaviorism and behavior therapy: Part 2 – 1960–1985. *Behavior Analysis: Research and Practice, 20*, 174–95.

Gurven, M., von Rueden, C., Massenkoff, M., Kaplan, H., & Lero Vie, M. (2013). How universal is the Big Five? Testing the five-factor model of personality variation among forager–farmers in the Bolivian Amazon. *Journal of Personality and Social Psychology, 104*, 354–70.

Gutchess, A. H., Welsh, R. C., Boduroglu, A., & Park, D. C. (2006). Cultural differences in neural function associated with object processing. *Cognitive, Affective and Behavioral Neuroscience, 6*, 102–9.

Hadleigh, B. (2007). *Broadway Babylon: Glamour, Glitz and Gossip on the Great White Way*. New York: Back Stage Books.

Haggerty, M. E. (1911). The nineteenth annual meeting of the American Psychological Association. *Journal of Philosophy, 8*, 204–18.

Hall, G. S. (1883). The contents of children's minds. *Princeton Review, 11*, 249–72.

Hall, G. S. (1885). The new psychology. *Andover Review, 3*, 242–59.

Hall, G. S. (1894). The new psychology as the basis of education. *Forum, 17*, 710–20.

Hall, G. S. (1901). The new psychology. *Harper's Monthly, 103*, 727–32.

Hall, G. S. (1904). *Adolescence: Its Psychology and Its Relations to Physiology, Anthropology, Sociology, Sex, Crime, Religion and Education*. New York: Appleton.

Hall, G. S. (1905). The negro in Africa and America. *Pedagogical Seminary, 12*, 350–68.

Hall, G. S. (1906). The question of coeducation. *Munsey's Magazine, 34*, 588–92.

Halperin, D. M. (2012). Homosexuality. In S. Hornblower, A. Spawforth & E. Eidinow (eds), *Oxford Classical Dictionary* (4th ed., pp. 700–3). Oxford: Oxford University Press.

Han, Q. (2019). Diasporic Chinese family drama through a transnational lens: *The Wedding Banquet* (1993) and *Saving Face* (2004). *International Journal of Media & Cultural Politics, 15*, 323–43.

Handel, G. (ed.). (1988). *Childhood Socialization*. New York: de Gruyter.

Hansen, R., & King, D. (2001). Eugenic ideas, political interests, and policy variance: Immigration and sterilization policy in Britain and the US. *World Politics, 53*, 237–63.

Hanson, N. R. (1958). *Patterns of Discovery: An Inquiry into the Conceptual Foundations of Science*. Cambridge: Cambridge University Press.

Haque, A. (2004). Psychology from Islamic perspective: Contributions of early Muslim scholars and challenges to contemporary Muslim psychologists. *Journal of Religion and Health, 43*, 357–77.

Harding, S. (1986). *The Science Question in Feminism*. Ithaca, New York: Cornell University Press.

Hardy, C. (Director). (2018). *The Nun* [Film]. New Line Cinema; Atomic Monster Productions; The Safran Company.

Harper, K. (2017). *The Fate of Rome: Climate, Disease, and the End of an Empire*. Princeton, New Jersey: Princeton University Press.

Harrell, W., & Harrison, R. (1938). The rise and fall of behaviorism. *Journal of General Psychology, 18*, 367–421.

Harris, B. (2009). What critical psychologists should know about the history of psychology. In D. Fox, I. Prilleltensky & S. Austin (eds), *Critical Psychology: An Introduction* (2nd ed., pp. 20–35). London: Sage.

Harris, B. (2011). Letting go of Little Albert: Disciplinary memory, history, and the uses of myth. *Journal of the History of the Behavioral Sciences, 47*, 1–17.

Harris, B. (2014). Rosalie Rayner, feminist? *Revista de Historia de la Psicología, 35*, 61–70.

Harris, R. A. (2005). *Rhetoric and Incommensurability*. Anderson, South Carolina: Parlor Press.

Harris-McCoy, D. E. (2012). *Artemidorus' Oneirocritica: Text, Translation, and Commentary*. Oxford: Oxford University Press.

Hartenstein, G. (ed.) (1850). *Johann Friedrich Herbart's sämmtliche Werke*. Leipzig: Leopold Voss.

Harvey, S. (2012). *Act Like a Lady, Think Like a Man: What Men Really Think about Love, Relationships, Intimacy, and Commitment*. New York: Amistad.

Haskins, C. H. (1922). Science at the court of the emperor Frederick II. *American Historical Review, 27*, 669–94.

Haslam, S. A., & Reicher, S. (2006). Stressing the group: Social identity and the unfolding dynamics of responses to stress. *Journal of Applied Psychology, 91*, 1037–52.

Hayes, S. C., Barnes-Holmes, D., & Roche, B. (2001). *Relational Frame Theory: A Post-Skinnerian Account of Human Language and Cognition*. New York: Kluwer.

Hayes, S. C., Strosahl, K. D., & Wilson, K. G. (2012). *Acceptance and Commitment Therapy: The Process and Practice of Mindful Change* (2nd ed.). New York: Guilford Press.

Heape, W. (1913). *Sex Antagonism*. London: Constable and Company.

Heilbron, J. L. (2010). *Galileo*. Oxford: Oxford University Press.

Henri, V., & Tawney, G. (1895). Ueber die Trugwahrnehmung zweier Punkte bei der Berührung eines Punktes der Haut. *Philosophische Studien, 11*, 394–405.

Henrich, J. (2008). A cultural species. In M. Brown (ed.), *Explaining Culture Scientifically* (pp. 184–210). Seattle: University of Washington Press.

Herbert, P. D. N., Penton, E. H., Burns, J. M., Janzen, D. H., & Hallwachs, W. (2004). Ten species in one: DNA barcoding reveals cryptic species in the neotropical skipper butterfly *Astraptes fulgerator*. *PNAS, 101*, 14812–17.

Herlihy, D. (1985). *Medieval Households*. Cambridge, Massachusetts: Harvard University Press.

Herrnstein, R. (1971). IQ. *The Atlantic, 228*(3), 43–64.

Herrnstein, R. J., & Murray, C. (1994). *The Bell Curve: Intelligence and Class Structure in American Life*. New York: Free Press.

Hickman, C. (2009). Cheerful prospects and tranquil restoration: The visual experience of landscape as part of the therapeutic regime of the British asylum, 1800–60. *History of Psychiatry, 20*, 425–41.

Hickok, L. P. (1854). *Empirical Psychology: Or, the Human Mind as Given in Consciousness*. New York: Ivison & Phinney.

Higher Education Statistics Agency. (2019). *Table 22 – HE Student Enrolments by Subject of Study and Domicile 2014/15 to 2017/18.* https://www.hesa.ac.uk/data-and-analysis/students/table-22 (accessed 1 June 2022).

Hilbig, B. E., & Moshagen, M. (2015). A predominance of self-identified Democrats is no evidence of a leftward bias. *Behavioral and Brain Sciences, 38,* e146.

Hillier, S. M., & Jewell, J. A. (1983). *Healthcare and Traditional Medicine in China, 1800–1982.* London: Routledge & Kegan Paul.

Ho, Y.-S., & Hartley, J. (2016). Classic articles in psychology in the *Science Citation Index Expanded*: A bibliometric analysis. *British Journal of Psychology, 107,* 768–80.

Hoffman, M. (2017). Psychoanalysis as science. In T. Schramme & S. Edwards (eds), *Handbook of the Philosophy of Medicine* (pp. 937–57). Dordrecht: Springer.

Hofmann, L., & Walach, H. (2011). Spirituality and religiosity in psychotherapy: A representative survey among German psychotherapists. *Psychotherapy Research, 21,* 179–92.

Holowinsky, I. Z. (1985). Soviet psychology and its view of American behaviorism. *Psychological Reports, 56,* 803–10.

Holy Office. (1961, 16 July). Monitum. *L'Osservatore Romano, 3.*

Hooker, E. (1993). Reflections of a 40-year exploration: A scientific view on homosexuality. *American Psychologist, 48,* 450–3.

Hoppenstand, G. (1992). Yellow devil doctors and opium dens: The yellow peril stereotype in mass media entertainment. In J. Nachmar & K. Lause (eds), *Popular Culture: An Introductory Text* (pp. 277–91). Bowling Green, Ohio: Bowling Green State University Popular Press.

Houston, R. A. (2014). A latent historiography? The case of psychiatry in Britain, 1500–1820. *Historical Journal, 57,* 289–310.

Houston, R. A. (2020). Asylums: The historical perspective before, during, and after. *Lancet Psychiatry, 7,* 354–62.

Hughes, B. M. (2012). *Conceptual and Historical Issues in Psychology.* London: Prentice-Hall.

Hughes, B. M. (2016). *Rethinking Psychology: Good Science, Bad Science, Pseudoscience.* London: Palgrave.

Hughes, B. M. (2018a). *Psychology in Crisis.* London: Palgrave.

Hughes, B. M. (2018b). Does psychology face an exaggeration crisis? *The Psychologist, 31,* 8–11.

Hughes, B. M. (2019). *The Psychology of Brexit: From Psychodrama to Behavioural Science.* Cham, Switzerland: Palgrave Macmillan.

Hull, C. L. (1943). *Principles of Behavior: An Introduction to Behavior Theory.* New York: Appleton-Century.

Hume, D. (1739). *A Treatise of Human Nature: Being an Attempt to Introduce the Experimental Method of Reasoning into Moral Subjects.* London: John Noon.

Huxley, A. (1932). *Brave New World.* London: Chatto & Windus.

Hyde, J. S. (2005). The gender similarities hypothesis. *American Psychologist, 60,* 581–92.

Hyde, J. S. (2014). Gender similarities and differences. *Annual Review of Psychology, 65,* 373–98.

Hyde, J. S. (2018). Gender similarities. In C. B. Travis, J. W. White, A. Rutherford, W. S. Williams, S. L. Cook, & K. F. Wyche (eds), *APA Handbook of the Psychology of Women: History, Theory, and Battlegrounds* (pp. 129–43). Washington, DC: American Psychological Association.

Hyde, J. S., Lindberg, S. M., Linn, M. C., Ellis, A. B., & Williams, C. C. (2008). Gender similarities characterize math performance. *Science, 321,* 494–5.

Hytner, N. (2004, 21 June). The truth behind the History Boys. *The Telegraph*: https://www.telegraph.co.uk/culture/theatre/drama/3619379/The-truth-behind-the-History-Boys.html (accessed 1 June 2022).

Iggers, G. G. (1959). Further remarks about early uses of the term 'social science'. *Journal of the History of Ideas*, *20*, 433–6.

Inbar, Y., & Lammers, J. (2012). Political diversity in social and personality psychology. *Perspectives on Psychological Science*, *7*, 496–503.

Inbar, Y., & Lammers, J. (2015). Increasing ideological tolerance in social psychology. *Behavioral and Brain Sciences*, *38*, e147.

Inglehart, R., & Welzel, C. (2005). *Modernization, Cultural Change, and Democracy: The Human Development Sequence*. Cambridge: Cambridge University Press.

Innamorati, M., Taradel, R., & Foschi, R. (2018). Between sacred and profane: Possession, psychopathology, and the Catholic Church. *History of Psychology*, *22*, 1–16.

Ioannidis, J. P. (2005). Why most published research findings are false. *PLoS Medicine*, *2*(8), e124.

Irigaray, L. (1985). *The Sex Which Is Not One*. Ithaca, New York: Cornell University Press.

Irwin, F. W. (1943). Edwin Burket Twitmyer: 1873–1943. *American Journal of Psychology*, *56*, 451–3.

Jackson, J. H. (1932). *Selected Writings of John Hughlings Jackson* (Vol. 2). London: Hodder & Stoughton.

Jacobson, M. F. (1999). *Whiteness of a Different Color: European Immigrants and the Alchemy of Race*. Cambridge, Massachusetts: Harvard University Press.

Jahoda, G. (2007). *A History of Social Psychology: From the Eighteenth-Century Enlightenment to the Second World War*. Cambridge: Cambridge University Press.

Jain, S. (2003). Psychiatry and confinement in India. In R. Porter & D. Wright (eds), *The Confinement of the Insane: International Perspectives, 1800–1965* (pp. 273–98). Cambridge: Cambridge University Press.

James, W. (1890). *The Principles of Psychology*. New York: Henry Holt.

James, W. (1892). A plea for psychology as a 'natural science'. *Philosophical Review*, *1*, 146–53.

Japanese Psychological Association. (2012). *Ethical Principles of Psychologists*. https://psych.or.jp/english/ethical (accessed 1 June 2022).

Jarius, S., & Wildemann, B. (2017). Pavlov's reflex before Pavlov: Early accounts from the English, French and German classic literature. *European Neurology*, *77*, 322–6.

Jarrett, C. (2014, 11 May). *What Neuro-revolution? The Public Find Brain Science Irrelevant and Anxiety-provoking*. Wired. https://www.wired.com/2014/11/neuro-revolution-public-find-brain-science-irrelevant-anxiety-provoking (accessed 1 June 2022).

Jastrow, J. (1927). The reconstruction of psychology. *Psychological Review*, *34*, 169–95.

Jay, M. (2016). *This Way Madness Lies: The Asylum and Beyond*. London: Thames & Hudson.

Jaynes, J. (1976). *The Origins of Consciousness in the Breakdown of the Bicameral Mind*. Boston: Houghton Mifflin.

Jensen, A. R. (1969). How much can we boost IQ and scholastic achievement? *Harvard Educational Review*, *39*, 1–123.

Jimenez, M. A. (1987). *Changing Faces of Madness: Early American Attitudes and Treatment of the Insane*. Waltham, Massachusetts: Brandeis University Press.

Jones, D., & Elcock, J. (2001). *History and Theories of Psychology: A Critical Perspective*. London: Hodder Education.

Jones, D. W. (2017). Moral insanity and psychological disorder: The hybrid roots of psychiatry. *History of Psychiatry*, *28*, 263–79.

Jones, E. E. (1998). Major developments in five decades of social psychology. In D. Gilbert, S. T. Fiske & G. Lindzey (eds), *Handbook of Social Psychology* (4th ed., Vol. 1, pp. 3–57). Boston: McGraw-Hill.

Jones, G. L. (1954). The history of the founding of the Eastern State Hospital of Virginia. *American Journal of Psychiatry*, *110*, 644–50.

Jones, K. (1993). *Asylums and After: A Revised History of the Mental Health Services from the Early 18th Century to the 1990s.* London: Athlone Press.

Jones, S. (1836). *Practical Phrenology.* Boston: Russell, Shattuck, & Williams.

Jordan, D. S. (1902). The higher education of women. *Popular Science Monthly*, *62*, 97–107.

Jouanna, J. (2012). The legacy of the Hippocratic treatise *The Nature of Man*: The theory of the four humours. In P. van der Eijk (ed.), *Greek Medicine from Hippocrates to Galen* (pp. 335–59). Leiden: Brill.

Judd, C. M., & Park, B. (1988). Out-group homogeneity: Judgments of variability at the individual and group levels. *Journal of Personality and Social Psychology*, *54*, 778–88.

Judge, M. (Director). (2006). *Idiocracy* [Film]. Ternion.

Justice, K. L. (1998). *Bestseller Index: All Books, by Author, on the Lists of Publishers Weekly and the New York Times through 1990.* Jefferson, North Carolina: McFarland.

Justice, S. (2008). Did the Middle Ages believe in their miracles? *Representations*, *103*, 1–29.

Kaalund, N. K. L. (2014). Oxford serialized: Revisiting the Huxley–Wilberforce debate through the periodical press. *History of Science*, *52*, 429–53.

Kahneman, D. (2012). *Thinking, Fast and Slow.* London: Penguin.

Kamber, N. K. (2016). Feminism and psychoanalysis. In N. Naples, R. C. Hoogland, M. Wickramasinghe & W. C. A. Wong (eds), *The Wiley Blackwell Encyclopedia of Gender and Sexuality Studies.* Hoboken, New Jersey: Wiley-Blackwell.

Kampen, N. B. (ed.) (1996). *Sexuality in Ancient Art: Near East, Egypt, Greece, and Italy.* Cambridge: Cambridge University Press.

Kant, I. (1785). *Grundlegung zur Metaphysik der Sitten.* Riga: Johann Friedrich Hartknoch.

Kant, I. (1786). *Metaphysische Anfangsgründe der Naturwissenschaft.* Riga: Johann Friedrich Hartknoch.

Kelemen, D. (2004). Are children 'intuitive theists'? *Psychological Science*, *15*, 295–301.

Keller, E. F. (1985). *Reflections on Gender and Science.* New Haven, Connecticut: Yale University Press.

Kemp, S. (1998). Medieval theories of mental representation. *History of Psychology*, *4*, 275–88.

Kemp, S. (2018). Quantification of virtue in late medieval Europe. *History of Psychology*, *21*, 33–46.

Kemp, S. (2019). Mental disorder and mysticism in the late medieval world. *History of Psychology*, *22*, 149–62.

Kenny, R. (2015). Freud, Jung and Boas: The psychoanalytic engagement with anthropology revisited. *Notes and Records*, *69*, 173–90.

King, D. B., Viney, W., & Woody, W. D. (2009). *A History of Psychology: Ideas and Context* (4th ed.). Boston: Pearson.

King, Jr, M. L. (1986). The power of nonviolence. In J. M. Washington (ed.), *A Testament of Hope: The Essential Writings of Martin Luther King Jr.* (pp. 12–15). New York: HarperCollins. (Original speech given 1957).

King-Hele, D. (1986). *Erasmus Darwin and the Romantic Poets.* Basingstoke: Macmillan.

King-Hele, D. (2005). Prologue: Catching up with Erasmus Darwin in the new century. In C. U. M. Smith & R. Arnott (eds), *The Genius of Erasmus Darwin* (pp. 13–29). Aldershot: Ashgate.

Kinsey, A. C., Pomeroy, W. B., & Martin, C. E. (1948). *Sexual Behavior in the Human Male.* Philadelphia: W. B. Saunders.

Kinsey, A. C., Pomeroy, W. B., Martin, C. E., & Gebhard, P. H. (1953). *Sexual Behavior in the Human Female.* Philadelphia: W. B. Saunders.

Klein, J. T. (1990). Across the boundaries. *Social Epistemology, 4,* 267–80.

Klein, R. A., Vianello, M., Hasselman, F., Adams, B. G., Adams, Jr, R. B., Alper, S., … Nosek, B. A. (2018). Many Labs 2: Investigating variation in replicability across samples and settings. *Advances in Methods and Practices in Psychological Science, 1,* 443–90.

Knox, H. A. (1915, 9 January). Measuring human intelligence: A progressive series of standardized tests used by the Public Health Service to protect our racial stock. *Scientific American, 112,* 52–3, 57–8.

Kočandrle, R., & Kleisner, K. (2013). Evolution born of moisture: Analogies and parallels between Anaximander's ideas on origin of life and man and later pre-Darwinian and Darwinian evolutionary concepts. *Journal of the History of Biology, 46,* 103–24.

Koch, S. (1969). Psychology cannot be a coherent science. *Psychology Today, 3,* 64–8.

Korean Psychological Association. (2004). *Korean Psychological Association Code of Ethics.* https://www.koreanpsychology.or.kr/eng/eng02_2.asp (accessed 1 June 2022).

Kostyleff, N. (1911). *La crise de la psychologie expérimentale.* Paris: Alcan.

Kotowicz, Z. (1997). *R. D. Laing and the Paths of Anti-psychiatry.* London: Routledge.

Kousoulis, P. (2011). The demonic lore of Ancient Egypt: Questions on definition. In P. Kousoulis (ed.), *Ancient Egyptian Demonology* (pp. ix–xxii). Leuven: Uitgeverij Peeters.

Kraepelin, E. (2007). On the question of degeneration. *History of Psychiatry, 18,* 399–404. [Originally published (1908) Zur Entartungsfrage. *Zentralblatt für Nervenheilkunde und Psychiatrie, 31,* 745–51.]

Krafft-Ebing, R. (1888). *Lehrbuch der Psychiatrie auf klinischer Grundlage für praktische Ärzte und Studirende.* Stuttgart: Ferdinand Enke.

Kravitz, D. A., & Martin, R. (1986). Ringelman rediscovered: The original article. *Journal of Personality and Social Psychology, 50,* 936–41.

Kren, M., Brunner, S., & Hessler, B. (Creators). (2020). *Freud* [TV Series]. Bavaria Fiction; Satel Film; Mia Film.

Krishnan, O. N. (2004). *In Search of Reality: A Layman's Journey through Indian Philosophy.* Delhi: Motilal Banarsidass.

Krstić, K. (1964). Marco Marulić: The author of the term 'psychology'. *Acta Instituti Psychologici Universitatis Zagrabiensis, 36,* 7–13.

Kruglanski, A. W., & Webster, D. M. (1996). Motivated closing of the mind: 'Seizing' and 'freezing'. *Psychological Review, 103,* 263–83.

Kugelmann, R. (2011). *Psychology and Catholicism: Contested Boundaries.* Cambridge: Cambridge University Press.

Kuhn, T. S. (1962). *The Structure of Scientific Revolutions.* Chicago: University of Chicago Press.

Kuijper, B., Pen, I., & Weissing, F. J. (2012). A guide to sexual selection theory. *Annual Review of Ecology, Evolution, and Systematics, 43,* 287–311.

Lackey, M. (2018). Ireland, the Irish, and biofiction. *Éire-Ireland, 53*, 98–119.

LaFortune, K. A. (2018). Eliminating offensive legal language. *Monitor on Psychology, 49*, 29.

LaFrance, M. (1983). Obituary: Clara Mayo (1931–1981). *American Psychologist, 38*, 112–13.

Lambert, J. (1948). Le sanglier néolithique trépané et mutilé de Roquefort (Alpes Maritimes). *Bulletin de la Société Préhistorique Française, 45*, 201–5.

Lambert, M. J., & Ogles, B. M. (2004). The efficacy and effectiveness of psychotherapy. In M. J. Lambert (ed.), *Bergin and Garfield's Handbook of Psychotherapy and Behavior Change* (pp. 139–93). New York: Wiley.

Landes, R. (1995). *Relics, Apocalypse, and the Deceits of History: Ademar of Chabannes, 989–1034.* Cambridge, Massachusetts: Harvard University Press.

Lashley, K. S. (1929). *Brain Mechanisms and Intelligence: A Quantitative Study of Injuries to the Brain*. Chicago: University of Chicago Press.

Laws, B. (2012, 3 March). Against Pinker's violence. *CTheory*.

Lazear, J. (1992). *Meditations for Men Who Do Too Much*. New York: Fireside.

Leahey, T. H. (1992). The mythical revolutions of American psychology. *American Psychologist, 47*, 308–18.

Leahey, T. H. (2001). *A History of Modern Psychology* (3rd ed.). Upper Saddle River: Prentice Hall.

Leaney, E. (2006). Phrenology in nineteenth-century Ireland. *New Hibernia Review/Iris Éireannach Nua, 10*, 24–42.

Le Bon, G. (1895). *Psychologie des foules*. Paris: Félix Alcan.

Lefebvre, A. (1866). *De la folie en matière de religion*. Paris: Putois-Cretté.

Leichsenring, F., & Steinert, C. (2017). Is cognitive behavioral therapy the gold standard for psychotherapy? The need for plurality in treatment and research. *JAMA, 318*, 1323–4.

Lejeune, D. (1993). *Les sociétés de géographie en France et l'expansion colonial au XIXᵉ siècle*. Paris: Albin Michel.

Letzter, R. (2016, 22 September). Scientists are furious after a famous psychologist accused her peers of 'methodological terrorism'. *Business Insider*. http://uk.businessinsider.com/susan-fiske-methodological-terrorism-2016-9 (accessed 1 April 2021).

Levy, J. (1972). Lateral specialization of the human brain: Behavioral manifestation and possible evolutionary basis. In J. A. Kiger, Jr (ed.), *The Biology of Behavior* (pp. 159–80). Corvallis, Oregon: Oregon State University Press.

Lewis, J., & Lewis, B. (2017). The myth of declining violence: Liberal evolutionism and violent complexity. *International Journal of Cultural Studies, 21*, 225–41.

Lewis-Williams, D. (2006). Building bridges to the deep human past: Consciousness, religion, and art. In F. LeRon Shults (ed.), *The Evolution of Rationality: Interdisciplinary Essays in Honor of J. Wentzel van Huyssteen* (pp. 149–66). Grand Rapids: Eerdmans.

Lexington. (2020, 21 March). Covid-19 is exposing America's resilience – and vulnerability. *The Economist*. https://www.economist.com/united-states/2020/03/21/covid-19-is-exposing-americas-resilience-and-vulnerability (accessed 1 June 2022).

Leydesdorff, L., & Rafols, I. (2009). A global map of science based on the ISI subject categories. *Journal of the American Society for Information Science and Technology, 60*, 348–62.

Liaudat, C. C., Vaucher, P., De Francesco, T., Jaunin-Stalder, N., Herzig, L., Verdon, F., Favrat, B., Locatelli, I., & Clair, C. (2018). Sex/gender bias in the management of chest pain in ambulatory care. *Women's Health, 14*, 1–9.

Libet, B., Gleason, C. A., Wright, E. W., & Pearl, D. K. (1983). Time of conscious intention to act in relation to onset of cerebral activity (readiness-potential): The unconscious initiation of a freely voluntary act. *Brain, 106*, 623–42.

Lin, L., Stamm, K., & Christidis, P. (2018). How diverse is the psychology workforce? News from APA's Center for Workforce Studies. *Monitor on Psychology, 49*, 19.

Lindberg, S. M., Hyde, J. S., Petersen, J., & Linn, M. C. (2010). New trends in gender and mathematics performance: A meta-analysis. *Psychological Bulletin, 136*, 1123–35.

Lippman, M. (1998). The convention on the prevention and punishment of the crime of genocide: Fifty years later. *Arizona Journal of International and Comparative Law, 15*, 415–514.

Littman, R. A. (1981). Psychology's histories: Some new ones and a bit about their predecessors – an essay review. *Journal of the History of the Behavioral Sciences, 17*, 516–32.

Loftus, E. F. (1979). *Eyewitness Testimony*. Cambridge, Massachusetts: Harvard University Press.

Lombroso, C. (1902). *Die Ursachen und Bekämpfung des Verbrechens*. Berlin: Hugo Bermühler.

Longino, H. E. (1987). Can there be a feminist science? *Hypatia, 2*, 51–64.

Lord, E. (1950). Experimentally induced variations in Rorschach performance. *Psychological Monographs: General and Applied, 64*, i–34.

Lovett, B. J. (2006). The new history of psychology: A review and critique. *History of Psychology, 9*, 17–37.

Lowe, R., & Yasuhara, Y. (2013). The origins of higher learning: Time for a new historiography? *History of Universities, 27*, 1–19.

Lubek, I. (1981). Histoire de psychologies sociales perdues: Le cas de Gabriel Tarde. *Revue Française de Sociologie, 22*, 361–95.

Lubek, I. (2000). Understanding and using the history of social psychology. *Journal of the History of the Behavioral Sciences, 36*, 319–28.

Lubek, I., & Apfelbaum, E. (2000). A critical gaze and wistful glance at *Handbook* histories of social psychology: Did the successive accounts by Gordon Allport and successors historiographically succeed? *Journal of the History of the Behavioral Sciences, 36*, 405–28.

Luborsky, L., Singer, B., & Luborsky, L. (1975). Comparative studies of psychotherapies: Is it true that 'everyone has won and all must have prizes'? *Archives of General Psychiatry, 32*, 995–1008.

Lucarelli, R. (2011). Demonology during the late Pharaonic and Greco-Roman periods in Egypt. *Journal of Ancient Near Eastern Religions, 11*, 109–25.

Luchte, J. (2009). *Pythagoras and the Doctrine of Transmigration: Wandering Souls*. London: Continuum.

Lynn, R., & Vanhanen, T. (2002). *IQ and the Wealth of Nations*. Westport, Connecticut: Praeger.

Ma, W. J., Husain, M., & Bays, P. M. (2014). Changing concepts of working memory. *Nature Neuroscience, 17*, 347–56.

Macaulay, T. ([1835] 1919). Minute by the Hon'ble T. B. Macaulay, dated the 2nd February 1835. In H. Sharp (ed.), *Selections from Educational Records, Part I (1781–1839)*. Calcutta, India: Superintendent, Government Printing.

Macdonald, D. A., & McAdams, N. N. (2001). *The Woolverton Family 1693–1850 and Beyond: Woolverton and Wolverton Descendants of Charles Woolverton, New Jersey Immigrant*. Rockport, Maine: Penobscot Press.

Madigan, S., & O'Hara, R. (1992). Short-term memory at the turn of the century: Mary Whiton Calkins's memory research. *American Psychologist, 47*, 170–4.

Mahalingam, R. (2007). Beliefs about chastity, machismo, and caste identity: A cultural psychology of gender. *Sex Roles, 56,* 239–49.

Maieron, M. A. (2017). The meaning of madness in ancient Greek culture from Homer to Hippocrates and Plato. *Medicina Historica, 1,* 65–76.

Makel, M. C., Plucker, J. A., & Hegarty, B. (2012). Replications in psychology research: How often do they really occur? *Perspectives on Psychological Science, 7,* 537–42.

Mamdani, M. (2001). *When Victims Become Killers: Colonialism, Nativism, and the Genocide in Rwanda.* Princeton, New Jersey: Princeton University Press.

Manning, R., Levine, M., & Collins, A. (2007). The Kitty Genovese murder and the social psychology of helping: The parable of the 38 witnesses. *American Psychologist, 62,* 555–62.

Manouvrier, L. (1884). Sur quelques erreurs dynamométriques. *Bulletins de la Société d'Anthropologie de Paris, 7,* 271–81.

Marchlewska, M., Cichocka, A., & Kossowska, M. (2018). Addicted to answers: Need for cognitive closure and the endorsement of conspiracy beliefs. *European Journal of Social Psychology, 48,* 109–17.

Markey, P. M., & Ferguson, C. J. (2017). *Moral Combat: Why the War on Violent Video Games Is Wrong.* Dallas: BenBella.

Marks, D. F. (2020). Increasing the transparency, openness and replicability of psychological research: Mandatory data sharing for empirical studies in the *Journal of Health Psychology. Journal of Health Psychology, 25,* 729–32.

Marschall, R. (ed.). (1990). *The Complete E. C. Segar Popeye: Dailies, 1935–1937.* Seattle: Fantagraphics Books.

Marx, K., & Engels, F. (1848). *Manifesto of the Communist Party.* London: J. E. Burghard.

Maslow, A. H. (1954). *Motivation and Personality.* New York: Harper & Row.

Mason, P. H. (2010). Degeneracy at multiple levels of complexity. *Biological Theory, 5,* 277–88.

Masson, J. M. (1984). *The Assault on Truth: Freud's Suppression of the Seduction Theory.* New York: Farrar, Straus and Giroux.

Matthey, A. (1816). *Nouvelles recherches sur le maladies de l'esprit, précédées de considerations sur les difficultés de l'art de guérir.* Paris: J. J. Paschoud.

Maudsley, H. (1865). On the method of the study of mind: An introductory chapter to *A Physiology and Pathology of the Mind. Journal of Mental Science, 11,* 257–61.

Maudsley, H. (1868). *The Physiology and Pathology of Mind.* London: Macmillan.

Maudsley, H. (1895). *The Pathology of Mind: A Study of Its Distempers, Deformities and Disorders.* London: Macmillan.

McCabe, D. P., & Castel, A. D. (2008). Seeing is believing: The effect of brain images on judgments of scientific reasoning. *Cognition, 107,* 343–52.

McCann, C. D., Higgins, E. T., & Fondacaro, R. A. (1991). Primacy and recency in communication and self-persuasion: How successive audiences and multiple encodings influence subsequent evaluative judgments. *Social Cognition, 9,* 47–66.

McDougall, W. (1908). *An Introduction to Social Psychology.* London: Methuen.

McDougall, W. (1914). Psychology in the service of eugenics. *Eugenics Review, 5,* 295–308.

McDougall, W. (1923). *An Outline of Psychology.* London: Methuen.

McEvedy, C., & Jones, R. (1978). *Atlas of World Population History.* Harmondsworth: Penguin.

McEvedy, C. P., & Beard, A. W. (1970). Concept of benign myalgic encephalomyelitis. *British Medical Journal, 1*(5691), 11–15.

McFadden, R. D. (2016, 4 April). Winston Moseley, who killed Kitty Genovese, dies in prison at 81. *New York Times*: https://www.nytimes.com/2016/04/05/nyregion/winston-moseley-81-killer-of-kitty-genovese-dies-in-prison.html (accessed 1 June 2022).

McGinnis, J. (2010). *Avicenna*. Oxford: Oxford University Press.

McLuhan, M. (1962). *The Gutenberg Galaxy: The Making of Typographic Man*. Toronto: University of Toronto Press.

McMahon, C. (2015). Why do we 'like' social media? *The Psychologist*, *28*, 724–9.

McNeil, J. T. (1951). *A History of the Cure of Souls*. New York: Harper & Row.

McNulty, J. K., & Fincham, F. D. (2012). Beyond positive psychology? Toward a contextual view of psychological processes and well-being. *American Psychologist*, *67*, 101–10.

McQueen, S. (Director). (2013). *12 Years a Slave* [Film]. Regency Enterprises; River Road Entertainment; Plan B Entertainment; New Regency Productions; Film4 Productions.

McShane, B. B., Gal, D., Gelman, A., Robert, C., & Tackett, J. L. (2019). Abandon statistical significance. *American Statistician*, *73*(S1), 235–45.

Mead, G. H. (1934). *Mind, Self, and Society from the Standpoint of a Social Behaviorist*. Chicago: University of Chicago Press.

Medawar, P. B. (1975). Victims of psychiatry. *New York Review of Books*, *21*, 17.

Mendrick, H., & Francis, B. (2012). Boffin and geek identities: Abject or privileged? *Gender and Education*, *24*, 15–24.

Menzies, W. C. (Director). (1936). *Things to Come* [Film]. London Film Productions.

Merleau-Ponty, M. (1942). *La Structure du comportement*. Paris: Presses Universitaires de France.

Merllié, D. (2012). Durkheim, Lévy-Bruhl, et la 'pensée primitive': Quel différend? *L'Anée sociologique*, *62*, 429–46.

Merton, R. K. (1996). The genesis and epicene character of the word *scientist*. In K. Erikson (ed.), *Sociological Visions* (pp. 226–54). New Haven, Connecticut: Yale University Press.

Metzger, N. (2013). Battling demons with medical authority: Werewolves, physicians and rationalization. *History of Psychiatry*, *24*, 341–55.

Meyer, I. H. (2003). Prejudice, social stress, and mental health in lesbian, gay, and bisexual populations: Conceptual issues and research evidence. *Psychological Bulletin*, *129*, 674–97.

Michael, M., King, L., Guo, L., McKee, M., Richardson, E., & Stuckler, D. (2013). The mystery of missing female children in the Caucasus: An analysis of sex ratios by birth order. *International Perspectives on Sexual and Reproductive Health*, *39*, 97–102.

Midgley, M. (1979). Gene-juggling. *Philosophy*, *54*, 439–58.

Milgram, S. (1963). Behavioral study of obedience. *Journal of Abnormal and Social Psychology*, *67*, 371–8.

Mill, J. S. (1859). *On Liberty*. London: John W. Parker & Son.

Miller, G. A. (1956). The magical number seven, plus or minus two: Some limits on our capacity for processing information. *Psychological Review*, *63*, 81–97.

Mischel, W., & Ebbesen, E. B. (1970). Attention in delay of gratification. *Journal of Personality and Social Psychology*, *16*, 329–37.

Mitchell, B., & Roberts, J. V. (2012). Sentencing for murder: Exploring public knowledge and public opinion in England and Wales. *British Journal of Criminology*, *52*, 141–58.

Mitchell, K. J. (2018). *Innate: How the Wiring of Our Brains Shapes Who We Are*. Princeton, New Jersey: Princeton University Press.

Mitscherlich, A., & Mielke, F. (1949). *Doctors of Infamy: The Story of Nazi Medical Crimes*. New York: Henry Schuman.

Mittman, A. S., & Kim, S. M. (2017). Monstrous iconography. In C. Hourihane (ed.), *The Routledge Companion to Medieval Iconography* (pp. 518–33). Abingdon, UK: Routledge.

Mix, L. J. (2018). *Life Concepts from Aristotle to Darwin: On Vegetable Souls*. Cham, Switzerland: Palgrave Macmillan.

Möbius, J. S. (1901). The physiological mental weakness of woman. *Alienist and Neurologist, 22*, 624–42.

Modelski, G. (1987). *Long Cycles in World Politics*. London: Palgrave Macmillan.

Moore, S. J. (1914). The articulation of the concepts of normal and abnormal psychology. *American Journal of Psychology, 25*, 283–7.

Moreau, J. (1843). *Recherches sur les aliénés, en orient: Notes sur les établissements qui leur sont consacrés a Malte (Ile de), au Caire (Égypte), a Smyrne (Asie-Mineure), a Constantinople (Turquie)*. Paris: Bourgogne et Martinet.

Morel, C. M. (2003). Neglected diseases: Under-funded research and inadequate health interventions. *EMBO Reports, 4*, s35–s38.

Morell, J. D. (1853). *Elements of Psychology, Part I*. London: William Pickering.

Morrow, P. A. (1904). *Social Diseases and Marriage: Social Prophylaxis*. New York: Lea Brothers & Co.

Mortimer, P. P. (2020). Royal Free Disease after 65 years: What was it and what has become of it? *Reviews in Medical Virology, 30*, e2096.

Morton, S. G. (1839). *Crania Americana; or a Comparative View of the Skulls of Various Aboriginal Nations of North and South America*. Philadelphia: J. Dobson.

Moscovici, S. (1972). Society and theory in social psychology. In J. Israel & H. Tajfel (eds), *The Context of Social Psychology: A Critical Assessment* (pp. 17–68). New York: Academic Press.

Moscovici, S. (1989). Preconditions for explanation in social psychology. *European Journal of Social Psychology, 19*, 407–30.

Moscovici, S., & Marková, I. (2006). *The Making of Modern Social Psychology: The Hidden Story of How an International Social Science Was Created*. Cambridge: Polity Press.

Münsterberg, H. (1898). The psychology of the will. *Psychological Review, 5*, 639–45.

Murdoch, J. E. (1975). From social into intellectual factors: An aspect of the unitary character of late medieval learning. In J. E. Murdoch & E. D. Sylla (eds), *The Cultural Context of Medieval Learning* (pp. 271–348). Dordrecht: Reidel.

Murphy, E. (2003). The administration of insanity in England 1800 to 1870. In R. Porter & D. Wright (eds), *The Confinement of the Insane: International Perspectives, 1800–1965* (pp. 334–49). Cambridge: Cambridge University Press.

Murray, C. (2020). *Human Diversity: The Biology of Gender, Race, and Class*. New York: Twelve.

Naaman, E. (2017). Maimonides and the habitus concept. *Journal of the American Oriental Society, 137*, 537–42.

Nacul, L., O'Boyle, S., Palla, L., Nacul, F. E., Mudie, K., Kingdon, C., Cliff, J. M., Clark, T. G., Dockrell, H. M., & Lacerda, E. M. (2020). How myalgic encephalomyelitis/chronic fatigue syndrome (ME/CFS) progresses: The natural history of ME/CFS. *Frontiers in Neurology, 11*, 826.

Nederlands Instituut van Psychologen (2015). *Beroepscode voor psychologen 2015*. Utrecht, Netherlands: NIP.

Nelkin, D., & Gilman, S. L. (1988). Placing blame for devastating disease. *Social Research, 55,* 361–78.

Netton, I. R. (1992). *Al-Fārābī and His School.* London: Routledge.

New Haven Register (2013, 11 May). Joe Dimow. *New Haven Register:* https://legcy. co/2Pk1Hfw (accessed 1 June 2022).

Newman, C. (2018). The good, the bad and the unholy: Ambivalent angels in the Middle Ages. In M. Ostling (ed.), *Fairies, Demons, and Nature Spirits: 'Small Gods' at the Margins of Christendom* (pp. 103–22). London: Palgrave Macmillan.

Ngun, T. C., & Vilain, E. (2014). The biological basis of human sexual orientation: Is there a role for epigenetics? *Advances in Genetics, 86,* 167–84.

Nguyen, C. T. (2020). Echo chambers and epistemic bubbles. *Episteme, 17,* 141–61.

Nickles, D. P. (2003). *Under the Wire: How the Telegraph Changed Diplomacy.* Cambridge, Massachusetts: Harvard University Press.

Nielsen, J. A., Zielinski, B. A., Ferguson, M. A., Lainhart, J. E., & Anderson, J. S. (2013). An evaluation of the left-brain vs. right-brain hypothesis with resting state functional connectivity magnetic resonance imaging. *PLoS One, 8,* e71275.

Nietzsche, F. (1886). *Jenseits von Gut und Böse: Vorspiel einer Philosophie der Zukunft.* Leipzig: C. G. Naumann.

Nina-Rodrigues, R. (1903). La paranoïa chez les nègres. *Archives d'Anthropologie Criminelle, de Criminologie et de Psychologie Normale et Pathologique, 118,* 609–55 and 689–714.

Nizamie, S. H., & Goyal, N. (2010). History of psychiatry in India. *Indian Journal of Psychiatry, 52* (Suppl. 1), S7–S12.

Northup, S. (1853). *Twelve Years a Slave.* Auburn, New York: Derby & Miller.

Oda, A. M. G. R., Banzato, C. E. M., & Dalgalarrondo, P. (2005). Some origins of cross-cultural psychiatry. *History of Psychiatry, 16,* 155–69.

O'Donnell, J. M. (1979). The crisis of experimentalism in the 1920s: E. G. Boring and his uses of history. *American Psychologist, 34,* 289–95.

O'Keeffe, C., & Wiseman, R. (2005). Testing alleged mediumship: Methods and results. *British Journal of Psychology, 96,* 165–79.

O'Leary, D. (2018). Why bioethics should be concerned with medically unexplained symptoms. *American Journal of Bioethics, 18,* 6–15.

Olivelle, P. (1998). *The Early Upaniṣads: Annotated Text and Translation.* New York: Oxford University Press.

O'Mara, S. M. (2015). *Why Torture Doesn't Work: The Neuroscience of Interrogation.* Cambridge, Massachusetts: Harvard University Press.

Open Science Collaboration. (2015). Estimating the reproducibility of psychological science. *Science, 349*(6251), aac4716.

Ornstein, R. E. (1972). *The Psychology of Consciousness.* San Francisco: Freeman.

Orwell, G. (1949). *Nineteen Eighty-Four: A Novel.* London: Secker & Warburg.

Osler, W. (1921). *The Evolution of Modern Medicine.* New Haven, Connecticut: Yale University Press.

Oxford Dictionaries. (2020). *Definition of Pneumonoultramicroscopicsilicovolcanoconiosis.* https:// www.lexico.com/definition/pneumonoultramicroscopicsilicovolcanoconiosis (accessed 11 January 2020).

Panico, R., Richer, J., & Powell, W. H. (1993). *A Guide to IUPAC Nomenclature of Organic Compounds.* Hoboken, New Jersey: Wiley-Blackwell.

Panteleakos, G., Poulakou-Rebelakou, E., & Koutsilieris, M. (2013). Anatomy and physiology in the work of Nemesius of Emesa 'On the Nature of Man'. *Acta Medico-historica Adriatica*, *11*, 319–28.

Paranjpe, A. C. (2006). From tradition through colonialism to globalization: Reflections on the history of psychology in India. In A. C. Brock (ed.), *Internationalizing the History of Psychology* (pp. 56–74). New York: New York University Press.

Parry, P. I., & Levin, E. C. (2012). Pediatric bipolar disorder in an era of 'mindless psychiatry'. *Journal of Trauma & Dissociation*, *13*, 51–68.

Pascal, B. (1669). *Pensées de M. Pascal sur la religion et sur quelques autres sujets*. Paris: Guillaume Desprez.

Pearson, K. (1894). Contributions to the mathematical theory of evolution. *Philosophical Transactions of the Royal Society (A)*, *185*, 71–110.

Pearson, K. (1901). *National Life: From the Standpoint of Science*. London: Adam and Charles Black.

Pearson, K. (1905). Skew variation, a rejoinder. *Biometrika*, *4*, 169–212.

Pearson, K., & Moul, M. (1925). The problem of alien immigration into Great Britain, illustrated by an examination of Russian and Polish Jewish children: Part II. *Annals of Eugenics*, *1*, 56–127.

Pease, A., & Pease, B. (2002). *Why Men Lie and Women Cry*. Buderim, Australia: Pease International.

Pedlar, V. (2003). Experimentation or exploitation? The investigations of David Ferrier, Dr Benjulia, and Dr Seward. *Interdisciplinary Science Reviews*, *28*, 169–74.

Penfield, W. (1975). *The Mystery of the Mind: A Critical Study of Consciousness and the Human Brain*. Princeton, New Jersey: Princeton University Press.

Penn, A. (2002). *Adventures in the Afterlife: The Secret Diary of Thomas Edison*. Los Angeles: Magic Hour Press.

Pereira, D. R. (2017). Revisiting the contributions of *The New Phrenology* to the brain–mind debate. *Journal of Theoretical and Philosophical Psychology*, *37*, 152–63.

Perry, G. (2013). Deception and illusion in Milgram's accounts of the obedience experiments. *Theoretical & Applied Ethics*, *2*, 79–92.

Perry, R. B. (1930). Psychology, 1876–1929. In S. E. Morison (ed.), *The Development of Harvard University since the Inauguration of President Eliot, 1869–1929*. Cambridge, Massachusetts: Harvard University Press.

Peterson, C., & Seligman, M. E. (2004). *Character Strengths and Virtues: A Handbook and Classification*. Oxford: Oxford University Press.

Pethes, N. (2016). *Psychicones*: Visual traces of the soul in late nineteenth-century fluidic photography. *Medical History*, *60*, 325–41.

Petroski, H. (1990). *The Pencil: A History of Design and Circumstance*. New York: Knopf.

Pew Research Center. (2014, 13 November). *Chapter 8: Religion and Science*. https://www.pewresearch. org/religion/2014/11/13/chapter-8-religion-and-science (accessed 1 June 2022).

Pew Research Center. (2015, 1 July). *Americans, Politics and Science Issues*. https://www.pewresearch. org/science/2015/07/01/americans-politics-and-science-issues (accessed 1 June 2022).

Pew Research Center. (2017, 10 May). *6. Science and Religion*. https://www.pewforum. org/2017/05/10/science-and-religion (accessed 1 June 2022).

Pew Research Center. (2019, 2 August). *Trust and Mistrust in Americans' Views of Scientific Experts*. https://www.pewresearch.org/science/2019/08/02/trust-and-mistrust-in-americans-views-of-scientific-experts (accessed 1 June 2022).

Philippeau, H. R. (1956). Exorcisme. In G. Jacquemet (ed.), *Catholicisme: Hier, aujourd'hui, demain* (Vol. 4, pp. 941–5). Paris: Letouzay et Ané.

Phillips, A. C., Ginty, A., & Hughes, B. M. (2013). The other side of the coin: Blunted cardiovascular and cortisol reactivity is also associated with negative health outcomes. *International Journal of Psychophysiology, 90*, 1–7.

Piaget, J. (1936). *Les origines de l'intelligence chez l'enfant.* Paris: Alcan.

Pickren, W. E. (2000). A whisper of salvation: American psychologists and religion in the popular press, 1884–1908. *American Psychologist, 55*, 1022–4.

Pickren, W. E. (2009). Indigenization and the history of psychology. *Psychological Studies, 54*, 87–95.

Pielke, R. A. (2007). *The Honest Broker: Making Sense of Science in Policy and Politics.* Cambridge: Cambridge University Press.

Pinel, P. (1806). *A Treatise on Insanity, in Which Are Contained the Principles of a New and More Practical Nosology of Maniacal Disorders Than Has Yet Been Offered to the Public.* Sheffield/London: W. Todd/Cadell and Davies.

Pines, M. (1989). On history and psychoanalysis. *Psychoanalytic Psychology, 6*, 121–35.

Pinker, S. (2011). *The Better Angels of Our Nature: Why Violence Has Declined.* New York: Viking.

Planck, M. K. (1950). *Scientific Autobiography and Other Papers.* New York: Philosophical Library.

Poldrack, R. A. (2012). The future of fMRI in cognitive neuroscience. *Neuroimage, 62*, 1216–20.

Pomeroy, E., Bennett, P., Hunt, C. O., Reynolds, T., Farr, L., Frouin, M., Holman, J., Lane, R., French, C., & Barker, G. (2020). New Neanderthal remains associated with the 'flower burial' at Shanidar Cave, Iraqi Kurdistan. *Antiquity: A Review of World Archaeology, 94*, 11–26.

Popper, K. R. (1965). *Conjecture and Refutation: The Growth of Scientific Knowledge.* New York: Harper & Row.

Porter, R. (1987). *A Social History of Madness: The World through the Eyes of the Insane.* New York: Weidenfeld & Nicolson.

Porter, R. (1990). Foucault's great confinement. *History of the Human Sciences, 3*, 47–54.

Potkay, A. (2019). Lucretius, Englishman: Meter, mortalism, and love in Dryden's translations from *De Rerum Natura. Eighteenth-Century Life, 43*, 1–22.

Priestley, J. B. (1960). *Literature and Western Man.* New York: Harper & Brothers.

Prioreschi, P. (1991). *A History of Medicine, Volume 1: Primitive and Ancient Medicine.* Omaha: Horatius Press.

Psychological Society of Ireland. (2010). *Code of Professional Ethics.* Dublin: Psychological Society of Ireland.

Psychological Society of South Africa. (2007). *South African Professional Conduct Guidelines in Psychology.* Johannesburg: Psychological Society of South Africa.

Quétel, C. (1990). *History of Syphilis.* Baltimore: Johns Hopkins University Press.

Quetelet, A. (1835). *Sur l'homme et le développement de ses facultés, ou essai de physique sociale.* Paris: Bachelier.

Quine, W. V. (1951). Two dogmas of empiricism. *Philosophical Review, 60*, 20–43.

Rad, M. S., Martingano, A. J., & Ginges, J. (2018). Toward a psychology of *Homo sapiens*: Making psychological science more representative of the human population. *PNAS, 115*, 11401–5.

Radhakrishnan, S. (2009). *Indian Philosophy* (2nd ed., Vol. 1). Oxford: Oxford University Press.

Radke, S., & de Bruijn, E. R. A. (2012). The other side of the coin: Oxytocin decreases the adherence to fairness norms. *Frontiers in Human Neuroscience, 6*, 193.

Ramirez Rossi, F., & Froment, A. (2018). Earliest animal cranial surgery: From cow to man in the Neolithic. *Scientific Reports*, *8*, 5536.

Randall, W. L. (2007). From computer to compost: Rethinking our metaphors for memory. *Theory & Psychology*, *17*, 611–33.

Rao, K. R., & Paranjpe, A. C. (2016). *Psychology in the Indian Tradition*. New Delhi: Springer.

Rashed, R. (2008). Ibn Al-Haytham (Alhazen). In H. Selin (ed.), *Encyclopaedia of the History of Science, Technology, and Medicine in Non-Western Cultures* (pp. 1090–3). Heidelberg: Springer-Verlag.

Ratcliffe, S. (ed.) (2016). *Oxford Essential Quotations*. Oxford: Oxford University Press.

Rauch, F. A. (1841). *Psychology: Or, a View of the Human Soul; Including Anthropology, Adapted for the Use of Colleges*. New York: M. W. Dodd.

Rawson, E. (1982). The life and death of Asclepiades of Bithynia. *Classical Quarterly*, *32*, 358–70.

Rayner Watson, R. (1930). I am the mother of a behaviorist's sons. *Parent's Magazine & Better Family Living*, *5*, 16–18, 67–8.

Rayner Watson, R. (1932, February). What future has motherhood? *Psychology*, 46–7, 63–6.

Redding, R. E. (2001). Sociopolitical diversity in psychology: The case for pluralism. *American Psychologist*, *56*, 205–15.

Reeves, H. T. (1938). The later years of a noted mental defective. *American Journal on Mental Deficiency*, *43*, 194–200.

Reich, D. (2018). *Who We Are and How We Got Here: Ancient DNA and the New Science of the Human Past*. Oxford: Oxford University Press.

Restak, R. (2000). *Mysteries of the Mind*. Washington, DC: National Geographic.

Reuber, M. (1998). Moral management and the 'unseen eye': Public lunatic asylums in Ireland, 1800–1845. In G. Jones & E. Malcolm (eds), *Medicine, Disease and the State in Ireland, 1650–1940* (pp. 208–33). Cork, Ireland: Cork University Press.

Reville, W. (2020, 5 November). Is it acceptable to use data from Nazi medical experiments? *Irish Times*: https://www.irishtimes.com/news/science/is-it-acceptable-to-use-data-from-nazi-medical-experiments-1.4388509 (accessed 1 June 2022).

Rheingold, J. C. (1964). *The Fear of Being a Woman: A Theory of Maternal Destructiveness*. New York: Grune & Stratton.

Richards, G. (2010). *Putting Psychology in Its Place: Critical Historical Perspectives* (3rd ed.). London: Routledge.

Richards, G. (2012). *'Race', Racism and Psychology: Towards a Reflexive History* (2nd ed.). London: Routledge.

Richards, R. J. (2009). Myth 19: That Darwin and Haeckel were complicit in Nazi biology. In R. J. Numbers (ed.), *Galileo Goes to Jail: And Other Myths about Science and Religion* (pp. 170–7). Cambridge, Massachusetts: Harvard University Press.

Riepe, D. M. (1982). *The Naturalistic Tradition in Indian Thought*. Santa Barbara, California: Praeger.

Riès, S. K., Dronkers, N. F., & Knight, R. T. (2016). Choosing words: Left hemisphere, right hemisphere, or both? Perspective on the lateralization of word retrieval. *Annals of the New York Academy of Sciences*, *1369*, 111–31.

Ring, K. (1967). Experimental social psychology: Some sober questions about some frivolous values. *Journal of Experimental Social Psychology*, *3*, 113–23.

Risen, J. (2014). *Pay Any Price: Greed, Power, and Endless War*. New York: Mariner Books.

Riskin, J. (2016). *The Restless Clock: A History of the Centuries-Long Argument over What Makes Living Things Tick*. Chicago: University of Chicago Press.

Roberts, J. H. (2009). Myth 18: That Darwin destroyed natural theology. In R. J. Numbers (ed.), *Galileo Goes to Jail: And Other Myths about Science and Religion* (pp. 161–9). Cambridge, Massachusetts: Harvard University Press.

Robins, R. W., Gosling, S. D., & Craik, K. H. (1999). An empirical analysis of trends in psychology. *American Psychologist, 54*, 117–28.

Robinson, A. (2016). The Marconi connection. *New Scientist, 3086*, 42–3.

Robinson, D. (1970, April). The 100 most important people in the world. *Esquire*, pp. 104–7.

Robinson, D. N. (1989). *Aristotle's Psychology*. New York: Columbia University Press.

Robinson, D. N. (2013). Historiography in psychology: A note on ignorance. *Theory & Psychology, 23*(6), 819–28.

Robinson, N. (1729). *A New System of the Spleen, Vapours, and Hypochondriack Melancholy: Wherein All the Decays of the Nerves, and Lownesses of the Spirits, Are Mechanically Accounted For*. London: Bettesworth, Innys, and Rivington.

Roca, A. L., Georgiadis, N., Pecon-Slattery, J., & O'Brien, S. J. (2001). Genetic evidence for two species of elephant in Africa. *Science, 293*, 1473–7.

Rodriguez, R. (Director). (2019). *Alita: Battle Angel* [Film]. 20th Century Fox; Lightstorm Entertainment; Troublemaker Studios; TSG Entertainment.

Rokeach, M. (1973). *The Nature of Human Values*. New York: The Free Press.

Rondi, B. (Director). (1963). *Il demonio* [Film]. Titanus; Vox Film; Les Films Marceau; Cocinor.

Rosenhan, D. L. (1973). On being sane in insane places. *Science, 179*, 250–8.

Rosenthal, R. (1966). *Experimenter Effects in Behavioral Research*. New York: Appleton-Century-Crofts.

Rosenthal, R. (1979). The file drawer problem and tolerance for null results. *Psychological Bulletin, 86*, 638–41.

Rosenzweig, S. (1936). Some implicit common factors in diverse methods of psychotherapy. *American Journal of Orthopsychiatry, 6*, 412–15.

Ross, E. A. (1908). *Social Psychology: An Outline and Source Book*. New York: Macmillan.

Ross, G. (Director). (2012). *The Hunger Games* [Film]. Color Force.

Ross, L. (1977). The intuitive psychologist and his shortcomings: Distortions in the attribution process. In L. Berkowitz (ed.), *Advances in Experimental Social Psychology* (pp. 173–220). New York: Academic Press.

Ross, L., Lepper, M., & Ward, A. (2010). History of social psychology: Insights, challenges, and contributions to theory and application. In S. T. Fiske, D. T. Gilbert & G. Lindzey (eds), *Handbook of Social Psychology* (5th ed., Vol. 1, pp. 3–50). Hoboken, New Jersey: Wiley.

Roux, S. (2005). Empedocles to Darwin. In E. Close, M. Tsianikas & G. Frazis (eds), *Greek Research in Australia: Proceedings of the Biennial International Conference of Greek Studies, 2003* (pp. 1–16). Adelaide: Flinders University.

Royce, J. (1895). Preliminary report on imitation. *Psychological Review, 2*, 363–7.

Rudnick, L. P., & Heru, A. M. (2017). The 'secret' source of 'female hysteria': The role that syphilis played in the construction of female sexuality and psychoanalysis in the late nineteenth and early twentieth centuries. *History of Psychiatry, 28*, 195–208.

Rush, B. (1812). *Medical Inquiries and Observations, upon the Diseases of the Mind*. Philadelphia: Kimber & Richardson.

Russell, W. L. (1941). A psychopathic department of an American general hospital in 1808. *American Journal of Insanity, 98*, 229–37.

Russian Psychological Society. (2012). Этический кодекс психолога. Moscow: Russian Psychological Society.

Rutherford, A. (2000). Radical behaviorism and psychology's public: B. F. Skinner in the popular press, 1934–1990. *History of Psychology, 3*, 371–95.

Sacred Congregation for the Doctrine of the Faith. (1975, 10 July). Christian faith and demonology. *L'Osservatore Romano* [English edition], pp. 6–10.

Sahlins, M. (1976). *The Use and Abuse of Biology: An Anthropological Critique of Sociobiology*. Ann Arbor, Michigan: University of Michigan Press.

Saint-Simon, H. (1825). *Nouveau Christianisme: Dialogues entre un conservateur et un novateur*. Paris: Bossange Père.

Saliba, G. (1994). *A History of Arabic Astronomy: Planetary Theories during the Golden Age of Islam*. New York: New York University Press.

Salsburg, D. (2001). *The Lady Tasting Tea: How Statistics Revolutionized Science in the Twentieth Century*. New York: Freeman.

Samelson, F. (1980). E. G. Boring and his history of experimental psychology. *American Psychologist, 35*, 467–70.

Samelson, F. (2000). Whig and anti-Whig histories: And other curiosities of social psychology. *Journal of the History of the Behavioral Sciences, 36*, 499–506.

Sanford, V. (1935). Pierre-Simon Laplace. *Mathematics Teacher, 28*, 111–13.

Santayana, G. (1905). *The Life of Reason: The Phases of Human Progress I. Introduction and Reason in Common Sense*. New York: Scribner's.

Santoro, G., Wood, M. D., Merlo, L., Anastasi, G. P., Tomasello, F., & Germanò, A. (2009). The anatomic location of the soul from the heart, through the brain, to the whole body, and beyond: A journey through Western history, science, and philosophy. *Neurosurgery, 65*, 633–43.

Sartre, J.-P. (1943). *L'Être et le néant: Essai d'ontologie phénoménologique*. Paris: Librairie Gallimard.

Sass, L. A. (2014). Delusion and double book-keeping. In T. Fuchs, T. Breyer & C. Mundt (eds), *Karl Jaspers' Philosophy and Psychopathology* (pp. 125–47). New York: Springer.

Sato, T., Mizoguchi, H., Arakawa, A., Hidaka, S., Takasuna, M., & Nishikawa, Y. (2016). History of 'history of psychology' in Japan. *Japanese Psychological Research, 58*, 110–28.

Saunders, N. J. (1994). Predators of culture: Jaguar symbolism and Mesoamerican elites. *World Archaeology, 26*, 104–17.

Schachter, S., Nuttin, J., De Monchaux, C., Maucorps, P. H., Osmer, D., Duijker, H., Rommetveit, R., & Israel, J. (1954). Cross-cultural experiments on threat and rejection: A study of the Organization for Comparative Social Research. *Human Relations, 7*, 403–39.

Schaffner, F. J. (Director). (1968). *Planet of the Apes* [Film]. APJAC Productions.

Scheidel, W. (2009). Population and demography. In A. Erskine (ed.), *A Companion to Ancient History* (pp. 134–45). Chichester: Wiley-Blackwell.

Schlotte, F. (1955). Beiträge zum Lebensbild Wilhelm Wundts aus seinem Briefwechsel. *Zeitschrift der Karl-Marx-Universität Leipzig, 5*, 333–49.

Schmidt, C. G. (1984). The group-fantasy origins of AIDS. *Journal of Psychohistory, 12*, 37–78.

Schmucker, S. S. (1842). *Psychology: Or, Elements of a New System of Mental Philosophy, on the Basis of Consciousness and Common Sense*. New York: Harper & Brothers.

Schönpflug, W. (2017). Professional psychology in Germany, National Socialism, and the Second World War. *History of Psychology, 20*, 387–407.

Schruijer, S. G. L. (2012). Whatever happened to the 'European' in European social psychology? A study of the ambitions in founding the European Association of Experimental Social Psychology. *History of the Human Sciences, 25*, 88–107.

Schur, M. (Creator). (2016–20). *The Good Place* [TV Series]. Fremulon; 3 Arts Entertainment; Universal Television.

Schwab, J. J. (2011). *The Birth of the Mob: Representations of Crowds in Archaic and Classical Greek Literature*. Berkeley: University of California.

Schwartz, S. H. (1992). Universals in the content and structure of values: Theory and empirical tests in 20 countries. In M. Zanna (ed.), *Advances in Experimental Social Psychology* (Vol. 25, pp. 1–65). New York: Academic Press.

Schwekendiek, D. (2009). Height and weight differences between North and South Korea. *Journal of Biosocial Science, 41*, 51–5.

Scott, R. (Director). (1982). *Blade Runner* [Film]. The Ladd Company; Shaw Brothers; Blade Runner Partnership.

Scull, A. (1983). The domestication of madness. *Medical History, 27*, 233–48.

Scull, A. (2015). *Madness in Civilization: A Cultural History of Insanity, from the Bible to Freud, from the Madhouse to Modern Medicine*. Princeton, New Jersey: Princeton University Press.

Scull, A. T. (1979). *Museums of Madness: Social Organization of Insanity in 19th Century England*. New York: St Martin's Press.

Sedlmeier, P., & Gigerenzer, G. (1989). Do studies of statistical power have an effect on the power of studies? *Psychological Bulletin, 105*, 309–16.

Seligman, M. E. P. (1972). Learned helplessness. *Annual Review of Medicine, 23*, 407–12.

Seligman, M. E. P. (1998). President's column: What is the 'good life'? *APA Monitor, 29*, 1.

Sensales, G., & Dal Secco, A. (2014). The rise of a science in the early twentieth century: The forgotten voice of Gualtiero Sarfatti and the first 'social psychology' volumes in Italy. *History of Psychology, 17*, 36–49.

Sersch, M. J. (2019). *Demons on the Couch: Spirit Possession, Exorcisms and the DSM-5*. Newcastle upon Tyne: Cambridge Scholars Publishing.

Shaffern, R. W. (2006). The pardoner's promises: Preaching and policing indulgences in the fourteenth-century English church. *The Historian, 68*, 49–65.

Shannon, C. E. (1948). A mathematical theory of communication. *Bell System Technical Journal, 27*, 379–423.

Shapira, M. (2013). *The War Inside: Psychoanalysis, Total War, and the Making of the Democratic Self in Postwar Britain*. Cambridge: Cambridge University Press.

Shapira, M. (2017). 'Speaking Kleinian': Susan Isaacs as Ursula Wise and the inter-war popularisation of psychoanalysis. *Medical History, 61*, 525–47.

Shapira, M. (2021). A case for a 'middle-way career' in the history of psychology: The work of pioneering psychoanalyst Marjorie Brierley in early 20th century Britain. *History of Psychology, 24*, 55–76.

Sherwood, H., & Giuffrida, A. (2017, 1 September). Pope reveals he had weekly psychoanalysis sessions at age 42. *The Guardian*: https://www.theguardian.com/world/2017/sep/01/pope-francis-psychoanalysis (accessed 1 June 2022).

Shields, S. A. (1975). Functionalism, Darwinism, and the psychology of women: A study in social myth. *American Psychologist, 30*, 739–54.

Shorter, E. (1997). *A History of Psychiatry: From the Era of the Asylum to the Age of Prozac.* New York: Wiley.

Shumway, D. R., & Messer-Davidow, E. (1991). Disciplinarity: An introduction. *Poetics Today, 12*, 201–25.

Sick, D. H. (2013). Oedipal complexes: Freud and Artemidorus. *Soundings: An Interdisciplinary Journal, 96*, 382–97.

Sighele, S. (1891). *La folla delinquente.* Turin: Bocca.

Silverman, I. (1977). Why social psychology fails. *Canadian Psychological Review/Psychologie Canadienne, 18*, 353–8.

Simmons, J., Nelson, L., & Simonsohn, U. (2011). False-positive psychology: Undisclosed flexibility in data collection and analysis allow presenting anything as significant. *Psychological Science, 22*, 1359–66.

Skaggs, E. B. (1933). The meaning of the term 'abnormality' in psychology. *Journal of Abnormal and Social Psychology, 28*, 113–18.

Skinner, B. F. (1948). *Walden Two.* Indianapolis: Hackett.

Skinner, B. F. (1957). *Verbal Behavior.* Acton, Massachusetts: Copley.

Skinner, B. F. (1971). *Beyond Freedom and Dignity.* Indianapolis: Hackett.

Skues, R. A. (2006). *Sigmund Freud and the History of Anna O.: Reopening a Closed Case.* Basingstoke: Palgrave Macmillan.

Sloan, T. (2009). Theories of personality. In D. Fox, I. Prilleltensky & S. Austin (eds), *Critical Psychology: An Introduction* (2nd ed., pp. 57–74). London: Sage.

Smaldino, P. E., & McElreath, R. (2016). The natural selection of bad science. *Royal Society Open Science, 3*, 160384.

Smedley, A. (1998). 'Race' and the construction of human identity. *American Anthropologist, 100*, 690–702.

Smedley, A., & Smedley, B. D. (2005). Race as biology is fiction, racism as a social problem is real: Anthropological and historical perspectives on the social construction of race. *American Psychologist, 60*, 16–26.

Smiles, S. (1859). *Self-Help: With Illustrations of Character and Conduct.* London: John Murray.

Smith, J. D., & Wehmeyer, M. L. (2012). Who was Deborah Kallikak? *Intellectual and Developmental Disabilities, 50*, 169–78.

Smith, P. M. (2013, 20 October). We can be heroes: 12 Years a Slave, Schindler's List, and the hero problem in American movies. *Slate*: https://slate.com/culture/2013/10/12-years-a-slave-and-schindlers-list-how-american-movies-valorize-those-who-escape-historys-tragedies.html (accessed 1 June 2022).

Sokal, M. M. (1981). *An Education in Psychology: James McKeen Cattell's Journal and Letters from Germany and England, 1880–1888.* Cambridge, Massachusetts: MIT Press.

Sondhaus, E., & Finger, S. (1988). Aphasia and the CNS from Imhotep to Broca. *Neuropsychology, 2*, 87–110.

Son Hing, L. S., Bobocel, D. R., Zanna, M. P., & McBride, M. V. (2007). Authoritarian dynamics and unethical decision making: High social dominance orientation leaders and high right-wing authoritarianism followers. *Journal of Personality and Social Psychology, 92*, 67–81.

Spellman, B. A. (2015). A short (personal) future history of Revolution 2.0. *Perspectives on Psychological Science, 10*, 886–99.

Stace, W. T. (1962). *A Critical History of Greek Philosophy.* New York: St Martin's Press.

Stachowski, R. (1993). *Roots of Polish Psychology*. Poznań: Institute of Psychology.

Staeuble, I. (2006). Psychology in the Eurocentric order of the social sciences: Colonial constitution, cultural imperialist expansion, postcolonial critique. In A. C. Brock (ed.), *Internationalizing the History of Psychology* (pp. 183–207). New York: New York University Press.

Stainton Rogers, W. (2009). Research methodology. In D. Fox, I. Prilleltensky & S. Austin (eds), *Critical Psychology: An Introduction* (2nd ed., pp. 335–54). Los Angeles: Sage.

Staub, M. E. (2016). The other side of the brain: The politics of split-brain research in the 1970s–1980s. *History of Psychology, 19,* 259–73.

Staum, M. S. (2003). *Labeling People: French Scholars on Society, Race, and Empire, 1815–1848.* Montreal: McGill-Queen's University Press.

Stelmack, R. M., & Stalikas, A. (1991). Galen and the humour theory of temperament. *Personality and Individual Differences, 12,* 255–63.

Stephens, M. (1998). *The Rise of the Image and the Fall of the Word*. Oxford: Oxford University Press.

Sternberg, R. J. (2019). A theory of adaptive intelligence and its relation to general intelligence. *Journal of Intelligence, 7,* 23.

Sternberg, R. J., Grigorenko, E. L., & Kidd, K. K. (2005). Intelligence, race, and genetics. *American Psychologist, 60,* 46–59.

Stevens, A., & Price, J. (2016). *Evolutionary Psychiatry: A New Beginning – Classic Edition*. Abingdon, UK: Routledge.

Stevens, S. S. (1973). Edwin Garrigues Boring. *Biographical Memoirs: National Academy of Sciences, 43,* 41–76.

Stigler, S. M. (1980). Stigler's law of eponymy. *Transactions of the New York Academy of Sciences, 39,* 147–58.

Stiglic, N., & Viner, R. M. (2019). Effects of screentime on the health and well-being of children and adolescents: A systematic review of reviews. *BMJ Open, 9,* e023191.

St John, P. B. (1844). The death blanket. *Chamber's Edinburgh Journal, 24,* 373–6.

Story, G. W., Vlaev, I., Seymour, B., Darzi, A., & Donan, R. J. (2014). Does temporal discounting explain unhealthy behavior? A systematic review and reinforcement learning perspective. *Frontiers in Behavioral Neuroscience, 8,* 76.

Stove, D. (1992). The demons and Dr Dawkins. *American Scholar, 61,* 67–78.

Strathern, A. (1994). Between body and mind: Shamans and politics among the Anga, Baktaman and Gebusi in Papua New Guinea. *Oceania, 64,* 288–301.

Stroebe, W. (2012). The truth about Triplett (1898), but nobody seems to care. *Perspectives on Psychological Science, 7,* 54–7.

Stromberg, R. N. (1988). The philosophes and the French Revolution: Reflections on some recent research. *History Teacher, 21,* 321–39.

Strube, M. J. (2005). What did Triplett really find? A contemporary analysis of the first experiment in social psychology. *American Journal of Psychology, 118,* 271–86.

Strupp, H. H., & Hadley, S. W. (1979). Specific vs nonspecific factors in psychotherapy. *Archives of General Psychiatry, 36,* 1125–36.

Student. (1908). The probable error of a mean. *Biometrika, 6,* 1–25.

Sutton, J. (2018). Tone deaf? *The Psychologist, 31,* 12–13.

Szasz, T. S. (1961). *The Myth of Mental Illness: Foundations of a Theory of Personal Conduct.* New York: Harper & Row.

Szreter, S. (1988). The importance of social intervention in Britain's mortality decline c. 1850–1914: A re-interpretation of the role of public health. *Social History of Medicine*, *1*, 1–37.

Tallis, R. (2021). *Freedom: An Impossible Reality.* Newcastle upon Tyne: Agenda Publishing.

Tannen, D. (1990). *You Just Don't Understand: Women and Men in Conversation.* New York: Ballantine.

Tarde, G. (1898). *Études de Psychologie Sociale.* Paris: Giard & Brière.

Tavris, C. (1993). The mismeasure of woman. *Feminism & Psychology*, *3*, 149–68.

Taylor, S. E. (1998). The social being in social psychology. In D. Gilbert, S. T. Fiske & G. Lindzey (eds), *Handbook of Social Psychology* (4th ed., Vol. 1, pp. 58–95). Boston: McGraw-Hill.

Taylor, S. E., Klein, L. C., Lewis, B. P., Gruenewald, T. L., Gurung, R. A. R., & Updegraff, J. A. (2000). Biobehavioral responses to stress in females: Tend-and-befriend, not fight-or-flight. *Psychological Review*, *107*, 411–29.

Teo, T. (2009). Philosophical concerns in critical psychology. In D. Fox, I. Prilleltensky & S. Austin (eds), *Critical Psychology: An Introduction* (2nd ed., pp. 36–54). London: Sage.

ter Hark, M. (2004). *Popper, Otto Selz and the Rise of Evolutionary Epistemology.* Cambridge: Cambridge University Press.

ter Hark, M. (2010). The psychology of thinking before the cognitive revolution: Otto Selz on problems, schemas, and creativity. *History of Psychology*, *13*, 2–24.

Terman, L. W. (1916). *The Measurement of Intelligence: An Explanation of and a Complete Guide for the Use of the Stanford Revision and Extension of the Binet–Simon Intelligence Scale.* Boston: Houghton Mifflin.

Thatcher, M. (1987, 31 October). AIDS, education and the year 2000. [Interview by D. Keay]. *Woman's Own*, 8–10.

Thomas, R. K. (2007). Recurring errors among recent history of psychology textbooks. *American Journal of Psychology*, *120*, 477–95.

Thoreau, H. D. (1854). *Walden; or, Life in the Woods.* Boston: Ticknor and Fields.

Thorndike, E. L. (1898). What is a psychical fact? *Psychological Review*, *5*, 645–50.

Thorndike, E. L. (1914). *Educational Psychology Briefer Course.* New York: Teachers College, Columbia University.

Thorne, S. R., Hegarty, P., & Hepper, E. G. (2019). Equality in theory: From a heteronormative to an inclusive psychology of romantic love. *Theory & Psychology*, *29*, 240–57.

Tibi, S. (2006). Al-Razi and Islamic medicine in the 9th century. *Journal of the Royal Society of Medicine*, *99*, 206–7.

Tiefer, L. (1992). Critique of the DSM-III-R nomenclature for sexual dysfunctions. *Psychiatric Medicine*, *10*, 227–45.

Tóibín, C. (2004). *The Master.* London: Picador.

Tolman, E. C., & Honzik, C. H. (1930). 'Insight' in rats. *University of California Publications in Psychology*, *4*, 215–32.

Tomlinson, S. (1997). Phrenology, education and the politics of human nature: The thought and influence of George Combe. *History of Education*, *26*, 1–22.

Tong, B. R. (2003). Taoist mind–body resources for psychological health and healing. In S. G. Mijares (ed.), *Modern Psychology and Ancient Wisdom: Psychological Healing Practices from the World's Religious Traditions* (pp. 175–98). New York: Routledge.

Tonquedec, P. J. (1938). *Les maladies nerveuses ou mentales et les manifestations diaboliques.* Paris: Beauchesne.

Tracey, T. J. G., Wampold, B. E., Lichtenberg, J. W., & Goodyear, R. K. (2014). Expertise in psychotherapy: An elusive goal? *American Psychologist, 69*, 218–29.

Trafimow, D., & Marks, M. (2015). Editorial. *Basic and Applied Social Psychology, 37*, 1–2.

Triplett, N. (1898). The dynamogenic factors in pacemaking and competition. *American Journal of Psychology, 9*, 507–33.

Tucker, W. H. (1994). *The Science and Politics of Racial Research.* Urbana, Illinois: University of Illinois Press.

Tuke, D. H. (1894). Increase of insanity in Ireland. *Journal of Mental Science, 40*, 549–61.

Turing, A. M. (1937). On computable numbers, with an application to the Entscheidungsproblem. *Proceedings of the London Mathematical Society, s2-42*, 230–65.

Tversky, A., & Kahneman, D. (1974). Judgment under uncertainty: Heuristics and biases. *Science, 185*, 1124–31.

Tversky, A., & Kahneman, D. (1983). Extensional versus intuitive reasoning: The conjunction fallacy in probability judgment. *Psychological Review, 90*(4), 293–315.

Twain, M. (1876). *The Adventures of Tom Sawyer.* Hartford, Connecticut: American Publishing Company.

Twain, M. (1885). *Adventures of Huckleberry Finn (Tom Sawyer's Comrade).* New York: Webster.

Twain, M. (1906). Autobiography of Mark Twain. In B. Griffin & H. E. Smith (eds), *Autobiography of Mark Twain* (Vol. 2, pp. 1–456). Berkeley: University of California Press.

Twelftree, G. H. (2010). *Jesus the Exorcist: A Contribution to the Study of the Historical Jesus.* Eugene, Oregon: Wipf and Stock.

Tyson, G. P. (1975). A found woman: Some recent biographies of Mary Wollstonecraft. *Eighteenth-Century Studies, 9*, 263–9.

Unger, M. F. (1994). *Biblical Demonology: A Study of Spiritual Forces at Work Today.* Grand Rapids, Michigan: Kregel.

Unsworth, A., & Voas, D. (2018). Attitudes to evolution among Christians, Muslims and the non-religious in Britain: Differential effects of religious and educational factors. *Public Understanding of Science, 27*, 76–93.

Uttal, W. R. (2001). *The New Phrenology: The Limits of Localizing Cognitive Processes in the Brain.* Cambridge, Massachusetts: MIT Press.

van der Zande, J. (2010). *Statistik* and history in the German enlightenment. *Journal of the History of Ideas, 71*, 411–32.

Vernon, M. D. (1965). Review of the book *A Short History of British Psychology, 1840–1940,* by L. S. Hearnshaw. *Eugenics Review, 56*, 212–13.

Vestrucci, A. (2020). Recalibrating the logic of free will with Martin Luther. *Theology and Science, 18*, 358–82.

Vinkers, C. H., Tijdink, J. K., & Otte, W. M. (2015). Use of positive and negative words in scientific PubMed abstracts between 1974 and 2014: Retrospective analysis. *BMJ, 351*, h6467.

Vitali, V. (1896). *Studi antropologici in servizio della pedagogia.* Forlì, Italy: Luigi Bordandini.

Volk, A. A., & Atkinson, J. A. (2013). Infant and child death in the human environment of evolutionary adaptation. *Evolution and Human Behavior, 34*, 182–92.

Von Hartmann, E. (1869). *Philosophie des Unbewussten: Versuch einer Weltanschauung.* Berlin: Carl Duncker.

Wachowski, L., & Wachowski, L. (Directors). (1999). *The Matrix* [Film]. Warner Bros.; Village Roadshow Pictures; Groucho II Film Partnership; Silver Pictures.

Wagner-Egger, P., Delouvée, S., Gauvrit, N., & Dieguez, S. (2018). Creationism and conspiracism share a common teleological bias. *Current Biology, 28*, R867–R868.

Wallace, A. R. (1864). The origin of human races and the antiquity of man deduced from the theory of 'natural selection'. *Transactions of the Anthropological Society of London, 1*, clviii–clxxxvii.

Walsh, A. A. (1972). The American tour of Dr. Spurzheim. *Journal of the History of Medicine and Allied Sciences, 27*, 187–205.

Walsh, R. (2015). What is wisdom? Cross-cultural and cross-disciplinary syntheses. *Review of General Psychology, 19*, 278–93.

Walsh, R. T. G., Teo, T., & Baydala, A. (2014). *A Critical History and Philosophy of Psychology: Diversity of Context, Thought, and Practice*. Cambridge: Cambridge University Press.

Wampold, B. E., & Imel, Z. E. (2015). *The Great Psychotherapy Debate: The Evidence for What Makes Psychotherapy Work* (2nd ed.). London: Routledge.

Wampold, B. E., Mondin, G. W., Moody, M., Stich, F., Benson, K., & Ahn, H.-n. (1997). A meta-analysis of outcome studies comparing bona fide psychotherapies: Empirically, 'all must have prizes'. *Psychological Bulletin, 122*, 203–15.

Watrin, J. P. (2017). The 'new history of psychology' and the uses and abuses of dichotomies. *Theory & Psychology, 27*, 69–86.

Watson, J. B. (1913). Psychology as the behaviorist views it. *Psychological Review, 20*, 158–77.

Watson, J. B., & Rayner Watson, R. (1928). *Psychological Care of Infant and Child*. New York: Norton.

Watters, E. (2010). *Crazy Like Us: The Globalization of the American Psyche*. New York: Free Press.

Wayland, F. (1854). *The Elements of Intellectual Philosophy*. Boston: Phillips, Sampson and Company.

Weaver, W., Snow, C. P., Hesburg, T. M., & Baker, W. O. (1961). The moral un-neutrality of science. *Science, 133*, 255–62.

Wegrocki, H. J. (1938). A critique of cultural and statistical concepts of abnormality. *Journal of Abnormal and Social Psychology, 34*, 166–78.

Weinberg, A. M. (1961). Impact of large-scale science on the United States. *Science, 134*, 161–4.

Weiskrantz, L. (1994). Donald Eric Broadbent. *Biographical Memoirs of Fellows of the Royal Society, 40*, 32–42.

Weiss, S. F. (2010). After the fall: Political whitewashing, professional posturing, and personal refashioning in the postwar career of Otmar Freiherr von Verschuer. *Isis, 101*, 722–58.

Weisstein, N. (1971). Psychology constructs the female; or, the fantasy life of the male psychologist (with some attention to the fantasies of his friends, the male biologist and the male anthropologist). *Journal of Social Education, 35*, 362–73.

Weld, H. P. (1931). Review of *A History of Experimental Psychology* by E. G. Boring. *Psychological Bulletin, 28*, 130–45.

Wellendorf, H. (2008). Ptolemy's political tool: Religion. *Studia Antiqua, 6*, 33–8.

Wertheimer, M. (1922). Untersuchungen zur Lehre von der Gestalt: I. Prinzipielle bemerkungen. *Psychologische Forschung, 1*, 47–58.

Westad, O. A. (2007). *The Global Cold War: Third World Interventions and the Making of Our Times*. Cambridge: Cambridge University Press.

Whewell, W. (1840). *The Philosophy of the Inductive Sciences, Founded upon Their History*. London: John W. Parker.

Whitman, J. Q. (2017). *Hitler's American Model: The United States and the Making of Nazi Race Law*. Princeton, New Jersey: Princeton University Press.

Whitmore, A. (2017). Fascinating *fascina*: Apotropaic magic and how to wear a penis. In M. Cifarelli & L. Gawlinkski (eds), *What Shall I Say of Clothes? Theoretical and Methodological Approaches to the Study of Dress in Antiquity* (pp. 47–65). Boston: American Institute of Archaeology.

Wickramasekera II, I. E. (2014). Early psychological knowledge. In T. Leahey, S. Greer, G. Lefrançois, T. Reiner, J. Spencer, I. Wickramasekera II & E. Willmarth (eds), *History of Psychology* (pp. 15–42). San Diego: Constellation.

Wilkinson, T. (2017). *Writings from Ancient Egypt.* London: Penguin.

Willis, T. (1664). *Cerebri anatome: Cui accessit nervorum descriptio et usus.* London: Joseph Martyn & James Allestry.

Willis, T. (1683). *Two Discourses Concerning the Soul of Brutes, Which Is That of the Vital and Sensitive of Man.* London: Thomas Dring.

Willy, R. (1897). Die Krisis in der Psychologie. *Vierteljahrsschrift für wissenschaftliche Philosophie, 21,* 227–353.

Wilson, D. (2017). *Superstition and Science: Mystics, Sceptics, Truth-Seekers and Charlatans.* London: Robinson.

Wilson, E. O. (1975). *Sociobiology: The New Synthesis.* Cambridge, Massachusetts: Harvard University Press.

Winnicott, D. W. (1949). Hate in the counter-transference. *International Journal of Psycho-Analysis, 30,* 69–74.

Winslow, F. (1853). Insanity in India. *Journal of Psychological Medicine and Mental Pathology, 6,* 356–67.

Wiseman, R. (2011). *Paranormality: Why We See What Isn't There.* London: Pan Books.

Wittgenstein, L. (1953). *Philosophische Untersuchungen.* Frankfurt: Suhrkamp.

Wojtila, K. [Pope John Paul II]. (1986). *Udienza generale. Mercoledì, 13 agosto 1986.* http://www.vatican.va/content/john-paul-ii/it/audiences/1986/documents/hf_jp-ii_aud_19860813.html (accessed 1 June 2022).

Wollstonecraft, M. (1792). *A Vindication of the Rights of Woman: With Strictures on Political and Moral Subjects.* London: J. Johnson.

Wollstonecraft, M. (1798). *Posthumous Works of Mary Wollstonecraft Godwin – Author of A Vindication of the Rights of Woman: In Four Volumes.* London: J. Johnson.

Wolpert, L. (1992). *The Unnatural Nature of Science.* London: Faber and Faber.

Woodward, I. (1979). *The Werewolf Delusion.* London: Paddington Press.

Woolley, H. T. (1910). Psychological literature: A review of the recent literature on the psychology of sex. *Psychological Bulletin, 7,* 335–42.

World Health Organization. (2018). *ICD-11: International Classification of Diseases 11th Revision.* https://icd.who.int/en (accessed 1 June 2022).

World Medical Association. (2013). World Medical Association Declaration of Helsinki: Ethical principles for medical research involving human subjects. *JAMA, 310,* 2191–4.

Worley, P. (2018). Plato, metacognition and philosophy in schools. *Journal of Philosophy in Schools, 5*(1), 76–91.

Wu, A. (Director). (2004). *Saving Face* [Film]. Destination Films.

Wundt, W. (1862). *Beiträge zur Theorie der Sinneswahrnehmung.* Leipzig: C. F. Winter'sche Verlagshandlung.

Wundt, W. (1863). *Vorlesungen über die Menschen-und Tierseele.* Leipzig: Voss.

Wundt, W. (1909). Das Institut für experimentelle Psychologie zu Leipzig. *Psychologische Studien*, 5, 289–93.

Yeomans, N. D. (2011). The ulcer sleuths: The search for the cause of peptic ulcers. *Journal of Gastroenterology and Hepatology*, 26, 35–41.

Yerkes, R. M. (1923). A foreword. In C. C. Brigham, *A Study of American Intelligence* (pp. v–viii). Princeton, New Jersey: Princeton University Press.

Yilanli, M. (2018). Muhammad ibn Zakariya al-Razi and the first psychiatric ward. *American Journal of Psychiatry Residents' Journal*, 13, 11.

Young, J. L. (2017). Numbering the mind: Questionnaires and the attitudinal public. *History of the Human Sciences*, 30, 32–53.

Young, J. L. (2020). Thinking in multitudes: Questionnaires and the composite cases in early American psychology. *History of the Human Sciences*, 33, 160–74.

Yü, Y.-S. (1987). 'O soul, come back!' A study in the changing conceptions of the soul and afterlife in pre-Buddhist China. *Harvard Journal of Asiatic Studies*, 47, 363–95.

Zachos, F. E. (2016). *Species Concepts in Biology: Historical Development, Theoretical Foundations and Practical Relevance*. Cham, Switzerland: Springer.

Zanchetta, B. (2015). Deconstructing 'declinism': The 1970s and the reassertion of American international power. *International Politics*, 52, 269–87.

Zapperi, R. (2013). *Freud e Mussolini: La psicoanalisi in Italia durante il regime fascista*. Milan: FrancoAngeli.

Zaretsky, E. (2005). *Secrets of the Soul: A Social and Cultural History of Psychoanalysis*. New York: Vintage.

Zarrintan, S., Shahnaee, A., & Aslanabadi, S. (2018). Rhazes (AD 865–925) and his early contributions to the field of pediatrics. *Child's Nervous System*, 34, 1435–8.

Zhu, Y., Zhang, L., Fan, J., & Han, S. (2007). Neural basis of cultural influence on self representation. *Neuroimage*, 34, 1310–17.

Zimbardo, P. (1971, 25 October). Statement. In *Hearings before Subcommittee No. 3, of the Committee on the Judiciary, House of Representatives, 92nd Congress, First Session on Corrections, Part II: Prisons, Prison Reform, and Prisoner's Rights: California* (Serial No. 15; pp. 110–21, 152–7). Washington, DC: US Government Printing Office.

Zinck, A. M. (1995). 'Doctrine by ensample': Sanctification through literature in Milton and Bunyan. *Bunyan Studies*, 6, 44–55.

INDEX